Manfred Rose (Ed.)

Heidelberg Congress on Taxing Consumption

Proceedings of the International Congress on Taxing Consumption, Held at Heidelberg, June 28-30, 1989

With Contributions by

Henry J. Aaron, Charles L. Ballard, Robin Boadway, Geoffrey Brennan
James M. Buchanan, Bernd Genser, John Kay, Gerold Krause-Junk
Joachim Lang, Charles E. McLure, Jr., Dennis C. Mueller
Peggy B. Musgrave, Richard A. Musgrave, Manfred Rose, Christian Seidl
Peter B. Sørensen, Richard E. Wagner, George R. Zodrow

With 18 Figures

Springer-Verlag Berlin Heidelberg New York
London Paris Tokyo Hong Kong

Professor Dr. Manfred Rose
Alfred-Weber-Institute
Faculty of Economics
University of Heidelberg
Grabengasse 14
D-6900 Heidelberg, FRG

ISBN-13: 978-3-642-75793-8 e-ISBN-13: 978-3-642-75791-4
DOI: 10.1007/978-3-642-75791-4

Softcover reprint of the hardcover 1st edition 1990

Printing: Weihert-Druck GmbH, Darmstadt
Bookbinding: T. Gansert GmbH, Weinheim-Sulzbach
2142/7130-543210

Preface

In June 1989 the Faculty of Economics of the University of Heidelberg and the Alfred Weber-Gesellschaft organized a congress on taxing consumption in Heidelberg. At this congress prominent academicians, tax policy experts, tax lawers, tax consultants, and business leaders met in order to analyze and discuss new issues about the pure economic merits, political economy, administrative complexity, legislative consequences, and international problems of consumption-based tax systems.

I should like to thank Benediktus Hardorp and Götz Werner who were unwavering in their support and encouragement to set up this congress. It is also gratefully acknowledged that Götz Werner and his company 'dm-drogerie märkte' generously provided the main funds for the congress and the publication of this volume. Of course, a further main obligation is to Wolfgang Köstlin and Karin Schlampp who had the local organization so well in hand and who were supported by a group of students of my seminar whom I would like to thank as well.

The scientific results of the congress will be published in two different volumes. The papers written in English are contained in this volume. The German papers and the papers dealing with topics which are of special interest to German readers will appear in a separate German volume. Both volumes also contain the comments of the formal discussants.

The papers published here are revised versions, taking into account the comments of the formal discussants as well as the comments of other congress participants. Their grouping runs parallel to the congress program according to the topics dealt with in the different working groups.

I am particularly grateful to Karin Schlampp, who directed the editing, to Tomas Farken, who provided assistance in solving word processing problems and to Irene Rößler for preparing accurate references.

Heidelberg
April 1990

Manfred Rose

Contents

PART TWO: Theoretical and Empirical Foundations of Taxing Consumption

Robin Boadway

John Kay

PART THREE: Taxing Consumption from a Public Choice and Constitutional Point of View

PART FIVE: Administrative Aspects of a Consumption-based Tax System

Charles E. McLure, Jr. and George R. Zodrow

PART SIX: Taxing Consumption from an International Point of View

Peggy B. Musgrave

Bernd Genser

PART ONE

Opening Lectures

Manfred Rose

The Superiority of a Consumption-based Tax System*

Every tax like every other social institution will outlive the period of its economic and psychological appropriateness. But as in all other social institutions, in tax systems rigidities will not live for ever: they will be washed-out gradually by the flow of time. Thus, income tax will disappear together with the economic system and mentality [of the bourgeois liberalism], to which it owes its existence.

Joseph A. Schumpeter[1]

I. Introduction

A major objective of setting up this congress was to further the academic and public debate on taxing consumption, but I especially hope that this congress will contribute to a more intensive consideration in the debate on the German tax reform of the opportunities, and of course risks, connected with the different approaches towards a consumption-based tax system.

---

* Slightly extended version of the lecture held at the opening ceremony of the congress. Some expositions refer especially to the German debate on the reform of the German tax system. I owe a special debt of gratitude to Antoinette Broek, who translated the German text. I would also like to thank Michael Ahlheim for helpful suggestions on an earlier version.

[1] Translated from Schumpeter ((1929/30) 1985, p. 132).

Although in my view scientific interest and commitment with regard to consumption-oriented tax regimes are increasing, the governments of many western countries pursue a strategy of tax reform which doesn't take this development into account. In the United States, for example the Tax Reform Act of 1986 is characterized by a reduction of the rates of income taxes at the household and the business level and a simultaneous broadening of the assessment bases of those taxes, not least avoiding losses of tax revenues. The recent important tax reform in 1990 in Germany was also characterized by a cut in the personal income and the corporation income tax rates. The financing of this project will probably turn out to be realized by a growth-determined increase of total tax revenues. In any case a systematic reform of the tax bases does not figure on the agenda of the present German tax policy.

From this we may conclude that one doesn't realize that only by applying tax rates to taxable bases will the desired tax revenue be produced. A focussing on tax rate reductions is therefore a most one-sided, I would even say, false procedure when it comes to creating a more efficient and just tax system. A tax reform policy, aiming at a growth of prosperity, should be a policy, in which the investigation of the base structure of our tax system should take precedence over the investigation of tax rates.[2] Such a policy, however, requires basic guidelines which would have to serve as a standard evaluation model for the precise assessment of the current system and the development of reform proposals. Such standard models, which shape current as well as theoretical tax systems, are undoubtedly the concept of (comprehensive) income taxation on the one hand and the concept of consumption taxation on the other hand.

The German tax system, the same holds good for many other European tax systems, is a mixed system of which one main part referring to the individual and the corporation income tax is income-based, and the other main part referring to the excise duties and the value-added tax is consumption-based. Tax-scientists, tax-policymakers and also people working in the tax administration require a reform especially of those taxes levied at the household and business level which one traditionally calls direct taxes. Looking at it from a systematic point of view the most important question is whether the system of direct taxes, i.e. personal income tax, corporation income tax,

---

[2] From a legislative point of view the reform of the assessment base of the German income tax takes constitutional precedence over its tax rates reform. See Lang (1985, pp. 27-29).

local business tax (municipal trade tax: 'Gewerbesteuer'), wealth tax and tax on inheritances and gifts is to be changed into a more comprehensive system of income taxation or into a system of overall consumption taxation. This question is fundamental and should be clarified beforehand, as any tax reform, however small it may be, may mean a first step towards a rational, less hybrid and more simply structured system.

Governments mostly avoid such decisions, because they are afraid of being tied down or hampered in their policy. But the negative consequences of such an indecisive policy will become manifest as soon as negative economic developments call for immediate action. It's even possible that such a situation already exists, considering the fact that the phenomenon of international competition in the field of tax systems is spreading.

These aspects also emphasize the urgent necessity of choosing a basic concept for setting up current and future tax reforms. And by doing so one should also consider the possibility of a consumption-oriented reform strategy. The ideal concept for reforming direct taxes would in my view be the requirement of aligning tax bases directly to consumed income, or to put it differently: to exempt saved and invested income from taxation.

II. Alternative Ways of Attaining a Consumption-based Tax System

Tax systems may be consumption based with respect to their direct taxes as well as their indirect taxes. In most countries of the European Community the value-added tax is the largest indirect consumption tax. Here a more consumption-oriented tax regime could be attained by increasing value-added tax rates and reducing direct tax rates, i.e. particularly personal income tax and corporation income tax. It's evident that in the United States a strategy of this kind would have to be preceded by an introduction of the European value-added tax, which is being employed increasingly all over the world. I will not, however, in my exposition on concepts for a more consumption-based tax system concentrate on the possible alternative of increasing the share of indirect consumption taxes, however interesting this may be, but on the alternatives of taxing consumption directly, which are less well-known in Germany. These considerations are directed at reforming the bases of the existing system of income taxation at the private household level and of profit taxation at the business level.

Special attention is paid to the consumed-income tax, a system which is favoured by many economists like for example Joseph Schumpeter. Referring to the cash-flow accounting procedure of calculating the consumable income and in accordance with the terminoloy of the Blueprints (1984) we call this net-income tax a cash-flow consumption tax. I would like to add that, according to Schumpeter only consumed-income tax (*'Verbrauchseinkommensteuer'*) is genuine income tax, "for in agreement with its fundamental meaning it is a tax raised from consumption funds and it will be clear to everybody that the whole argument in favour of the income tax will collapse if it has to be paid out of newly born capital."[3] When assessing the cash-flow consumption tax one has to apply the tax rate schedule to the difference between the taxpayer's cash receipts from various sources and the total transfers to all kinds of reserve funds, i.e. to saving accounts, life-insurance reserves, pension funds, deposits of securities etc. Attaining a consumption-oriented income implies that all reductions of reserve funds are dealt with as taxable cash inflows.[4] Because taxable income is calculated by substracting the total net-savings from the gross- incomes a tax payer receives during the year, I would prefer to speak of a *saving-exclusive income tax*. Regarding further voluntary transfers to other households (gifts etc.) as negative personal receipts[5], it's generally true that the tax payer finances his purchases on consumption goods and his tax payments out of the funds which total up to taxable net-of-saving-income in each period.

A business tax which ideally harmonizes with the cash-flow consumption tax should be designed as a tax on dividends providing full credit to domestic shareholders.

---

[3] Translated from Schumpeter ((1929/30) 1985, p. 125).

[4] For technical details concerning the assessment of the cash-flow consumption tax see especially Bradford (1984) and Lodin (1978).

[5] The taxation of gifts given would imply that they are in this case considered a kind of consumption by the donor. This is in accordance with the present income tax law because there are no allowances for transfers like gifts. Principally, the question of taxing given gifts is discussed controversially in relevant literature. See, for example, Bradford (1986, pp. 15-31).

Mitschke (1985) proposes to supplement the consumed-income tax by an accrual-wealth tax ('Reinvermögenszuwachssteuer') on wealth in stock at the end of life. "By taxing consumption in each year of life, and by additionally taxing wealth arising from annual savings at the end of life, one totally taxes lifetime income". Translated from Mitschke (1985, p. 53). Of course, this tax regime calls for taxing gifts etc. given, meaning that the donor filling in his tax form is not allowed to deduct such kinds of voluntary transfers.

Consequently, the saving-exclusive income tax system is mainly directed at taxing consumption personally at the household level.

The scientific discussions on a consumption-based tax system also focus on another approach. Exempting interest from taxation at the household level may finally lead to a taxation of personal lifetime consumption including gifts and bequests given. Since under this tax regime the taxes on present savings represent prepayment of taxes on future consumption so to speak, it is usually called the tax prepayment approach to direct taxation of consumption. I would however prefer to call this new tax model the *interest-exclusive income tax* or lifetime consumption tax.

A business tax would be consistent with this consumption-based personal tax if normal returns to capital are exempt from tax. Consequently, the business tax base is to be designed in such a way that returns of financial and real investments are tax burdened only if their rates exceed on the average the market rate of interest.

Contrary to the two briefly described consumption-based tax systems the existing income tax regimes are more adjusted to the *accretion-approach of taxing income*, generally defined as "the money value of the net accretion to one's economic power between two points in time".[6] Compared to the saving-exclusive and the interest-exclusive income tax the *classical income tax* is in the ideal case directed at taxing the gross-incomes which a household receives during the year.

The relative virtues of the classical and consumption-oriented approach of defining income for tax purpose have been debated at length in literature.[7] I do not intend to present this whole debate on this occasion, since many of the pros and cons to be brought forward will be discussed in detail in the various congress papers on this subject. However, a provoking claim like "Consumption Oriented Revision of the Tax System" ('Konsumorientierte Neuordnung des Steuersystems') cannot but incite the participants of this congress to ask themselves which main arguments speak in favour of precisely this reform approach. Taking up this question as a starting point, I would now like to call your special attention to those arguments, which in my view are strong enough to justify the establishment of a consumption-based tax system.

---

[6] Haig (1921, p. 59). For the accretion theory of taxing income see also Schanz (1896), Simons (1938), and Shoup (1984).

[7] For a summary of the principal arguments see, for example, Bradford (1986).

III. Principal Reasons for Favouring the Consumption Approach in Taxation

In order to prove that a consumption-based tax system will be advantageous it will be useful to focus first of all on the different processes by which the direct money burdens of taxes are changed into ultimate real burdens.

A. Tax Incidence and the Real Burden of Taxation

The process which leads from the tax payments of firms and households to the final incidence is still a matter of theoretical and empirical research. However, one fundamental truth concerning this topic is quite obvious and should be kept in mind when evaluating tax systems, namely the fact that the final burden of every tax usually takes on the shape of a personal sacrifice in consumption. Consequently, the private households are the main carriers of the burden which the current tax system is bringing about continuously. There is no doubt whatsoever that individuals are forced by way of personal taxes to renounce consumption. In the case of business taxes, especially taxes on profits which are used as equity funds to finance real investment, the forced renunciation of the consumption of private goods is not immediately recognizable. If on the one hand this kind of taxation is neutral with respect to investment, the reduction in private consumption will arise from shifting the taxes forward to the consumers via higher prices of consumption goods. If on the other hand business profit taxes cannot be shifted partly or totally and if this leads to a reduction in private investment and in the real capital stock, there will be less consumption possibilities available in the future. Although it's true again that the private households will be the main carriers of the tax burden taking the shape of consumption sacrifices, like in the case of shifting in prices, it will not be possible to identify out of the community of all consumers those people who bear the tax and their individual tax-burden share.

Assuming that the real burden of all taxes finally occurs at the household level in the form of utility losses from reduced consumption the following scenarios and figures may be interesting. To provide documentary evidence of the overall level of tax burden from a national economy point of view the relevant tax coefficient is traditionally calculated as the ratio of total tax revenue to gross national product. In the Federal Republic of Germany this coefficient varies between 23 and 25 per cent. Taking into consideration, however, that taxes are regarded as burdens in consumption, the gross national product including government expenditures on common services and private investments is not a very suitable reference base. The only appropriate base serving to express total tax burden by means of rate figures seems to be the level of aggregate private consumption. When applying such a concept the German statistics of national income show that the German treasurer charges the private households with a sacrifice which on average amounts up to 54 % of current consumption of private goods. Besides one may regard the compulsary social security contributions paid by employees and employer to the social security funds under the effective control of government as taxes and therefore as consumption sacrifices forced upon the private households by the government. Furthermore, transfer payments are made by the Government and out of legislative social security funds to provide income maintenance to the unemployed, to the poor ensuring them access to a minimum level of consumption, and to the retired. Regarding these income transfers, to simplify matters, as consumption of the receiving households and deducting the relevant aggregate figure from aggregate consumption, one obtains an approximation reflecting the consumption of all persons who are liable to taxes or similar contributions. The annual consumption sacrifices forced upon these persons by the state for the provision of public goods and social security has reached on average a level of almost 140 per cent in the past ten years. The average German taxpayer, spending 25000 DM a year on consumption goods could in principle spend as much as 60000 DM on consumption and retirement provisions in the same period if he need not pay taxes.

It becomes already quite obvious from this rough calculation that the burden created by the German tax system is considerable. Yet, these figures do not cover the whole spectrum of tax burdens. Less well-known to the general public are the deadweight losses of taxation which often constitute a main issue in the academic discussion on tax reforms. Before I go on discussing this topic, I would like to show that we can already draw some interesting conclusions with respect to our main question from the aforementioned facts concerning the real burden of taxation.

B. Functional Efficiency Virtues of Taxing Consumption

The realization that real tax burdens always represent sacrifices in consumption obtains a special meaning from the viewpoint of target-oriented tax policy. In principle it holds good for all target-instrument problems that the target effectiveness of instrument application should be as direct as possible. Looked upon it this way a rational, good tax system should be characterized by the closest possible relation between the aimed at tax effect and the actual tax effect. Before answering the question as to what extent a consumption-based tax system justifies this claim, we'll have to consider the basic functions which taxes must normally perform in industrial states with a democratic-political system and a free-enterprise economy.

Following the traditional dogmas the main function of taxes is to raise money in order to finance government expenditures. Thus taxes serve the administration of government budgets, i.e. they have an *administrative function*. Adolph Wagner (1890) emphasized the importance of the social policy function of taxation which guides the modern fiscal system of income redistribution. For this reason one has to take a *redistributive function* of taxation into account. Furthermore, we have learned from Abba Lerner (1951) that the *economic function* of taxes is directed at demand management in order to help government to allocate the disposable resources of an economy between the private and the public sector without simultaneously producing inflation and/or unemployment. Last but not least, taxes are also an essential component of the set of all the instruments which a democratic political system needs to work out well, i.e. taxes have - as Wicksell (1896) pointed out - also a general *political function*. Thus taxes should inform the voting consumer on the real costs of the budget which the government is continuously carrying out and of new fiscal policy programs which parties offer for example on the occasion of elections. It is one of the sad facts of life that politicians and the people from the tax administration usually accept only the (administrative) function of financing and neglect the importance of the other main functions which should guide good tax systems.

We must now distinguish between the aforementioned tax functions and *principles of taxation*. Like for example, the equity-oriented principle of a fair way of taxing and the output/input-oriented principle of an efficient way of taxing they are applied in order to evaluate different kinds of taxes and different shapes of assessing taxes with respect to fulfilling tax functions and other fiscal policy targets.[8]

[8] Basic principles of a rational tax system referred to here are dealt with comprehensively in the pioneering works of Haller (1964) and Neumark (1970).

Thus we can speak of a *(functional) efficient* tax system if it is impossible to reach a higher degree of realization of all tax functions at the condition of given resources employed in tax policy and tax administration. In this case I am referring to the ability to control the aimed at tax effect, necessary for the realization of tax functions. For if this ability with respect to a specific tax instrument is not (or not completely) given, the tax function concerned will not achieve its highest possible effectiveness, implying that the *criterion of functional efficiency* is not (completely) satisfied. Thus we shall have to assess tax instruments with respect to their suitability necessary to produce the aimed at effect in a clear-cut manner.

Now I would like to call your attention to various aspects of functional efficiency, which - in my opinion - have not sufficiently been taken notice of in the recent discussion on consumption-oriented tax reforms.

On the Administrative Function of Taxes

It's obvious that in a state with parliamentary democracy, a free market economy, protection of private property and an autonomus central bank the government needs the revenue from taxation in order to finance public expenditures. Thus, from a pure budget-administrative point of view the only reason for taxation is to provide the government with money which for some reason or other it wishes to spend. The desired effect which each tax should bring about here is the effect of contributing to the financing power of those governments who are not allowed to use the money press. I cannot see any fundamental difference between a consumed-income tax and an accrual-income tax when it comes to raising the required revenue in a controllable way.[9] Under both

[9] Schumpeter held the interesting view that the technical problems arising from levying a personal consumption tax would hardly be bigger than the problems are as a matter of fact already occurring permanently: "The technical difficulties arising from allowing the creation of reserves to be deductible are big, but not nearly as big as it is stated. They are namely of exactly the same dimension as the difficulties arising from the assessment of income tax. The self-employed and the wage earners would have to be demanded to provide proof of investment. Proof which could ninety times out of a hundred be furnished without great effort or loss of time through saving-accounts and deposit-registrations. The case of investing in one's own company is completely equivalent to the case of depreciation allowances. In addition, there would also be a considerable saving of effort for all parties resulting from the fact that the fight for depreciation allowances as far as income tax is concerned, could be stopped and the hunt for the

systems the understandably imperfect tax legislation and administration provide specific opportunities for more or less substantial tax evasion. These facts of tax evasion, which will vary considerably, are to be evaluated not only with respect to efficiency but also with respect to fairness in taxation.

On the Redistributive Function of Taxes

Adolph Wagner states that "next to the pure financial, but inherent purpose of taxation there is the possibility of setting up a second, social-policy oriented purpose by influencing the distribution of national income and wealth and in this way bring about a change of the primary distribution coming out of the free market process."[10] In the case of a function of redistribution specified in this way there is no doubt as to the kind of effect aimed at. The incomes of households are to be reduced in accordance with the distribution target. Consequently, this basic fiscal policy target can only be realized to a sufficient extent on the basis of an income-oriented tax system. This, however, does not inevitably require a comprehensive annual income tax as defined by Schanz-Haig-Simons. When redistributing primary incomes arising from factor payments, one should avoid a *double taxation of saving* by means of exempting interest income from taxation.[11] As already mentioned above, such an interest-exclusive annual tax base would automatically imply a taxation of the comprehensively defined lifetime consumption by persons, i.e. a lifetime-consumption-based part of the tax system. This implies that the redistributive function of taxation is oriented towards a redistribution of lifetime consumption between private households.

---

hidden investment would partly become redundant and partly easier, since every investment would find its way to the tax collector automatically." Translated from Schumpeter ((1929/30) 1985, p. 125-126).

[10] Wagner (1890, p. 207).

[11] This argument will be discussed below where we shall deal with the excess burden topic.

The German tax policy of levying compulsary contributions providing social assistance to the unemployed and the retired is socially responsible policy, which undoubtedly entails essential elements of an ideal regime of redistribution by taxation. The purpose of these social budgets which are institutionally separated from the ordinary government budgets is to provide workers and salaried staff belonging to the lower-income classes with a reasonable benefit in the case of unemployment and a fair pension in retirement. As the income from wages of many employees paying compulsory social security contributions in fact represents the main source of income and as these household-groups have little left for savings one may say that the payments into the contributory pension system equals a tax on the income, which would otherwise possibly be consumed.

Apart from the budgets of the social security institutions which are designed to bring about a redistribution of income but which in fact bring about a redistribution of consumption funds on a large scale there are social policy activities financed with means of the ordinary government budgets - providing people having no or very low income with a subsistence minimum fund allowing them to satisfy their basic needs in consumption. In the Federal Republic of Germany especially the budgets of the communities serve the purpose of such income maintenance programs. It's clear that the task of the state in this respect lies in the redistribution of private consumption and that taxation in this case has the function of absorbing private purchasing power of high-income-earners. Consequently, it will be necessary to set up tax bases directed at the taxation of annual consumption in order to guarantee the largest possible correspondence between the aimed at tax effect and the actual tax effect (i.e. the effective tax incidence).

On the Economic Function of Taxes

In my view the elaboration of the economic function of taxation is due to Abba Lerner and his functional finance approach. In accordance with this framework taxation should be judged by the way in which it functions in contributing to the prevention of inflation and deflation. Thus, "taxation must be regarded not as the government's way of earning its living, but as a device for reducing the incomes and thereby the expenditures of members of society."[12] The optimum rate of private investment will come into effect by maintaining the corresponding rate of interest. The appropriate fiscal instruments here are public borrowing and lending. Thus, taxation is mainly deviced to adjust private consumption expenditures. This rule is to be seen in connection with all the activities the government has to undertake to provide the public with all the goods and services which the private economy for whatever reasons does not or should not bring about.

Referring to the achievement of this target, the main fiscal-policy task in free-market-type economies is to establish a new allocation of resources between the private and the public sector without getting an inflationary or deflationary change of the tax-exclusive price level of consumer goods, i.e. of that price level which economists usually call an index of the producer prices, and without getting additional unemployment. In order to bring about the desired reallocation, simultaneously avoiding 'extra' changes in the value of money and in employment, private consumer demands must be pushed from the market in an adequate manner and to an adequate extent in order to withdraw resources for private use and to make room for public demands.

Thus, the economic function of taxation with respect to supporting the government's allocation branch in solving its basic tasks of reallocating resources efficiently calls for a controllable and directly occuring tax incidence in form of a reduction of private expenditures for consumption goods.

To begin with, taxing capital income at the business level is a typical case in which the form of assessing the tax does not correspond with the aimed at tax incidence effect. Thus the purchasing power of private households is not absorbed as directly as demanded. There is no doubt that the real burdens of business profit taxes, like those of all other taxes, always represent individual sacrifices in consumption. But capital income taxes levied at the business level usually do not reduce private consumption directly. The money burdens of business income taxes are only changed into real burdens for certain consumers in the course of a complex and empirically hardly identifiable process. The recognition that business profit taxes lead to losses in private consumption though not in a direct and controllable way gives the impression that these instruments, from an efficiency point of view, are not very useful when it comes to enabling the government to handle its basic reallocation task. Especially the taxes on re-

[12] Lerner (1951, p. 11)

tained profits serving the financing of real investment are inefficient instruments with respect to achieving the government's reallocation targets in a clear-cut manner.

Product taxes, excise duties etc. levied at the business level and a general turnover tax of the consumption type - such as the European value-added tax - which also has to be paid by firms do not always primarily result in absorbing private consumption expenditures to the same extent. An incomplete shifting due to a high price elasticity of demand on specific markets may cause a financial burden and have a disincentive effect on the concerned firms and in this way result at first in a lower rate of investment.

The best way of regulating the rate of private consumption, necessary to achieve the government's targets with respect to the allocation of resources and stabilization, is to tax the purchasing power for consumption purposes directly at the household level. Obviously the most appropriate instrument for really supporting those targets which are directed at the provision of public goods and services, the avoidence of inflation, and the maintainance of a reasonable level of employment is the annual consumed-income tax as favoured by Schumpeter. Here the tax base coincides almost completely with the tax target objects of the allocation branch and the stabilization branch, so that the actual tax effect can be brought into correspondence with the aimed at tax effect as closely as possible.

On the Political Function of Taxes

If consumers are asked to vote on bundles of options combining a complete set of government budgets and tax shares in accordance with Wicksell's political-fiscal approach[13], they must be well informed about the true real tax burden they will finally have to bear. It is obvious that the direct taxation of households will meet this requirement much better than any form of indirect taxation which is applied at the business level. Furthermore, a consumption-based direct tax system is as a matter of fact the best device to reveal to every individual tax payer and voter the real burden which he will have to bear as soon as the government budget program in question is set up.

For our current capital income tax system it holds that the suffering consumer in general is unaware that his or her tax burden lies well above his or her tax payment contribution. Especially consumers have no information whatsoever about the part they

[13] With this interpretation I follow Musgrave (1985, p. 10).

bear of those taxes which they do not pay themselves. Fiscal burden illusion exists particularly with respect to the corporation income tax, the personal income tax on profits retained in personally held companies and the local business tax (Gewerbesteuer). In this way, German consumers are not adequately provided with the information they need in order to evaluate the net advantages of being provided with public goods and services. The same applies of course to consumers of other countries employing a similar business income tax system. For our democratic society this doubtlessly implies an inefficiency with respect to the political voting system which is based on the idea of perfectly informed voters.

Thus, tax reforms towards a direct taxation of private consumption would mean a better source of information as to tax-induced losses in private consumption for each tax paying voter and actually improve his decision basis when it comes to weighing the benefits from public expenditures against the utility losses from taxation.
The direct taxation of consumption at the household level ensures the best prerequisites for adjusting the actual tax burden to the aimed at tax burden in a noticeable and thus informative way and would - compared with the political inadequacy of the current tax regime - significantly improve the democratic voting process with respect to the amount of resources which the government draws from the common pool.

C. Minimizing Excess Burdens by Taxing Consumption

Apart from the criterion of functional efficiency there is a more traditional efficiency principle, aiming at the ensurance of the lowest possible level of tax burden. In accordance with this approach a tax system can be regarded as efficient if it is impossible to reach the actual degree of realization of each of the tax functions at a lower level of tax burdens. From this it follows that one has to give preference to the tax system which minimizes tax burdens. Thus the *burden-minimizing criterion of efficiency* confronts us with the question as to which real tax burdens result from levying specific taxes or from a total tax system.

It is hardly known to the public that taxes in addition to the 'normal' burdens discussed above, which arise from the imposed payments, may also bring about excess losses in economic welfare which in the literature of public finance are often called dead-weight losses of taxation. The diversity of such extra burdens, which can also be ultimately identified as sacrifices in consumption, is enormous. This phenomenon always arises in those cases in which taxation results in making the consumption of specific goods, specific kinds of investment, the use of one of the factors of production or even the location of production in relation to other comparable economic activities and alternatives artificially more (or less) expensive, thus giving rise to discriminations. It's the reaction of all economic decision units concerned to those changes in relative prices which brings about these excess burdens. In such cases taxation distorts the decision of firms and households, so to speak and as a result of the response mentioned the economically best possible allocation of the disposable resources does not come into effect. Looking at it from this point of view one may also say that the more excess burdens a tax system causes the more inefficient it is with respect to the rate of economic utilization of resources.

This brings us, in view of our topic, to the discussion of a special group of unwanted side-effects of taxation. It's the elimination or - if this is not possible - the reduction of these side-effects on which particularly academic reform proposals often focus. Although the total lump-sum burden of taxation may be fixed on the basis of a given level of public expenditure, one could by means of a reform of the assessment bases at least succeed in bringing about a considerable reduction of the existing deadweight losses. It's true however, that the concepts of standardization and measurement of such burdens have not yet been developed to such an extent that they will make the fiscal-policymakers fully realize the dimension of the welfare benefits to be gained from reducing such burdens. It goes without saying that it is even more difficult to convince the public of the fact that a certain reform of the old tax system is particularly worthwhile, since the new system will not bring about a decrease in the total tax payment but only(!) lead to the disappearance of a range of discriminative facts of taxation.

In the following section, further emphasizing the superiority of a consumption-based tax system, I will discuss two phenomena of excess tax burdens, which in my view are of great importance for the comparison of tax systems.

Direct Effects on Individual Welfare

The discrimination of savings for future consumption purposes, brought about by the traditional income taxation, constitutes a long standing argument against an income-based tax system and, at the same time, in favour of a consumption-based tax system, not involving such discrimination. Joseph Schumpeter describes this most clearly as follows: "The benefit the saver will get out of the saved income part is the return on his investment. This return is, however, diminished twice as a result of the ruling (tax) practise. Firstly, the income tax levied on savings will cause the return to be smaller than it would have been without taxation. Secondly, this return already diminished by income tax is burdened once more by income tax."[14]

Now, the modern theory of optimal taxation shows that even a personal consumption tax is not completely efficiency-neutral, meaning that it will not exclude distortions on the individual household level. Like a comprehensive income tax, an expenditure tax will, though not to the same extent, implicitly lead to a relative lowering of the price of leisure. It's a common fact that only a tax base including the fictive expenditure on leisure in addition to the expenditure on consumption goods acquired on markets would be completely free of distortions and consequently also of excess burdens.[15] It is clear that the value of leisure cannot be taxed in a direct way. Here the theory of optimal taxation comes into effect, stating that the tax system strived for is the system which, at the condition of a given tax revenue and of an exclusion of taxing leisure directly, will bring about the smallest possible loss of utility for the consumer. The second best solution, so to speak, would be to tax leisure indirectly by taxing those goods higher which are more complementary to leisure. Applying this basic rule to our problem one obtains the recommendation to burden consumption in the (earlier) years of working higher than consumption in (later) retirement because of its higher relative complementarity to

[14] Schumpeter (1929/30, p. 125).

[15] Of the total time a consumer has at his disposal (twenty-four hours a day) he needs a certain part for satisfying his essential needs, such as eating, sleeping and consulting a doctor. This is time, he does not freely dispose of. The remaining part he divides between working hours on the one hand and leisure time on the other which means that the product of wage rate and leisure is to be regarded as forgone income from labour and/or equivalent to this, expenditure on "consumed" leisure time. This fictive expenditure should as a matter of fact, within the framework of a rational consumption-based tax system, be taxed to the same extent as other consumption expenses are.

leisure in the working phase. Consequently, the price of future consumption in present value terms should be reduced relatively to the price of present consumption. This can be effected best by increasing the net-rate of interest by means of which the price of future consumption is discounted in order to get its present value.

These considerations lead us to the optimal-tax theorem that income from interest has to be subsidized.[16] But, this should not be understood as a definite taxreform proposal. It's, however, a useful consequence in view of the demand for assessment bases which satisfy the tax-burden minimizing criterion of efficiency best, a demand which will certainly be often brought forward in the course of this congress. Starting from the assumption, that it's optimal to subsidize income from interest, we are nearer to the optimum with a consumption-based income tax than we would be with an accrual-income tax which, completely contrary to the optimal tax rule, implies a taxation of interest.

We may now draw the following conclusion: with regard to the decisions concerning intertemporal consumption and the decisions between consumption and leisure, the traditional income tax leads to bigger individual welfare losses than a personal consumption tax would.

This view is even underlined by the special effects emanating from the tax on business profits, which are levied within the framework of the classical system of taxing income.

In the case of shifting forward all capital income taxes paid by firms nearly all consumer prices will change. Uncontrolled excess burdens may arise for each consumer group from the implied change of relative prices of goods. But there is not the slightest chance that this effective tax incidence can at least be roughly adjusted according to those rules which were developed for the optimal commodity taxation so as to minimize deadweight losses.

If profit taxes paid by firms are not shifted forward, they must be borne by the shareholders, and the distortion of intertemporal decisions of households with respect to consumption as discussed above will arise. This negative efficiency effect in the utility space was recently stressed again by Ekkard Wenger (1988). Focussing on the statutory rates of all taxes in Germany reducing the rate of return of an equity financed asset

[16] For a similar reasoning see also Sinn (1987, p. 281-282).

invested by a corporation, he calculated that the formal incidence with respect to the current price of 1 DM future consumption may amount to a rise of 827 %. This calculation was based on a reasonable time span of thirty years between the working phase and the retirement phase. Such formal incidence effect is to be assessed with respect to the rule of optimal taxation in an intertemporal setting calling for higher taxes on consumption in present working phases than on consumption in future retirement.

In order to cancel the existing discrimination of savings which provide for future consumption it is not necessary to design the personal income tax as a cash-flow consumption tax, i.e. to allow the exemption of any saving amounts of which the tax payer has furnished evidence. Taxing lifetime consumption via a tax on the interest-exclusive annual income will bring about approximately the same result, i.e. the removal of the discrimination of future consumption involved in the existing income system.

Dynamic Market Effects

It was Schumpeter again, who pointed out another relative efficiency advantage of a consumption-based tax system. In his work on the crisis of the tax state, which was published in 1918, he indicated that the taxation of pure entrepreneurial profits, associated with the taxation of income, is detrimental to precisely that element in the economic process "which at present is by far the most important individual motive for work towards industrial progress."[17] The pure entrepreneurial profit - as distinct from interest, from the risk premium and from the wages of the entrepreneur - "arises in the capitalist economy whereever a new method of production, a new commercial combination or a new form or organization is successfully introduced. It is the premium which capitalism attaches to innovation."[18]

Taxation of profits from innovations may lead to a reduction of innovative activities in the business sector and at the same time to a lessening of the dynamic competition, which constitutes a determining factor in the development of our economy. In the long run, such effects can not but result in consumption sacrifices. Consequently, excess tax burdens in the form of missed consumption opportunities will accrue.

---

[17] Schumpeter ((1918), p. 22).

[18] Schumpeter ((1918), p. 22).

Even if we are right in assuming that the business sector as a whole is successful in shifting forward the profit tax with the aid of additional government expenditures on and demands for goods and labour, this is not necessarily true for each single firm. The effect in question may be quite different for firms in the same branch, which means that competitive disadvantages could arise. Furthermore, big firms usually have no difficulty in switching to more debt financing. As everybody knows such options are much more restricted for the small and medium-sized firms. Thus profit taxation may not only reduce the rate of growth of our economy but also stimulate the process of concentration.

In contrast, a strictly consumption-oriented tax system will not touch business profits as long as these serve the financing of new investments. This also implies that there will be no obstructions whatsoever as to the dynamic incentives and effects of the free-market economy. The decision to be taken by the domestic firms with respect to the kind and extent of capital formation, the capital-labour ratio, the retention rate, the debt-equity ratio and last but not least the goods and services to be produced are almost completely detached from taxation. So if, for whatever reason, a taxation of business profits cannot be avoided, it will at least have to be assessed in such a manner that there will be no tax burdens in the case of retaining returns for real investment purposes. For this reason a consumption-based tax system is optimally compatible with a taxation of business profits which ultimately only burdens earnings distributed to domestic households for consumption purposes or to foreign shareholders.

D. Equity Virtues of Taxing Consumption

A tax system does not only bring about unwanted side effects in the case of misallocation, waste or even obstruction of the quantitative as well as qualitative development of productive resources. It also runs counter to national goals, when it generates a distribution of burdens, which is not compatible with the prevailing public opinion regarding distributive justice. Taxation resulting in different shares of tax burdens for persons in 'equal circumstances' implies an unfair incidence result, i.e. a loss in horizontal equity. In the same way a given vertical distribution of tax burdens may be regarded by the majority of the concerned members of society as an infringement upon their views with respect to justness in taxation.

It is of utmost importance, when discussing the issue how to distribute total tax burden, to take the fact into account that the burden arising from levying the traditional income tax is attached to what each tax payer contributes to the national product available for the society as a whole in each period. How much he will thereby draw from the total production fund for his own consumption, in other words, how far he will burden society, so to speak is, however, irrelevant.

Furthermore, our present income tax regime brings about the discrimination of those who have a greater preference for future consumption, by means of the extra taxation of savings due to taxing income from debt-claims of every kind, in contrast to those who prefer present consumption. In view of these facts I cannot but fully agree with David Bradford's statement that "the extra discrimination against savers that is added by an accrual-income tax is anything but a disadvantage in equity terms."[19] On the occasion of the debate on the withholding tax levied on interest, which was introduced in 1989 and repealed in the same year, the West-Germans became once more fully aware of this unfairness.[20]

Besides, it becomes clear from the tax effects that a taxation of income according to the accretion approach will by no means generate the sharing of tax burdens one hopes for in accordance with traditional views of fairness and vertical equity. The comprehensive taxation of business profits, inherent to traditional income taxation, namely is justified by the equity-oriented argument that in this way a taxation of 'rich' shareholders and a simultaneous alleviation of tax burdens for lower-income groups will be achieved. This would also lead to a redistribution of the annual total accretion of wealth in our economy, allowing business income taxes to work against the concentration of private wealth. But it is a fact that the real burden of business profit taxes are borne by all consumers, probably in particular by the private households belonging to the lower-income groups. The shifting process is, moreover, so confusing that there is

---

[19] Bradford (1986, p. 315).

[20] The failed experiment of introducing a fully credited withholding tax on interest payments in 1989 - there was only a designed rate of 10 % - clearly showed how the statutory, accrual-typed form of taxing income had already been made ineffective via tax-resisting motivated tax evasion and in fact turned into a more consumption-oriented tax regime. This change is considerable, as can be concluded from the observed immense flight of capital.

hardly any possibility of identifying the groups bearing the real burdens nor the distribution of forced consumption sacrifices.

In the case of a consumption-based tax system, however, the individual will be taxed in accordance with the part he draws from the total amount of goods available to society[21], and the claim for a (vertical) just distribution of tax burdens may be complied with by means of a progressive rate schedule. Besides, there will be no more discrimination against those citizens who prefer future consumption to present consumption, because the saved income parts are taxed only once. From this it follows that in accordance with the fairness principle the level of the tax burden will be independent from the individual intertemporal preference with respect to consumption.

In this connection it becomes even relevant to ask whether it wouldn't be fairer to burden the persons preferring present consumption with higher taxes, since they will also have their share of the increase in welfare brought about by the fact that other people prefer saving and investing to immediate consuming.[22] "It is only by spending, not by earning or saving, that an individual imposes a burden on the rest of the community in attaining his own ends. In all his other activities his own interests and the interests of the community run not counter to one another but parallel."[23]
This argument also supports the concept of the dynasty view of tax equity based on the principle of completely exempting gifts and bequests given until these funds are used for consumption purposes by any member out of the group of recipients.

IV. Strategies in Favour of a Consumption-based Tax System

In the final section of this introduction I would like to devote a few words to the meaning the congress papers may have for those who expect practicable recommenda-tions for modern tax reform. The first general conclusion one may draw is that no proposal

[21] "An Expenditure base would tax people according to the amount which they take out of the common pool, and not according to what they put into it." [Kaldor (1965, S.53)].

[22] A similar suggestion has been made by Sievert: "Who does not save and invest should be delighted at savings and investments made by others; for he will share in the addition of welfare arising out of it. Why should he prevent the others from doing what is best for all by taxing?" Translated from Sievert (1988, p. 87).

[23] Kaldor (1965, p. 65).

concerning an exclusively consumption-based tax system can be said to be matured to such a degree that it could be turned into law. On the other hand ideas will be brought forward which could serve as rational concepts for the future reform of present tax systems. In brief, I would say that the strategy of tax policy should be directed at the following two main reform targets:

- the detachment of enterpreneurial investment decisions and with it the formation of real capital from business taxation;
- the adjustment of the actual effects to the optimal effects of taxes (with respect to efficiency and equity) by means of a consumption-oriented design of private household taxation.

There is no doubt that the introduction of a cash-flow business tax[24] would mean an important step towards detaching investment decisions from taxation. The allowance for immediate depreciation of real assets combined with full loss offset will result in complete tax-deductibility of the overall cost of both real capital and labour. This means that, again in present value terms, the return from marginal investment will be exempt from tax and that in this way an essential prerequisite for investment neutrality even in circumstances of inflation will be provided for. The fact that a cash-flow tax base is determined by the difference between realized receipts and payments, meaning that they can easily be identified by firms and controlled by tax authorities, also proves to be advantageous. This would be an important improvement upon the prevailing system of business taxation in the Federal Republic of Germany. The oppressing problems connected with making up the balance sheet and carrying out the valuation of assets for tax purposes would all disappear at once.

However, a practical, politically realizable tax reform policy will - always taking the historical law system as a starting point - seek to realize the new tax system by means of piecemeal measures. In this connection it is advisable to strive for intermediate forms of new tax system structures, which are realizable as stage-targets so to speak, taking into account the restrictions in the political field. From this it follows that a direct transition into a cash-flow-tax would be too great a leap forward. On the one hand one would, in

[24] The virtues of a cash-flow business tax are especially discussed in the paper of Charles McLure / George Zodrow contained in this volume and in the papers of David F. Bradford, Wolfram Richter / Wolfgang Wiegard, Franz W. Wagner, and Peter Swoboda contained in the German congress volume [Rose (1990)].

accordance with the prevailing German tax mentality, tend to regard the immediate write-off allowance as a tax privilege for firms and their shareholders and for this reason oppose them with equity arguments. On the other hand one should take into account losses of tax revenues from a budget-administrative point of view, which will certainly occur long years after the year in which the allowance of 'expensing' is introduced.

The concept of taxing the interest-exclusive business profit brought forward by Boadway and Bruce (1984) in the international debate on an investment-neutral tax system will probably be more acceptable than the cash-flow business tax approach. This tax model will also allow the realization of the indisputable efficiency advantages of a cash-flow tax, being neutral in its effects on the investment decisions of firms with or without inflation, by means of a different taxation method, a method which will be in line with all depreciation schemes and therefore also with the revenue-target of the treasury.

Starting from each existing form of taxing the yield of real investment, the interest-exclusive business profit tax can be brought about by a simple reform measure. In future, not only interests on debts can be deducted, but also interest on equity capital as indicated in the balance sheet made up for tax purposes. For the calculation of these costs of capital one could use the rate of interest on long-term public bonds.
This also seems to be advisable in view of the transition to an interest-exclusive personal income tax, a reform target having the greatest perspective of being realized in the near future.
With

- the European value-added tax burdening consumption indirectly,
- an interest-exclusive, progressive personal income tax and
- a proportional tax on the interest-exclusive profits of firms (regardless of their legal form of organization) with a dividend relief according to the full imputation system

as main pillars, one would make considerable progress on the road to an ideal consumption-based tax system.

As also clearly shown by the congress papers on the administrative and legal problems connected with the establishment of consumption-oriented tax regimes, the personal consumed-income tax - which I would assess as the ideal form of taxing consumption directly - requires an even more intensified scientific analysis, in order to reveal its practicability in politics and society in a convincing way. However, ideal concepts may already serve as rational models on the road which one follows by piece-meal tax reforms, small as they may be. This road should lead to a tax system which is perfectly compatible with our social market economy ('soziale Marktwirtschaft') implying in its turn that the fundamental alignment to consumption or, put differently, the tax exemption of investments and savings cannot be dispensed with.

References

Boadway, R. / Bruce, N. (1984), A general Proposition on the Design of a Neutral Business Tax, Journal of Public Economics 24, pp. 231-239.

Bradford, D.F. / The U.S. Treasury Tax Policy Staff (1984), Blueprints for Basic Tax Reform, 2nd ed., Washington, D.C.: Tax Analysts. (Orig. pub. as U.S. Treasury Department, 1977).

Bradford, D.F. (1986), Untangling the Income Tax, Cambridge, Massachusetts, and London, England: Harvard University Press.

Haig, R.M. (ed.) (1921), The Federal Income Tax, New York: Columbia University Press.

Haller, H. (1964), Die Steuern, Tübingen: J.C.B. Mohr (Paul Siebeck).

Kaldor, N. (1965), An Expenditure Tax, 4th impression, London: Unwin University Books.

Lang, J. (1985), Reformentwurf zu Grundvorschriften des Einkommensteuergesetzes, Köln: Verlag Dr. Otto Schmidt KG.

Lerner, A.P. (1951), Economics of Employment, New York: McGraw-Hill.

Lodin, S.O. (1978), Progressive Expenditure Tax - An Alternative?, Report of the 1972 Government Commission on Taxation, Stockholm: LiberForlag.

Mitschke, J. (1985), Steuer- und Transferordnung aus einem Guβ, Baden-Baden: Nomos Verlagsgesellschaft.

Musgrave, R.A. (1985), A Brief History of Fiscal Doctrine, in: A.J. Auerbach/M. Feldstein (eds.), Handbook of Public Economics, Vol. I, pp. 1-59, Amsterdam: North-Holland.

Neumark, F. (1970), Grundsätze gerechter und ökonomisch rationaler Steuerpolitik, Tübingen: J.C.B. Mohr (Paul Siebeck).

Rose, M. (ed.) (1990), Konsumorientierte Neuordnung des Steuersystems, Berlin und Heidelberg: Springer-Verlag.

Schumpeter, J.A. ((1918) 1954), The Crisis of the Tax State, in: A.T. Peacock et.al. (1954), International Economic Papers, pp. 5-38. Translation of "Die Krise des Steuerstaates", Graz und Leipzig 1918.

Schumpeter, J.A. (1929/1930), Ökonomie und Soziologie der Einkommensteuer, Der deutsche Volkswirt, Bd. 4, pp. 380-385, reprinted in: W.F. Stolper/Chr. Seidl (ed.) (1985), Joseph A. Schumpeter, Aufsätze zur Wirtschaftspolitik, Tübingen: J.C.B. Mohr (Paul Siebeck), pp. 123-132.

Shoup, C.S. (1984), The Schanz Concept of Income and the United States Federal Income Tax, Finanzarchiv 42, pp. 433-444.

Sievert, O. (1988), Änderung der Steuerstruktur in Richtung auf mehr Ausgabenbesteuerung ?, in: H. Zimmermann (ed.), Die Zukunft der Staatsfinanzierung, Stuttgart: Wissenschaftliche Verlagsgesellschaft, pp. 85-103.

Simons, H. (1938), Personal Income Taxation: The Definition of Income as a Problem of Fiscal Policy, Chicago: University of Chicago Press.

Sinn, H.-W., (1987), Capital Income Taxation and Resource Allocation, Amsterdam and New York: North-Holland.

Wagner, A. (1890), Lehr- und Handbuch der politischen Ökonomie, 4. Hauptabteilung, Finanzwissenschaft, 2. Teil, Theorie der Besteuerung, Gebührenlehre und allgemeine Steuerlehre, 2. Aufl., Leipzig: C.F. Winter'sche Verlagshandlung.

Wenger, K. (1988), Besteuerung und Kapitalbildung als intertemporales Optimierungsproblem, in: H. Hax/W. Kern/H.H. Schröder (eds.), Zeitaspekte in betriebswirtschaftlicher Theorie und Praxis, Stuttgart, pp. 279-295.

Wicksell, K. (1896), Finanztheoretische Untersuchungen nebst Darstellung und Kritik des Steuerwesens, Jena.

Richard A. Musgrave

On Choosing the "Correct" Tax Base - A Historical Perspective

Debate over the "correct" tax base is of long standing and my assignment is to view it in its historical perspective[1]. The literature is endless, and a variety of approaches may be distinguished[2]. Since they overlap in time, no neat sequential story can be told. I therefore present a brief review of each of the key approaches, keeping in mind their significance for the current debate over income versus expenditure tax.

In so doing, I will be concerned with the development of ideas regarding the "good" or "correct" tax base, not with the way in which the use of tax bases has in fact developed and tax structures have changed. I do so even though the two stories are obviously related. The early appearance of an income tax in Britain (1798) interacted with the attention of classical economists to income as tax base. The development of the Prussian income tax in the 1880s interacted with the extensive discussion of income concepts in Germany's fiscal literature of that time. Early if brief appearances of income taxation in the U.S. in 1862 and 1894 led to a discussion of income as tax base

---

[1] Looking back at how the theory of "good taxation" has developed, three major approaches may be distinguished. One, traditionally referred to as the benefit theory, holds that people should pay in line with benefits received. Another, reflecting the Wicksellian tradition (1896), views taxation as an instrument needed to secure preference revelation for public goods. A third views taxation as independent of the expenditure side and calls for contributions to be imposed in line with standards of equity and/or efficiency. The questions of how to best design the tax base may be raised in each of these contexts. For purposes of this conference, the third perspective is the most relevant one and hence followed here.

[2] For surveys of the tax base literature see Meyer (1884), Wilke (1921), Wueller (1938, 1939), Simons (1938). Historical studies are also included in many of the other contributions.

[Seligman (1911)] and its much later rise to prominence in World War II coincided with Henry Simons' beatification of the Schanz concept of accretion [Simons (1938)]. The current debate over expenditure tax may similarly foreshadow replacement of income by expenditures as the major base for personal taxation. However this may be, the development of tax structure is not my theme. Rather, it is the development of ideas regarding what constitutes the "correct" base.

I. National Income or Output as Potential Base

A first approach, dating back to François Quesnay's Tableau (1758) views the tax base in terms of national income. It is thus net income or output, viewed as the sum of factor shares, which constitutes the potential base from which tax revenue may be drawn. But not all of this base is available for taxation. According to the physiocrat's view, the only share that can in fact be reached is the rent of land, so that a sensible tax system might as well rely on rent as a single tax. With Smith (1776) and Ricardo (1817), other factor shares came to be allowed for. Ricardo's theory of distribution among factor shares is closely linked to his view of taxation, hence the title of his treatise. While wage income (or most thereof) was still needed for subsistence and thus not available as tax base, capital income could now be taxed. But it should be drawn on only sparingly, lest accumulation and thence employment will decline. Rent as a return to land again remained the ideal source of taxation.

This key role of rent reappears in various forms throughout the history of the tax base debate, including the single-tax doctrine of Henry George (1869) and Gunnison Brown (1937), as well as the later efficiency proposition that taxing the rent of land (or other forms of surplus income) is optimal [Lerner (1944)], as its supply is inelastic and thus avoids dead-weight loss. Nor came this support from economic quarters only. Taxation of rent also followed from John Locke's philosophy of property rights (1690), according to which a person is entitled to the fruits of his or her labor, while land and its return is held in common.

Up to the 1860s or so, the classical focus on net national income (as we call it today) as tax base also dominated the voluminous German literature on base definition, with Lotz (1821) among the earlier and Rau (1864) among its later proponents. Net national income sets the limit of what can be consumed (then known as Konsumtions-

Fond-Theorie) and hence what can be taxed away. This spirit of the national income approach, we might add, reappears in the current supply-side view of taxation, with its stress on output effects, rather than on the burden share of the individual taxpayer in the overall system.

II. Personal Income as Index of Taxable Capacity

The latter moves to the center of the stage as we turn to Adam Smith (1776) and his first maxim of taxation: "The subjects of every state", so he tells us, "ought to contribute towards the support of the government as nearly as possible in proportion to their respective abilities; that is, in proportion to the revenue which they respectively enjoy under the protection of the state". A key requirement of the good tax system thus becomes one of equity or fair distribution. The good tax system, as Adam Smith well recognized, and more clearly so than does our contemporary discussion, is not a matter of economics only. It is also a matter of distributive justice. The citizen is to contribute in line with his capacities and, so Adam Smith tells us, his revenue is to be taken as index thereof. But though net income or revenue is the norm, Smith found it difficult to be reached in practice. A broadly based consumption tax, so he suggested, may therefore have to serve as a second-best solution.

Nevertheless, and following Smith's first maxim, revenue or income came to be accepted widely as the best index of capacity to pay. In line with this, Edgeworth (1897), Cohen Stewart (1889), and others examined the implications of alternative (equal absolute, proportional, or marginal) sacrifice rules by reference to the marginal utility of a person's income. German authors similarly turned from the national income perspective of the classical approach to a personalized concept of income as the appropriate tax base. But though this change in direction was widely shared, there remained the question of just how income should be definded for this purpose. Must gains be regular to be recognized as income, must increases in the value of assets be realized as called for by the traditional accounting concept of cash flow, should gambling gains or gratuities received (gifts or bequests) be included, what permissible deductions were to be recognized as cost of earning, and so forth? These and similar questions were debated intensively, especially in the German literature of the 1870s and 1880s, with most prominent economists of the period participating therein, including Schäffle

(1861), Schmoller (1863), Meyer (1884), and Wagner (1892), to mention but a few.[3] Seligman (1919) was a major contributor in the United States. Valuable insights as well as confusion emerged, as the debate moved slowly away from the view of income as accounting proceeds or as shares in factor earnings. The goal was a generalized concept of gain, as reached finally in Schantz' seminal contribution (1896). "Income", so he argued, "equals the accumulation of wealth during a given time period, including the value of services received from others". With this formulation, the modern concept of income as accretion was coined, and many of the earlier issues - such as regularity, realization, or being part of national income became irrelevant. Once definded as accretion - or, which is the same, as addition to wealth plus consumption - personal income would be independent of regularity, realization, or source. Undistributed profits and gratuitous receipts became income, no less than dividends or factor earnings. Indeed, there was no longer a need for the sum of personal incomes to equal aggregate, national income, or factor earnings. All gains are to be included in the tax base. Thirty years later, the same concept was offered in the United States, apparently independently so, by R.M. Haig (1921);[4] but its final bloom, as noted before, came with the contribution of Henry Simons (1938 and 1950). His exposition of accretion soon became the bible of income tax reformers, extending through the decades of the 1950s, 1960s, and 1970s, on into the recent U.S. tax reform of 1986, perhaps its last gasp as some may hope and I fear.

But though the norm had been established, there remained the task of translating it into actual practice. Some improvements were made, most recently in the U.S. reform of 1986, but much remains to be done, be it in the U.S. or - and it seems even more so - in European income taxes. This story cannot be told here, but a few of the more frequent shortcomings may be noted. Whereas the accretion concept calls for full taxation of captial gains, unrealized gains remain excluded and realized gains are frequently taxed on a preferential basis. Tax-exempt interest on debt issued by lower levels of government is allowed. Imputed rent from owner-occupied residences which should be included remains usually overlooked, while mortgage interest is permitted as

---

[3] For a succinct analysis of the German debate, see Simons (1938).

[4] Even though Haig's position is generally linked to accretion, careful reading of his own paper suggests that his basic preference may have been for consumption. I am indebted to Professor David Wildasin for this point.

a deduction. Receipts from gifts and bequests are not in the base. Depreciation which should be allowed in line with the asset's exhaustion is frequently granted on an accelerated basis. Retained earnings of corporations which should be imputed to the shareholder are left out, and corporate source income which should be integrated with that of the shareholder is frequently subjected to an extra tax. In addition to these more basic problems, many other loopholes or tax preferences might be noted, reflecting the political pressures of the day. At the same time, other practices result in an undue tax burden. In particular, inflation adjustmens in the determination of capital income are imperfect or absent. The modern income tax is thus far from complying with the accretion norm. Yet without that norm, there would be no guide to income tax reform, and no logic by which arbitrary abuse could be restrained.[5]

III. The Case for Consumption as Tax Base

I now turn to the case for consumption rather than income as the "correct" tax base. While currently seen as a new and revolutionary idea, it also has its long-standing tradition. To begin with, two moralistic arguments in its favor may be noted. Hobbes' Leviathan (1654), and almost a century ahead of Adam Smith, required tax burdens to be distributed equally; but that equality of imposition was to call for consumption not income as tax base. "For what reason is there", so he argued, "that he who labors much should be charged more than he though living idly gets little and spends all that he gets? But when the impositions are laid upon those things which men consume, everybody pays equally for what he uses; nor is the Commonwealth defrauded by the luxurious waste of private men". A further case for the taxation of consumption rather than accumulation followed from the spirit of asceticism and its Puritan ethics as described by Max Weber (1905). With saving seen as virtue, there follows a moralistic case for taxing consumption as vice. Such feelings may or may not remain present in the current debate.

Morals aside, the economist's case for the consumption base, as far as I can see, was made first by John Stuart Mill (1848). Smith's requirement that the tax base be

[5] For the U.S. debate over tax reform in recent years, see Goode (1976), U.S. Treasury (1978), U.S. Treasury (1984), and Pechman, ed. (1977).

imposed in line with abililty to pay is translated into the dictum that individuals should be made to suffer an equal sacrifice. This, so Mill held, calls for proportional taxation, adding thereto the mistaken conclusion that thereby total sacrifice would be minimized. More important in our context is Mill's further proposition that equality of sacrifice requires consumption and not income as tax base. "The proper method of assessing an income tax", so he argues, "would be to tax only that part of income devoted to expenditure, exempting that which is saved. For when saved and invested it henceforth pays income tax on the interest which it brings, not withstanding that it has already been taxed on the principal. Unless, therefore, savings are exempted from income tax, the contributors are taxed twice on what they save and only once on what they spend... The difference thus created to the disadvantage of prudence and economy is not only impolitic but unjust". Choice of the consumption base, on the contrary, assures that the law will not distort "the natural competition between consumption and saving". The consumption base, therefore, is more in line with the equity requirement of equal treatment. And since it does not distort the choice between consumption and saving, it is also - to use modern terminology - preferable on efficiency grounds. Mill thus poses the subsequent argument at the outset. At the same time, Mill did not think that imposition of a personal consumption tax would be practicable. An income tax with lower rates on high saving groups is seen as the more feasible solution. Mill thus reverses Smith's earlier view as to which base is best and second best.

The case against the income base as imposing a double taxation of saving then came to be supported by major economic theorists, including (so I gather from only a brief reference) Alfred Marshall (1917), as well as careful treatment by Einaudi (1914) and Pigou (1928). The latter again faults the income tax with discrimination against saving and future consumption, but now with emphasis on the resulting inefficiency (dead-weight loss) rather than on Mill's primary concern with equity. The weight of the modern argument thus shifts away from equity and to the efficiency case for the consumption base.

This takes us to Irving Fisher (1937, 1942), that most emphatic early advocate of the modern expenditure tax. His case for consumption as tax base builds on his earlier contributions to captial theory, the theory of interest and time preference. A person's income, as traditionally defined (let me call it Y') may be either consumed or saved. The value of the capital in which the saving is invested then equals the discounted value of the future consumption stream to which it gives rise. With that stream seen as income (let me call it Y"), value is determined by income of the Y" type. The part of Y' which is saved in addition to capital, as Fisher sees it, and has to be excluded from what *he* calls the income base. The term income is thus used in two different ways, with Y' corresponding to incomings of the income tax concept (i.e., as incoming gains or accretion) and Y" corresponding to what is ordinarily called consumption. Terminological confusion aside, the main point once more is that defining the tax base as Y' results in double taxation of saving, the basic point made a century earlier by John Stuart Mill and in more straightforward terms.

All this, however, was not Fisher's main contribution to the tax base discussion. His main contribution was to demonstrate how the base of a consumption tax may be computed in practice. Consumption is to be arrived at not by collecting grocery bills but in an indirect fashion. All cash proceeds are added (be they from wages, dividends, interest, borrowing, sale of assets, or withdrawals from financial accounts) and all non-consumption uses of cash outlays (be they for investments, debt repayment, or addition to financial accounts) are deducted. His basic formula was thus quite in line with later formulations [Kaldor (1955); Meade Report (1978); Blueprints for Basic Tax Reform (1984)] and only refinement has been added. Fisher's demonstration that a person's aggregate consumption can thus be determined revolutionized the face of consumption as tax base. The earlier notion that consumption as tax base had to be impersonal or "objective" - as was the case of the retail sales and value-added tax - was dispelled; and, along with it, the notion that consumption-based taxes had to be regressive. Progressive rates and personal exemptions could be applied as under the income tax, and the taxation of consumption would no longer have to be second-rate. As a result, the politics of the consumption base was also changed, with Kaldor's case for a progressive expenditure tax aimed precisely at reaching England's upper classes which, though income-poor, could finance their tax-free consumption by liquidation of assets.

While critique of the income tax thus leads to an expenditure base, this was only one of two possible outcomes. The crucial objection, from Mill over Fisher, rested on the proposition that the taxation of interest (or capital) income discriminates against saving and hence future consumption. Such discrimination is avoided by exempting saving and moving to a consumption or expenditure base. But it may be avoided also, and it would seem more directly so, by exempting interest (the return to capital) from the base of the income tax. Using certain simplifying assumptions and disregarding transition problems, this would leave us essentially with an income tax on wage and rent income only. Why then has there been so little attention to putting the case against discrimination in these terms, emphasizing that the expenditure tax (with rent relativeley minor) is essentially similar to an income tax on wage income?[6] I find it puzzling to offer a convincing answer. Can it be that the case for taxing consumption (see our earlier reference to Hobbes and the Puritan ethics) sounds a lot more appealing than would that for singling out wages as the prime base for income taxation? Surrendering leisure is, after all, no less and may well be more burdensome than waiting. Indeed, is there not a long-standing tradition which, if anything, would view the return to labor as more (not less) deserved than that of captial income? I am reminded in this context of a paper on Thomas Aquinas which some fifty-seven years ago I wrote as a student in this university for Professor Bergsträsser's seminar. Your university itself is thus to be blamed or credited with my offering this linkage of fiscal economics and theology.

Back to economics. Here the problem is oversimplified by concern with the choice between present and future consumption only. Interference with work-leisure choice also imposes a dead-weight loss, whatever the timing of consumption. While the expenditure base bypasses discriminiation against saving, but both bases interfere with the choice of leisure, a choice which (contrary to what theorists conveniently assume) is not unrelated to that between present and future consumption. The problem clearly is more complex than is suggested by focusing on the timing of consumption only, and by viewing it as independent of the choice of leisure.

A further oversimplification arises by assuming that all accumulation is for purposes of future consumption only. Benefits derived from the holding of wealth - be they viewed in terms of security, power, or prestige - are neglected. Once they are included, as Henry Simons (1938) rightly urged that they should be, full exemption of interest or of saving is no longer neutral but biases the system in favor of saving. A two prongued system of consumption and wealth (or capital income) is thus called for.

Finally, it should be noted that not all savings need be eventually consumed. Instead, they may be passed on as gifts or be left as bequests. Their inclusion in the tax base of the donor and donee is thus essential if the tax base is to be neutral between all

[6] See for instance Stiglitz (1986), p. 533.

uses. The proper base should thus be viewed as encompassing all potential uses and not only consumption. In short, the case for the consumption base is less clear cut then may appear at first sight.

At a more practical level, I am also concerned that current proposals - referred to as cash-flow tax, modified income tax, and so forth - leave the public with a confused picture of what the acutal tax base is about. The public is told that there will be a business tax, and will like to hear this, but it hardly understands that this very tax (by granting expensing) is designed to leave capital income essentially untaxed. Other plans call for a so-called pre-payment tax which, at closer consideration, turns out to be a wage tax only. Lacking transparency may have political merit, but for tax policy to play its proper role in a democratic society, the concept of tax base and its index of ability to pay should be evident and easy to interpret.

IV. Minimizing Dead-Weight Loss

One further approach need be noted, now calling for the choice of tax base or, rather, of tax bases so as to minimize dead-weight loss. This concern now is applied not only to the timing of consumption but to all economic choices. In whatever way the tax bill is to be distributed across taxpayers, this should be done to collect the needed amount from any given payee so as to minimize his/her burden. Only a tax sadist would wish to do otherwise. The problem arises because taxes, when imposed on economic activity, cause a taxpayer to react to resulting changes in relative prices or returns. This response imposes a dead-weight loss or excess burden, so that the resulting burden exceeds the amount of tax that is paid. Such an excess burden could be avoided by the use of lump-sum or head taxes, but that solution is unacceptable as a matter of tax equity. While all taxpayers have only one head, they nevertheless differ in capacity to pay. The problem then is (1) to use those tax bases which minimize dead-weight loss, and (2) to distribute the resulting burden (including the remaining dead-weight loss) in an equitable fashion. In optimal tax terminology, this means to minimize total sacrifice, with individual burdens weighted by a postulated social welfare function.

Developed in recent years from the foundations laid by Pigou (1928) and Ramsey (1927) some fifty years ago, this approach - referred to, perhaps somewhat self-servingly, as optimal taxation - is now the generally accepted norm among the younger generation of tax theorists. Professor Rose and his students, as you well know, have been in the forefront of this development. Minimizing dead-weight loss establishes a presumption in favor of taxing products which are inelastic in demand, and of services which are inelastic in supply.

Salt and beer outrank yachts and champagne in eligibility as product tax bases; and the rent of land or other rent-like incomes once more reigns as the ideal base on the sources side. But the choice of tax bases also affects the burden distribution among income groups. Products which are inelastic in demand also tend to carry a low-income elasticity, and the services of unskilled workers may be more price elastic than those of wealthy professors and business executives. In order to minimize total sacrifice, the choice of bases thus becomes intertwined with the application of welfare weights, and this qualifies that choice.

While the optimal solution would suggest the use of multiple bases, the resulting task of reconciling efficiency and distributional considerations thus becomes highly complex. In the end, the better part of wisdom may well be to return to a uniform base, be it in terms of income or consumption.

This, as I see it, is the story which I was asked to tell. In doing so, I have focussed on how the "correct" tax base is to be defined, looking at the good tax system "an sich". (I am using this Kantian terminology because it fits well, even though my American colleagues will question it as typically German). The normative, of course, is only one part of the problem. Ranking income and consumption while assuming both to be implemented in perfect fashion is not the same as ranking them after difficulties of implementation are allowed for. As has been pointed out in recent years, and will be discussed at length in this conference, consumption bypasses certain difficulties inherent in the income base, including in particular the treatment of capital gains, of depreciation, and of inflation adjustments to capital income. But other troubles remain, such as the treatment of imputed rent. Still others are certain to emerge, should an outright expenditure tax be implemented. In particular, there is the problem of drawing a creditable line between what constitutes consumption and investment. The expenditure tax with its personalized approach to the consumption base is surely vastly superior to the value-added tax, not withstanding the latter's popularity in Europe and, potentially also in the United States. At the same time, I am not sure that expenditure tax administration will have such easy sailing as compared to the income tax.

The final choice has to be made among feasible options and not pure norms. My focus on the latter, therefore, gives not the entire picture. But it is not rendered irrelevant thereby. As J.S. Mill (1848) put it so nicely, perfect taxation, "like other standards of perfection, cannot be realized; but the first objective in every practical discussion should be to know what perfection is". At both these levels, the debate over income versus consumption is still open; and I would suggest may well remain so even after this conference is over.

References

Edgeworth, F.Y. (1897), The Pure Theory of Taxation, Economic Journal, reprinted in: R.A. Musgrave / A.Peacock (eds.) (1958), Classics in the Theory of Public Finance, London: Macmillan.

Einaudi, L. (1914), Corso di sciences delle finanze, 2nd ed., Turino.

Fisher, I. (1937), Income in Theory and Income Taxation in Practice, Econometrica 5, pp. 1-55.

Fisher, I. / Fisher, H. (1942), Constructive Income Taxation, New York: Harper.

George, H. (1869), Progress and Poverty, reprinted (1954), New York: Schalkenbach Foundation.

Goode, I.R. (1976), The Individual Income Tax, Washington, D.C.: The Brookings Institute.

Gunnison Brown, H. (1932), The Economic Basis of Tax Reform, Columbia: Lucas.

Haig, R.M. (1921), The Concept of Income, in: R.M. Haig (ed.), The Federal Income Tax, New York.

Hermann (1870), Staatswirtschaftliche Untersuchungen, München.

Hobbes, Th. (1654), Leviathan; C.B. McPherson, (ed.) (1968), New York: Penguin Books.

Kaldor, N. (1955), An Expenditure Tax, London: Allen & Unwin.

Lerner, A. (1944), The Economics of Control, Ch. 19, New York: Macmillan.

Locke, J. (1690), Two Treatises on Government; P. Laslett (ed.) (1963), Book II, Ch. 5., New York: New American Library.

Lotz (1837), Handbuch der Staatswirtschaftslehre, Erlangen.

Marshall, A. (1917), The Equitable Distribution of Taxation, reprinted in: A.C. Pigou (ed.) (1925), Memoirs of Alfred Marshall.

Meade, J.E. (1978), The Structure and Reform of Direct Taxation, London: Allen & Unwin.

Meyer, R. (1884), Die Principien der gerechten Besteuerung in der neueren Finanzwissenschaft, Berlin.

Mill, J.S. (1848), Principles of Political Economy; W.J. Ashley (ed.) (1921), London: Longman's, pp. 813-814.

Mills, O.L. (1921), The Spendings Tax, National Tax Journal.

Pechman, J.A. (ed.) (1977), Comprehensive Income Taxation, Washington, D.C.: The Brookings Institute.

Pigou, A.C. (1928), A Study in Public Finance, Ch. 10, London: Macmillan.

Quesnay, F. (1758), Le Tableau Économique.

Ramsey, F.P. (1927), A Contribution to the Theory of Taxation, Economic Journal XXXVII, pp. 47-61.

Rau, K.H. (1864), Grundsätze der Finanzwissenschaft.

Ricardo, D. (1817), The Principles of Political Economy and Taxation, London.

Schanz, G. (1896), Der Einkommensbegriff und die Einkommenssteuergesetze, Finanzarchiv 13, p. 1-88.

Schmoller, G. (1863), Die Lehre vom Einkommen in ihrem Zusammenhang mit den Grundprincipien der Steuerlehre, Zeitschrift für die gesamte Staatswissenschaft 19, pp. 1-86.

Seligmann, R.A. (1911), The Income Tax, New York: Macmillan.

Seligmann, R.A. (1919), Are Stock Dividends Income?, American Economic Review 9, pp. 517-536.

Simons, H. (1938), Personal Income Taxation, Chicago: University of Chicago Press.

Simons, H. (1950), Federal Tax Reform, Chicago: University of Chicago Press.

Smith, A. (1776), The Wealth of Nations, Vol. II.; E. Cannon (ed.) (1904), New York: Putnam.

Stiglitz, J. (1986), Economics of the Public Sector, New York: Norton.

U.S. Treasury Dept. (1978), Blueprints for Basic Tax Reform. Also see 2nd edition, Bradford, D. (ed.) (1984), Arlington: Tax Analyst.

U.S. Treasury Dept. (1984), Tax Reform for Fairness, Simplicity, and Economic Growth, Vol. 2, Washington, D.C..

Wagner, A. (1892), Grundlegung der Politischen Ökonomie, 3rd ed., Leipzig.

Weber, M. (1905), Die Protestantische Ethik und der "Geist" des Kapitalismus, Archiv für Sozialwissenschaft und Sozialpolitik, Vol. 4.1, pp. 1-54 and Vol. 4.2, pp. 1-110.

Wicksell, K. (1896), Finanztheoretische Untersuchungen, Jena: Fischer.

Wilke, G. (1921), Die Entwicklung der Theorie des Staatlichen Steuersystems in der deutschen Finanzwissenschaft des 19. Jahrhunderts, Finanzarchiv 38, pp. 1-108.

Wueller, P.H. (1938), Concepts of Taxable Income, Parts I and II, Political Science Quarterly 53, pp. 83-110 and pp. 557-583.

PART TWO

Theoretical and Empirical Foundations of Taxing Consumption

Robin Boadway

The Short Run and Long Run Welfare Effects of Implementing a Practical System of Consumption Taxation

I. Introduction

Tax reform seems to be a perpetual item on the policy agenda of governments around the world, reflecting the fact that we still do not seem to have it "right". There are many reasons for this. One is simply that judgments about what is the right tax system vary immensely across observers, even well-informed ones. This is inevitable given the value judgments involved. Another is that the reform process is itself potentially painful. Although tax reform may improve the efficiency of the economy and lead to some net gains, it is almost always the case that it also involves a reallocation of the tax burden among taxpayers with some gaining and others losing. Moreover, it also often involves transitional or short run windfall gains and losses. Governments apparently place great weight on these transitional effects. One of the main purposes of this paper is to investigate the interaction of these transitional gains and losses with longer run effects from a dynamic welfare economics point of view.

Tax reform can be disaggregated into two separate aspects, both conceptually and operationally. These are the choice of the base and the choice of the rate structure.[1]

[1] The distinction may not be so clear cut in the case of differential commodity taxation. We shall avoid the difficulties raised in this case by restricting our discussion to broadly-based taxes with proportional tax rates. It is not hard to come away from the optimal tax literature with the sense that differential commodity taxes do not add much of practical importance to the policy arsenal of governments over and above personal

Our discussion will concentrate entirely on the choice of the base. Ultimately, the choice of the tax base revolves around the treatment of asset income. There are three main types of taxes used by governments - personal taxes, general commodity taxes, and payroll taxes.[2] The latter two effectively exempt asset income from the tax base, while including non-asset income. From a tax base point of view, they are essentially equivalent to using consumption as a tax base. As for the personal tax, the treatment of asset income is the essence of the debate over whether the personal base should be consumption or some form of income. Thus, in general, we can pose our discussion equivalently as the choice between a consumption versus an income base, or the choice between taxing asset income or not.

The fact that the treatment of asset income is the essential tax base reform issue means that the associated problems are inherently dynamic in nature. Yet the literature on tax reform has evolved more or less independently of the literature on dynamic welfare analysis. This paper represents an exploration in the relationships between the two literatures, with a particular interest in determining what practical lessons can be learned from the theory. Much of the discussion will be heuristic rather than technical, despite the fact that the relevant literature is itself very technical. Much of it will also be synthetic in nature. The nature of the underlying technical arguments will be indicated where appropriate. An indication of the difficulty of the technical analysis is that, in that part of the the tax reform literature which emphasizes dynamic consequences, virtually all qualitative results have relied on simulation rather than analytical techniques.[3]

---

taxes and general commodity taxes. Apart from the usual separability arguments against differentiated commodity taxes (as outlined, say, in Atkinson and Stiglitz, 1980), there are equally compelling arguments based on ignorance of what the true underlying preference structure be. See the recent paper by Bruce (1989).

[2] Some might think of the corporation income tax as being yet another major separate tax. I prefer to think of it as an adjunct to the personal tax, which it is in those countries which use the imputation principle. Its inclusion in the discussion would make no substantial difference.

[3] A good summary of the state of the literature in this area may be found in Kotlikoff (1984). There are, of course, many results of the effects of tax reforms in a dynamic steady state setting. However, being steady state, they avoid many of the interesting dynamic effects by assumption.

We proceed as follows. A brief review is presented of the design issues involved in implementing a consumption base at the personal level, either alone or alongside commodity and/or payroll taxes. The emphasis will be on those design issues of relevance for the implementation of policy objectives of a dynamic welfare theoretic nature. Next, an equally brief review will be given of the sorts of welfare results that have been obtained in the tax reform literature. Then, a review of the theory of welfare economics as it has been developed in dynamic economies will be given. Attention will be restricted primarily to full information, perfect certainty settings. The problems of conducting dynamic welfare analysis in these economies are formidable enough. The extension of the analysis to stochastic economies with or without perfect information is still in its infancy. Following this, the welfare economics of personal tax reform will be considered in light of the welfare theory. Some attempt will be made to place the existing welfare results of tax reform in the broader perspective. Finally, the practical steps required to achieve dynamic welfare objectives will be considered.

II. Main Issues in the Design of a Feasible Consumption Tax Base

The literature on designing and administering a practical consumption tax base at the personal level is well-developed so we need not spend too much time on it here.[4] Instead, we simply reiterate some of the key issues which will be of relevance for our discussion of the welfare effects and which will relate consumption taxation at the personal level with payroll and commodity taxes as well as with personal income taxation.

The key feature which distinguishes these general tax bases is their treatment of assets. To see this, consider the following stylized definition of a consumption base:

$$C \equiv E + rA - \Delta A + (I-B) \qquad \text{(a)}$$

where C is consumption, E is current (non-capital) earnings, A is asset wealth, r is the rate of return on asset wealth, I is inheritances (or gifts received) and B is bequests (or

[4] See, for example, U.S. Treasury (1977).

gifts given).[5] This might be distinguished from the comprehensive income base, usually defined to be consumption plus the net accrual of wealth, or

$$Y \equiv C + \Delta A \equiv E + rA + (I-B) \qquad \text{(b)}$$

Thus, the consumption base should deduct additions to wealth but include all capital income. The income tax should only do the latter. Note at the outset that asset income which is saved rather than consumed has no current implications for the consumption tax base, while for the income base, it does. This immediately raises administrative difficulties for the income base since it means that accrual accounting and indexing will generally be required for capital income, while cash accounting can generally be used for the consumption tax. At the same time, the use of cash accounting for asset transactions requires that records be kept of asset holdings.

The treatment of assets as in (a) may not be suitable for all assets for a variety of reasons. For one, assets whose return rA takes an imputed form and is consumed when "earned" would impose measurement problems since rA is not observable on any market.[6] For another, the costs of record keeping could be quite high for liquid assets or assets which are held only for short periods of time. Also, the tax base defined by (a) may not be smooth over time and this could cause horizontal equity problems if marginal tax rates are not constant. Finally, there may be compliance costs with including I-B in the base.

Fortunately, as is well known from the literature, there is an alternative way of treating assets which is equivalent in present value terms and which avoids these

---

[5] In including net inheritances or gifts as consumption, we are implicitly assuming that the giving of bequests and gifts is not being interpreted as an act of consumption. If it were, *B* would not appear on the righthand side of (a), at least that part of *B* which constituted ***intentional bequests***. Then, if *B* were treated as part of the consumption of the donor, one could argue that *I* should not be treated as part of the consumption of the recipient for tax purposes. The issues of whether or not to include *B* and *I* in the tax base apply whether one is using consumption or income as the norm. We need not try to resolve the issue here. There are, of course, lots of other problems that are common to both. The non-taxability of leisure and household production and the treatment of the family would be two.

[6] This is also a problem for the income tax, and one which can not be avoided in the manner discussed below.

problems. It is simply to ignore all transactions involving the asset for tax purposes. For assets treated in this way, the flow terms $rA-\Delta A$ do not appear in the tax base. The taxes are said to be *prepaid* on the asset in the sense that its acquisition cost is not tax-deductible, but future interest and principle repayments are not taxable.

If capital markets function well, the present value of $rA-\Delta A$ will be zero for any asset. For assets treated on a tax-prepaid basis, there are no tax consequences whatsoever from transactions in them. Note that, if all assets were tax-prepaid, the tax system would be equivalent to an income tax system with capital income exempt, or, ignoring net bequests, to a labour income tax system.

For various reasons, it is desirable to require that some types of assets be treated on a consumption basis (or *designated* basis to use the term of the U.S. Treasury, 1977) and others on a tax-prepaid basis. Those that should be treated on a tax-prepaid basis include owner-occupied housing and other consumer durables, cash balances, and insurance policies, or any other asset which provides consumption services in the imputed form. On the other hand, assets in unincorporated businesses should be treated as designated and taxed on a cash flow basis. Otherwise, there would be a requirement to distinguish capital income (which is not taxable) from labour income, and firms would have an incentive to masquerade the latter as the former. Also, investment in human capital should be treated on a cash flow basis. To treat it as tax prepaid would require including forgone earnings in the tax base, that being one of the main costs of acquisition of human capital, and excluding income from accumulated human capital from the base. The latter is notoriously difficult to measure. Some have also argued that equity income might be treated as a designated asset [Economic Council of Canada (1987)]. The argument is that windfall gains and rents that are consumed are taxed under a designated base but not under a tax prepaid base. Equity assets are relatively more susceptible to receiving these forms of returns.

Apart from these requirements for individual assets, taxpayers should be given the choice as to which assets to prepay taxes on and which to designate. Such choice will enable them to economize on compliance costs, for example, by treating liquid assets as tax prepaid. It will also enable them to engage in self-averaging over the life cycle so as to avoid the disadvantages of a lumpy tax base when marginal tax rates are not constant or to overcome liquidity constraints. Variations in the marginal tax rate can be due either to a progressive tax structure or changes in the levels of tax rates over time.

Thus, the main implementation problems with taxing consumption according to the strict definition used in (a) can be avoided by suitable use of the tax prepaid method. That constitutes the main administrative advantage of consumption taxation over comprehensive income taxation. The latter is simply not a feasible tax base. Apart from the requirement to use accrual accounting for capital income and to index fully, the requirement to measure rA cannot be avoided. This poses insuperable problems in the case of human capital investments, unincorporated businesses, insurance, cash balances, and consumer durables. It is, therefore, not surprising that most so-called income tax systems are, in fact, much closer to consumption tax systems; that must inevitably be the case.

The above discussion makes clear the relationship between the personal consumption tax base and the other main taxes. General commodity taxes are basically like consumption taxes. Assuming they apply cash flow principles to *all* consumer purchases, they incorporate some elements of designated treatment and some of tax prepaid treatment. Consumer durables and other assets yielding consumer services in kind are effectively taxed on a prepaid basis. Most other assets are taxed on a designated basis, including human capital and unincorporated business investments. Unlike with a personal consumption tax, the taxpayer has no discretion as to which assets to treat on which basis. Similarly, payroll taxation is basically like the tax-prepaid method of taxing consumption. As such, it does not avoid the problems involved in taxing assets on a tax prepaid basis, problems which required certain assets to be designated under a personal consumption tax.

III. The Effects of Personal Tax Base Reform on Saving and Welfare

There has now developed a considerable literature on the welfare effects of reform of the personal tax base, particularly reforms which involve moving from an income base to a base which exempts asset income. Two variants of the latter are the wage tax and the so-called consumption tax. These correspond with treating assets on a tax-prepaid basis and a designated basis respectively. In this section, we summarize what positive and normative analysis there has been of moving from an income tax to a tax which exempts asset income in one of these two ways.

As Kotlikoff (1984) has stressed, the economic effects of tax reforms can be disaggregated into relative price effects and income effects. In the context of changes in the tax treatment of asset income, the relative price effects involve the removal of the tax distortion on capital income, or equivalently on the relative price of future consumption in terms of present consumption. As with all price changes, the effects of changes in the after-tax interest rate have ambiguous effects *a priori* on saving behaviour because of offsetting income and substitution effects.[7] However, in the case of saving behaviour, in addition to the usual income and substitution effects, there are some additional effects at work, one of which is that referred to by Summers (1981) as the *human wealth effect*. This effect refers to the reduction in the present value of lifetime earnings when the interest rate increases. Its effect is to reduce the perceived wealth of consumers and thus reduce current consumption and increase the interest elasticity of saving. Summers argued that taking it into account properly could increase the aggregate interest elasticity of saving from the previously-estimated upper limit of about 0.4 [Boskin (1978)] to the region of 2.0-4.0.[8]

The magnitude of the interest elasticity of saving is increased even further by taking account of another effect which might be termed the *human capital accumulation effect*. This effect reflects the fact that when the after-tax rate of interest rises, human capital investment is induced to fall as households substitute physical capital accumulation for human capital accumulation.[9] I know of no empirical estimates of this effect. Overall, taking account both of the human wealth effect and the human capital accumulation effect, we might expect the interest elasticity of saving to be positive and perhaps of significant magnitude.

The human capital accumulation effect arises because of the existence of an asset (human wealth) which is untaxed under the income tax system. Presumably a similar

---

[7] Although the effect on saving is ambiguous, the effect on future consumption is generally not. This distinction was analyzed in Feldstein (1978).

[8] Corroboration of this empirically is very difficult since it requires lifetime earnings and asset accumulation profiles by household and these are not available. An attempt to construct them from taxation statistics may be found in Beach, Boadway and Bruce (1988). Elasticities of savings estimated on the basis of these latter data were between 1.0 and 2.0 providing some support to the importance of the wealth effect.

[9] The effect of capital tax changes on human capital accumulation has been noted by Driffill and Rosen (1983) and Davies and St. Hilaire (1987).

effect applies with regard to consumer durables, which also tend to be tax sheltered under income tax systems. The removal of the tax on capital income reduces the incentive to hold wealth in this form as opposed to business capital and thus increases the interest elasticity of demand for the acquisition of other assets.[10] This effect, like the human wealth effect relies on capital markets being well-functioning, particularly on the absence of liquidity constraints. Little work has been done in this area. Overall, the combined effect of the substitution effect, the ordinary income effect, the human wealth effect, the human capital accumulation effect, and this consumer durable effect might be expected to result in a rather large interest elasticity of demand for saving in assets other than human capital and consumer durables.

In addition to the relative price effect of income tax reform, there are also income effects. The nature of these income effects depends upon the budget constraint imposed on the government during the tax reform. A common assumption is to require the tax reform to be revenue-neutral in each time period. In this case, the income effects are purely redistributive in each period. However, again following Kotlikoff (1984), it is useful to think of disaggregating the redistributive effects of the tax reform along two dimensions - an income and an age dimension. The former are referred to as *intragenerational* income effects and refer to the redistribution of the tax burden across similar aged persons in different (lifetime) income classes. Intragenerational income redistribution is affected largely throught the progressivity of the rate structure. The latter are called *intergenerational* income effects and refer to the redistribution of purchasing power among different age cohorts. Since we are discussing reform of the base rather than the rate structure, most of the interesting income effects are intergenerational ones, and we concentrate on these. Indeed, to avoid intragenerational effects, we will typically deal with proportional taxes applied to different bases.

Revenue-neutral reforms of the personal tax base have important intergenerational income effects which turn out to be important for welfare analysis. These can be deduced from comparing the life cycle profile of tax liabilities under various tax bases. Taxes on wage income are concentrated in the pre-retirement period of the life cycle. Taxes on capital income follow the pattern of asset accumulation which, according to

---

[10] Indeed, in countries which allow interest deductibility on the acquisition of consumer durables, the effect will presumably be even stronger.

the life cycle theory, should be hump-shaped. An income tax is a combination of these two. A tax on consumption follows the profile of consumption which is expected to rise over the life cycle. Comparing these various taxes, wage tax liabilities occur earlier in the life cycle relative to the tax on income, which, in turn, are earlier than those under the consumption tax.

These timing effects determine the intergenerational income effects from tax reform. Thus, substitution of an income tax for a wage tax has as one of its effects an ongoing transfer from older to younger cohorts. The substitution of a consumption tax for an income tax has a similar effect. Each has the same intergenerational impact as a reduction in the size of unfunded public pensions or a reduction in the size of the public debt. The incentive effect of these intergenerational income effects on saving should be unambiguous. Since, according to the life cycle theory, the propensity to consume out of wealth rises with age, a redistribution from older to younger cohorts should increase savings, and vice versa.

The magnitude of the intergenerational income effect is, of course, an empirical question, and one which is made more ambiguous by the presence of other effects. For one, to the extent that bequests are planned and are for altruistic reasons, the intergenerational transfer effects of tax reform on saving behaviour will be undone by offsetting bequests. This effect, the so-called *Ricardian equivalence theorem*, is well known in the context of public debt and unfunded public pensions [See Barro (1974)]. But, precisely the same effects are at work in tax reform. Another effect that may be present is that of imperfect capital markets which impose liquidity constraints on individual borrowing behaviour [Hubbard and Judd (1987)]. If households are liquidity-constrained early in life, the substitution of, say, a consumption tax for a wage tax may not increase savings since the marginal propensity to consume out of liquid funds early in life may be very high. Finally, uncertainty about the length of life combined with the absence of full annuity markets has been shown to have implications for the effect of intergenerational transfers on saving behaviour [Abel (1985); Hubbard and Judd (1987)]. In the case of public pensions, the benefits paid have the characteristics of an annuity. By providing a form of insurance against uncertainty in the length of life, they reduce the need to hold wealth for precautionary (self-insurance) purposes. This is wealth which partly ends up being transferred to the next generation through unintentional bequests. Thus, public pensions, whether or not funded reduce saving for this purpose. The same effect should be present with intergenerational transfer effects resulting from tax reforms. This effectively increases the responsiveness of capital accumulation to the intergenerational redistributive component of tax reforms.

As well as saving effects from income tax reform, there are likely to be effects on other factor markets. The income tax and the consumption tax both distort the labour-leisure margin. Since the base of the income tax is larger, its tax rate should be smaller and the distortion imposed on labour markets should therefore also be smaller than the consumption tax. Essentially, the consumption tax avoids the distortion on saving at the expense of a larger one on labour supply. Much of the literature essentially ignores the implications of the labour supply distortion, largely because, as will be evident below, the savings distortion effect is thought to be of much larger consequence in a dynamic setting. Our discussion below will also largely ignore the labour market distortions.

Given the parcity of reliable empirical evidence on the effects of tax reform on saving behaviour and the difficulty of doing either econometric or analytical work in the context of dynamic models, much of the analysis of tax reforms has relied on simulation modelling. The results from these models turn out to be highly suggestive and at the very least indicate that potentially large effects on capital accumulation, consumption and welfare can be obtained from major income tax reforms. It is worth reporting and trying to understand the reasons for these results. The starting point is the well known article by Summers (1981). Summers simulated the steady state effects of revenue-neutral changes from an income tax to each of a consumption tax and a wage tax in a single-sector overlapping-generations neo-classical growth model with identical households which save according to the life-cycle hypothesis with no bequests. The parameters of the model are chosen to correspond roughly with the stylized facts of the U.S. economy and tax system. Of particular importance, under the income tax, the tax rate on capital income was assumed to be 50 % and on wage income 20 %. The rate of growth of the economy was taken to be 3.5 % and the pre-tax rate of return on capital 10.5 %. Wages were assumed to rise exponentially over the life cycle. Household utilities were taken to be additively separable over time with instantaneous utility functions having constant elasticities of marginal utility.

The results of Summers' simulations were startling. They indicated that the substitution of a wage tax for the income tax would cause the following steady state changes for a typical case: the capital-output ratio would rise by about 40 %; per capita consumption would rise by about 13 %; and per capita lifetime utility would rise by about 5 %. The substitution of a consumption tax for an income tax would cause even bigger changes: the capital-output ratio by about 53 %, per capita consumption by about 16 %, and per capita utility by about 12 %. These are very big numbers when set against the sort of welfare changes one normally associated with tax reforms in static economies (and presumably they dwarf the welfare effects of changes in the labour market distortion).

The reasons for numbers of these magnitudes are easy to fathom, taking account of the relative price effects and the intergenerational income effects mentioned above. The move from the income tax to the other two taxes causes a rise in the after-tax rate of return on saving. Given the large human wealth effect built into the model, especially by the rising age-earnings profile, the interest elasticity of savings is quite high. Indeed, it is high enough to swamp an adverse intergenerational transfer effect involved in the change to the wage tax. Since the latter is collected earlier in life relative to the income tax, the intergenerational income effect of the change works against saving. Nonetheless, aggregate saving clearly rises as indicated by the rise in the capital intensity. The magnitude of the intergenerational income effect is apparent when we compare the consumption tax result with the wage tax result since the difference between these is identically equivalent to the effect of a transfer from older to younger cohorts. A substitution from a wage tax to a consumption tax would cause saving to rise, as indicated by the substantially higher capital intensity under the consumption tax.

The consequence of these rises in capital intensity for per capita consumption and welfare is another matter. As is well known, and as is discussed in the next section, an increase in capital intensity along the steady state path will cause consumption and welfare to rise if the pre-tax rate of return on investment exceeds the rate of growth of the economy. Furthermore, the rise will be larger the larger is that difference.[11] In the Summers world, the pre-tax rate of return exceeds the rate of growth by a considerable

[11] One way to see this is to consider the consequences for a representative cohort of a perpetual redistribution from the old to the young. Imagine the simple case were the only source of growth is population and cohorts live for only two periods. A tax of t per old person whose proceeds are transferred to the young yields $t/(1+n)$ per young person where n is the population growth rate. This transfer will cause lifetime wealth to rise by $t/(1+n) - t/(1+r)$, or $(r-n)t/[(1+n)(1+r)]$, where r is the rate of interest. The greater is r relative to n, the larger will this gain be.

margin, and that is the reason why the increase in capital intensity causes such an increase in consumption and utility.

The Summers analysis has spawned a considerable further literature on the long run effects of income tax reform. Basically, it has gone in two directions. One is to conduct the same sort of simulations under different sorts of assumptions or with richer models. The other is to simulate the full path from one steady state to another in response to tax reforms. Consider each briefly in turn.

Summers' results are based on simulations in the context of a specific model and obviously the results would vary with changes in the model or its parameters. We can do no more here than to indicate the direction in which effects would change if different assumptions were adopted. The first, and most dramatic, case to consider is the case in which bequests are allowed. Basing bequests on a crude utility-of-bequest function does not alter the results fundamentally [see Seidman (1983)], but basing them on an operative altruistic bequest motive does. In this case, all intergenerational income effects of the tax change are undone leaving only the relative price effects. The magnitudes of the welfare change associated with the move to the consumption tax would be reduced accordingly.

Allowing for different labour market assumptions also affects the quantitative results obtained. Auerbach, Kotlikoff and Skinner (1983) have adopted a number of different assumptions. Changing the age-earnings profile from exponentially increasing to strictly concave reduces the magnitude of the human wealth effect and therefore reduces the interest elasticity of savings. Allowing for a labour-leisure choice reduces the welfare gain from the changes to a wage or consumption tax. In fact, they are able to show that long run welfare may be reduced by the switch to a wage tax if labour supplies are elastic enough. Making retirement age variable can also reduce the welfare gains from the reforms. Also, allowing the tax system to have increasing marginal rates tends to exaggerate the magnitude of the existing results.

The Summers analysis has also been extended to an open economy setting by Gauthier (1988). In this case, the interest rate is fixed exogenously by world capital markets. One would expect, therefore, that the saving and welfare effects are correspondingly greater because the general equilibrium feedback of the interest rate is removed. This is, in fact, what happens unless the international tax crediting arrangements are such as to dissipate the gains. Another extension in the open economy setting has been presented by Boadway and Bruce (1988), though not with simulations. They have argued that in an open economy a perfect income tax system is very difficult to achieve. A corporate tax is needed to withhold from foreign corporations, assuming that corporations are taxed on the origin (source) principle. The corporate tax must be integrated with the personal tax to prevent distortions in the financing of firms. However, since the integration must be done at the personal level, and since world capital markets effectively segment the saving and investment sides of domestic capital markets, integration ends up undoing the tax on capital income at the personal level. The consequence is that small open economies which apply the imputation system to corporate source income are already treating it on a consumption tax basis at the personal level. Thus, the formal move to a consumption tax system would have minimal further impact.

An interesting extension is to allow for other assets in the economy besides reproducible business capital. Davies and Whalley (1989) have recently amended Summers' model to allow for human capital investment financed by forgone earnings and produced according to a technology which is strictly concave in time invested. Since human capital is basically treated on a consumption basis under the income tax, the tax system induces persons to substitute human capital for business capital whose return is fully taxable. When the tax substitutions are performed, the opposite occurs. Business capital is substituted for human capital. However, this causes the interest rate to fall, thus inducing more human capital to accumulate. In their simulations, they find that the interest rate after the tax substitution has occurred is not too different from the after-tax interest rate before the tax substitution. As a result, the quantity of human capital in the long run has not changed and the long run effect of the tax substitution on consumption and welfare has not been affected by the presence of human capital.[12]

Human capital is not the only sort of capital which tends to be sheltered from tax. Other sorts of capital are as well. One major form is consumer durables, including housing, automobiles, etc. As with human capital, these assets are substituted for non-sheltered capital under an income tax system. When the tax substitution is done, previously-taxable capital will be substituted for them. Again, the induced fall in the

[12] See, however, the discussion below concerning the transition. Here, human capital is important.

interest rate will minimize the extent to which consumer durables end up being reduced in the new tax situation. As with human capital, the presence of consumer durables may not affect the qualitative results of Summers in the long run. However, as discussed earlier, it may serve to reinforce the positive response of (business) capital accumulation to interest rate changes. No explicit analyses of this case appear to have been done.

Finally, we have mentioned above the possibility of liquidity constraints affecting the analysis. The substitution of a wage tax for an income tax may serve to tighten the liquidity constraint facing the consumer and effectively increase the saving response (by reducing dissaving). This is an extension of the analysis of Hubbard and Judd (1987). By the same token, a hypothetical change from a wage tax to a consumption tax may not have the saving-enhancing effect that would be predicted for it on the basis of the presumed difference in the propensity to consume in different age brackets. Again, no explicit simulations have been done of this.

The discussion so far has been about the long run (steady state effects) of tax reforms. The upshot tends to be that substituting a consumption-type tax for an income tax might be expected to increase saving significantly. And, given that the rate of return on investment is greater than the rate of growth of the economy, per capita consumption and welfare should rise significantly. The magnitudes will be greater to the extent that the assets are treated on a designated basis rather than a tax prepaid basis. The force of these results is reduced considerably when one takes into account transitional effects as has been done in a number of papers. The message of the transition is often quite clear. The long run gains of tax reform must often be accompanied by short run losses making the policymakers task very difficult.

A clear representation of the consequences of the transition in the Summers' model may be found in Auerbach, Kotlikoff and Skinner (1983).[13] They simulate the path of transition for the two cases of substituting a wage tax and a consumption tax for an income tax. Households are assumed to have perfect foresight about the future path of the economy so that they can foresee all relevant prices correctly over their life cycles. Policy changes are, of course, taken to be surprises. The results of the simulations are quite interesting and informative. Let us concentrate on the effect of the tax

[13] See also more extended versions reported in Auerbach and Kotlikoff (1987) and in Kotlikoff (1984).

substitutions on lifetime utility levels by age cohort or generation. In the case of the wage tax substitution, older cohorts alive at the time of the change obtain a windfall gain of sizeable proportions. For younger and future cohorts, the gain diminishes with time of birth and actually becomes negative in the long run.[14] The opposite occurs for the consumption tax substitution. Older generations lose and younger and future generations gain.

The source of the difference in the two cases is easy to see. Both tax substitutions have a relative price effect as a result of eliminating the tax on capital income. However, the wage tax collects income earlier in the life cycle than the consumption tax and this results in less demand for asset wealth. Equivalently, the difference between the wage tax and the consumption tax is essentially a continuing intergenerational transfer, in favour of older cohorts in the case of the wage tax. It is well known from, say, the literature on unfunded public pensions, that the introduction of an ongoing transfer from young to old causes a windfall gain to the older generations when instituted (and a corresponding loss to the old when extinguished).

This recognition that the intergenerational transfer component of tax reform is responsible for the initial windfall loss from instituting a consumption tax suggests the possibility that tax reform accompanied by appropriate lump sum transfers might be made Pareto-improving. Auerbach, Kotlikoff and Skinner show that this is indeed the case. By combining intergenerational lump sum transfers in the transition with a substitution of a consumption tax for an income tax (all in a period by period revenue-neutral way), the transition to the new steady state with higher per capita utility can be accomplished such that no cohort is made worse off as compared with the alternative income tax path.

Even this is not the end of the story. Once it is recognized that the essential difference between a wage tax and a consumption tax is an intergenerational transfer, it is readily apparent that the scheme of compensating intergenerational transfers in Auerbach, Kotlikoff and Skinner can be replicated by an appropriate mix of wage and consumption taxation along the adjustment path. Gauthier (1988) has indeed shown this to be the case. His simulations of the adjustment path in a Summers-type model show

[14] The long run loss is due to the endogeneity of labour supply and retirement age. As mentioned, in Summers' simulation of the same case, per capita utility rises in the steady state.

that a Pareto-improving move from an income tax to a consumption tax steady state can be accomplished by first instituting a wage tax and then gradually increasing the consumption tax and reducing the wage tax in a revenue-neutral way.[15] We return to the implications of these results in the last section of the paper.

Transitional analyses have also been conducted in other settings. An interesting case involves the model with human capital analyzed by Davies and Whalley (1988). As mentioned earlier, they found that in the long run the existence of human capital investment (whose return is untaxed under both actual income and consumption tax systems) does not significantly affect the long run equilibrium towards which the economy tends after a tax reform. However, the transition path is affected. The presence of endogenous human capital formation serves essentially to speed up the path of transition of the stock of business capital as households substitute it for human capital. Despite that, the transitional path of per capita utilities is remarkably similar to those found in Auerbach, Kotlikoff and Skinner (1983).[16]

The above analysis is essentially positive in nature in the sense that it reports the effects of tax changes on utility levels by cohort without making judgments or prescriptions. In fact, the literature on the normative analysis of income tax reform is relatively sparse. Almost all of it is done in the context of steady state or stationary state settings. A familiar result in the latter setting applies optimal tax theory to a single consumer in a life cycle setting. In the simplest case, consider a consumer choosing among three goods - present consumption, future consumption and leisure. Suppose the government can tax labour income and capital income at separate rates. Given a pre-determined government requirement, what are the set of optimal tax rates on capital and labour income?[17] In general, the optimal tax rates will mirror neither an income tax system (where the tax rate on capital and labour incomes are identical) nor a consumption tax system (where the tax rate on capital income is zero). The latter will be optimal if compensated cross price elasticities of demand for both present and future consump-

---

[15] Gauthier uses static expectations in his analysis as regards to both the future path of prices and the path of government policy. Presumably the analysis would survive other expectational assumptions.

[16] This is so despite the fact that static expectations rather than perfect foresight are assumed.

[17] This is equivalent to allowing the taxes to be levied on present and future consumption at different rates and solving for the optimal rates.

tion with respect to the wage rate are zero and the compensated elasticity of labour supply is zero.[18] Alternatively, the consumption tax will be optimal if present and future consumption are equally substitutable with leisure.[19] In general, the tax rates on labour income and capital income will differ. If future consumption is more complementary with leisure than is current consumption, it should be taxed more heavily (i.e., $t_r > 0$). Whether an income tax offers the appropriately higher rate is an empirical question. A global comparison between the two may or may not yield an income tax superior even in these circumstances. If it is not known which of present or future consumption is more complementary with leisure, an equal ignorance argument along the lines of Bruce (1989) would argue in favour of proportional taxation (i.e. consumption taxation).

The above argument can be extended to a dynamic setting by restating it in terms of a representative consumer in the steady state. King (1980) has shown that the same three-good setting as above extended to a steady state setting will yield an optimal commodity tax rule which is similar to the static case but contains one extra term. Precisely, the optimal tax structure is given by:

$$t_r r(-\sigma_{22}+\sigma_{H2})/(1+r) = t_w(\sigma_{HH}-\sigma_{2H})/(1-t_w) + (r-n)/(1+n)$$

where n is the rate of growth of the economy. Again, neither a pure consumption tax nor a pure income tax would in general be optimal.

Unfortunately, these optimal tax exercises do not capture the essence of the problem since they effectively abstract from the truly dynamic aspects. Income tax reforms (like debt policy and pension policy) are inherently dynamic in their effects and have consequences stretching far into the future. One of the purposes of this paper is to review the literature on dynamic welfare economics with a view to assessing its relevance for the tax reform debate. The next section sets the stage by presenting a review

---

[18] The exact formula for the rate structure is given by $t_r(1-t_w)/t_w = -(\sigma_{HH}-\sigma_{2H})(1+r)/[(\sigma_{22}-\sigma_{H2})r]$ where t_r and t_w are the factor tax rates, σ_{HH} is the compensated elasticity of labour supply σ_{22} is the compensated elasticity of demand for future consumption and σ_{2H} and σ_{H2} are compensated cross price elasicities. (See Sandmo, 1985). If $\sigma_{HH}=0$, $t_r=0$ at the optimum.

[19] Thus, $t_r=0$ if $\sigma_{HH}=\sigma_{2H}$, which in turn requires that $\sigma_{1H}=\sigma_{2H}$.

of some of the key results that have been derived in the literature, particularly results on dynamic efficiency.

IV. Dynamic Welfare Economics: A Cursory Review of the Literature

The literature on dynamic welfare economics has a long history going back to the growth theory of the 1960s. It is both an extensive and at times a difficult literature and we cannot do full justice to it here. It is also in many ways an incomplete literature. Most results are derived from very simple dynamic models, often single sector or even exchange economies, and almost always assuming perfect foresight and the absence of uncertainty. The focus is exclusively on efficiency issues rather than equity. Generally speaking, the idea is to investigate how well the two theorems of welfare economics hold up in a dynamic setting. Our survey will basically state relevant results rather than proving them.

We begin with some notation. A dynamic model specifies sequences of consumption $\{c_t\}$, capital stocks $\{k_t\}$, and primary factors of production $\{l_t\}$ over time, given initial stocks. The sequences $\{c_t\}$, $\{k_t\}$, $\{l_t\}$ are together referred to as a path P. The present value price sequence associated with commodities is denoted $\{p_t\}$. Special cases of dynamic economic models we consider include:

i) Single sector growth models (Solow-Swan neo-classical type)
ii) Exchange economy growth models
iii) Overlapping generation (OLG) models, with and without bequests
iv) Steady (or stationary) state growth paths along which per capita variables are constant.

What follows is simply a summary of the results obtained for a variety of welfare criteria in a variety of models.

1. Dynamic Production Efficiency

The concept of dynamic production efficiency and the derivation of results on it are due to Samuelson (1960) and Dorfman, Samuelson, Solow (1958). The results can be simply stated. Consider two paths P and $\bar{P}$ such that:

a) $\{c_t\} = \{\bar{c}_t\} \quad \forall\, t$

b) At a terminal date T, the stocks of all commodities but one are the same.

c) P has a larger terminal stock of that commodity than does $\bar{P}$.

Then $\bar{P}$ is dynamically inefficient. If no feasible P satisfies a) - c), then $\bar{P}$ is dynamically efficient.

Theorem: [Samuelson (1960); Dorfman, Samuelson, Solow (1958)]
A competitive allocation is dynamically production efficient.

2. Short-run Consumption Efficiency

A feasible path $\bar{P}$ is short-run consumption efficient over the time horizon $t = 1,....,T$ if there does not exist another feasible path P over the same horizon such that:

a) $c_t \geq \bar{c}_t$ for all $t = 1,...,T$ and $k_T > \bar{k}_T$

b) for some period τ $(1 \leq \tau \leq T)$, either $c_\tau^i > \bar{c}_\tau^i$ for some good i, or $k_T^i > \bar{k}_T^i$ for some capital stock k^i.

Theorem: [Cass, (1972)]
If a dynamic path is short-run consumption efficient, it is also a competitive path.

3. Consumption Efficiency

A path $\bar{P}$ is consumption efficient over the infinite horizon $t = 1,2,..., \infty$ if there does not exist any alternative feasible path P along which:

a) $c_t \geq \bar{c}_t$ for all t

b) for some $\tau \geq 1$ and for some consumption good i, $c_\tau^i > \bar{c}_\tau^i$ (given k_0).

Theorem: [Phelps, (1965) for single sector growth models]

Suppose k^* is the golden rule capital-labour ratio (i.e., the capital-labour ratio for the steady state which maximizes per capita consumption). Consider a path along which $k_t \geq k^* + \in$ for some $\in > 0$, all $t > t_0$ This is a consumption inefficient path.

Note that this theorem implies (using the result under 4. below) that steady state paths such that the interest rate is less than the rate of growth ($r < g$) are consumption inefficient. This is the case of *capital overaccumulation*. Such paths could, in principle, be competitive ones. An alternative way to put it is that the economy is dynamically inefficient if it invests (or saves) more than the return to capital in steady state. It is dynamically efficient if it invests no more than the return to capital.

Cass (1972) has generalized this result using an economy with a production technology:

$$k_{t+1} = f(k_t) - c_t$$

where $f(k_t)$ is a gross output function. (In this economy, the golden rule steady state is that for which $f'(k^*) = 1$.)

Theorem: [Cass, (1972) for single sector growth models]

Suppose capital stocks are bounded away from 0 and ∞ and that $f''(k_t) < a < 0$ for all k_t. A path satisfying that will be consumption inefficient if and only if

$$\lim_{t \to \infty} \sum_{s=0}^{t} \pi_s < \infty$$

where

$$\pi_s = \prod_{h=0}^{s-1} f'(k_h) \text{ (the future value of a unit of capital).}$$

Note that $1+R_t = (\pi_t)^{1/t}$ is a rate of interest. Cass has also generalized this to the many-commodity case.

4. Golden Rule Consumption Efficiency

A steady state path is golden rule consumption efficient if it generates a per capita consumption level that is higher than along any other steady state path.

Theorem: [Phelps, (1961)]

If there is a steady state path on which the net rate of return on investment (r) equals the rate of growth (g), then this steady state produces a path of consumption which is uniformly higher than the consumption path associated with any other steady state.

5. Golden Rule Optimality

This applies to OLG models and is the per capita utility equivalent of golden rule consumption efficiency. A steady state is golden rule efficient if there is no other steady state path which is Pareto-preferred by a representative generation.

Theorem: [Samuelson, (1958); Starrett, (1972)]

If a steady state consumption path is golden rule optimal, then the rate of growth is the associated interest rate; furthermore, if a competitive price system has g as its interest rate, then it is golden rule optimal.

Note that this theorem applies regardless of the number of commodities and of the number of time periods in each cohort's life.

6. Dynamic Pareto Optimality

A path of consumption vectors accruing to households indexed by date of birth t is called $\{c_t\}$. A path $\{\bar{c_t}\}$ is dynamically efficient if there exists no other consumption path $\{c_t\}$ such that :

a) $u_t(c_t) \geq u_t(\bar{c}_t) \quad t = 0,\ldots,\infty$

b) $u_\tau(c_\tau) > u_\tau(\bar{c}_\tau)$ for some $\tau \geq 0$

c) no more resources are used at any date for households $t = 0,\ldots,\infty$.

Note that this rules out generations $t = 0,\ldots,\infty$ from exploiting previous generations.

Theorem: [Starrett, (1972)]

a) If $r \geq g$ along a steady state path $\{\bar{c}_t\}$, then $\{\bar{c}_t)$ is dynamically efficient.

b) If $r < g$ along a steady state path $\{\bar{c}_t\}$, then $\{\bar{c}_t\}$ is dynamically inefficient.

This generalizes Phelps (1965) from dynamic consumption efficiency to dynamic Pareto optimality. The following result is for exchange economies only.

Theorem: [Balasko and Shell, (1980)]

Consider an exchange economy of two-period overlapping generations in which the sequence of $\{c_t\}$ is bounded from above. (This implies that the long run growth rates in endowments of all commodities are non-positive.) Given some mild uniformity conditions on consumer preferences, a consumption sequence $\{c_t\}$ is dynamically Pareto optimal if and only if:

$$\sum_{t=0}^{\infty} \frac{1}{|p^t|} = 0.$$

Note that this roughly translates into the idea that a growth path is dynamically Pareto optimal if long run interest rates do not exceed long run growth rates. It generalizes Cass (1972) in a sense.

7. Weak Pareto Optimality (WPO)

This is a concept defined by Balasko and Shell for exchange economies. A path $\{\bar{c}_t\}$ is weakly Pareto optimal (WPO) if there is no alternative path $\{c_t\}$ with the properties:

a) $\Sigma\, c_t = \Sigma\, \bar{c}_t$

b) $c_t = \bar{c}_t$ except for a finite t

c) $u_t(c_t) \geq u_t(\bar{c}_t)$ with at least one inequality.

Theorem: [Balasko and Shell, (1980)]

If $\{\bar{c}_t\}$ is dynamically Pareto optimal, then it is also WPO (but not necessarily the reverse).

8. Short-run Pareto Optimality (SRPO)

This is also defined by Balasko and Shell for exchange economies. A path $\{\bar{c}_t\}$ is SRPO if there are no alternative $\{c_t\}$ and $t' \geq 0$ such that:

a) $\Sigma\, c_t = \Sigma\, \bar{c}_t$

b) $c_t = \bar{c}_t$ for every $t \geq t'$

c) $u_t(c_t) \geq u_t(\bar{c}_t)$ with at least one strict >.

Theorem: [Balasko and Shell, (1980)]

$\{\bar{c}_t\}$ is SRPO if and only if it is WPO.

Theorem: [Balasko and Shell, (1980)]

Every competitive allocation is WPO; every WPO allocation is a competitive allocation associated with some suitably-assigned endowments.

9. Dynamic Pareto Optimality in an Uncertainty Setting

In a recent paper by Abel, Mankiw, Summers and Zeckhauser (1986), the Starrett (1972) result on dynamic Pareto optimality has been extended to a growing economy with uncertain production technology. Define individual expected utility functions as:

$$u(c_t^y) + E_t v(c_{t+1}^0)$$

where c_t^y is consumption of the young in period t, c_{t+1}^0 is the consumption of the old in t+1 and E_t is the expectation conditional on information available at t. Households work a fixed amount when young and receive a wage which is partly saved. Savings go to purchase equity in firms, the only asset available. Asset market equilibrium requires:

$$E_t \left[\frac{v'(c_{t+1}^0)R_{t+1}}{u'(c_t^y)} \right] = 1$$

where $R_{t+1} = (V_{t+1} + D_{t+1})/V_t$ for the market portfolio, with V_t the value of shares in t and D_t the value of dividends. The production technology is a general one and is given by:

$$Y_t = F(I_{t-1}, I_{t-2}, \ldots, I_{t-n};\ N_t, \theta_t)$$

where I_t is investment, N_t is population and θ_t is the state of nature in period t.

The concept of dynamic Pareto optimality is defined in terms of expected utilities. Let

$$\Omega(\theta_t) = u(c_t^y(\theta_t)) + E(v(c_{t+1}^0(\theta_{t+1}))|\theta_t)$$

be expected utility for generation t born in state of nature θ_t. An initial equilibrium is dynamically inefficient if it is possible to increase $\Omega(\theta_s)$ for some θ_s without decreasing $\Omega(\theta_t)$ for any other θ_t. If such a Pareto improvement is impossible, the equilibrium is dynamically efficient.

Theorem: [Abel, Mankiw, Summers, Zeckhauser (1986)]
If $D_t / V_t \geq \epsilon > 0$ in all periods and all states of nature, then the equilibrium is dynamically efficient. If $D_t / V_t \leq -\epsilon < 0$ in all periods and all states of nature, then the equilibrium is dynamically inefficient.

This result can be stated in an alternative way by defining

$$G_{t+1} \equiv V_{t+1} / V_t \quad .$$

Recall that R_{t+1} was the rate of return on the market portfolio as defined earlier.

Theorem: [Abel, Mankiw, Summers, Zeckhauser (1986)]
If $R_t / G_t \geq (1 + \in) > 1$ in all periods and all states of nature, then the equilibrium is dynamically efficient. If $R_t / G_t \leq (1 - \in) < 1$ in all periods and all states of nature, then the equilibrium is dynamically inefficient.

The above result applies for the market rate of return. They also show that the result holds for the rate of return on any arbitrary asset.

This completes our summary of the literature on dynamic efficiency. What remains now is to consider the consequences of it for the issue of income tax reform. While we couch our discussion in terms of tax reform, it should be obvious that much of the same discussion can be applied to pension and government debt reform.

V. The Relevance of Dynamic Welfare Theory for Tax Reform

We have seen in section III that moving from an income base to a consumption-type base involves two distinguishable effects - a relative price effect and an intergenerational transfer effect. The relative price effect could increase or decrease saving depending on the relative sizes of the substitution and various income and asset substitution effects. However, of all these effects, only the ordinary income effect works to reduce the saving response to a rise in the after-tax interest rate. The substitution effect, the human wealth effect, the human capital accumulation effect and the consumer durable asset substitution effect all increase the responsiveness of saving to removal of the tax on capital income. Thus, we might expect the relative price effect to increase capital accumulation. By the same token, we might expect the static efficiency gain of removing the capital income distortion to be large relative to any increased distortion that might be imposed on labour markets due to the higher effective tax on labour income.[20] As for the intergenerational transfer effect, in the absence of fully operative bequests and with reasonably functioning capital markets, saving will increase if the tax change involves a transfer in favour of younger generations, and vice versa. The use of designated asset treatment will involve a redistribution in favour of the younger cohorts augmenting the saving response, while tax-prepaid treatment will redistribute in favour of older ones.

The consequences of these changes in saving for welfare have been the subject of keen interest in the literature. The prominence given to Summers' startling result of the enormous potential gain in per capita welfare reflects this. What is important to recognize is that the large gain in steady state utility in moving from the income tax to the consumption tax is attributable largely to the assumed difference in the pre-tax rate of return on investment r (10.5 %) and the rate of growth in the economy g (3.5 %). Similar long run gains would accrue from other policies designed to increase the saving rate, including reducing unfunded public pensions or reducing the government debt, both of which operate through intergenerational redistributive effects.

The policy question is whether the observed difference between r and g can be used to make an unambiguous case for policies which increase the saving rate. Feldstein (1977a) has essentially argued for increasing the saving rate on precisely these grounds. One suspects that the consensus among, say, U.S. economists that the saving rate is too low, that social security should be funded, and that the public debt is too high are all ultimately based on similar arguments about the long run effects of increasing the capital stock. However, what is equally clear from the welfare economic discussion of the previous section is that a case for increasing the saving rate can *never* be made solely on the basis of dynamic inefficiency.[21] Indeed, dynamic inefficiency can only

---

[20] Auerbach, Kotlikoff and Summers (1983) argued that this need not necessarily be the case. However, their simulations did not include, for example, the endogenous human capital accumulation effect. Driffill and Rosen (1983) have argued that the endogeneity of human capital formation adds considerably to the deadweight cost of income taxation relative to consumption taxation. Their findings have been supported by Davies and Whalley (1989).

[21] A similar point has recently been made in the context of unfunded public pensions by Breyer (1989). He has shown that when $r > g$, an economy with an unfunded public pension is Pareto efficient. *A fortiori*, regardless of whether r is greater or less than g, unfunded public pension schemes can never be eliminated in a Pareto-improving way.

apply when there is too much capital rather than too little, and then only under rather restrictive considerations. Thus, if attention is restricted to a finite horizon setting or if r is not less than g forever, dynamic inefficiency no longer applies.

In the absence of dynamic inefficiency, policies based on purely redistributive transfers across generations cannot be Pareto-improving. Thus, deficit reduction, the funding of social security and the move from a wage tax to a consumption tax in a world with fixed labour supplies cannot be Pareto-improving. Some other arguments must be brought to bear. One possible one would be to use equity arguments based on an inter-generational social welfare function. Thus, a permanent redistribution from the old to the young would increase the capital stock. If $r > g$, per capita utility would rise in the long run, albeit at the expense of welfare of older cohorts. To justify this on equity grounds would require that the marginal social utility of income gains to the younger exceeds that to the older, something which might be hard to subscribe to if per capita utilities are rising over time.[22] Some other argument is required.

Efficiency-based arguments for increasing the saving rate can only be realized when the policy involves the elimination of "static" distortions. However, in a dynamic setting the possibilities become quite interesting. This can be seen by reconsidering and extending the transitional analyses of Auerbach, Kotlikoff and Skinner (1983) and Gauthier (1987). Recall that these authors have shown that a move from an income tax to a consumption tax can be accomplished in a Pareto-improving way if, in the case of Auerbach, Kotlikoff and Skinner, lump sum transfers are permitted during the transition, or if, as in Gauthier, the transition is made first from the income tax to the wage tax and then gradually to the consumption tax. Understanding the mechanisms at work will help to show how much more widely these arguments can be applied. The following diagrammatic treatment can be shown to apply more rigourously algebraically.

Figures 1 and 2 depict lifetime utility by cohort indexed by age of birth under various tax regimes. Consider Figure 1 first. The lines labelled C-tax, Y-tax and W-tax represent the steady state per capita lifetime utility levels achieved under the pure consumption tax (all assets treated on a designated basis), the income tax and the wage tax (all assets treated on a tax-prepaid basis), respectively. The diagram abstracts from

---

[22] On the other hand, simply summing up the monetary gains in lifetime consumption over time would show a positive amount if $r > g$. The greater monetary gain to the younger may outweigh their lower marginal social utilities of income.

technical change and also assumes that, as in Auerbach, Kotlikoff and Skinner but unlike Summers, that steady state utility under the income tax exceeds that under the wage tax. The discussion below actually applies more vigourously when the opposite is the case. The curves labelled a, b and c represent the path of per capita utility by cohort resulting from immediate transitions from the income tax to the wage tax, the income tax to the consumption tax, and the wage tax to the consumption tax. The former two involve both relative price effects on capital markets and intergenerational transfers, while the latter is a purely intergenerational transfer. For simplicity, let us ignore distortions on labour markets by assuming that labour supply is fixed. In fact, all that is required is that there be a static welfare gain from the substitution of a consumption-type tax for an income tax.

Figure 1 also shows a series of dashed lines, each one flatter than the other. These lines represent transitional paths from a wage tax to a consumption tax done more and more gradually. Along one of these paths, the move is made from the wage tax to the consumption tax gradually by allowing an increasing proportion of assets to be treated as designated rather than tax-prepaid. The slower is the transition, the flatter is the curve. As the transition is made slower and slower, the per capita losses to the older generations becomes less and less, but losses are spread out among more generations. If the transition is made slow enough, the per capita losses can be made indefinitely small, but for a large number of generations. It is this ability to reduce the per capita losses from intergenerational redistributive policies that accounts for the possibility of Pareto-improving tax reforms as simulated by Auerbach, Kotlikoff and Skinner (1983) as well as Gauthier (1987). These possibilities are depicted in Figure 2.

In Figure 2, a fourth steady state per capita utility level is added - that in the Golden Rule steady state where $r=g$. Of course, the Golden Rule path generally involves more than tax policy; it will also likely involve some explicit redistribution from older to younger cohorts, the opposite of social security or debt financing. Again the other curves represent transitional paths. In interpreting these transitional paths, note that moving from either C-tax or W-tax to the Y-tax can be done gradually enough to make per capita utilities fall for losing generations by arbitrarily small amounts. (Such paths are not depicted on the diagram.) The path labelled a corresponds with that simulated by Auerbach, Kotlikoff and Skinner (1983). They allowed for an immediate switch from an income tax to a consumption tax accompanied by a series of intergenerational transfers designed to ensure that the older generations were just compensated for their additional tax burden. Gauthier (1987) showed that their transition could also be accomplished by changing first to a wage tax and then gradually to a consumption tax. This would have an equivalent effect to the cohort specific transfers of Auerbach *et al.*

However, it is apparent that there are an indefinite number of paths of transition from the income tax to the consumption tax which would be Pareto-improving for all generations. For example, path b illustrates the case where the transition is slower from the wage to the consumption tax. The older generations gain more, at the expense of the later generations. Obviously, a whole sequence of such paths could be chosen. Which one will be preferred depends on interpersonal lifetime utility comparisons.

The potential for Pareto-improving policy changes is much wider still. There is no reason to restrict the end point to be the consumption tax steady state. In Figure 2, the transition path c represents a Pareto-improving move right to the Golden Rule steady state. This will be possible because of the fact noted earlier that a move from the C-tax steady state to the Golden Rule can be made gradually so as to reduce the loss to an arbitrarily small amount. Of course, the transition to the Golden Rule will be longer than to the C-tax path. Other end points are obviously also possible. Thus, there will be an extremely large number of possible paths which can only be ranked by some sort of intergenerational utility comparisons. Again, while the marginal utility will be lower on paths closer to the Golden Rule, the monetary measure of gains in moving from the income tax will also be larger.

In light of the discussion of the previous section, it is clear that the possibility for these dynamic Pareto-improving policy changes cannot be a result of dynamic inefficiency as that term is understood. Rather, they exist because of traditional static deadweight losses. In the case of the income tax, there is a static deadweight loss which persists over time. Eliminating the deadweight loss and "investing" the proceeds in a higher capital stock can give rise to significant long run gains with no loss in short run utility levels.

The transitional paths described above require the elimination of the capital market distortion combined with a phasing in of the intergenerational redistributive component of the policy change. As has been pointed out, the latter can be done by the complementary use of lump sum transfers as in Auerbach *et al*, or it may be done by a gradual change in the proportion of assets treated on a tax prepaid basis and on a designated basis as proposed by Gauthier. The latter is the only way of proceeding practically. However, the implementation of the gradual transition is not a trivial problem. Most proponents of a personal consumption base would presumably like to decentralize the decision as to which assets to hold in which form to the households, subject to certain constraints. As we have seen, consumer durables and other assets which yield an imputed return would have to be treated on a tax prepaid basis, while unincorporated business assets and human capital investment at the very least would have to be designated. Otherwise, taxpayers might be given freedom decide how other assets might be treated so as to allow their tax liabilities to vary appropriately over the life cycle and to minimize transaction costs. It would be practically very difficult for the government to exercise wide discretion as to which proportions of assets should be treated in which way, especially since, during the transition, the proportions would have to vary with the age of the person. Moreover, as should be obvious, allowing a completely decentralized determination of those proportions will not generally result in a Pareto-improving path.[23]

Apparently, the government could not rely solely on a personal consumption tax during the transition. It would have to use supplementary instruments. Such instruments are available in the form of indirect consumption taxes (i.e., general sales taxes such as the VAT) and payroll taxes. The transition from an income to a wage to a consumption tax would have to be achieved by instituting a payroll tax and gradually replacing it with a general sales tax.

Things would be further slightly complicated by the existence of many types of assets. The simulation models reported above largely relied on a single asset model whose return varied instantaneously. Equity ownership of business capital would be an example of this. However, the existence of other asset types whose tax treatment varies gives rise to windfall gains or losses due to asset revaluation effects.[24] Attempts to introduce Pareto-improving tax changes must take these into account. An important class of such assets would be consumer durables such as housing which are tax-shel-

[23] The actual path would obviously depend upon how expectations of households were formed about the path of the tax rate over the life cycle.

[24] This phenomenon was first pointed out by Feldstein (1977b) in the context of the land tax.

tered and are used partly as a store of wealth. A tax change which removed the tax on capital income and increased the after-tax return on capital would reduce the price of housing thereby imposing a sudden windfall loss on existing homeowners. Since equity ownership in housing tends to increase with age, this increases the loss suffered by these persons from a switch directly to a tax on consumption from a tax on income. Furthermore, the use of a wage tax during the transition may not be enough to offset the loss to the older generations. Thus, the transition may require a gradual switch from an income to a wage tax in the first instance before the consumption tax is phased in. The switch would have to be slower the more durable the stock of housing. Redistributional problems during the transition may also be encountered in other assets. For example, holders of fixed interest securities would get a windfall gain as interest rate reductions would increase the market value of their assets (assuming, of course, that the tax change is unanticipated).

A natural final question that arises is whether the transition should be really required to satisfy the Pareto principle. Knowing that a move to the Golden Rule path could be accomplished by an appropriate phasing in of the tax reforms, could we not simply advocate moving there directly by tax policies which immediately increase the saving rate? Those who might argue in favour of that point of view might use two sorts of arguments. The first is the "traditional" applied welfare economics arguments in favour of treating efficiency arguments separately from equity ones as espoused, say, by Harberger (1971). Harberger has argued forcefully that policymakers should simply tote up the monetary gains and losses, and pursue policies which maximize the net gain. This has sometimes been justified on the basis of hypothetical compensation criteria of the Kaldor-Hicks variety. However, accepting the compensation criterion amounts *de facto* to making an interpersonal welfare comparison strongly in favour of the *status quo*. This amounts to an extreme version of existing property rights. I do not find the compensation criterion a compelling ethical argument.

The separation of efficiency from equity considerations might also be justified on the argument that instruments for redistribution may be separated from those for equity. While that may be an appropriate view to take when evaluating projects, it seems not to be so when evaluating changes which have intergenerational redistributive consequences, such as a substitution of a consumption tax for a wage tax. The reason is that the latter policy is, in fact, equivalent to the policy which the government would be using as the equity instrument. Thus, the separation of equity from efficiency considerations in this context makes no sense.

One other position that could be taken is that in the dynamic context it is not at all clear which path to take as the *status quo* against which to require that policy changes be Pareto-improving. After all, the paths involve utility levels of future generations and it is hard to imagine expectations concerning those utility levels being binding on existing government policies. At most, one might argue that currently-alive generations be made no worse off by the policy changes. Taking this point of view, therefore, does not compel policy changes to be Pareto-improving forever.

Whether or not Pareto-improvements are a necessary condition for dynamic policies, the requirement to make intergenerational welfare comparisons cannot be avoided if one is to take a position on which policies are to be preferred. For such normative comparisons, some sort of intergenerational social welfare function is needed. It is obviously very difficult to imagine how policy prescriptions based on an such a social welfare function could ever be implemented, even more so than the use of social welfare functions in a purely static setting. Actual governments of the day interested only in the welfare of alive generations will obviously have an incentive to redistribute in their own favour at the expense of future generations, at least in the absence of an operative bequest motive. Surely this is one of the most important policy dilemmas of all time.

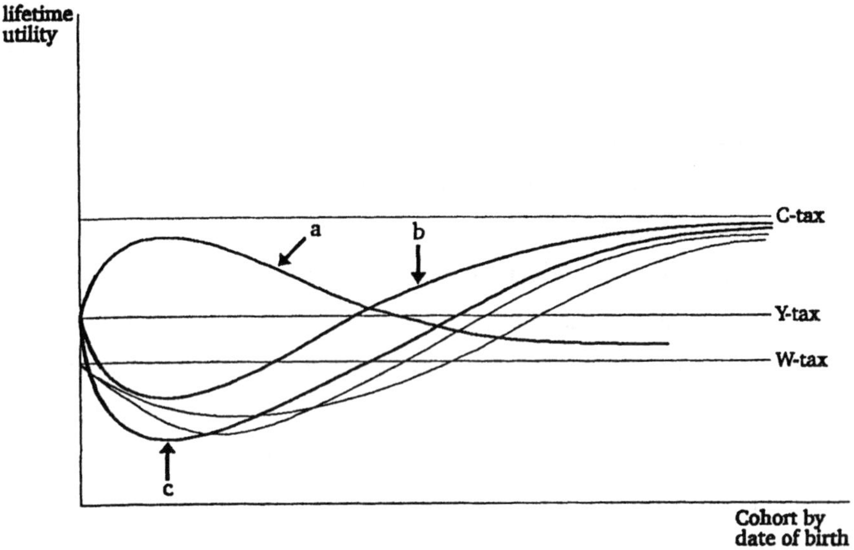

Figure 1

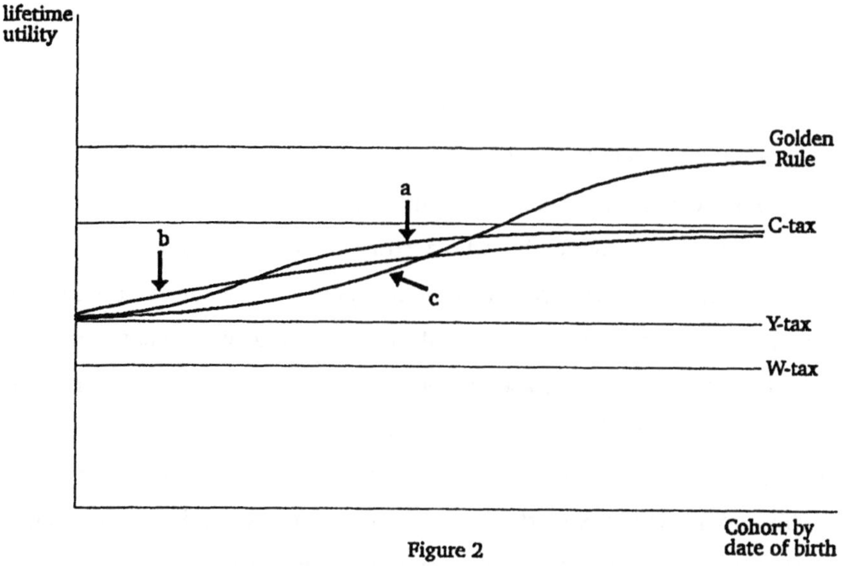

Figure 2

Comments by Michael Ahlheim

The paper by Robin Boadway can be divided into four main parts. In the first part the concept of a personal consumption tax and its most important properties are introduced to the reader, and the differences between this tax and a comprehensive income tax are elaborated. This part draws a very clear and concise picture of the whole idea of a consumption tax and its variants which is understandable also for readers who have not worked on this subject before.

After this introduction the author turns to the problems of tax reform, i.e. to the economic consequences of substituting a consumption tax or a wage tax (which is the so-called tax prepayment version of a consumption tax) for an income tax. Though some of the effects arising from such a tax reform work against saving most of them encourage it and so the result (as stated on page 58) is that "substituting a consumption type tax for an income tax might be expected to increase saving significantly". At this point my first question arises: At the beginning of this chapter it is said that effects like the human wealth effect, the human capital accumulation effect and the consumer durables effect are increasing the interest elasticity of saving and not just saving itself, as a naive reader would have guessed. My problem is that I could not find an argument which supports this thesis in general. The only cases I could think of were examples where this effect depended - via the income elasticity and the substitution elasticity - on the special features of the respective preference ordering. So, this effect should be made clear a bit more detailed, as I think.

This point seems to be of some relevance since such a rise in the interest elasticity of saving could easily reverse the whole story of a consumption tax raising private saving: The increase in private savings as it is expected to occur as an immediate result of such a tax substitution tends to lower interest rates in a general equilibrium setting so that with the higher interest elasticity of saving the first-round effect of increasing private saving could easily be off-set or even reversed. So the final effect of a consumption tax on private saving could be much more uncertain than the literature on consumption tax normally suggests. I think it is one of the merits of this chapter that it makes very clear the ambiguity of the arguments which are commonly stated in favour of a consumption tax.

The next chapter is called "Dynamic Welfare Economics: A Cursory Review of the Literature" and it has all the advantages and disadvantages of a review which is really cursory. To start with the advantages this chapter gives a rather comprehensive collection of the criteria of dynamic efficiency and of dynamic Pareto optimality which are known from the literature.

The disadvantage of such a cursory review is necessarily that the concepts to be dealt with cannot be explained in a satisfactory way. The author states definitions and theorems concerning nine different kinds of efficiency and Pareto optimality most of which stem from different articles with different basic assumptions. Since there are nearly no additional explanations with respect to the economic meaning and relevance of the different concepts a reader who is not already an expert in this special field might feel a bit lost. Looking for a device to help him out of this fix he could have a look at the next chapter to see which of these concepts are really used to support the economic reasoning there.

Concerning efficiency I got the impression that in principle the concept of David Starrett (1972) as cited on page 66 is the most important one for the understanding of the last chapter. It simply says that a steady state path is dynamically efficient if and only if it is associated with an interest rate that is not smaller than the growth rate of the economy. The economic intuition behind this theorem seems to be rather obvious since in common growth models of the Swan-Solow type in these cases per capita consumption could not be raised without raising the capital intensity of the economy. So there is no overaccumulation of capital and no unnecessary saving as would be the case if the interest rate were smaller than the growth rate of the economy. This concept also seems to correspond to the theorem on consumption efficiency by Phelps which is stated on page 64 and it surely has some connection with the other concepts of efficiency stated in this chapter. But I think that such a connection is far from being obvious, e.g. in the case of the efficiency theorem of David Cass as stated on page 64. So some additional remarks on the relations between the various definitions and theorems would be of great value here.

Turning to the concept of Pareto optimality I got the impression that the definition that fits best into the reasoning of the last part of this paper is not stated here at all. I am talking of the definition given by Balasko and Shell (1980, p. 286) which says that a consumption path c is Pareto optimal if there is no other path that is associated with the same aggregated life-time consumption but which leads at least in one period to a higher utility level and in no period to a lower utility level than path c. So this definition consists only of conditions a) and c) of the definition of weak Pareto optimality as stated on pages 66 and 67 by Boadway. I think that this definition fits better into the discussion of the following chapter than the one stated on page 66. Besides, there seems to be a mistake in the definition given by Boadway: The present values of the norms of the period price vectors associated with a Pareto optimal consumption path should converge to zero so that the sum of their reciprocal values goes to infinity. This, again, corresponds to the idea that the long run growth rate of the economy should not exceed the long run interest rate, which is exactly the opposite to Boadways interpretation (on p. 66).

In section 9 of this chapter we find two theorems on "Dynamic Pareto Optimality in an Uncertainty Setting" though the reasoning throughout the whole paper relies completely on perfect information, as I understand. So the question arises why these rather complicated theorems are quoted here at all.

Summing-up I must admit that this chapter is not my favourite one. The purpose of such a chapter could be to give an impression of the state of the art. But this target cannot be reached by merely quoting the main theorems if these are of a highly technical nature and can hardly be understood without the theory surrounding them. Some additional explanations would be helpful here. Another purpose could be to prepare the theoretical ground for the following discussion. To reach this target it would have been sufficient to state one theorem on dynamic efficiency and one on dynamic Pareto optimality and to build the economic arguments of the following chapter around these theorems. The chapter here seems to be a compromise of both ideas which leaves the reader a bit frustrated.

The last chapter of the paper deals with problems of transition arising when a consumption tax or a wage tax is substituted for an income tax and examines the relevance of dynamic welfare theory for the evaluation of such tax reforms. As a first result it is pointed out that in a real world economy, normally the interest rate will never be smaller than the rate of growth so that these economies will always be efficient in the sense of the afore-mentioned criterion. So, as the author puts it, a case for increasing the saving rate by substituting a consumption tax for an income tax can never be made solely on the basis of dynamic efficiency under real world conditions. This means that the concept of dynamic efficiency is irrelevant for the evaluation of such a tax reform.

But it is shown that the elimination of static inefficiencies like the deadweight loss that is caused by an income tax through the discrimination of future consumption can lead to Pareto improving tax policies. It is demonstrated how the life time per capita consumption and utility gains which accrue from the substitution of a consumption or a wage tax for an income tax can be redistributed in a way that is Pareto superior to the income tax situation. The working of the respective policies proposed by Auerbach/Kotlikoff/Skinner (1983) on the one hand and by Gauthier (1987) on the other is described in a very comprehensive and easy-to-understand way in this chapter. Nevertheless, since these policies rely heavily on measures that are not feasible in practice, like e.g. lump-sum transfers, the author seems to be rather pessimistic with respect to the practical use of these Pareto improving policies.

So the conclusion of this chapter and of the whole paper (which, however, is not stated there explicitly) seems to be that the different concepts of dynamic welfare economics are only of little or no importance for the evaluation of real-world tax reform policies. Or, applying this result to the subject of our congress: There is no hope that a tax reform towards a consumption tax which is feasible in practice can be justified by arguments of dynamic efficiency or dynamic Pareto optimality.

References

Abel, A.B. (1985), Precautionary Saving and Accidental Bequests, American Economic Review 75(4), pp. 777-91.

Abel, A.B. / Mankiw, N.G. / Summers, L.H. / Zeckhauser, R.J. (1986), Assessing Dynamic Efficiency: Theory and Evidence, National Bureau of Economic Research Working Paper No. 2097.

Atkinson, A.B. / Stiglitz J.E. (1980), Lectures on Public Economics, New York: McGraw-Hill.

Auerbach, A.J. / Kotlikoff L.J. (1987), Dynamic Fiscal Policy, New York: Cambridge University Press.

Auerbach, A.J./ Kotlikoff, L.J. / Skinner, J. (1983), The Efficiency Gains from Dynamic Tax Reform, International Economic Review 24(2), pp. 81-100.

Balasko, Y. / Shell K. (1980), The Overlapping-Generations Model, I: The Case of Pure Exchange without Money, Journal of Economic Theory 23(3), pp. 281-306.

Barro, R.J. (1974), Are Government Bonds Net Wealth?, Journal of Political Economy 82(6), pp. 1095-1118.

Beach, Ch.M. / Boadway R.W. / Bruce N. (1988), Taxation and Savings in Canada, Ottawa: Economic Council of Canada.

Boadway, R.W. / Bruce, N. (1988), Problems with Integrating Corporate and Personal Taxes in an Open Economy, Queen's University Discussion Paper No. 735.

Boskin, M.J. (1978), Taxation, Saving and the Rate of Interest, Journal of Political Economy, 2 (2, part 2), pp. 3-27.

Breyer, F. (1989), On the Intergenerational Pareto Efficiency of Pay-as-you-go Financed Pension Schemes, Journal of Institutional and Theoretical Economics, forthcoming.

Bruce, N. (1989), Efficient Tax Reform Without Lump-Sum Taxation: An 'Equal Ignorance' Argument for the Level Playing Field, mimeo.

Cass, D. (1972), On Capital Overaccumulation in the Aggregative, Neoclassical Model of Economic Growth: A Complete Characterization, Journal of Economic Theory 4 (April).

Davies, J.B. / St-Hilaire, F. (1987), Reforming Capital Income Taxation in Canada, Ottawa: Economic Council of Canada.

Davies, J. / Whalley, J. (1989), Taxes and Capital Formation: How Important is Human Capital?, mimeo.

Dorfman, R. / Samuelson, P. / Solow, R. (1958), Linear Programming and Economic Analysis, New York: McGraw-Hill.

Driffill, E.J. / Rosen, H.S. (1983), Taxation and Excess Burden: A Life-Cycle Perspective, International Economic Review 24(3), pp. 671-83.

Economic Council of Canada (1987), Road Map for Tax Reform, Ottawa: Ministry of Supply and Services.

Feldstein, M.S. (1978), The Rate of Return, Taxation and Personal Savings, Economic Journal 88 (September), pp. 482-87.

Feldstein, M.S. (1977a), Does the United States Save Too Little?, American Economic Review Papers and Proceedings 67 (February), pp. 116-21.

Feldstein, M.S. (1977b), The Surprising Incidence of A Tax on Pure Rent: A New Answer to an Old Question, Journal of Political Economy 85 (April), pp. 349-60.

Gauthier, D. (1988), Taxation and Savings: A Study of Tax Alternatives Using an Applied Dynamic Life Cycle Growth Model, Ph.D. Thesis, Queen's University, unpublished.

Harberger, A.C. (1971), Three Basic Postulates of Applied Welfare Economics: An Interpretive Essay, Journal of Economic Literature 9(3), pp. 785-97.

Hubbard, R.G. / Judd, K.L. (1987), Social Security and Individual Welfare, American Economic Review 77(4), pp. 630-46.

King, M.A. (1980), Saving and Taxation, in: G.A. Hughes / G.M. Heal (eds.), Essays in Public Policy, London: Chapman and Hall, pp. 1-35.

Kotlikoff, L.J. (1984), Taxation and Savings: A Neoclassical Perspective, Journal of Economic Literature XXII(4), pp. 1576-1629.

Phelps, E. (1961), The Golden Rule of Accumulation, American Economic Review 51(3), pp. 638-43.

Phelps, E. (1965), Second Essay on the Golden Rule of Accumulation, American Economic Review 55(3), pp. 783-814.

Samuelson, P.A. (1958), An Exact Consumption-Loan Model of Interest with or without the Social Contrivance of Money, Journal of Political Economy 66(6), pp. 467-82.

Samuelson, P.A. (1960), Efficient Paths of Capital Accumulation in Terms of the Calculus of Variations, in: K. Arrow / S. Karlin / P. Suppes (eds.), Mathematical Methods in the Social Sciences, Stanford: Stanford University Press.

Sandmo, A. (1985), The Effects of Taxation on Savings and Risk Taking, in: Alan J. Auerbach / Martin Feldstein (eds.), Handbook of Public Economics, Vol.I, Amsterdam: North-Holland, pp. 265-311.

Seidman, L.S. (1983), Taxes in a Life Cycle Growth Model with Bequests and Inheritances, American Economic Review 73(3), pp. 437-41.

Starrett, D.A. (1972), On Golden Rules, the "Biological Theory of Interest", and Competitive Inefficiency, Journal of Political Economy 80(2), pp. 276-91.

Summers, L.H. (1981), Capital Taxation and Capital Accumulation in a Life Cycle Growth Model, American Economic Review 71(4), pp. 533-44.

United States Treasury (1977), Blueprints for Basic Tax Reform, Washington: U.S.G.P.O..

John Kay

Consumption and Income Taxation: Horizontal Equity and Life Cycle Issues*

I. Introduction

"What reason is there, that he which laboureth much, and sparing the fruits of his labour, consumeth little, should be more charged, than he that liveth idlely, getteth little, and spendeth all he gets: Seeing the one hath no more protection from the commonwealth than the other?"

Hobbes, *Leviathan*, Ch. XXX

If Hobbes were alive today, he would be required to express himself somewhat differently. Consider two individuals, one of whom laboureth much, supplying labour l_m, while the other, living idlely, supplies l_i. Both face the same wage, w, while m but not i spares a fraction s of the fruits of his labour.

Now contrast an income tax, at rate x_y, with a consumption tax imposed at rate x_c. Under the income tax, individual m consumes an amount $(1-x_y)(1-s)wl_m$ and i an amount $(1-x_y)wl_i$. If the two individuals have identical utility functions in consumption and labour u(c,l) with $u_c > 0$, $u_l \leq 0$, they enjoy respective utilities

* I am grateful to Syed Ahsan and Wilhelm Pfähler for discussion of an earlier version.

$$m: u((1-x_y)(1-s)wl_m, l_m) \qquad i: u((1-x_y)wl_i, l_i)$$

and pay respective taxes

$$m: x_y wl_m \qquad i: x_y wl_i \quad .$$

Since $l_m > l_i$, m makes a greater tax payment although if, for example, $s > 1 - \frac{l_i}{l_m}$, then i enjoys higher utility.

Under a consumption tax at rate c, however, utilities achieved by the two individuals are now

$$m: u(\frac{(1-s)wl_m}{1 + x_c}, l_m) \qquad i: u(\frac{wl_i}{1+x_c}, l_i)$$

and respective tax payments

$$m: \frac{x_c}{1+x_c}(1-s)wl_m \qquad i: \frac{x_c}{1+x_c} wl_i$$

If $u_l = 0$, then $u_m > u_i$ if tax payments by m are greater than tax payments by i, and the inequities of the income tax are avoided.

This formulation is at once longer and less elegant than that of Hobbes, but it does have the advantage of focussing attention immediately on a number of issues which have been central to the subsequent literature on equity questions in the choice between income and consumption taxes.

First, note that Hobbes anticipates not only a number of fiscal policy arguments, but also the Keynesian consumption function. He which laboureth much spareth the fruits of his labour, while he that liveth idly chooses, or is compelled to, spend all he gets. Thus the average propensity to consume diminishes with income, at least in cross-section data. The distribution of income is more unequal than the distribution of consumption: correspondingly, the distribution of tax payments based on income is more egalitarian than the distribution of tax payments based on consumption, if the two tax schedules are the same.

Next, observe that, as presented, sparing the fruits of one's labour is simply irrational. He which laboureth much would enjoy unambiguously higher utility by ceasing to spare the fruits of his labour. This problem can be dealt with in one of two ways. We might assume that the spared fruits of labour generate utility just as do the consumed fruits. Thus the utility function becomes u(c,s,l) with $u_s > 0$ and in this case respective utilities under the income tax may be written

$$m: u((1-x_y)(1-s)wl_m, (1-x_y)swl_m, l_m)$$
$$i: u((1-x_y)wl_i, 0, l_i)$$

with tax payments as before. Although the inequity which was the subject of earlier concern is not now impossible, the case in which the arguments of m's utility function are simply dominated by those of i can now be excluded. This "spot" view of intertemporal choice - in which current utility depends on potential as well as consumption in the current period as well as actual consumption in that period - underlies much discussion of the comprehensive income tax.

An alternative means of resolution is to observe that m may well be sparing the fruits of his labour with a view to enjoying retirement in which he spares also the labour itself. Here consumption is c_1 in period 1 and c_2 in period 2 with utility function $u(c_1,c_2,l)$. Fruit spared in period 1 is enhanced at a rate r by period 2 but this enhancement is, of course, subject to income tax. Now we have under the income tax respective utilities of

$$m: u((1-x_y)(1-s)wl_m, (1+(1-x_y)r)s(1-x_y)wl_m, l_m)$$
$$i: u((1-x_y)wl_i, 0, l_i)$$

and tax payments

$$m: x_y wl_m((1+rs)(1-x_y)) \qquad i: x_y wl_i$$

while under the consumption tax utilities are

$$m: u\left(\frac{(1-s)wl_m}{1+x_c}, \frac{(1+r)swl_m}{(1+x_c)}, l_m\right) \quad i: u\left(\frac{wl_i}{1+x_c}, 0, l_i\right)$$

and tax payments

$$m: \frac{x_c}{1+x_c} wl_m(1+rs) \qquad\qquad i: \frac{x_c}{1+x_c} wl_i$$

We may note here that if $x_y = \frac{x_c}{1+x_c}$, then the tax payments by m and i are identical under both income and consumption taxes. Since $l_m > l_i$, individual m pays more in both cases. In the life cycle model, the potential inequity is that he which laboureth much pays more tax than he that liveth idly, and this is true whether he which laboureth much chooses to spare the fruits of his labour or not.

Whether there is indeed inequity may depend on the role played by l_i and l_m. If $u_l = 0$, then m enjoys unambiguously higher utility than i, and it is difficult to disagree with an outcome in which this is reflected in higher tax payments. Our concern is that labour involves disutility and hence that i may achieve higher utility levels. The key problem is our inability to tax leisure and that is common to both income and consumption taxes.

But this should alert us to a broader problem in the treatment of equity issues. If m and i indeed have identical utility functions, why does one labour much while the other liveth idlely? If, on the other hand, they are different, what is the basis of the comparisons under which horizontal equity - the equal treatment of similar individuals - is to be assesed?

Hobbes' model therefore introduces us to the principal issues of equity in the choice between income and consumption taxes. Is equity to be judged from a "spot" or "life cycle" perspective? Do we rank individuals by reference to the consumption possibilities available to them over their lifetime, or over some shorter interval? How should an equitable tax system respond to differences between individuals in the tradeoff between goods and leisure? How, if at all, should the principle of horizontal equity be interpreted? And what are the distributional implications of consumption or income based taxation? Subsequent sections of this paper consider these issues. Sections II and III develop a framework for analysing equity issues over the life cycle. Section IV explores the implications for horizontal equity.

II. Income and Consumption Taxes in a Simple Life Cycle Model

The life cycle framework is a useful means of exploring the choice between income and consumption taxation. Auerbach and Kotlikoff (1987) and Zodrow (1989) have developed simulation models by employing specific assumptions about income patterns and utility functions. The approach adopted here is closer to that of Bradford (1980), Graetz (1980) and Bradford (1986) who consider the relations between alternative tax structures under general assumptions about earnings profiles and preferences. Although their arguments are now well enough known to be described by Zodrow as "the standard paradigm", no rigorous or comprehensive explanation of these relationships appears to exist. In this section I seek to develop a framework for that purpose.

Over his lifetime (O,L) an individual receives labour income w(t) and spends at a rate z(t). He accumulates assets A(t) and, in the absence of gifts and bequests, A(O) = A(L) = 0. In any period, incomings are therefore (w+rA) and outgoings z, so that in the absence of taxes

$$(1) \qquad \mathring{A} = w + rA - z$$

and hence

$$(2) \qquad A(t) = \int_t^L (z-w)e^{-r(y-t)}dy \int_0^t (w-z)e^{r(t-y)}dy \; .$$

Proposition 1

In the absence of gifts and bequests, and given a fixed and certain return on capital, a consumption tax x_c and a tax on labour income x_L are identical if $x_L = x_c / (1+x_c)$.

With a tax on labour income at rate x_L, (1) becomes

$$(3) \qquad \mathring{A} = (1-x_L)w + rA - z$$

and with a tax on consumption at rate x_c, (1) becomes

$$(4) \qquad \mathring{A} = w + rA - (1+x_c)z \ .$$

With a tax on labour income, a consumption plan z(t) is feasible if

$$(5) \qquad \int_0^L \{(1-x_L)w + rA - z - \mathring{A}\}e^{-rt}dt \geq 0$$

ie. if

$$(6) \qquad \int_0^L (1-x_L)we^{-rt}dt \geq \int_0^L z(t)e^{-rt}dt$$

since

$$A(0) = A(L) = 0$$

Under a consumption tax z(t) is feasible if

$$(7) \qquad \int_0^L (w + rA - (1+x_c)z - \mathring{A})e^{-rt}dt \geq 0$$

as above if

$$(8) \qquad \int_0^L we^{-rt}dt \geq \int_0^L (1+x_c)z(t)e^{-rt}dt \ .$$

Thus the sets of feasible consumption plans are identical under the two taxes if and only if $(1-x_L) = \frac{1}{(1+x_c)}$ so that $x_L = \frac{x_c}{1+x_c}$ as in section I.

Hence if this condition holds, the same consumption plan z(t) will be chosen under both tax regimes. Moreover, under the labour income tax the present value of revenue is

$$x_L \int_0^L we^{-rt}dt \; ,$$

while under the consumption tax it is

$$(9) \qquad x_c \int_0^L ze^{-rt}dt = \frac{x_c}{1+x_c} \int_0^L (w+rA-\dot{A})e^{-rt}dt \text{ from (4)}$$

$$(10) \qquad = \frac{x_c}{1+x_c} \int_0^L we^{-rt}dt$$

and hence the two taxes yield identical revenue.

With a comprehensive income tax at rate x_y, (1) becomes

$$(11) \qquad \dot{A} = (1-x_y)(w + rA)-z \; .$$

Consider first an individual with a fixed pattern of lifetime labour income w(t). Then under the labour income tax the present value of lifetime tax payment is

$$X = \int_0^L x_L we^{-rt} \, dt$$

and under the comprehensive income tax

$$X = \int_0^L x_y (w+rA)e^{-rt}dt$$

Proposition 2 follows immediately.

Proposition 2

A comprehensive income tax raises more or less revenue than a labour income tax at the same rate, or an equivalent rate consumption tax, as the average discounted value of lifetime assets $\int_0^L Ae^{-rt}\,dt$ is greater or less than zero.

The value of $\int_0^L Ae^{-rt}dt$ reflects, in a loose sense, how late in a lifetime an individual chooses to consume. We might seek to make this more precise.

Figure 1 illustrates two alternative consumption paths, each with the same present value. z_1 is, in an obvious sense, later than z_2 and this is reflected in Figure 2, which compares cumulative values. The analogy with Lorenz dominance is obvious [see Atkinson (1970)]. The relationships in Figure 1 and Figure 2 are straightforward but, as Figures 3 and 4 show, the dominance pattern shown in Figure 2 is consistent even with a much more ambiguous pattern than that displayed in Figure 1.

Thus a consumption plan z is unambiguously *later* over the lifetime than an alternative z_2 with the same present value if

$$\int_0^L z_1 e^{+r(\tau-t)}dt \le \int_0^L z_2 e^{r(\tau-t)}dt \quad \forall\ \tau \in (0,L)\ .$$

We are also, however, interested in comparing profiles with different present values. Consider the patterns z_2' and z_2'' in Figure 5. z' is, we might suggest, later than z_2' (although it is mainly smaller than z_2') and it might also be seen as later than z_2''. If we adopt this definition then we have a more general concept.

Definition 1

A consumption plan $z_1(t)$ is later than an alternative $z_2(t)$ if

$$\int_0^{\tau} z_1 e^{+r(\tau-t)} dt \leq \int_0^{\tau} z_2 e^{r(\tau-T)} dt \text{ for some } \tau_0 \text{ and } \forall\ \tau \leq \tau_0.$$

We can now look at the effect of earlier or later consumption plans on tax liabilities and on the value of lifetime consumption.

Proposition 3

For a fixed time pattern of labour income w, an individual with a later consumption plan pays more tax under a comprehensive income tax, and enjoys a lower present value of lifetime consumption.

With a comprehensive income tax, we have

$$(12) \qquad \mathring{A} = (1-x_y)(w+rA)-z$$

and with fixed w

$$(13) \qquad \mathring{A}_1-\mathring{A}_2 = (1-x_y)r(A_1-A_2)-(z_1-z_2) \ .$$

Hence:

(14)

$$\int_{T_1}^{T_2} (\mathring{A}_1-\mathring{A}_2)e^{-rt}dt = (1-x_y)r\int_{T_1}^{T_2} (A_1-A_2)e^{-rt}dt - \int_{T_1}^{T_2} (z_1-z_2)e^{-rt}dt$$

and so

(15)

$$[(A_1-A_2)e^{-rt}]_{T_1}^{T_2} = -x_y r \int_{T_1}^{T_2} (A_1-A_2)e^{-rt}dt - \int_{T_1}^{T_2} (z_1-z_2)e^{-rt}dt \ .$$

We show first that the single crossing case (as z_2'' in Figure 5) cannot arise where w is the same on both consumption paths.

Suppose there is some $\hat{\tau}$ such that

$$\int_0^{\hat{\tau}} (z_1-z_2)e^{+r(\hat{\tau}-t)}dt = 0 \ .$$

Then by setting $T_2=\hat{\tau}$ and $T_1=0$ in (15), we have

$$(16) \qquad [A_1-A_2]e^{-r\hat{\tau}} = - x_y r \int_0^{\hat{\tau}} (A_1-A_2)e^{-rt}dt$$

and also by setting $T_2=L$ and $T_1=\hat{\tau}$

$$(17) \qquad -(A_1-A_2)e^{-r\hat{\tau}} \le - x_y r \int_{\hat{\tau}}^{L} (A_1-A_2)e^{-rt}dt \ .$$

Hence

$$\int_0^L (A_1-A_2)e^{-rt}dt \le 0 \ .$$

Now set $T_2 = L$ and $T_1 = 0$ in (15) and find

$$(18)\qquad x_y r \int_0^L (A_1 - A_2)e^{-rt}dt = \int_{T_1}^{T_2} (z_2 - z_1)e^{-rt}dt$$

which makes

$$(19)\qquad \int_{T_1}^{T_2} z_2 e^{-rt}dt > \int_{T_1}^{T_2} z_1 e^{-rt}dt \ .$$

Thus we need only consider cases like z_2 in Figure 5 where

$$\int_0^{\tau} (z_1 - z_2)e^{-rt}dt < 0 \ \forall \ \tau \text{ in } (0,L) \ .$$

Then set $T_1=0$ and $T_2=L$ in (15) and it is immediate that z_2' involves a higher present value of lifetime consumption and a lower present value of lifetime tax payment.

Now relax the assumption of fixed w and consider individuals who differ in their lifetime earnings profile. We can define early and late earnings patterns in essentially the same way as we have defined early and late consumption patterns. Thus:

Definition 2

An earnings profile $w_1(t)$ is later than an alternative $w_2(t)$ if

$$\int_0^{\tau} w_1 e^{-r(\tau-t)}dt \le \int_0^{\tau} w_2 e^{-r(\tau-t)}dt \text{ for some } \hat{\tau} \text{ and } \forall \ \tau < \hat{\tau} \ .$$

The comprehensive income tax penalises late consumers among those with the same pattern of lifetime earnings: it also penalises early earners among those with the same pattern of lifetime consumption. This can be expressed in

Proposition 4

For a fixed time pattern of consumption z, an individual with a later earnings profile pays less tax under a comprehensive income tax and requires a lower present value of lifetime earnings.

The proof is essentially similar to that of proposition 3.

We start from the relation

$$\mathring{A}_1 = (1-x_y)(w+rA)-z$$

and since z is fixed we can now write

$$(20) \qquad \mathring{A}_1-\mathring{A}_2 = (1-x_y)((w_1-w_2)+r(A_1-A_2)) \ .$$

Hence

$$(21) \qquad [(A_1-A_2)e^{-rt}]_{T_1}^{T_2} = (1-x_y)\int_{T_1}^{T_2}(w_1-w_2)e^{-rt}dt$$

$$- x_y r\int_{T_1}^{T_2}(A_1-A_2)e^{-rt}dt \ .$$

Again, we show that the single crossing case w_2'' cannot occur and hence that all unambiguous comparisons between early and late earnings profiles are as between w_1 and w_2''. Hence Proposition 4 follows.

III. Extensions to the Basic Model

The framework presented in Section II assumes that individuals enter and leave the world with $A(O) = A(L) = 0$ so that there are no gifts or bequests. If these assumptions are relaxed we have

Proposition 5

A tax on labour income at rate x_L, combined with a tax on accessions at the same rate, is equivalent to a tax on consumption at rate x_c, combined with an equal rate tax on bequests, if $x_L = x_c / (1+x_c)$.

From (3) and (4) we have

$$\dot{A} = (1-x_L)w+rA-z$$

and

$$\dot{A} = w+rA-(1+x_c)z$$

under the income and consumption taxes respectively. In the income tax case, assume a tax on accessions $\hat{A}$ at rate x_L so that $A(O) = (1-x_L)\hat{A}$, so that a consumption plan is feasible if

$$(22) \qquad (1-x_L)\hat{A} + \int_0^L (1-x_L)we^{-rt}dt \geq \int_0^L z(t)e^{-rt}dt + \hat{B}$$

where $\hat{B}$ is planned bequests.

In the consumption tax case with bequests charged at rate x_c, z(t) is feasible if

$$(23) \qquad \hat{A} + \int_0^L we^{-rt}dt \geq \int_0^L (1+x_c)z(t)e^{-rt}dt + (1+x_c)\hat{B} .$$

It follows that the sets of feasible consumption plans are again identical if $x_L = x_c / (1+x_c)$ and it can easily be shown that tax revenue is the same in the two cases.

Advocates of expenditure based taxation rarely suppose that a pure consumption tax is feasible. Almost all commodities are, to a degree, durable (think not only of refrigerators, but also of haircuts and meals in fine restaurants) and it is therefore necessary to tax either the expenditure at the time of purchase (as is usual with sales taxes) or the imputed income derived from the commodity (as is sometimes done for owner occupied housing under the income tax although almost never for other goods). Denote the expenditures associated with a given consumption stream by s(t) and define the stock of durable goods held as $S(\tau)$ where

$$S(\tau) = \int_0^{\tau} \{s(t)-z(t)\}e^{-r(\tau-t)}dt \geq 0$$

and S(O) = S(L) = O. Thus durable stocks are necessarily non-negative but over a lifetime the present value of consumption is equal to the present value of expenditures.

This implies

Proposition 6

An expenditure tax and a consumption tax are equivalent.

But also

Proposition 7

Under a comprehensive income tax, a given consumption plan is feasible with a lower earnings schedule if it is associated with a higher stock of durables.

A "lower" earnings schedule is a schedule $w_2(t)$ such that $w_2(t) < w_1(t) \; \forall \; t$.

Consider a consumption tax and an expenditure tax at rate x. A consumption tax implies

$$\mathring{A} = w+rA-s-xz$$

while an expenditure tax requires

$$\mathring{A} = w+rA-(1+x)s \; .$$

Thus a consumption plan is feasible under a consumption tax if

$$(24) \quad \int_0^L we^{-rt}dt \geq \int_0^L se^{-rt}dt - x\int_0^L ze^{-rt}dt - (1-x)\int_0^L se^{-rt}dt$$

and under an expenditure tax if

$$(25) \quad \int_0^L we^{-rt}dt \geq (1-x)\int_0^L se^{-rt}dt \ .$$

Hence choices and revenues are again the same and 8 follows.

With a comprehensive income tax, consider two means to the same consumption plan z(t) involving respective expenditures s_1 (t) and s_2(t). Then since

$$(26) \quad \mathring{A} = (1-x_y)(w+rA)-s$$

$$(27) \quad \Delta\mathring{A} = (1-x_y)(\Delta w+r\Delta A)-\Delta s$$

where Δ denotes the difference between the consequential paths of w, s and A. Now set

$$(28) \quad \Delta w = -r\int_0^{\tau} se^{r(\tau-t)}dt$$

noting that if $\Delta S > 0 \ \forall t$ then $\Delta w < 0 \ \forall t$

Then

$$(29) \quad \Delta\mathring{A}-\Delta\mathring{S} = (1-x)r(\Delta A-\Delta S)$$

and since A(0) = S(0) = A(L) = S(L) this equation can hold with $\Delta A = \Delta S$ throughout, verifying proposition 7.

Now consider the impact of uncertainty in the absence of taxes. The instantaneous budget constraint now becomes

$$(30) \qquad \mathring{A} = w+rA+\sigma-z$$

for some random variable σ with mean O. An obvious development of Proposition 1 is

Proposition 8

Two individuals with the same expected present values of lifetime receipts or consumption have the same expected value of tax payments under a labour income tax at rate x_L and a consumption tax at equivalent rate $(x_c / (1+x_c))$.

Of more significance, however, is

Proposition 9

If two individuals have the same earnings profile, an individual with a higher present value of windfalls pays more tax under a consumption tax than under a labour income tax.

Since (1) and (2) are now

$$\mathring{A} = (1-x_L)w+rA+\sigma-z$$

and

$$\mathring{A} = w+rA+\sigma-(1+x_c)z$$

integrating and rearranging as before gives

$$(31) \qquad (1-x_L)\int_0^L we^{-rt}dt = \int_0^L ze^{-rt}dt$$

and

$$(32) \qquad \int_0^L we^{-rt}dt = \int_0^L \sigma e^{-rt}dt + (1+x_c)\int_0^L ze^{-rt}dt$$

from which the result follows.

We might note, however, as an immediate corollary

Proposition (12)

If a labour income tax is also imposed on windfall income, then a consumption tax and a labour income tax are equivalent even under uncertainty.

Part of the interest of this result arises because a comprehensive income tax *does* fall on windfalls. Thus it appears to move the labour income tax base towards the consumption based tax. Typically, however, it overcompensates. It falls on capital income as well, and those with a higher present value of windfalls will also generally have a higher present value of capital income. I say generally because here the characteristics of the CIT in discriminating between late and early earners interacts with its discrimination between windfall and non windfall earners.

To see these issues as distinctly as possible, consider an individual with constant non- windfall wage income w and a Hicksian consumption plan - thus, in the absence of taxes, he faces a budget constraint:

$$(33) \qquad \dot{A} = w+rA+\sigma-z$$

and sets z(t) so that it satisfies this differential equation for constant z, $\sigma=0$ and A(O) = A(t). Thus consumption plans are constantly adjusted to spread the benefit of windfall income over the residual lifetime. In such a framework we have

Proposition 13

An individual with a higher present value of adjusted windfall income has a higher present value of income from capital, where the adjustment transforms the windfall into an equivalent perpetuity. (The adjustment is required because a "late" windfall is more valuable than an "early" windfall).

Since

$$\mathring{A} = w + rA + \sigma - z$$

z is chosen such that

(34)

$$\int_T^L \mathring{A}e^{-rt}dt = w\int_T^L e^{-rt}dt + r\int_T^L Ae^{-rt}dt - z\int_T^L e^{-rt}dt \;\; \forall\, \tau \le L \, .$$

Hence

$$(35) \qquad z - w = \frac{rA(T)e^{-rT}}{e^{-rT} - e^{-rL}}$$

and substitution back into (33) gives

$$(36) \qquad \mathring{A} = rA + \sigma - \frac{rAe^{-rT}}{e^{-rT} - e^{-rL}}$$

which, with rearrangement and integration, implies

$$(37) \qquad r\int_0^L Ae^{-rT}dT = \int_0^L \sigma(e^{-rT} - e^{-rL})dT \, .$$

IV. Principles of Horizontal Equity

The concept of horizontal equity plays a somewhat uneasy role in discussions of public finance issues. Loosely, the principle is that similar individuals should be taxed similarly. The operational value of this principle rests on some capacity to determine what is meant by similarity.

The strongest statement of this would seem to be that of Feldstein (1978) who proposes a utility based definition: individuals obtaining the same utility should pay similar taxes. This has apparent precision and, Feldstein argues, the further merit of being required by efficiency as well as equity considerations. (In fact, this turns out not to be the case, requiring convexity properties in the set of opportunities available: Kay and King (1986) and Bradford (1986), following Stiglitz, cite the example of two men in a lifeboat with water enough only for one: apparently the only horizontally equitable outcome is that both die). But the real weakness of Feldstein's concept is the weight it places on utilitarianism in precisely those areas where utilitarianism is weakest. If individuals are identical (whatever that means) then the principle of horizontal equity has limited operational significance, certainly in the present context. But if individuals are different, how do we make comparisons? Is Croesus as happy as St Francis of Assisi and how would we know? And supposing there were some means of establishing this (perhaps, for example, everyone, including Croesus and St Francis agreed that St Francis was happier, although they would also have to agree that they meant the same thing) would we actually wish to take that into account, by imposing higher taxes on St Francis than on Croesus? It seems very unlikely that this is what many people would feel they meant by the achievement of horizontal equity.

We might then assess horizontal equity by reference to the opportunities available, rather than to the utilities achieved. This is not simply, as Zodrow (1989) suggests, a practical expedient adopted for lack of information available, but an alternative and apparently superior measure. We would like to tax Croesus precisely because we observe that the resources available to him are very great and that if he is not happy in spite of it that is his problem, not ours. However, this is less helpful than it might appear because the interpretation of horizontal equity then rests on the definition of equivalent opportunities. Are individuals similarly placed if they enjoy the same endowment at a point in time, or over their whole lifetime? This is an intelligible question but it is one which the principle of horizontal equity is intended to help us resolve, not one which ought to need to be resolved in order to determine what is meant by horizontal equity. We are telling the principle what to do rather than having it tell us.

This impasse has, of course, been reached before. Indeed, we look back to the giants of the income/consumption tax debate and find their comments on precisely this issue. Musgrave observes that "the only meaningful way in which the terms double taxation or under taxation can be used in connection with equity is to indicate discrimination for or against particular taxpayers in terms of a given index of equality. It is this index that must be decided upon first to prove that double taxation or under taxation occurs, rather than the reverse order". [Musgrave (1959, p. 163)]. Kaldor comments that "the substance of the matter is not disposed of by defining the term Income in one way or another; nor can the relative merits of the two different systems of taxation be decided by asking which of them has the right to the coveted title of 'income tax'." [Kaldor (1985, p. 81)].

Thus we arrive at Kaplow's (1985) characterisation of horizontal equity as "a measure in search of a principle". It does not follow from that, however, that the issues to be found in most textbooks (or in this paper) under the subtitle of horizontal equity are of no significance. Rather the heading of horizontal equity is a convenient label for grouping discussion of which issues may properly be taken into account in determining tax burdens, and which may not. We reject random taxation because we think random taxation is wrong, and, fundamentally, there is nothing more to it than that. But we do not think it is lexicographically wrong, and might accept that the two men in a lifeboat might toss a coin to see who should survive, recognising that this is not arbitrary, or Pareto inferior, even if it is random. Or we might allow certain kinds of discrimination: the cry "women and children first" is probably (still) acceptable, even if the cry of "white men first" is not.

In common with public opinion generally, I think that the tax system may properly take account of residence, nationality, age, disability and family responsibilities in determining liability: that it should not take account of race, political opinion, height or weight; and that sex, marital status and education are borderline characteristics, the propriety of whose inclusion is open to argument. I cannot find any easy criterion for distinguishing these characteristics and note that the groupings have changed over time: it is, for example, more acceptable than in earlier periods to take account of disability or education and less acceptable to take account of political opinion, sex or marital status. The selection of appropriate and inappropriate criteria is a matter on which judgement should be made directly, on the basis of prevailing social values.

If this approach is accepted, the proper task for the economist charged with helping resolve horizontal equity issues is the following. Establish for each proposed tax base the factors which are included and excluded, in the calculation of liability. A comparison of the legitimacy of the inclusions, and validity of the exclusions then provides a basis for an - inescapably subjective - assessment of the relevant measure of ability to pay.

Drawing on the results of Sections II and III for this purpose, the main principles to emerge appear to be the following:

(a) a tax on labour income and a tax on consumption are largely identical as between those with the same value of lifetime resources; the main differences arise in relation to the treatment of uncertainty and the taxation of bequests

(b) with uncertainty, a labour income tax equalises tax burdens on those with equal ex ante resources and a consumption tax on those with equal ex post resources

(c) the equivalence is restored if windfalls are taxed in a labour income tax and if accession forms part of the labour income tax base and bequests of the consumption base

(d) a comprehensive income tax, relative to either of these, discriminates against late consumers, early earners, low consumer durable stocks, and high windfall income.

If lifetime resources are seen as an appropriate criterion in assessing tax liability, the additional factors introduced into the computation by the comprehensive income tax seem - at best - irrelevancies. The comparison between the labour income tax and the consumption tax is less clearcut (but less important). The treatment of gifts and bequests is a matter for divergent views (and has been). (See, for example, Aaron and Galper, 1985).

Within the framework presented here, then, an attack on the horizontal equity properties of the consumption tax must be based on the judgement that lifetime resources are themselves an inappropriate component of the tax base and that the much sorter time perspective of the comprehensive income tax corresponds better to common perceptions of fairness. This is, for example, the position of Goode (1980) who stresses, in particular, the imperfection of capital markets and the myopia of individuals. For Goode, and those who share his view, the redistribution of income across the life cycle is much the same issue was the redistribution of income between individuals. If it were impossible to transfer resources between points in time, then this would clearly be the case. But even if there were not capital markets at all, this extreme counter perspective could not be defended: you do not have to open all the tins in the store cupboard today. What is the proper time period for making distributional comparisons - a day, a year, a lifetime? This is, in part, an empirical question and in part a matter for value choices.

V. Conclusions

It is in the nature of a paper on horizontal equity that there can be no conclusions: the task of the writer is to set out the issues for the reader's judgement. But the major judgements which I draw from the analysis here are the following. First, the case for the comprehensive income tax appears very weak. It is difficult to understand why for so long it should have dominated the literature as the basis from which deviations should be measured in judging the equity of a tax system. Second, the principle of horizontal equity is a weak crutch, and few decisive arguments one way or another are to be derived from it. More powerful rationales for consumption taxation are to be found elsewhere.

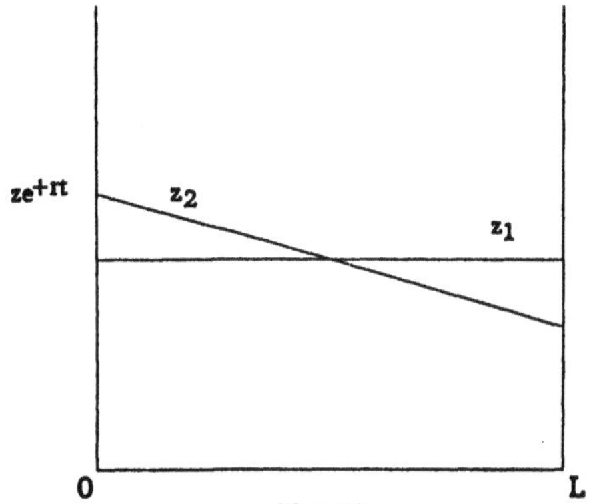

Figure 1

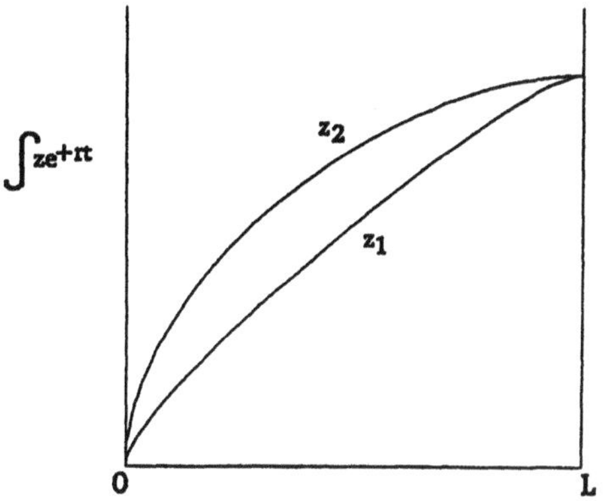

Figure 2

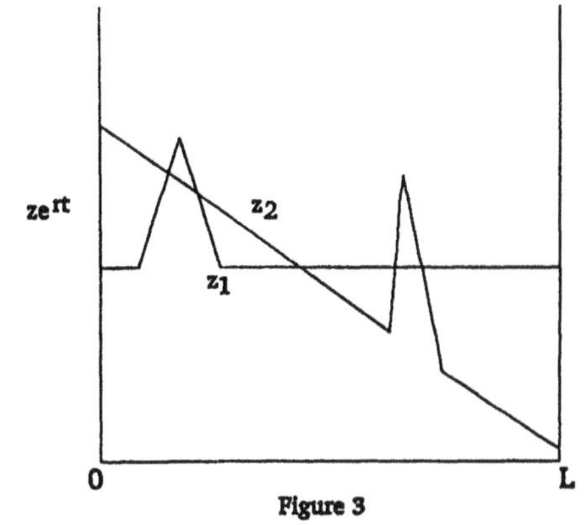

Figure 3

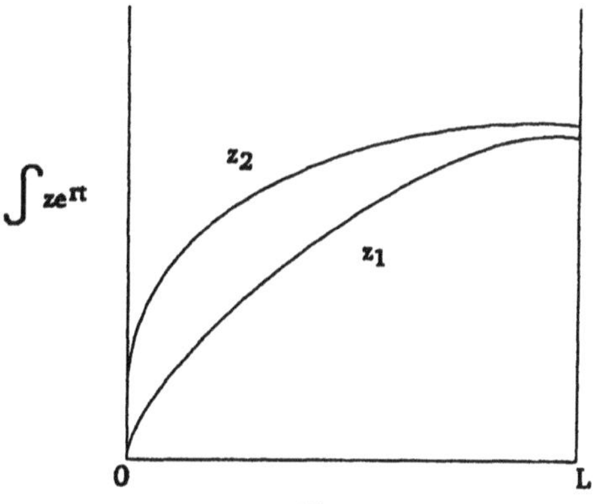

Figure 4

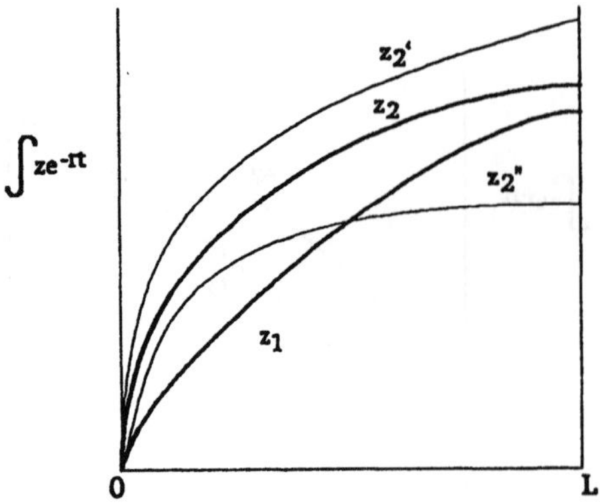

Figure 5

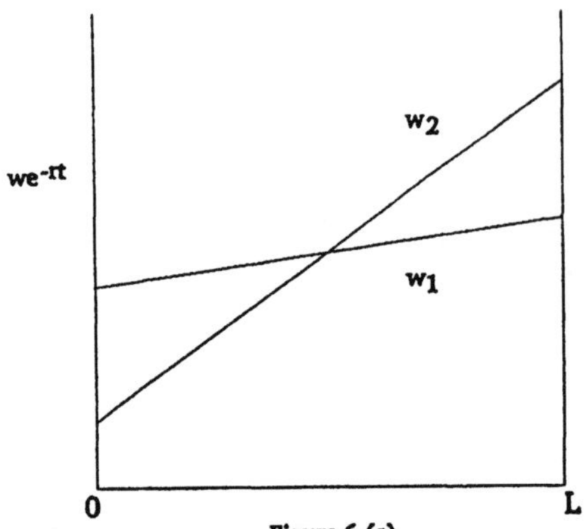

Figure 6 (a)

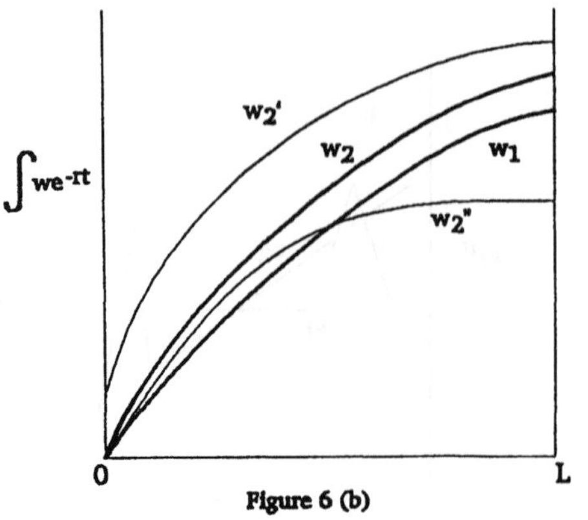

Figure 6 (b)

Comments by Syed M. Ahsan

I. Overview

I find John Kay's (1990) paper most stimulating. It makes three distinct contributions. First, he shows that the value of life-time tax payments may differ depending on whether the tax base is consumption or income if we admit differences in the time profile of earnings and consumption over the life-cycle. Next, he extends the basic life-cycle model to analyze the impact of the introduction of uncertainty, of bequests and durables. Finally, he provides a rather illuminating discussion of the principle of horizontal equity, and how in principle an economist is to interpret it. Since I mostly agree with this latter discussion, and the conclusion I draw from it helps to focus on the analysis that preceded it, let me dwell on it first.

II. Horizontal Equity

Kay discards Feldstein's (1978) position that individuals obtaining the same utility should pay the same tax. If individuals are "identical" then the principle has limited applicability but he correctly observes, how do we make comparisons when they are different. This difficulty leads him to consider the "opportunities" available to an individual as the basis for assessing tax liability and for measuring horizontal equity. This view requires a definition of "equivalent opportunities" to be practicable. He suggests that an economist's task is to "establich for each proposed tax base the factors which are included and excluded in the calculation of liability", and in so doing resolve the issue of horizontal equity. Evidently, this choice must be a subjective one (e.g., issues of marital status, education and sex). In summary then, Kay would appear to favour "life-time resource" as an appropriate criterion in assessing tax liability with the taxable amount determined by considerations such as the family situation etc. to be determined somehow. Perhaps one can be a little more specific on the latter issue. I believe a proper role of the economist would be to spell out the equity (and efficiency) aspects of inclusion of specific factors (e.g., marital status, age, disability, education), and let the political process resolve which ones are relevant for a particular society at a point in its history. In the following I will assume that life-time resource is the measure of horizontal equity.

III. The Standard Paradigm

Kay develops a framework that captures what is sometimes referred to as the "standard paradigm" in the tax reform literature. The underlying model is a simple life-cycle one with a fixed horizon, and initially without inheritance and bequests. It would be helpful for our discussion to restate some of the key relationships of his model in a simpler notation. Let $V_r(w)$ denote the present value of the *endowment* (here wage income) stream, where *r* is the appropriate rate of discount. We let this present value be the same for all agents. For the three taxes considered, we may express the present value of tax payments as follows:

$$(3.1)\quad X(1) = x_1 V_r(w) ,$$

$$(3.2)\quad X(c) = x_c(1+x_c)^{-1} V_r(w) , \text{ and}$$

$$(3.3)\quad X(y) = x_y [V_{\tilde{r}}(w) + V_{\tilde{r}}(r,S)] ,$$

where x_1, x_c and x_y denote, respectively, the proportional tax rates on endowment, consumption and comprehensive income. Capital letters, X(.), denote the corresponding present values from each tax. Also note that in (3.3), the appropriate rate of discount, $\tilde{r} = (1 - x_y)r$, is the net-of-tax interest rate on investment. Evidently the $V_{\tilde{r}}(r,S)$ denote the present value of capital income. Note that two individuals facing an identical wage stream, may save differently and under a comprehensive income tax (CIT) will face unequal tax burdens. This led Feldstein to conclude, "a tax on consumption satisfies horizontal equity that is violated by a general tax on income" (p. 49)[1]. Evidently the consumption tax and endowment tax are equivalent.

The nice thing about Kay's development of the life-cycle framework is his interpretation of what we sum up as $V_{\tilde{r}}(r,S)$, the evolution of capital income through time.

---

[1] Even if individuals had identical tastes (as they do in Feldstein's analysis), savings paths may still differ if the endowment (wage) profiles differ.

Two interesting results are obtained when he specifies the conditions that characterize the *timing* of earnings and of consumption. In particular, he shows, given an identical w(t)-profile, *late* consumers would pay more tax under CIT than under a consumption tax (Proposition 4). Similarly, for two agents pursuing an identical consumption path, C(t), *late* earners would pay less under a CIT than under a consumption (or endowment) tax (Proposition 6). Although these are established rigorously, no intuitive discussion is offered. The rationale for the first result would perhaps run as follows: with a given w(t)-profile, late consumers accumulate assets early in life, and would therefore be burdened with tax on interest income accruing to this capital under a CIT. Behind proposition 6 lies a parallel reasoning; early earners must lend (while others borrow or lend less) and thus incur interest income tax while everyone pursues the given C(t)-path. If this is a correct description, the two results are much like two sides of the same coin - an identical borrowing-lending strategy triggers both results.

Several minor remarks are in order. First, we observe that the "wage tax" referred to in the standard paradigm is really a tax on the flow of endowment (i. e., inheritance plus wage incomes); thus letting initial assets, A(O), be nil is too restrictive. A wage tax would not be horizontally equitable vis-a-vis a consumption tax unless the initial assets are taxed in period-1. After all, a primary difference among individuals in the real world is in the value of their initial physical endowment.

More serious perhaps is Kay's use of the same discount rate for CIT as for consumption and wage taxation. Clearly, the correct discount rate under the former is $r(1-x_y)$. With this modification, his proposition 2 need not hold; comparing equations (3.1) and (3.3) above, we see that should $x_1 = x_y$ (as he does) given $\tilde{r} < r$, $V_r(w) < V_{\tilde{r}}(w)$.[2] However, in a rather special case of a two-period model with endowment appearing in period-1 only, this result goes through.

IV. Uncertainty

The section of the paper dealing with extensions to the basic model specifically considers inheritance and bequests, consumption of durables and a windfall component to

[2] Kay's proposition 2 essentially says that should $x_y = x_1$, a CIT raises more or less revenue than a wage tax (or an equivalent consumption tax) as the average discounted value of lifetime assets is greater or less than zero.

the endowment stream. I find the treatment of bequests and durables useful, and some new results are obtained (e.g., proposition 9). It is in the treatment of uncertainty that I believe lies the potential of extending the standard paradigm. The weakness of the windfall representing uncertainty is that the former cannot affect behaviour and would thus be of limited interest. There are at least two interesting types of modelling one can pursue. First, we have wage and/or length of life uncertainty and within this context one may incorporate decisions such as work-leisure, retirement and human capital accumulation. Alternatively, one can pursue portfolio decisions within the consumption-saving framework and analyse the consequences of capital risk. The present discussant has attempted the latter in a simple two-period context [Ahsan (1989)], and this is seen to offer new insights on both the choice of tax base and on the question of horizontal equity.

With choice between safe and risky assets, the present value of tax payments described earlier (equations 3.1. to 3.3.) can be seen to be modified as follows:

$$(4.1)\quad X(1) = x_1 V_r(w)\ ,$$

$$(4.2)\quad X(c) = x_c(1+x_c)^{-1}[V_r(w)+V_r(g)]\ , \text{ and}$$

$$(4.3)\quad X(y) = x_y[V_{\tilde{r}}(w)+V_{\tilde{r}}(r,S)+V_{\tilde{r}}(g)]\ ,$$

where the last terms in equations 4.2. and 4.3. measure the present value of capital gains (losses).[3] A number of new results emerge from this extension. First

Proposition 1
In a world of capital risks and asset choice, the endowment (or wage income) tax and the consumption tax are not equivalent.

This is evident by comparing equations (4.1) and (4.2). Recall that in the certainty case, absent taxes, individuals consume their life-time endowment $V_r(w)$. With asset

[3] Strictly speaking, in a two-asset world this is the present value of differential return from risky investment. This has been interpreted as capital gains by several public finance writers. See Ahsan (1989) for additional details.

choice, the value of life-time consumption equals the sum of the present value of the endowment stream *and* of risky capital gains/losses.

Cash-Flow and Tax Pre-payment Debate

The preceding result opens up new issues on the equivalence of the two methods of implementing a consumption tax, namely, the cash-flow and the tax pre-payment alternative. In the absence of portfolio choice, the latter option is effectively a tax on endowment (or, wage tax). There seem to be two possible ways the equivalance between the two accounting procedures may be re-established. One would be to exempt capital gains from the consumption tax base. This would lead to

$$(4.2a) \quad X(c) = x_c(1+x_c)^{-1}V_r(w) .$$

Alternatively, we could propose a new tax (x_a) that applies to $V_r(w)$ and $V_r(g)$ uniformly:

$$(4.4) \quad X(a) = x_a[V_r(w)+V_r(g)] .$$

Elsewhere I have called it a "wealth" tax (as it falls on the total life-time wealth). Evidently, equations (4.4) and (4.2) are equivalent but are based on seperate accounting procedures.

Proposition 2

In a world of capital risks and asset choice, a proportional wealth tax is equivlent to a general consumption tax. Alternatively, if the capital gains are exempt from the consumption tax base, the latter becomes equivalent to a tax on endowment alone.

We may argue the wealth tax to be a *de facto* pre-payment tax while the consumption tax is its cost-flow equivalent. However, an important difficulty arises; even if individuals were to pre-pay tax on endowment, they face additional future tax liability on capital gains and hence the need for registered accounts.[4] Thus the once perceived ease of administering a pre-payment tax is greatly compromised.

Leaving aside accounting difficulties, the above result (proposition 2) has interesting implications for horizontal equity. Concern that election of the pre-payment method would induce horizontal inequities in the presence of uncertainty since those lucky with a high realized return will benefit [e.g., see Graetz (1980)], disappears in our set up. Capital gains are to be treated the same under both methods. By the same token, the debate on the appropriateness of equity in the *ex-ante* or *ex-post* sense [e.g., see Bradford (1980)] also becomes irrelevant in the choice of tax boxes.

Perhaps the life-cycle framework proposed by Kay could be expanded to examine the issues arising out of asset choice (e.g., the cash-flow versus pre-payment options and of horizontal equity) in greater detail.

References

Aaron H. / Galper H. (1985), Assessing Tax Reform (Brookings Institution, Washington, D.C.).

Ahsan, S.M. (1989), Risk-Taking, Savings and Taxation: A Re-Examination of Theory and Policy, Canadian Journal of Economics, (forthcoming).

Atkinson A.B. (1970), On the Measurement of Inequality, Journal of Economic Theory.

Auerbach A.J. / Kotlikoff L.J. (1987), Dynamic Fiscal Policy (Harvard University Press, Cambridge, Mass.).

Bradford, D.F. (1980), The Case for a Personal Consumption Tax, in: Pechmann, J. (ed.) (1980), *op. cit.* .

[4] Note that even if one were to go the route of exempting capital gains from the consumption tax base in order to make it strictly equivalent to an endowment (wage) tax, the accounting difficulties are just as relevant. Not only do we need to have savings registered, future movement of asset values need to be monitored (as they are de-registered for presumed consumption).

Bradford D.F. (1986), Untangling the Income Tax (Harvard University Press, Cambridge, Mass.).

Feldstein, M.S. (1978), The Welfare Cost of Capital Income Taxation, Journal of Political Economy, LXXXVI, pp. 29-51.

Goode R. (1980), The Superiority of the Income Tax, in: Pechman, J. (ed) (1980).

Graetz, M.J. (1980), Expenditure Tax Design, in Joseph Pechmann, ed., (1980), *op. cit.* .

Kaldor N. (1955), An Expenditure Tax (Allen & Unwin, London).

Kaplow L. (1985), Horizonal Equity: Measures in Search of a Principle, NBER Working Paper 1679.

Musgrave R. (1959), The Theory of Public Finance (McGraw Hill, New York).

Musgrave R. (1976), ET, OT and SBT, Journal of Public Economics 6.

Pechman J. (ed.) (1980), What Should Be Taxed: Income or Expenditure? (Brookings Institution, Washington, D.C.).

Zodrow, G.R. (1989), The Individual Tax Base - Annual, Lifetime or Consumed Income, ISPE Conference, Rotterdam.

Peter Birch Sørensen

Taxation of Income, Consumption, and Wages in an Open Economy*

I. Introduction

During the 1970s and 80s public finance economists devoted increasing attention to the taxation of consumption and wages as an attractive alternative to the existing income tax systems, which are widely believed to discourage savings and capital formation. Despite the ongoing internationalization of the western economies, most of these studies of the macroeconomic effects of tax reform have assumed a closed economy. As Slemrod (1988) has noted, economists have only recently begun to realize that the effects of tax policy may change markedly as the economy is opened up to international trade in goods and assets.

To illustrate the importance of openness, consider the effects of a general uniform capital income tax the revenue of which is redistributed to the private sector in the form of lump-sum transfers. Such a tax will tend to reduce private savings, and in a closed economy the real rate of interest will therefore tend to go up, causing a partial shifting of the tax burden onto wage earners via a fall in the capital intensity of production.[1] In principle, it makes no difference for this result whether the tax is collected at the source

* All results reported but not explicitly derived in this paper are demonstrated in a technical appendix available from the author. Comments from Pierre Pestieau and Wolfram Richter are gratefully acknowledged, but all remaining errors and shortcomings are of course my own responsibility.

[1] This effect of a capital income tax is implied by a standard neoclassical growth model in which the overall savings rate varies positively with total disposable income and the after-tax rate of return. In an overlapping-generations model, the effect of a capital income tax will vary according as the old generation or the young generation receives the tax revenue, since the two groups have different propensities to consume.

of capital income, i.e. as a business tax, or whether it is collected at the household level as a personal income tax. By contrast, a business tax and a personal tax on capital income will have very different effects in an open economy with high international mobility of capital. Since the business tax is levied on capital *invested* in the domestic economy, it will tend to induce an *export* of capital to other countries which are now offering relatively higher after-tax rates of return to investment. This process of domestic disinvestment will continue until the domestic pre-tax rate of return has risen to such an extent that the after-tax return is again competitive with the net rate of return in the rest of the world. If the domestic economy is small and capital mobility is perfect, the business tax will be fully shifted in this way. On the other hand, a personal tax on the return to *all* capital owned by domestic residents will not affect the relative attractiveness of domestic and foreign assets and therefore will not tend to reduce domestic investment, but will instead discourage domestic savings, thereby inducing an *import* of capital. In the small economy with perfect capital mobility, the pre-tax rate of interest will not be affected at all, and the burden of the tax will be borne fully by domestic wealth owners.

This example suffices to indicate the importance of allowing for openness in the discussion of tax reforms. On this background, the present paper attempts to illuminate the macroeconomic effects of taxes on income, consumption, and wages in a small open economy. The framework of analysis is an extended open-economy version of the well-known model developed by Blanchard (1984, 1985) in which consumers optimize their consumption and asset accumulation over finite expected lifetimes. As an alternative, one might have chosen to work with the popular model of a representative household optimizing over an infinite horizon, used for instance by Hodrick (1982) and Sen and Turnovsky (1988). However, in that model a stationary state can be attained only when the after-tax rate of interest equals the exogenous consumer rate of time preference. Thus, in a small open economy with perfect capital mobility where the interest rate is exogenously given from abroad, there is no market mechanism to ensure convergence to a long-run equilibrium in the infinite horizon model, i.e. equilibrium can be upheld in the model only if one is prepared to assume that the net rate of interest is for some unexplained reason *always* in line with the exogenous rate of time preference. In Blanchard's finite horizon model we shall see that this problem does not arise, since equilibrium can be reached even if the net rate of interest deviates from the rate of time preference.

In the following three sections we describe the household, business and government sectors of our model. We then carry out a balanced-budget incidence analysis of the impact, dynamic, and steady-state effects of taxes on income, consumption, and wages, assuming exogenous terms of trade but endogenous savings and labor supply. The last part of the paper endogenizes the terms of trade in order to study the effects of tax policy on this important variable, assuming for simplicity that labor supply is given. In the final section, the main conclusions are summarized.

II. The Household Sector

The general characteristics of our household sector are identical with those described in Blanchard (1985), although we extend his model to allow for endogenous labor supply and for more than one consumer good. Each agent faces a constant probability of death p throughout his life, so the expected remaining lifetime of an agent of any given age is 1/p. At any instant of time, a large cohort, whose size is normalized to be p, is born. Taken together, these assumptions imply that population is constant and equal to unity. All consumers are identical except that they have been born at different times and therefore have different levels of non-human wealth. There are no bequests, so a new-born individual has zero financial wealth.

Throughout the paper, the notation x(s,v) will indicate the value of variable x at time v, for a person born at time s ($s \leq v$). At any point in time, instantaneous utility for the individual is given by the log-linear utility function

$$(1) \quad u(s,v) = \alpha \log(c^d(s,v)) + \beta \log(c^i(s,v)) + \gamma \log(L^* - L(s,v))$$

where c^d is consumption of a domestically produced good, c^i is consumption of an imported good, and L^*-L is leisure time, with L^* being the total time endowment, and L indicating the amount of work. At any time z, the consumer strives to maximize expected discounted utility over his lifetime horizon. Given the constant probability of death p, and given an exogenous rate of time preference θ, this is equivalent to maximizing

$$(2) \qquad U \equiv \int_{z}^{\infty} u(s,v)e^{-(\theta+p)(v-z)}dv \quad .$$

To derive the consumer's budget constraint, we invoke Blanchard's assumption that life insurance companies offer an annuity to each consumer on the condition that they can take over his wealth when he dies. Given perfect competition and zero profits in annuity markets, the bonus per period received by the consumer will equal his expected wealth transfer to the insurance company which is the probability of his death (p) multiplied by his stock of non-human wealth (a). With a dot indicating a derivative with respect to time v, and using the imported good as numéraire, we may then write the consumer's dynamic budget constraint as

$$(3) \qquad \dot{a}(s,v) = (\rho+p)a(s,v) + \omega(v)L(s,v) + \tau(v) - (1+t^c)[q(v)c^d(s,v) + c^i(s,v)]$$

where ρ and ω are the after-tax rates of interest and wages, respectively, τ is a government transfer, t^c is the proportional tax rate on consumption, and q denotes the terms of trade, i.e. the price of domestically produced goods in terms of imported goods. Note that ω and τ have not been indexed by s, reflecting our assumption that all agents receive the same wage rate and the same government transfer payment. Equation (3) simply defines the individual's savings as the difference between his total income from all sources minus his total expenditure on consumption and tax payments. In addition to (3), the consumer must also satisfy the following intertemporal solvency constraint which prevents him from borrowing indefinitely to pay interest and principal on his debt:

$$\lim_{v \to \infty} a(s,v)e^{-(\rho+p)v} \geq 0 \quad . \tag{4}$$

Inserting (1) into (2) and maximizing the resulting expression subject to (3), one can show that the first-order conditions imply the following relationships, where $c \equiv qc^d + c^i$ equals *total* consumption measured in terms of the numéraire:

$$c^d(s,v) = \alpha c(s,v)/q(v)(\alpha+\beta) \tag{5}$$

$$c^i(s,v) = \beta c(s,v)/(\alpha+\beta) \tag{6}$$

$$\omega(v)(L^*-L(v)) = \gamma c(s,v)(1+t^c)/(\alpha+\beta) \tag{7}$$

$$\dot{c}(s,v) = (\rho-\theta)c(s,v) \quad . \tag{8}$$

Equation (8) restates the familiar condition that the individual's total consumption will be rising or falling over time, according as the rate of time preference is lower or higher than the net rate of interest. (7) specifies the "consumption" of leisure, measured in equivalent units of the numéraire, as a fraction of total material consumption, while (5) and (6) indicate the relation between total consumption and consumption of the two individual goods. We now wish to derive a relationship between total consumption and total wealth. For this purpose, we rewrite (3) as

$$\begin{aligned} \dot{a}(s,v) = {} & (\rho+p)a(s,v) + \omega(v)L^* + \tau(v) \\ & - (1+t^c)c(s,v) - \omega(v)(L^*-L(s,v)) \end{aligned} \tag{9}$$

Integrating (9), using (4), we get

$$(10)\qquad \int_v^{\infty} [(1+t^c)c(s,z) + \omega(z)(L^*-L(s,z))]e^{-(\rho+p)(z-v)}dz$$

$$= a(s,v) + h(v)$$

where

$$(11)\qquad h(v) \equiv \int_v^{\infty} [\omega(z)L^* + \tau(z)]e^{-(\rho+p)(z-v)}dz$$

is "potential" human wealth, i.e. the discounted value of future transfers plus the future labor income which might be earned if the individual spent all his time working. Thus equation (10) simply says that the discounted value of the sum of the individual's material consumption and his "consumption" of leisure must equal the sum of his non-human wealth and his potential human wealth. According to (8) we have

$$(12)\qquad c(s,z) = c(s,v)e^{(\rho-\theta)(z-v)}, \qquad z \geq v$$

Substituting (7) and (12) into (10), and calculating the resulting integral, we find that

$$(13)\qquad c(s,v) = \eta[a(s,v) + h(v)] ,$$

$$\eta \equiv (\alpha+\beta)(\theta+p)/(1+t^c)(\alpha+\beta+\gamma) > 0$$

In other words, total material consumption at any time is proportional to total wealth at that time.

This concludes our discussion of individual consumer behavior. To derive aggregate household behavior, we note that the relation between any aggregate variable X(v) and its individual counterpart x(s,v) is given by

$$(14) \qquad X(v) = \int_{-\infty}^{v} x(s,v)pe^{p(s-v)}ds$$

since a cohort born at time s has a size of $pe^{p(s-v)}$ as of time v. Applying the rules of aggregation explained by Blanchard (1985, pp. 228-29) to the individual equations derived above, one finds that

$$(15) \qquad L = L^{*} - \gamma(1+t^{c})C/(\alpha+\beta)\omega$$

$$(16) \qquad C = \eta(A+H) \quad , \qquad C \equiv qC^{d}+C^{i}$$

$$(17) \qquad \dot{H} = (\rho+p)H - \omega L^{*} - \tau$$

$$(18) \qquad \dot{A} = \rho A + \omega L + \tau - (1+t^{c})C$$

where we have dropped the time index for notational convenience, and where L is of course aggregate labor supply. Notice that an analogue of the term *pa* in the individual budget constraint (3) does not appear in the aggregate equation (18). In other words, whereas individual financial wealth accumulates, for those alive, at rate $\rho + p$, aggregate financial wealth accumulates only at rate ρ, because the amount pA is a transfer, via life insurance companies, from those who die to those who survive.

To complete the description of our model, we may now turn to the business and government sectors.

III. The Business Sector

To avoid imposing an excessively complex dynamic structure on our model, we assume that firms can instantaneously and costlessly adjust their capital stock to its desired level. For the business sector as a whole, this is only possible if firms can instantly buy and sell capital equipment in the world market. We therefore assume that the imported good demanded by consumers can also be used for domestic capital investment. Thus the business sector produces domestic output Y by means of imported capital goods K plus labor.[2] The relation between inputs and output is given by a standard constant-returns production function F(•) with positive, but diminishing marginal productivities of capital and labor (we continue to drop the time indexes whereever this should cause no misunderstandings):

$$(19) \qquad Y = F(K,L), \qquad F_K>0,\ F_{KK}<0,\ F_L>0,\ F_{LL}<0,\ F_{KL}=F_{LK}>0 \quad .$$

For simplicity we abstract from depreciation, assuming capital goods to be immortal. However, all our results will go through if we interpret Y as output *net* of depreciation and assume that the tax code allows true economic depreciation. Since we are interested in comparing the various types of taxes in their "pure" form, we shall assume that the government levies a uniform non-discriminating capital income tax at rate t^i on business profits as well as interest income. If *i* is the rate of interest before tax, we then get the arbitrage condition

$$(1-t^i)qF_K(K,L) = \rho \equiv i(1-t^i) \qquad \text{or}$$

$$(20) \qquad qF_K(K,L) = i$$

[2]The assumption that domestic output is not used for investment purposes is in fact quite unimportant for all the results derived in section VI. The reason is that the model in section VI assumes exogenous terms of trade and therefore works like a one-good model in which domestic and foreign output is identical and may be used for investment as well as consumption.

stating that the net return on business investment must equal the net return obtainable on passive financial investment. Note that when debt interest is tax deductible, (20) will hold in the case of debt finance as well as equity finance of business investment. The fact that t^i does not appear in the final version of (20) reflects the well-known result that a genuine Schanz-Haig-Simons capital income tax (allowing true economic depreciation) is investment neutral.[3]

If w is the wage rate before tax, measured in units of the imported numéraire good, we have the familiar additional optimum condition

$$(21) \qquad qF_L(K,L) = w$$

saying that - given tax deductibility of wage costs - firms will hire labor until the value of its marginal product equals the wage rate before tax.

The small economy will be unable to influence the absolute price of its imports, but if it produces a differentiated product, it will face a downward-sloping world demand curve for its output. Hence the relative price of domestic output will be a declining function of net exports (Y-C^d):

$$(22) \qquad q = g(Y-C^d) \quad , \quad g' < 0 \quad .$$

In the alternative textbook case of a small open economy producing a standard, undif-ferentiated good traded in the world market, the prices of exports as well as the prices of imports are given from abroad, and the terms of trade are simply exogenous. We shall consider both cases below.

IV. The Government

Let us finally turn to the government sector. The government is assumed to balance its budget, spending all tax revenue on identical lump-sum transfers to each individual. Since population has been normalized at unity, total transfer payments are simply τ.

[3] See Sinn (1987, ch. 5) for an elaboration of this theorem.

We may also recall from (20) that financial assets and business assets yield the same pre-tax rate of return *i* and are subject to the same income tax rate t^i . Hence we may write the balanced-budget constraint as

$$(23) \qquad t^i iA + t^w wL + t^c C = \tau$$

where t^w is the tax rate on labor income, and the first term on the left-hand side is the revenue from the capital income tax.

Throughout our analysis, we shall treat all tax rates as exogenous policy variables, assuming the level of transfers to adjust passively to balance the budget. The analysis will thus be of the balanced-budget-incidence variety.

V. The Model with Exogenous Terms of Trade

We now have all the building blocks to set up a full scale macro model in order to study the macroeconomic effects of tax policy. As a preliminary, recall that since the production function is homogeneous of degree one, the marginal productivities are homogeneous of degree zero in labor and capital. Defining $k \equiv K/L$, we may therefore rewrite the profit maximum conditions (20) and (21) as

$$(24) \qquad qF_K(k,1) = i$$

$$(25) \qquad qF_L(k,1) = w \quad .$$

Since capital mobility is perfect, and the capital income tax is based on the residence principle, the domestic rate of interest before tax must equal the world rate of interest given from abroad, so the variable *i* in (24) is exogenous. In the popular case of a small open economy selling a standard product, the terms of trade q are likewise exogenous, and equations (24) and (25) will then determine the wage rate before tax. In other words, given the investment neutral capital income tax, factor prices before tax will be quite independent of the tax rates, and the burden of a tax on any of the two factors will be borne fully by the owners of that factor.

The model may now be reduced to two simple dynamic equations. First, insert (23), (20), and (15) into (18) and utilize the definition $\omega \equiv w(1-t^w)$ to find

$$(26) \qquad \dot{A} = iA + wL^* - \phi C, \qquad \phi \equiv 1+[\gamma(1+t^c)/(\alpha+\beta)(1-t^w)] .$$

Next, eliminate L, H and $\dot{H}$ from the system (15) through (18) to get

$$(27) \quad \dot{C} = [i(1-t^i)-\theta]C - \psi pA, \quad \psi \equiv (\alpha+\beta)(\theta+p)/(\alpha+\beta+\gamma)(1+t^c) .$$

With i and q being exogenous, and w being predetermined from (24) and (25), the system (26) and (27) makes up a pair of autonomous, linear differential equations in C and A, provided all tax rates are taken to be exogenous constants. The steady state corresponding to this dynamic system can be shown to be a saddlepoint, if

$$(28) \qquad i[i(1-t^i)-\theta] - p\phi\psi < 0 .$$

At first sight, this condition may not look very informative, but if we set all tax rates equal to zero and exploit the definitions of ϕ and ψ, (28) simplifies to $i<\theta+p$, i.e. the interest rate should be lower than the sum of the rate of time preference and the death rate. If (28) is violated, the system will be entirely unstable, but that case will be excluded here. Moreover, we shall assume that $i(1-t^i)>\theta$, implying from (27) that the steady-state level of non-human wealth is positive for positive levels of consumption. With these restrictions on parameter values, the adjustment of the economy to a steady-state equilibrium where $\dot{C}=\dot{A}=0$ can be illustrated by means of figure 1, where the curve $\dot{C}=0$ was derived from (27), and the $\dot{A}=0$ curve was found from (26). In the short run, the stock of non-human wealth is predetermined by past accumulation, so when the economy is exposed to a shock which changes its equilibrium position E, consumption will "jump" so as to place the system on the stable trajectory corresponding to the new equilibrium. To see that movement along the stable arm of the saddlepoint is the only adjustment which is both optimal *and* feasible, notice that if the system starts out in a point below the stable arm, consumption will become negative in finite time, whereas if the economy takes off from a point above the stable branch, A will converge on minus infinity, i.e. the country's net foreign debt will sooner or later exceed the finite stock of wealth owned by the rest of the world, which is likewise impossible.

Note that while the total stock of wealth is predetermined at any point in time, our assumption of costless adjustment of the capital stock implies that wealth owners can instantaneously reallocate their portfolios between real capital and financial assets. For instance, if some policy measure reduces the desired stock of capital, investors can instantly sell capital goods in the world market and buy international bonds instead.

With these observations in mind, let us now use the model consisting of (24) through (27) to study the effects of alternative tax instruments when the terms of trade are exogenous.

VI. The Effects of Tax Policy when the Terms of Trade are Exogenous

Table 1 summarizes the short-run and long-run incidence of the various tax instruments when the tax revenue is redistributed as lump-sum transfers to the private sector. Note that the impact effects refer to *unanticipated* policy changes. Since A is predetermined in the short run, the instantaneous effect on this variable will of course always be zero. Besides showing the effects of the tax instruments already introduced, table 1 also reports the effects of a comprehensive Schanz-Haig-Simons income tax, i.e. a uniform tax on wages, interest and profits, collected at rate t^*.

Since the policy effects on C^d and C^i are all directly proportional to the effects on C, only the latter effects have been reported in the table.

Consider now the impact effect of a rise in the capital income tax rate t^i. As shown in figure 2 (where E_0 is the initial steady state and E_1 is the new steady state), such a policy change will cause a short-run increase in consumption by lowering the net reward to saving. Because of the log-linearity of the utility function, consumers will wish to consume leisure and material goods in fixed proportions as long as relative prices are constant. This is reflected in equation (15) which predicts that a rise in material consumption will ceteris paribus be followed by a fall in labor supply. Since we see from (24) that optimal capital intensity is constant, the fall in labor supply and employment will be accompanied by a proportional cut in capital input and hence by an equiproportional drop in output. With a drop in domestic output and income and a simultaneous rise in consumer demand, net savings (which were zero in the initial steady state) turn negative. Over time, the resulting decumulation of assets will reduce the stock of wealth, and according to figure 2 this will cause a long-run *decline* in consumption. Hence the short-run effects on labor supply, capital input and output will be reversed in the long run. The increase in steady-state labor supply reflects the fact that consumers adjust to the lower level of wealth partly by reducing material consumption and partly by taking less leisure.

Let us turn next to the effects of a wage tax, t^w. This is of some interest, since several tax economists have argued that a combination of a wage tax with a business tax on "pure" profits would offer an attractive alternative to personal taxes on comprehensive income or expenditure, mainly on administrative grounds.[4] As illustrated in figure 3, the wage tax causes a short-run decline of consumption, because it reduces potential human wealth. The fall in potential human wealth is the net result of a decline in the present value of potential labor income which is not fully offset by a rise in the present value of government transfers. Essentially, the transfers financed by the tax revenue from the tax on *actual* labor income cannot compensate for the tax-induced fall in *potential* labor income, since actual labor supply is less than potential labor supply. Despite the fall in consumption, we see from figure 3 that the wage tax will nevertheless initiate a process of dissaving because it discourages labor supply, thereby inducing a fall in output and income which is even greater than the fall in consumption. Over time, dissaving will be brought to halt, partly via a further fall in consumption, and partly via a gradual recovery of labor supply and output. However, it can be shown that the new steady-state values of labor supply, capital input, and domestic output will remain below their initial equilibrium values, provided the system is saddlepoint stable even if our parameter γ is zero, i.e. even if labor supply were exogenous (according to (15) we have $L = L^*$ when $\gamma = 0$).

The effects of a comprehensive income tax may be seen as the sum of the effects of a capital income tax and a tax on wages. Whereas the substitution effects of the higher

[4] See, for instance, Hall and Rabushka (1983), Bradford (1988), and McLure and Zodrow (1988). An early Danish statement of similar arguments was given by Thorlund Jepsen (1975).

taxes on capital tend to stimulate current consumption at the expense of future consumption, we have just seen that the wage tax component of a comprehensive income tax will have a negative human wealth effect which will tend to reduce both current and future consumption. While the impact effect on current consumption is thus uncertain, the short run effect on savings is unambiguously negative, so the stock of wealth will be lower in the new long run equilibrium. As a result of this, consumption is also sure to be lower in the new steady state.

Figure 4 illustrates the effects of the comprehensive income tax just mentioned. The figure shows the case where the negative human wealth effect of the higher tax rate on wages dominates the positive substitution effect of the higher tax rate on capital income, resulting in a short-run fall in consumption. As we pointed out, it is also possible that the impact effect on consumption is positive. Because of offsetting substitution and wealth effects, the comprehensive income tax will have uncertain long-run effects on labor supply and hence on output and the capital stock.

Consider finally the effects of our consumption tax parameter t^c, which may be interpreted as a general VAT or as a direct proportional expenditure tax. A consumption tax reduces the purchasing power of wages and in this respect it works like a wage tax, making for a short-run decrease in consumption, labor supply, and output, and tending to initiate a process of dissaving. However, the consumption tax also reduces the effective purchasing power of accumulated non-human wealth, and in this way it works like a capital levy on existing financial wealth. In order to at least partially restore the purchasing power of their wealth, consumers will respond by reducing their level of consumption even more. It can be shown that the fall in consumption will be sufficiently large to call forth a positive level of savings, despite the reduction of labor supply and output. As illustrated in figure 5, the private sector will thus start to accumulate assets and will end up with a larger stock of non-human wealth in the new steady state equilibrium. It can also be shown that, while the steady-state effect on consumption is uncertain, the negative effects of the consumption tax on labor supply, capital input and output will persist in the long run, although these long-run effects will be smaller numerically than the corresponding impact effects.

One final comment on the consumption tax seems worthwhile: In textbooks on Public Finance it is often claimed that a tax on consumption is "equivalent" to a wage tax. The analysis above makes clear that this is not correct. While both types of tax imply a zero marginal effective tax rate on the return to saving, the consumption tax differs from the wage tax by imposing a capital levy on existing non-human wealth. The two taxes are therefore fully equivalent only for a "new-born" (young) person entering the economic sphere with no financial wealth.[5]

So far we have considered only the effects of *un*anticipated changes in tax policy. It should be mentioned that not only the quantitative, but also the qualitative short-run effects of ***anticipated*** shifts in policy may sometimes differ from the impact effects of policy changes that take the private sector by surprise. This is illustrated in figure 6, which shows the effect of an anticipated increase in the wage tax rate. Initially the economy is in equilibrium in point E_0. The government then announces that it will raise the tax rate on wage income at some future time t″. Consumers will start to adjust to this already at the time of announcement, so there will be an immediate drop in consumption to point E′. From then on, the economy will start following the unstable dynamics governing behavior in the area below the two curves $\dot{A}_0 = 0$ and $\dot{C}_0 = 0$ until at time t″, when the tax hike is implemented, it reaches point E″ on the stable trajectory corresponding to the new steady state equilibrium. The important point is that, during the period when the economy moves from E′ to E″, savings will be *positive* and will turn negative only after point E″ has been reached. By contrast, figure 3 shows that savings will be negative throughout the intire adjustment period, when the tax increase is unanticipated.

VII. Tax Policy and the Terms of Trade

The effects of various policy measures on international competetiveness and the terms of trade are often considered quite important in economic policy debates. In the rest of the paper we shall therefore drop the assumption of exogenous terms of trade and assume instead that the domestic economy can expand its net exports only by accepting a lower relative price of its output, as specified in (22). On the other hand, to avoid problems of analytical intractability, we shall now make the simplifying assumption that labor supply is exogenous, i.e. we shall set our parameter γ equal to zero, implying from

[5] The reader might also consult Auerbach and Kotlikoff (1987, ch. 5) for a good explanation of the differences between the two types of taxes in a life cycle framework.

(15) that $L=L^*$. With inelastic labor supply, a wage tax will work like a lump sum tax and becomes entirely neutral, if the revenue is redistributed as a lump sum transfer to the private sector. Consequently, the effects of a comprehensive income tax, which is a combination of a wage tax and a tax on capital income, will be identical with the effects of the capital income tax itself. Below we shall therefore consider only the comprehensive income tax vis á vis the consumption tax.

Given the assumptions just mentioned, we end up with the following version of our model (to be explained below):

$$(29) \qquad g(F(K,L^*) - \alpha C q^{-1}(\alpha+\beta)^{-1}) - q = 0$$

$$(30) \qquad qF_K(K,L^*) - i = 0$$

$$(31) \qquad q[F(K,L^*)-F_K(K,L^*)K] - wL^* = 0$$

$$(32) \qquad \dot{C} = [i(1-t^*)-\theta]C - p(\theta+p)(1+t^c)^{-1}A$$

$$(33) \qquad \dot{A} = iA + wL^* - C \quad .$$

Equation (29) is simply the demand curve (22) in which we have inserted the aggregated analogue of (5) plus the production function (19). Equation (30) restates the arbitrage condition (20), and (31) is obtained from the marginal productivity condition (21), using the linear homogeneity of the production function. (32) and (33) follow immediately from (27) and (26), once we set $\gamma=0$.

Relations (29) through (31) may be used to derive the equilibrium values of q, K, and w, for any given value of C. The reader may easily verify from these equations that

$$(34) \qquad \partial q/\partial C > 0, \qquad \partial K/\partial C > 0, \qquad \partial w/\partial C \equiv w_c > 0 \quad .$$

From the last inequality in (34) it is seen that w is a rising function of C. Using this relationship to eliminate w from (33), one obtains an autonomous pair of non-linear differential equations in C and A. Linearizing this system around its steady state, one finds that it will display saddlepoint stability (and otherwise be totally unstable) in the neighborhood of equilibrium, if

$$(35) \qquad i[i(1-t^*)-\theta] + (w_c L^* - 1)p(\theta+p)(1+t^c)^{-1} < 0 \quad .$$

(35) is the analogue of condition (28) in the previous version of our model, and we shall assume that it is met, just as we continue to assume that $i(1-t^*) > \theta$ to ensure a positive equilibrium level of non-human wealth.

On this background, it is possible to derive the impact and steady state effects of tax policy reported in table 2. We see that the qualitative effects of the two tax instruments are exactly opposite to each other. Consider first the effects of a rise in the comprehensive income tax rate. Because it reduces the net reward to saving, such a policy change induces consumers to increase their present consumption at the expense of future consumption. The ensuing short-run rise in demand for domestic consumer goods will tend to reduce net exports, thereby driving up the relative price of domestic goods and improving the terms of trade. This in turn will make it profitable for domestic producers to install more (imported) capital goods and expand their output. Because of a higher capital intensity of production improving their marginal productivity, workers will be offered a higher wage rate (in terms of the numéraire).

So much for the short run. In the long run, we see from table 2 that all of these effects of a higher income tax rate will be reversed. The reason is that the decumulation of assets caused by the short-run fall in savings will lead to a lower steady state level of wealth which depresses domestic consumer demand. As a result of this weakening of the domestic market, domestic producers increase their exports, but this leads to a deterioration of the terms of trade, which in turn induces firms to reduce their demand for capital and labor.

As already indicated, the qualitative effects of a higher tax rate on consumption are exactly opposite to those of the income tax hike. In the short run, a higher consumption tax rate is contractionary (even though the revenue is transferred back to the private sector), as consumers start to save in order to partially restore the *after-tax* purchasing power of their existing assets. This leads to an accumulation of assets, and over time the ensuing increase in wealth provides the basis for a *higher* level of consumption which will in turn *improve* the terms of trade via higher demand for domestic goods.

VIII. Summary and Conclusion

In this paper we have studied the short-run and long-run macroeconomic effects of tax policy in a small open economy, with special emphasis on a comparison between income and consumption taxes. We considered an economy inhabited by intertemporally optimizing consumers with finite expected lifetimes. Capital was taken to be perfectly mobile internationally, and a distinction was made between an imported good, which could be used for consumption as well as investment, and a domestic good, used for domestic consumption and exports. With this set-up, the terms of trade could be uniquely defined by a single relative price.

In the first version of the model, the small economy was assumed to produce a standard internationally traded good the relative price of which it could not control. Despite this simplifying postulate of exogenous terms of trade, some complexity was introduced via an assumption of endogenous labor supply. This model was used to study the impact, dynamic and steady state effects of taxes on capital income, wages, consumption, and comprehensive income, assuming the tax revenue to be redistributed to the private sector in the form of lump-sum transfers. Not surprisingly, the taxes on wages and income were found to reduce the long-run levels of consumption and national wealth, because of the distortions they introduce in the markets for labor and capital. However, because of offsetting effects deriving from taxes on capital and taxes on labor, the long-run effects of the comprehensive income tax on the inputs of capital and labor and hence on domestic output were found to be uncertain. By comparison, a consumption tax was found to reduce the steady-state levels of employment, capital input, and output, to increase the steady-state level of national wealth, and to have an uncertain effect on the steady-state level of consumption.

The last section of the paper introduced endogenous terms of trade, but in order to derive unambiguous policy effects, it became necessary to postulate inelastic labor supply. With these modifications of the model, another balanced-budget incidence analysis of income and consumption taxes was carried out. It turned out that the two types of taxes had exactly opposite qualitative effects. In the short run, a comprehensive income tax would be expansionary and improve the terms of trade, but in the long run it would be contractionary, worsen the terms of trade and reduce national wealth. A consumption tax, on the other hand, would have the reverse effects. Thus this analysis suggested that if labor supply is relatively inelastic, as many economists believe it to be, a switch from income to consumption taxes could have rather favorable long-run macroeconomic effects, although such a reform would be likely to have some unpleasant contractionary effects in the short run.

To return to the theme of the introductory section, the present paper has hopefully helped to illuminate the importance of openness for the effects of tax policy. For instance, in the closed economy tax-induced changes in non-human wealth are equivalent to changes in the physical capital stock. By contrast, our analysis of the open economy with endogenous labor supply revealed that a capital income tax will tend to *increase* the domestic stock of capital in the long run, even though it will *reduce* the *total* stock of non-human wealth (via a fall in net foreign assets). Similarly, the model with endogenous labor supply implied that a consumption tax will reduce the steady-state capital stock despite the fact that it will increase equilibrium national wealth. As a final example, while a capital income tax might be shifted to a considerable degree in a closed economy, the presence of capital mobility in the open economy significantly reduces the scope for shifting.

Needless to say, the technical analysis in this paper could be expanded and improved in many directions. One major limitation, as far as the short-run analysis is concerned, was the simplifying assumption that firms could instantaneously and costlessly adjust their capital stock to its desired level. Attempts at introducing the realistic phenomenon of gradual adjustment of the capital stock have been made by Matsuyama (1987) and Nielsen and Sørensen (1989), although only within models with exogenous labor supply and exogenous terms of trade. It would of course also be interesting to extend the analysis to the case of large open economies, perhaps along the lines suggested by Nielsen (1989). As a final caveat, we should also mention that a highly aggregated model like the present one cannot illuminate what is probably one of the most important arguments in the debate on income versus consumption taxes: This is the argument that any real world system of capital income taxation is bound to introduce substantial *intersectoral* distortions in the allocation of capital, because of a host of practical problems of ensuring a uniform, non-discriminating taxation of all the different types of capital income.

Table 1

Balanced-budget incidence of alternative tax instruments in a small open economy with exogenous terms of trade

Rise in / Effect on	Impact effects				Steady-state effects			
	t^i	t^w	t^*	t^c	t^i	t^w	t^*	t^c
C	+	-	?	-	-	-	-	?
$\dot{A}$	-	-	-	+	0	0	0	0
A	0	0	0	0	-	-	-	+
L	-	-	-	-	+	-[1]	?	-
K	-	-	-	-	+	-[1]	?	-
Y	-	-	-	-	+	-[1]	?	-

Note: The impact effects refer to *unanticipated* policy changes. All effects on i and w are zero. The effects on C^d and C^i are proportional to the effects on C.

1. A sufficient condition for this result to hold is that the system is saddlepoint stable even when labor supply is exogenous ($\gamma = 0$).

Table 2

Balanced-budget incidence of alternative tax instruments in a small open economy with endogenous terms of trade

Rise in / Effect on	Impact effects		Steady-state effects	
	t^*	t^c	t^*	t^c
q	+	-	-	+
C	+	-	-	+
K	+	-	-	+
Y	+	-	-	+
W	+	-	-	+
$\dot{A}$	-	+	0	0
A	0	0	-	+

Note: The results are derived on the assumption that labor supply is exogenous.

Figure 1. The dynamics of consumption and asset accumulation in a small open economy

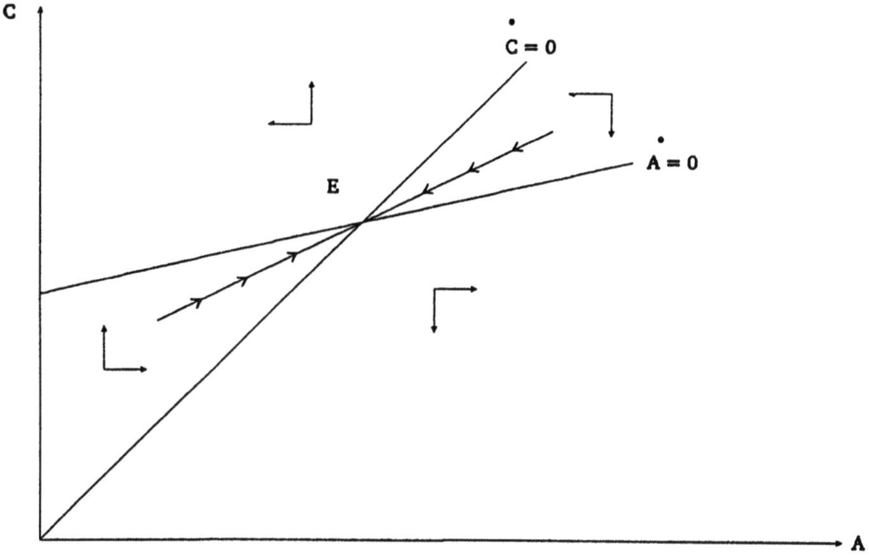

Figure 2. Effects of an unanticipated rise in the capital income tax rate

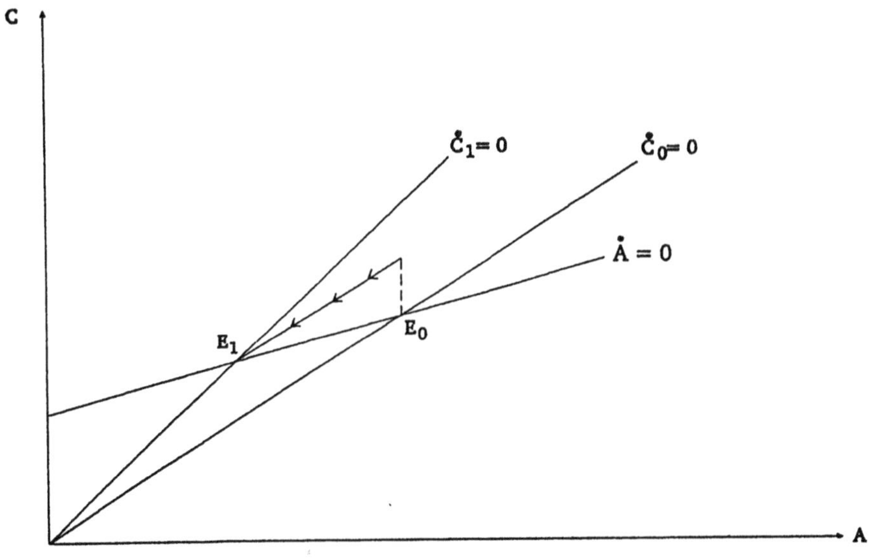

Figure 3. Effects of an unanticipated rise in the wage tax rate

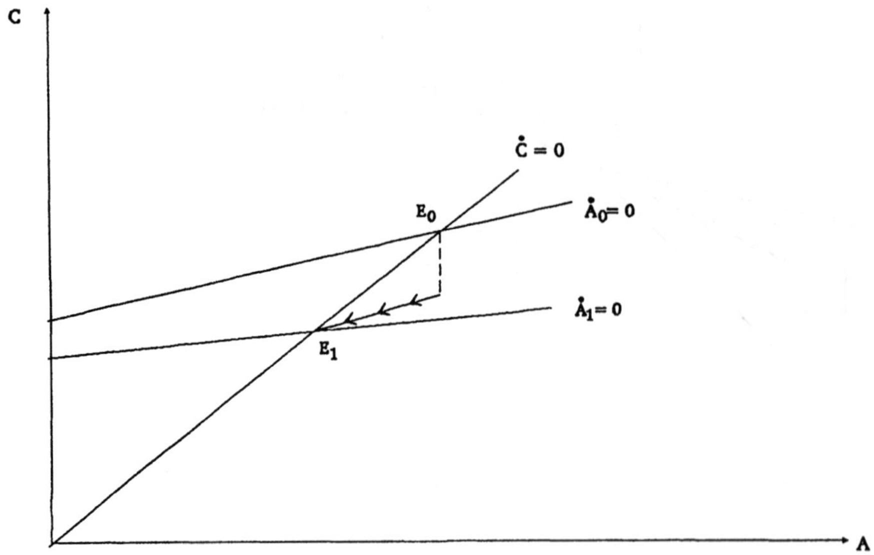

Figure 4. Effects of a comprehensive income tax

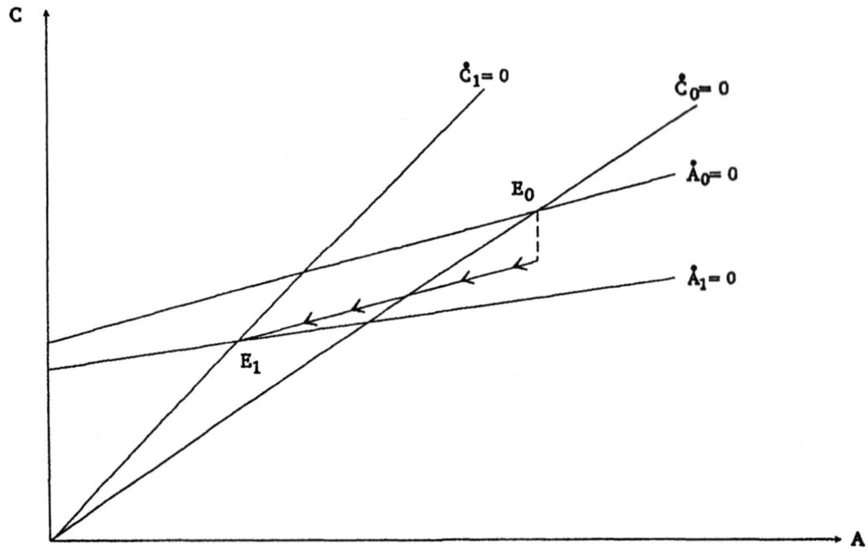

Note: The impact effect on C could also be positive

Figure 5. Effects of a consumption tax

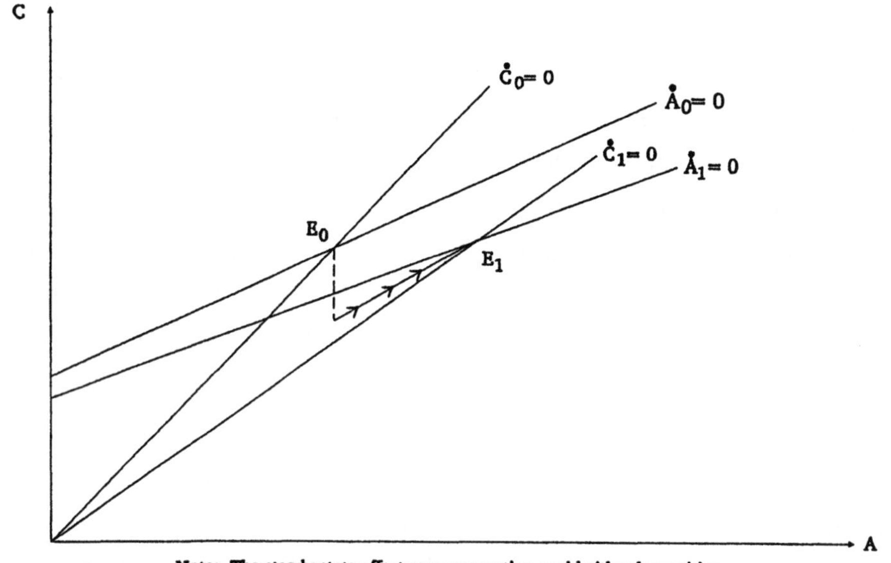

Note: The steady-state effect on consumption could either be positive or negative

Figure 6. Effects of an anticipated permanent rise in the wage tax rate

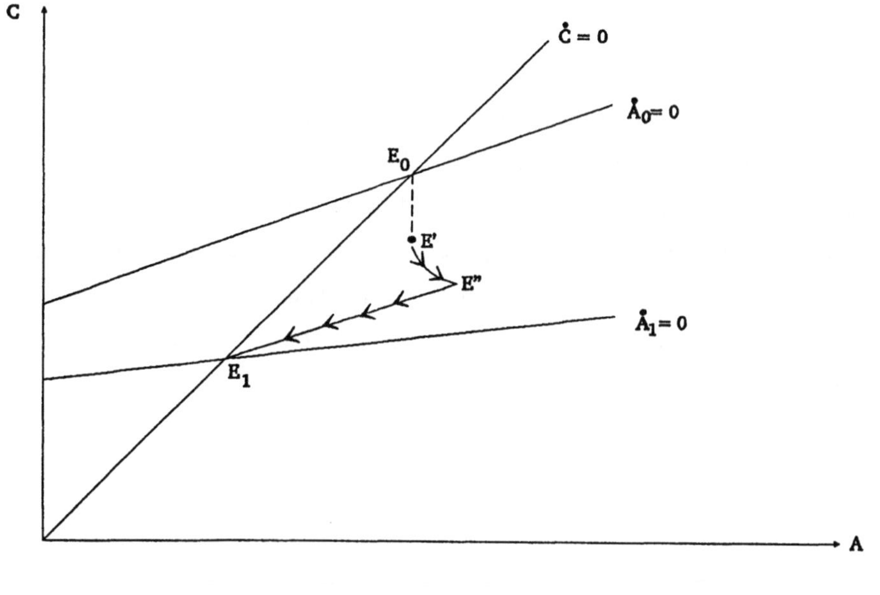

Comments by Pierre Pestieau

This is an excellent piece of research. I must praise the author for the clarity and the neatness of his presentation. The analysis is well-done, the reasoning develops straightforwardly and the results are derived and interpreted correctly. With such a paper, the task of a discussant is to deal with the basic assumptions of the model, its specification and its relevancy.

My first remark, which is perhaps a bit provocative, concerns the dynamic approach and the analytic framework of this model which is in the tradition of optimal growth theory à la Ramsey and Cass. What do we get from that as opposed to the static model à la Corlett and Hague? I agree with the author when he underlines the importance of analyzing an open economy to grasp correctly the incidence of income versus expenditure taxation. In that setting, the possibility of investing abroad, of importing consumption and capital goods has to be taken into account. Introducing openness surely modifies what we know about the comparative merits of expenditure and income taxation. My question rather concerns the dynamic approach which is intellectually tempting but brings little, considering that it is hard to see through what is going on. Not only the intuition of the results is hard to grasp, but is it not paradoxical to focus on steady-state tax incidence results whereas tax reform tends to be at best a medium run issue?

We are given two alternative models: one with given terms of trade but elastic labor supply and one with flexible terms of trade but inelastic labor supply. The key results of either model can be summarized in the following table.

There is something a bit mechanical with fixed labor supply. In the short run, $\dot{A}$ and C go opposite each other and in the expected direction. In the long run, C and A go in the same direction determined by the sign of $\dot{A}$ in the short run. With endogenous labor supply, substitution and income effects bring some ambiguity which in my view is more interesting.

Endogeneous terms of trade
Exogeneous labor supply

	income tax		consumption tax	
	SR	LR	SR	LR
C	+	−	−	+
$\dot{A}$	−	0	+	0
A	0	−	−	+

Exogeneous terms of trade
Endogeneous labor supply

	income tax		consumption tax	
	SR	LR	SR	LR
C	?	−	−	?
$\dot{A}$	−	0	+	0
A	0	−	0	+

I now turn to two other basic features of this paper: Blanchard's model and the macroeconomic content. Blanchard's model is very ingenious; it gives the illusion of heterogeneity but ultimately it is not much different from a single infinitely lived individual's model. The alleged reason to use it is to avoid assuming that, in the steady state, the after-tax rate of interest equals the rate of time preference. In my view, models of small open economies are often too casual about the requirement of a steady-state world market general equilibrium. Such an equilibrium could indeed lead to that unwanted condition.

Finally, I want to come back to the purpose of this exercise. The paper talks indifferently of tax incidence and of macroeconomic effects. In my view, there is little macroeconomics in this paper even though the dynamics of consumption, employment and capital stock is dealt with. The basic ingredients of macroeconomic questions are indeed assumed away: inflation and unemployment. To put it in other words, we have here a typical general equilibrium setting. In that respect, even though this is not the purpose of the paper, what would be the optimal tax policy? Zero tax? Less generally, when reading the tax incidence tables, what are the desirable variations? An increase in consumption and a decrease in labor supply? This is too serious a question to be left to policymakers.

References

Auerbach, A. / Kotlikoff, L. (1987), Dynamic Fiscal Policy, Cambridge: Cambridge University Press.

Blanchard, O.J. (1984), Current and Anticipated Deficits, Interest Rates and Economic Activity, European Economic Review 25, pp. 7-27.

Blanchard, O.J. (1985), Debt, Deficits, and Finite Horizons, Journal of Political Economy 93, pp. 223-247.

Bradford, D. (1988), What are Consumption Taxes and Who Pays Them?, Tax Notes, April 18, 1988.

Hall, R.E. / Rabushka, A. (1983), Low Tax, Simple Tax, Flat Tax, New York: McGraw-Hill.

Hodrick, R.J. (1982), On the Effects of Macroeconomic Policy in a Maximizing Model of a Small Open Economy, Journal of Macroeconomics 4, pp. 195-213.

Matsuyama, K. (1987), Current Account Dynamics in A Finite Horizon Model, Journal of International Economics 23, pp. 299-313.

McLure, C.E. / Zodrow, G.R. (1988), Implementing Direct Consumption Taxes in Developing Countries, Working Paper on Public Economics (WPS 131), Washington D.C.: World Bank.

Nielsen, S.B. (1989), Capital Income Taxation in A Growing World Economy, Paper presented at the Nordic Workshop on Financial Markets, Investment, and Taxation in Tampere, Finland, April 7-8, 1989.

Nielsen, S.B. / Sørensen, P.B. (1989), Capital Income Taxation in A Growing Open Economy, Paper presented at the Nordic Workshop on Financial Markets, Investment, and Taxation in Tampere, Finland, April 7-8, 1989.

Sen, P. / Turnovsky, S.J. (1988), Deterioriation of the Terms of Trade and Capital Accumulation: A Reexamination of the Laursen-Metzler Effect, NBER Working Paper No. 2616.

Sinn, H.-W. (1987), Capital Income Taxation and Resource Allocation, Amsterdam: North-Holland.

Thorlund Jepsen, G. (1975), Skatterne Foer, Nu og i 1985, Albertslund: Det Danske Forlag.

Charles L. Ballard

On the Specification of Simulation Models for Evaluating Income and Consumption Taxes*

I. Introduction

Economists have emphasized a number of possible advantages of consumption taxation over income taxation.[1] One of the most important of these has to do with dynamic efficiency. It is often asserted that increased reliance on consumption taxation would result in welfare gains.[2] However, from the perspective of the policymaker, it may not suffice merely to assert that consumption taxation is *better*. In order to have much chance of

* My interest in this subject was first stimulated by David Starrett. My greatest debt is to Larry Goulder, for much help over a long period. I also have had helpful discussions with Tim Bresnahan, Larry Kotlikoff, Larry Martin, Joe Pechman, Karl Scholz, John Shoven, and Kun-Young Yun. I thank Neil Bjorksten for fine research assistance, and Lori Austin for her excellent work in preparing the manuscript. The support of the National Science Foundation (Grant 84-20283) is gratefully acknowledged.

1 William Andrews (1974), David Bradford (1980), and Henry Aaron and Harvey Galper (1985) are among those who have emphasized the administrative advantages of a personal expenditure tax. Under such a tax, there is no need either to worry about accruing wealth or to make certain types of inflation adjustments. I acknowledge that these issues are of great importance. In this paper, however, I focus narrowly on the effects of different configurations of taxes on capital accumulation and welfare within a computational general equilibrium model.

2 However, except in the very simplest models, it is not possible to prove any theorems about the superiority of consumption taxation. For example, see Anthony Atkinson and Agnar Sandmo (1980). In general, the question of whether consumption taxation is superior will depend on the structure and parameters of the model.

overcoming the inertia of the political system, it may be necessary for economists to show that the efficiency gains are, in some sense, *large*.

In fact, several simulation studies have found substantial welfare gains.[3] However, the results of any simulation study are believable only to the extent that the underlying model is believable. For example, an economist who has contributed to this literature once referred to a simulation model "by saying it is a characteristic of these models that saving is highly elastic".[4] In this paper, we shall see that this statement is true of many simulation models, especially those in which *human wealth effects* play an important role. If the actual saving behavior of consumers in the real economy is highly elastic, then these models may do a good job of guiding our understanding. However, if real-world consumers are not very elastic, these models are of limited usefulness.

In fact, there is great controversy about the size of the elasticity of savings with respect to the real net rate of return.[5] It is not my purpose to resolve that controversy. However, I will show that the simulation models that have been used are quite capable of producing *extremely* elastic intertemporal responses. In my view, these responses ought to be looked upon with caution. If the simulation models are indeed overly sensitive in their intertemporal responses, then the welfare gains suggested by the models may be upwardly biased.

The primary purpose of this paper is to provide an insider's view of the simulation models that have been used to assess questions of dynamic tax policy. I will discuss the strengths and weaknesses of some of the models, and will point out some of the pitfalls encountered when economists use dynamic simulation models. I will analyze three basic types of dynamic model. The first is a model in which the consumer chooses between

---

[3] For example, see Don Fullerton, John Shoven, and John Whalley (1983), Alan Auerbach and Laurence Kotlikoff (1983), Auerbach, Kotlikoff, and Jonathan Skinner (1983), and Dale Jorgenson and Kun-Young Yun (1986). All of these are discrete-time simulation models. In this paper, I deal exclusively with the properties of such models. Of course, there is a substantial literature based on continuous-time models. It is hoped that, in the future, the continuous-time models of Kenneth Judd (1985, 1987) and others can be analyzed in the same way as the discrete-time models are analyzed here.

[4] Kotlikoff, speaking in seminar at the National Bureau of Economic Research, Stanford, CA.

[5] Among the better-known pieces in the literature are Michael Boskin (1978), Philip Howrey and Saul Hymans (1980), Lawrence Summers (1981), and Alan Blinder and Angus Deaton (1985).

present and future consumption, and repeats the choice every year for infinite time. The second is a true *infinite-horizon* model, in which the consumer maximizes an infinite stream of consumption, subject to an infinite-horizon wealth constraint. The third is an overlapping-generations life-cycle model, in which each generation maximizes lifetime utility, subject to a lifetime wealth constraint. Each of these three structures of consumer dynamics forms a part of a computational general equilibrium model of the United States economy and tax system. In order to facilitate comparisons, all of the calculations will be based on the same data set (for 1983) and the same model treatment of the various taxes in the economy.

The three model types are described in the next section. The third section reports results. I provide substantial analysis of the sensitivity of the results with respect to model structure and parameters. Different methods of controlling the intertemporal responsiveness of the models are analyzed. In the final section of the paper, I draw some conclusions, and suggest avenues for future research.

II. The Simulation Models

A. A Model with a Simple Present/Future Choice

The first type of dynamic model that I will consider is the GEMTAP model originally developed by Don Fullerton, John Shoven, and John Whalley.[6] It contains a rich intersectoral structure, but its dynamics are fairly simple. In this model, the consumer makes a choice in every period between present and future consumption. The consumer repeats this choice for an infinite number of periods, so that welfare calculations are made with respect to an infinite stream of consumption. However, this model differs significantly from the *infinite-horizon* models that will be described below. In any period

[6] This model has a long history of application to consumption taxation issues. The first evaluation of the effects of a personal consumption tax using this model appeared in Fullerton, Shoven, and Whalley (1983). Ballard (1987) assessed the sensitivity of those results to changes in the specification of consumer foresight. Ballard, John Karl Scholz, and Shoven (1987) used the model to assess the effects of introducing a value-added tax. Douglas Bernheim, Scholz, and Shoven (1988) performed a systematic analysis of the sensitivity of the model.

within the GEMTAP model, the consumer's choices are made subject to a single-period income constraint, rather than an intertemporal wealth constraint.

The dynamic structure of the GEMTAP model is thus somewhat limited. However, the model does have one important advantage. Because of the simple nature of its dynamic structure, the model can be calibrated to any desired degree of intertemporal responsiveness. The investigator can specify the desired elasticity of saving with respect to the rate of return, and this can be done simply and precisely. Thus, if the investigator believes that the *true* savings elasticity is low, or even negative, that belief can be put into the model.

Since the GEMTAP model has been described elsewhere on several occasions, the description here will be brief. A very detailed description can be found in Ballard, Fullerton, Shoven, and Whalley [BFSW (1985)]. In each period, consumers maximize a nested utility function:

$$\text{(a)} \qquad U = U(H(C_0(X_1, X_2, \ldots, X_n), l), C_F) \quad .$$

The outer nest involves the choice between H, a composite of current consumptions, and C_F, a composite of a future consumption stream (C_1, C_2,...). Specifically, C_F is the annual consumption from a perpetual annuity made possible through the current period's saving. The demand for C_F thus results in a derived demand for saving. This is useful for purposes of calibrating the model, since saving data are a part of the observed data set, whereas C_F is not directly observable. The middle nest of the three nests in the utility function divides H between current leisure, l and C_0, a composite of consumption for the various current consumption commodities. A problem with this model of the labor/leisure choice is that it is dynamically inconsistent. Future leisure is not valued now, but when the future period arrives, leisure at that time is valued. The H and U nests are both specified in constant elasticity of substitution (CES) form.

The inner nest divides C_0 among current consumption commodities, such as food, housing, appliances, etc. The C_0 nest is specified as a Cobb-Douglas function. In the case of the data set used here, this function is defined over 17 consumption commodities. These 17 commodities are shown in Table 1, along with the 19 industrial sectors. (The production sectors classification and the consumer goods classification are different because of differences in the classifications used in the data. A fixed-coefficient transition matrix is used to transform between consumer and producer goods.)

The elasticity of substitution in the outer nest of the utility function determines the elasticity of saving with respect to the real net rate of return. The investigator using this model chooses a desired value for the savings elasticity, and then chooses the elasticity of substitution that yields the desired savings elasticity. Similarly, there is a one-to-one relationship between the elasticity of substitution in the middle nest of the utility function, and the elasticity of labor supply with respect to the real net wage rate. Details of the calibration procedures can be found in [BFSW (1985), especially Chapter 6]. In many of the papers based on this model, the *central case* values are 0.4 for the savings elasticity and 0.15 for the labor supply elasticity. Those are chosen as the central case elasticities here, as well, but sensitivity analysis is provided. In addition, a value of -0.20 is chosen here for the total income elasticity of labor supply, which yields a central case compensated elasticity of 0.35. This is a somewhat smaller income elasticity than has been used in most earlier papers.

Most of the details of the consumer side of the GEMTAP model, described above, will not be duplicated in the other models. However, the structure of production and the modeling of taxes are the same across all three model types. In any single period, there are 19 producer-good industries that use capital and labor in CES value-added functions. They also use the outputs of other industries through a matrix of fixed input-output coefficients. The tax rates on labor for each industry are derived by taking payroll taxes and other contributions as a proportion of labor income, while the tax rates on capital for each industry are derived by taking corporate income, corporate franchise, and property taxes as a proportion of capital income.

Each of these 19 producer goods is used directly for investment, for net exports, and for exhaustive government expenditures. In this regard, it is important to note two things. First, the investment demand is satisfied in a passive way. When the desired saving by consumers increases, the investment sectors in these models meet the demand without incurring any special adjustment costs. The inclusion of adjustment costs would, presumably, reduce the welfare gains associated with the switch to a consumption tax. Secondly, although there is international trade in the model, there are no international capital flows. If the world is actually characterized by a perfect international capital market, then the gains associated with adopting a consumption tax might be greatly reduced. Lawrence Goulder, Shoven, and Whalley (1983) use the GEMTAP model (in a version fairly similar to the one used here) to analyze the sensitivity of the results with respect to changes in the specification of international flows of goods and capital. While they find that the specification of goods flows has rather little effect on the results, the specification of capital flows can have large effects. In some cases, the adoption of a consumption tax actually leads to substantial *losses* in the Goulder-Shoven-Whalley study. Unfortunately, there is substantial controversy about the degree of perfection of the international capital market. [See, for example, Martin Feldstein and Charles Horioka (1980) and Arnold Harberger (1980)]. Until that controversy is resolved to a greater degree, it will be difficult to draw definitive conclusions with respect to the effects of the switch from income taxation to consumption taxation. Nevertheless, it should be clear that this is another area where most of the simulation models employed thus far may be biased in the direction of larger welfare gains, since most abstract from international capital flows. [Another very good discussion of these issues can be found in Joel Slemrod (1988)].

The same data set is used for all three model types. Previous applications of the GEMTAP model used a general equilibrium data set for 1973. [See BFSW (1985), especially Chapters 4 and 5.] In this paper, I employ an updated data set for 1983. The basic sources of the data are very similar to those for the earlier data set. Details on this new data set can be found in Karl Scholz (1987).[7] This data set allows one to perform calculations for each of 14 consumer groups. However, for our purposes here, this disaggregation is of little value. I follow standard procedures to aggregate into a single consumer group.

---

[7] The Scholz data have been amended in one way. A new Z matrix of transition between producer goods and consumer goods is used, based on data from the May, 1984, Survey of Current Business.

B. Infinite-Horizon Model

The second type of dynamic model considered here is the infinite-horizon model, in which a single consumer maximizes the utility from an infinite stream of consumption, subject to an infinite-horizon wealth constraint.[8]

The entire approach to specifying these infinite-horizon models is fundamentally different from the approach in GEMTAP. In GEMTAP, the approach is to specify the actual behavioral responses of consumers in the model. In the case of certain applications of the infinite-horizon model (as well as certain applications of overlapping-generations life-cycle models), the approach is to specify certain parameters of the utility function, which may yield a wide variety of behavioral responses.

Frank Ramsey's pathbreaking article (1928) was the first to use the infinite-horizon consumer to describe intertemporal consumption choice. Since Ramsey's time, a variety of justifications have been given for the use of these models. One reason to use this type of model is that the equilibrium path of prices under perfect foresight will be unique, whereas it may not be unique in the case of an overlapping-generations life-cycle model with perfect foresight. Infinite-horizon models are also justified on occasion by appealing to the work of Robert Barro (1974), who described conditions under which a dynasty of consumers with finite life might behave as if they were a single infinitely-lived consumer. A third reason for the infinite-horizon scheme (and probably the most important) is its simplicity and tractability.[9] However, no one has ever justified the use of these models on the basis of the realism of the intertemporal responses that they generate.[10]

The large degree of intertemporal responsiveness that is typical for infinite-horizon models arises from what Summers calls *human wealth effects*. If the rate of return increases as a result of a change in tax policy, the present value of the consumer's

---

[8] Infinite-horizon simulation models include Jorgenson and Yun (1986a, 1986b), Ballard and Lawrence Goulder (1985), and Goulder and Summers (1987).

[9] Having had experience with both types of models, I can attest to the fact that infinite-horizon models are substantially simpler from a computational standpoint than are overlapping-generations life-cycle models.

[10] In fact, most articles written with models in which lifetime utility is maximized subject to a lifetime wealth constraint do not discuss the problem of intertemporal responsiveness at all. An exception is Ballard and Goulder (1985), although this issue was not the central focus of that paper.

wealth decreases. The consumer is now poorer, and decreases his consumption. Even a small percentage change in consumption can lead to a very large swing in saving. The effect is larger when the proportion of the consumer's lifetime wealth accruing in the future is greater. Obviously, the extreme case is the one where the consumer's stream of earnings stretches into the infinite future. When the consumer in the model has an infinite earnings stream, and when that stream can be allocated freely, the savings responses can be very large indeed.

Before proceeding to the model, it is important to deal with an issue of semantics. Infinite-horizon models of the type pioneered by Ramsey share the characteristic that the steady-state rate of return is determined uniquely. If a change in tax policy shocks the system, the original steady-state rate of return will eventually be re-established. This model characteristic is sometimes described as implying that the *long run savings rate is infinitely interest elastic*.[11] This statement is of limited value for two important reasons. First, the statement reflects an unusual interpretation of the meaning of an elasticity. It is essentially a general equilibrium elasticity, in that it refers to the behavior of the rate of return that occurs in general equilibrium when capital stocks are allowed to adjust. However, when economists think of elasticities, their thinking is usually partial equilibrium in nature. (When we discuss the elasticity of labor supply with respect to the net wage, we do not typically refer to the general equilibrium change in wages that might occur if sufficiently large numbers of workers were to alter their labor supply in response.) However, it is certainly possible to perform an experiment which would yield a more conventional, partial equilibrium elasticity measure. In such an experiment, we would ask what would occur if the consumer believed that the rate of return were to be increased permanently by a small proportion. In this case, the elasticity could not be infinite, even if the very long run. Experiments of this type are performed in this paper, and the resulting elasticities are reported. Second, it would be easy (but incorrect) to infer from the above quote about the infinite interest elasticity that (a) the welfare cost of capital taxation is infinite in such a model, or (b) even if the welfare cost is finite, the welfare cost of taxation is the same regardless of the specific parameterization. In fact, the welfare effects of taxation in models of this type do respond to the *short-run* speed

[11] This quote is from Summers (1981, p. 537). See David Starrett (1988, esp. p. 241) for more discussion.

of adjustment to the new steady state. The speed of adjustment can differ widely, depending on parameters. In this paper, I will report in detail on some of these differences.

The calculations presented here are based on modified versions of the infinite horizon model developed by Ballard and Goulder (1985). The simplest case involves no labor/leisure choice, so that consumption is the only choice variable. In this case, the behavior of the single consumer is characterized by the additively separable utility function:

$$\text{(b)} \qquad U = \sum_{t=1}^{\infty} \frac{1}{(1-Pt)^{t-1}} U_t(C_t) \quad ,$$

where Pt is the subjective rate of time preference and C_t is consumption in period t. David Starrett (1982) first suggested that a Stone-Geary formulation of the instantaneous utility or *felicity* function would be useful in studying the behavior of life-cycle consumers. The Stone-Geary formulation is followed here.
Let C_t^* represent minimum required consumption in period t. Then define

$$\text{(c)} \qquad \hat{C}_t \equiv C_t - C_t^*$$

as discretionary consumption in period t. For the instantaneous felicity function, U_t, it is customary to choose a single isoelastic form for all periods:

$$\text{(d)} \qquad U_t = \begin{cases} \dfrac{\hat{C}_t^{\,1-\delta}}{1-\delta} \; , & \delta \neq 1 \\ \ln \hat{C}_t \; , & \delta = 1 \end{cases} \quad , \text{ all } t \quad ,$$

The parameter δ is the inverse of the intertemporal elasticity of substitution for $\hat{C}_t$.

Combining the above expressions, we can write a given consumer group's lifetime utility (from year 1, in the non-logarithmic case) as

$$\text{(e)} \qquad U = \sum_{t=1}^{\infty} \frac{1}{(1+Pt)^{t-1}} \; \frac{\hat{C}_t^{1-\delta}}{1-\delta} \; .$$

Consumers maximize U subject to the constraint that the present value of lifetime consumption must not exceed the present value of lifetime resources. This constraint can be written as

$$\text{(f)} \qquad \sum_{t=1}^{\infty} \frac{P_t C_t}{\prod_{s=1}^{t} (1+r_s)} = W_1 + \sum_{t=1}^{\infty} \frac{w_t L_t + Y_t}{\prod_{s=1}^{t} (1+r_s)} \; ,$$

where $r_1 \equiv 0$, and where W_1 is the value of inherited capital, L_t is labor supply in period t (which is exogenous in this case), Y_t is the value of transfers received in period t, r_s is the rate of return in period s, and P and w denote the prices of consumption and labor, respectively. Expression (f) thus states that the present value of lifetime consumption must not exceed the value of inherited capital plus the present value of lifetime earnings and transfers. For purposes of expositional simplicity, equation (f) abstracts from taxes. The inclusion of taxes is straightforward.

Combining (e) and (f), we can write the consumer's Lagrangean function. Manipulation of the resulting first-order conditions yields an equation of motion for consumption:

$$\text{(g)} \qquad C_t = C_{t-1} \left[\left(\frac{P_t}{P_{t-1}}\right) \left(\frac{1+Pt}{1+r_t}\right) \right]^{\frac{-1}{\delta}}$$

The equation of motion, (g), can be manipulated and substituted into the wealth constraint, (f), and this will yield a solution for first-period consumption.

In the steady state, with constant prices, P, the growth of consumption depends on the rate of return, rate of time preference, and intertemporal substitution elasticity. This relationship between r, Pt and δ places severe constraints on the ability of the investigator to analyze the sensitivity of the model. If we accept data on the capital stock and the net saving rate, then the steady-state growth rate will be determined by the data. If the growth rate is thus given by the data, then the relative sizes of C_t and C_{t-1} are predetermined. Then, if the rate of return is given a particular value, any change in δ must be matched by a change in Pt. This has implications for the model which will be discussed below.

An alternative approach to model specification is the approach taken by Summers (1981). (Although Summers referred specifically to an overlapping-generations life-cycle model, his approach could just as well be applied in an infinite-horizon context.) He chooses different combinations of Pt and δ, without reference to any constraint given by data. Starrett (1982) was the first to point out the problems associated with this approach. Each parameter combination is consistent with a unique saving rate, and some of these saving rates are extremely unusual. It might be tempting to liberate ourselves from the data in the manner of Summers. However, my view is that we *must* calibrate our models to the data if we are to have any hope of achieving realistic results. Within the class of models characterized by equations of motion like (g), if we calibrate to the data *and* also desire to specify the degree of intertemporal responsiveness, it will generally be necessary to employ additional model features. One such feature is the Stone-Geary minimum consumption level. Others will be discussed below.

A second variant of the infinite-horizon model allows for variable labor supply. In this case, the utility function becomes (in the non-logarithmic case):

$$\text{(h)} \qquad U = \sum_{t=1}^{\infty} \frac{1}{(1+Pt)^{t-1}} \frac{\left[\hat{C}_t^{\alpha} \, l_t^{1-\alpha} \right]^{1-\delta}}{1-\delta} ,$$

where l_t is leisure in period t, and α is a weighting parameter. The manipulation of the first-order conditions, calibration of parameters, etc., are very similar to those shown above. [See Ballard and Goulder (1985) or Ballard (1988)].

C. Overlapping-Generations Life-Cycle Model

The problem with the two preceeding models is that they are not capable of analyzing a number of important issues. Since they abstract from the simultaneous existence of many generations of different ages, these models cannot consider the redistribution of the tax burden across cohorts. The intergenerational distribution of the tax burden is interesting by itself, and it also has important implications for dynamic efficiency, as stressed by Alan Auerbach and Laurence Kotlikoff (1983, 1987). These two authors have been the leaders in the development of overlapping-generations life-cycle (OLG) simulation models for the evaluation of dynamic tax policies.

Despite the ability of OLG models to analyze a wider range of issues, they are not without problems. They are much more cumbersome from a computational standpoint, and they do not necessarily remove the possibility of very large intertemporal responses. Even when the length of economic life is only 50 or 55 years, the human wealth effects can be very substantial. Consider the results from the first paper by Auerbach and Kotlikoff (1983). In their Figure 13.6, they show that the immediate effect of an unanticipated switch to a consumption tax is an increase in the savings rate from 10% to about 42 %. Neither the article by Auerbach and Kotlikoff nor the comment by Joseph Stiglitz (1983) seems to indicate any surprise at the large magnitude of this response, but I would assert that many economists would find this response highly unusual.[12]

In this paper, I report briefly on some calculations based on the OLG model developed by Ballard and Goulder (1987). At present, this model does not have a version with no labor/leisure choice, and it lacks a Stone-Geary feature. In the future, these extensions will allow us to make further comparisons between infinite-horizon and OLG models. For now, however, it is still possible to learn some interesting lessons.

Each cohort has an economic life of 55 years, and a new cohort is *born* each year. Thus, in any year, there are 55 cohorts of different ages making household decisions. Households derive utility from consumption, leisure, and bequest-giving. The utility function for any given cohort takes the following additively separable form:

(i)

$$U = \frac{1}{1-\delta} \sum_{t=1}^{T} \frac{1}{(1+Pt)^{t-1}} \left(C_t^{1-\sigma} + \alpha_t l_t^{1-\sigma}\right)^{\frac{1-\delta}{1-\sigma}} + \frac{1}{1-\delta} \frac{1}{(1+Pt)^T} b^{\delta} B_T^{1-\delta} .$$

[12] The jump of saving in the more recent work of Auerbach and Kotlikoff (1987) is not so spectacular, but it still involves a near tripling of the saving rate. Part of the reason for this is that the original level of savings is lower in the data set used in this later work. See Starrett (1982) for discussion of the relationship between the level of saving and the amount of responsiveness of saving.

In the above expression, T is the index for the last year of life, C_t and l_t are consumption and leisure in year t, and B_T is the bequest left at the end of year T. The parameter Pt indicates time preference, while σ and δ are elasticity parameters. The parameter σ is the inverse of the elasticity of substitution between C and l in a given period. Similarly, δ is the inverse of the elasticity of substitution between bundles of C and l across periods. The elasticity of substitution between any C-l bundle and bequests is also $1/\delta$. The distribution parameter α influences the intensity of demand for leisure at given relative prices.

The parameter b determines the strength of the bequest motive. When b is zero, individuals derive no benefit from bequest-giving and leave no bequests. The larger the value of b, the greater the fraction of lifetime resources left by individuals to succeeding generations. This treatment of bequests has a certain appeal, positing a plausible motivation for bequests - satisfaction from the act of bequest giving itself. This type of structure has been used, for example, by Alan Blinder (1974). However, it should be noted that other plausible explanations for bequests have been proposed and evaluated. [See, for example, James Davies (1981)].

Each cohort maximizes utility subject to an intertemporal wealth constraint. Again suppressing taxes for expositional convenience, we can write the wealth constraint from time t = 1 as:

$$\text{(j)} \qquad \sum_{t=1}^{T} \frac{P_t C_t}{\prod_{s=1}^{t} (1+r_s)} + \frac{B_T}{\prod_{s=1}^{T} (1+r_s)} = W_1 + \sum_{t=1}^{T} \frac{w_t L_t + Y_t + IN_t}{\prod_{s=1}^{t} (1+r_s)} .$$

This is the same as the wealth constraint in the infinite-horizon case (equation (f)), with three exceptions. First, of course, the horizon stops at T=55 years. It is assumed that there is no uncertainty about date of death. [See Davies (1981) for extensive discussion.] Second, B_T is the value of the bequest left by the cohort at death. Third, IN_t is the inheritance received in any period t. If b from equation (i), the bequest weighting parameter, is 0, then B_T and IN_t will not enter the wealth constraint.

Each cohort has a given endowment, H^*, of potential labor time which is allocated to working and leisure: $H^* = L_t + l_t$. The value of H^* is constant over the lifetime of a given cohort. The hourly wage, w_t, can be written as

$$w_t = \hat{w}_t e_h \quad ,$$

where $\hat{w}_t$ is the prevailing wage per unit of effective labor, and e_h is the ratio of effective labor to labor hours for a cohort of age h. The labor efficiency ratio e changes over the lifetime of a given cohort, reflecting changes in skills and physical stamina associated with the extent of work experience and age. Several studies indicate that e follows a hump-shaped pattern over the life cycle, rising over most of economic life but falling in the last portion. This model incorporates exogenous values for e based on the study by Ronald Oaxaca (1973).

Although the details differ, the basic thrust of the mathematics of the consumer's maximizing choices is very similar to that described above for the infinite-horizon case. [See Ballard and Goulder (1987) for details].

III. Results

The results reported here are arrived at in the following manner. First, consistency adjustments are made for the 1983 data set. The original raw data are taken from many different sources, and are not mutually consistent. The adjustments assure, for instance, that total factor payments by industry equal total factor incomes for consumers. Second, the parameters of the model are *calibrated* to the data set. The calibration procedures ensure that, in the absence of any policy changes, the model will replicate the 1983 data set. Dynamic calibration procedures further ensure that, in the absence of any policy changes, the model will generate steady-state growth. [See BFSW (1985), especially Chapters 6 and 7 and Ballard and Goulder (1987), for details on these techniques.]

After the calibration has been completed, the model is ready to perform simulations. The first is a *base-case* simulation, which simply replicates the original data set and then produces a steady-state growth path. Various data on prices and quantities are saved from the base case run, so that they can be compared later with the data that emerge from a *revised-case* simulation, which is based on the same behavioral parameters, but with a different configuration of taxes.

For the revised-case simulation, we wish to specify a tax policy change that moves in the direction of greater reliance on consumption taxation, and less on income taxation. As is well known, this can be accomplished either by taxing consumption itself (as with a value-added tax) or by offering deductions for saving within the income tax. In this paper, I concentrate on the latter. A further comparison between the personal expenditure tax (studied here) and the value-added tax (not studied here) is left for future research. [See Ballard, Scholz, and Shoven (1987) for some comparisons based only on the GEMTAP model with 1973 data.]

The move to a full consumption tax is modeled in the same way in which it has been modeled for earlier papers, such as Fullerton, Shoven, and Whalley (1983), Ballard (1987), and Ballard, Scholz, and Shoven (1987). This involves increasing a parameter that specifies the percentage of new financial saving that is deductible from the personal income tax. This model treatment is problematic, since it abstracts from difficult issues of the transition. If consumers have pre-existing assets that can earn the deduction when transferred to a qualified account, then it will be possible for them to avoid taxation without actually undertaking any saving.[13] This possibility is ignored by the simple model treatment used here. The model treatment of saving deductions also abstracts from the fact that the United States government has attempted to reduce its revenue losses by placing a ceiling on the amount that can be deducted in any one year. This raises the possibility that, in the case of consumers who planned to save more than the ceiling (even in the absence of any saving incentives), the government would lose revenue without providing any marginal incentive to save. By abstracting from these issues and employing a very simple model treatment of the consumption tax, we once again may impart an upward bias to the welfare gains.

Every simulation reported here is a *differential incidence* simulation, in which the level of government exhaustive expenditure is held constant. In order to maintain equal government revenue yield, it is necessary to alter some tax rate. Here, the personal income tax rates are altered. In the early years of a sequence of equilibria, it is nearly always the case that the tax rates must be increased. Sometimes, in the later years, the

[13] See Feldstein and Daniel Feenberg (1983) for some information on the size of these pre-existing transferable assets. In the case of a majority of the households in their survey, the amount of these assets was very small. However, for an important minority, the amount of such assets was quite substantial. This could lead to severe problems along the transition.

economy has grown sufficiently rapidly that lower tax rates are possible than those of the base case.

In several of the earlier papers in this literature, the equilibrium calculations were spaced more than one year apart, in order to reduce computational expense. Here, however, the equilibria are calculated annually.[14]

In all of the sequences of equilibria reported here, the adoption of a consumption tax leads to capital deepening, and thus to a decrease in the relative price of capital services over time.[15] The approach to the new steady state is most rapid in the early years of the transition. Eventually, there is an asymptotic approach to the new steady state. For the purposes of some of the calculations reported in this paper, it is best to have a very close approximation of the new steady state. In the case of the GEMTAP model, the approach to the new steady state can be fairly slow, so that I calculate sequences stretching 200 years into the future. For the other models employed here, the approach to the new steady state is typically much more rapid, so that shorter sequences (e.g., 100 years) are sufficient.[16]

All of the sequences calculated here employ the assumption of myopic expectations regarding prices. [See Ballard and Goulder (1985) for extensive discussion of the role played by expectations of future prices in an infinite-horizon model similar to the one used here.] Ballard (1987) includes similar discussion with respect to a version of GEMTAP that is similar to the one used here. In both cases, it is shown that perfect foresight reduces the welfare gains compared with myopia. The reason is that, under perfect foresight, consumers correctly anticipate the decrease in rates of return brought

[14] With the computational technology that is currently available, annual calculations do not present a great problem. The calculations reported here were performed on a *386*-type personal computer. The sequences of equilibria typically took only a few minutes for GEMTAP and the infinite-horizon model, and about an hour for the overlapping-generations model. For some discussion of the effects of different spacing of equilibria, see Ballard (1987).

[15] This is true even in the case of a negative savings elasticity. It is important to recall that savings is an amount of expenditure (expressed in dollars). This should not be confused with the actual quantity of new capital, which is saving divided by the *price of saving*. See Charles McLure (1980).

[16] For welfare evaluation in GEMTAP and the infinite-horizon model, it is necessary to calculate *termination terms*, which project the utility stream to the infinite future. As long as the economy has reached a close approximation of the true steady state, these projections are highly accurate. See BFSW for discussion.

about by capital deepening, and this slows down the adjustment to the new steady state. However, the differences in the welfare results are not very large, especially when annual calculations are made. On the other hand, the savings in computational time from using myopia are very substantial.[17]

Let us begin with the results from the *central case* of the GEMTAP model, in which the savings elasticity is 0.4 and the uncompensated labor supply elasticity is 0.15. In this case, as in every other case investigated here, the base case net savings rate is about 6.27 % of base case GNP. Initially, the savings rate rises to about 6.41 %. As is typical in these steady-state models, the savings rate then falls, but remains always above its base-case value. Its new steady-state value is about 6.33 %.

The speed of convergence to the new steady state can be measured along many dimensions. These include the capital/labor ratio (which eventually rises by about 17 % above its base case value), the relative price of capital services (which eventually falls by about 15 %), and the size of the capital stock (which eventually rises by about 18 % in this case). The model produces detailed information on all of these. Here, we focus on the capital stock. The transition is rather slow. The ratio of revised-case capital stock to base-case capital stock increases halfway toward its new steady-state after 29 years. Only after 117 years does this ratio move 95 % of the way toward its new steady state.

One problem with interpreting the welfare results that emerge from these models is that the welfare numbers are reported in a variety of different ways. In many of the papers written using the GEMTAP model, the welfare gain is either reported in dollars, or as a percentage of the entire present value of base-case welfare, where welfare includes the value of leisure. The problem with the dollar numbers is that they are not compared to any yardstick, so that their relative size is difficult to determine. The problem with comparing with the present value of base-case welfare is that the yardstick itself is not constant. If the leisure endowment is specified differently, then there will be an effect on the level of base-case welfare. In order to avoid these difficulties, I report the welfare gains as a percentage of the present value of the base-case GNP

---

[17] In all of the simulations reported here, it is assumed that the policy change is unanticipated. The policy change occurs precisely at the beginning of the revised-case simulation. Consumers believe (correctly) that the new policy will hold forever. Under these circumstances, the effects of expectations are not great. If we desire to consider announcement effects or the difference between permanent and temporary policies, then it would certainly be appropriate to devote more attention to expectations.

stream. (The calibration procedures ensure that base-case GNP is the same in every simulation reported here.)

The welfare gain in the GEMTAP central case is about 1.20 % of the GNP stream. Different readers may reach different conclusions about whether this seems *large* or *small*. It strikes me as moderately large - it is certainly of sufficient size to be worried about.

This central case result was calculated using a version of the model with one consumer, 19 production sectors, and 17 consumer goods. The disaggregation on the production side makes rather little difference to the results. The movement halfway to the new steady state takes 33 years in this case, compared with 29 years in the disaggregated version. The welfare gains are virtually identical.[18]

Table 2 presents details on the speed of convergence and the welfare gains in the GEMTAP model, for a wide variety of savings elasticities. Not surprisingly, higher elasticities lead to faster convergence and to higher welfare gains. Two things are interesting to note in connection with Table 2. First, the welfare gain is still positive, even for a negative savings elasticity. [See Feldstein (1978) and Charles McLure (1980)]. Second, note that the marginal effect on welfare of further increases in the savings elasticity is diminishing. The economy can only adjust so fast, so that there is effectively an upper asymptote for the welfare gain.

Even though Table 2 indicates that the adjustment to the new steady state takes a very long time for the lower values of the savings elasticity, it should be remembered that the policy change being simulated here is a very large one. It might reasonably be expected that the adjustment to a large shock would take many years. On the other hand, very large savings elasticities lead to very rapid adjustment, even given the large size of the change. In the case of a savings elasticity of 7.0, the economy moves halfway to the new steady state in only five years, and 80 % of the way in only ten years. This is accom-plished by very large increases in saving. In the first period of the revised-case

[18] James Davies, Robert Hamilton, and Whalley (1985) argue that the difference between the factor intensities of the capital goods and consumption goods sectors is an important determinant of the results. They therefore argue that the results of one-sector models, such as those of Auerbach, Kotlikoff, and Skinner, are likely to be biased in an important way. While I acknowledge the point of Davies, *et. al.*, it does appear (in this application, at least) that this effect is rather small.

simulation with a savings elasticity of 7.0, the savings rate jumps to 14 percent, which shows an increase of more than 120 % over the base case.[19]

Next, I report results for the infinite-horizon model. Although the model is specified in Stone-Geary form, it is still possible to have an instantaneous utility function that is homothetic, simply by setting the *minimum required consumption* parameter equal to zero. This makes the model more comparable to that of Jorgenson and Yun, who do not use any such method.

We start with the case of no labor-leisure choice, with no minimum required consumption, and $\delta = 1.1$.[20] In this case, in order to meet the conditions of steady-state growth, the rate of time preference is approximately 1.85 %. This specification is *highly* elastic in its intertemporal responses. If we simulate the response of the consumer to a small increase in the rate of return that is believed to continue forever, we find an *impact elasticity* (elasticity of first-period saving) of about 18.18. When a consumption tax is simulated, the effect is of an explosion of capital accumulation in the first few periods. The savings rate in the first period is about 20.34 %, which is more than triple its value in the base case. After this huge first-period response, the savings rate declines rapidly. By the eighth year, it is back below 7 %. By that time, however, the transition to the new steady state is more than 96 % complete.

Compared with any of the GEMTAP simulations, this is a very rapid adjustment. In spite of this, the welfare gain is 1.43 % of the base-case GNP stream, which is smaller than in many of the GEMTAP runs. The structures of utility in the two models are not comparable, so that there is no standard of measurement through which we can transform from one model to another. Throughout the simulations reported here, however, it is almost always true that, for any *given* model structure, faster adjustment leads to a higher welfare gain.

---

[19] The results for the consumption tax are not greatly affected by the labor supply elasticity. Unfortunately, it was not possible to push the calculations to higher values of the savings elasticity, because of computational problems.

[20] This value of δ was chosen by Ballard and Goulder (1985) as their central case value. It is associated with an intertemporal substitution elasticity that may be on the high side of the empirical literature, but is consistent with the work of Lars Peter Hansen and Kenneth Singleton (1982). Support for higher values of δ (and therefore lower values of the elasticity) can be found in the survey of the literature in James Davies (1981), and in Robert Hall (1985). We shall turn to higher values of δ shortly.

One way to alter the intertemporal responsiveness of the model is to adopt a minimum required consumption level, as suggested by Starrett. In order to maintain the steady state, it is necessary that this level must grow over time. Thus, its level is conveniently expressed as a percentage of base-case consumption. In Table 3, we see that it takes a very high level of minimum required consumption in order to slow down the responses very much. Even when the required consumption is 80 % of base-case consumption, it still takes only 10 years to approach halfway toward the new steady state.

The above results are for the infinite-horizon model with no labor-leisure choice. In this case, the increased income tax rates necessary to maintain equal government revenue yield cannot have a distortionary effect on labor supply. If we allow for variable labor supply, then it is at least possible that the labor supply distortion would reduce the gains from the switch to a consumption tax. This point was emphasized by [Stiglitz (1983)] in his critique of the first Auerbach-Kotlikoff paper, which was based on a model with no labor-leisure choice.

However, in practice, the specification of a model with an endogenous labor supply choice is surprisingly tricky. With no labor-leisure choice, the human wealth effects merely cause the consumer to reduce his consumption of goods. With a labor-leisure choice, as in the case of the utility function in equation (h), the human wealth effects cause the consumer to reduce his consumption of the composite of goods and leisure. Thus, saving now rises for two reasons: Goods consumption is reduced, and leisure is also reduced, which means that labor supply increases.

This effect can be very large if the model is specified such that the total time endowment is large relative to base-case labor supply, such that large increases of labor are possible. (In fact, the elasticity of labor supply with respect to the rate of return is often much larger than the elasticity of labor supply with respect to the real net wage in models of this type.) In this model, we specify the time endowment as a fixed multiple of the base-case labor supply. If this ratio is 1.2 (with $\delta = 1.1$ and no minimum required consumption), first-period labor supply rises by 3.9 % relative to its base-case value. This makes the increase in saving even greater than before. If the ratio of time endowment to base-case labor supply rises, this effect rises as well. If the ratio is 2.0, first-period labor supply rises by 22.9 % relative to the base case. The ratio of saving to GNP soars to 27.3 % in the first period in this case, and the transition to the new steady state is 98.8 % complete after only five years. Some further details can be found in Table 3.

Note that the welfare gains are substantially larger in the case of variable labor supply than they were in the case of no labor-leisure choice. In the case of no labor-leisure choice, the economy always moves to the same steady-state capital stock. In the case of endogenous labor supply, the increase in labor makes it necessary for the economy to have a larger steady-state capital stock. The larger degree of capital accumulation leads to larger welfare gains.

The infinite-horizon experiments reported thus far have been based on a value of 1.1 for δ. One obvious possibility for controlling the model is to increase δ (and therefore to decrease the intertemporal substitution elasticity.) However, this also causes a problem. As mentioned above, any change in δ requires that we also change Pt. If we accept the steady-state growth rate implied by the data, and if we hold constant the base-case rate of return, then increases in δ are associated with decreases in Pt. While a higher value of δ would tend to reduce the intertemporal sensitivity, a lower value of Pt would tend to do the opposite. Thus, if we wish to calibrate the model, it is simply not possible to perform an unconstrained sensitivity analysis with respect to one parameter, while holding all other parameters constant. In fact, the effect of δ tends to be stronger here, so that increasing δ does reduce the overall speed of adjustment. However, as δ rises, it eventually becomes necessary to use negative values of Pt, which many economists may find unappealing. Many simulations were run, and a few of these are reported in Table 3.

Finally, let us turn to some results for the OLG model. Models of this type are more complicated than the models discussed earlier. Consequently, the OLG models potentially offer the investigator more degrees of freedom in the calibration process. For example, in the infinite-horizon models, the steady state requires that the base-case labor supply and earnings of the infinitely-lived consumer must grow at a constant rate. This rules out the possibility of borrowing constraints. In an OLG model, there are many generations alive at one time, and they may each have a hump-shaped earnings profile. In principle, this will allow for borrowing constraints.

In practice, however, the OLG models can have problems of their own. The simplest case has no bequests, as in the models used by Auerbach and Kotlikoff. In this case, the problem lies in calibrating the behavior of consumers so that the observed captial stock is explained through the endogenous savings decisions of the consumers. In the infinite-horizon model, the consumer is *born* with the existing capital stock, and it is only necessary for the consumer to save enough to allow that capital stock to grow at the steady-state rate. In the OLG model with no bequests, consumers are born without any capital and die without any capital. But they must somehow save enough during their lifetimes to generate the observed capital stock. In practical terms, this requires that consumers do a tremendous amount of saving early in life, followed by very rapid dissaving late in life. This has important effects. First, it once again removes any possibility of borrowing constraints.[21] Second, it leads directly to the results emphasized by Auerbach and Kotlikoff on the intergenerational distributional effects of the switch to a consumption tax: Since the older cohorts in a model of this type desire to dissave rapidly, they are harmed by the adoption of a consumption tax.

Unfortunately, this no-bequest model does not fit the facts very well. Kotlikoff and Summers (1981) are among those who suggest that bequests explain a large portion of the capital stock. Elsewhere, there is ample evidence that elderly cohorts do not dissave a great deal. Thus, we must view with caution the conclusions reached by a model of this type regarding the welfare effects on different cohorts.

The OLG model employed here cannot duplicate the results of Auerbach and Kotlikoff precisely, because of data differences, etc. However, the models are sufficiently similar in structure that the details presented here are probably relevant to an understanding of the earlier work by Auerbach and Kotlikoff. In addition, these results are interesting in themselves.

I begin with a no-bequest variant of the model, in which $\sigma = 2$ and $\delta = 2.5$ (and therefore the intertemporal subsitution elasticity is 0.4).[22] Here, in the base case, each cohort saves 25.3 % of its disposable income in the first year of its economic life (which might be considered as corresponding to a chronological age of about 20 or 25). Saving continues to be very strong early in life, peaking at nearly 29 % of disposable income in the 13th period.The savings rate then drops, and finally goes negative in the 37th year of the consumer's 55-year economic life. In the last year of life, 85 % of consumption is financed by dissaving. Others may draw their own conclusions, but I find these profiles to be very unusual. And yet, the profiles follow inevitably from the assumptions made in the model, and the need to calibrate to the observed data.

---

[21] A fine bibliography and good discussion of the borrowing constraints literature can be found in the article by Glenn Hubbard and Kenneth Judd (1987).

[22] These values were chosen as the central case by Ballard and Goulder (1987).

Because of these profiles, the generations that are middle-aged or old at the time of the transition to the new policy are harmed by the change. In this case with no bequests, the 38 oldest generations all suffer welfare losses. In proportionate terms, the largest of these losses occurs for the cohort that is in its 36th year of economic life at the time of the switch. Its welfare loss amounts to 0.46 % of the present value of its lifetime resources.

If bequests are allowed, then the model will be calibrated with less rapid saving early in life, and less rapid dissaving later. This mitigates the harmful effects on the welfare of those who are old at the time of the change. The bequest weighting parameter, b, has no intrinsic meaning independently of the other parameters of the model. In the case considered here, b=6 implies that a bequest equal to about 8 % of average annual consumption is left to heirs. Here the younger cohorts still do substantial saving, but less than in the no-bequest case. The youngest cohort has a savings rate of about 19.7 % and saving goes negative in the 45th year of economic life. In this case, the oldest 33 cohorts still suffer losses, but the largest of these losses is substantially smaller, at 0.36 % of lifetime resources. With b=9, only 28 cohorts lose, and the largest loss is 0.26 %.

It should be noted that the evaluation of welfare presents some problems in the model with bequests. Since bequests are in the utility function, an increase in bequests will increase the utility of the generation leaving the bequest, *ceteris paribus*. However, this will increase the capital stock of subsequent cohorts, which will tend to increase their utility as well. Thus, there is an inherent element of double counting in the welfare evaluations based on this model. For this reason, I will not emphasize the welfare results for the OLG model with bequests. Suffice it to say that, in spite of the welfare losses for the cohorts that are oldest at the time of the policy change, the present value of the welfare gain is still positive for every parameter combination studied here.[23]

As mentioned above, even in the case of a substantial bequest motive, the calibration procedures still yield lifetime profiles in which the youngest cohorts do a substan-

[23] In the simulations reported here, there is no estate tax in the base case or in the revised case. Many advocates of consumption taxation view the consumption tax as including a tax on bequests, as if they were consumption at the moment of death. Clearly, this could have important effects on the results. The analysis of different configurations of estate taxes is an interesting and important topic for future reseach.

tial amount of saving. Thus, borrowing constraints do not emerge as an issue. In the future, it may be possible to develop simulation models in which there are many age groups, as well as intracohort variation in lifetime wealth. If each age group had a *rich* group with a bequest motive, plus a *poor* group without any such motive, it might be possible to generate more realistic simulations. Fullerton and Diane Rogers are currently working in this direction. [See Rogers (1988)].

Next, I shall discuss some of the calibration issues that arise in the OLG context. It was mentioned above that the OLG model affords the investigator more degrees of freedom in calibration than does the infinite-horizon model. In the infinite-horizon model, essentially all variables are growing at the steady-state rate, and this leaves the researcher very little discretion to specify the parameters of the model. In the OLG model, it is possible for each cohort to have base-case earnings, consumption, and saving profiles that do not grow at the steady-state rate, so long as certain consistency conditions *across* cohorts are met. See [Ballard and Goulder (1987), especially the Appendices] for an extended discussion. This allows the potential for a variety of different schemes to be used in order to calibrate the model. Here, we fix the rate of time preference at 1 %, and alter the time endowment in order to generate acceptable profiles. This has the advantage of avoiding the negative rates of time preference that we saw in the infinite-horizon case. However, as explained above, changing the time endowment has important implications for the model. Moreover, there are some sets of parameters which simply cannot be calibrated using this procedure. That is, for some sets of parameters, there is no positive amount of leisure that would be consistent with replicating the base-case data and generating a steady-state growth path. For example, I attempted to use values of δ over the full range investigated earlier for the infinite-horizon case. However, with $b=0$ and $\sigma=0.5$ it was simply not possible to calibrate the model with δ less than 1.4.

Simulations were run for the no-bequest version of the model, for values of δ ranging from 1.4 to 3.0. The impact elasticities of savings with respect to the rate of return range from about 1.74 for $\delta=1.4$ to about 3.48 for $\delta=3.0$.[24] This seems coun-

[24] These overall elasticities can be decomposed into separate elasticities for each cohort. Not surprisingly, the largest effects come for the youngest cohorts, who have the largest human wealth effects. For example, when $\delta=3$, the youngest cohort has an impact elasticity of 2.54, while the middle-aged cohort (in the 28th year of economic

terintuitive, since δ is the inverse of the intertemporal substitution elasticity. However, the calibration procedures lead to a higher value for the time endowment in the case of $\delta=3.0$, so that the labor supply response is much greater. This larger labor supply response means that, in the early years of the simulation, a lower equal-yield tax increase is necessary when $\delta=3.0$, even though the subsidies paid to savings are greater. Since the tax increases are lower, the damage to the cohorts that are old at the time of the policy change is less when $\delta=3.0$. The difference is nearly a factor of two for the very oldest cohort, but the relative difference shrinks when we move to younger groups. In the long-run steady state, the welfare effects in the two cases are rather close to each other. The present value of the welfare gains is between 1 % and 2 % of the present value of base-case GNP for all of these values of δ.

The point of this discussion is not to emphasize specific results. Rather, it is to show the reader some of the difficulties that can be encountered in specifying a dynamic model of this type. Every simulation model used to date has problems. Some of these problems are well known; others are not at all well known. Only with a fuller appreciation of the problems can we interpret the existing results properly and move on to build better models in the future.

IV. Conclusion

Economists have devoted a great deal of time and energy to the development of simulation models for the purpose of investigating questions about dynamic tax policies. Much has been learned from these efforts. However, it should be clear that much remains to be done.

Most of the simulation models suggest that greater reliance on consumption taxation would lead to welfare gains. That conclusion is echoed by the results reported here.

---

life) has an elasticity of 1.48. The positive effect on saving continues to shrink as we go to older cohorts. The oldest 19 cohorts have negative saving in the base case. Saving does increase for most of these cohorts, and the increased saving induced by the higher rate of return is measured as a negative elasticity. Finally, the oldest five cohorts actually have negative savings responses. When all of these are combined, the aggregate elasticity is about 3.48.

However, it has repeatedly been necessary to urge caution in interpreting these results, because of the many special assumptions employed in the models. The case for a consumption tax remains persistent but uneasy.

The original GEMTAP work showed a concern for the importance of specifying the speed of dynamic adjustment. However, that model has an unusual dynamic structure that is difficult to interpret, and it cannot address intergenerational issues. The papers written by Jorgenson and Yun use an infinite-horizon model. The papers do not give evidence that the speed of adjustment was an important concern of the authors. The papers do not report details on the speed of adjustment, so that the results should be interpreted with caution.[25] More recently, Goulder [writing with Summers (1987) and with Barry Eichengreen (1988)] has developed infinite-horizon models with a concern for the speed of intertemporal response. By discounting future human wealth at a high rate and by using adjustment costs in investment, these papers achieve a measure of control over the speed of capital accumulation. However, none of the infinite-horizon models employed to date is capable of moderate to slow adjustment, and these models also cannot address intergenerational issues.

Because of their ability to address intergenerational issues, the overlapping-generations life-cycle models are probably the most promising. However, the pioneering work by Auerbach, Kotlikoff, and Skinner has produced models that tend to be very sensitive in their intertemporal responses. Once again, this leads me to urge caution in interpreting the results.

Since there are many problems with the econometric literature on savings reponses, it is difficult to make a final judgement about the *correct* size of these reponses. Therefore, it is *possible* that responses as large as those that are typical of the infinite-horizon and OLG models could actually occur. However, I consider this a low-probability prospect.

On the basis of the observations made here, I would like to sketch out a set of characteristics of the *overlapping-generations life-cycle model of the future*. If we are to increase the confidence that we attach to estimates of the welfare effects of income and consumption taxes, we must move toward more sophisticated models. The model

---

[25] However, in the discussion following a seminar at the National Bureau of Economic Research, Cambridge, MA, (August 5, 1985), Yun suggested that the intertemporal responses in his model are very rapid.

features listed below do represent items on my own research agenda, but I hope that other economists will join me in the effort to build models capable of giving more reliable answers to dynamic tax policy questions.

Adjustment costs in investment.

There is now a large literature on this subject. [See, for example, Auerbach (1988) and the discussion of the literature contained therein. Also, the book by Auerbach and Kotlikoff (1987) includes some calculations with adjustment costs.] Unfortunately, however, the use of this very realistic feature is still unusual in tax policy simulation models of the type discussed here.

Bequests.

Bequests add to the realism of the model, in and of themselves. More importantly, bequests can generate a large proportion of the capital stock in the model. Thus, they can allow us to avoid having to explain the existing capital stock solely out of intragenerational life-cycle saving. With bequests explaining much of the capital stock, we would not have to require the consumers in the model to save frantically in their early years, and then dissave just as frantically later on. If consumers no longer were modeled as saving large amounts early in life, it would be possible to incorporate borrowing constraints.

Uncertainty.

The vast majority of the dynamic simulation literature is based on completely deterministic models. And yet, it would be foolish to assert that this is a realistic way to model the environment in which consumers make their decisions. Uncertainty about date of death, health status, future earnings, etc., all may have important effects on our understanding of dynamic tax policies, and yet these have scarcely been employed at all.

New structures for the felicity function.

In many ways, this may be the most exciting possibility of all. The assumption of intertemporal additive separability pervades the literature, but its realism is highly questionable. It has been said that *anticipation is the greater pleasure*. And yet the person with these simple forms of intertemporal additive separability cannot experience anticipation, has no memory, no habits, and no capacity to learn. Much of the richness of human experience is ruled out by these highly restrictive assumptions. It is especially bizarre to see models with additive separability and perfect foresight. This combination of assumptions yields models in which people have tremendous understanding of the external world and its prices, but little understanding of themselves. In the future, economists may want to consider incorporating richer structures of consumer dynamic behavior into their simulation models. The ideas of W.M. Gorman (1967), Hersh Shefrin and Richard Thaler (1988), and others may serve as starting points for these efforts.

Table 1

Producer Goods (Industries)	**Consumer Goods** (Expenditure Categories)
1. Agriculture, forestry, and fisheries	1. Food
2 Mining	2. Alcohol
3. Crude petroleum and gas	3. Tobacco
4. Contract construction	4. Household foods and utilities
5. Food and tobacco	5. Shelter
6. Textiles, apparel, and leather	6. Furnishings
7. Paper and printing	7. Appliances
8. Petroleum	8. Apparel
9. Chemicals, rubber, and plastics	9. Public transportation
10. Lumber, furniture, stone, clay, and glass	10. New and used cars, fees and maintenance
11. Metals, machinery, instruments, and miscellaneous manufacturing	11. Cash contributions and personal care
12. Transportation equipment and ordinance	12. Financial services
13. Motor vehicles	13. Reading and entertainment
14. Transportation, communications, and utilities	14. Household operations
15. Trade	15. Gasoline and motor oil
16. Finance and insurance	16. Health care
17. Real estate	17. Education
18. Services	
19. Government enterprises	

Table 2

Effects of the Adoption of a Consumption Tax in the GEMTAP Model

Savings Elasticity	1 year	Percentage of Adjustment to New Steady State After: 5 years	20 years	50 years	Welfare Gain as Percentage of Base Case GNP Stream
-0.2	1.37%	6.70%	24.44%	51.28%	0.69%
0.0	1.72	8.30	29.48	58.83	0.89
0.2	2.09	10.01	34.52	65.64	1.06
0.4	2.48	11.78	39.43	71.56	1.20
0.6	2.88	13.58	44.13	76.59	1.32
0.8	3.30	15.41	48.57	80.80	1.43
1.0	3.73	17.24	52.71	84.86	1.52
2.0	6.02	26.35	69.29	94.28	1.86
3.0	8.54	35.09	80.19	97.90	2.07
4.0	11.27	43.22	87.21	99.22	2.21
5.0	14.22	50.63	91.70	99.71	2.31
6.0	17.38	57.25	94.59	99.89	2.39
7.0	20.50	62.73	96.38	99.96	2.45

Table 3

Effects of the Adoption of a Consumption Tax in the Infinite-Horizon Model

A. δ = 1.1, no labor-leisure choice, Pt = 1.85 %

(Required Consumption)/ (Base-Case Consumption)	Impact Savings Elasticity	Percentage of Adjustment to New Steady State After 1 year	5 years	20years	Welfare Gain as Percentage of Base-Case GNP Stream
0.0	18.18	45.06%	91.08%	99.99%	1.45%
0.2	14.17	30.84	83.45	99.92	1.45
0.4	10.16	21.99	72.35	99.51	1.43
0.6	6.14	14.38	55.92	97.15	1.38
0.8	2.13	7.19	32.43	83.01	1.23

B. δ = 1.1, endogenous labor-leisure choice, no minimum required consumption, Pt = 1.85 %

Time Endowment/ (Base-Case Labor Supply)	Impact Savings Elasticity	Percentage of Adjustment to New Steady State After 1 year	5 years	20 years	Welfare Gain as Percentage of Base-Case GNP Stream
1.2	20.73	44.78	93.13	100.00	1.65%
1.6	25.83	51.54	97.41	100.00	1.88
2.0	30.92	62.15	99.62	100.00	2.02

C. Variable δ, Pt, no labor-leisure choice, no minimum required consumption

δ	Pt	Impact Savings Elasticity	Percentage of Adjustment to New Steady State After 1 year	5 years	20 years	Welfare Gain as Percentage of Base-Case GNP Stream
1.1	1.85%	18.18	45.06%	91.08%	99.99%	1.45%
2.0	-0.13%	9.14	20.82	69.31	99.17	1.42
3.0	-2.28%	5.45	13.83	53.26	95.76	1.37

Comments by Gunter Stephan

Why should dynamic and computable equilibrium models be applied, if it is intended to analyze the economic effects of a change in the taxation scheme? From my viewpoint there are at least two important reasons: First, computable equilibrium models provide a framework that is logically consistent and allows to study both on a theoretical and on an empirical level, how a change in policy affects the allocation of resources and the distribution of income. To my knowledge no other tool available has the same ability. Second, economic systems evolve over time, hence dynamic efficiency is an important issue to be considered. Of course, one can gain some insight into the distributional and allocational impact of a policy change by doing comparative statics. But equally important is the question: How do economic systems adjust over time? Answering this question requires a truly dynamic model.

The time path of adjustment depends heavily upon the expectations economic agents have formed. Economic theory has developed a vast variety of models using different assumptions about the individuals' expectations. In his paper, Charles Ballard discusses just three in a non-technical fashion: the GEMTAP model which has a recursive structure with myopic agents on one side, the infinite horizon approach which leads to a fully intertemporal model of the Ramsey type where the economic agents are clairvoyant on the other side, and, in the middle between these two poles, the overlapping generations framework.

It is important to memorize that these three types of models rely upon different assumptions regarding the organization of the economy and the intertemporal decision making behavior of the economic agents. The infinite horizon model is simply an intertemporal version of the Arrow-Debreu framework. There is a complete set of perfect and well-organized future markets at which plans are coordinated at the beginning of the time horizon. As such an infinite horizon model can be used only to analyze gradual long-term adjustment and economic development which is based upon long-run equilibrium price formations. In particular, elasticities must be interpreted as long-run elasticities. I will return to this issue below.

Recursive models like the GEMTAP one employed two central assumptions: First, in each period there are well-organized spot-markets, but second, no complete set of well-organized future markets exists; or if it exists, economic agents make no use of it. This means especially that economic decisions are based upon expectations which are derived solely from the information available during the current period and future plans are never passed on markets or coordinated over time. Hence, the economy is running in a sequence of period-related but intertemporally uncoordinated flow equilibria and the reaction of the economy to a policy change has to be interpreted as short-run rather than a long-run response.

It can be argued that a recursive structure is a more realistic approach, since economic agents are myopic rather than clairvoyant with respect to the future and since the assumption that a complete set of future markets exists is a complete fiction. But the recursive model can produce Cobb-Webb cycles and intertemporally inconsistent as well as inefficient results. Only if prices do not change rapidly over time, this type of model generates a relatively good approximation to an intertemporal equilibrium.

Like the recursive approach overlapping generations models lack from the existence of a complete set of future markets. Given the sequential structure of the generations it is simply impossible to assume that all economic plans can be coordinated at the beginning of the time horizon of the economy on future markets. But, in contrast to the recursive approach, economic agents do not act myopically. They plan at date of their birth for their whole life time.

Having the different structures underlying the different types of the models in mind, it is obvious that these models cannot be transformed into each other and the results computed for the different types cannot be compared directly. In particular, the savings elasticities have different meanings. In the infinite horizon model it is logically consistent only to talk about long-run elasticities whereas the GEMTAP models has short-run elasticities. A look at the results reported in the Ballard paper (see Tables 2 and 3) shows that the elasticities for the infinite horizon model are systematically higher than the ones for the GEMTAP model. Moreover, the elasticities of the infinite horizon model are derived ones. They are implicitly specified, if the steady state values are given, whereas the model builder can freely chose elasticities for the GEMTAP models.

Given these considerations I have some problems to understand what is meant when the Ballard paper says that reducing the degree of myopia decreases the welfare gains of a tax reform. Reducing the degree of agent's myopia leads to an increase in saving elasticities which in turn imply higher welfare gains. The only way to interpret this result is: Suppose that for the GEMTAP and the infinite horizon model the same elasticities are specified numerically, then the GEMTAP models produce higher welfare gains. But, as far as I can see, both types of models rely upon completely different assumptions about the organization of the economy and the intertemporal behavior of economic agents! My conclusion is that analyzing the dynamic effects of a change in the tax system requires a careful investigation on which of the models fits best in the existing real world situation.

Finally, I should like to mention some minor points:

1. For each type of model a counterfactual analysis is employed to evaluate the economic impact of a change in the tax system. However, why does the policy change have to happen at the beginning of the time horizon? My experience with dynamic computable equilibrium models shows that a better insight in to the adjustment process is provided, if it is supposed that a change in policy takes place during the time horizon.
2. I do not share the author's view that an overlapping generations model is the most promising approach. Of course, overlapping generations models enable to analyze the impact of changing the tax system upon the distribution of income between young and older people. But this type of model still shows theoretical problems and the computational effort is higher than in any alternative case.
3. From my viewpoint the innovation and the substitution of techniques is also an important issue to be considered. Any change of the tax system affects the demand and supply of the consumers. This changes the market conditions to which the production side has to react which in turn feeds back into the consumers' decisions. In a dynamic context it seems therefore important to me to study not only the behavior of the consumers in detail but also the adjustment potential of the economy's supply side.
4. More than one type of labor should be considered. Economic theory tells us that switching from income to consumption taxation might imply a shift from unskilled to skilled labor. Households simply invest more in human capital. This leads to a different distribution of income and a set of reactions in the whole economy.

Despite these critical comments let me conclude at a highly positive note. Charles Ballard's paper represents an instructive synthesis of what has been learned about dynamic tax models. His presentation is transparent and can be cross-checked by others. As such his work has the potential to stimulate further research and fruitful discussions.

Comments by Karl W. Roskamp

The subject Professor Ballard discussed in his paper is of considerable economic and social interest. I am glad that he addressed the problem of specification, once simulation models are to be set up to evaluate intertemporal effects of income and consumption taxes. I should like to single out a particularly important specification to which a good deal of attention has recently been given in the literature on intertemporal optimization models but which is not mentioned in Professor Ballard's paper.

Economists try to buttress their arguments about intertemporal effects of taxes on consumption and savings by resorting to mathematical models. These are dynamic models and they imply optimization over time. There is usually an objective function to be maximized subject to a number of differential equation and (or) integral equation constraints. Used are in this case the tools of calculus of variations or more generally the Maximum Principle. Sometimes economists prefer to use a simpler variant of the calculus of variation for their analyses, namely the so-called isoperimetric method. Professor L.H. Summers e.g. used the latter in his widely cited 1981 American Economic Review article entitled "Capital Taxation and Accumulation in a Life Cycle Growth Model" [A.E.R. 71 (1981, pp. 533-544)]. Professor Ballard uses the same method on pp. 155-156 of his paper. This notwithstanding, the calculus of variations method is in all cases involved.

Calculus of variations is a time-honored maximization method, going all the way back to John Bernoulli's work on the brachystochrone in 1697. What was new with this method was that one need for the solution of a problem boundary conditions or, more generally, transversality conditions. One had to state how an intertemporal timepath would begin and how it would end. It is the transversality condition problem to which I should like to draw attention.

In many of the intertemporal optimization models which one can now find in the economic literature the reference is to *infinite time horizon* models. Professor Ballard too uses this type of model in his paper. Resorting to such models certainly has a great advantage. The problem of transversality conditions, and they are often the most difficult ones to come to grips with, can be greatly reduced. Infinite time horizon models is a facile way to sidestep the latter - or so it seems. Sometimes the whole problem of transversality conditions is simply relegate to a footnote in which the reader is advised to examine the size and sign of a discount factor and thus to satisfy himself that the former are met.

Unfortunately mathematics and for that matter calculus of variations, is not that simple. There is now among mathematicians as well as economists an uneasy feeling that with infinite time horizon models often an inadmissible shortcut is taken which deprives us of needed knowledge concerning the stability of the model. So says for instance Walter P. Heller in a wellknown Econometrica article: "It is a curious fact that while most finite horizon economic models are stable, almost all infinite time horizon models are unstable" [Econometrica (Vol. 45, No. 1, Jan. 1975 pp. 65 seqq.)]. That is indeed more then disconcerting because with unstable models one can do nothing.

Thus it seems that if authors use an infinite time horizon model they should not only *assume* but actually *prove* that the transversality conditions are fulfilled. More specific, they should prove that there is indeed a steady state convergence over the whole timepath from here to infinity. Such a proof is admittedly often rather difficult as it requires a close examiniation of the characteristic roots of the system of differential equations generating the various timepaths. However, without such a proof one cannot be sure what the system will do. It may well be unstable.

In view of these inherent difficulties I believe that economists would do well if they were to study the problems discussed in this session with the aid of finite horizon models rather than infinite time horizon ones. The former can be completely solved. With them one would be on much safer ground. Also, empirical testing is facilitated if computable, finite time horizon models are used.

For those who feel that something still lies beyond a finite time horizon - which can of course span the whole liftime of a person - there is the possibility to introduce bequests into the terminal boundary conditions. This should go a long way to assuage their concerns.

I should finally like to give, for the sake of comparison, the results of another Michigan simulation study on the replacement of the U.S. individual income tax by a consumption tax. Used was in this case a continuous, finite time horizon model. It was found that over 45 years real consumption could be 8 % higher with a consumption tax than with an equal yield income tax. This is considerably higher than Professor Ballard finds in his steady state study. Thus the choice between a finite time horizon or infinite time horizon optimization model is certainly important. It could turn out to be *the* specification problem.

References

Aaron, H.J. / Galper, H. (1985), Assessing Tax Reform (Washington, D.C.: The Brookings Institution).

Andrews, W.D. (1974), A Consumption-type or Cash Flow Personal Income Tax, Harvard Law Review 87, pp. 1113-88.

Atkinson, A.B. / Sandmo, A. (1980), Welfare Implications of the Taxation of Savings, Economic Journal 90, pp. 529-49.

Auerbach, A.J. (1988), Tax Reform and Adjustment Costs: The Impact on Investment and Market Value, Mimeo, University of Pennsylvania.

Auerbach, A.J. / Kotlikoff, L.J. (1983), National Savings, Economic Welfare, and the Structure of Taxation, in: M. Feldstein, ed., Behavioral simulation methods in tax policy analysis (Chicago: University of Chicago Press for the National Bureau of Economic Research), pp. 459-93.

Auerbach, A.J. / Kotlikoff, L. J. (1987), Dynamic Fiscal Policy (Cambridge, England: Cambridge University Press).

Auerbach, A.J. / Kotlikoff, L.J. / Skinner, J. (1983), The Efficiency Gains from Dynamic tax Reform, International Economic Review 24, pp. 83-100.

Ballard, C.L. (1987), Tax Policy and Consumer Foresight: A General Equilibrium Simulation Study, Economic Inquiry 25, pp. 267-84.

Ballard, C.L. (1988), On the Specification of Tax Policy Simulation Models with Infinite Horizon, Mimeo, Michigan State University.

Ballard, C.L. / Fullerton, D. / Shoven, J.B. / Whalley, J. (1985), A General Equilibrium Model for Tax Policy Evaluation (Chicago: University of Chicago Press for the National Bureau of Economic Research).

Ballard, C.L. / Goulder, L.H. (1985), Consumption Taxes, Foresight, and Welfare: A Computable General Equilibrium Analysis, in: J. Piggott and J. Whalley, eds., New developments in applied general equilibrium analysis (Cambridge, England: Cambridge University Press), pp. 253-82.

Ballard, C.L., / Goulder, L.H. (1987), Tax Incidence Calculations with an Overlapping Generations General Equilibrium Model, Mimeo, Michigan State University.

Ballard, C.L. / Scholz, J.K. / Shoven, J.B. (1987), The Value-Added Tax: A General Equilibrium Look at the Efficiency and Incidence, in: M. Feldstein, ed., The effects of taxation on capital accumulation (Chicago: University of Chicago Press for the National Bureau of Economic Research), pp. 445-74.

Barro, R.J. (1974), Are Government Bonds Net Wealth?, Journal of Political Economy 82, pp. 1095-1117.

Bernheim, B.D. / Scholz, J.K. / Shoven, J.B. (1988), Consumption Taxation in a General Equilibrium Model: How Reliable are Simulation Results?, Mimeo, Stanford University.

Blinder, A.S. (1974), Toward an Economic Theory of Income Distribution (Cambridge, MA: MIT Press).

Blinder, A.S. / Deaton, A. (1985), The Time-Series Consumption Function Revisited, in: Brooking Papers on Economic Activity 1985: 2, pp. 465-511.

Boskin, M.J. (1978), Taxation, Saving, and the Rate of Interest, Journal of Political Economy 86, pp. S3-S27.

Bradford, D. (1980), The Case for a Personal Consumption Tax, in: J.A. Pechman, ed., What should be taxed: Income or expenditure? (Washington, D.C.: The Brookings Institution), pp. 75-113.

Davies, J.B. (1981), Uncertain Lifetime, Consumption, and Dissaving in Retirement, Journal of Political Economy 89, pp. 561-77.

Davies, J. / Hamilton, R. / Whalley, J. (1985), Capital Income Taxation in a Two-Commodity Life-Cycle Model: The Role of Factor Intensity and Asset Captialization Effects, Mimeo, University of Western Ontario.

Feldstein, M. (1978), The Welfare Cost of Capital Income Taxation, Journal of Political Economy 86, pp. S29-S51.

Feldstein, M.S. / Feenberg, D.R. (1983), Alternative Tax Rules and Personal Saving Incentives: Microeconomic Data and Behavioral Simulations, in: M. Feldstein, ed., Behavioral simulation methods in tax policy analysis (Chicago: University of Chicago Press for the National Bureau of Economic Research), pp. 173-209.

Feldstein, M. / Horioka, C. (1980), Domestic Savings and International Capital Flows, Economic Journal 90, pp. 314-29.

Fullerton, D. / Shoven, J.B. / Whalley, J. (1983), Replacing the U.S. Income Tax with a Progressive Consumption Tax, Journal of Public Economics 20, pp. 3-23.

Goulder, L.H. / Shoven, J.B. / Whalley, J. (1983), Domestic Tax Policy and the Foreign Sector: The Importance of Alternative Foreign Sector Formulations to Results from a General Equilibrium Tax Analysis Model, in: M. Feldstein, ed., Behavioral simulation methods in tax policy analysis (Chicago: University of Chicago Press for the National Bureau of Economic Research), pp. 333-64.

Goulder, L.H. / Eichengreen, B. (1988), Savings Promotion, Investment Promotion, and International Competitiveness, in: R.M. Feenstra, ed., Trade policies for international competitiveness (Chicago: University of Chicago Press).

Goulder, L.H. / Summers, L.H. (1987), Tax Policy, Asset Prices, and Growth: A General Equilibrium Analysis, National Bureau of Economic Research Working Paper No. 2128.

Gorman, W.M. (1967), Tastes, Habits, and Choices, International Economic Review 8, pp. 218-22.

Hall, R.E. (1985), Real Interest and Consumption, National Bureau of Economic Research Working Paper No. 1694.

Hansen, L.P. / Singleton, K.J. (1982), Generalized Instrumental Variables Estimation of Nonlinear Rational Expectation Models, Econometrica 50, pp. 1269-86.

Harberger, A.C. (1980), Vignettes on the World Capital Market, American Economic Review 70, pp. 331-37.

Howrey, E.P. / Hymans, S.H., The Measurement and Determination of Loanable-Funds Saving, in: J.A. Pechman, ed., What should be taxed: Income or expenditure? (Washington, D.C.: The Brookings Institution), pp. 1-31.

Hubbard, R.G. / Judd, K.L. (1987), Social Security and Individual Welfare: Precautionary Saving, Borrowing Constraints, and the Payroll Tax, American Economic Review 77, pp. 630-46.

Jorgenson, D.W. / Yun, K.Y. (1986a), The Efficiency of Capital Allocation, Scandinavian Journal of Economics 88, pp. 85-107.

Jorgenson, D.W. / Yun, K.Y. (1986b), Tax Policy and Capital Allocation, Scandinavian Journal of Economics 88, pp. 355-77.

Judd, K.L. (1985), Redistributive Taxation in a Simple Perfect Foresight Model, Journal of Public Economics 28, pp. 59-83.

Judd, K.L. (1987), The Welfare Cost of Factor Taxation in a Perfect-Foresight Model, Journal of Political Economy 95, pp. 675-709.

Kotlikoff, L.J. / Summers, L.H. (1981), The Role of International Transfers in Aggregate Capital Accumulation, Journal of Political Economy 89, pp. 706-32.

McLure, C.E., Jr. (1980), Taxes, Saving, and Welfare: Theory and Evidence, National Bureau of Economic Research Working Paper No. 504.

Oaxaca, R. (1973), Male-Female Wage Differentials in Urban Labor Markets, International Economic Review 14, pp. 673-709.

Ramsey, F.P. (1928), A Mathematical Theory of Saving, Economic Journal 38, pp. 543-59.

Rogers, D.L. (1988), A Computable General Equilibrium Model of Lifetime Tax Incidence, Mimeo, University of Virginia.

Scholz, J.K. (1987), Documentation for the 1983 General Equilibrium Data Set, Mimeo, Stanford University.

Shefrin, H.M. / Thaler, R.H. (1988), The Behavioral Life-Cycle Hypothesis, Economic Inquiry 26, pp. 609-43.

Slemrod, J. (1988), Effects of Taxation with International Capital Mobility, in: H.J. Aaron, H. Galper, and J.A. Pechman, eds., Uneasy Compromise: Problems of a Hybrid Income-consumption Tax (Washington, D.C.: The Brookings Institution), pp. 115-48.

Starrett, D.A. (1982), Long Run Savings Elasticities in the Life Cycle Model, Factor Markets Workshop Research Paper No. 24, Stanford University.

Starrett, D.A. (1988), Effects of Taxes on Saving, in: H.J. Aaron, H. Galper, and J.A. Pechman, eds., Uneasy Compromise: Problems of a Hybrid Income-consumption Tax (Washington, D.C.: The Brookings Institution) pp. 237-59.

Stiglitz, J.E. (1983), Comment, in: M.S. Feldstein, ed., Behavioral simulation methods in tax policy analysis (Chicago: University of Chicago Press for the National Bureau of Economic Research), pp. 493-98.

Summers, L.H. (1981,) Capital Taxation and Accumulation in a Life Cycle Growth Model, American Economic Review 71, pp. 533-44.

PART THREE

Taxing Consumption from a Public Choice and Constitutional Point of View

Geoffrey Brennan and James M. Buchanan

Consumption Taxation and Democratic Process

I. The Public Choice Approach to Tax Issues

The object of this paper is to examine consumption taxation from a constitutionalist public choice perspective. This perspective is characterized by several distinctive features. In the first place, and most conspicuously, the perspective places in the analytical foreground, the fact that decisions about the bases upon which, and rates at which, taxes are to be levied are *political* decisions. In the second place, the perspective emphasizes the essential connection between the tax and expenditure sides of the budget. In the third place, the perspective identifies tax arrangements as part of the institutional/constitutional fabric within which other political determinations are made, rather than merely as ordinary outcomes of political process.

These features are distinctive. The standard approach to tax analysis, familiar from the public finance textbooks, involves the direct application of normative criteria - horizontal and vertical equity, efficiency and so on - to the evaluation of alternative tax options. This application proceeds with virtually no explicit attention to questions of political reality. The whole exercise takes place within an equi-revenue framework that explicitly rules out the possibility of any connection between tax instruments and expenditure levels. And the exercise deals with tax choices as if they were no different from other policy choices, thereby denying any special status to tax questions.

The three distinctive features of the public choice approach are related. The public choice claim is that, once political feasibility is taken seriously, different tax institutions are bound to affect expenditure levels: changing tax arrangements will change the prices that different voters-citizens have to pay for collectively provided goods,[1] and is thereby likely to change the levels of spending that the different voters demand. Only under very special circumstances will the emergent political equilibrium be invariant to such changes in voters' demands. Furthermore, if particular tax regimes generate the "prices" that different voters pay for public spending, then the tax regime must be specified *before* voter preferences on spending levels can be registered. Tax decisions are *not* just like any other policy decisions; they are rather part of the *framework* or *structure* within which those other policy decisions are made. [Brennan and Buchanan (1980, 1983)]. Tax decisions must be viewed as logically prior to decisions in other policy areas.

If the equi-revenue setting assumed in the orthodox tax reform analysis is descriptively inaccurate - if, that is, changes in tax arrangements *do* affect expenditure levels - then the policy recommendations stemming from the orthodox analysis are potentially misleading, even if one accepts the standard normative framework. That is, the standard analysis should incorporate the possible feedback effects of tax choice on expenditure levels, because in at least some cases orthodox policy conclusions can be significantly modified. For example, consider a tax arrangement that generates revenues to finance a flat per person subsidy. The shift from a proportional to a progressive income tax would, in the normative framework, be approved on "vertical equity" grounds (whatever its standing by reference to other criteria): but if such a shift causes a reduction in expenditure levels, then the per person subsidy will decline and the net effect may well be to reduce the redistributive impact of the fiscal program. The orthodox approach ought, then, to embody a recognition of the substantive invalidity, as distinct from the analytical convenience, of the equi-revenue method.

It goes without saying that normative tax theorists ought more generally to be concerned about political structure. Public finance specialists will, for example, occasionally rail against the influence of special interest groups in securing differentially favorable treatment in tax legislation. And practitioners will often respond to theorists' calls for, say, inclusion of imputed rent on owner-occupied dwellings in the income tax base, or for full taxation of capital gains (and losses) on an accruals basis, by reference

[1] A point emphasized in early public choice/public finance contributions by Wicksell and Lindahl.

to "what's on" politically. Yet the question of whether some tax bases are likely to be more immune from special interest pressures than others is rarely posed explicitly. And questions as to just how much complexity can be permitted in a democratically viable tax system,[2] and how this constrains "tax design" are rarely mentioned in standard discussions. In the context of the central topic of this conference, for example, the case for consumption taxation is often set against the case for a fully comprehensive income tax system of the Haig-Simons kind, as if the latter were fully feasible - whereas our fiscal history surely suggests that the prospects for, say: proper tax treatment of durable consumption goods (housing, most notably); or for properly differential indexation of labor and capital incomes under inflation; or for genuinely equivalent tax treatment of interest income and capital gains; are all hopelessly remote.[3] Moreover, there is a question as to of whether normative criteria would dictate a truly neutral (and horizontally equitable) tax system when the economy is riddled with so many other distortions, many of which are themselves government imposed.

The point here is that public finance specialists who work within the standard evaluative framework and with the standard analytic tools have good reason to take the issues of political feasibility seriously. And, for the economist taking a matter "seriously" means to focus on it with all the analytic firepower available. Hence, the ultimate rationale for the analytical input of public choice in tax analysis.

There is, however, a difficulty involved in simply grafting public choice analysis on to the orthodox approach. The difficulty is that, once the *empirical* relevance of political "constraints" is admitted, their *normative* relevance tends to obtrude as well. Specifically, although public finance economists may turn out to be closet technocrats who regard the whole political apparatus as an unfortunate barrier to their own capacities to "do good, fiscally speaking", there is surely something slightly odd about that attitude. If the analytic framework includes the institutional structure within which tax reform proposals are advanced, and within which those proposals themselves must ultimately be legitimated and operationalized, then, by necessity, the proposals become "political",

---

[2] Vickery's ingenious proposal for the taxation of lifetime income, for example, has always struck most observers as infeasible politically simply because taxpayers would not understand it! [See Vickery (1947)].

[3] The Meade Committee's discussion of the case for consumption taxation recognizes, more than most, the inordinate difficulties of a truly comprehensive 'income tax'.

not only in the context of positive analysis but also in terms of the normative approach adopted. It is, for example, a characteristic of democratic governance that policies (including tax policies) that are too complicated to be understood by ordinary citizens are unlikely to prevail. And this characteristic is not, in itself, undesirable because it limits the extent to which citizens can be exploited by unscrupulous governments. Such citizens' feedback may, of course, be a source of irritation to those who want to direct citizens for their own "good", but that is an irritation that true democrats readily accept.

The strictures noted are applicable to all policy analysts, and in particular, are applicable to tax policy. Democratic political constraints need not be viewed implicitly as unfortunate barriers to the implementation of ideally designed fiscal arrangements, but as part of an institutional apparatus that is itself widely endorsed and makes a strong claim to normative authority. We do not, of course, claim here that electoral constraints, and democratic political processes more broadly, operate "perfectly": indeed, much of public choice scholarship seems to indicate how imperfect that operation may be. Our point is, rather, to insist that the normative criteria adopted for tax policy analysis, whatever precisely those criteria are, have to be of the same kind as, and consistent with, those that are used to evaluate the institutional setting within which tax policy decisions are made. In short, the approach to tax policy must be "constitutional". Once political considerations are allowed to obtrude - as properly they must - in tax policy analysis, they do more than add to the set of relevant constraints: there is more at stake than merely adding an extra equation or two to the system. The whole framework of analysis must shift gears into constitutional overdrive.

This methodological admonition is essentially independent of the particular model of political processes that is adopted. Public Choice analysis offers its own family of such models, with certain common features. Such models, or significant aspects of them, might be rejected as implausible, uncongenially abstract, or logically incoherent. But a basic public choice *approach* must remain: political considerations are relevant, however one happens to model them; interconnections between tax instruments and revenue levels arise in a wide variety of scenarios; and the need for a "constitutional window" remains, however political decision structures are deemed to work.

The particular model of political processes chosen will, of course, be relevant to the analysis of particular tax alternatives and to the normative ordering of these alternatives. Accordingly, the proper starting point for tax analysis must be a consideration of alternative political models. To discuss alternative tax policies *before* the logically prior issues of political process are addressed is to get the cart before the horse. In the next Section, we shall develop the particular political model to be used in the remainder of the paper. Only when this is done shall we move on to deal with the specific issue of consumption taxation. To this point, all that we have tried to establish is that some such political model is necessary. In doing so, however, we have already distanced ourselves considerably from public finance orthodoxy, as it appears in both the tax reform literature and in the standard undergraduate and graduate texts.

II. The Political Model: Modified Leviathan

In the previous section, we argued that the public choice *approach* is consistent with a wide variety of models of political process, of which the more familiar public choice models make up only one possible set. For purely illustrative purposes, we did make appeal at various points to features of a model in which an "as if" majority rule is taken to constrain electoral outcomes in line with the demands of the median voter. In such a model, equilibrium levels of public expenditure are taken to be the result of a set of demand-supply calculations by individual citizen-voters. The tax institutions chosen determine the supply prices of public spending to the separate, individual citizens, and thereby the median of the individual equilibria in the polity. This kind of model is familiar in public choice, particularly in applications to issues in public finance [see for example Bergstrom & Goodman (1973), Borcherding & Deacon (1972), and Meltzer & Richard (1981)]. In these models, the tax-price assumptions made are often rather simple ones (e.g. that the tax is a proportional income tax, so that cost shares are constant over output and equal to individuals' income shares). To the extent that it is possible to speak of a mainstream thrust in an area as new, professionally unorthodox, and counter-cultural as public choice, this model is clearly part of it. Relevant analytics have been developed elsewhere [Buchanan (1967) and Brennan et al (1983) among others], and will be referred to later as they bear on the consumption tax issue.

However, we propose to *begin* analysis here with a different model, one which we developed jointly some years ago [Brennan and Buchanan (1980)] and which is summarized under the rubric 'Leviathan'. Like the demand-driven median voter model, this model also exhibits the two characteristics relevant to our critique of public finance orthodoxy: that is, changes in tax arrangements do affect expenditure levels; and tax arrangements are properly to be evaluated in constitutional terms - as elements in a fiscal constitution. Unlike the median-voter model, however, tax constraints become operative directly, in the form of limits on the taxing power itself, rather than indirectly, via feedback from the electoral process. The model of politics involved in this Leviathan approach is, quite explicitly, *non-democratic* - although the criteria by which alternative fiscal constitutions are evaluated remain consistent with and emerge from the liberal democratic tradition.[4]

Both in our original paper [Buchanan & Brennan (1977)] and in the subsequent book-length treatment [Buchanan & Brennan (1980)] we made relatively little attempt to justify the usefulness of this model of politics, nor did we specifically ground it in a public choice base.[5] This neglect is in part explained by our intention to use the Leviathan model for rhetorical rather than descriptive purposes. After all, the orthodox tradition in normative public finance presupposes government discretion in policy choice - such a presupposition was not of *our* devising. We were concerned simply to impose a certain coherence in the assumed motivations of political and market agents, and then to see where the analytical logic would lead. In retrospect, it may seem disin-

---

[4] Our initial objective in developing this Leviathan model was to replace the model of politics and governance implicit in public finance orthodoxy - namely, the benevolent despot model - with one that was minimally different. We retained the assumption that governments exercise discretion over political outcomes, that political agents do indeed hold some "power to govern". But we replaced the assumption of benevolence with a motivational structure congruent with that used elsewhere in economics (a motivational structure which, incidentally, is taken for granted in the derivation of citizen response to tax changes and underlies the whole analysis of tax incidence and tax efficiency in mainstream public finance). That is, we modelled government as a non-benevolent agent. Although we did not model government as directly *male*volent, and indeed we even allowed for the possibility of some altruism on government's part [see, for example, Brennan and Buchanan (1980, section 7.4, pp. 148-150)], we did assume that any discretionary power available to political agents would be exploited to the same extent and in the same way as analogous power in markets is assumed to be exploited - that is, governments act to maximize surplus in the same manner as (other, more conventional) monopoly enterprises. And because the monopoly model of the firm is a tool familiar to economists, we had ready to hand technical constructions that could be readily extended to the constitutional choice among tax instruments.

[5] We did attempt justificatory argument in our later book (1985).

genuous to say that we wished to make as large a concession as possible to the orthodox model of government behavior, but it is worth noting here that the Leviathan model is in one sense much closer to the political model implicit in public finance orthodoxy than is the median voter/cost share model of mainstream public choice.

In any event, there is no great difficulty grounding Leviathan in familiar public choice soil. For example, the McKelvey (1976) model of the manipulative agenda-setter is one version of the cycling-majority problem that generates precisely the central Leviathan result - namely, that majoritarian electoral "constraints" do not in fact *constrain* at all. In the McKelvey model, the ultimate equilibrium is the agenda-setter's private optimum. It should perhaps be noted that this model does not treat electoral considerations as entirely irrelevant. The path by which the final equilibrium is attained is critically influenced by the preferences of citizen-voters: the agenda-setter requires considerable knowledge about what citizens' preferences are before the necessary sequence of majority-approved policy packages can be put together. Nevertheless, the preferences of citizen-voters *are* irrelevant to the policy position characterizing the final equilibrium, and in that sense electoral constraints are ineffective. In such an environment, one must look to other constraints to secure outcomes more in line with those citizen-voters desire. If the agenda-setter is taken to be a rational egoist, in line with standard motivational assumptions in economics, surplus-maximization (and hence revenue-maximization from available tax instruments) emerges as the logical behavioral postulate. Restricting available tax choice seems the most natural and effective means of restraining the agenda-setter, although it is not the only means.

The model in which electoral constraints are ultimately nonbinding, and in which the *only* operative constraints on government behavior are those imposed by the natural revenue limits of constitutionally assigned tax powers, is clearly a *limiting* case. Such limiting cases have their analytic uses, and this can be so even when the limit itself is quite implausible as a description of reality. Economics is, after all, replete with them: the Samuelsonian model of "pure" public goods, and the conventional monopoly model are two examples that spring to mind. The analytic virtue of such limiting cases is that they allow one to focus on the logical implications of particular assumptions without unduly cluttering the discussion.

Nevertheless, many commentators seem to have found the revenue-maximizing model of government behavior too extreme to be taken seriously and have rejected the whole analysis on such grounds. This is perhaps not surprising because the model does turn many of the central results in the tax-reform orthodoxy on their heads. In particular, it calls into question the standard claim that broader-based taxes are necessarily normatively superior to more narrowly-based ones. It is not unreasonable to require that any such challenge to the most cherished principles of tax reform be grounded in a model of political process that is tolerably plausible.

There are two observations to be made here. First, the fact that the virtue of tax base broadness emerged in normative tax policy debate only after a long intellectual struggle is itself instructive. Broadness may commend itself to public finance orthodoxy, but it is often greeted with deep suspicion among taxpayers themselves. It can be difficult to convince taxpayers that base-broadening measures are not merely additional means of increasing the tax take. It is all very well for the public finance economist to dust off the equi-revenue framework, and to point out that a broader tax base can lead to rate reductions leaving everyone potentially better off. The economist can properly insist that there is no *logical* relationship between base-broadening and revenue levels. But the equi-revenue comparison is merely an analytic device, nothing more. It makes no claim to descriptive reality, and it has never, to our knowledge, been advanced on such grounds. Indeed, to be so advanced would require precisely the sort of model of political process that has been so conspicuously absent in the orthodox public finance literature.

It is also notable that the standard normative framework conceives of tax *justice* as a matter solely of the relative treatment of individual taxpayers. If the government confiscates the assets of only one citizen, without adequate compensation, it violates precepts of horizontal equity: it is acting "unjustly". But the injustice can be removed if government confiscates the assets of all citizens equally: precepts of horizontal equity will then be fully satisfied. If government exploits its citizens it may or may not be guilty of "inefficiency" depending on how the exploitation is effected, but in the standard framework it can never be accused of acting "unjustly". In the standard normative account the possible dimension of fiscal justice between government and citizen-taxpayers as a group is simply ignored, or, more disturbingly, deemed to be irrelevant. With such an obvious gap, citizen-taxpayers are right to view the recommendations of the public finance experts with some skepticism. There are rival intuitions involved in the broadness issue, and without wanting to make any concession to taxpayer populism, we should not simply assume that the economist-expert's judgments are authoritative.

The second observation about the plausibility of the Leviathan model is that the central policy conclusions can be derived from models less extreme than that used in *The Power to Tax*. Certainly tax-revenue maximization is not required. What is crucial is the validity of the following two propositions:

(i) equilibrium revenue-take is positively related to maximum revenue yield, *ceteris paribus* (so that, roughly, the easier one makes it to raise revenue, the more will be raised):

and

(ii) revenue levels tend to be "too large" in some normatively defensible sense.

Within the limits set by these two assumptions, almost any concession can be made to critics. Revenue-maximization can be dropped; electoral constraints can be reintroduced; some benevolence on the part of political agents can be admitted. We do not assume of course that such concessions will stifle all criticism. The two crucial propositions [(i) and (ii) above] are substantial ones; they are potentially controversial and certainly need justificatory argument. But focussing on these assumptions will at least direct criticism to that which is logically necessary rather than peripheral to the argument.

In what remains of this Section, we shall attempt to argue briefly for each of these propositions. In each case, the central question for us is this: under what models of political process will these two propositions be valid? If the set of such models is appropriately broad, and their assumptions suitably plausible, then the tax implications of the simpler version of the Leviathan model will be vindicated: limits on the assignment of taxing powers will remain a critical piece of any proper normative tax analysis.

Consider, then, proposition (i) above. We know that that proposition follows automatically in the simple Leviathan model. Broader-based taxes generate larger *maximum* revenue than do narrower-based taxes, so if government is appropriately modelled as a revenue-maximizer, broadening the tax base will automatically lead to higher revenue. And this result will remain valid if government *cannot* maximize revenue by virtue of other constraints imposed by the system, provided that those constraints are not specified directly or indirectly in revenue terms. Suppose, for argument's sake, that government can only acquire *half* the maximum revenue from any assigned tax base because, say, electoral constraints bite beyond that point. Clearly, proposition (i) will still obtain. In fact, however, proposition (i) also follows in entirely *non*-Leviathanesque models - in models, that is, that are entirely "demand-side" driven. Consider, for example, the standard median-voter model, in which allowance is made for the excess burdens of alternative tax regimes. Standard analysis assures us that, *ceteris paribus*, the broader the tax base the smaller the excess burden generated for any given revenue. Alternatively expressed, the marginal cost of raising a dollar of revenue, including the excess burden generated, is lower for broader based taxes, other things equal. Since the aggregate demand curve for public expenditure is downward-sloping, the reduction in the marginal cost of public expenditures means that total expenditure will tend to be higher for broader based taxes. Note, however, that such a presumption might be upset by changes in tax incidence: if the narrower tax base involves a lower tax-price (including excess burden) for the median voter than does the broader based tax, then the median voter will choose a higher level of expenditure under the narrower-based tax. In general, however, tax-price considerations seem likely to establish a further, independent reason for a positive association between base-broadness and expenditure levels. If broadening the base gathers up a larger number of citizens in the tax net, then the costs of public spending will tend to be spread more evenly over the set of voters, and *ceteris paribus* this will tend to lower the tax-price of the median voter. There is, however, and interesting discontinuity here which is worth noting. A tax may be so narrowly focussed that a majority of citizens pay less than average tax. In this event, the median voter will have a *lower* tax-price under the narrower tax than under some broader one. Once the tax base is broad enough to include a majority of citizens in paying taxes more or less equally, then extending the tax net will reduce tax payments for all the others at any given level of aggregate tax revenue, and there must be a presumption that the equilibrium level of expenditure will increase.

In addition to these "real" factors - cost-share effects and excess burden considerations - it seems plausible to argue that fiscal illusion will tend to establish a positive association between base broadness and expenditure level. Consider a fisc that is seeking to raise revenue, and is faced with two prospects: increasing the tax rate on an existing base; or leaving the tax rate constant and broadening the base. In general, the latter seems likely to confront less political flak - partly because taxpayers tend to be less aware of base redefinition than of tax rate hikes. For most taxes, the tax *rate* is a salient feature of the fiscal regime - and charges in that rate are conspicuous. Not so for base changes, which can often be minor, covert and/or apparently rationalizable on other grounds. There are of course countervailing considerations: a tax rate change involves all taxpayers paying a little more, whereas a base change often falls quite specifically on a restricted number of taxpayers for whom the co-ordination problems involved in organizing special interest lobbying are smaller. Nevertheless, tax rate changes are readily identified by voters for what they are, and the electoral cost of base-broadening per dollar of revenue raised is likely to be smaller than for a tax rate hike. Accordingly, larger revenue increases are likely to arise if base-broadening is used, and *ceteris paribus* tax take will tend to be larger in political equilibrium under a more broadly-based tax system.

In summary, then, in a wide variety of reasonably plausible political models, broadness of tax base and total tax revenue are positively related: proposition (i) seems to be fairly robust. To be sure, we can devise cases where proposition (i) fails. In particular, if the tax base is narrow *enough*, in the sense that the tax falls predominantly on a minority of taxpayer-citizens, then increased broadness may *reduce* electoral demands for public spending. But this seems a rather special case, and probably irrelevant to the sorts of tax systems typical in contemporary democracies. Accordingly, we shall take proposition (i) as given.

Consider now proposition (ii) - the claim that revenue levels tend to be "super-optimal". This is clearly a contentious claim, and has been debated with some vigour in the literature. The arguments *for* the proposition are essentially of two kinds. The first kind focuses on the nature of electoral pressure: it is a "demand-side" argument. The argument is that, under majority rule, with general taxation, special interest coalitions will tend to form to promote projects whose benefits are enjoyed predominantly by the decisive majority. [See Tullock (1959) and Buchanan & Tullock (1962) for the classical statements]. Because taxation is general, majority members will pay less than the full cost of the projects they particularly desire (and in the limit only half), and hence push those projects to a level beyond that which efficiency norms would dictate. Now, it would seem that those projects preferred by special interest groups composing the minority will tend to be under-expanded. However, with log-rolling, it is possible that all special interest groups will be members of some majority coalition, and hence that every special interest project will command majority support. Each project will then be expanded beyond the optimal size. Of course, the over-expansion will not occur for pure public goods. Moreover, if the special interest projects in question include tax breaks as well as spending projects then public goods expenditure will tend to be too low. We should then concede that, in principle, the demand-side argument might go either way. In practice, however, if there are forces (both explicitly constitutional and otherwise) that tend to keep tax bases reasonably broad, the balance of the argument seems to support the aggregate over-expansion conclusion.

The second line of argument for proposition (ii) is a supply-side one. It depends on the judgment that electoral competition under majority rule is a very loose constraint on the conduct of political agents: that there are political profits in electoral equilibrium. The "benevolent despot" construction would have us believe that such political profits will be spent in the public interest - or, at least, in the politician/bureaucrats' perception(s) of the public interest - but any economic model will presumably want to treat political agents as rational in roughly the same terms as other players in the socio-economic game. Now, in standard models of monopolistic markets, profits are appropriated by restricting output and raising price. The net effect of profit creation is to reduce total expenditure. That is, in the market, profits and total revenue are inversely related in the neighborhood of equilibrium, and it must remain a matter for conjecture whether the presence of rents implies excessive total revenue. We certainly *know* that, perfect discrimination aside, positive market profits imply *under*-expanded output. Electoral competition, however, is quite different. Because parties/candidates offer competing, mutually exclusive policy packages, the appropriation of citizen-surplus takes a different form.

Consider, for example, a party that seeks only maximum political profits. In settling on its offer to citizens, profits and output are independent. Consequently, the best strategy for the party is to offer a public spending package that leaves citizen surplus as large as possible, and to set taxes at a level that leaves profit at a level it thinks it can get away with. To offer any other spending package would leave scope for a competitive party to obtain more votes *and* more profit; setting the optimal spending level would allow a marginally higher profit without leaving voters any worse off. Electoral competition will, on this reading, focus on tax levels - with both parties choosing expenditure packages with the same expected voter support. Accordingly, positive political profits imply excessive tax revenues. In other words, proposition (ii) is upheld *unless* electoral constraints are totally binding: the situation of zero political profits emerges as a limiting, and in our view, not very plausible, case.

However, the normative implications of this argument, unlike those of the earlier demand-side argument, are unclear. In the earlier argument, there was a one-to-one connection between revenues and expenditures: if public revenues were over-expanded, so would public expenditures levels be, and vice versa. In the supply-side argument, public goods supply can be optimal, while public revenues are over-expanded. This fact invites the question: if expenditure levels are optimal, should we *care* about tax levels? The answer to this question is not entirely clear cut[6] our view is that the level of political profits should be of concern to the citizenry, and hence that constitutions should be designed to minimize transfers from citizens to political agents.

"Supply-side" arguments of this kind sometimes take the additional step of arguing that political profits are likely to be spent on higher levels of public goods supply. This

[6] It would be possible to extrapolate directly from the analogous private monopoly model and to treat all political surplus as an addition to the net consumer - and producer-surplus enjoyed by citizens from the provision of private and public goods. One might attempt to justify this position constitutionally by observing that, behind the veil of ignorance, any one individual is as likely to be a recipient of this surplus as any other, and hence the surplus will *ceteris paribus* be positively valued in the constitutional calculus. [This is essentially the line taken by Corke and West (1980) for example]. If this claim should be accepted, it would only be to the extent that higher political surplus generated larger excess burdens, or gave rise to resource-destroying rent-seeking, that a persuasive normative case against Leviathan could be mustered. Rent-seeking may, of course, arise to exhaust political surplus partially or totally. But even if there should be no rent seeking, we believe that the normative case against redistributives from citizen-voters to political agents is persuasive. To take the opposite view is to claim that dictatorship is no worse than democracy, because all that is at stake is the redistribution of surplus from citizens to rulers. One would, on these grounds, entirely neutralize the normative thrust of the McKelvey theorem: once the manipulative agenda-setter is included in the set of normatively relevant persons, majority rule becomes efficient precisely *because* the agenda-setter is dictatorial.

But our object here and in *The Power To Tax* has been to derive a fiscal constitution for a basically liberal political order: for these purposes we accept liberal principle that government should be in the interests of the governed though of course it remains to be determined just what institutional and fiscal structure best supports that principle.

is, for example, the line adopted by Niskanen (1971) in his well-known treatment of bureaucracy. Niskanen's claims are: first, that bureaus are able to appropriate political profits by virtue of their superior access to knowledge about costs of public output; and second, that these bureaus are impelled by their internal logic and/or moral zeal to spend revenues obtained on higher output levels. Alternatively, one could perhaps argue that most of the political profit is secured by political *parties* who expend that profit on projects of high ideological value to themselves, though of negligible value to citizens. Certainly, there is not much evidence of politicians or bureaucrats taking political profits out in the form of *cash*: only small profits in aggregate would be required to secure enormous personal fortunes for all politicians in national assemblies, for example, and though politicians seem to do well enough by the standards of ordinary mortals, they do not seem to be making a fortune. Accordingly, one might argue that, after all, loose electoral constraints do lead to excessive levels of public goods supply. We ourselves find this connection plausible, but we do not see our whole argument to hinge upon it. That is, we do not see the only reason for opposing enormous political profits to lie in the possibility that they might be spent on excess public goods and services: in our view, general liberal principles imply that such profits are objectionable *per se*.

The main conclusion to be drawn from the broad ranging discussion of this section, is that in a wide variety of political models, the traditional public finance argument for broader based taxes is at risk: beyond some point, increased broadness is likely to be undesirable. Consequently, the assignment of taxing powers must take proper account. not only of the efficiency and equity of alternative tax systems, but also of the ways in which those tax systems interact with the political structure to deliver electoral decisions about levels of public goods supply and to generate different levels of political profit.

III. Tax Substitution: Consumption *versus* Income Taxation

We can now turn to the particular tax matters that are the central preoccupations of this conference.

In the conventional normative treatment, consumption taxes are discussed in two different settings. In the first place, there is the question of whether, within a "comprehensive tax" framework, consumption expenditure or income represents the better tax base. In other words, what is the appropriate tax treatment of savings? This first question is something of a chestnut in public finance economics, and we have relatively little to contribute directly on it. However, since the question is indirectly relevant for our concerns, we shall say *something* about it.

In the second place, there is the question of whether, when an income tax is subject to various loopholes with significant evasion and avoidance, the fisc might do better to rely on an appropriate *mix* of taxes rather than on a single tax. In this context, a case is often made for the consumption tax specifically, not as an alternative to an income tax, but as a supplement to it. Here, the consumption tax is usually advanced in its indirect rather than direct form - say as a wholesale or retail sales tax, or a value-added tax of the consumption type. The sorts of issues that are raised in this tax *supplementation* context are rather different from those raised in the 'income versus consumption' setting, and the implications within our modified Leviathan model are also different. Accordingly, we shall postpone the tax supplementation questions until the next section, and focus here on the tax substitution debate.

Suppose the choice to be made is between a conventional income tax and a consumption-expenditure tax of the Kaldor or Andrews kind. Which is to be preferred? In answering this question, we shall attend to several subsidiary questions. Specifically, what are the effects of replacing an income tax with a consumption tax on: the distortions of choice induced by the tax system among private goods (i.e. excess burdens as traditionally understood); the structure of cost shares (or 'tax prices'); the extent of fiscal illusion; the time profile of revenues; and the prospectivity/retroactivity of the various tax systems. We examine the first three of these matters *in this section*. Questions of the time profile of revenues and the degree of retroactivity introduced are set aside in the interests of space.

A. Consumption Tax and Tax Efficiency

Within its own terms, the charge that the income tax involves 'double taxation' of savings, and therefore distorts the inter-temporal allocation of consumption decisions is compelling. Taken on its face, the intertemporal neutrality of the consumption tax implies that the marginal cost of public funds will be lower under a consumption tax than an equi-revenue income tax, and hence that both the median voter's desired level of public goods supply and the predicted level of political surplus would be *larger* under the consumption tax alternative. Or, at least, this would be so in the absence of fiscal illusion (which we shall discuss separately below).[7]

It should be clear from our earlier discussion that we consider the terms of this debate to be excessively abstracted from fiscal real-politic. The truth of the matter is that no income tax currently in existence much resembles the Haig-Simons ideal, and especially so in connection with the taxation of capital income. That is, capital income is taxed in a highly non-uniform manner - with imputed rent on housing exempt, capital gains taxed on a realizations rather than accruals basis and often at lower rates than interest income, and superannuation contributions often tax exempt or even subsidized, while ordinary dividend income is inadequately indexed for inflation and often subject as well to tax at the corporate level. Even if one were an income-base proponent *in principle*, one might well argue that consumption taxation is more efficient, because entrenched popular perceptions and/or political interests make uniform taxation of various kinds of capital income virtually inconceivable, and because uniformity of tax treatment of capital is more important from an efficiency viewpoint than "roughly" proper treatment of savings versus consumption (as an income-tax proponent would see it). Equally, however, consumption-base proponents ought to recognize that the intro-

---

[7] The defense of income base proponents against the double taxation charge has tended to take the following forms:

a) although strict efficiency considerations support the consumption tax, horizontal equity considerations support the *income* base, because income represents a superior index of 'ability to pay';

b) future consumption is a leisure complement. Hence 'second best' considerations suggest differently heavy taxation of future consumption (which is what the income tax achieves);

c) the consumption-base argument depends critically on the implausible assumption that all saving is for future consumption; if pure accumulation as a motive for saving is admitted, the case for the income tax is restored.

As one of us has argued elsewhere, (c) is only half correct - when accumulation is a motive for saving, the consumption tax is not ideal, but neither is the income tax, and the question of which is superior becomes an empirical one of some complexity. [See Brennan and Nellor (1982)].

duction of a consumption base is likely to create strong pressure for a supplementary tax on wealth - either in the form of explicit wealth taxation or estate and gift duties - and that such taxes not only undermine the consumption base ideal but may also turn out to be even more haphazard than is the (implicit) taxation of wealth embodied in the income tax.

Moreover, it is difficult to see how the question of the appropriate tax treatment of savings can be divorced from other public policies that bear on savings, most notably those connected with unfunded government social security programs. If, as we believe, private savings *are* significantly reduced by such social security schemes (notwithstanding argument by Barro and others to the contrary) then to treat tax questions in isolation from that fact seems extraordinary, and though one might argue that the ideal response is to moderate the social security program, the quasi-contractual nature of government obligations under those programs makes significant change on this front politically unlikely.

With all this in mind, it does seem persuasive to argue that from an efficiency viewpoint the consumption base is a superior option, say, for the United States currently, even if the efficiency arguments are less conclusive more generally. This superior tax efficiency means that, fiscal illusion and cost share effects aside, the consumption tax would lead to larger demands for public spending and larger political surplus than would the income tax.

B. Cost Share Effects

It is difficult to see any significant aggregate cost-share effects associated with a shift from income to consumption taxes. Both are broad general taxes, and though the more uniform treatment of capital income under the consumption base would doubtless moderate avoidance/evasion activities, the effects of this on total voter demand for public spending are unlikely to be significant.

It is however the case that the distribution of consumption in any taxpaying period (say a year) will predictably be less dispersed than the distribution of income. Accordingly, with an identical rate structure (say proportional) the cost-share of the median voter is likely to be somewhat higher under the consumption tax than under the income tax. Of course, expenditure base proponents often have in mind that rate structures will be altered to maintain roughly the same distributional effect (this is clearly Kaldor's view, for example) and such changes would seem to wash out most of any cost-share modification. The difficulty here is however that progressive rate structures do not generate determinate *marginal* cost-share arrangements, and the shift from one progressive rate scale to another may well alter marginal cost-shares in an unpredictable way. [See Brennan (1977) and Brennan *et al* (1984) VI for a fuller discussion]. Definite predictions here would require a fuller specification of the precise rate structures involved, and how these would be likely to vary as revenue demands alter. In the absence of that fuller specification, it seems safe to conclude that cost-share effects are unlikely to be large but probably involve the median voter facing a rather higher cost-share under the consumption base. This higher cost-share will *ceteris paribus* reduce demands for public spending, and also reduce political surplus: the electoral cost of a dollar's extra surplus.

C. Fiscal Illusion

Because the income and expenditure taxes are both direct taxes, likely to be paid and collected under identical arrangements, there would seem to be little role for differential fiscal illusion. There are, however, two considerations that are relevant here. The first relates to *perceptions* of base broadness; the second to the role of the corporate income tax in the income tax system. The discussion in sub-section A. above suggests that the consumption tax is *broader* in the relevant efficiency dimension than the income tax. The income tax involves *two* rates, one of t on present consumption and one of $(2t-t^2)$ on future consumption[8]; the consumption tax levies an effective rate of t^1 on both. It may make little sense to talk of relative "broadness" in this context, but it is clear that rational, fully informed taxpayers would recognize the high rate of tax on future consumption and moderate their behavior in the light of it - including, say, their behavior in taking risks, working hard, etc. In fact, however, because the *timing* of revenue streams under the income tax is as it is, the current tax rate required under the income tax is lower than under an equi-revenue consumption tax. The consumption tax delays payment of tax on the principal of any savings until the future when the savings are spent on consumption; the income tax on the other hand taxes the principal currently.

[8] 2t is an adequate approximation in most cases - hence 'double taxation'.

Accordingly, the *current* equi-revenue income tax rate is lower. To the extent that taxpayers focus on the current rate of tax - which is a natural enough focus - it will seem to then as if the consumption base involves higher overall taxation in generating the same period-by-period revenue. And citizen-voters may well respond to that higher perceived tax rate by reducing the demand for public spending. In other words, although the true welfare cost of the income tax may be higher than for an equi-revenue consumption tax, our conjecture is that the *apparent* cost to taxpayers of any given public project will be higher, under the consumption tax and hence that total public revenue (both public goods expenditure and political surplus) will be lower under the consumption tax.

A further source of fiscal illusion under the income tax relates to the role of the corporate income tax. Although typically rationalized as a second-best alternative to accruals-based capital gains tax, and hence an integral part of the income tax system, the company income tax is a significant revenue source in its own right. There would be no case for the company tax in a consumption base system, and the consumption tax would have to cover company tax revenue as well. The relevant rate of consumption tax would therefore be higher than under an equi-revenue income tax - and again it seems likely that taxpayers would be induced to vote for a smaller overall revenue take.

D. Summary

In this section, we have examined briefly the effects of substituting the consumption base for the income base in the direct tax system. Because other participants at this conference will focus on the pure tax effects - the efficiency and equity of the two taxes per se - we have directed attention instead to the likely effects on public spending levels. And on this matter, the different considerations lead in opposite directions. According to simple excess burden logic, the consumption tax presents the voter-taxpayer with a lower tax-price than does the income tax, because the former is less distorting. Consequently, the voter-taxpayer will prefer a higher level of public goods spending under the consumption tax; and equally, political agents will be able to extract a larger amount of fiscal surplus. By contrast, fiscal illusion considerations suggest that the *apparent* burden (for any level of revenue) will be higher for the consumption tax. Hence, the consumption tax will lead voter-taxpayers to demand lower levels of government outlay and will restrict the potential for political agents to appropriate surplus. We suspect that the effects of fiscal illusion here will predominate - and hence we conjecture that substituting the consumption base for the income base will lead to greater electoral pressure for reduction in the total tax take.

IV. Tax Supplementation: Consumption Tax and the Tax Mix

In the previous section, we examined the question of the consumption base as an alternative to the income base - much in the same terms as a textbook discussion might have it, though with an eye to relevant political/public choice considerations. In much contemporary policy discussion, however, the consumption tax issue arises in a different setting. The policy choice conceptualized is not a total but a marginal one: that is, the issue is whether the consumption tax should be used as a *supplement* to the income tax over some range. To put the question in conventional equi-revenue terms, should a reduction in personal income tax rates be financed by introducing (or increasing rates of a pre-existing) consumption tax? The consumption tax involved here will typically be an *indirect* tax, say a retail sales tax or v.a.t., and the conjecture is that adjusting the tax mix in this way would reduce evasion and avoidance - that the effective tax base of using these two taxes (income tax and sales tax) together is broader than if either were used on its own.

This argument depends on an implicit judgment that the distinction, long since regarded as essentially irrelevant in public finance circles, between direct and indirect taxation is one of substance. The argument is not that a direct income tax and a direct consumption expenditure tax used in tandem will make for a broader effective base. If a direct expenditure tax provides less scope for avoidance and evasion, this would be an argument for the expenditure tax *simpliciter*. The argument is rather that with both a direct (income or expenditure) tax and an indirect tax (of consumption *or* income type) avoidance and evasion would be reduced.

In its heuristic version, the argument is simply this - that, in the presence of a consumption tax, someone who evades or avoids the income tax will, at least, have to pay *some* tax when his income tax savings are spent. And analogously, someone who consumes relatively little of goods heavily taxed under the consumption tax will nevertheless have to pay some income tax. In other words, what the fisc loses on the income tax swings, it picks up on the consumption tax roundabouts - and vice versa. This argument is a pure 'tax *mix*' argument. It does not depend on either tax (indirect consumption tax or direct income tax) being broader in coverage than the other. It depends rather on the proposition that you are likely to get more water by dipping into the stream with two leaky buckets, one inside the other, than if you used using either bucket on its own.[9]

It should be clear that any such argument depends critically on the buckets being in different places - that is, on the direct income tax having a different incidence from the indirect consumption tax. And this in turn hinges on the distinction between direct and indirect taxation. The argument would go ahead even if the direct tax had a consumption base, or if the indirect tax included capital goods in its base. And the argument would fail if the two taxes were both direct, but on different bases. It is surely implausible to argue that a taxpayer who, say, under-reports her income for tax purposes would not under-report that income if there were a tax deduction for all savings (i.e. a consumption base). The tax-mix argument, at least as usually advanced in the tax policy literature, depends upon the proposition that direct and indirect taxes differ in some policy relevant way.

Yet, here, the public finance specialist seems to confront a puzzle. One of the most basic incidence results in the literature asserts that incidence is independent of the side of the market on which the tax is levied. A tax imposed on producers of X has exactly the same incidence at a tax imposed on consumers of X. A proper analysis of the "swings and roundabouts" argument, therefore, would seem to suggest that the whole construction is inconsistent. Take a simple case. Suppose that taxi-cab drivers systematically pay less income tax than others: there are, we may suppose, differential opportunities in the taxi-cab industry for under-reporting of income. All the same, so the argument goes, the taxi-cab driver will pay *some* tax on the consumption goods he buys - the extra meat, fancier clothes, and more up-to-date videos that he obtains with his ill-gotten gains. Whereas under a single income tax system, taxi-cab drivers will pay *nothing* on unreported income, they will now pay *something* via the subsidiary income tax. But of course, this line of reasoning depends on income taxes being paid by factors of production and indirect taxes being fully forward shifted onto consumers - and this

[9] A more formal treatment of this issue is offered in Brennan (1988).

asymmetry of incidence assumptions cannot be allowed to pass unquestioned. If we are to take it that indirect taxes on meat, clothes, videos etc., are fully shifted forward to consumers of those products, then we must equally take it that the lower effective tax in the taxi-cab industry will be fully forward-shifted to consumers of taxi-cab services. That is, the tax advantages of under-reporting potential in the taxi-cab industry will attract workers into the industry until effective net-of-tax returns are equalized across all employments. As a result of such movements, relative wages will shift to wipe out any differential tax advantages. Alternatively, if the benefits of differential evasion opportunities are enjoyed by taxi-cab drivers, then the indirect tax must be analogously treated: the tax on meat, clothes, videos, etc. must be assumed to be fully borne by butchers, clothiers, and other factors of production in those taxed industries, and the taxi-cab driver will pay *no* extra tax when he consumes these "taxed" goods. In short, the tax-mix argument appears to depend on popular misconceptions about tax incidence - misconceptions which a systematic incidence analysis clearly reveals, and which properly educated public finance specialists should have long since abandoned.

If this is so, however, there is a further puzzle - this one, for the *public choice* theorist. If the tax incidence of direct and indirect taxes (or tax concessions) is essentially identical, why do the politically viable tax bases for direct and indirect taxation seem to differ so markedly? If a special interest coalition is able to secure favorable tax treatment of some good X under indirect taxation, why not equally under direct taxation? More generally, if the prevailing coalition of interests generates a political equilibrium that secures tax arrangement A under indirect taxation, why should not that same arrangement prevail under direct taxation? If the distinction between direct and indirect taxation is irrelevant *economically*, how can it be relevant politically? It might be added in this connection that armchair empiricism suggests that direct and indirect taxes do tend to generate different political coalitions. For example, most real-world indirect tax systems have exemptions for particular goods: food, prescription drugs, childrens' clothing, and more generally for particular goods that suggest themselves as especially "worthy" in some way. Direct tax systems almost never do; though clearly it would not be impossible, by any means, to give an income tax exemption for expenditure on specific items. We observe that the sorts of exemptions and concessions that are common under the income tax are different from the exemptions and concessions common under the sales tax (or indirect equivalent)[10]. Whether we are to explain such exemptions/concessions in terms of special interest coalitions or of the requirements of professionally accepted fiscal norms, such differences seem difficult to rationalize. One might, of course, argue that, because direct taxes typically adopt a progressive rate structure and indirect taxes do not, indirect taxes require some differentiation in rates between 'luxuries' and 'necessities'. It is, however, notable that although many countries in the recent past have substantially modified the degree of progression in their direct tax systems, they have not introduced a new range of direct tax *concessions* (on say food expenditure).

There is at stake in all this a matter of general interest to public finance scholars - namely, the basis of a general "theory of indirect taxation" that restores the distinction between direct and indirect taxes as a meaningful and potentially significant one in public finance analysis. Armed with such a theory, we might lend some analytic respectability to the tax mix argument. However, although we shall argue that adjusting the tax mix *can* alter the effective broadness of the tax system, we do not believe that this broadening is necessarily a good thing: the total revenue take emerging in political equilibrium will predictably increase under such broadening, and that increase must be considered in any proper normative evaluation.

Our theory of indirect taxation consists of the following propositions:

1. a direct tax will in general have a different incidence from an indirect tax with a nominally identical base and rate;
2. direct taxes will in general have a different base from indirect taxes in political equilibrium.

In the argument that follows we try briefly to defend these two propositions.

The standard theory of tax incidence, as we have noted, asserts that it is irrelevant who has the legal responsibility to hand revenue over to the fisc. That irrelevance proposition is based on the presumption that the legal tax base is entirely clear and totally enforceable. In fact, however, the precise legality of various activities and the legal definition of the tax base are often unclear and leave room for interpretation by the revenue 'collector'. Moreover, there is typically some scope for under-reporting or patently "illegal" activity where the risks of discovery are not too great. Of course, it is

[10] Though some exemptions/concessions are common - most notably, medical services.

possible to tack the possibility of avoidance and evasion onto the theory of incidence, but this is often done in a context where all agents are taken to be identical in their avoidance/evasion activities. For example, we might postulate that all taxpayers are natural tax-minimizers (the direkt obverse of the notion that all are net-of-tax wealth maximizers) and that all have identical attitudes to risk. Then, although there may be differential opportunities to evade and avoid in different occupations, these will be fully fleshed out in standard incidence terms. Factors of production will move into those industries where *effective* net-of-tax returns are higher and consumers will tend to buy more of those products where effective gross-of-tax prices are lower. To be sure, indirect taxes may be more or less robust against tax evasion/avoidance than direct taxes, but that is merely an argument for the more robust form *simpliciter*, not for the tax mix line that we are concerned with here.

The simple wealth-maximizing postulate seems, however, to be more than usually strained in the evasion/avoidance setting. The possibility of a self-reporting system operating at all depends on a sufficient spread of taxpayer morality in the community, a morality which we should note is not abundant enough in some countries to make direct taxation at significant rates feasible. If taxpayers are differentially attuned to the relevant moral dictates, then some will rationally pay more tax on the same legal base than others. Of course, if some industries, employments, forms of business organization etc. offer greater opportunities for evasion/avoidance activities than others, one would expect a preponderance of lower-morality taxpayers in those areas, and concomitant effects on product and factor prices. However, the pattern of tax payments will predictably differ according to who is appointed to do the reporting. The shift from direct taxes, where the legal liability to hand revenue over to the fisc lies with the individual, to indirect taxes, where that legal liability lies with firms, involves a redistribution of effective tax burdens across taxpayers even when the nominal legal base (say aggregate consumption) is the same, and even where there are no rate structure complications (i.e. the direct tax is proportional).

But are tax bases likely to be the same under direct and indirect taxation in political equilibrium? We believe the answer is no. And there are two reasons. First, direct taxes offer prospects for a finer-grained pattern of discrimination among taxpayers than do indirect. The most conspicuous offering on this smorgasbord is opportunity for a progressive rate structure, but progression is not unique here. A direct tax (or subsidy) can more readily distinguish taxpayers according to marital status, family size, age, and other personal characteristics. This richer set of possibilities makes certain political coalitions salient that would be much less salient under indirect taxes. Consider, for example, the case of progression. The availability of progression isolates as a conspicuous dimension of political process the conflict of interest between 'richer' and 'poorer' (whether in income, consumption or some other terms). Under indirect taxation that conflict becomes somewhat muddied: it may still be relevant, but different coalitions tend to emerge - say between the poor and food-producers - and somewhat different dimensions of political conflict are exposed. To mention another increasingly relevant example, direct taxation offers the possibility of overt discrimination between taxpayers on the basis of sex - a dimension of possible political conflict that is largely suppressed under indirect taxation. *In principle* direct taxes can give policy expression to *any* pattern of discrimination available under indirect: expenditure on any item or output could be favorably treated or penalized under the income tax. But beside the point. If there are political coalitions viable under direct taxation that would not be viable under indirect, then those that are viable under indirect will be so much less potent under direct. Potent political coalitions may determine the (public) choice of policy instruments; but equally the choice of policy instruments can determine which political coalitions are potent.

Nor is this the whole story (as our earlier remarks about the influence on equilibrium tax bases of recent changes in progressivity suggest). Fiscal illusion may be substantially irrelevant in isolating the actual incidence of different taxes, and hence for the assessment of the 'equity' of alternative tax systems, but it is central to the determination of political equilibria. Whether taxpayer beliefs about incidence are right or wrong is irrelevant for their behavior as voters: what is relevant is the content of those beliefs. If (most) taxpayers believe that all indirect taxes are fully forward shifted, and all direct taxes are 'backward shifted', they may well vote for a sales tax exemption for food and vote against an income tax exemption for food expenditure (believing that the latter will be enjoyed largely by workers in the food industry). Accordingly, direct and indirect *bases* will tend to differ.

Public finance specialists would surely admit that tax incidence is one area where counter-intuitive propositions abound (and hence, of course, where our professional expertise is most valuable). But it is precisely for that reason that non-experts may believe many things that "ain't so". The general equivalence propositions in public finance orthodoxy that assert, among other things, the irrelevance of the direct/indirect tax distinction are among the more counter-intuitive in public finance theory. If many taxpayers believe the direct/indirect tax distinction is a relevant one, this belief will influence their votes and render the distinction politically relevant. In politics, more perhaps than elsewhere, 'believing makes it so'.

To summarize. Direct and indirect taxes tend to have different bases in political equilibrium; and even with identical nominal bases will tend to have different effective incidence. The two claims are independent, but the second bears upon the first, because even without fiscal illusion and an independently structured set of political coalitions, that different incidence would give reasons for different voter behavior. The clear implication is that a shift from a single (or overwhelmingly predominant) direct tax system to a multiple tax system, with extensive reliance on some new broad-based indirect tax, *will* broaden the effective tax base. It is, we believe, a predictable implication of such base-broadening that total tax revenues will increase, and conceivably quite significantly. Any such tax-induced revenue increases must be a significant part of any proper normative evaluation of the underlying tax change; and it certainly cannot be presumed that such revenue increases are desirable. Whether they are so or not must ultimately depend on whether citizen-taxpayers want them - and specifically *not* on whether they serve the particular normative preconceptions, ideological commitments and/or interests of those who exercise political power or those who advise them.

V. In Summation

Our assignment was to discuss consumption taxation in a constitutional perspective. As the main text of preceding Sections indicates, this assignment has proven to be a difficult one. Despite its full quarter-century life, the research program in public choice, and particularly the sub-program in constitutional economics, has not been incorporated in the standard analyses of fiscal institutions. To an extent, therefore, any particular application, to consumption taxation or anything else, must start from scratch, as it were, and lay the groundwork through a generalized methodological critique. Section I is little more than an extended plea for the recognition that fiscal choices are *political* and must be analyzed as such. But such recognition comes at a cost. If the political economy of taxation is to be addressed at all, even in cursory fashion, some model of how politics works must be introduced.

Constitutional issues arise only if and when politics are presumed to operate less than perfectly. If we could, somehow, rest content with the romantic delusion that government, through the behavior of political agents, works always in furtherance of the "public interest" and in full knowledge of what this interest is, there could be no supportable arguments for the imposition or existence of constitutional constraints on governmental authority, fiscal or otherwise. Alas, however, governments are neither omniscient nor always benevolent, and, when we recognize such reality, the whole set of issues raised by constitutional constraints emerge.

The constraints that will be preferred depend on the way that differing political structures are predicted to work, and making such predictions involves much work that has hardly commenced. In one sense, the whole of our Section II may seem foreign to the purpose of our paper. But we judged it necessary to suggest the outlines of the general model of politics that informs our ultimate constitutional perspective, especially since our earlier model of revenue-maximizing Leviathan has been subjected to much criticism.

Only with Section III, more than midway through the text, did we begin to address directly the issues of the conference. The discussion in Sections III and IV is in many respects non-controversial, but we have tried to place the familiar analysis in the nonfamiliar constitutional context and to suggest how implications might be derived. Our ultimate position on consumption taxation is, predictably, nihilistic. We hope that our argument, here and elsewhere, demonstrates that the conventional normative case for broad-based taxation rests on questionable foundations, when a constitutional perspective is taken. But this argument offers no particular grounds in support of *any* particular set of tax arrangements. How much should the taxing authority of governments be constrained and by what instruments over and beyond electoral feedbacks? Answers to these questions depend on how much government spending is preferred, how individuals and groups differ in their demands for both public and private goods, how politics is predicted to work, how constitutional constraints impose their limits, and where nations are in their evolving fiscal histories.

Comments by Peter Bernholz

The paper by Brennan and Buchanan consists of three parts. In a first part the necessity to use the public choice approach when analyzing tax issues is discussed. The second part tries to prove that the monopoly model of a state, formulated in earlier work by the authors, i.e., of a state in which politicians exploit citizens, is relevant as an approach to reality in spite of the critique raised against it. The third part (Sections III and IV) tries to derive conclusions concerning the relative merits of income vs. consumption taxes or of a mix of such taxes as seen from the public choice and the constitutional perspectives.

I have no problems with the general message of the first part. The best ideas on what an efficient tax system should look like, are not very helpful if constitutional and other restrictions on political and bureaucratic processes are not such that politicians, bureaucrats, voters and interest groups are motivated to accept such a tax system. Moreover, if one starts from the normative premise of a free society, then the constitutional framework should not only allow an efficient system but also a system favoring as much as possible the wants of its citizens as perceived and expressed by themselves. But if this premise is accepted, then a separate discussion of taxes and expenditures must remain a somewhat doubtful procedure.

I would even propose that one should move farther than Brennan and Buchanan in two respects. First, one could argue that the present complex and broad tax system with many gaps and loopholes is just the result one would expect, given the politico-economic tendencies in a system of indirect democracy in which spending and tax decisions are not directly connected and in which the powers of parliaments to tax and to spend are scarcely limited by the constitution. I myself, years ago, tried to explain from a public choice perspective, why certain tax and expenditure patterns and certain levels of taxes and expenditures develop favoring the expansion of government activities in such democracies [Bernholz (1979, chapter 5); see also Bernholz and Breyer (1984, chapter 3)].

But if politico-economic forces are at work in nearly unlimited indirect democracies to develop specific tax and expenditure systems too complex and broad to be controlled by citizens, then another problem arises which has not been mentioned by

Brennan and Buchanan. How and under which conditions could constitutional rules be implemented which would allow an efficient tax and expenditure system allowing voters to express their own wishes? A system which would prohibit the misuse of taxing and spending powers by shifting coalitions of minorities and majorities as well as by interest groups and bureaucracies. For why should the political forces profiting from a nearly unlimited democratic system be willing to agree to a tax and expenditure constitution limiting their own influence? [This problem has been explicitly mentioned in Buchanan (1985)].

The second part of the paper presented by Brennan and Buchanan appears to be more controversial. Not that I doubt that politicians do have a broad range of discretionary power concerning tax and expenditure decisions which can be exploited by them. Voters are, in fact, rationally uninformed about most matters which do not strongly concern them, their families or friends, since the small influence they can exert on the outcome of elections does not warrant to incur sizable costs of informing themselves. Also, citizens may lack the education to understand relationships in a complex society and may hold politicians responsible if their own situation deteriorates even if they do not understand the causal relationships. Finally, the argument derived by the authors from the possibility of implicit logrolling as a reason of a broad range of discretion is certainly acceptable, though it is not clear who can exploit this range of discretion, politicians holding government office or interest groups [Bernholz (1977)].

But I am not at all sure whether "surplus-maximization (and hence(?) revenue maximization from available tax instruments) emerges as the logical behavioral postulate" (pp. 197 seqq.) for the rational agenda setter, e.g., the politician. Brennan and Buchanan stress themselves that the surplus cannot usually be directly appropriated by politicians. But then, how and by whom is it appropriated? What does it mean then, that "a party seeks only maximum political profits" (p. 202). What is meant by "political profits"? Could it not be that a maximum of such profits is reached at a level of revenues which is not maximal? For it might be possible that a politician could only maximize his income or that of his family or friends by introducing regulations or rules creating hidden rents from which he would profit directly or indirectly. And that in doing so he might even lower indirect taxes, let's say, on a good, the import of which would be reduced by a regulation? The latter with the purpose to compensate consumers and to maintain their support as voters?

The problems raised do not become less difficult if one assumes that taxation is used to confer benefits on special interest groups which may perhaps form logrolling coalitions to get the necessary majorities (with imperfect information of voters this may even not be necessary). For why should politicians, who do not benefit themselves, be interested in revenue maximizing for this purpose, if political competition for votes does not drive them into this direction? But then one would have to prove that the activities of interest groups and competition for votes lead by themselves to revenue maximization. This would, however, imply that government politicians don't have the discretion to secure a maximal surplus for their own benefit.

To make a long story short, one would have liked to see in the paper the development of some conditions under which propositions (i) and (ii) (p. 199) are true. For only then would one know under which conditions the application of the exploitative model of government to the problem of the relative merits of income and consumption taxes were warranted. Perhaps in contrast to the authors, I suspect that the rule of non-appropriation of revenues by politicians offers some useful protection against an exploitative maximization of tax revenues.

In the third part of their paper, Brennan and Buchanan try to apply their model to the question of income vs. consumption taxes or vs. a mix of these taxes. The arguments and conclusions presented there seem to be valid though probably not exhaustive. E.g., I suspect that the progressiveness of income taxes makes it easier for politicians to increase tax revenues over time than a sales, turnover or value added tax. It is true that tax payers probably have a somewhat better knowledge of the income taxes than of the indirect taxes they have to pay. And this fact would tend to lead to stronger resistance to increases of income tax *rates* compared to increases of indirect taxes. But income taxes increase more than proportionately compared to GNP because of *bracket creep* caused not only by inflation but also by increasing real per capita incomes connected with economic growth. There is thus no need for politicians to raise income tax *rates*, which would be a highly visible action. I suspect that the higher taxes caused by growth will not be perceived by taxpayers if their incomes are subject to a withholding tax and if they are not obliged to declare their incomes. This is especially true since real disposable incomes are growing in spite of higher taxes, so that people feel better off. Even in Switzerland, where income taxes have to be declared by everybody, it took about forty years until the severe bracket creep caused by *inflation* was felt to be a burden by the population. Only then the threat of a popular initiative forced the government to introduce the automatic bracket adjustment postulated by the constitution years ago, when the Federal income tax was introduced during World War II. But no such initiative has even been discussed concerning the higher percentage to be paid out of income by nearly everybody because of strongly increased per capita incomes.

Brennan and Buchanan point out that their "ultimate position on consumption taxation is, predictably, nihilistic". Given the fact that public choice theory has only just started to analyze the important problems which are the subject of this conference, it is perhaps not surprising that no clear-cut results can be presented. It may even be true that different results opposing each other can be derived, of which we only know the directions but not the magnitudes, so that a total result cannot be derived. Whether this is true or not can only be answered in the future with more specific and empirically supported models. The analysis given by Brennan and Buchanan is a stimulating first step in that direction.

Comments by Frans van Winden

This paper by Brennan and Buchanan which I have read with great interest, consists of two parts that are approximately of equal length: (a) a methodological part, and (b) a part dealing with tax issues that are of particular concern of the conference. Their central point in the first part is that a constitutionalist public choice perspective is needed for the tax issue - consumption taxation - at stake, and that this perspective is likely to lead to different conclusions than the traditional public finance approach. Using this perspective in the second part of the paper, they ultimately arrive at a "nihilistic" position, of the "it all depends" type, on consumption taxation which they relate to the existing lack of knowledge concerning political structures and processes.

Given this ultimate position and the space constraint, I will concentrate in my comment on the methodological part of their paper. More particularly, I will first focus on the advocated constitutionalist public choice perspective, and, subsequently, on the descriptive quality of their "modified Leviathan" model.

The constitutionalist public choice perspective is characterized by the following features: (a) decisions about taxes are political decisions; (b) the tax and expenditure sides of the budget are essentially connected; (c) tax arrangements are part of the institutional/constitutional fabric within which other political decisions are made, rather than merely outcomes of political process.

Although the first two features may almost seem to be truisms, I agree with the authors that their message has unduely been neglected in the standard public finance approach to tax analysis which focuses on normative aspects of equity and efficiency, typical within an equi-revenue framework, paying insufficient attention to questions of political reality.

I have difficulty, however, with the third feature and some of the consequences and interpretations that the authors relate to it. First, although I subscribe to the view that tax arrangements or systems (instead of tax rate adjustments, for example) are of a structural/institutional character, I am not convinced that they cannot be considered as ordinary outcomes of political process. In my view such arrangements (institutions) are of a similar nature as capital goods - albeit social instead of physical or human -, built up by investments that are ordinary outcomes of decisionmaking processes. As in case of the latter, matters such as the length of the time-horizon, maintenance and depreciation costs (think of administration, avoidance, evasion, erosion), initial costs, and the possibility of innovations play a role here [see Van Velthoven and Van Winden (1989), for an explanation of tax reform along these lines]. To suggest a real dichotomy here is to suggest more than there seems to be to it, and may direct research in the wrong direction. Second, given the essential connection between tax and expenditure sides of the budget, why not also allow for expenditure arrangements under the third feature? Take, for instance, the installment of pay-as-you-go (instead of funded) social security schemes. As the authors themselves note, such schemes appear to entail quasi-contractual government obligations. I find it hard to see then why, from a constitutionalist public choice pespective, "Tax decisions must be viewed as logically prior to decisions in other policy areas". More generally, given the aforementioned essential connection, I do not understand how the tax regime is to be specified before preferences on spending levels are registered, as the authors assert.

The "modified Leviathan" model discussed by the authors is meant to be descriptive, in contrast with their well-known Leviathan model which, according to them, was used for rhetorical rather than descriptive purposes. Instead of tax-revenue maximization this model is based on the following two propositions: (a) equilibrium revenue-take is positively related to maximum revenue yield, ceteris paribus; (b) revenue levels tend to be "too large" in some normatively defensible sense.

As regards the first proposition, my critique is that the authors seem to neglect here the importance - from a public choice perspective - of how politicians and bureaucrats are affected themselves by tax arrangements. Compare, for the sake of argument, an income tax, to be paid by politicians and bureaucrats as well, with a profit tax or land tax. Although the maximum yield under the former may be much higher, for obvious reasons self-interested politicians and bureaucrats may prefer a smaller revenue-take under such a regime than in case of the latter. Regarding the second proposition, the problem is, of course, what should be considered as normatively defensible. (Almost) anything seems to go here. I, for one, find the arguments of the authors, put forward in a footnote, contra the addition of political surplus (reaped by political rulers) to the net consumer - and producer-surplus enjoyed by citizens (non-rulers) as such not particularly convincing. The surplus of other social groups could as well be contested.

"Despite its full quarter-century life, the research program in public choice, and particularly the subprogram in constitutional economics, has not been incorporated in the standard analyses of fiscal institutions". Although political economists should always be aware of the fact that other than scientific factors may play a role here - after all, research in this area is heavily dependent on the financial support of those whose behavior is analyzed and criticized - the scientific prospects of public choice or modern political economy may in my view be improved if much more effort is put in the following directions. First, general formal models should be developed for a rigorous analysis of government behavior (such as the functioning and viability of different tax-structures), taking account of its interaction with behavior in the private sector, and employing a richer model of political decisionmaking. Second, a richer model of political decisionmaking demands a much stronger focus on pressure group activity; political reality is at odds with the emphasis on elections and majority decisionmaking in the public choice literature. Third, a richer model of political decisionmaking should further allow for a more sophisticated view of the interests of politicians and bureaucrats. Apart from the fact that it cannot a priori be excluded that through self-selection in the labor market the interests of agents in the public sector may be different from those of agents in the private sector, it should be acknowledged that in reality the (self-)interests of politicians and bureaucrats are shaped by, and become more other-directed through: (a) multiple positions (through the ownership of stocks, for example, they may also partly share the interests of capitalists); (b) mobility (think of the insurance motive); (c) pressure by other (private sector) agents. Even while retaining self-interest as point of departure such considerations invoke the use of weighted representations of different utility functions, also referring to social groups in the private sector [see Van Winden (1983)].

References

Bergstrom, T.E. / Goodman, R.P. (1973), Private Demands for Public Goods, American Economic Review 63 (June, 1973), pp. 280-296.

Bernholz, P. (1977), Dominant Interest Groups and Powerless Parties. Kyklos 30, Fasc. 3, pp. 411-420.

Bernholz, P. (1979), Grundlagen der Politischen Ökonomie, Vol. 3, Tübingen: J.C.B. Mohr (Paul Siebeck).

Bernholz, P. / Breyer, F. (1984), Grundlagen der Politischen Ökonomie, 2nd, thoroughly revised edition, Tübingen: J.C.B. Mohr (Paul Siebeck).

Borcherding, T.E. / Deacon, R.T. (1972), The Demand for Services of Non-Federal Governments, American Economic Review 62, pp. 891-901.

Brennan, G. (1977), A Note on Progression and Public Sector Size, Public Choice 32 (Winter, 1977), pp. 123-124.

Brennan, G. (1988), Equity and Feasible Tax Reform, ch. 7, in: G. Brennan / Greval / Gronewegen (eds.), Taxation and Fiscal Federation. Sydney: ANU Press.

Brennan, G. / Buchanan, J.M. (1980), The Power to Tax, Cambridge: Cambridge University Press.

Brennan, G. / Buchanan, J.M. (1983), Tax Structure and Social Overhead Capital, Public Finance and Economic Growth, in: K. Roskamp (ed.), Detroit: Wayne State University Press.

Brennan, G. / Buchanan, J.M. (1985), The Reason of Rules, Cambridge: Cambridge University Press.

Brennan, G. / Buchanan, J.M. (1983), Predictive Power and the Choice Among Regimes, Economic Journal 93, pp. 89-105.

Brennan, G. / Nellor, D. (1982), Wealth, Consumption and Taxation, National Tax Journal XXV No. 4, pp. 427-436.

Brennan, G. / Bohanon, C. / Carter, R. / et al. (1984), Public Finance and Public Prices, Public Finance/Finances Publiques XXXIX No. 2, pp. 157-181.

Buchanan, J.M. (1967), Public Finance in Democratic Progress, Chapel Hill: University of North Carolina Press.

Buchanan, J.M. / Tullock, G. (1962), The Calculus of Consent, Ann Arbor: University of Michigan Press.

Buchanan, J.M. (1986), The Relevance of Constitutional Strategy, Cato Journal 6, pp. 513-518.

Browning, E.G. (1977), A Hidden Welfare Cost of Taxation, National Tax Journal 30, pp. 89-90.

Corke, G. / West, E.G. (1980), Tax Constraints on Leviathan, Journal of Public Economics 13, pp. 395-401.

Lindahl, E. (1919), Die Gerechtigkeit der Besteuerung, Lund: Gleerumska.

McKelvey, R. (1976), Intransitivities in Multidimensional Voting Models and Some Implications for Agenda Control, Journal Economic Theory 12, pp. 472-482.

Meade, J.E. / et al. (1978), The Structure and Reform of Direct Taxation. London: Institute for Fiscal Studies.

Meltzer, A. / Richard, S. (1981), A Rational Theory of the Size of Government, Journal of Political Economy 89 No. 5, pp. 914-927.

Musgrave, R.A. (1981), Leviathan Corneth - or Does He?, in: H. Ladd / T.N. Tideman (eds.), Tax and Expenditure Limitations, Washington: Urban Institute Press, pp. 121-138.

Tullock, G. (1959), Some Problems of Majority Voting, Journal of Political Economy 67, pp. 571-579.

Velthoven, B. van / Winden, F. van (1989), A Behavioral Model of Tax Reform, University of Amsterdam.

Winden, F. van (1983), On the Interaction between State and Private Sector, A Study in Political Economics, Amsterdam: North-Holland

Vickery, W. (1947), Agenda for Progressive Taxation, New York: Ronald Press.

Wicksell, K. (1896), Finanztheoretische Untersuchungen, Jena: Gustav Fischer.

Dennis C. Mueller

Public Choice and the Consumption Tax

The study of taxation in economics has traditionally been the province of public finance. Much of the analysis of taxation in public finance has been normative. The question posed is, What taxes ought the polity employ to raise revenue? Answers to this question have been derived using two alternative principles of taxation: (1) that those who benefit from a government provided good or service should pay for it, or (2) that individuals should be taxed according to their ability to pay [Musgrave (1959, chs. 4, 5)]. The former principle sees government as an institutional analog to the market, achieving Pareto optimal allocations of resources by providing public goods and internalizing externalities. This principle receives one of its earliest and still most eloquent statements in Knut Wicksell's (1896) *quid pro quo* theory of government.

Where the benefit principle seeks only Pareto optimality in the allocation of resources, those advocating ability to pay formulae seek to go beyond Pareto optimality and satisfy some additional criterion of distributive justice. Explicit in most of these analyses, and implicit in all is a utilitarian ethic which allows individual welfares to be compared and aggregated, as in a Benthamite social welfare function.

The subdiscipline of public choice has arisen in part as an effort to complement the normative analysis of traditional public finance theory with a positive analysis of how government does actually function. For example, the expenditure side of public finance describes much of the work of government as the provision of public goods and internalization of externalities, the kind of outcomes that public choice predicts would arise if polities followed Wicksell's advice and used the unanimity rule. But no country uses anything which comes close to a unanimity rule, and most use the simple majority rule in conjunction with other political institutions. These lead to quite different predictions about the composition and scale of government output. As one extreme example, Meltzer and Richard (1981, 1983) employ the median voter theorem to explain the entire growth of government in this century as a result of redistribution from rich to poor under majority rule. A public choice analysis of the consumption tax must involve both a description of the incidence of the tax to identify the gainers and losers, and an analysis of the political institutions under which the tax will be instituted.

I. Public Choice Considerations

Unfortunately for the question at hand, the public choice literature has been heavily concerned with the analysis of the expenditure side of government, with very little attention having been paid to taxation.[1] To some extent then, we need to charter new ground. To begin, we need to discuss the likely incidence of a consumption tax vis-a-vis the tax it would displace, presumably the personal income tax. Since political debate on the nature of a consumption tax is not very far advanced in the United States, one can only speculate as to the form such a proposal would take, if it were ever to surface. I consider three polar cases.

(1) The consumption tax as pure public good. One can envisage designing a consumption tax such that all taxpayers paid essentially the same tax bill as under the personal income tax,[2] and yet all individuals were made better off through the substitution of the consumption tax for the personal income tax. There are at least two arguments for why this might come about. First, the consumption tax would remove the distortion between present and future consumption that exists under the personal income tax and should, therefore, stimulate saving and investment. All citizens would be expected to benefit from the additional investment and growth stimulated by the changed incentives under the consumption tax. Alternatively, the costs of administering the consumption tax are thought by many[3] to be considerably lower than for the income

[1] Exceptions being Brennan and Buchanan (1980), and Hettich and Winer (1988).

[2] Both Geoffrey Brennan and Frans van Winden pointed out at the conference that the task of giving everyone the same tax bill would not be simple, particularly over a transition period in which the elderly would need special treatment to avoid their being triple taxed.

[3] See the paper in this volume by McLure and Zodrow.

tax, and thus a substantial savings in administrative costs should accompany such a substitution. If incidence is the same as under the income tax, all benefit from the substitution of the consumption tax for the income tax, and the decision to exchange the two taxes has all of the attributes of a pure public good.

(2) The consumption tax as a change in tax progressivity. It is possible to envisage the consumption tax as largely a change in tax progressivity relative to an income tax. For example, a flat tax on *all* consumption raising equal revenue to current income taxes would be a more regressive tax than an income tax excluding lower incomes and/or with rates rising with income.

(3) The consumption tax as a tax reduction for certain groups. As with all taxes, one can envisage certain exceptions to the tax (loopholes) being included so that some groups achieve tax reductions under a new formula. The kinds of exceptions that are possible and groups which can be benefitted are as boundless as a tax lawyer's imagination.

The first type of consumption tax could in principle be implemented even if the polity employed the unanimity rule. All that would be required is to inform the polity of the tax's desireable properties and its implementation would be forthcoming. But the fact that no polity uses the unanimity rule changes one's prediction as to the nature of a consumption tax that would actually pass in a parliamentary vote. If the parliament uses the majority rule to make decisions, some members of the parliament have an incentive to rewrite a tax proposal of the first type to make it look like a proposal of the second or third type. In so doing, the parliamentary majority could benefit its supporters to a still greater extent than under a proposal of type 1. Public Choice would predict, therefore, that an elected Parliament operating under some form of qualified majority rule would pass a form of consumption tax that was at best a combination of the type 1 consumption tax and types 2 and/or 3.

Without question the most frequently employed analytic tool of public choice used to analyze public sector outcomes is the median voter theorem. It has been used to explain the composition of government expenditures and their aggregate level.[4] It was used by Meltzer and Richard (1981, 1983) to explain the growth of government as a manifestation of the redistributional potential of majority rule.

[4] See Mueller (1989, chs. 10, 17).

To apply the median voter theorem to analyze the outcomes under majority rule one needs to have issues with but a single dimension of saliency. Meltzer and Richard tailor the income tax to fit this mold by making it a flat rate tax on income coupled to a per capita subsidy. The vote on a consumption tax could be treated as a single-dimensional issue, if one assumed that it was constrained to raise a given amount of revenue, T, by a combination of say an exclusion of x dollars of consumption and a flat tax t on the remainder. The necessity of raising T dollars of total revenue would tie the choice of x and t, and reduce the choice to the single one of choosing x or t. The higher the excluded consumption x the more progressive the incidence of the tax.

While one can construct a tax formula in such a way so that the choice of formula is a single-dimensional issue, tax formulae actually in use do not resemble this simple structure. More than one rate is applied depending on the height of income. Such formulae add dimensions to the issue space as do the various options for defining taxable income. Once the issue space has more than one dimension, however, the equilibrium provided by the median voter theorem vanishes, and the power of this analytical tool disappears.

Fortunately, other classes of public choice models exist which describe equilibria with multidimensional issue spaces [Mueller (1989, chs. 10, 11)]. In one particularly relevant class of these, two parties or candidates are assumed to compete for votes by promising platforms defined over multidimensional issue spaces. The key assumption employed in establishing the existence of an equilibrium is the inherently plausible one that candidates or parties are uncertain to a degree about how individuals will vote, and thus expect that an increase in the benefits promised a particular voter increases only the probability that that voter votes for the candidate. In a variant of this class of models, Peter Coughlin, Peter Murrell and myself (1988) show that two party competition for the votes of interest groups leads to an equilibrium platform which maximizes a weighted sum of the utilities of the different interest group members, where the weights depend on the size of an interest group and its ability to promise votes to a party.

Models such as this one help to explain why some groups fare better than others under political outcomes. This model would predict the kinds of loopholes benefitting particular interests under a consumption tax as exist now under the income tax. Is tuition at private schools consumption? Donations to charities? Donations to political candidates? The reasoning of economists and other social scientists and social reformers is only one, and not necessarily the most important, input into answering these questions.

What then does public choice predict regarding the implementation of a consumption tax? At a first pass, I would say that the actual tax introduced, if any were to be introduced, would certainly have elements of the second and third forms of consumption tax, and if the premises underlying the first form are valid, could have elements of all three. It is hard for any economist to argue that anyone will pass up opportunities that make some or all better off, and harm no one. Certainly no vote maximizing politician should pass up such an opportunity. Thus, if a consumption tax can be designed with incentive effects that enlarge the social pie, then vote seeking politicians can be expected to incorporate those effects into any tax changes they make.

But political competition is also colored by a left-right, poor-rich dichotomy. Left-wing parties the world over are to be found trying to enhance the interests of workers, the poor, etc., while right-wing parties represent business, and upper income groups generally. That these economic and class interests would not step forward to shape the design of a fundamental revenue source for government is hardly to be expected.

Finally, there are the special interests with their lobbyists and lawyers, the termites of democracy, who can be seen boring away at democratic institutional structures wherever they are found. Their work is evident in the expenditure patterns and tax structures of every democracy in the world. It is impossible to believe that they would not exert their influence in shaping the structure of a consumption tax were one introduced.

More specific predictions would require more detailed analysis of the particular institutional structure of a given country. For example, local interests are favored by the geographic mode of representation used in the United States more so than under the proportional representation systems used in most European parliamentary systems. The long and expensive political campaigns of the United States give more scope for organized interest group influence than is available in the United Kingdom. We shall return to these questions later, but first let us consider some reasons why one perhaps should not take the public choice analyst's predictions so seriously.

II. Flies in the Public Choice Ointment

Before one places much weight on the predictions of public choice, perhaps one should ask how well this methodology fares in predicting outcomes and other characteristics of the political process.

The distinguishing feature of public choice analysis is the assumption that all participants in the political process - voters, politicians, and bureaucrats - act rationally and in their own self interest. To give this assumption predictive power, self-interest must be defined rather narrowly. Thus, candidates are assumed to be ideological chameleons willing to adopt any platform that will win more votes [Downs (1957, pp. 21-31)]. Bureaucrats seek only the personal gains that come with expansions in the size of their bureaus [Niskanen (1971, pp. 36-42)]. The individual voter is concerned with only the consequences of her vote on her narrowly defined personal interests [Mueller (1989, ch. 18)]. Not one of these assumptions receives resounding confirmation in the empirical public choice literature.

In analyses of the voting records of members of Congress, ideology, as measured by the character of the past votes of an individual representative, emerges as a resilient predictor of the future votes of a representative, which no accounting for the interests of a representative's constituents can expunge.[5] Models, which assume that parties pursue ideological goals, whenever the public opinion polls give them a comfortable lead, have also received a fair amount of empirical support [Frey and Schneider (1978a, b, 1979, 1981a); Schneider and Pommerehne (1980)].

Attempts to account for the growth of government in Western democracies using public choice theories have met with mixed success even in the hands of sympathetic observers [Borcherding (1985); Mueller (1987)]. Neither the public choice theory of bureaucracy nor any other leading public choice hypothesis as to why governments grow offers an adequate account of the growth of government in recent years.

But the most spectacular failing of public choice theory comes, of course, in predicting the behavior of the individual voter. In a large electorate, no rational and narrowly self-interested citizen would bother to vote, since the probability that her vote

---

[5] See Kau and Rubin (1979); Kau, Keenan, and Rubin (1982); Chappell (1982); and Kalt and Zupan (1984). For a valiant, but I believe unsuccessful attempt to demonstrate the unimportance of ideology, see Peltzman (1984).

affects the outcome, and thus her welfare, is so low. Yet even in the United States half of the electorate, nearly 100 million people, turned out in the recent presidential election, and in Europe relative turnouts are much higher.

The single most important explanation for this seemingly irrational behavior on the part of voters appears to be that they are motivated by a sense of public or civic duty. They vote in the belief that their vote supports not only the candidate or party for whom they vote, but the strength of the democratic institutions of their country. At least that is the impression one gains from the divers surveys of voters [Riker and Ordeshook (1968); Ashenfelter and Kelley (1975); Mueller (1989, ch. 18)]. Further confirmation of this impression is obtained from the responses of voters to questions of why they voted for the particular candidate or party for whom they voted. Some individuals vote against incumbents, not because they themselves have been made worse off by the incumbent's policies, but because they believe the country has been made worse off. For example, high unemployment can cost an incumbent president the votes of even those who have not been hurt by unemployment and do not expect to be hurt by it [Fiorina (1978); Kiewiet (1981, 1983); Kirchgässner (1985)].

Thus, both the decision to vote, and the decision for whom to vote seem to be at least in part, or for a part of the electorate, explained by an individual's conception of what is in the 'public interest' and not just what is in her own, narrow self-interest. This conclusion implies that the outcomes of the political process, even if candidates slavishly bowed to voter preferences, would in part reflect general perceptions of what is in the public interest [Tullock (1984); Mueller (1989, ch. 18)]. When one adds to this consideration, the likelihood that representative voting is affected by their own ideological positions, the possibility increases that decisions on whether to introduce a consumption tax or not will be affected by whether such a change is viewed as being in the broad public interest. Our ability to predict the possibility that a consumption tax would be enacted and the form it would take, using the public choice methodology, appears to be considerably circumscribed. Rather than press on further with deductive analyses of what might happen, it is perhaps useful to pause and reexamine an event in political history that resembles in its importance the adoption of a consumption tax, the decision in the United States to enact a personal income tax.

III. The Adoption of the Personal Income Tax in the United States

The federal income tax was first enacted in 1861 as a source of revenue to finance the Union's effort against the South in the Civil War [Waltman (1985, p. 3); Carson (1977, p. 26)]. While neither the war nor the tax were universally popular, both were endorsed by a substantial fraction of the population and the combination of war expenditures and income tax to finance them comes about as close to the provision of a public good coupled to a method to pay for it as this country has come. The revenue raised by the tax was by no means enough to cover all of the costs of the war, however, and as usual much of these were covered by the issuance of debt. The vote in Congress on the 1861 measure was along the predictable lines of economic interest. The obvious alternative to the income tax was a tax on land. Representatives from the Western states voted for the income tax, consistent with their constituents' interests. Farmers in the West were long on land and short on cash. Votes against the income tax came from representatives from the higher income Eastern states. Much of the debate surrounding the introduction of this first income tax was over whether it was the rich or poor who should pay for the war [Carson (1977, ch. 3)]. With the close of the war, this debate continued and intensified. While some favored retaining the income tax on distributional-equity grounds, without the public good-war justification it could not be sustained. The first United States income tax was repealed in 1872 [Waltman (1985, p. 3)]. It is worth noting that a case regarding failure to pay the income tax worked its way up to the Supreme Court, which in 1880 declared the tax constitutional since it was *not* a direct tax [Carson (1977, pp. 41-2)].

Debate over the income tax ebbed and flowed during the remainder of the 19th century and on into the early part of the 20th. This was an era in which corporate capitalism first began to have a major and visible impact on the economic landscape. This development fostered the birth of numerous radical political movements and the popularity of several radical political philosophies. Edward Bellamy's Utopian tract, *Looking Backward 2000-1887*, advocating state ownership of production, became a best seller [Ratner (1942, p. 162)]. Henry George proposed a single tax on rent, and came in second in the race for mayor of New York in 1886, outpolling Theodore Roosevelt [Ratner (1942, pp. 153-4)]. Among the many political parties that got started, the Populists, Socialists, and later the Progressives had the most success. All favored reenacting the individual income tax.

Perhaps at no other time in the history of the United States have economic interests aligned themselves along geographic lines as they did during the last quarter of the 19th century and the beginning of the 20th. Railroad, banking, manufacturing and commercial interests were concentrated in the East, farming interests in the South and Midwest. This geographic division of economic interests coupled with our geographic system of political representation combined to facilitate making the classic division of economic class interests into a major political issue of the day, with the farmer-poor interests being joined by the increasingly important labor-union interest groups.

Throughout this period, demands to reenact the income tax were typically coupled with proposals to lower tariffs which were seen by their critics as tailored to protect and benefit the manufacturing interests of the East, while raising the prices paid by farmers and the prices of necessities for the poor. On October 1, 1890, the Republican controlled Congress passed the McKinley Tariff Act raising the average import duty from 44 to 48 percent, and providing other benefits for business. The political reaction to the bill was swift and dramatic. One month later, the Democrats and Populists won three fourths of the seats in the House [Ratner (1942, pp. 159-60)]. This victory helped shift the balance of political power in Congress and lead to a bill cutting tariffs and introducing a tax of 2 percent on personal and corporate incomes over $4,000. This would be equivalent to a tax of 2 percent on incomes over $56,000 measured in 1989 dollars. Votes on the bill were along party and economic-geographic lines. Voting for the final tariff measure with the accompanying income tax amendment were 196 Democrats and 8 Populists. Voting against were 122 Republicans, 17 Democrats, and 1 Populist. Votes for came from the South and Midwest, votes against from the Northeast and Far West [Ratner (1942, pp. 180-1)].

In 1895, the Supreme Court declared the new income tax law unconstitutional. Joseph H. Choate, one of the leading advocates of the day, was paid a reported $200,000 (the equivalent of $2,800,000 in 1989 dollars) to argue the case against the income tax before the Supreme Court [Carson (1977, p. 60)]. In doing so, he interpreted the tax as an attack on the institution of private property, and thus a threat to civilized government.

I have thought that one of the fundamental objects of all civilized governments was the preservation of the rights of private property...that it was the very keystone of the arch upon which all civilized government rests, and that this once abandoned, everything was at stake and in danger. [Ratner (1942, p. 200)].

Choate characterized the principles upon which this attack on private property was launched as "communistic, socialistic [and] populistic". He asserted rather prophetically that if the tax were not declared unconstitutional there would be nothing to halt a "communistic march" by Congress leading from tax rates on income of 4 percent to tax rates on income of 20 percent [Carson (1977, p. 59)].

It would edify the intellect if the Supreme Court had decided the issue as one of rich against poor, private property against the communistic hoard. But, as is the Court's wont, it chose to decide the issue using a contorted reading of the Constitution. In so doing, it declared the tax unconstitutional. The Constitution requires that direct taxes be apportioned among the states on the basis of population. The income tax fell on income from land, and, according to the Court's interpretation of the intent of the drafters of the Constitution, they had intended that a tax on land be called a direct tax. Since the income tax was not apportioned among the states according to population, it was unconstitutional [Ratner (1942, pp. 200-08); Waltman (1985, p. 4)]. Where the Supreme Court of 1880, wishing not to overturn the income tax of 1865, found it to be an excise tax, the Court of 1895, seeking a different outcome, declared it to be a direct tax.

It would be comforting to those who have faith in the detached wisdom of the Supreme Court, if one could account for the Court's reversal on the constitutionality of the income tax between 1880 and 1895 as resulting from a more profound and penetrating reading of the Constitution. But other evidence suggests that the Court's majority was deeply conservative and voted to protect the economic interests threatened by the tax.

The amendment to the tariff bill of 1894, which introduced a tax on personal and corporate income, was but one of several reform measures stemming from the populist and progressive response at the end of the 19th century to the emergence of corporate capitalism. These would include the creation of the ICC in 1887 to regulate railroads and the passage of the Sherman Antitrust Act in 1890. The Court's decision on the income tax in 1895 was one of a series of convoluted opinions of that era that served to protect corporate and wealthy interests from the social tide of that day. These decisions would include its

(1) 1886 decision in *Santa Clara* in which the Court went out of its way to grant 14th Amendment protection to corporations. With this decision, the Court interpreted an Amendment to the Constitution originally passed to protect black citizens from discriminatory actions by whites, as one which protects corporate "citizens" from discriminatory tax treatment by the citizens of a state.

(2) 1895 decision in *E. C. Knight* in which the court concluded that manufacturing was not commerce and thus that the mergers and actions of the Sugar Trust were not in violation of the Sherman Act.

(3) 1895 decision in the contempt charges brought against the socialist union organizer Eugene V. Debs.[6]

Certainly Justice Field must have expressed the true reasoning underlying the Court's decision when he said in reference to the income tax

> *The present assault upon capital is but the beginning. It will be but the stepping stone to others, larger and more sweeping, till our political contests will become a war of the poor against the rich [Waltman (1985, p. 4)].*

The proposal to amend the Constitution to allow Congress to tax income received the required two thirds majorities in both Houses of Congress with the help of votes of opponents of the tax, who thought it would fail to be ratified by the required three fourths of states' legislatures. But it was, and the federal government began taxing incomes once again in 1913 [Ratner (1942, chs. 13, 14); Waltman (1985, pp. 4-6)].

IV. Conclusions

What inferences can one draw from the United State's experience with the individual income tax regarding the likely fate and form of a personal consumption tax? One impression is clear from the long and acrimonious struggle to introduce the income tax. Both it's supporters and its opponents viewed the tax as a device for shifting the burden of paying for government onto upper income individuals and corporations (or their

---

[6] On the *Debs* and *Knight* cases, see Ratner (1942, pp. 193-95). On *Santa Clara*, see Horwitz (1987).

owners). The left-right, poor-rich dichotomy captures much of the ideological content of the debate over the income tax. The simplifying analytic device of depicting political positions as lying along a single dimensional issue space seems adequate for characterizing the positions taken on this issue.

The assumptions underlying the public choice models of politics seem reasonably consistent with the history of this tax. Representatives from districts with concentrations of corporate interests and economic wealth opposed the tax. Representatives from rural, farming districts favored it. Representatives appeared to have voted as their constituents would want them to on the assumption that these constituents prefer not to pay taxes.

Can one garner any support for the public interest view of politics from the record of the income tax? This question is more difficult to answer, in part because one must define what a voter's view of the public interest is. The first tax was enacted to pay for the Union's expenses in waging the Civil War. Moreover, some members of Congress favored the Constitutional Amendment allowing Congress to tax income, although they opposed the tax itself, because they thought that Congress should have the power to raise revenue in this way in times of fiscal crisis [Ratner (1942, ch. 14)]. Much of the writing for and against the tax can be interpreted as narrowly partisan, but some writers defended the tax on grounds of fairness and burden sharing that may have convinced even those who would have to pay it that its introduction was good for the country [Ratner (1942, p. 149)].

As noted above, Meltzer and Richard have claimed that the growth of government is a consequence of the redistributive activity of government. The arguments of Brennan and Buchanan (1980) would certainly imply that citizens wishing to hold Leviathan in check would have been wise *not* to have granted Congress the power to tax income. Did a citizen of the United States in 1913 foresee the future fiscal consequences of this new source of revenue for Congress?

The 1913 tax fell on less than one percent of the population [Carson (1977, p. 3)]. Given the small fraction of the population who paid the tax, and the initial level of the rate, it is a wonder that it did not roll through Congress with almost no opposition. One infers that many who paid nothing or relatively little under the first tax realized that it was only the initial crack throwing open the fiscal doors. On the other hand, even Choate at the rhetorical heights of his argument against the income tax in front of the

Supreme Court could envisage a tax rate on personal income of no more than 20 percent, less than one fourth of the maximum rates of a half century later.

If the end of the 19th century in the United States can be called the Age of Populism and Progressivism, then the end of the 20th century is the Age of Regressivism. Where reformers of the earlier era sought to constrain the power of the "trusts", reformers of today preach deregulation and a repeal of the antitrust laws. Where reformers of the earlier era sought to expand the government's capacity to raise revenue and increase equity by taxing the income of the rich, reformers today seek smaller government and a reduced, relative tax burden on the rich. These policies were the heart of the Reagan Revolution, and they remain popular today. In his first week in the Presidency, George Bush proposed cutting the capital gains tax from 33 to 15 percent, claiming that it would raise tax revenue and the incomes of the less well to do. A more complete about face from the prevailing ideology of 100 years ago one could not imagine.

The saliency of the tax progressivity issue is such that one must anticipate that the introduction of a personal consumption tax would be yet another occasion for great debate over the proper progressivity of the tax structure. Since the consumption tax would replace the income tax, each taxpayer would, of course, be interested in her payments under the new consumption tax compared to her payments under the income tax. But any change in the tax code can be the occasion for a change in overall incidence, one expects that a change so fundamental as replacing the income tax with the consumption tax would reopen this debate. Given the currently prevailing ideological winds in the United States, any change in tax progressivity must be anticipated to be in the direction of increased regressivity.

An actor missing from the historical drama leading up to the enactment of the income tax was the special interest group. In general, interest groups prefer to play not on center stage during the great ideological debates of the day, but offstage in the corridors of Congress. Their mark has been made on our tax structure through the many seemingly minor changes that have been introduced down through the years.

Given that the consumption tax would replace the income tax, interest groups would be forced into the debate right from the start, each seeking to protect and enlarge its membership's benefits under the present code.

Considering the intense struggle that ensued during the recent reform of the tax code in the United States, the mind boggles at the thought of the lobbying activity that would accompany the replacement of the income tax with a consumption tax. The public good benefits of the tax would need to be large indeed to offset the transaction costs inherent in such a structural change.

Comments by Bengt-Arne Wickström

Introduction

Dennis Mueller discusses both efficiency and political-feasibility aspects of the introduction of a consumption tax. Most of his arguments build on the analogies one might find in the history of the introduction of the income tax in the United States. Although these certainly are both enlightening and interesting, there are some clear theoretical conclusions that can be drawn from fairly simple public-choice models. In this comment, I will outline such a public-choice argument based on the median-voter model. First, however, I would like to comment on the efficiency aspect of a consumption tax.

Efficiency of a Consumption Tax

In Mueller's essay there seems to be an implicit assumption that there are possible Pareto improvements to be had from the introduction of a consumption tax as a replacement for an income tax. I would like to take issue with this point.

An income tax gives rise to two main distortions. The choice between leisure and other consumption is distorted, since leisure is left untaxed while other consumption is taxed through the income tax. Also the choice between consumption today and consumption in the future is distorted, since the capital market is distorted with a lower rate of return on savings than the relevant rate of substitution in production.

This latter distortion is removed in the case of an expenditure tax, whereas the former distortion is left unchanged. However, if there are positive net savings in the economy, the tax base is also reduced. Hence, in order to leave the tax revenue constant, the tax rate in the case of an expenditure tax has to be higher. That is, the distortion in the choice between consumption and leisure is increased. The choice of the optimal tax is then not clear. The alternatives are two small distortions versus one big one.

From the theory of optimal taxation we know that the choice of an optimal tax will depend on the demand elasticities, in this case the elasticity of demand for leisure and the elasticity of demand for future consumption. In the polar case of a very inelastic demand for future consumption, the income tax is to be preferred. In the other polar case of a very inelastic demand for leisure, the expenditure tax is to be preferred. Thus, the efficiency properties of the two taxes are an empirical issue.

The Median Voter and the Consumption Tax

In a public-choice analysis, one normally attempts to analyze the impact of a certain policy proposal, like the introduction of an expenditure tax, on specific agents or groups of agents, and subsequently draw conclusions about their actions in the political arena. I feel some of this missing in Mueller's discussion, where he could have tried to analyze the impact of the two taxes on individuals and from such an analysis drawn some conclusions on the feasibility of implementation of an expenditure tax.

Several interesting results can be had from fairly simple assumptions. Thus, for instance, in an economy with positive net savings and savings linearly dependent on income, any voter with an income below the average-income voter (and, hence, also the median voter under any realistic income distribution) will prefer the income tax under an equal revenue constraint if the average tax rates of the two alternatives are proportional to one another and if the tax is progressive. This is a consequence of the fact that consumption is more equally distributed than income and that the tax rate in the case of an expenditure tax has to be higher than in the case of an income tax, because of the narrower base.

Of course, the distributional characteristics of the two alternatives could be very different, making any prediction impossible. It seems rather unlikely, though, that big changes in distributional characteristics would occur. If the political agents are in some kind of equilibrium before the introduction of the expenditure tax, one could expect that this equilibrium would prevail also after the introduction of the expenditure tax.

The analysis so far, however, builds on a certain amount of fiscal illusion. If one assumes perfect foresight on the individuals in the economy, the conclusion is no different. In fact, it is much stronger. In an economy where each individual is a saver at the beginning and a dissaver at the end of its life cycle, the conclusion follows under fairly general assumptions about tax schedules.

Let, for instance, the two alternative tax systems be such that the (properly discounted) tax burden over the life cycle is exactly the same under the expenditure tax as under the income tax. That is, any individual at the beginning of the life cycle would be indifferent between the two alternatives. The time profiles of the tax payments are very different, though. Since, *ex hypothesi*, at the beginning of the life cycle the individual is a saver, the income tax would then be higher than the expenditure tax, whereas at the end of the life cycle, when the individual is a dissaver, the opposite is true.

For a middle-aged individual, however, the beginning of the life cycle is history and only the future matters, and future taxes based on consumption exceed future taxes based on the income basis by the same amount that in the past an income based tax would have exceeded a consumption based one. Hence, even though at the beginning of the life cycle each individual is indifferent between the two taxes, as time goes by it will prefer the income tax more and more strongly. That is, in the population everyone except the youngest individuals will have a preference for the income tax if the life-time incidence of the two alternatives is the same.

It is hence, for every proposed consumption-tax schedule, possible to find an income-tax schedule which brings in the same revenue and which is preferred by almost all individuals in the economy. Under the income tax the young will pay more than under the expenditure tax and the old will pay less than under the expenditure tax, thus keeping the revenue the same. The fact that time moves in only one direction, however, makes everyone except the very youngest individuals to give more weight to old age than youth, which is already past and hence irrelevant for the calculation of the life-time tax payments.

This model, of course, has to be made more precise, taking account of age distribution, population growth, economic growth, interest rate, and net life-time savings. The basic conclusion, though, is based on very simple assumptions and is quite robust. It can be expected to remain unaltered, and an expenditure tax would be politically unstable as compared to an income tax.

Conclusion

My conclusion is thus that there are strong reasons why an expenditure tax will not meet with popular approval and a simple public-choice model leaves little hope for the proponents thereof.

References

Ashenfelter, O. / Kelley, S. Jr. (1975), Determinants of Participation in Presidential Elections, Journal of Law and Economics 18, pp. 695-733.

Borcherding, T.E. (1985), The Causes of Government Expenditure Growth: A Survey of the U.S. Evidence, Journal of Public Economics 28, pp. 359-382.

Brennan, G. / Buchanan, J.M. (1980), The Power to Tax: Analytical Foundations of a Fiscal Constitution, Cambridge: Cambridge University Press.

Carson, G. (1977), The Golden Egg, Boston: Houghton Mifflin.

Chappell, H.W. Jr. (1982), Campaign Contributions and Congressional Voting. A Simultaneous Probit-Tobit Model, Review of Economics and Statistics 64, pp. 77-83.

Coughlin, P. / Mueller, D.C. / Murrell, P. (1988), Electoral Politics, Interest Groups, and the Size of Government, Mimeo, University of Maryland.

Downs, A. (1957), An Economic Theory of Democracy, New York: Harper and Row.

Fiorina, M.P. (1978), Economic Retrospective Voting in American National Elections: A Micro-Analysis, American Journal of Political Science 22, pp. 426-443.

Frey, B.S. / Schneider, F. (1978a), An Empirical Study of Politico-Economic Interaction in the U.S., Review of Economics and Statistics 60, pp. 174-183.

Frey, B.S. / Schneider, F. (1978b), A Politico-Economic Model of the United Kingdom, Economic Journal 88, pp. 243-253.

Frey, B.S. / Schneider, F. (1979), An Econometric Model with an Endogenous Government Sector, Public Choice 34(1), pp. 29-43.

Frey, B.S. / Schneider, F. (1981a), A Politico-Economic Model of the U.K.: New Estimates and Predictions, Economic Journal 91, pp. 737-740.

Hettich, W. / Winer, S.L. (1988), Economic and Political Foundations of Tax Structure, American Economic Review 78, pp. 701-712.

Horwitz, M.J. (1987), Santa Clara Revisited: The Development of Corporate Theory, in W.J. Samuels / A.S. Miller (eds.), Corporations and society, New York: Greenwood Press, pp. 13-63.

Kalt, J.H. / Zupan, M.A. (1984), Capture and Ideology in the Economic Theory of Politics, American Economic Review 74, pp. 279-300.

Kau, J.B. / Rubin, P.H. (1979), Self-Interest, Ideology, and Logrolling in Congressional Voting, Journal of Law and Economics 22, pp. 365-384.

Kau, J.B. / Keenan, D. / Rubin, P.H. (1982), A General Equilibrium Model of Congressional Voting, Quarterly Journal of Economics 97, pp. 271-293.

Kiewiet, D.R. (1981), Policy-Oriented Voting in Response to Economic Issues, American Political Science Review 75, pp. 448-459.

Kiewiet, D.R. (1983), Macroeconomics and Micropolitics, Chicago: University of Chicago Press.

Kirchgässner, G. (1985), Causality Testing of the Popularity Function: An Empirical Investigation for the Federal Republic of Germany, 1971-1982, Public Choice 45(2), pp. 155-173.

Meltzer, A.H. / Richard, S.F. (1981), A Rational Theory of the Size of Government, Journal of Political Economy 89, pp. 914-927.

Meltzer, A.H. / Richard, S.F. (1983), Tests of a Rational Theory of the Size of Government, Public Choice 41(3), pp. 403-418.

Mueller, D.C. (1987), The Growth of Government: A Public Choice Perspective, International Monetary Fund Staff Papers 34(1).

Mueller, D.C. (1989), Public Choice II, Cambridge: Cambridge University Press.

Musgrave, R.A. (1959), The Theory of Public Finance, New York: McGraw-Hill.

Musgrave, R.A. / Peacock, A.T. (eds.) (1958), Classics in the Theory of Public Finance, New York: St. Martin's Press.

Niskanen, W.A. Jr. (1971), Bureaucracy and Representative Government, Chicago: Aldine-Atherton.

Peltzman, S. (1984), Constituent Interest and Congressional Voting, Journal of Law and Economics 27, pp. 181-210.

Ratner, S. (1942), American Taxation, New York: W.W. Norton.

Riker, W.H. / Ordeshook, P.C. (1968), A Theory of the Calculus of Voting, American Political Science Review 62, pp. 25-42.

Schneider, F. / Pommerehne, W.W. (1980), Politico-Economic Interactions in Australia: Some Empirical Evidence, Economic Record 56, pp. 113-131.

Tullock, G. (1984), A (Partial) Rehabilitation of the Public Interest Theory, Public Choice 42(1), pp. 89-99.

Waltman, J.L. (1985), Political Origins of the U.S. Income Tax, Jackson: University Press of Mississippi.

Wicksell, K. (1896), A New Principle of Just Taxation, Finanztheoretische Untersuchungen, reprinted in: Musgrave / Peacock (1958), pp. 72-118.

Richard E. Wagner

Fiscal Principle, Fiscal Politics, and Consumption Taxation*

This paper uses consumption taxation as a vehicle for examining questions of political process and constitutional order. The fiscal politics of consumption taxation is my main concern here; I do not seek to contribute directly to any of the predominant streams of economic literature on consumption taxation, but rather seek to refract this literature through some public choice principles regarding the operation of political processes.[1] The theory of public choice seeks to apply an economic logic to political processes, and this paper seeks to apply that logic to consumption taxation in particular. According to that logic, tax policy is the outcome of what can be called a "market" for tax legislation, and the operation of this market is constrained by a set of constitutional rules within which fiscal and political processes operate and through which tax programs emerge.[2]

Actual political outcomes may diverge significantly from those outcomes that seem to be supported by normative reasoning. This may happen because of problems of knowledge: even a benevolent despot seeking to implement certain normative principles may fail to do so because of a lack of knowledge. This may also happen because of the nature of political incentive: the incentive to implement normative tax programs may be weak compared with the incentive to award tax privileges to politically powerful groups while imposing tax penalties on politically weak groups. This paper explores some

* I am grateful to the Lynde and Harry Badley foundation for financial support.

[1] For a seminal treatise on issues that arise in seeking to develop an explanatory approach to fiscal processes, see Buchanan (1967). Some relationships between public finance and public choice are surveyed in Buchanan (1975).

[2] For a wide-ranging survey of the market for legislation, see Tollison (1988). For interesting efforts to place taxation into the context of a market for legislation, see Doernberg and McChesney (1987) and Hettich and Winer (1988).

aspects of how the fiscal politics of consumption taxation might be placed within a logic of collective action, including a consideration of how a constitutional perspective might be brought to bear on political processes and fiscal choice.

I. Fiscal Principle and the Grammar of Tax Advocacy

It is surely accurate to say that the bulk of the literature on public finance supports broad-based over narrow-based forms of taxation, regardless of whether the tax base is income or consumption.[3] Much of that support is grounded in notions of tax neutrality. A truly broad-based tax would avoid the injection of tax-induced biases into the structure of economic activity. To be sure, any practical tax would have some exemptions from the tax base. For instance, even the most broadly based consumption or income tax would surely exclude leisure. And other exclusions would be likely as well. Hence, the structure of economic activity will unavoidably be influenced by taxation. Indeed, it is doubtful whether the construct of neutral taxation is anything other than pure fantasy, for even the fabled head tax would surely inspire people to intensify their efforts to avoid the census takers as the amount of tax rose.

Even though a truly broad-based, non-distortionary tax may be unattainable, there is surely much scholarly sentiment, considerations from the theory of second best notwithstanding, that a tax system with a relatively broad base would be superior to one with a relatively narrow base, because the range of tax-related sources of discrimination and distortion would be diminished. To be sure, the apparently strong normative appeal of the ideal of tax neutrality has some puzzling features. For whatever nonneutralities that may be eliminated through a program of broad based taxation can be restored through an offsetting program of public expenditure. A value added tax that imposes a lower rate on agricultural products will be discriminatory relative to one that taxes all transactions at the same rate. But what difference does this make if the proceeds from a non-discriminatory form of value added tax are used to finance some program of agricultural subsidies? A discriminatory tax without agricultural subsidies or a nondiscrimi-

[3] For contrary support for narrow-based over broad-based taxation, based on public choice reasoning, see Brennan and Buchanan (1980). Such support is also mustered on the grounds that narrow-based taxation allows people greater flexibility in timing their tax payments over their lifetimes, in Buchanan and Forte (1964).

natory tax with agricultural subsidies would seem to leave little to choose from on a priori grounds. Any pattern of distortionary or discriminatory taxation can be accomplished alternatively through the expenditure side of the budget in the presence of nondiscriminatory taxation.

Within the context of broad-based taxation, there is considerable controversy over the merits of income and consumption as alternative bases. Yet such controversy should be kept in perspective, for it seems relatively minor in comparision to the apparent extent of agreement over the general merits of broad-based taxation. After all, any examination of alternative approaches to broad-based taxation must start from a recognition that in many respects alternative forms of broad-based taxation are economically equivalent [e.g., Mieszkowski (1967)]. In light of the basic identity that income is the sum of consumption and saving, a consumption tax is equivalent to an income tax that excludes saving. And in a life cycle model where saving is deferred consumption, lifetime income and lifetime consumption are identical. Further, this identity can be preserved even when people make bequests, by treating those bequests as consumption by the testator. Comprehensive tax bases may, in turn, be applied to either the sources or the uses side of the market. Hence a proportional tax on personal income is equivalent to a value added tax that provides for the depreciation of capital goods. And a proportional tax on personal consumption is equivalent to a value added tax that provides for the expensing of capital goods.

Despite this general or first-order identity among broad-based taxes, there are plenty of second-order differences to generate controversy. A consumption tax eliminates the discrimination against saving that an income tax possesses, so it would eliminate a distortion in the capital market. But the lower base of a consumption tax means it will have to carry a higher rate to yield the same revenue as an income tax, and this higher rate would intensify the distortion in the labor market. On standard welfare grounds a comparison of such distortions is ambiguous and, hence, open to controversy.[4]

---

[4] Such second best considerations also arise in comparing reforms of existing tax systems with the design of new tax systems, as Feldstein (1976) explains. Hettich and Winer (1985) survey how different approaches to public finance lead to different implications for tax reform.

Some also argue that a consumption tax would shift tax burdens away from people with higher incomes to people with lower incomes. Whether this might be so, however, depends on whether the tax would be imposed on factor-market or on product-market transactions. Taxes imposed on product-market transactions cannot be designed with any great sensitivity to reflect the economic circumstances of the taxpayer. Granted, a VAT of either the consumption type or the income type could impose higher rates on products used predominately by people with higher incomes than it imposes on products used predominately by people with lower incomes. But efforts to do this would complicate tax administration, and would also generate a great deal of horizontal inequity because the consumers of any such product would typically cover a relatively broad portion of the income distribution. The use of a progressive rate structure would seem to require that the tax be levied on factor-market transactions; however, such a personal tax could as easily be based on consumption as on income.

The comparative merits of progressive and flat-rate tax structures is, of course, a topic of long-standing controversy. But that controversy is independent of the comparative merits of consumption or income as alternative tax bases; support for (or opposition to) progressivity is essentially irrelevant to the choice between income and consumption as alternative tax bases, and rather supports the principle that whichever base is selected, tax liability should be imposed on the sources of income. Since questions of the distribution of the tax burden are conceptually independent from questions concerning the form of the tax base, I shall abstract from distributive questions here by taking a flat-rate tax on consumption as the point of analytical departure. Hence, I shall treat as equivalent a personal tax on consumption and a VAT of the consumption type. In light of the first-order equivalence among broad-based taxes and given the acceptance of some principle of broad-based taxation, it seems to me that differences in particular implementations of broad-based taxation are of secondary consequence. Or at least they are with respect to the issues I wish to address here, so I shall treat various approaches to broad-based taxation as equivalent in order to concentrate on fiscal politics and fiscal choice.

II. Optimal Discrimination through Political Processes?

It is important to note that fiscal principle does not universally support broad-based over narrow-based taxation. Arguments about optimal commodity taxation aside, the Pigovian-type arguments about corrective taxation view government as seeking to correct, through a set of discriminatory, narrow-based taxes, market failures that are presumed to result because of some divergence between social cost and private cost [e.g., Baumol (1972); but see Lee (1985) for a consideration of how exogenous politics might disrupt the standard Pigovian reasoning]. In the absence of such Pigovian taxes, a competitive market processes may lead to excessive outputs in cases where private and social cost diverge. To be sure, the literature on corrective taxation explores such distinctions as whether taxes are imposed on outputs, inputs, or product characteristics. While there are many complexities in the theory of corrective taxation, not the least of which is its range of applicability in light of the critiques by Coase (1960) and Turvey (1963), such complexities are peripheral here, for I wish only to note that fiscal principle can also be brought to bear in support of narrow-based, discriminatory forms of taxation.

When considerations in support of a broad-based tax system are combined with Pigovian considerations, what results is a discriminatory, nonneutral tax system in which some sources or uses of income are taxed more heavily than others. What does this combination of considerations do to the ability to judge how closely fiscal practice conforms to fiscal principle? A principle of broad-based taxation is starkly simple, so it is straightforward to judge the extent to which it is being followed or violated. Any exclusion from the base, whether income or consumption, or any differentiation in rates among items of consumption or sources of income, violates the principle, and that is all there is to the matter. But this simplicity in judging the degree to which practice adheres to principle vanishes once some principled support for discriminatory taxation is allowed to enter the picture.

The ability to justify some complex format of discriminatory taxation as representing some combination of neutral taxation and corrective taxation does not ipso facto imply that actual fiscal processes operate to implement such a tax program. The deviation from a broad base that actual fiscal processes exhibit may represent efficiency responses, such as characterized by the Pigovian framework. But they may also represent the redistributive outcomes of rent-seeking processes, under which politically influential groups are able to reduce their tax burdens by imposing higher burdens on relatively uninfluential groups. A logic of welfare economics need not coincide with a logic of collective action. Recognition of this possibility raises in turn a set of questions as to the ability to distinguish between these explanations of observed tax structures. It also raises questions concerning the extent to which different constitutional rules promote or impede the different types of outcome, for the degree to which the justificatory argument may reasonably characterize actual fiscal outcomes will be influenced by the constitutional framework within which fiscal choices emerge.

With two quite different interpretations being possible with respect to particular cases of differential rates or exclusions from the tax base, it becomes necessary to ask to what extent it is possible to judge which interpretation better suits existing tax practices. To approach this kind of question requires some shift away from a logic of welfare economics to a logic of collective action. The central focus must be on the arguments or explanations for movements away from a broad tax base. What is at issue is the plausibility of going from an observed pattern of differential taxation to a conclusion that those deviations from the nondiscriminatory pattern of a broad-based tax represent Pigovian-like corrections of market processes and not the rent-seeking outcomes of political processes.

Consider, for instance, the taxation of cigarettes. Such taxes are commonly justified as representing a form of corrective taxation, in response to the argument that smokers impose substantial costs on society. The extent of those costs depend upon presumptions made about the negative health consequences of smoking. A survey by the Office of Technology Assessment (1985) for the United States placed these costs in the range of $2 to $3 per pack of cigarettes. Such a line of argument has been used to advocate cigarette taxes in this range, as one particular application of the Pigovian tax program.

However, this line of argument is contested sharply in Tollison and Wagner (1988). They argue that whatever might be the economic reflections of the health consequences of smoking, those costs are borne by smokers and not by nonsmokers.[5] Tollison and Wagner argue that, economically, smoking is essentially indistinguishable from any

[5] For a basically similar conclusion, though reached from a somewhat different line of reasoning, see Manning, et al. (1989).

other type of activity that might have some risk associated with it. A person might choose to prune trees using a chain saw instead of a hand saw, despite the greater riskiness of the chain saw, because the positive valuation placed on the saving of time and energy exceeds the negative valuation placed on the risk of an accident. The cost of severed limbs from chain saw accidents is reflected in the market for chain saws, and there is no way that those lost limbs could be adduced as being evidence of a discrepancy between private cost and social cost. And it is the same for smoking. People smoke because the benefit they associate with smoking exceeds the cost they have to bear, a cost that includes whatever health consequences they anticipate having to bear.[6]

Cigarette taxation may be more readily understandable as a process by which some people are successful in shifting taxes onto others. Suppose the alternative to a cigarette tax is an increase in some broad-based tax. Compared with the broad-based tax, the cigarette tax allows a concentration of tax burdens on a relatively small subset of the population. In the United States, for instance, around 30 percent of adults smoke. Moreover, the average incomes of smokers is less than that of nonsmokers, and smokers have disproportionately heavy representation in blue-collar occupations, so smokers would seem to be generally less influential politically than nonsmokers. Hence, a cigarette tax may not so much reflect the operation of Pigovian-like processes as it reflects the operation of rent-seeking or wealth-transfer processes, through which nonsmokers are able to transfer some of what otherwise would be their tax burden onto smokers.

---

[6] Tollison and Wagner (1988) also argue that the Pigovian arguments are inapplicable to environmental tobacco smoke. Even though this might appear to look like an externality problem, Coasian resolutions are readily available. People are not generally forced into an association with smokers. For the most part, any such association is voluntary. Whatever cases of involuntary association might exist would normally be of short duration, where no questions of negative health consequences seem to arise anyway. And with largely voluntary exposure, it would seem to be a case of people choosing to expose themselves to tobacco smoke because their negative evaluations of doing so are less than their positive evaluations of what they would gain from maintaining the associa-tions of which the exposure to environmental tobacco smoke are part.

III. Self Interest, Political Incentive, and Consumption Taxation

Recognition that governmental processes are no more grounded on a principle of benevolence than are market processes renders even weaker the normative case for discriminatory taxation. But at the same time, the actual imposition of discriminatory taxation becomes more understandable once it is recognized that governmental processes are as much driven by self interest as are market processes. Within an interest group model of government, the market for legislation is viewed as a process in which the legislature brokers wealth transfers among the citizenry [e.g., McCormick and Tollison (1981)]. Some people are net gainers in this process and others are net losers. There are, to be sure, many particular markets and margins through which the market for legislation can operate. One of these is the market for tax legislation.

Conceptually, it is useful to distinguish two facets of the market for tax legislation, even though both facets are dealt with simultaneously in the legislative process. One facet relates to the ultimately inescapable truism that increased expenditure requires increased taxation, either currently or in the future. The other facet refers to the desire of people to receive favorable tax status and to have taxes paid by other people instead of by themselves. These two facets suggest a two-stage conceptualization of the market for tax legislation. The first stage is essentially uniform and nondiscriminatory; the second stage is particular and discriminatory. The first stage can be thought of as a process through which a revenue committee drafts a broad-based, flat-rate tax to raise a particular amount of revenue. The second stage can be thought of as a process through which the revenue committee revises its initial draft in response to lobbying efforts by different interest groups. The revision that emerges will contain exemptions from the tax base as well as perhaps having a variety of tax rates.

Consider first the enactment of the initial tax measure - the first draft of the legislation the tax committee will ultimately submit to the legislature. At this stage there will be no exclusions from the tax base, aside from matters of "practicality", and the tax rate will be uniform. There are, to be sure, several ways the tax burden could be distributed in conformity with this general notion. One way would be a head tax, where the amount of revenue to be raised is simply divided by the number of people available to be taxed. Another would be a flat-rate income tax. Still another would be a personal consumption tax. And yet another would be a uniform tax on value added. In keeping with the theme of this conference, suppose the tax is either a personal consumption tax or a value added tax of the consumption type.

Within the context of a logic of collective action, this first stage can be illustrated by a model in which the tax rate is put up for auction through the political process. A status quo rate is paired with some alternative, higher rate. Some people bring pressure to bear in support of the higher rate, while others bring pressure to bear in opposition. The higher rate will be enacted if supporters are able to exert more pressure than opponents, which, in turn, is to say that they are willing to pay more in political currency than are opponents. Figure 1 provides a simple illustration of this process. The three members of the community, A, B, and C, who differ in their private consumption opportunities, face a choice of what tax rate to select, given that the base will be broad and the rate flat. As shown in Figure 1, A, B, and C prefer the tax rates, and the levels of public spending that those rates make possible, A_1, B_1, and C_1 respectively.

So long as the tax rate is below A_1, a motion to increase the tax rate will encounter no opposition. The marginal political cost to a politician of sponsoring a tax increase would be zero. But at higher tax rates opposition will commence. An increase in the tax rate from A_1 to B_1 will make A worse off, as illustrated by *aa*. In turn, *aa* can be thought of as representing the maximum amount that A would bid to oppose the tax increase. But B and C will be better off with the higher tax, as illustrated by *bb* and *cc* respectively. These magnitudes represent the maximum amount B and C would bid to get the tax rate increased from A_1 to B_1.

It is straightforward to conceptualize in marginal terms the political benefits and political costs of alternative tax rates. This is illustrated in Figure 2, where the equilibrium tax rate, T, results when the marginal political benefit (MPB) from taxation equals the marginal political cost (MPC). As Figure 2 is constructed, there is an initial range over which there is no political cost to higher taxation. This corresponds to the case where the tax rate is less than A_1 in Figure 1. For higher tax rates, MPC represents the increase in the aggregate value of the losses illustrated by *aa* in Figure 1. In similar fashion, MPB represents the increase in the aggregate value of the gains from higher taxation illustrated by *bb* and *cc* in Figure 1. The tax rate will be what it is and not something else because at any other rate political pressures will be predodminately on the side of pushing it up or pulling it down.

To be sure, much work remains to be done in bringing a logic of collective action to bear on taxation. It is possible to conceptualize tax policy as being produced within a market for legislation, in which the willingness of market participants to pay for legislation is reflected in the strength of the political pressure they exert on the fiscal process. It is easy to imagine a world of perfect representation, in which tax rates are put up directly for auction, the currency through which the auction is conducted is the willingness to pay illustrated in Figure 1, and in which everyone's bid for or against a proposed rate would be registered.

But there are also some significant differences between the market for fiscal legislation and ordinary markets. Tax rates are not subject to any kind of direct auction, and the currency in which transactions take place is only partly pecuniary. There clearly are cases where monetary payments are made directly to secure policy measures, and even campaign contributions may be a moderately close substitute for such direct payments. But much of the currency in the market for legislation takes such forms as hiring lobbyists, running newspaper advertisements, and organizing letter-writing campaigns. Political pressure is far more ambiguous than is the market pressure of willingness to pay, though it is surely no less real. Thus there are likely to be several reasons why actual tax rates might deviate from what would result in a world of perfect representation.[7]

In market processes individual demands are aggregated without any discrimination other than that of willingness to pay. But this is not so in political processes, for some people are able to pursue collective action more effectively than others. Interest group processes require individuals to invest in the promotion of the collective interest of the group's members. As Olson (1966) explains, latent pressure will not automatically be transformed into actual pressure. In terms of Figure 1, the extent of opposition or support will be more fully reflected into the MPB and MPC of Figure 2 for some people and groups than for others. Among other things, groups that face lower organization costs will be more predominant in fiscal outcomes than those that face higher

---

[7] The theory of fiscal illusion [e.g., Pommerehene and Schneider (1978) and Wagner (1976)] argues that such choices as that between a personal consumption tax and a VAT of the consumption type, may influence taxpayer perceptions of cost. In terms of Figure 2, MPC for a VAT may lie below MPC for a personal consumption tax. If so, a VAT would yield a larger public sector than the personal consumption tax.

costs. Hence, .conclusions reached about the equilibrium properties of a model of collective action are not necessarily identical with conclusions reached about the equilibrium propeties of a model of welfare economics.

To be sure, an examination of tax policy in terms of a logic of fiscal politics need not be orthogonal to such an examination in terms of a logic of welfare economics. Even if we ask not how high the tax rate should be, but rather ask how high it will be, the answer to the positive question may not be totally unrelated to the answer to the normative question. One aspect of the political benefit surely reflects perceived external costs that people think they are bearing. If external costs are present, these costs will surely translate into some form of political benefit or demand. For instance, suppose Figure 2 reflects an aggregation over n distinct product markets. All of these markets are identical, save that one is a source of external cost. In terms of Figure 2, this would surely translate into a higher MPB for any particular tax rate, which in turn would lead to a higher level of taxation on that product than on other products, as illustrated by MPB^* and T^*.

But such external costs are not the only source of such political demand. Spending constituencies desire revenues, and these form a source of political demand that would exist even if external costs were zero. Tax increases, of course, go into a general fund, for which various spending constituencies compete. Such a framework was implicit in the construction of Figure 2. Both the support for and the opposition to tax increases are conditioned by the public goods nature of tax revenues. However, if the revenues from a particular tax can be earmarked for a particular expenditure program, tax revenues would be transformed into a private good, for a property right would have been created in the tax revenue. Consequently, the political demand for taxation should rise, as illustrated by the shift from MPB to MPB^* in Figure 2. In this manner rent seeking can also enter the logic of fiscal politics.

More generally, the first draft, nondiscriminatory tax code is unlikely to survive the political process by which tax legislation is enacted.[8] Questions of external cost aside, the first-draft, broad-based tax is unlikely to survive the political process without modification. Such survival would result only so long as the relationships between marginal

[8] See, for instance, Becker (1983). Moreover, the essential identity of fiscal politics and regulatory politics is examined in Posner (1971).

political benefit and marginal political cost were the same for all relevant markets and margins. Survival would result, as it were, only if a disaggregation of Figure 2 in terms of categories of expenditure (for a tax on the sources side) or types of markets (for a tax on the uses side) led to the same MPC-MPB relationship for each particular category that could be subject to differential tax treatment.

But if the participants in those various markets differ in such things as the costs of organization and the degree of geographical concentration, those interest groups that are relatively effective at political organization will, by raising the marginal political cost of taxation, be able to secure tax reductions. These reductions could occur through lower rates or they could occur through exclusions from the tax base, but in any event a pattern of differential taxation will emerge. More effectively organized groups will secure lower tax burdens than less effectively organized groups, because more effectively organized groups raise the marginal political cost of taxation.[9] With legislation being a process of brokering wealth transfers, interest groups that are relatively effective in this process will be able to secure wealth transfers, which in the case of taxation will be various types of exclusions, exemptions, and deductions. And for those groups that are relatively less effective in this process, the result will be a rise in taxes. Winners in the market for tax legislation will pay lower taxes; losers will pay higher taxes.

In what particular way the tax increase takes place surely depends on the form of taxation in question, for the form of taxation will constrain the agenda that the market for tax legislation will follow. With respect to personal taxes on income or consumption, losers in the market for legislation cannot directly be given a higher tax rate than winners. So the winners gain through the acquisition of exclusions, exemptions, and the like, and the tax rate that is applied to the base of the tax increases in consequence. The losers in the market for tax legislation pay a higher tax in this manner. The winners are taxed at the same, higher rate, but this higher tax is more than offset by the value of the exclusions and other privileges.

With respect to taxes on the uses of income, there is probably more scope for the market for tax legislation to operate through the creation of differential tax rates. A

[9] It is, of course, possible, that such a tax base could be earmarked for a particular spending program, which would also increase the marginal political benefit from taxation. The effect on the tax rate is indeterminate in this case, though the amount of political activity will increase on both sides of the transaction.

value added tax can more easily give lower rates to favored groups than could a personal tax on income or consumption. Once the principle of a flat-rate tax has been breached, and the Pigovian principle provides a convenient bridge, there is no unambigous way that lower tax rates in some markets can be used as evidence of tax favoritism, because some plausible rationalization in terms of social value can surely be created. Similarly, a higher tax rate cannot unambiguously be used as evidence of tax discrimination, because a rationalization in terms of social cost can also be constructed. The cost to most people of seeking to distinguish among such arguments surely exceeds the value, so variation in rates seems unlikely to elicit much political opposition to the rate differential.

But it seems different with personal taxation. Although there is considerable disagreement about the merits or the desirable extent of progressive taxation, it is widely accepted that the variation in rates is legitimate only across incomes. There is no sense that tax rates should differ according to occupation or interest group. Yet effective rates do differ in this way, but do so through the operation of such things as special provisions for depreciation that could, conceptually though perhaps not politically, have been accomplished by a lower tax rate.

IV. Fiscal Politics in Constitutional Perspective

Once it is recognized that the outcomes of fiscal politics conform to an economic logic, the problem of fiscal reform becomes a constitutional one of seeking to change the constraints within which fiscal choices are made. Within democratic political systems one important function of constitutional rules is to contain what Ostrom (1987) calls the republican disease, which refers to the ability of winning coalitions to gain advantages for their members by imposing disabilities upon others - and which refers to government as a partisan in rent-seeking processes rather than a provider of public goods.

To be sure, it is difficult to make sense of many constitutional provisions without a presumption that government is dominated by self-interest, and that the operation of in-period politics is likely to have undesirable consequences without appropriate constitutional constraints. The presence of a first amendment guarantee in the American constitution, for instance, embodies the presumption that Congress otherwise would be likely to abridge freedom of the press, religion, and speech. Similarly, the last clause of the fifth amendment is inexplicable, save for the presumption that Congress would otherwise be likely to countenance the taking of private property without paying just compensation, and would do so for private and not just for public use.

It is instructive to note the American constitution contains a number of constraints on the use of fiscal authority. The first clause of article I, section 8 limits Congress by insisting that tax revenues be used only to "provide for the *common* defense and *general* welfare", and it requires that "all duties, imposts and excises shall be *uniform* throughout the United States". The emphasis should surely be on the adjectives: common, general, uniform, for these suggest a recognition that in-period politics would otherwise be subject to the republican disease. Surely, if there were no presumption that fiscal discrimination would be likely to emerge through ordinary democratic processes, there would have been no point to such a requirement of uniformity. The uniformity clause has been interpreted as applying geographically, particularly as requiring uniform rates of federal taxation throughout the United States. But it is easy to see that without that limitation, the use of tax discrimination on a regional basis might have emerged. But budgets are two-sided entites, and expenditure discrimination can substitute for tax discrimination, as noted earlier. In similar fashion, the restrictions provided by the "*common* defense" and the *general* welfare" can likewise be understood as reflecting a recognition that constitutional constraints on fiscal authority are necessary to control the republican disease.[10]

At the same time, to articulate limitations on governmental processes, out of a recognition that otherwise those processes will undertake the proscribed activities, does not itself assure obdience to those limits, as Wagner (1987) explores. The opportunity for discriminatory taxation points to some severe constitutional questions for democratic political systems. Bruno Leoni (1960) points out that "no taxation without representation" originally meant no taxation without the consent of the taxpayer. A principle of non-discrimination would seem very much to be a related element of a constitutional approach to taxation, as Hutt (1966) argued in his review essay on *The Calculus of Consent*. While it is reasonable to think of democracy as a process, among other things, of self-taxation, in that we choose to tax ourselves, it is unreasonable to think of it legit-

---

[10] Buchanan (1964) argues that a combination of flat-rate taxation and expenditure programs are of general or common benefit may be one that leads to approximate unanimity about the size of the public sector.

imately as a process by which some people choose to tax others. A tax measure that gets a two-thirds majority may be fine when the majority are among the taxpayers. But when the taxes are concentrated among the minority, what may result is a system of a majority chosing to tax not themselves but to tax other people, and a severe conflict with the principles of constitutional goverment becomes quickly apparent.

The extent to which the actual tax enactments of actual governments can be reconciled with the normative vision of constitutional government would seem to depend on the extent to which the constitutional rules that constrain political processes prevent the use of government as a means of imposing disabilities on some people for the benefit of others. In short, the more fully constitutional processes work in the direction of requiring the consent of taxpayers, as illustrated by the Wicksellian principle, the more likely it is that normative visions and positive explanations will become congruent.[11] The less fully constitutional controls operate to constrain the market for tax legislation, the more likely it seems that tax legislation will be an on-going process through which the legislature serves as an arena for brokering wealth transfers. Such legislative activity does, of course, run strongly contrary to the view that one of the most important tasks for government is to provide a framework of stable rules and to secure rights, for the continual churning of the tax code by the legislature injects instability into the economic process, along with associated economic costs, and diminishes the security of individual rights.

[11] For an examination of the Wicksellian principle in this light, see Wagner (1988).

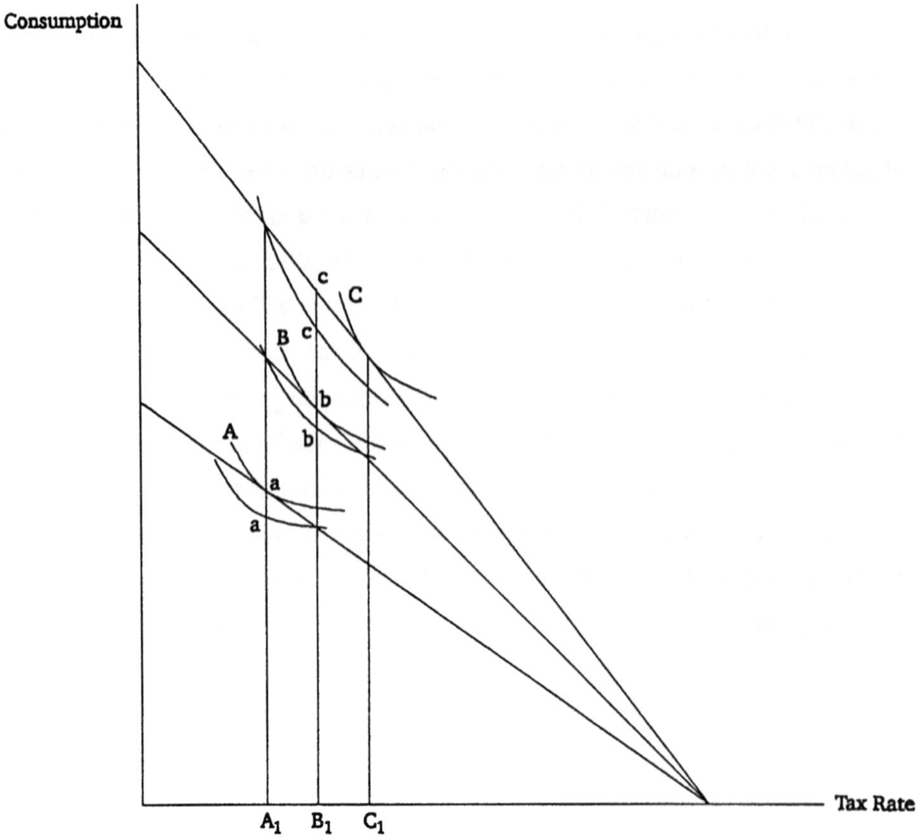

Figure 1

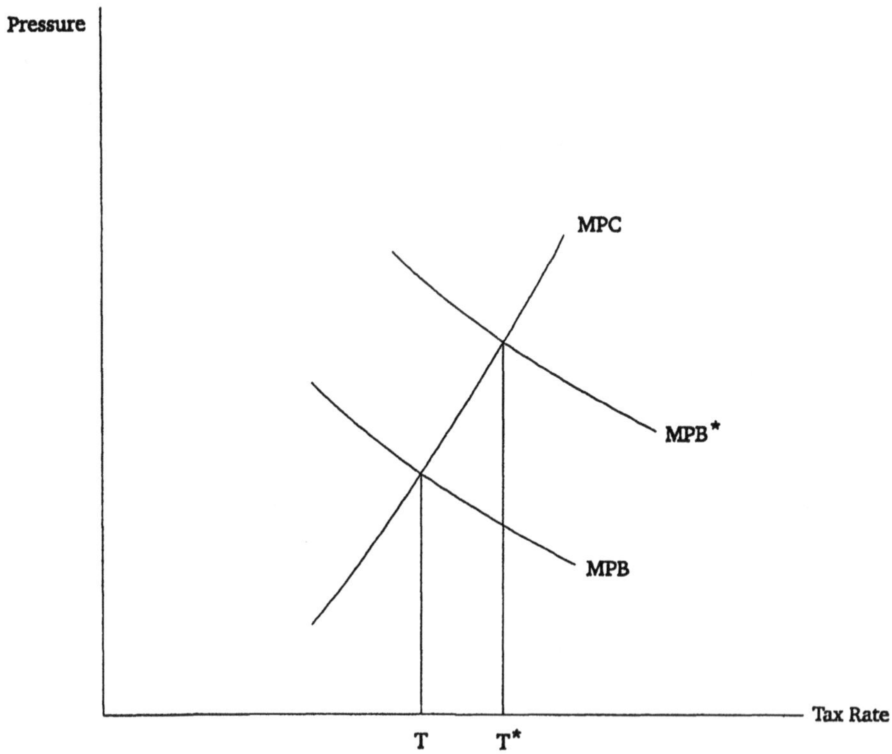

Figure 2

Comments by Charles B. Blankart

The Stages of Analysis

The paper by *R.E. Wagner* is very interesting and stimulating. I agree with most of its content and its conclusions. I only want to raise some questions which in a careful analysis, have to be raised though they may not overthrow the results. This should be kept in mind when I emphasize my points of disagreement. *Wagner's* paper can be divided into four analytical parts: The *first part* describes the traditional public finance point of view on tax systems. Since it is mostly a record of the actual state of the art there is little scope of disagreement. The *second* is on the political economy of broad based taxes. On this point I disagree with the author in the sense that I do not believe so much in the positive aspects of this system as he does. The *third* part is on the political market of tax legislation. Here I disagree for the opposite reason: I do not fully believe that the political market is such a bad institution as the author believes it to be. In the *fourth* part the author calls for constitutional reforms. I agree, but I think that the point should be more deeply elaborated. In the following remarks I shall abstain from commenting on the first part of the paper. For little can be said against its logic of welfare economics when one accepts its underlying assumptions. I shall rather turn directly to the second part.

The Political Economy of Tax Auctions

The author suggests: "It is easy to imagine a world of perfect representation in which tax rates are put up directly for auction... and everyone's bid for or against a proposed rate would be registered."

I doubt that such an auction system is so easy to imagine. I rather believe that there are more problems implied than the author suggests. First of all the rules of the auction should be specified more clearly. If the author means (what I do not really believe) that the auction is a mechanism to elicit individuals' willingness to pay for a public good, he is clearly wrong. For here we encounter the classical textbook free rider problem where the bids will be zero. From his exposition one could also conclude that he means that the tax schedules are fixed ex ante and that only the tax rates and hence the amount of public good supply is put for auction. But even under these circumstances preferences will not be revealed correctly. There will be overstatements by high demanders and understatements by low demanders. From the so-called demand revealing process we know that money bids will only represent undistorted demands if the decisive bidder has to pay the clarke tax. Thus, my general impression is that the pure auction system as suggested by the author will not be suitable to elicit undistorted demands. This is why I find that the politicical economy of broad based taxes ("stage 1" in *Wagner's* exposition) is not so attractive as characterized by the author.

The Market for Tax Legislation

Broad based taxes will, however, not yet be the definite outcome of the political process, as the author explains. Taxes decided in the first stage of *Wagner's* analysis will be restructured in the second stage on the market for tax legislation. My impression is that the market for tax legislation is not such a bad institution as characterized by the author. After all, a market brings exchange and exchange is a basically good thing. Clearly, a market for tax legislation would only be fully satisfactory under unanimity rule. Under these conditions, bargaining on the market for tax legislation is even a necessary condition to achieve consent and hence efficiency. This is what *Knut Wicksell* tought us nearly 100 years ago. Bargaining becomes suspect, however, when we go off the unanimity rule. But even under these conditions, some bargaining on taxation may be multilaterally advantageous. For under pure voting on the supply of public goods the outcome may be inefficiently low or inefficiently high. A good illustration of this type of inefficiency resorts from the median voter model where the quantity decided may be below or above the paretooptimal output. The defect of the voting system could be overcome through bargaining. Clearly, when bargaining on taxation goes beyond that narrow scope and results in shifting tax burdens on minorities, the outcome is no more multilaterally advantageous and it is difficult to draw the border line. But I only wanted to object that all tax bargaining is necessarily an evil.

The Necessity of Constitutional Reforms

In the last part the author suggests that the evils of the market for tax legislation should be eliminated by a revision of the rules of the game laid down in the constitution. This is probably the most difficult part of the paper, because it requires the design of constitutional rules.

The basic idea of the constitutional reform is clear: If a set of stable rules can be imposed on the politicians, the outcome of the political process will change in a predictable and hopefully improving way. But what are stable rules? The author gives some examples - the requirements of *common* defense, *general* welfare and *uniform* taxation - but no theory on what the general characteristics of stable rules are. Such a theory is, however, necessary in my view for the constitutional approach to be more than an intellectual excercise. If we do not know how to design constitutional rules, the approach cannot help to overcome the actual deficiencies of the political process.

My guess is that those rules will be stable in a constitution which are so general that the individual remains continuously behind the veil of ignorance. I mean rules which the individual is unwilling to abolish because the advantage for him or her to do so is very short run and might turn out to be a disadvantage immediately after the situation has changed. Rules of such a kind may be some of the human rights and the principle of equality before the law. They tend to be self-enforceable. Rules securing long term rights of individuals in a particular position, however, are likely to be unstable in the post-constitutional world. They will be subject to discussion and eventual revision under the pressure of the oppinio communis. In this latter group of rules we find typically tax laws. Therefore the prospects of restructuring tax rules in order to restrain the market for tax legislation have to be judged rather pessimistically. But I think that more research is needed in this field.

References

Baumol, W.J. (1972), On Taxation and the Control of Externalities, American Economic Review 62, pp. 307-322.

Becker, G.S. (1983), A Theory of Competition Among Pressure Groups for Political Influence, Quarterly Journal of Economics 98, pp. 371-400.

Brennan, G. / Buchanan, J.M. (1980), The Power To Tax, Cambridge: Cambridge University Press.

Buchanan, J.M. (1975), Public Finance and Public Choice, National Tax Journal 28, pp. 383-394.

Buchanan, J.M. (1964), Fiscal Institutions and Efficency in Collective Outlay, American Economic Review 54, pp. 227-235.

Buchanan, J.M. (1967), Public Finance in Democratic Process, Chapel Hill: University of North Carolina Press.

Buchanan, J.M. / Forte, F. (1964), Fiscal Choice through Time: A Case for Indirect Taxation?, National Tax Journal 17, pp. 144-157.

Coase, R.H. (1960), The Problem of Social Cost, Journal of Law and Economics 3, pp. 1-44.

Doernberg, R.L. / McChesney, F.S. (1987), On the Accelerating Rate and Decreasing Durability of Tax Reform, Minnesota Law Review 71, pp. 913-962.

Feldstein, M.S. (1976), On the Theory of Tax Reform, Journal of Public Economics 6, pp. 77-104.

Hettich, W. / Winer, S. (1985), Blueprints and Pathways: The Shifting Foundations of Tax Reform, National Tax Journal 38, pp. 423-445.

Hettich, W. / Winer, S. (1988), Economic and Political Foundations of Tax Structure, American Economic Review 78, pp. 701-712.

Hutt, W.H. (1966), Unanimity Versus Non-Discrimination (As Criteria for Constitutional Validity), South African Journal of Economics 34, pp. 133-147.

Lee, D.R. (1985), Rent Seeking and its Implications for Pollution Taxation, Southern Economic Journal 51, pp. 731-744.

Leoni, B. (1960), Freedom and the Law, Los Angeles: Nash.

Manning, W.G. / et al. (1989), The Taxes of Sin: Do Smokers and Drinkers Pay Their Way?, Journal of the American Medical Association 261, pp. 1604-1609.

McCormick, R.E. / Tollison, R.D. (1981), Politicians, Legislation, and the Economy, Boston: Martinus Nijhoff.

Mieszkowski, P. (1967), On the Theory of Tax Incidence, Journal of Political Economy 75, pp. 250-262.

Office of Technology Assessment (1985), Smoking-Related Deaths and Financial Costs, Washington D.C.: Office of Technology Assessment.

Olson, M. (1965), The Logic of Collective Action, Cambridge: Harvard University Press.

Ostrom, V. (1987), The Political Economy of a Compound Republic, 2nd ed., Lincoln: University of Nebraska Press.

Pommerehne, W.W. / Schneider, F. (1978), Fiscal Illusion, Political Institutions, and Local Public Spending, Kyklos 31, pp. 381-408.

Posner, R.A. (1971), Taxation by Regulation, Bell Journal of Economics 2, p. 22-50.

Tollison, R.D. (1988), Public Choice and Legislation, Virginia Law Review 74, pp. 339-371.

Tollison, R.D. / Wagner, R.E. (1988), Smoking and the State, Lexington, MA: D. C. Heath.

Turvey, R. (1963), On Divergencies between Social Cost and Private Cost, Economica 30, pp. 309-313.

Wagner, R.E. (1976), Revenue Structure, Fiscal Illusion, and Budgetary Choice, Public Choice 25, pp. 45-61.

Wagner, R.E. (1987), Parchment, Guns, and the Maintenance of Constitutional Contract, in: Ch. K. Rowley (ed.), Democracy and Public Choice: Essays in Honor of Gordon Tullock, pp. 105-121, Oxford: Basil Blackwell.

Wagner, R.E. (1988), The Calculus of Consent: A Wicksellian Retrospective, Public Choice 56, pp. 153-166.

PART FOUR

Legal Aspects of Taxing Consumption

Joachim Lang

Taxing Consumption from a Legislative Point of View*

I. Introduction

In all States with developed tax systems is a widespread wish to carry out fundamental tax reforms. In 1985, the President of the United States tried to enlist support with the programme "Reduce tax rates, reduce complexity, increase fairness, and increase growth"[1]; with it, he created not only a national, but also an international trend towards fundamental reforms[2]. Indeed, the American President's programme came out against defects which the taxpayers in all developed "tax states" complain about:

The tax burdens are considered to be too high. Hence, the citizens begin to think how one could fetter the Leviathan's, i.e., the State's, insatiable hunger for tax revenue by compelling the State to justify its taxes[3], and by introducing a constitutional limitation of the bases of tax assessment (the so-called tax bases) and of the structures of the tax rate schedules[4]. Taxation has reached such a degree of complexity that even tax experts cannot comprehend the system any longer. This is why in the Federal Republic of Germany even the associations of the tax consultants and of the tax officials advocate to simplify the tax system, although the experts have, normally, an interest in keeping the special knowledge - from which they make their living - to themselves and, if possible, in

* Translated by W.E. Weisflog, Brighton.

1 Cf. U.S. Treasury Department (1985).

2 Numerous articles and papers on tax reform have also been published in Germany. [See e.g. Lang (1987) and Tipke (1986)].

3 Cf. Vogel (1988, p. 19).

4 Cf. Brennan/Buchanan (1980).

excluding the layman from it! The taxpayers too find taxation unjust, unfair, and inequitable. Frequently, citizens in equal economic circumstances carry dramatically different tax burdens, because the tax bases are not based on clear, comprehensible principles and rules[5]. Democratic distribution policies and resistance to high tax burdens give rise to a great number of tax privileges for certain groups of electors or voters, as well as to tax loopholes and tax incentives as a premium for a certain governmentally approved conduct. The assumption that the fairness of taxation can be increased by greater differentiation is not sound, since most differentiations spring from special provisions which impair the equality of taxation. Next to the inequality of the laws are the inequalities as regards the *implementation* of the unequal laws: the well-informed citizens, and those well-advised by specialists, know how to get round the inscrutable system better than the non- or badly informed citizens.

This present state of the taxation raises the question of whether the tax systems have not developed in the wrong direction; if so, only a fundamental change of direction should initiate the recovery. This is where the movement "*Taxing Consumption*" comes in. The criticisms, i.e., the high tax rates, the complexity and the inequity of the tax bases, are mainly laid at the door of the *income tax*, and the question of a malformation is being raised in particular in the case of this type of tax. The alternative of the so-called *personal expenditure tax* charges the consumed income only and exempts the savings. Is this concept the better one for the future? At the end of the twentieth century this question will be answered differently than at the end of the nineteenth century, i.e., during the labour pains of the modern industrial society. At the end of the twentieth century we know that the citizens of the industrial societies consume too much, and this at the expense of the environment, at the expense of the developing countries and at the expense of future generations. We know that we will need a great degree of productivity in order to solve the problems of excessive consumption. Hence, does it not suggest itself to spare the savings, i.e., the invested income - which is the basis of the productivity - from tax and to make *consumption* more expensive?

---

[5] "They can't understand the logic or equity of people in seemingly similar situations paying dramatically different amounts of tax....." [U.S. Treasury Department (1985, p. 264)].

II. Constitutional Fundamentals of Taxation

A. Taxation in a Democratic State Based on the Rule of Law

The States in Western Europe, North America and Japan, whose tax systems are being discussed here, are democratic States governed by the rule of law, including the fundamental principles of justice, moral principles, fairness and due process. Therefore, the constitutional fundamentals of taxation in these states are the legality of taxation[6] and the exercise of the legislative power by the organs of the representative democracy[7].

1. The Rule of Law

Legality of taxation means that taxation must have a basis in law. For this reason principles of taxation are *legal* principles; actual rules of taxation are legal rules; actual taxation institutions such as types of tax, tax bases, and tax rates are legal institutions. Therefore, theoretical concepts of taxation have to attend how law originates and how it develops.

The rule of the law identifies the laws with the justice[8]. Therefore the laws must not merely be an instrument of the State for the purpose of exercising its power; rather, they must at the same time be "law" in the sense of a norm which orders society in accordance with generally comprehensible ethical maxims[9].

2. Reform of the Tax Law in a Democracy

2.1. Stable and Unstable Elements of the Law in a Democracy

The law and its maxims are, like the societies which they order, subject to a continuous change. However, one can perceive that there are legal institutions which enjoy a very high stability. Such stable elements of the law are often not tied to a specific

---

[6] Cf. Tipke/Lang (1989, pp. 34 seqq.).

[7] Cf. Böckenförde (1987, pp. 29 seqq.).

[8] The closest connections between the economic theories of taxation on the one hand and the law on the other have probably been made by F.A. von Hayek in his fundamental work "The Constitution of Liberty" (1960).

[9] According to article 20, para. 3, of the "Grundgesetz": "... the executive and the judiciary shall be bound by law and justice".

socialorder. Rather, they outlast the individual social order and become part and parcel of several social orders, as Comparative Law demonstrates. On the other hand, there are unstable elements of the law which have been stamped with the spirit of a certain social order or epoch and which - due to the change in the social views - are re-introduced into the political decision process. It is only these *un*stable elements of the law that are, in fact, the object of the democratic legislative power. The difference between stable and unstable elements of the law can be observed in particular in the "classical" spheres of law. The rules on the passage of the risk from seller to buyer are thousands of years old. No politician would dare to touch such stable elements of the law! However, the practice of selling goods at one's doorsteps has given rise to a special need for some legal protection of the buyer. By catering for this need, a part of the law on the sale and purchase of goods has become unstable. Therefore, the democratic legislator in the Federal Republic of Germany for instance, passed 1986 a law on the revocation of "doorstep sales" and similar transactions[10].

On the whole, the law aims at continuity. The lasting application of principles, rules and concepts is of prime importance for the solidification of the law. In the Anglo-American legal systems, the democratic decision field is already marked out by the institutional difference between the "statute law" passed by the parliaments and the "common law" which is - as is, of course, well-known - to a large extent customary law developed by the judges. In fact, the legislative act is also enveloped in legal custom. The codes of law in European legal history since the Codex Justinianus are the result of a long legal tradition which began casuistically unstable and has become stabilized in the course of time by means of structuring the case law by dogmatic jurisprudence. Even the Code Napoleon - in spite of its revolutionary elements - preserved in the main the continuity of the dogmatically highly developed French civil jurisprudence.

The modern democratic legislative policy proceeds on surprisingly traditional lines. In the preparatory stage of the legislation, politicians and commissions like to flirt with revolutionary ideas and let themselves be fascinated by novel and progressive proposals. However, at the latest at the bill stage, the legal tradition overtakes the belief in progress and forsakes the latter. Seen in the cold light of day, the "Tax Reform Act of 1986" - which has been effusively feasted in the United States as a "tax revolution" - has

[10] Cf. Law of 16.1.1986, Bundesgesetzblatt Teil I, p. 122.

altered the US income tax law only marginally and selectively. The rules of the Internal Revenue Code have become neither clearer nor simpler. Its complexity has not been reduced, and similar facts are still being taxed dissimilarly. In the Federal Republic of Germany too, the aim of the tax reform 1990, "to create an equitable and simpler tax system"[11] has remained unfulfilled. Admittedly, - like in the USA - a reform of the income tax *rate* schedule has been achieved, but neither in the USA nor in Germany has the "tax legislator" succeeded in bringing about a fundamental reform of the income tax *assessment* bases, - a reform which is considered to be necessary by fiscal experts for both, economic and legal, reasons.

The introduction of the value added tax in the Federal Republic in 1968 was, on the other hand, revolutionary in its economic effects, and undoubtedly very progressive. However, this economic progress has only been achieved because it was possible to take over the concepts and terms of the old turnover tax system.

2.2. Juridico-Economic Perspectives of Tax Reforms

Economic Attempts at Reform Versus Stability of The Fiscal Law

The demand for a fundamental reform of the taxation raises the following question: Which elements of the taxation have already become so stable that they have by now become inaccessible to the democratic decision process? Closely connected with this question is another one: In which way is it possible to utilize theoretical economic knowledge and findings? If one intends to make good use of such findings with a view to taking them into consideration when formulating legislative policy, then mainly two obstacles stand in one's path:

a) Firstly, theoretical models of optimal taxation are based on mathematically definable, but compared with the reality idealized and greatly simplified assumptions. Hence, the results of the analyses must be judged under the proviso that the irrationality of human co-existence will considerably dent the fascinating evidential value of the mathematically transparent connections between cause and effect.

---

[11] Cf. Bundestags-Drucksache 11/2157, p. 116. On the Tax Reform Law 1990 of 25.7.1988 (Bundesgesetzblatt Teil I, p. 1093) see Tipke/Lang (1989, pp. 188 seqq.) (with further references).

b) Secondly, the realization of an optimal taxation, however conceived, presupposes that the legislator has powers which, in fact, he does not have and never had. For, as outlined above, the legislator is in a straitjacket made of a more or less stable legal reality, - a legal reality which stays the same over relatively long periods and, similarly, can (unfortunately) only be altered over relatively long periods. This is a fact of legal life which is verbalized e.g. in the saying "an old tax is a good tax"[12].

The recommendation of Brennan and Buchanan (1980), namely to incorporate the tax bases and the tax rate schedules into the constitution in order to "tame" the Leviathan, assumes a power of the democratic legislator which is not at his disposal. Besides, the assumption that decision-making bodies of the State would, in the interest of maintaining or increasing their own power, strive for the maximization of the revenue is contrary to the demand for a constitutional fixing of the taxation. Such decision-making bodies of the State would never work towards a constitutional reform which would deprive them of their powers.

Stable and Unstable Institutions in the Field of Taxation

What will happen in the end is that which G. Brennan and J.M. Buchanan (1980) suggested, though not through an unlikely tour de force of the democratic legislator, but by the force of the historical development of jurisprudence. Fiscal law, which has developed in conjunction with the free enterprise industrial society, has a relatively short legal tradition, - too short in order to have stabilized sufficiently. On account of this, tax law is a permanent subject of legislative policy. In the Federal Republic, one tax reform plan follows another, one tax amendment law another tax amendment law. These are the symptoms of an instability which, however, offers on the other hand the opportunity to develop taxation in the right direction. To be sure, the arduous business of supporting the legislator scientifically requires patience, tenacity and an ability to cope with frustrations and setbacks, and this is precisely so, because the process of changing law is lengthy and only allows him to proceed in small steps. However, one fine day in the future too, fiscal law will belong to the "old" laws! At that moment in time, the

[12] Cf. Buchanan (1967, pp. 58 seqq.) (Existing Institutions and Change: The Effects of Time in Fiscal Decisions, "An old tax is a good tax").

institu-tions of the fiscal law will then be so consolidated in all civilized countries, or even internationally, like the institutions of the "classical" Private Law today.

However, the present restlessness in the sphere of tax policy does not extend over the whole fiscal law . Like each law the fiscal law consists of stable and unstable elements. In this context the following should be noted:

a) As is well known, the earliest forms of taxation put the burden on consumption. Indirect taxes on consumption were already levied in antiquity and contribute a substantial part of the tax revenue up to this day. Since their administration is relatively simple, they are used as the main source of tax revenue particularly in countries with inefficient fiscal administrations. In the European Community, the harmonization of the indirect taxes is expressly stipulated in Article 99 of the Rome Treaty. The harmonization of the value added taxes has made the biggest strides. Exactly because of this supra-national treaty commitment, the value added tax in the EC-countries can be regarded as a stable institution, especially since the tax base is to a great extent fixed. On the other hand, the alignment of the value added tax *rates* is still a bone of contention.

The special taxes on consumption, the so-called *excise duties*, particularly on petrol and other hydrocarbon oils, on tobacco products and certain alcoholic drinks enjoy a high degree of stability thanks to their administrative convenience and their high revenue-producing capacity. No government can seriously consider to abolish them. In the Federal Republic, the tax on hydrocarbon oils and the tobacco tax were increased considerably, and a new tax on natural gas has been introduced in order to finance, i.e. to make up for, the reduction of the income tax rate schedule in the Tax Reform Law 1990[13]. The EC-Commission would like to retain the excise duties on tobacco products, hydrocarbon oils, spirits, wine and beer and to harmonize them, but wants to abolish the remaining indirect taxes on consumption[14].

The Achilles' heel of the excise taxes is the arbitrary manner in which goods are being taxed. Up to now, no economically or legally consistent system of indirect taxation exists which selects and delimits the tax objects in accordance with general criteria of "special taxation-worthiness", like for instance a general rule according to which one

[13] Cf. Verbrauchsteueränderungsgesetz 1988 of 20.12.1988, Bundesgesetzblatt Teil I, p. 2270.

[14] Proposed Directive of 7.3.1972, Amtsblatt EG Nr. C 43 of 29.4.1972.

should tax all types of alcoholic drinks and other consumption goods owing to the detrimental social effects of their consumption. The above mentioned element of arbitrariness results in the instability of the excise duties from a legislative policy point of view. Since a system of special taxation has not yet been established, the conglomerate of excise duties is fair game for all sorts of taxing purposes; particularly promising would appear to be their use for environmental protection purposes[15]. In this sphere a considerable extension of the excise duties can be expected to take place in the future.

b) Meanwhile, the centres of gravity of present and future fiscal policy are in the field of the law appertaining to taxes on earnings and profits, and particularly in the field of income tax law. The comprehensive (accretion-model) income tax, the inheritance and gift tax, as well as the taxes on the income from specific assets (German "Soll-Ertragsteuern", i.e., the trade capital tax, the wealth tax, and the real property tax) are based on the redistribution-politically coloured idea of equity which liberated man from the fetters of the feudal State and emancipated him in the modern State. Article 13 of the French Declaration of the Rights of Man and of the Citizen of 6.8.1789 tied the ability to pay taxes to property, i.e. to wealth (and not to consumption); the "general levy" demanded in this Article was meant to "be spread out equally over all citizens by taking into account their fortunes (wealth)".

aa) It took progressive income tax no more than a century, in order to assert itself institutionally beside the indirect consumption taxes, and this not so much owing to the legislator thinking in terms of equity, but mainly thanks to its revenue yield. The first income tax on the aggregate income was introduced in 1799 in order to finance England's war against Napoleon[16]. The beginnings of income taxation on German soil too had their origins in the need for finance caused by the war. Karl Freiherr vom Stein propagated 1806 a progressive war tax on the total income. In his view, this tax was "the most uniform and most lucrative levy". Under his influence the said tax was introduced in 1808 in Prussia, Lithuania and Königsberg[17].

---

[15] On environmental protection and the tax system of the Federal Republic see Dickertmann (1988, pp. 91 seqq.).

[16] According to Sabine (1966, p. 26), William Pitt's "general tax upon all the leading branches of income" was "a war that beat Napoleon".

[17] Cf. Großfeld (1981, pp. 29 seqq.).

The justification of the income tax based on legal ethics developed in the course of the 19th century in view of the bad social conditions during the transition of the feudal agrarian society to the industrial society. The theory of progressive taxation in accordance with the "ability to pay" - the progressivity principle, and the "ability to pay"-principle - was elaborated[18]. The fundamental socialist social criticism[19] contributed greatly to the view that taxation of the consumption was unjust. The shifted burden of the indirect consumption taxes tended to fall - so it claimed - on the basic necessities of life and, at the same time, disproportionately on the economically weaker classes of society, whereas the "general progressive capital tax whose percentage rate increases with the size of the capital"[20] guaranteed the equitable and uniform distribution of the tax burden. The unrestrained development of the capitalist economy induced, however, also middle-class politicians and scientists to rethink their socio-political ideas, as a result of which the thought of a socially just taxation based on the "ability to pay" was soon not restricted any more to members of the socialist movement, but entered also the minds of the middle-class social reformers[21]. When minister of finance, Johannes von Miquel introduced in 1891 in Prussia the modern progressive income tax, he met with general approval and was able to say: "This favourable mood is mainly due to our German sense of fairness. One does not complain so much about high taxes, if one considers them as being just, but may well do so, if they are unequal"[22].

bb) In the industrial societies at the end of the twentieth century the mood is a completely different one. The fiscal yieldingness and lucrativeness of the taxes on income[23] has eroded the "equity value" of the income taxation, i.e., its value as an instrument of social justice and fairness. The resistance against high tax burdens, strate-

---

[18] Cf. Birk (1983, pp. 14 seqq.).

[19] On this cf. the postdoctoral thesis by Mesmer (1976).

[20] Thus Friedrich Engels [as quoted by Mesmer (1976, p. 215)].

[21] Thus Birk (1983, p. 15) (based on C.Frantz and Adolph Wagner).

[22] Quoted by Pausch (1964, p. 33).

[23] In the Federal Republic, in 1987 the four (for the Revenue!) most "profitable" taxes on income, namely (1) the income tax, (2) the corporation tax, (3) the church tax, and (4) the trade tax, produced together 57 percent of the total tax revenue of 481,209 million Deutschmark. The trade tax (Gewerbesteuer) is, however, not only based on the trading profits, but also on the trading capital, hence has the characteristics of a tax on the anticipated (potential) profits (so-called "Soll-Ertragsteuer" in German).

gies of tax avoidance, submissiveness of politicians to the so-called "lobby", as well as the policy of the State to use taxes for regulatory purposes have enormously complicated the income tax laws and have made holes into the tax base. Hence, the social consensus in favour of a *reform* of the income taxation, is aptly circumscribed by the initially mentioned programme "Reduce tax rates, reduce complexity, increase fairness".

In spite of failures in the field of legislative policy, the efforts to achieve a fundamental reform of the income tax continue. The Annual Conference of the German Jurists, during which fiscal themes are normally very rarely discussed, looked in 1988 into the question of whether the income tax law should be reformed in order to remove unequal tax treatment and in order to simplify it[24].

From the complexity and inequity of the taxes on income in today's fiscal law the conclusion can be drawn that, as far as the taxes on income are concerned, we are not dealing with "stabilized law", and hence a fundamental reform of the income tax must be carried out sooner or later. In that case the programme "lowering of the tax rates by means of a widening of the assessment basis", which is being discussed at present, will probably not be realized in the direction of a "comprehensive tax base". The so-called "net wealth addition theory" or "accretion theory" (Haig/Simons/Schanz concept)[25] has not gained acceptance in law, since it is practically impossible to include into the tax base all those types of income (benefits and uses, etc.) which are not part and parcel of the income that has been gained in the "market" (in other words, types of income which are not money income, but income or accumulation *in kind*, in "natura"). The definition of the "gross income" in the German Income Tax Law (Paragraph 2, section 1 - 3 EStG) includes as a matter of principle only the income which has been earned (German "erwirtschaftet") and realized in the "market" ("am Markt realisiert")[26], in other words, only the so-called "market income" ("Markteinkommen"). In the writer's opinion, one can safely agree with this limitation of the tax bases, since it is a practicable way of

---

[24] Cf. Discussion of the 57th "Deutscher Juristentag" on the theme: "Should the income tax law be reformed in order to remove unequal treatment and in order to simplify it?" [Deutscher Juristentag (1988), vol II., Proceedings N, as well as Kirchhof (1988)].

[25] Cf. Haig (1921), Simons (1938), and von Schanz (1896, p.1).

[26] See Kirchhof (1988, pp. 20 seqq.), as well as Lang (1981/88), and Lang (1985), in which I have tried to formulate the rules of the "market income", as developed in the legal practice, in a draft for a new (reformed) law.

achieving at least a degree of tax equality[27]. Proceeding in this direction, the aim must be to close the loopholes in the taxation of the "market income", for instance by taxing also the interest and the capital gains which are not derived from business assets (in other words, also the interest and capital gains of *non*-business taxpayers). What matters in this connection is, that an admittedly limited, but on the other hand practicable assessment basis is applied consistently and uniformly. The above limitation to the "market income" has already become "stabilized" in today's fiscal law to such a degree that G. Brennan's and J.M. Buchanan's proposal[28] to limit the taxbase *constitutionally* to the "money income" has, in fact already become part and parcel of the legal reality (i.e., without the need for a special provision in the Constitution).

cc) The legal instability of the taxes on income may, in the coming decades, very well have an effect on the tax law concerning *business enterprises* (German "Unternehmenssteuerrecht"). In Bonn, the seat of the West German government, the reform of the taxation of business enterprises is being discussed intensively, - which is somewhat surprising since, after the disappointing "success" of the Tax Reform Law 1990 with the voters, one rather expected that the politicians would turn to other themes than those connected with taxation policy. It appears that the need for tax reform is particularly urgent in the field of taxation of business enterprises. The increasing economic interdependence of the national economies in a world economy forces the various countries to adopt international standards of taxation - particularly business taxation. This pressure results in advantages and draw-backs for the aim of a fundamental tax reform. Advantageous is the pressure on the national democracies to alter their tax systems and to bring them into line with that which has been internationally recognized as being right. Thanks to this, tax reforms are pushed in the direction of stable legal structures in fiscal law, too, - structures which, like those in the "classical" fields of law, are universally accepted. Disadvantageous is, on the other hand, the enormous extension of the decision basis. A national democracy cannot any longer fundamentally reform its tax system on its own, so to speak as a "solo run". The national democracies

---

[27] For further details see Kirchhof (1988, pp. F20 seqq.).

[28] Cf.Brennan/Buchanan (1980).

are tied up in a relatively stable system of international treaties, above all the treaties for the avoidance of double taxation[29].

The subject of international standardization of the taxation of business enterprises will become topical mainly after the completion of the EC Internal Market. Up to now, the EC-Commission and the national governments have only very vague ideas on the harmonization of the *direct* taxes. However, already now, we can see the first signs of a de facto harmonization, triggered off by the competition of lower corporation tax rates in the various countries. The relatively high tax burden on the profits of German enterprises makes the politicians in Bonn visibly nervous, but, alas, does not further their willingness to study more thoroughly the problem of a far-reaching reorganization of the taxation of business enterprises!

In the Federal Republic, the following taxes are at present above all the subject of reform discussions:

(1) the income tax, which taxes the profits of limited and unlimited partnerships, including the so-called "Mitunternehmerschaften", progressively[30],

(2) the corporation tax, which taxes the income of joint-stock (incorporated) companies proportionally[31], and

(3) the particularly controversial municipal trade tax ("Gewerbesteuer") with two assessment factors, namely (a) the tax on trading profits ("Gewerbeertragsteuer"), a supplementary tax on trading profits, and (b) the tax on the trading capital ("Gewerbekapitalsteuer"), a supplementary tax to the wealth tax ("Vermögensteuer") and the municipal real property tax[32]. As to the wealth tax, the suggestion is to limit it to the private fortunes. A shift of the municipal tax revenue from the trade tax to the real property tax is considered to be possible, since at present the taxable values for real property are set at unrealistically low levels[33].

---

29 On this see Vogel's comments, this volume.

30 Up to the end of 1989: 0 - 56 percent. From 1990 onwards, the Tax Reform Law 1990 [see fn. 11] lowers the top rate by 3 (!) points to 53 percent.

31 Up to the end of 1989: 56 percent. From 1990 onwards according to the Tax Reform Law 1990: 50 percent.

32 On the state of the political discussion see the references in Tipke/Lang (1989, pp. 500 seqq.).

33 Cf. Lang (1989a, p. 3, p. 17).

c) The still outstanding reform of the taxation of business enterprises offers a good opportunity for taking a step in legislative policy towards the realization of the *personal expenditure tax* - which has been the main topic at the recent Congress on "Taxing Consumption" at Heidelberg. The administrative implementation of the personal expenditure tax[34] could, cum grano salis, be carried out with one stroke of the pen of the legislator. He would only have to "zero-rate" the corporation tax rate, and as a consequence, every taxpayer would establish a corporation for all his productive, i.e., gainful activities. Solicitors and doctors would be employees of their corporation. The private management of property, i.e., of a taxpayer's fortune, would also be organized on corporate lines, and owners of rented property, insurance policies and savings books would be turned into corporations, too. Only those amounts, which the taxpayers would draw out for their private consumption, would be subject to the progressive income tax. Hence, in that case the income tax would become in the main a tax on the *consumed* wages and dividends.

Such a solution has serious deficiencies, as we shall see later on. But it shows that the international trend towards a lowering of the corporation tax rates moves in the direction of taxing the *invested* income *lower* than the consumed income.

Concealed in this international competition of the developed industrial nations to reduce the tax burden on *retained* profits, a train of thought comes to the fore which has been pushed aside by the redistribution ethics of the 19th century. This train of thought, as is by now well-known, was formulated centuries ago by Thomas Hobbes in his "Leviathan":

> *"What reason is there, that he which laboureth much, and sparing the fruits of his labour, consumeth little, should be more charged, than he that liveth idely getteth little, and spendeth all he gets: seeing the one hath no more protection from the commonwealth than the other?"*[35]

The idea to mete out the income tax according to the *consumed* income collides with the 19th century postulate that the State ought to play a role in the ongoing accumulation of capital as a redistributor of incomes, in order to mitigate, or even to stop, the drifting apart of "rich" and "poor". Next, John Stuart Mill put forward the thesis that

---

[34] On this see the papers of McLure/Zodrow and Seidl in this volume.

[35] Hobbes (1651, ch. xxx).

taxing the income from capital, which has been accumulated out of *taxed* income, was a "double tax on savings"[36], and this line of thinking too did not meet with the approval of the redistribution adherents. According to the philosophy underlying the current income tax, i.e., of the so-called "accretion-model income tax", the income from capital (in British terms the "unearned" income!) is *new* income. He who saves much and consumes little increases his future ability to consume by the income from the invested income. The citizen with a small income who consumes it - or rather *has* to consume it in order to subsist! - lags more and more behind the wealth of the citizen who has sufficient income to accumulate a fortune, "wealth", and who can continually enlarge his sources of income. In the 19th century, the moral of the fable of the indolent grasshopper and the thrifty ant[37] did not convince, since the sections of the population who deserved social protection were precisely hard-working ants without hope for a better future.

The ideology of equity which underlies the "accretion-model income tax" is so entrenched in fiscal policy that up to now all proposals and models for a personal expenditure tax[38], be they ever so brilliant, have not advanced any further than into the antechamber of legislative policy[39].

However, the fiscal-ethic thinking is, I believe, in a phase of radical change. This is - and I am convinced of that - the hour of an interdisciplinary cooperation between economists and jurists who are open-minded about the economic analyses of the *effects* of taxation and as regards new economic concepts of taxation[40]. The economic arguments for a consumption-orientated reform of the tax system[41] have in the meantime

---

36 On this see McNulty (1989, pp. 120, 123-124).

37 De La Fontaine (1901).

38 Fisher/Fisher (1942), Kaldor (1965), and Meade (1978).

39 Cf. Bradford (1984), as well as Weisflog (1985, p. 257). The failed experiments with the expenditure tax in India in 1957 and in Sri Lanka in 1959 do not contribute anything useful as far as legislative policy is concerned.

40 In the Federal Republic, so far anyhow, the jurists have, unfortunately not been greatly interested in new reform concepts such as the personal expenditure tax. But the subject has been dealt with by the journal "Steuer und Wirtschaft" in a German translation of Andrew's (1974, pp. 1113 seqq.), A Consumption-Type or Cash-Flow Personal Income Tax, and the contribution by McNulty (1989, pp. 120, 123 seqq.).

41 Compiled by Rose (1989, p. 191). See also Kay/King (1986, pp. 90 seqq.), Mitschke (1985), and the contributions in Pechmann (1980).

become so well founded that it would be positively silly to neglect them in legal policy. In this connection, two aspects are, in my view, of special importance:

1) On the one hand, modern industrial society tends towards growth and towards increasing the wealth. Therefore the income must be taxed lowly during the investment phase. The ecologically harmful consequences of the economic growth do not by themselves cast doubt upon the idea of growth; rather, they give grounds for instituting a qualitative transformation of the economic growth. This transformation is at present being discussed under the still rather vague formula "ecological alteration of the economy". A rational "Eco-tax-system", which has been sufficiently researched as to its economic effects, must, among other things, also contribute towards this end.

2) On the other hand, the citizens, and the consumptive potential of their households, are the ones on whom all tax burdens fall at the end of the line. Hence, it seems only economically rational, to connect the tax bases directly to private consumption. Not yet fully researched is the disparate development of the fortunes (i.e., the accumulated capitals) which might occur, if the accumulation of wealth were completely tax-exempt. In an industrial society with widely dispersed wealth, this problem has, however, not the same dramatic importance which it would have had in the societies of the 19th century. Inspite of this, it must, of course be solved convincingly in such a lego-ethical manner that the solution is capable of overturning the legal tradition of a century.

Juridico-Political Limitations when Trying to Materialize Economic Objectives

Having said all that, we come up against the following limitations when trying to materialize economic objectives:

a) A tax reform can, in principle, only be achieved in small steps, in "increments". Owing to this limitation, models of optimal taxation, which start out from the premise that they can be realized overnight, are eliminated. The results of economic research rather have the function of a signpost: a rational tax reform concept cannot be developed without tax effect analyses which are as precise as possible[42]. Furthermore, the "tax policy of the small steps" - "incrementalism" (Lindblom) - in particular requires a rational tax reform concept, for without "signposts" each small step may be a step back-

[42] On this see Mann (1987).

wards. In that case, fiscal legislation becomes aimlessly operating forward-reverse tax legislation.

b) As far as legislative policy is concerned, the success of an economic reform concept mainly hinges on one point: to what extent can it fall back on existing legal concepts, terms and norms? The long-term social consensus on legal rules consolidates in the practical application of the law through a multitude of decisions on individual law (court) cases, each of which removes a small piece of conceptual vagueness and semantic ambiguity, but may, on occasion, also produce new obscurities. Thus, the clarification of the content of legal concepts and delimitations is so laden with conflict, so lengthy and laborious, that every conceptual change meets with considerable resistance. Experts of the fiscal practice (tax officials, tax consultants, judges) will use their influence in government ministries and federations always forcefully *against* conceptual changes. Admittedly, falling back on familiar concepts and terms which have been clarified in the law of the land by the judges, is also required for reasons of upholding the "certainty of law" (German "Rechtssicherheit"). Even the terminologically conservative turnover tax reform had to be carried through against the resolute resistance of the tax practitioners[43].

Nevertheless, just this (turnover tax) reform demonstrates clearly that economic objectives can be realized even with a relatively minor alteration of the legal concepts. Hence two tasks have to be connected between the two disciplines, economics and law: First of all, one has to establish which economic objectives ought to be taken into consideration in legislative policy. Following that, one has to examine which particular elements in the existing juridico-conceptual apparatus are suitable for translating the economic objectives into the legal reality. Anybody who believes that "one only has to know what one wants to do, and then one can translate it straightaway into the legal reality", clearly underestimates the inertia of the latter. The inertia of the legal reality is the main problem of the branch of jurisprudence which deals with the various legal aspects of "legislation", in particular with the process of its enactment (German "Gesetzgebungswissenschaft").

Hence, it does not come as a surprise to a jurist that the US "Tax Reform Act of 1986", as well as the German "Tax Reform Law 1990", were in essence tax *rate* schedule

---

[43] Cf. Heilmann (1975, pp. 91 seqq.).

reforms. While a reform of the bases of assessment includes the system of legal concepts of a tax and requires the introduction of new legal institutions (e.g. in the case of the turnover tax reform the so-called "tax credit for input tax" (German "Vorsteuer-abzug")), there is no need for an alteration of the legal concepts where a mere alteration of the tax *rate* schedule is being carried out. For this reason, reforms of the tax rate schedule can be realized relatively easily from a legislative policy point of view, since in their case they are not opposed by the might of the legal tradition. As to the latter, we must remember that the existing legal institutions are not only being defended by the politically influential tax practitioners, but by all those who are in danger of losing legally defined advantages - privileges -, like, for instance, the tax deduction for entertaining expenses. Such tax advantages or tax privileges are seen by the taxpayer affected as "his right" and their removal as "injustice".

For this reason, the - above mentioned - international lowering of the corporation tax rates could be the first realistic step towards a consumption-orientated taxation. This assessment of the situation leads to the approach (which I shall put forward in more detail in section III.D of this paper) to extend the existing corporation tax to a general tax on the saved income, including invested income and retained profits. When proceeding in this way, the consumed income would be delimited in legal terms (i.e., so to speak "juridically separated" from the invested income). Hence the consumed income could be subjected to separate taxation.

c) The most important precondition for a lego-political success of an economic reform concept is, in the end, its power to convince from the point of view of legal ethics. The classical science of economics has based its conception of what constitutes an economically "correct" taxation in essence not so much on economic efficiency criteria, but rather on criteria derived from *social ethics*[44]. By using this approach, the classical economists had an extremely successful impact on the development of the taxation in the 19th century. Legal systems are normative systems which want to transmit a system of (legal) values based on justice, fairness and equity[45]. Thus, for a jurist it goes without saying that economic effects must be valued from the angle of *individual* equity. But

[44] Thus, as Musgrave says in his Historical Perspective: "As Adam Smith recognized clearly - even more clearly than our present discussion - : a good tax system is not simply a question of economics; it is also a question of (re)distribution equity."

[45] On this, more detailed, see Lang (1989b, p. 201).

also the work of the politician to convince the electors or voters of the rightness of his party's proposals, etc. will only be successful, if it is based on generally convincing tax-ethical arguments, - unless, of course, the politician in question merely applies tactics of persuasion by election promises, in other words, tactics based on "election bribery"!

There is no doubt that the arguments for selecting *consumption* as an assessment basis are gaining in lego-ethical persuasiveness. The central point is the present waste of resources at the expense of future generations. However, from a legislative policy viewpoint I agree with Richard A. Musgrave[46] that the tax-ethical discussion on "income versus consumption" is still open, and that a "dual system, consisting of consumption taxation and wealth taxation (or taxation of the income from capital)" is necessary.

Therefore, we have to offer the tax legislator a concept which meets the old and the new thinking. He needs leeway for the adaptation of the legislation to the new way of thinking, and at the same time his path for a possible retreat from the new thinking must be left open, so that he can take it, if it should prove that tax-exemption for capital formation should create social tensions. For this reason, one cannot altogether dispense with the taxation of capital formation for the time being. Rather, initially we have to institute a "*dualism of the income taxes*", in other words a system whereby the consumable incomes and the saved incomes are being taxed *separately*. Once this dualism has been set up, the tax legislator has the opportunity to tax-exempt capital formation step by step by reducing the income tax rate on the latter (accumulation-model income tax!) or - conversely - to put a brake on the capital formation by increasing the tax rate, should the said capital formation cause undesirable socio-political side effects.

2.3. Fundamental Reform of the Tax Law in a Democracy?

Viewed from the angle of political realism such a reform of income taxation is so fundamental that it raises the question of whether a democracy is at all capable of such a reform feat.

The experiences with the fiscal legislation in the Federal Republic of Germany lead one also to the realization that public-choice mechanisms in a "horsetrading-

[46] Cf. Musgrave's paper in this volume.

democracy", the latter has been excellently described by F.A. von Hayek[47]) do not normally bring about an income tax reform whose extent is as wide as that envisaged in this paper[48]. Again and again, the competition of the political parties in the field of tax policy has encouraged them to misuse the fiscal law as an instrument of social engineering. In consequence, the unstable elements of the tax law have been continually fissured and driven further and further apart from that which one could call a "rational tax system".

In spite of this, a democracy too has a chance of being able to carry out a fundamental reform, namely when the pressures of political circumstances or events put a stop to the competition for votes, and when the political forces, which normally work against each other, line up in one direction. Thus, extraordinary historical situations give rise frequently to a common effort by all democratic forces. At that particular moment, quite often great political personalities with charisma, and capable of integrating the various factions and political forces, enter into the political arena.

Great reform movements of this kind have also occured in the history of taxation, like e.g. the introduction of the income tax in England by William Pitt on the occasion of the war against Napoleon, or the introduction of the Prussian income tax by Johannes von Miquel which was precipitated by the unbearable social misery at the end of the 19th century.

At the end of the twentieth century, political pressures are developing which - as far as I can see - enhance the chances for a fundamental tax reform. The following is my assessment of the situation:

a) The state of the present fiscal law is becoming more and more unedifying, in practice as well as in the theory. In particular, in spite of all political endeavours, the tax reformers have up to now not been able to reverse the increased complexity of the law into a trend towards simplification. This statement is also valid in respect of the tax law of the United States. Nevertheless, the initially mentioned tax reform programme of the American President was a historic signal. As is well-known, the tax reform attempts of the Reagan administration have triggered off one of the biggest lobby-campaigns in American history. This campaign failed, however, owing to the all-party conviction that

---

47 Cf. Hayek (1979).

48 On the situation in the Federal Republic see Raupach/Tipke/Uelner (1985), as well as Tipke (1989a, pp. 291 seqq.).

the tax law required urgent improvement. This exemplary victory of the democratic forces over the mighty chiefs of the federations, associations and syndicates was a first historical sign that the time is ripe for a fundamental reform of taxation.

b) This sign has international importance, since the already mentioned interdependence of the national economies in the world economy, in particular their involvement in a relatively stable system of double tax treaties, exerts a pressure to align tax systems and reforms internationally. This pressure ought to contribute greatly to the promotion of mutual understanding between the democratic parties of a country. Especially the above mentioned completion of the EC Internal Market might considerably increase the political pressure to carry out a fundamental reform.

c) Finally, the dramatic deterioration of the natural living conditions (pollution, ozone hole, etc.) produces - at least in West Germany - a willingness, reminiscent of the war years, to accept tax increases for the protection of the environment. The generally recognized need to do something for its protection gives in the Federal Republic at present rise to a hectic discussion on the so-called eco-taxes. Providing these discussions will be channelled in the right direction, a fairly wide field of all-party cooperation opens up, namely in respect of taxing consumption in conformity with environmental protection.

B. Equality, Liberty and Social Solidarity as Constitutional Fundamentals for a Consumption-orientated Reform of Tax Systems

1. On the Constitutionally Guaranteed Basic Consensus as regards Equality, Liberty and Social Solidarity

Reflexions on internationally aligned reforms of the law on taxation make it necessary to find out about the legal principles which are prevalent in all States with developed tax systems. The jurist first of all thinks of the (written) constitutions of the democratic States which are governed by "the rule of law".

From a juridical point of view, these constitutions restrict the room for manoeuvre of the democratic legislator. Owing to this, - at least where *written* constitutions exist - taxes cannot be created or invented "as you (or, rather, the tax legislator!) like it". For instance, the introduction of the personal expenditure tax would require an alteration of the German "fiscal constitution"[49]. The institution of the German Federal Constitutional Court ("Bundesverfassungsgericht") makes sure that the democratic legislator remains within the boundaries of the "Grundgesetz" (i.e., the constitution of the Federal Republic of Germany).

The control of the legislator by the Federal Constitutional Court is, however, in turn restricted by the principle of the separation of powers. For this reason, the Federal Constitutional Court practices, like the United States Supreme Court, the principle of judicial self-restraint vis-a-vis the legislator: the judge must not rule over the legislator. In line with this precept, the Federal Constitutional Court gives the tax legislator very considerable leeway[50], in consequence of which a rational, sensible tax law cannot be invalidated.

However, the Federal Constitutional Court has developed a system of constitutional tax principles, which can be more than a mere instrument of controlling of whether the constitutional limits have been observed; rather, it is a system of principles which forms and outlines the substantive constitutional basic conditions, i.e. requirements, to which a rational tax system must conform. By this approach, the fiscal jurisprudence is being challenged to develop principles sustaining the system of fiscal law, - principles which thereupon must also be used as standards of legislative policy[51].

This approach, namely adherence to the principles which emanate from the constitutional basic values, leads inevitably to the international plain, since the fiscal law touches on fundamental values that are enshrined in all constitutions of the democratic States governed by "the rule of law". Put in a nutshell: these are the fundamental values of equality, liberty and social solidarity ("fraternité") which two hundred years ago were formulated in the "Déclaration des droits de l'homme et du citoyen" and which form to this day the basic political consensus of societies with a developed tax system.

For a consumption-orientated tax reform the system of constitutional tax principles means the following:

---

[49] On this see Birk (1990).

[50] Cf. Herzog (1988, p. 289).

[51] The theory on the principles sustaining the system of fiscal law (German "sytemtragende Prinzipien") has been developed by Tipke (1973, pp. 18 seqq.), and Tipke/Lang (1989, pp. 24 seqq.). On the approach from the angle of legislative policy cf. Lang (1989b, pp. 206 seqq.).

2. Equality

2.1. System-Consistent Taxation in Accordance with the Ability to Pay

It is internationally accepted that tax equality is linked to the principle of taxation in accordance with the ability to pay[52]. Hence, a reform concept must be able to claim that it has put the ability-to-pay principle into concrete form. In the 19th century the said principle was developed in support of the class struggle as a principle for the justification of tax progression. The validity of this argument is now disputed. According to the findings of contemporary fiscal jurisprudence, the ability-to-pay principle does not tell us how to structure tax rate schedules[53].

On the other hand, as a *legal* principle, the ability-to-pay principle can play a useful role in particular in connection with the "privilege-free" formulation of the bases of taxation, i.e., to ensure that these bases do not confer privileges on certain selected groups of taxpayers. When trying to formulate the assessment basis in line with the above, the method of "systems consistency", i.e., consistent application of the system (German "Systemkonsequenz"), developed by K.Tipke[54] is particularly useful. This method ist to be carried out in two steps: In a first step, the rule, which is from a legal and economic viewpoint appropriate to the circumstances that have to be regulated, is being established. In a second step, the rule, which has been recognized as being pertinent to the matter in hand, is consistently implemented within its field of application, - taking, however, into account any other rules which collide with the one that has been established. As regards to the first step, it is, for instance, not to be recommended to realize the Haig-Simons-Schanz-concept of income in its pure form, because this concept is not suitable for the legal subject-matter under review. Appropriate to the legal subject-matter under review, - in other words: objective and fair -, is only the market income theory[55], since in the legal practice - as opposed to the legal theory - only the market income can be accurately ascertained, valued and taxed.

---

[52] See the references in Tipke/Lang (1989, pp. 27 seqq.).

[53] On this see Schmidt (1960).

[54] See for instance Tipke (1981).

[55] Cf. Kirchhof (1988, pp. F20 seqq.), and Lang (1985).

When proceeding to the second step, i.e., the implementation of the market income theory, the legislator has to see to it that the market incomes are taxed, if at all possible, without leaving loopholes and without giving tax preferences[56].

2.2. Consumption as a Fair Indicator of a Person's Ability to Pay Taxes

The traditional view, as formed in the 19th century, assigns the task of the taxation in accordance with the ability to pay first and foremost to the *income tax*[57]. This role of the income tax as "upholder" of the ability-to-pay principle is not restricted to the progressive tax rate schedule, but comprises also the comprehensive (accretion model!) assessment basis; the tax base "income" is considered to be the ideal indicator of the ability to pay .

However, it is exactly this view of the ideal indication of the ability to pay which has proved to be too narrow. Rather, the *whole* tax system ought to be governed by the ability-to-pay principle. In principle, three ability-to-pay indicators can be distinguished: (1) the dynamic indicator "income", (2) the static indicator "wealth", and (3) the dynamic indicator "consumption"[58]. As regards taxes on consumption, the Federal Constitutional Court[59] has declared that the latter are "taxes on the economic ability to pay, which manifests itself in the use of the income for the personal necessities (wants/needs) of life".

---

[56] There is indeed a special need to reduce or even to get rid of exempt amounts (deductions/allowances), exemption limits, lump-sum deductions for expenses, and gaps/loopholes in the law which apply to *particular* types of incomes only, since such exemptions etc. give rise to completely different income concepts and to different tax charges (tax burdens) in the tax base. For instance, only one quarter of the income from old age pensions (retirement pensions) is being charged to tax, and capital gains of private individuals are not taxed at all. On this see Deutscher Juristentag (1988), Tipke (1989b, p. 186), and Raupach/Tipke/Uelner (1985), Tipke/Lang (1989, pp. 232 seqq., pp. 323 seqq.). In Lang (1989a) I have attempted to formulate the legal rules for the market income without leaving any gaps or loopholes and without granting any privileges.

[57] Thus the decisions of the Federal Constitutional Court of West Germany (Bundesverfassungsgericht - BVerfG -). See the following decisions in the official compilation (Entscheidungen des Bundesverfassungsgerichts): BVerfGE 43, 104, 120; 61, 319, 343; 66, 214, 223.

[58] Cf. Tipke/Lang (1989, pp. 160 seqq.), Birk (1988, pp. 43-44).

[59] See Bundesverfassungsgericht BVerfGE 65, 325, 326.

Earlier on we have stated that, at the end of the day, the citizens and the consumptive potential of their households are the bearers of all tax burdens. This justifies not only the type of tax on the consumed income, but indicates also that already the *existing* income tax comprises elements of the ability to consume. The historical intention of the progressive tax rate schedule is, to tax the citizen in accordance with his "ability to make a sacrifice", an ability which is judged by the availability of income for one's personal consumption[60]. It is therefore logically quite consistent that the assessment basis of the existing income tax has been conceived as "private consumption fund" (German "privater Konsumfonds"). This follows from the existence of tax deductions (or "personal allowances"/"personal reliefs" (UK)) for the essential consumption expenditure. Hence, the assessment basis of the income tax is, in principle, dualistically constructed: first, the market income is defined. Secondly, from this (gross) income, that particular part of the income, which is not available for the tax payment is excluded by means of granting tax deductions (personal allowances/personal relief(s)) for the necessary private expenditure[61].

Hence, it would appear that the ability-to-pay indicator no. 3 - "consumption" - is already an integral element of the existing income tax law, and therefore the question can be raised, whether the *saved* income should not be eliminated from the assessment basis of a tax rate schedule which rests on consumption-theoretical foundations.

3. Liberty and Social Solidarity

3.1. The Concept of the "Social Market Economy"

In the eyes of economics and public law, taxation is an "institution of liberty": taxation is a form of partnership of the State in private economic activities[62], in other words, is not tantamount with collecting State-owned property[63]. The liberally organized State is not a beehive, out of which the beekeeper creams off, so to speak, the whole national

---

[60] When shaping the progression, the legislator has considerable leeway, since the "just" tax rate schedule cannot be determined exactly.

[61] On this see Tipke/Lang (1989, pp. 198 seqq.).

[62] In the German literature on Public Law, this aspect of the taxation has been dealt with mainly by Kirchhof in various papers of his, [see e.g. Kirchhof (1981, p. 213)].

[63] The latter is the view expressed by Friedrich Engels (1846).

income, in order to return solicituously to the bees that which they need in order to survive. Rather, in liberally organized States, the national income is private property, from which two types of contribution have to be made: (1) the price for the protection of the citizen and his property by the State[64], and (2) the obolus of social solidarity which the State demands from the citizens who carry on economic activities[65].

The historical origin of the income tax as a war tax proves that the State may have exceptionally great financial requirements which cannot be ignored and which justify high taxes that dig deep into the pockets, i.e., into the wealth, of its citizens. In so far as this is the case, the loss of the economic freedom of action owing to the impact of the taxation cannot be kept within absolute limits. In the extreme case, the price for the protection by the State may (e.g. in the case of a lost war) even eat up, so to speak, the economic livelihood of the citizens. The first-mentioned justification for taxes, namely the price for the protection by the State, does at present not appear to be a problem that falls within the theme: "the Leviathan's insatiable hunger for tax revenue" which we have touched on at the beginning of section I of this paper.

The present discussion on the justification of taxes[66] is rather directed towards questions which are difficult to deal with on a juridical level, namely questions on the tense relationship between economic freedom of action and social solidarity. How much solidarity can the community, i.e., the society, call for from the citizen who is actively engaged in a free enterprise economy? Which tasks should be the responsibility of the State, and which ones not? And, as an inevitable follow-up question: how much income and wealth may and should be redistributed by taxation?

The West German Constitution (Grundgesetz) contends no answers to these questions, because it is not based on a particular economic structure[67]. However, a fundamental political consensus exists in fact, according to which the economy of the

---

[64] Thus the justification of the taxes, based on the natural law, from Thomas Hobbes to Adam Smith's first maxim of taxation.

[65] Thus the justification of the taxes, based on the concept of the "social State"/Welfare State, and originating with the "Déclaration des droits de l'homme et du citoyen" of 1798.

[66] In the Federal Republic this theme has been dealt with mainly by Vogel (1988, p.19). See also Tipke/Lang (1989, pp. 178 seqq.).

[67] On the politico-economic neutrality of the Grundgesetz cf. Bundesverfassungsgericht, BVerfGE 4, 7, 17 f; 7, 337, 400; 14, 19, 23; 30, 292, 315; 50, 290, 337.

Federal Republic of Germany has to be a "social market economy" (German "soziale Marktwirtschaft"), hence has to operate on the basis of a free enterprise system with a social security component. Thanks to this concept, the West German economy prospers, and similarly the Japanese one. The close ties between the achievement-orientated mentality and the need for security, in other words, the identification of the workforce with the place of work, based on a feeling of security, are the elementary mental conditions which have contributed or even ensured the Japanese and German economic successes. That is why the components of the Welfare State are very marked, very pronounced. Whilst the West German Constitution merely contains a declaration that the Federal Republic is a "social federal state"[68], without defining the latter, the Japanese constitution[69] formulates precisely the aims of its social State.

However, a discussion on international standards of taxation cannot restrict itself to a review of national mentalities and characteristics, since the relationships between the two values of liberty and social solidarity have developed differently in the individual countries. The conception of liberty of the American society, which is based on the Virginia Bill of Rights of 12.6.1776, and which, as a matter of principle, gives priority to the private welfare over the public one, will have to deal with the subject of fiscal redistribution differently than an industrial society (like West Germany, for instance) with a more or less pronounced system of State welfare.

The theme, which these societies have in common, is not the measure of social solidarity that befits the individual industrial societies, but the defects or redistribution of incomes and wealth, but the inefficiency of the government machinery, the take-over of State functions that private enterprise would perhaps carry out cheaper (maybe even more equitable)[70], the misdirected allocation of the production factors by the economy owing to the proliferation of State subsidies, and a faultily constructed tax system. As regards the last-mentioned point I wish to make the following comments.

---

[68] Art.20, para. 1, Grundgesetz: "The Federal Republic of Germany is a democratic and social federal state".

[69] Art.25 Jap. constit.:"All people shall have the right to maintain the minimum standards of wholesome and cultured living. In all spheres of life, the state shall use its endeavours for the promotion and extension of social welfare and security, and of public health."

[70] Thus Vogel (1987, p. 1151, p. 1180).

3.2. Adequacy of Consumption Taxation within a Free Enterprise System

Both, on the level of legal politics as well as on the level of the application of the law, the existing progressive income tax has triggered off so much tax resistance that its equity value exists nowadays only on paper. Innumerable breaches in the (ideally comprehensive) tax base, the "art" of tax avoidance, excessive time, energy and money that has to be spent on administration and consultancy, a flood of court cases, "tax flight" and tax evasion syndromes, deficits as regards the sense of right or wrong, and inappropriate formulation of contracts, are the hallmarks of the present income tax law[71].

Hence, from the juridical point of view too, one can argue that the loss of economic freedom of action caused by the present progressive taxation of the "market income" is too great. This loss has led to unacceptable social conditions. Compared with the above, the loss of economic freedom of action would be far smaller, if the *consumed* income were the tax base, since the tax would not claim its share of the income in the phase during which the income is earned.

The taxation of the consumption is economically adequate since the "motive forces" of the free enterprise system would not be interfered with taxwise[72], and since the market-economic result would be taxed at a time when it is consumed. Hence, it seems only appropriate and fair, to let the State partake in the economic result of the citizen, if and when the citizen *consumes* i.e., enjoys the fruit of his labours. The time of the consumption of the fruit would also from an ethical point of view appear to be a more plausible time of sharing it out than the time of its growing[73]!

3.3. Neutrality of Consumption Taxation

The concept of not burdening the earning process with tax, guarantees a high (I do not wish to claim an "absolute") degree of *fiscal neutrality*. For a limited period of time, that

---

[71] Cf. Raupach (1985, p. 15).

[72] Cf. Rose (1989, p. 191).

[73] On this see also Hardorp (1990).

is, up to the consumption of the economic result, one could say that the so-called Edinburgh (McCulloch) "leave-them-as-you-find-them" rule of taxation[74] applies.

The Edinburgh rule is entirely based on values derived from economic ("laissez-faire") liberalism; it is not compatible with the Welfare State-principle[75]. But it does not exclude the component of the Welfare State-principle, if it is applied only for a limited time and not for all tax types, e.g. when the Welfare State carries out a one-off redistribution of the wealth by means of the inheritance and gift tax[76].

The fiscal practice shows that the existing taxation gives rise to the most glaring infringements of the principle of fiscal neutrality. Hence, there is an urgent need to give in the sphere of income taxation priority to the principle of fiscal neutrality over the Welfare State-principle. It is the incomes *of individuals* which, after all, have the most comprehensive and the closest connection with the permanent economic activity of the citizen, owing to which fact his economic freedom of action is affected most of all by the taxation of his *personal* income.

For jurists the fiscal neutrality of the taxation is closely related to the principle of equality, especially in the shape of the "competitive neutrality", i.e., the fiscally neutral treatment of competitors (German "Wettbewerbsneutralität")[77] and in the shape of the neutrality (i.e., neutral treatment) of legal forms[78]. As mentioned above, the principle of equality demands that the bases of assessment are formulated in accordance with the principle of "systems consistency" (German "systemkonsequent"), which means: the taxation of the "market income", without loopholes or tax privileges[79]. If this condition

---

[74] Cf. Walker (1887, p. 491). See also Groves (1974, p. 96).

[75] Cf. Tipke/Lang (1989, p. 50).

[76] Mitschke (1985) proposes a combination of an annual consumption tax and a single, non-recurring incremental net wealth tax ("Reinvermögenszuwachssteuer").

[77] This theme is being discussed in connection with the reform of the taxation of associations ("Vereine").

[78] This theme was the subject of discussions on the occasion of the 33rd "Deutscher Juristentag" in 1924 at Heidelberg and of the 53rd "D.J." in 1980 in Berlin, in both instances, however, without the Juristentag formulating any concrete proposals for a taxation which is neutral as regards the legal forms of enterprises. [Deutscher Juristentag (1925), Deutscher Juristentag (1980)].

[79] Cf. Deutscher Juristentag (1988), Tipke (1989b, p. 186), Raupach/Tipke/Uelner (1985), Tipke/Lang (1989, pp. 232 seqq., pp. 323 seqq.), and Lang (1985).

were fulfilled, then a great number of the reasons, owing to which taxation becomes the main decision-making factor, would fall by the wayside.

The principle of neutrality of legal forms (German "Rechtsformneutralität") requires that any economic activity, regardless of which legal form under which it is being carried out, should be taxed equally. Up to now, the legal discussion has not yet reached a clear answer to the question of which premises must be fulfilled, in order that neutrality of legal forms may be achieved. Generally, the view is held that different legal forms justify different forms of taxation[80]. At this point, we must differentiate, however, more accurately. We must ask ourselves, in which way legal forms, owing to their juridical construction, give rise to different economic facts. For instance: a business loss has to be borne only by the partner of an unincorporated business, but not by the shareholder of a corporation, at least not directly. The financial situation of a shareholder depends directly on the market value of the share and only indirectly on the profits or losses made by the corporation. Hence, the so-called "partnership tax" (German "Teilhabersteuer")[81] (where the total profits are imputed to the shareholders, and the latter are taxed under the individual income tax; in other words, where shareholders are treated for tax purposes as if they were partners in an unincorporated business) has met with fierce rejection by the jurists, since the tax does not sufficiently take into account the economic-juridical realities of a corporation[82].

Hence, from the juridical point of view, neutrality of the legal forms can only mean: equal tax burden in case of the same economic-juridical realities[83]. In order to meet this demand, much still needs to be done. For instance, it is not clear to anybody, why profits from partnerships are being taxed progressively, profits from corporations proportionally. This different way of structuring the tax rates has, in principle, nothing to do with the legal form. Furthermore, the different taxation of capital gains, the different tax rates of the various types of taxes on gross or net assets (property/capital), the different recognition of contracts between partners and the partnership, - all these are

---

80 Thus, e.g. the expert's opinion ("Gutachten") by Walz (1980).

81 Cf. Report of the Canadian Royal Commission of Taxation (1967, vol.4, pp. 3 seqq., Appendix H, pp. 661 seqq.).

82 Gutachten der Steuerreformkommission (1971, paper 17, Tz. II 100 seqq.).

83 On this approach see Lang (1989a, p. 3).

annoying discriminations which are due to the tax law (i.e., public law), and have nothing to do with economics or the private law[84].

From the point of view of neutrality of the legal form, one must, in principle oppose strongly the above-mentioned actions of those States which reduce (or have reduced) corporation tax rates only. Rather, a type of taxation should be set up, which taxes all retained "market incomes" independently of the legal form of the business enterprise *proportionally*, since the progressive tax rate schedule is not an appropriate and fair form of taxation for incomes that are not available to the "private consumption fund" (German "privater Konsumfonds"). The economic freedom of action is being restricted without socio-political necessity, if the taxpayer is practically forced to form a corporation or to fulfill other technical, i.e., formal-juridical, conditions at considerable bureaucratic expense, only in order to obtain the appropriate taxation, that is, tax exemption for the capital accumulation. For these reasons, the above-mentioned tax on the saved income must be open, i.e., available, for all forms of economic activity, including activities which are not carried out within the framework of legally independent forms of organization, such as private saving, letting of houses, etc., - in short: also for all non-consumption activities.

3.4. Prerequisites for Social Solidarity

On the Postulate of Redistribution: Old and New Responsibilities

From such a widely conceived tax on the saved income to the taxation of consumption, it is only a very short step, a step which could relatively easily be taken by "zero-rating" the tax on the saved income.

Alas, the redistribution postulate, which was developed in the 19th century and was extended into the Welfare State, is opposed to such stroke of the pen of the legislator. The following objections could be raised against a complete tax exemption of the accumulation of capital:

a) As mentioned already, the problem of a potential excessive disparate development of the accumulated capitals has not yet been solved satisfactorily. The differences between "rich" and "poor" might become so great that even in those States where the wealth of

---

[84] For a more detailed treatment of this aspect see Lang (1989a).

the nation is widely spread and where, in consequence, the social classes live in peace and harmony, social tensions might erupt. If at the end of a taxpayer's life a tax on the capital accumulation were imposed as a supplement to an annual consumption tax[85], this problem would still not be solved convincingly. Firstly, I have some reservations based on legal ethics: is it right, if the State lets the citizens save and invest (or even encourages them to do so) up to the end of their lives, only in order to seize a substantial part of the accumulated wealth by means of a progressive tax rate, - like a cat that plays with a mouse before he carries it off and eats it? Secondly, a tax-payer, who has accumulated a large fortune tax-free, will find ways and means in order to fend off the one-off tax raid on the wealth which he has assembled free of tax.

b) In the cases of very high incomes, the measure "ability to pay tax" proves to be too small in order to provide "social justice". If, for instance, a successful entrepreneur, filmstar or sports personality has got an annual income of 15 million Deutschmark and consumes 3 mill. DM of that, then even an expenditure tax amounting to 3 mill. DM (= tax rate of 100 %) does not sufficiently take into account the ability to pay of the tax-payer in question. This objection - insufficient taxing of the ability to pay - is not only pertinent in the case of luxury consumption which only forms a small fraction of the earnings, but also in the case of an extremely small rate of consumption where under an expenditure tax a rich Mr. Scrooge might possibly be taxed even less than his employees[86]. Hence, even with a tax rate of over one hundred percent, the problem of insufficient taxing of the taxable capacity cannot be solved satisfactorily either.

Admittedly, here we are discussing extreme cases which form statistically a negligent group compared to the great mass of the taxpayers who consume more than 90 percent of their incomes. But the fairness of taxation cannot be brushed aside by statistical data. Fairness is a legal value that refers to the *individual* person, and therefore a legal institution must regulate fairly also the exceptional particular case[87]. Experience shows that just such exceptional cases become the focal point of parliamentary debates;

---

[85] Thus Mitschke's (1985) proposal [see footnote 76].

[86] Mr. Scrooge, the proverbial miser in Dickens (1843) .

[87] I am rather surprised that Andrews (1984, p. 1113) deals with the redistribution effects only very generally, and that he treats the - from the juridical and parliamentary point of view very important and potentially "explosive" - cases of the "very high-income taxpayers" as cases of negligible importance only, by stating briefly that there were "other ways of effectively taxing such persons".

therefore, in the end a compensatory solution must be offered by the legislator, one which does tax the accumulation of wealth[88].

c) Finally, I fear that dispensing with the taxation of the capital accumulation cannot be realized in a revenue-neutral manner. The calculations, which have been done up to now, are questionable. Above all, the theoretical ideas as regards comprehensive tax bases are, in my view, not realizable. Much would be achieved already, if the "market incomes" were taxed without loopholes and tax privileges[89].

Anyhow, relinquishing State functions and tax revenue is easier said than done. The problem of the "Leviathan" can be solved with the greatest difficulties only, if one merely puts forward scientific (constitutional and economic) arguments. At the end of the day, social trends and mentalities determine the scope of the State functions and the efficiency of the public administration. He who wants to cut down the State functions and wants to strengthen the "self-responsibility" of the citizens, will be able to achieve this not so much by scientific analyses, but rather by political means, that is, by persuading the sceptics or those who hold different opinions.

The reality of today's Welfare State has its roots in social responsibilities which the State took on in the 19th century. The value system of the Welfare State, with the "dignity of man" at its centre, is obliged to get rid of poverty. There is no exculpation for rich industrial States, if there is poverty within their borders. Even in rich industrial States, this responsibility of the Welfare State has, however, remained unfulfilled in spite of the increase of the gross national products and of the increased proportion which the taxes take from the latter. In the meantime, new responsibilities have been added to the old ones. The ethics of the Welfare State extend now to the whole social life of man in a contemporary national community. Moreover, the philosopher Hans Jonas[90] has demonstrated that entirely new responsibilities have sprung up , namely those vis-a-vis the developing countries.

---

[88] The inheritance and gift tax is not suitable for this purpose, owing to the many possibilities of transferring capital abroad. Multinational enterprises, filmstars and sport personalities will not accept a rigorous inheritance and gift tax (i.e., will avoid it), hence, in practice, we are left only with the possibility of taxing accumulations of wealth *currently*.

[89] Cf. Deutscher Juristentag (1988), Tipke (1989b, p. 186), Raupach/Tipke/Uelner (1985), Tipke/Lang (1989, pp. 232 seqq., pp. 323 seqq.), and Lang (1985).

[90] Cf. Jonas (1979). Cf. also Jonas (1977).

In view of such new responsibilities, a reduction of the State functions and of the tax revenues does not seem to be a serious possibility. However, these new responsibilities might very well give grounds for carrying out a consumption-orientated reform of the tax system, since the productivity of the national economies will not be able to concentrate in future solely or mainly on furthering the consumption requirements of the private households. Rather, the national economies will have to cope with other tasks (e.g. the protection of the environment, help for third world countries, fighting the drug traffic, etc.), all of which cause huge costs, and, whilst the citizen satisfies his needs, he will have to learn to carry an appropriate share of these - to him so to speak "external" - costs. He will have to learn to think in terms of "socio-ethics"!

Tax Exemption of the Consumption Necessary for One's Existence

The more consumption might have to be taxed, the more it is imparative to exempt that part of the consumption which is necessary for a socio-cultural minimum standard.

In the Federal Republic a citizen has a constitutional claim to a socio-cultural subsistence minimum which is provided by the social security[91]. This claim must be transferred to the fiscal law: the State must not take from the citizen that which the State must give to the citizen, if the latter doesn't have it[92]. In this sense there exists a constitutionally connected "unity of values", a concord, between the social security law and the fiscal law. This "unity of values" (German "Werteinheit") means the following:

a) In the case of the direct taxes on income and on wealth, it must be ensured as a matter of principle that those parts of the income or the wealth, which are necessary for upkeeping a socio-cultural minimum standard, are exempt from tax. This means as regards to the income tax: from the total income (which should be defined, if at all possible, in a way that does not leave any gaps or loopholes), in other words, from the "gross income from whatever source derived" [I.R.C. Sec. 61 (a)], that part of the income should be exempted which is used in order to pay for the basic necessities of life

[91] On this see Bundesverfassungsgericht, BVerfGE 40, 121, 133; Bundesverfassungsgericht of 21.6.1977, BVerfGE 45, 187, 228.

[92] Cf. Birk (1983, p. 137), Kirchhof (1988), Lang (1985), Pezzer (1989, pp. 223 seqq.), Söhn (1988), p. 154).

(German "indisponibles Einkommen" = the income over which the taxpayer cannot freely dispose).

Since the beginning of the Seventies, the German fiscal jurisprudence has been occupied intensively with the question of how these unavoidable subsistence expenses should be taken into account in income taxation in a way that is appropriate to the realities of the situation[93].

This type of expenses cannot be taken into acount accurately by a so-called "zero-zone" (German "Nullzone") in the tax rate schedule. Hence, in all countries, the "zero-zones" in the income tax rate schedules do not make allowance for a realistic subsistence minimum. By starting out from this situation, the German fiscal jurisprudence works on a dualistic structure of the income tax base, namely on that which assesses in a first step the *complete* "market income", and then in a second step eliminates that part of income, which is used for the necessary consumption (German "indisponibles Einkommen")[94]. According to this theory, the "zero-zone" in the tax rate schedule should be replaced by a "basic tax allowance" ("Grundfreibetrag") in the tax *base*. The purpose of this "basic tax allowance" would be to take full account of the regular basic needs of the taxpayers which can be expressed in a lump sum[95].

Following the direction of this development in legal dogmatics in the field of the income tax base, the annual conference of German jurists (Deutscher Juristentag) decided in 1988 with a large majority, to recommend that only that particular part of the earnings should be subject to the income tax, which is effectively available (German "disponibel") to the taxpayer[96]. Hence, the unavoidable subsistence expenses ought to be tax-deductible from the gross income and should not merely be taken into account by means of an unrealistically low tax-exempt amount in the tax rate schedule[97]. By making this proposal, the German "Juristentag" wants the tax legislator to fix the "subsi-

---

93 On this see the references in Tipke/Lang (1989, pp. 210 seqq.), and Söhn (1988).

94 See the references in Tipke/Lang (1989, pp. 198 seqq.), and in Lang (1981/88, p. 34 seqq.).

95 On this see my proposal for a new law in Lang (1985, p. 99).

96 Resolution of the 57th "Deutscher Juristentag", in: Deutscher Juristentag (1988, p. N214).

97 However, the tax base of the income tax must not only comprise, i.e., take into account, the unavoidable subsistence expenses, but also any maintenance payments for defraying essential living expenses, as well as any other special transfer payments.

stence income" at such a level, that this tax-exempt amount is *above* the subsistence level fixed in the social security law[98]. At present, however, the subsistence level in the German tax law is still below that fixed in the German social security law[99]; hence, it would be already a great success of legislative politics, if the fiscal subsistence minimum were raised by the legislator to the social security level!

Social tranfers (i.e. the various types of social security payments) are financed by the solidarity imposed on the taxpayer in favour of the financially needy citizens. This solidarity is perverted, if the fiscal existence minimum is fixed below the social security level. As far as this contradiction is concerned, there exists a definite requirement to harmonize taxes and social transfer payments.

Within a tax based on the *consumed* income, the concept of "subsistence income" could certainly be realized more accurately than in the case of the existing "market income tax". In particular, the setting off (in other words, the "clearing") of social transfers could be carried out better in a consumption tax system[100] than in a system which taxes the market income.

b) The *in*direct taxation of the consumption by a value added tax and special consumption taxes, for instance on alcohol or tobacco, or the "eco-taxes" (see above), are, as is well-known, not capable of taking into account the personal circumstances of the one who, at the end of the day, bears the tax burden. Hence, the socialist criticism of the indirect taxes on consumption, as formulated in the 19th century, still holds. We must add, however, that the disproportionate tax burden imposed on the socially weaker sections of the society by the indirect consumption taxes is at present still compensated by the direct (and progressive) taxation of the incomes, - which is entirely in line with the aspirations of the socialists at the end of the 19th century!

In theory, the following two possibilities exist in order to tax-exempt the essential consumption:

---

98 CF. Deutscher Juristentag (1988, p. N215).

99 In the reform draft Lang (1985, pp. 70 seqq.), I have pointed out the following inconsistency. From an amount of wages, which is equal to the amount of social security that a family of four received in Darmstadt in 1985, DM 2,662 "Lohnsteuer" (income tax on earnings, similar to the Brit. Paye) was deducted at source.

100 Cf. Mitschke (1985).

aa) *(Exemption method)* Firstly, by not taxing the essential goods, i.e., those which are necessary for one's existence, from the start. For instance, sugar taxes or salt taxes are taxes on essentials, hence these taxes should not be charged.

The existing German turnover tax contains e.g. objective tax exemptions for the letting of land (§ 4, no. 12a UStG), for medical services (§ 4, no. 14 UStG) and for social services (§ 4, no. 15 seqq. UStG), but on foodstuffs half the standard turnover tax rate is being levied (§ 12, sec. 2, no. 1, annex no. 2 seqq. UStG). These types of tax reliefs are rudimentary approaches to a system designed to exempt the necessities of life.

The exemption method has, however, the drawback of being very inaccurate, since it also exempts consumption which is not absolutely essential for one's existence. This is because of the peculiarities of indirect taxation, which cannot take into account the *personal* circumstances.

bb) In contrast, the method of tax-exempting the consumption by means of *tax rebates* to the consumer allows an exact relief of the essential necessaries at the consumer stage. The value added tax is, from a technical point of view, particularly well suited to realize the tax exemption of the essential necessities, since the value added tax system allows to determine relatively exactly what the tax burden of the final consumer should be. The tax rebate method causes a lot of administrative work at first sight only. The tax rebates can be fixed in the form of lump-sums, based on the statistical average prices, and can be paid out within the framework of (i.e., as a deduction from) the tax demands. If a citizen does not pay taxes to the tax collector owing to the former being unemployed, then the tax rebates could be paid out by the Ministry of Social Security together with the various other social transfer payments (social security, unemployment benefit, housing benefit, child allowances, etc.). This is the moment where the proposal comes in, to unify social transfers and taxation administratively[101].

The problem of a socially unjust taxation will be intensified especially by the trend to indirect taxation for the purpose of protecting the environment. The postulate of a socially just, i.e., equitable, taxation in accordance with the ability to pay may collide with the "regulatory" justification of taxes. Such a collision is unlikely to occur in the case of goods which do not come within the range of "essential" consumption that has to be spared from taxation because of the tenets of the "social State". As regards the indi-

---

[101] Cf. Mitschke (1985).

rect taxes on tobacco and alcohol , the objection that they cause social injustice cannot be raised, in my opinion. However, taxes on alcohol should not be charged arbitrarily on some types of drinks only; rather, these excise duties should tax *all* alcoholic beverages in accordance with their alcohol level. The tax on hydrocarbon oils, on the other hand, falls also on essential consumption, like for instance in the case of fuel or in the case of car journeys in connection with a person's occupation. Here, "green" arguments for an increase of the tax on hydrocarbon oils collide with the claim of the citizen to have his livelihood and existence protected by the Welfare State.

Such collisions will have to be solved at the expense of the claim for social protection. All citizens of industrial States, also the needy citizens, must be made aware that their way of living gives rise to costs which they have not borne up to now. These "external" costs will move closer and closer into focus, not only from the point of view of economics, but also from that of social ethics and jurisprudence. Taxation can contribute to accustoming the consumer to a solidarity which encompasses not only the present, but also the future generations. In this respect, there is only an apparent, but not a real conflict between an indirect consumption taxation, designed to protect the environment, on the one hand, and a Welfare State or "social State", which is understood as being the font of social solidarity, on the other.

Assuming the Social Responsibility for the Family by Taking Maintenance Obligations Accurately Into Account When Assessing the Tax

Finally, the ability to pay tax is also reduced, if the taxpayer has to support a family. Therefore, there is probably international agreement that the family must be taken into account by the tax legislator in some way or another, be it by means of personal allowances, exemptions, personal deductions, or by a special tax rate schedule for married persons or for the whole family. So far, however, an international consensus on the "right" taxation of the family has not been reached.

The reason for this is in the main that the economic income theory has directed its attention mainly to the definition of income as a, if ever possible, comprehensive tax base, but has neglected the question of "unavailability" (German "Indisponibilität") of the income, one reason of this omission being that "income" and "consumption" are from the purely economic point of view different things. Therefore, among politicians[102] too, there is a widespread view that the deductions for maintenance expenses, like the child tax allowance were social incentives or subsidies and not necessary elements to indicate the ability to pay tax.

The German fiscal jurisprudence and, in line with it, the German "Juristentag"[103] has abandoned this view to qualify deductions for maintenance expenses as social subsidies. It has developed the above outlined dualistic structure of the income tax base, an approach which also takes into account any maintenance obligations that may exist[104]. From the point of view of economics, this approach is only comprehensible, if one recognizes in principle, that the taxable income should not be considered as being identical with the income as defined by the economists (i.e., the "economic" definition of income), but that the "fiscal" definition of income should also take into consideration those uses of the income which *reduce* the ability to pay. Hence, the "right" tax base should, looked at from an economic viewpoint, be a "mixed" value derived partly from income and partly from consumption. The decisive starting-point for the taking into account of maintenance obligations by the tax system is the responsibility which society has for the family as the nucleus of the co-existence of people within a State. Like so many other constitutions, the German Federal one, puts marriage and family under the special protection of the State (Art. 6, para.1, GG). Therefore, the Federal Constitutional Court deduces from the ability-to-pay principle the postulate that maintenance obligations must be taken into acount in a manner which meets the realities of the case[105]. Hence, maintenance obligations have not got the same quality as other uses of income, e.g. expenditure on leisure. Rather, they belong to the "unavailable" parts of the income[106].

Maintenance payments reduce the economic ability of the payer and increase that of the recipient of the payment. In consequence, maintenance obligations should be taken into account by allowing the payer to deduct legally enforceable maintenance

---

[102] See for instance, Matthäus-Maier (1988, p. 252).

[103] Cf. resolution of the 57th "Deutscher Juristentag", in: Deutscher Juristentag (1988).

[104] Cf. Tipke (1983, p. 39), Söhn (1988), Pezzer (1989).

[105] See Bundesverfassungsgericht, BVerfGE 61, 319; 66, 214; 67, 290; 68, 143, 152 seq. - See also the resolution passed by the "Deutscher Juristentag", in: Deutscher Juristentag (1988, p. N215).

[106] Cf. the references in Tipke/Lang (1989, pp. 215 seqq.).

payments from the total income (gross income) and by correspondingly charging them to tax in the hands of the recipient (so-called "family-real-splitting")[107].

To sum up: in the Federal Republic, legal institutions have been worked out which are in principle suitable as buildings blocks for an income tax based on the ability to consume.

III. Approaches to a Consumption-orientated Reform of the German Tax System

A. Necessity for a Multiple Tax System Based on Diverse Ability-to-pay Indicators

First of all it must be said that it appears impossible to obtain the tax revenue of the leading industrial States (in 1989 in the Federal Republic, for instance, over 500 billion DM) from a single type of tax. The classical principle of "maxim of convenience", which was formulated by Adam Smith and which is still indispensable in legislative policy, requires that the tax revenue spring from several types of tax with different ability-to-pay indicators. On account of this, the alternatives, namely a (personal) expenditure tax as a "single tax", or orientating the tax system exclusively on consumption, must be ruled out a priori.

B. Juridico-Institutional Framework

The juridico-institutional limitations do not allow the total reconstruction of the tax system. Rather, the democratic legislator can only fulfill current political reform requirements and can only reform the tax system in small steps ("increments"!) which, furthermore, extend to relatively few tax types only.

a) In connection with the above remarks, the following are typical current reform requirements:

Urgently in need of reform is the taxation of the personal incomes, and this is in respect of two points, namely (a) the tax bases, and (b) the tax rate schedules. The symptoms of tax resistance in particular make it necessary to reduce considerably the tax revenue from the taxation of these incomes.

Futhermore in need of reform is the taxation of the business enterprises. In the Federal Republic of Germany, this is being discussed particularly with an eye to the (-

107 On this in more detail: Lang (1981/88, pp. 545 seqq., pp. 650 seqq.).

as international comparisons show -) very high tax burden of the German enterprises[108]. From the economic[109] and the juridical point of view, the international differences of the tax burdens are, however, only one section of the need for reform. This need exists also as regards the entirely different tax burdens of the German business enterprises owing to different legal forms (see footnote 33), the special fiscal charges of the municipal trade tax, as well as the loopholes and tax privileges in the tax bases (see footnote 56).

Finally, from (a) the necessity to reform the taxation of the personal incomes and especially the taxation of business enterprises, and (b) the necessity to reduce the revenue from income taxation considerably, follows the *consumption-orientated* reform of the tax system, which I wish to outline in greater detail in the following pages.

As regards such a consumption-orientated reform of the tax system there are the following alternatives:

aa) The theme of the present discussion particularly in Heidelberg is the reconstruction of the direct income taxes from income taxes on the capital accumulation into taxes on the consumed income.

bb) Object of the contemporary political discussion is to shift the tax revenue from the income taxes to the indirect consumption taxes[110]. This procedure seems correct, provided the direct taxes on income are being substituted by indirect consumption taxes that are in principle suitable and destined to cover the general financial requirements of the State. Seen in this light, particularly the value added tax, being a general tax on consumption, appears suitable for compensating for the income tax: it is, admittedly, less "just", i.e., less equitable, than the income tax, because it cannot take into account personal circumstances, but it is, on the other hand, imperceptible and practicable, hence it triggers off relatively little tax resistance[111]. Last but not least, it is, like the income tax, capable of producing a high tax revenue, and its "equity deficit" can be reduced considerably by means of the above-mentioned tax rebates to the consumer.

---

[108] See for example: Fuest/Kroker (1989, p. 260).

[109] Cf. Schneider (1989).

[110] On this see: Bundesministerium für Finanzen (1989, pp. 81 seqq.), as well as Tipke/Lang (1989, p. 183).

[111] Cf. Tipke/Lang (1989, pp. 184/185).

cc) A further alternative is the substitution of the income tax by excise taxes. Here, attention is to be paid to the fact that excise taxes are based on the social harmfulness of the consumption. For this reason these taxes would be fully achieved if and when their tax revenue had fallen to zero! Consequently, their regulatory justification cannot really be reconciled with the fiscal purpose of these taxes, which is, to help cover the general financial requirements of the State.

However, the conventional excise taxes or duties, in particular the excise duties on tobacco, hydrocarbon oils and alcohol (which ought to be harmonized, according to the view of the EC-Commission)[112] do not serve exclusively for regulatory purposes, but also for meeting the general financial requirements[113]. Their tax revenue[114] is high, so that they fulfill their fiscal purpose very well. For this reason it is to accept, that the West German legislator has compensated income tax reductions by increasing excise taxes through the "Verbrauchsteueränderungsgesetz 1988"[115] (Excise Taxes Amendment Act 1988). However, my recommendation would be to remove the above-mentioned arbitrary selection of tax objects. Above all, the existing taxes on alcoholic drinks should be extended to a general alcohol tax which comprises *all* types of drinkable alcohol. Such a global alcohol tax would fulfill the criteria of equity, because it would no longer discriminate certain alcoholic products.

In contrast to excise taxes with a regulatory *and* a fiscal purpose, excise taxes with only a regulatory purpose, like the much discussed special "eco-taxes" for the protection of the environment, are unsuited as a permanent substitute for taxes with a fiscal purpose. One could employ them, if need be, in a transitional phase, for instance when one wants to prune the overall tax revenue of the much maligned "Leviathan". In that case, one could temporarily compensate the loss of tax revenue owing to income tax reductions by the introduction of special "eco-taxes" and to "slim down" the Tax State thanks to the effectiveness of these new taxes.

---

[112] Cf. proposed Directive of 7.3.1972, Amtsblatt EG Nr. C 43 of 29.4.1972, p. 23.

[113] Cf. for example Schmölders (1956, p. 635).

[114] In 1987 the tax revenues were as follows: tax on hydrocarbon oils DM 26,136 m, tobacco tax DM 14,507 m, taxes on spirits DM 4,072 m, and beer tax DM 1,280 m.

[115] Cf. Verbrauchsteueränderungsgesetz 1988 of 20.12.1988, Bundesgesetzblatt Teil I, p. 2270.

b) The juridico-institutional limitations force the democratic legislator to restrict the reform of the tax system to as few as possible tax types and to utilize at the same time the instability of the institutions of the fiscal law which shows up in the current reform requirements.

Bearing in mind these preconditions, it is highly likely that in the near future (i.e., in the next decade) the main emphasis of a reform of the German tax system will be on the *taxes on income and wealth*. The current reform discussion concerns above all the following taxes:

	tax revenue 1987:
(1) the income tax	DM 202,751 m
(2) the corporation tax	DM 27,302 m
(3) the trade tax (Gewerbesteuer)	DM 31,438 m
(4) the wealth tax (Vermögensteuer)	DM 5,422 m

In case of the above taxes, there is a particularly urgent requirement for a structural reform. When reforming them, one should start out from the assumption that the remaining taxes of the German tax system (total tax revenue of the latter in 1987: DM 481,209 m) will not be changed structurally as far as the fiscal facts (i.e., the tax objects) are concerned, and this goes especially for the indirect taxes on consumption (value added tax and excise duties on hydrocarbon oils, tobacco and alcoholic drinks) which are the subject of the EC-harmonization proposals.

A reduction of the present tax revenue from the above-mentioned four types of taxes means that other taxes must inevitably be increased. The candidates are mainly the value added tax and the excise taxes. The present consensus of opinion would appear to make an increase of the tax on hydrocarbon oils and of the motor vehicle tax (a direct consumption tax on the use of motor vehicles) politically especially acceptable (in order to "save the German forest"!). Within the framework of the EC tax harmonization one should also give thought to my suggestion to introduce global excise taxes. I suppose that it would be very difficult to push new types of "eco-taxes" with a single regulatory purpose through the legislative process, and this in spite of the present strong environmental awareness.

Another possibility might be the above-mentioned shifting of the municipal tax revenue from the trade tax to the real property tax. In the Federal Republic, a cutting down of the municipal tax revenues is neither desirable nor politically negotiable; for this reason, every reform proposal must at least see to it that the municipalities are, also after a reform, not worse off than before.

C. Substitution of the Income Tax, the Corporation Tax, the Trade Tax (Gewerbesteuer) and the Wealth Tax (Vermögensteuer) by a General Tax on the Consumed Income and a General Tax on the Saved Income

The above outlined approach, namely to reconstruct the existing dualism of income tax and corporation tax in a consumption-orientated manner, leads to the proposal of

a) a general tax on the *consumable income*, and

b) a general income tax on the *saved income* (including invested income and retained profits).

This proposal would prove to be particularly useful in the case of a reform of the *municipal taxes*. The existing trade tax (Gewerbesteuer) charges to tax merely a fraction of the "value added" (German "Wertschöpfung") in a municipality. For this reason the "Gewerbesteuer" corresponds only insufficiently to the municipal expenditure on its infrastructure. Therefore, it has been suggested by several study groups to replace the present trade tax by a general tax on the net product created by a business enterprise in a municipality (i.e., by a so-called "Wertschöpfungssteuer")[116].

The general tax on the saved income, proposed in this paper would charge this "added value" or "net product" comprehensively. As a result, the way could be opened for a fiscal participation of the municipalities in the "net product", if the "Gewerbesteuer" were be abolished in favour of a general tax on the saved income, and if the municipalities were also allocated a share of this new tax[117].

Together with the "Gewerbesteuer", the "Vermögensteuer" should also be abolished, in order to reduce the - from the economic point of view particularly undesirable

---

[116] Thus for example by the "Wissenschaftlicher Beirat beim Bundesministerium der Finanzen" (1982).

[117] Cf. also the "Frankfurter Institut für Wirtschaftspolitische Forschung" (1989).

- "tax burden on the substance"[118] which plagues the German tax system. In comparison with its relatively meagre tax revenue, the "Vermögensteuer" gives, furthermore, rise to disproportionately high, even excessive administrative expenses, since the existing tax requires periodic statements of assets and liabilities.

On the whole, the conclusion can be drawn that the income tax, corporation tax, trade tax and wealth tax should all be replaced by the two proposed new income taxes. Any tax revenue losses caused by this proposal could partly be recouped by formulating the tax bases of the two new income taxes in a way which leaves, if ever possible, no loopholes and contains no tax privileges (see footnote 56). Besides, tax revenue would have to be shifted to the real property tax (German "Grundsteuer") and to the indirect taxes on consumption. Admittedly, the real property tax, being another tax on the substance, is also open to criticism from the economic point of view, but this tax is, on the other hand, adequately justified by the benefit principle of taxation.[119]

D. Extension of the Corporation Tax to a General Tax on the Saved Income

1. Approach: Separate Taxation of Saved Income and Consumable Income

The technical task of the legislative is to realize the dualism of the tax on the consumable income and the tax on the saved income under the precondition that the existing legal institutions should, if at all possible, be left intact.

a) We have already indicated what could be the starting point: a corporation tax with a tax rate of zero would have the effect that the whole capital formation would be organized within the framework of corporations. However, this solution would, in the main , have two drawbacks:

aa) Firstly, the result would be that the other legal forms of economic activity would be pushed completely into the background. The principle of fiscal neutrality requires, however, neutrality as regards the legal form of enterprises. Hence, as already mentioned earlier on, an income tax on the saved income must be open to *all* forms of economic activity. For instance, the owner of a savings book should not be forced to start up a corporation and to endow this corporation with the minimum capital

---

[119] See, for instance, Nachtkamp (1989, p. 185).

[119] Cf. Lang (1989a, pp. 16 seqq.).

prescribed by law. For the purpose of taxation, it must, in principle, be sufficient, if he keeps a record of his savings and can prove it.

bb) A corporation tax with a tax rate of zero would exempt the capital accumulation completely from tax. The consequences of such a renunciation of incomes redistribution cannot yet be foreseen today.

b) For this reason, legal institutions must be offered to the legislator which leave him the freedom of action to tax the saved income as well as the consumable income, but with two *different* types of taxes. In that case, the legislator has the possibility of structuring the tax rate schedules differently. On this, we have stated already earlier on that by means of a progressive tax rate schedule the ability to *consume* is, in principle, to be charged to tax. Hence, it would be wrong anyway, to tax the saved income progressively. Therefore, it would be advisable not to tax the capital accumulation differently, depending on the legal form (as is the case at present), namely either progressively (partnerships!) or proportionally (corporations!), but *uniformly proportionally*.

Such a general taxation of the capital accumulation would cut out the whole saved income including the invested and retained income from the so-called consumption income tax. This way saved income and consumable income would be taxed separately; thereby it is not yet determined, whether the non-saved income is really consumed.

Now, this idea of separation raises two questions: (a) how to determine the saved income, and (b) how to treat the consumption which is paid for out of the savings?

aa) The, from a practical juridical point of view, irrefutable objection against the expenditure tax is the practical impossibility of establishing the private consumption of a taxpayer by means of book-keeping. Hence, all proposals which want to make the personal consumption expenditure and the consumption goods in their entirety the assessment basis of a tax are, in my opinion (which has been rather reinforced in Heidelberg), doomed to failure from the start.

I am convinced that, from a practical juridical angle, the only possibility is to cling to the tax base "market income", and to see to it that any loopholes and tax privileges (see footnote 56) can be removed. If the saved income is cut out of the comprehensive tax base "market income", then the result is the residual figure of the *consumable* income, i.e., the income that is not being saved, invested or retained by the taxpayer, but is available to his private "consumption fund" ("Konsumfonds"). Hence, the existing income tax can, in principle, be left the way it is, and this is so, because it takes on the characteristics of a progressive tax on the consumable income, if the saved income is extracted from the tax base of market income. By applying this procedure, the economic effect of the (personal) expenditure tax is achieved, without one having to record the personal consumption expenditure comprehensively.

bb) If and when the savings are consumed, at that moment the postulate of tax equality demands that this consumption has to be subjected to the progressive tax on the consumable income. That is why transfers from the still proportionally taxed savings must increase the tax base of the progressive tax on the consumable income. In this case the double taxation must be eliminated by crediting the proportional tax to the progressive tax on the consumable income. Here too, we can, in principle, take the existing dualism "income tax/imputable corporation tax" as a model.

2. The General Tax on the Saved Income as a "Business Tax" ("Betriebsteuer"); Technicalities

A first approach to a taxation which conforms to the principle of "legal form neutrality" is a business tax, in Germany discussed in very different variants under the term "Betriebsteuer"[120]. Compared with the corporation tax, the "Betriebsteuer" extends the special taxation of the retained business income considerably, but is on the other hand capable of improving the "legal form neutrality" and the "investment neutrality" only slightly. In the present discussion on the reform of the taxation of business enterprises, the concept of the "Betriebsteuer" is decidedly being rejected, since the "Betriebsteuer" gives privileged tax treatment to the business incomes, a fact which is incompatible with an equal taxation in accordance with the ability-to-pay-principle.

Hence, I have developed the concept of a global "business tax", which encompasses *the entire non-consumption-sphere* in the extent as outlined above, and which has therefore the characteristics of a *global* tax on the saved income[121].

The terminological *starting point* of my "business tax"-concept is an already existing term, namely the term "*Gewerbebetrieb*". This term is defined in paragraph 15, sec. 2/1 of the German Income Tax Law (EStG): (approx. translation) "An independent (self-employed) lasting (permanent) activity, which is carried out with the intention of

---

[120] On this see Elschen (1989), Lang (1989a, p. 3, pp. 8 seqq.).

[121] Cf. Lang (1989a, p. 3, pp. 8 seqq.).

making a profit, and which appears to be a participation in the general economics traffic (trade), is a 'Gewerbebetrieb', if the activity cannot be regarded as practising farming and forestry, nor as practising a profession or vocation, nor as any other independent (self-employed) work (activity)."

If one strips this legal definition of the ballast of legal demarcation, one is left with the core definition of the "Betrieb" as "the independent, permanent participation in the market, with the intention of making profits". In accordance with this core definition, the "business tax", as conceived by me, taxes the "market income" derived from *any* independent (self-employed) permanent (lasting) economic (business) activity including all trade and professional activities, farming and forestry, letting, leasing and all types of private investments, shares, saving books, insurances, etc. In the existing income tax law the incomes from all these activities are devided up into various schedules of income, and in consequence taxed entirely differently (see footnote 56). Hence, it is urgently required to subject the incomes from the above business activities to a uniform taxation.

According to my concept, the incomes from the above-mentioned business activities would, however, only be subject to the "business tax", where the minimum requirements as regards rendering of accounts are being fulfilled, so that a credit or imputation procedure can be applied.

3. Relationship between the Proportional "Business Tax" and the Progressive Tax on the Consumable Income

In those cases where the minimum accounting requirements are not fulfilled, the incomes from the above-mentioned business (trading) activities would be subject to the progressive tax on the consumable income. This legal consequence is based on the following relationship between the proportional "business tax" and the progressive tax on the consumable income.

a) My "business tax" concept starts out from the idea that the tax on the consumable income is the *main* tax, i.e., the tax which shall take the citizen's ability to pay into account once and for all. Hence, the function of the "business tax" is only that of a "pre-tax" (German "Vorsteuer") which shall tax the saved income up to the moment of the transfer of the income into the private "consumption fund". As long as the business or trading profits remain part and parcel of the business assets, they are to be charged to tax at the proportional business tax rate only. Profit distributions out of the trading assets are, on the other hand, withdrawals of money which are subject to the progressive consumption income tax; the previously paid "business tax" must, however, be credited to the consumption income tax[122].

b) The concept of a "business tax" with a low proportional tax rate in the form of a "pre-tax" to the progressive consumption income tax should be realized as follows:

aa) First of all, the tax base of the consumption income tax must be designed in such a way that the non-available income, and in particular maintenance obligations, will be taken fully into account. In this respect I refer to the above outlined findings of the German fiscal jurisprudence and of the resolutions of the German "Juristentag".

bb) If, according to this procedure, the taxable income takes the taxpayer's ability to consume into account in a realistic manner, then the tax rate schedule of the tax on the consumable income can start with a proportional tax rate which coincides with the tax rate of the "business tax". The progressive tax rate schedule could then start from an income level which is high enough to allow the taxpayer to save. For this purpose (i.e., in order to establish this level), statistical data on the savings behaviour could be consulted. The "business tax", as conceived by me, should therefore have the effect that, when saving takes place, the initial "tax step" of the proportional tax rate is prolonged in accordance with the size of the saved income, and hence that the progression only starts later on. This effect will not only induce the taxpayer to save, but also act as an incentive to meet the minimum accounting requirements laid down as regards the "business tax", in order to avoid that the saved income is subjected to the progressive tax charge.

cc) In practice, those taxpayers who are not going to consume the whole of their market income, will form a "participation enterprise", into which all payment-flows to enterprises, in which the taxpayer is a participant, are concentrated (see the diagram of the fields of application of the income tax and the "business tax" at the end of my paper). The purpose of such a "participation enterprise" is to delimit (as a matter of fiscal technique) the two "charging spheres", namely the progressive tax on the consumable income and the proportional "business tax", from each other.

The "participation enterprise" can be established informally, without legal complications or expense. In principle, it suffices to keep and render accounts from which can

---

122 Cf. Lang (1989a, p. 3, p. 14).

be seen which participations, stocks and shares, savings accounts, insurances, etc. are being administered by this enterprise. These accounts can be compiled with the assistance of a home computer. Keeping the accounts could also be a banking service.

As long as the "market income" is retained as part of the trading assets of corporations, partnerships, sole proprietorships , etc., or retained in the "participation enterprise" as any kind of private investments (capital assets, savings books, insurance policies, etc.), it will be charged to tax at the low, proportional tax rate of the "business tax". In the case of profits distributions from one enterprise to another, the credit method comes into play, with the consequence that the proportional tax burden is not doubled. In this way, the distributed amount of income will bear only a relatively small tax burden. On the other hand, drawings and distributions from the "participation enterprise" into the "consumption fund" will be subject to the full rigour of the progressive tax on the consumable income, bearing in mind, however, that the "business tax" will be credited to the latter.

dd) The payment-flows between the business tax sphere/"participation enterprise" on the one hand and the progressive consumption income sphere on the other can, in principle, be defined as follows:

Payments into the "participation enterprise" are to be qualified as deposits (German "Einlagen"). In the case of these deposits, two legal consequences can be distinguished:

- If the deposit is made out of income which is subject to the tax on the consumable income, then that particular amount of income has to be exempted from the tax on consumable income and to be added to the profit that is subject to the "business tax". Main example is the employee who wants to save a part of his earnings. The part of the salary which is, e.g. paid into a savings book, can be exempted from the tax on the consumable income and then forms part of the profit that is taxable under the "business tax". This way, the employee also participates in the proportional "business tax". Hence he can opt for the "business tax", but, unless he excercises this option, he is not subject to it. This type of flexible solution for employees seems to be appropriate and fair.
- If, however, the deposit is not made out of income, but out of already taxed assets, then it is to be treated as "profits-neutral" (German "erfolgsneutral").

Payments out of the "participation enterprise" are to be treated analogously to the procedure for payments into it. This means, that withdrawals or distributions out of the "participation enterprise" are subject to the tax on consumable income. On the other hand repayments of deposits have to be treated as "profits-neutral".

E. On the Legislative Realization of the Concept

I sincerely believe that the effect of the expenditure tax can only be achieved step by step, if the saving is recorded in the books and if it is taxed separately by a "business tax" in the form of a non-consumption tax. It is, of course, a matter of the legislative decision-competence, in how far the legislator will in future practice redistribution policy, or in how far he wishes to benefit from the advantages of a consumption taxation.

In the Federal Republic, many employees have no contact with the tax office, since the income tax is deducted from the salaries and paid to the fiscal authorities by the employer. This very practical procedure should be retained by all means. If no "business tax"-declaration is filed and no proof of any saving from the earnings can be furnished, then it can safely be assumed that the income from employment will be put entirely into the private "consumption fund", i.e., used up for consumptive purposes.

Finally, the "business tax"-concept introduced in this paper allows all systems of accounting. Both, Public Finance and Management Science[123], are called to develop a system of accounting which displays best the liquidity that is required for the tax payment. The discussions which are currently taking place in this connection hinge mainly on the question of a taxation based on the cash flow[124].

IV. Summary

The present state of the taxation of the income from business enterprises justifies the conclusion that the tax systems have developed in the wrong direction and that only a fundamental change of direction can initiate the recovery of them.

The present taxation of the income from business enterprises, and the principles involved, in particular the ability-to-pay principle, are marked by the redistribution ideology of the 19th century. The phenomena of the resistance against high tax burdens

[123] Cf. Schneider (1978, p. 27).

[124] On this see Wagner (1990), and Bradford (1990).

have hollowed out the equity value of the income tax. Owing to this, there is an urgent requirement for the tax system to be more consumption-orientated. Moreover, the economic arguments in favour of a personal expenditure tax point also in the direction of a consumption-orientated tax system.

The main problem, with which we are confronted first of all, is the high stability of legal institutions. Hence, tax systems can only be changed in small steps ("increments"). However, it is exactly the legislation of the small steps ("incrementalism") that needs a concept which indicates the direction, since without signposts, each step can be a step backwards. In that case, the tax legislator is aimlessly operating forward-reverse legislation. In this respect the economic theories of optimal (income) taxation do have a signpost function.

The jurist, who is engaged in work in the field of legislative policy, must take note of these theories and must give thought to the question of which institutions of the existing law are suitable in order to realize the tax effects which have been recognized by the science of economics as being the right ones. At the same time it is imperative for the practical legislative policy to use conceptual systems with which everybody is familiar, so that the effort of learning new concepts and terms may be minimized.

Furthermore, tax reforms can only be realized, if they are basically in agreement with the constitutionally and socially fixed conditions of equality, liberty and solidarity. In the case of a consumption-orientated reform of the tax system, the postulate of redistribution must, above all, be discussed anew. At present, it would appear that it is impossible from a legislative policy point of view to relinquish the taxation of the capital accumulation completely. However, the economic arguments for the personal expenditure tax encourage the jurist, who works in the field of legislative policy, to work out those legal institutions which will enable the legislator to move step by step towards a time when it will be possible to do without the taxation of the capital accumulation. Here, the legislator needs institutional freedom of action. He must also have the possibility of turning back, if the path to a consumption-orientated tax system should prove to be impassable.

As for the German tax system, I recommend to replace the income tax, the corporation tax, the trade tax and the wealth tax by a dual system of a proportional tax on the saved income (in form of a "business tax") and a progressive tax on the consumable income. The "business tax" encompasses the whole saved income including the invested income and retained profits. The tax on the consumable income encompasses the whole market income without the saved income; thereby only the available income is subject to the progressive tax rate schedule. In order to be able to delimitate the unavailable income, the German fiscal jurisprudence has already developed legal institutions which have been approved in 1988 by the German "Juristentag" by a large majority.

Diagram: Field of application income tax/business tax

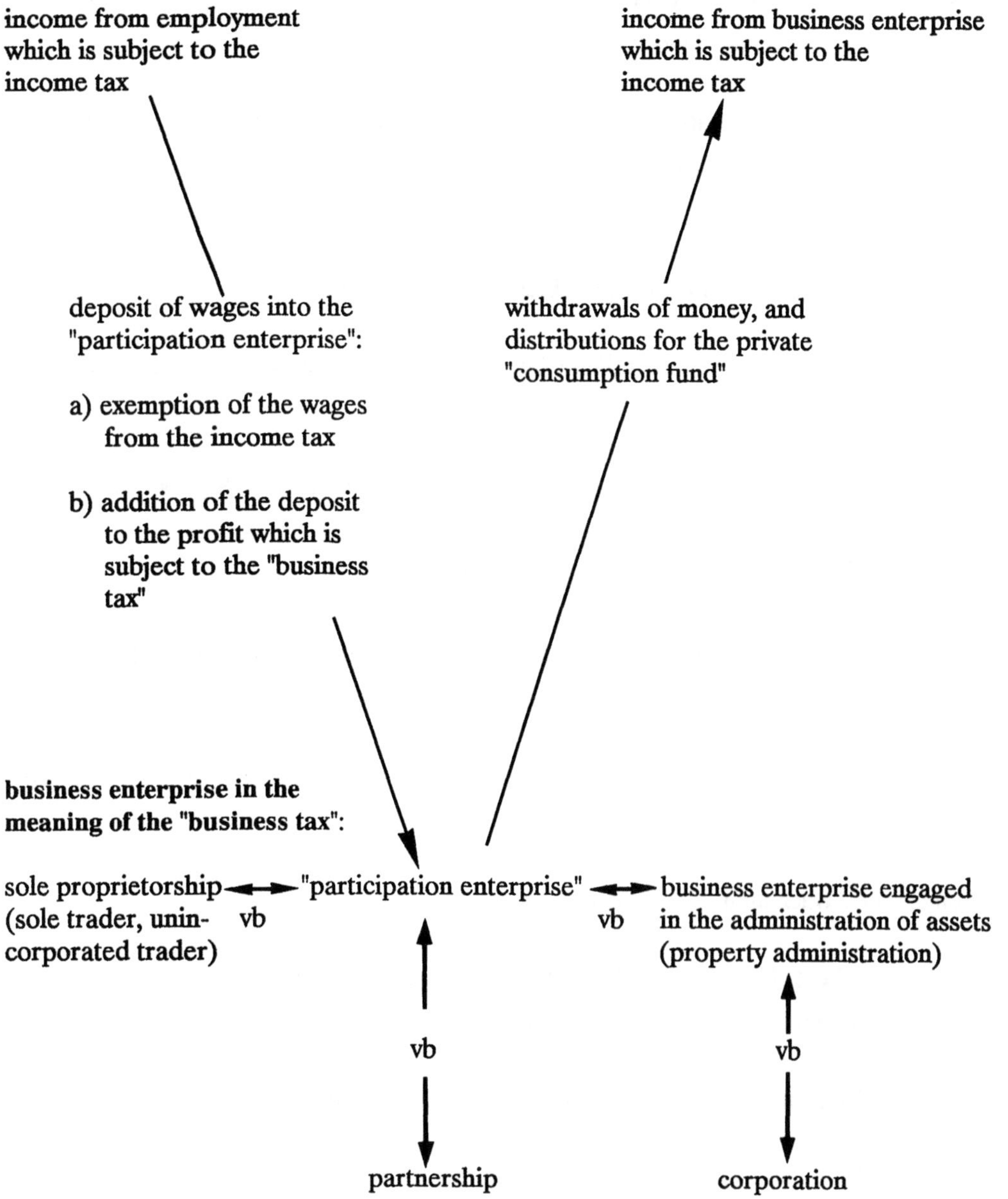

vb = asset relationships in the field of application of the "business tax" which is not affected by the progressive income tax charge

References

Andrews, W.D. (1974), A Consumption-Type or Cash Flow Personal Income Tax, Harvard Law Review 87, pp. 1113 seqq.

Birk, D. (1983), Das Leistungsfähigkeitsprinzip als Maßstab der Steuernormen, Ein Beitrag zu den Grundfragen des Verhältnisses Steuerrecht und Verfassungsrecht, Köln.

Birk, D. (1988), Steuerrecht I, Allgemeines Steuerrecht, München.

Birk, D. (1990), Verfassungsrechtliche Grenzen der Konsumbesteuerung, in: M. Rose (ed.) (1990), op. cit..

Böckenförde, E.-W. (1987), Demokratische Willensbildung und Repräsentation, in: J.Isensee/P.Kirchhof (eds.) (1987), Handbuch des Staatsrechts der Bundesrepublik Deutschland, vol. II., pp. 29-48, Heidelberg.

Bradford, D.F. (1984), Blueprints for Basic Tax Reform, U.S.Treasury Tax Policy Staff, Arlington.

Bradford, D.F. (1990), Die X-Steuer: Weg zur Steuervereinfachung, in: M. Rose (ed.) (1990), op. cit..

Brennan, G. / Buchanan, J.M. (1980), The Power to Tax, New York.

Buchanan, J.M. (1967), Public Finance in Democratic Process, Fiscal Institutions and Individual Choice, North Carolina.

Bundesministerium für Finanzen (ed.) (1989), Finanzbericht 1989, Bonn.

Deutscher Juristentag (1925), Verhandlungen des 33. Deutschen Juristentages, Berlin.

Deutscher Juristentag (1980), Verhandlungen des 53. Deutschen Juristentages, München.

Deutscher Juristentag (1988), Verhandlungen des 57. Deutschen Juristentages, München.

Dickens, Charles (1843), A Christmas Carol, London.

Dickertmann, D. (1988), Maßnahmen für den Umweltschutz im Rahmen des bestehenden Steuersystems, in: K. Schmidt (ed.) (1988), Öffentliche Finanzen und Umweltpolitik I, pp. 91-227, Berlin.

Elschen, R. (1989), Institutionale oder personale Besteuerung von Unternehmensgewinnen?, Hamburg.

Engels, F. (1846), Das Fest der Nationen in London, Rheinische Jahrbücher zur gesellschaftlichen Reform, vol. II, pp. 1-19.

Fisher, I. / Fisher, H. (1942), Constructive Income Taxation, A Proposal for Reform, New York, London.

Frankfurter Institut für Wirtschaftspolitische Forschung (1989), Reform der Unternehmensbesteuerung, Bad Homburg.

Fuest, W. / Kroker, R. (1989), Unternehmensbesteuerung im internationalen Vergleich, Kritische Anmerkungen zum DIW-Gutachten, Steuer und Wirtschaft 1989, pp. 260-266.

Großfeld, B. (1981), Die Einkommensteuer, Geschichtliche Grundlage und rechtsvergleichender Ansatz, Tübingen.

Groves, H.M. (1974), Tax Philosophers, Wisconsin.

Gutachten der Steuerreformkommission 1971, Schriftenreihe des Bundesministeriums der Finanzen (BMF), Heft 17, Bonn.

Haig, R.M. (1921), The Concept of Income, in: R.M. Haig (ed.) (1921), The Federal Income Tax, New York.

Hardorp, B. (1990), Konsumsteuer und Gesellschaft - Zum erforderlichen steuersystematischen Bewußtseinswandel, in: M. Rose (ed.) (1990), op. cit..

Hayek, F.A. von (1960), The Constitution of Liberty, Chicago.

Hayek, F.A. von (1979), Law, Legislation and Liberty, vol. III: The Political Order of a Free People, London.

Heilmann, M. (1975), Die Umsatzsteuerreform in der Bundesrepublik Deutschland, Die Entstehung des Umsatzsteuergesetzes von 1967, Frankfurt.

Herzog, R. (1988), Der Weg zum Bundesverfassungsgericht, Das Verhältnis zwischen Verfassungsgerichtsbarkeit und Steuergerichtsbarkeit, Deutsche Steuer-Zeitung 1988, pp. 287-291.

Hobbes, Th. (1651), Leviathan or, the Matter, Forme and Power of a Common-wealth Ecclesiasticall and Civil, London.

Jonas, H. (1977), The Concept of Responsibility: An Inquiry into the Foundations of an Ethics for Our Age, in: H.T. Engelhardt / D. Callahan (eds.) (1977), Knowledge, Value and Belief, New York.

Jonas, H. (1979), Das Prinzip Verantwortung, Versuch einer Ethik für die technologische Zivilisation, Frankfurt.

Kaldor, N. (1965), An Expenditure Tax, London.

Kay, J.A. / King, M.A. (1986), The British Tax System, Oxford.

Kirchhof, P. (1981), Besteuerung und Eigentum, in: Veröffentlichungen der Vereinigung der Deutschen Staatsrechtslehrer, vol. 39.

Kirchhof, P. (1988), Empfiehlt es sich das Einkommensteuerrecht zur Beseitigung von Ungleichbehandlungen und zur Vereinfachung neu zu ordnen?, Gutachten, in: Verhandlungen des 57. Deutschen Juristentages Mainz 1988, vol. I, Gutachten F, München.

La Fontaine, Jean de (1901), La cigale et la fourmi, in: L.Sanard (ed.) (1901), Fables de La Fontaine, Paris.

Lang, J. (1981/88), Die Bemessungsgrundlage der Einkommensteuer, Köln.

Lang, J. (1985), Reformentwurf zu Grundvorschriften des Einkommensteuergesetzes, Köln.

Lang, J. (1987), Die einfache und gerechte Einkommensteuer, Ziele, Chancen und Aufgaben einer Fundamentalreform, Köln.

Lang, J. (1989a), Reform der Unternehmensbesteuerung, Steuer und Wirtschaft 1989, pp. 3-17.

Lang, J. (1989b), Verantwortung der Rechtswissenschaft für das Steuerrecht, Steuer und Wirtschaft 1989, pp. 201-211.

Mann, H. (1987), Theorie und Politik der Steuerreform in der Demokratie, Frankfurt.

Matthäus-Maier, I. (1988), Für einen gerechten und einfachen Familienlastenausgleich, Zeitschrift für Rechtspolitik, pp. 252-258.

McNulty, J.K. (1989), The Basic Structure and Characteristics of the U.S. Income Tax and Future Reform Possibilities. Publ. as a German translation in: Steuer und Wirtschaft 1989, pp. 120-137.

Meade, J.E. (1978), The Structure and Reform of Direct Taxation, London.

Mesmer, B. (1976), Steuerreform als Übergangsmaßnahme, Die Rezeption der Forderung nach progressiver Besteuerung in den frühsozialistischen Programmen, Berne.

Mitschke, J. (1985), Steuer- und Transferordnung aus einem Guß, Entwurf einer Neugestaltung der direkten Steuern und Sozialtransfers in der Bundesrepublik Deutschland, Baden-Baden.

Nachtkamp, H.H. (1986), Allokationswirkungen der Bestandsbesteuerung, Finanzarchiv 44, pp. 185-223.

Pausch, A. (1964), Johannes von Miquel, Sein Leben und Werk, Stuttgart.

Pechmann, J.A. (1980), What Should Be Taxed: Income or Expenditure? Washington, D.C.: Brookings Institution.

Pezzer, H.-J. (1989), Familienbesteuerung und Grundgesetz, Steuer und Wirtschaft 1989, pp. 219-226.

Raupach, A. (1985), Der Niedergang des deutschen Einkommensteuerrechts, Möglichkeiten der Neubesinnung, in: A. Raupach / K. Tipke / A. Uelner (eds.) (1985), Niedergang oder Neuordnung des deutschen Einkommensteuerrechts?, pp. 15-132, Köln.

Raupach, A. / Tipke, K. / Uelner, A. (eds.) (1985), Niedergang oder Neuordnung des deutschen Einkommensteuerrechts?, Köln.

Report of the Canadian Royal Commission of Taxation (1967), vol.4, pp. 3 seqq., Appendix H, pp. 661 seqq.

Rose, M. (1989), Argumente zu einer "konsumorientierten Neuordnung des Steuersystems", Steuer und Wirtschaft 1989, pp.191-193.

Rose, M. (ed.) (1990), Konsumorientierte Neuordnung des Steuersystems, Berlin, Heidelberg.

Sabine, B.E.V. (1966), A History of Income Tax, London.

Schanz, G.von (1896), Der Einkommensbegriff und die Einkommensteuergesetze, Finanzarchiv 13, pp. 1-87.

Schmidt, K. (1960), Die Steuerprogression, Tübingen.

Schmölders, G. (1956), Das Verbrauch- und Aufwandsteuersystem, in: W. Gerloff / F. Neumark (eds.), Handbuch der Finanzwissenschaft, vol. II, pp. 635-720, Tübingen.

Schneider, D. (1978), Steuerbilanzen, Rechnungslegung als Messung steuerlicher Leistungsfähigkeit, Wiesbaden.

Schneider, D. (1989), Reform der Unternehmensbesteuerung aus betriebswirtschaftlicher Sicht, Steuer und Wirtschaft 1989, pp. 328-339.

Simons, H.C. (1938), Personal Income Taxation, Chicago.

Söhn, H. (1988), Verfassungsrechtliche Aspekte der Besteuerung nach der subjektiven Leistungsfähigkeit im Einkommensteuerrecht: Zum persönlichen Existenzminimum, Finanzarchiv 46, pp. 154-171.

The decisions of the Federal Constitutional Court of West Germany (Bundesverfassungsgericht - BVerfG -), in: Entscheidungen des Bundesverfassungsgerichts (BVerfGE).

Tipke, K. (1973), Steuerrecht, Ein systematischer Grundriß, Köln.

Tipke, K. (1981), Steuergerechtigkeit in Theorie und Praxis, Vom politischen Schlagwort zum Rechtsbegriff und zur praktischen Anwendung, Köln.

Tipke, K. (1983), Neuordnung der Familienbesteuerung, Steuerberater-Kongress-Report 1983, pp. 39-89, München.

Tipke, K. (1986), Einkommensteuer-Fundamentalreform, Notwendigkeit und Möglichkeiten, Zum Vorbild des amerikanischen Reformverfahrens, Steuer und Wirtschaft 1986, pp. 150-169.

Tipke, K. (1989a), Lehren aus der Steuerreform 1990, Steuer und Wirtschaft 1989, pp. 291-310.

Tipke, K. (1989b), Über Steuervergünstigungen - Abbautheoretische Überlegungen, Finanz-Rundschau 1989, pp. 186-191.

Tipke, K. / Lang, J. (1989), Steuerrecht, Ein systematischer Grundriß, Köln.

U.S. Treasury Department (1985), The President's Tax Proposals for Fairness, Growth and Simplicity, Washington, D.C., also publ. in Steuer und Wirtschaft 1985, pp. 264-267.

Vogel, K. (1987), Der Finanz- und Steuerstaat, in: J. Isensee / P. Kirchhof (eds.) (1987), Handbuch des Staatsrechts der Bundesrepublik Deutschland, vol. I, pp. 1151-1186, Heidelberg.

Vogel,K. (1988), The Justification for Taxation: A forgotten question, American Journal of Jurisprudence 33, pp. 19-59.

Wagner, Franz W. (1990), Der Einfluß einer cash flow-Steuer auf Finanzierung und Rechnungslegung, in: M. Rose (ed.) (1990), op. cit..

Walker, F.A. (1887), Political Economy, New York.

Walz, W.R. (1980), Empfiehlt sich eine rechtsformunabhängige Besteuerung der Unternehmen?, Gutachten, in: Verhandlungen des 53. Deutschen Juristentages Berlin 1980, vol. I, Gutachten F, München 1980.

Weisflog, W.E. (1985), Amerikanische Steuerreform, Steuer und Wirtschaft 1985, pp. 160-171, pp. 247-264.

Wissenschaftlicher Beirat beim Bundesministerium der Finanzen (1982), Gutachten zur Reform der Gemeindesteuern in der Bundesrepublik Deutschland, Schriftenreihe des Bundesministeriums der Finanzen, Heft 31, Bonn.

PART FIVE

Administrative Aspects of a Consumption-based Tax System

Charles E. McLure, Jr. and George R. Zodrow

Administrative Advantages of the Individual Tax Prepayment Approach to the Direct Taxation of Consumption

I. Introduction

One of the most important fiscal developments of the past twenty years has been the worldwide growth in reliance on the value-added tax (VAT). Following its adoption by the European Common Market in the 1960s, the VAT has become the "workhorse" of fiscal systems throughout the world. At least forty countries now levy VATs, and many others use other forms of broad-based general sales taxes, as well as more selective taxes on consumption.[1]

The tantalizing question for the 1990s is whether the next sea change in tax policy will involve a worldwide shift from income taxation toward direct taxes on consumption. No country currently levies such a tax, although both India and Ceylon (now Sri Lanka) experimented briefly with such a tax during the 1950s [Eigner (1959), Goode (1960)]. Comprehensive studies of consumption-based direct taxation have been prepared in Sweden [Lodin (1974)], the United Kingdom [Institute for Fiscal Studies (1978) - the "Meade Committee Report"], the United States [U.S. Department of the Treasury (1977)], Canada [Economic Council of Canada (1987)], and Colombia [McLure, Mutti, Thuronyi and Zodrow (1988)]. Stimulated by the work of Kaldor (1955), these reports draw, *inter alia*, on the work of Andrews (1974), Mieszkowski (1977, 1980), Hall and Rabushka (1983, 1985), Aaron and Galper (1985), and Bradford (1986). Proposals for

---

[1] See McLure (1987a), Shoup (forthcoming), and Tait (forthcoming).

expensing (first-year write-off) of capital goods, an important component of a consumption-based tax, have been made for such diverse countries as Malawi and Mexico.

The earliest arguments for a consumption-based tax were couched in philosophical terms. Thus it was argued that tax should be based on what one "takes out of the pot" (consumption), rather than what one "puts into it" (income). These arguments were never fully persuasive, and latter-day advocates of consumption taxes have relied more heavily on economic arguments to support their case.

Representatives of business have been among the strongest advocates of expensing, commonly arguing that more generous tax treatment of investment encourages capital formation and stimulates economic growth. However, such advocacy generally has not been in the context of a conceptually consistent tax on consumption; in particular, business representatives have not suggested that expensing be accompanied by the changes in the treatment of debt and interest described in Section II below. A wide variety of academic economists have also expressed support for direct taxes based on consumption, and quite a few researchers, including those cited above, have developed conceptually consistent approaches to the direct taxation of consumption in recent years.

Early economic discussions of consumption-based direct taxes have commonly focused on the relative advantages of taxes based on income and on consumption, in terms of the criteria of economic efficiency and equity. The earliest studies of the relative efficiency properties of the two taxes stressed two factors. On the one hand, a proportional tax on consumption does not discriminate against saving for future consumption, while the taxation of interest income under a proportional income tax raises the price of future consumption and thus distorts the individual present-future consumption choice. On the other hand, a consumption tax is likely to involve greater disincentives for work effort, since a higher tax rate is generally required under a consumption tax than under an income tax. Although the efficiency costs of the consumption tax due to distortions in the labor-leisure choice may be sufficiently large to offset the benefits of neutrality toward the saving-present consumption choice, such an outcome appears to be unlikely under most specifications of the economic models used in these analyses.[2]

In terms of the criterion of horizontal equity, advocates of a tax on consumption stress that a taxpayer with a given present value of lifetime earnings will pay the same amount of tax, in present value terms, under a proportional consumption tax regardless of when during life income is earned and when it is consumed. In contrast, under the income tax, the tax burden is greater in present value terms the earlier income is earned and the later it is consumed.[3] Proponents of the income tax counter that this advantage of a consumption-based tax is either irrelevant (because annual income is a better indicator of ability to pay than is the present value of lifetime earnings) or much less important than the defects of consumption taxes from the point of view of vertical equity. On the latter score, income tax advocates argue that the consumption tax is quite inferior, because it would be less progressive than the income tax. Consumption tax supporters respond that any degree of progressivity can be achieved by changing the rate structure. In addition, many argue that vertical equity should be measured with respect to an individual's "lifetime endowment" - the present value of lifetime earnings plus all gifts and inheritances received[4] - rather than on annual income or lifetime consumption; in this case, a consumption-based tax regime may not actually be substantially less progressive than an income tax, even with a given rate schedule.

Many recent discussions of the choice between income and consumption taxes have focused on the simplicity advantages of the consumption-based tax. This is perhaps no more clearly seen than in a recent report to the government of Colombia [McLure, Mutti, Thuronyi and Zodrow (1988)], in which the term "Simplified Alternative Tax" (SAT) was chosen to highlight these simplicity advantages. Prepared for a developing country in which administrative capabilities are extremely scarce, that report (p. 361) stressed that "the Simplified Alternative Tax is superior to the income tax in terms of the simplicity criterion in most areas."

---

[2] A wide variety of recent studies have both amplified and challenged this basic result on the relative superiority of a consumption tax in terms of the efficiency criterion. See Zodrow (forthcoming) and Boadway (in this volume) for surveys.

[3] See Zodrow (forthcoming) for an evaluation of the relative advantages of income and consumption taxes in terms of the criterion of horizontal equity within the context of a multi-period life-cycle model of individual behavior.

[4] This treatment of gifts and bequests is discussed in the appendix.

This paper, which draws heavily on Zodrow and McLure (1988), examines the relative administrative advantages of the income tax and two forms of consumption-based direct taxation.[5] It focuses on two prototypical schemes for taxing consumption. The first combines a tax on individual cash flow with a business tax on real and financial cash flows (the Meade Committee R+F base) and is termed the "ICF/RF" consumption tax; it most closely follows the "qualified accounts" approach described in *Blueprints for Basic Tax Reform* [U.S. Department of the Treasury (1977)] and in Aaron and Galper (1985). The second combines a tax base requiring individual tax "prepayment" with a business tax on real cash flows (the Meade Committee R base) and is termed the "ITP/R" consumption tax; it is most closely related to the flat tax of Hall and Rabushka (1983, 1985), the X-tax of Bradford (1986), and the SAT cited above. (These terms are defined further in the next section.) These two alternatives capture most of the major features of the various consumption tax plans that have been proposed.[6,7]

The paper is organized as follows. A description of the characteristics of income taxation and the two types of consumption-based direct taxes in Section II is followed by comparisons of the administrative features of consumption and income taxes in Section III. Section IV considers the advantages of the ITP/R consumption tax relative to the ICF/RF version, and problems of the ITP/R approach are discussed in Section V. Brief concluding remarks are presented in Section VI.

II. Main Features of Income and Consumption Taxes

Before examining the relative administrative advantages of the income tax and the ITP/R and the ICF/RF versions of the consumption tax, it will be useful to have a brief

---

[5] See also Zodrow (1987).

[6] The S base examined by the Meade Commission is the major exception; it has not received a great deal of attention in the literature and is not discussed in this paper.

[7] It has sometimes been suggested that it might be possible to allow both ICF and ITP treatment of saving to co-exist in the same tax system; see, for example, U.S. Department of the Treasury (1977). However, such an approach would create opportunities for abuse that could not readily be prevented [see Graetz (1979)].

description of the most important features of each prototypical tax. Additional details and some illustrative numerical examples are provided in the appendix.

A. The Income Tax

Under the income tax, the principal amount of a loan has no tax consequences for either the borrower or lender. Individuals pay tax on interest receipts, as well as on labor income. Business interest expense is allowed as a deduction for both individuals and corporations. Though many countries also allow deductions for interest on home mortgages, such treatment is not consistent with a conceptually sound income tax unless the imputed rental income from owner-occupied housing is subject to tax. The same argument applies to other consumer interest. Even countries that attempt to tax imputed income from owner-occupied housing do not extent that principle to other consumer durables.

Some countries employ the "classical system", under which income attributable to equity-financed investments of corporations is taxed both under the corporate income tax and the individual income tax, when distributed as dividends to shareholders. By comparison, some countries provide relief from such double taxation of dividends, either by allowing shareholders a tax credit for corporate income tax attributable to their portion of distributed corporate income or by applying a different tax rate to corporate profits that are retained rather than distributed or allowing corporations a deduction for dividends paid; no country attempts complete integration of the corporate and individual income taxes, which would require the attribution of undistributed corporate profits to shareholders for tax purposes.[8]

The gain on capital assets - the difference between the adjusted basis (commonly acquisition cost less depreciation, perhaps adjusted for inflation) and the amount realized from the sale of an asset - is subject to tax under an income tax. In principle, capital gains should be taxed on an accrual basis, but for administrative and other reasons, such gains are taxed only upon realization. Capital gains are often taxed preferentially, and sometimes are entirely exempt from taxation; such provisions are commonly justified as a means of offsetting inflation, mitigating the effects of progressive taxation (when the realization of a relatively large amount of gains

---

[8] See McLure (1979) for a more complete discussion of integrating the corporate and personal income taxes.

artificially increases annual income), preventing the "locking-in" of unrealized gains, or stimulating capital formation.

Under a conceptually correct income tax, depreciation allowances reflect economic depreciation; similar statements apply to related items such as depletion of natural resources and amortization of the expense of creating intangible assets. The cost of goods sold by businesses is determined by appropriate inventory accounting.

If the measurement of real income is not to be distorted by the effects of inflation, it is necessary to provide inflation adjustment of depreciation allowances, the cost of goods sold from inventory, interest income and expense, and the basis of capital assets employed in calculating capital gains. These adjustments are conceptually distinct from the necessity of indexing amounts stated in nominal terms (such as personal exemptions and bracket limits in the rate schedule) which arise under any of the three alternatives considered here. Accelerated depreciation, last-in, first-out (LIFO) inventory accounting, and preferential treatment of capital gains are commonly used as ad hoc substitutes for explicit inflation adjustment. Ad hoc adjustments for interest income and expense are substantially less common. Only in highly sophisticated systems, such as the "integrated" approach used in Chile, is inflation adjustment provided in a systematic and conceptually sound manner.[9]

Consistent application of income tax principles to fringe benefits would have the following characteristics. First, contributions to retirement plans would be made from after-tax income. Second, the income earned on assets in retirement accounts would be taxed on an accrual basis. Third, retirement benefits could be withdrawn without tax consequences. In actual practice, taxation of such benefits is commonly more generous, in that deductions may be allowed for contributions to retirement plans and income may be allowed to accumulate tax free, with both principal and interest being taxed only upon withdrawal; this is essentially the treatment required under the ICF/RF version of the consumption tax described below. An intermediate approach is to allow tax-free accumulation of income, but to allow no deductions for contributions; in this case, a distinction must be made between tax-free return of contributions and taxable distribution of income at retirement.

---

[9] See McLure, Mutti, Thuronyi and Zodrow (1988, chapter 7) for a detailed discussion of inflation adjustment, including a description of the Chilean approach.

Some income tax advocates believe that gifts and inheritances received should be included in the recipient's tax base, but that no deduction should be allowed for the making of gifts and bequests. Others would find the double taxation of gifts and bequests implied by this definition of taxable income over-reaching; they would recommend either only inclusion in the tax base of the recipient, or perhaps taxation only to the donor as a proxy for taxation of the recipient.

B. The ICF/RF Consumption Tax

Under the ICF/RF version of the consumption tax, individuals are taxed on the basis of their net cash flow. Thus they are allowed a deduction for saving in "qualified accounts" and pay tax on the return of principal upon disposition of assets in qualified accounts, as well as on the withdrawal of earnings on assets in such accounts. Similarly, the proceeds of loans are included in the tax base, and both repayment of principal and interest expense are deductible on a cash flow basis.

Gifts and inheritances received are included in the tax base of the recipient. Deductions are not allowed for gifts or bequests transferred to other individuals if one accepts the lifetime endowment view of tax equity, while deductions for such transfers are allowed if one accepts the "dynastic" view of equity under which such transfers are taxed only if actually used for consumption. (Alternatively, under the dynastic approach, gifts and bequests can be taxed only to the donor by disallowing a deduction for such transfers and excluding them from the base of the recipient; in this case, taxation of the donor serves as a proxy for taxation of the recipient.)

Under the RF base, the business tax accords cash flow treatment to both real and certain financial assets. That is, there is immediate expensing of all business-related purchases, including those of capital goods, depletable assets, expenditures creating intangible assets, and purchases of inventories. Thus there is no need for special provisions for either depreciation or inventory accounting. Consistent with the cash flow treatment of debt at the individual level, businesses also include loan proceeds in the tax base and are allowed deductions for both interest expense and repayment of principal. By comparison, the tax base does not include proceeds from new share issues and no deduction is allowed for dividends paid. Moreover, there is no deduction for equity investments in other firms, and intercorporate dividends received from such investments are not taxable to the receiving firm.

C. The ITP/R Consumption Tax

Under the ITP/R approach, capital income (e.g., interest, dividends and capital gains) is not included in the individual tax base, and individuals do not receive a deduction for saving. As shown in the appendix, such treatment is under certain circumstances equivalent in present value terms to ICF treatment. Specifically, relative to ICF treatment, the benefit of the tax exemption of capital income under the ITP approach is equivalent in present value terms to the cost of not receiving a tax deduction for saving; thus, the tax that would be due upon withdrawal of principal and interest under the ICF approach is "prepaid" through the denial of a deduction for saving under the ITP approach. Consistent with the exemption of interest income, interest expense is not deductible under the ITP approach. The treatment of gifts and bequests is as in the ICF/RF tax.

As under the business portion of the ICF/RF tax, businesses are accorded cash flow taxation of real flows, including expensing of all business-related purchases. However, consistent with the ITP approach at the individual level, business loans have no tax consequences, and interest expense is not deductible. As under the RF base, the proceeds of new share issues are not included in the business tax base and dividends paid are not deductible; in addition, there is no deduction for equity investment in other firms, and intercorporate dividends are not taxable to the recipient firm.

III. A Comparison of Consumption and Income Taxes

As noted in the introduction, many advocates of consumption-based direct taxation focus on its simplification benefits, compared to the taxation of income. However, administrative considerations do not all favor consumption-based alternatives. This section specifies the administrative advantages and disadvantages of taxation based on consumption and on income. It generally applies to both forms of consumption-based taxation. The section that follows examines the relative simplicity advantages of the two forms of consumption-based taxation described above.

A. Relative Advantages of Consumption-based Taxation

Under the generally accepted Schanz-Haig-Simon definition of income, the basis for income taxation is consumption plus the change in net wealth during the accounting period. Measuring changes in net wealth pose difficult problems of valuation - problems that can be lumped together under the heading of "timing issues".[10] In essence, the question is when income should be realized for tax purposes and when deductions should be allowed for expenses. If income is recognized too late (too soon) or deductions are accelerated (postponed) taxable income falls short of (exceeds) economic income in the early years of an investment and exceeds (falls short of) it in later years.

The deferral of tax liability associated with delayed recognition of income or accelerated deductions can be of substantial value, especially during times of high inflation. Thus there are (or should be) complex rules dealing with such issues as when to recognize income from long term contracts, when to recognize interest income on debt securities issued at a discount, and when to tax income from installment sales. Similarly, rules must be devised to ensure that deductions are allowed only for items that reflect reductions in net wealth during the period.

The proper pattern of depreciation allowances is perhaps the best known timing issue. Income for tax purposes reflects economic income only if depreciation allowances for tax purposes accurately track economic depreciation - the decline in the real value of depreciable assets. If depreciation allowances for tax purposes are too rapid (slow), income for tax purposes will understate (overstate) economic income in present value terms.

Unfortunately, it is extremely difficult to determine the rate at which various assets depreciate. Moreover, there may be a tendency to specify depreciation known to be more rapid than economic depreciation in order to stimulate investment or to offset the effects of inflation (if deductions for depreciation are not indexed for inflation). In any event, depreciation allowed for tax purposes is always somewhat arbitrary and in some cases may not closely reflect economic depreciation. Similar problems occur in the case

[10] For more on timing issues, as well as a discussion of problems of inflation adjustment, see McLure (1988).

of depletion allowances for natural resources and amortization of intangible assets. Of course, income will also be understated if consumption tax principles are used in the calculation of the business tax base - that is, if capital expenditures are deducted immediately rather than being capitalized and recovered over time, for example through depreciation allowances or proper accounting of the cost of goods sold from inventory.

All these timing issues (and others) disappear under a consumption-based tax. Since all purchases of real assets are expensed, questions of the proper pattern of depreciation allowances, depletion, amortization, and inventory accounting simply do not arise. Financial transactions either have no consequences for tax purposes (e.g., borrowing and lending and interest payments and receipts under the ITP/R tax), or they are treated on a simple cash flow basis (e.g. deductions for saving, repayment of principal and interest expense and taxation of the proceeds of loans and withdrawals of principal and interest income under the ICF/RF tax). In either event, timing issues do not arise.

The failure to employ cash flow accounting under the income tax is particularly problematical under inflationary circumstances. Depreciation allowances that would reflect economic depreciation in a world without inflation fail to allow tax-free recovery of capital in an inflationary environment. The same is true of first-in, first-out (FIFO) inventory accounting; the historical costs of goods added to inventory at an earlier time of lower prices will fail to reflect the current value of such assets. Taxation of nominal capital gains - gains calculated by subtracting the adjusted historical basis of assets from the amount realized, without adjusting basis for inflation - results in the taxation of fictitious inflationary gains. Indeed, tax liability may exist even though a real (inflation-adjusted) loss has been realized. Finally, inclusion of nominal interest income in the tax base (full deduction of nominal interest expense) results in taxation (deduction) of the inflationary component of interest, as well as the real component. In essence, taxation (deduction) is being applied to (allowed for) the repayment of principal, contrary to the rules of income taxation.

Inflation adjustment is one of the most complex aspects of a conceptually sound income tax. Only a tax system that is based on inflation adjustment of balance sheets, such as that used in Chile, is likely to be truly satisfactory in accurately measuring economic income. Such an approach would add considerable complexity to the income tax; it would be especially problematical for individuals and small businesses, who are unlikely to have the detailed balance sheet information necessary for implementation of this scheme.[11] Conceptually less satisfactory approaches, such as the ad hoc proposals contained in the 1984 recommendations of the U.S. Treasury Department to President Reagan [U.S. Department of the Treasury (1984)] illustrate the difficulty of alternative methods of inflation adjustment, especially for interest income and expense.

These problems of inflation adjustment also do not arise under a consumption-based tax. Because a given transaction either has no tax consequences or results in immediate recognition of income or deduction of expenses, inflation does not distort the measurement of the tax base. The only real problem arises if inflation rates are so high that the measurement of the tax base is distorted due to the time lag between the earning of income and incurring of expenses and the filing of tax returns. There is no truly satisfactory solution to this problem at high rates of inflation, although it can be alleviated through more frequent filing (for example, by using quarterly filing, as is done under many VATs). In any event, this problem is no worse under a consumption-based tax than under the income tax.

Taxation of capital gains is inevitably complicated under an income tax. Records must be kept of the dates of acquisition and the initial value of assets, which must then be adjusted for depreciation and inflation. Where homogeneous or economically equivalent assets are involved, it is necessary to have conventions for identifying particular assets or presumptive ordering rules (e.g., FIFO or LIFO) that specify the order in which assets are presumed to be sold. Administration is difficult because of problems of verification of costs and dates of acquisition and monitoring compliance.

By comparison, capital transactions pose no problems under the consumption-based tax. In the case of real assets, immediate expensing implies that the tax basis for such assets is always zero. In the case of financial assets, either the disposition of such assets has no tax consequences or such assets also have a zero basis. In both cases, the appropriate tax treatment under a consumption tax is far simpler than under the income tax.

[11] Note that such a balance sheet approach to inflation adjustment would not necessarily be fully consistent with generally accepted accounting principles in those countries where such principles exist.

If deductions for depreciation do not reflect real economic depreciation under an income tax, complex adjustments or "recapture" rules are required to deal with the disposition of business assets. If depreciation for tax purposes is accelerated, the excess of tax depreciation over economic depreciation must be included in the tax base to prevent purely tax-motivated selling by taxpayers. Alternatively, if tax depreciation is slower than real economic depreciation, a compensating adjustment must be made to prevent over-taxation. In marked contrast, there is no need to apply recapture rules upon disposition of capital assets under a consumption-based tax. The entire proceeds of such dispositions are simply included in the tax base.

As demonstrated in the appendix, under the appropriate conditions, a consumption-based tax results in a marginal effective tax rate (METR) on capital investment of zero. This feature may provide a lower limit on marginal effective tax rates under the consumption tax, since any tax preferences providing more generous treatment would automatically result in a negative METR, i.e., government subsidization of investment. By comparison, the METR on equity-financed investment under a conceptually pure business income tax is simply the statutory rate, so there is ample room for tax preferences that create METRs that lie between zero and the statutory rate.[12] Thus, there is some chance - though this is merely political speculation - that the range of METRs might be smaller under the consumption-based tax than under the income tax. Such a reduction in the range of METR differentials would result in a more efficient allocation of capital among competing investments. In addition, relatively small METR differentials should help to restrict opportunities for tax arbitrage (e.g., borrowing and taking interest deductions at the statutory tax while investing in an asset that yields income that is effectively taxed at a lower rate).

Integration of the corporate and personal income taxes is a particularly complicated issue under most income taxes. Complete integration, or attribution of all corporate earnings (and any corporate taxes paid) to individual shareholders, is generally viewed to be infeasible [McLure (1979)]. Even partial integration schemes designed to provide relief only from double taxation of dividends add considerable complexity. This is particularly true under the shareholder credit or imputation method

[12] Note that tax preferences can result in negative METRs on debt-financed investment; for example, see McLure, Mutti, Thuronyi and Zodrow (1988, chapter 4).

- by far the most popular means of providing dividend relief - if various tax preferences result in effective corporate taxation at a rate lower than the statutory rate. In this case, complex techniques are customarily devised to provide dividend relief only to the extent that tax has actually been paid at the corporate level. Alternatively, firms can be allowed a deduction for dividends paid. However, many countries are reluctant to provide such generous treatment if the shareholder is a foreigner or a tax-exempt institution, and identifying such shareholders for the purpose of denying the deduction (or assessing a special tax on distributions) is also very difficult from an administrative standpoint.

In contrast, integration of the corporate (or business) and individual taxes causes few problems under a consumption-based tax. The issue of double taxation of marginal investments does not arise, since the METR on capital investment is zero. Moreover, double taxation generally is not a problem. This is easiest to see under the ITP/R tax; since there is no taxation of dividends at the individual level, double taxation cannot occur. However, under the ICF/RF approach, double taxation of the returns to entrepreneurship can arise if such returns are taxed under the business cash flow tax and as dividends or capital gains under the individual cash flow tax; this issue is discussed further below.

B. Relative Disadvantages of the Consumption-based Tax

As noted above, considerations of administrative and compliance simplicity do not all favor a consumption-based tax over the income tax. Several advantages of the income tax in terms of the criterion of simplicity are described in this section.

Perhaps the most striking difference between the two taxes is that the treatment of debt transactions and interest income and expense under either version of the consumption-based tax would be quite different from that under the income tax. Thus an extensive educational campaign would probably be required to gain taxpayer acquiescence and familiarity with either form of the consumption tax. Taxpayers would need to know and accept the fact that interest is neither taxable nor deductible under the ITP/R approach, or that borrowing (lending) results in an addition to (deduction from) the tax base under the ICF/RF tax. (The question of which of these approaches would be more acceptable is discussed further in the following section.)

The simplicity advantages of the consumption-based tax may be largely illusory if information not required for implementation of the consumption tax is nonetheless needed for purposes for financial accounting.[13] In developed countries this probably is not a major consideration, since sophisticated business taxpayers would have little difficulty in dealing with two quite different concepts of "income"; moreover, they would almost certainly welcome the opportunity to utilize the simpler consumption-based measure of the tax base, alongside whatever financial accounting is required for other reasons, in lieu of the substantially more complicated accounting required for income tax purposes.[14] Moreover, this issue would not arise for most individuals, since they have little reason to prepare income statements aside from those required by the fiscal authorities.[15] However, the problem of "conformity" between income and tax accounting is likely to be more important in developing countries, where there may be relatively little in the way of generally accepted accounting principles aside from those found in the tax law. Adoption of a consumption-based tax, by breaking the link between tax and financial accounting, might impede the development of the latter.

Although expensing under a consumption-based business tax is much simpler than accounting for depreciation (and depletion, amortization, etc.), it nevertheless creates several potential problems. One such problem arises because losses for tax purposes are likely to be experienced much more commonly under a consumption-based tax that allows expensing than under an income tax that allows deductions only for depreciation. If tax policy is not adjusted to take account of this, new firms will be put at a competitive disadvantage relative to established ones, and there will be undesirable tax-motivated incentives for mergers and acquisitions, especially if interest rates are high. This problem is mitigated if loss-carryforwards with interest are available, although the determination of the appropriate interest rate might be a difficult and contentious issue. For existing firms with prior taxable income, the possibility of loss-carryback is more satisfactory from an economic point of view, but more demanding of resources for

---

[13] Note that this issue would also arise in countries that utilize elements of accrual accounting in the administration of a VAT.

[14] Note that the methods used for financial and tax accounting seldom coincide even under an income tax.

[15] However, as noted by Aaron (in this volume), income records would have to be maintained by individuals qualifying for income-tested transfer programs.

compliance and administration. More problematical is the fact that some companies may never be profitable and thus may never be able to use carryovers unless they merge with a profitable firm.

Note also that individuals generally would be precluded from utilizing such losses to offset labor income. Such a "schedular" approach has the obvious advantage of obviating the need for complex anti-shelter provisions. Nevertheless, strict application of separate tax regimes to labor income and income from business and capital yields undesirable results in the case of business activities involving legitimate losses. It might thus be desirable to devise techniques through which legitimate losses could be passed through to individual taxpayers under certain circumstances.[16] However, such provisions would create additional complexity under a consumption-based tax system and might open up avenues for tax abuse.

Expensing also accentuates some opportunities for tax abuse. For example, there is greater potential for losses on such activities as "hobby farms". Monitoring and enforcement could be difficult, especially if an attempt is made to use income-based rules to distinguish hobby activities from legitimate business ventures.

A second form of abuse involves disposition of expensed depreciable assets without reporting the proceeds of sale. The need for monitoring would be greater under the consumption-based tax than under the income tax, because the gains to such abuse would be greater with expensing than with depreciation, even if the latter is accelerated. On the other hand, the deduction for expensing of real asset purchases by a buyer will be reflected in the taxable income of the seller (if it is an entity subject to the business tax). This makes possible a form of cross-checking that is much more difficult under the income tax, since deductions for purchases of real assets are spread out over many periods.

Land may be especially problematical under a consumption-based tax system, especially during the transition from an income-based tax system to a consumption tax. There may be great resistance to allowing expensing of land; after all, land is not a depreciable item under the income tax. (It should be recognized that, except for differences in marginal tax rates, there is no net benefit resulting from transactions in land

[16] For example, it might be deemed desirable to allow such "pass through" treatment of losses for relatively low-income individuals whose only business activity is investing in land or real estate.

between taxpayers; the buyer takes an immediate deduction for the purchase price, while the seller includes the whole proceeds of the sale in the tax base, without any deduction of basis which is identically zero.) But if no deduction is allowed for the purchase of land (and making the reasonable assumption that no attempt is made to segregate receipts attributable to land from other receipts), the income to land is effectively taxed at the statutory rate. As a result, there would be considerable pressure on the distinction between land and improvements that would give rise to complexity and monitoring problems in response to taxpayer attempts to recharacterize land as structures.

Some of the most vexing problems related to consumption (and income) taxation involve trans-national investment and flows of income across national borders. For example, many countries, especially those in the third world, might be expected to resist the notion of allowing consumption-based tax treatment of income earned by foreign investors. Techniques such as separate income taxation and withholding taxes could be used in an attempt to impose taxes on foreign investment income higher than the zero marginal effective tax rate applied to income from domestic investment. (It should perhaps be recognized, however, that consumption-based taxation, with its marginal effective tax rate of zero, would actually be less generous than the current "income tax" treatment provided foreign investment in many countries; the combination of investment allowances, accelerated depreciation, full deduction of nominal interest expense, and tax holidays commonly reduces marginal effective tax rates on income from foreign investment to below zero.) Any such attempt would presumably be opposed by foreign investors and their countries of residence.

A second potential problem in this area involves the question of whether a consumption-based business tax and any withholding taxes that might accompany it would be creditable in capital-exporting countries such as the United States, which allows credits only for taxes levied on net income. In principle, one might argue that a country that is willing to allow credits for an income tax should be willing to allow credit for consumption-based taxes, which are even less generous than income taxes. (The rationale for limiting credits to income taxes is to prevent credits from being claimed for such payments as royalties, production taxes, and other forms of taxation not related to net income.) Be this as it may, a consideration of the issue that focused on crediting only taxes on *net* income might concentrate on the absence of interest deductions (under the ITP/R base) or the inclusion of proceeds of borrowing in the tax base (under the ICF/RF base) in ruling a consumption based tax to be non-creditable. One is almost led to conclude that the creditability of consumption-based taxes might even depend on the skill and wording with which the first request for foreign tax credits was presented to the U.S. Internal Revenue Service.

Recent changes in U.S. tax law suggest that the issue of creditability might actually be less important than it appears at first sight. Because of changes in rules used to determine the source of income, the increased use of "baskets" to segregate foreign source income for purposes of calculating limits on the foreign tax credit, and the reduction in U.S. corporate tax rates, many more firms will be in an excess foreign tax credit position than under pre-1987 law. To the extent this is true, it would make relatively little difference whether credits are allowed for a consumption-based tax; neither that tax nor the income tax would actually give rise to credits against U.S. tax liability, even if only the latter is legally a creditable tax.

IV. Advantages of the ITP/R Tax over the ICF/RF Tax

It appears that the ITP/R method of implementing a direct tax based on consumption has substantial administrative advantages over the ICF/RF approach. These are discussed in this section; problems of the ITP/R approach that create a relative advantage for the ICF/RF plan are discussed in the section that follows. It will be convenient in the present section to focus first on those differences that affect primarily the taxation of individuals, because of the differences in the ITP and ICF techniques. The discussion then turns to differences in business taxation resulting from the choice of the R base rather than the RF base.

A. Individual Issues

Perhaps the most obvious difference between the two forms of consumption taxation is that the ICF approach requires substantially more record-keeping than does the ITP approach. Compliance would require precise records on all transactions involving savings, loans, the receipt of capital income including interest income, dividends and capital gains, interest payments and the repayment of principal on loans, and all withdrawals from qualified accounts; a tax audit would require strict monitoring of all such transactions. By comparison, compliance with and administration of the ITP approach would be considerably simpler, since none of these capital transactions has any tax consequences. Note also that, since all capital transactions are excluded from the individual tax base under the ITP approach, withholding would be much more accurate than under either the ICF consumption tax or the income tax.

The treatment of loans provides perhaps the best example of the relative simplicity advantages of the ITP approach over the ICF approach. Under the latter method, ensuring that all individual interest income is reported would present the same monitoring and enforcement problems that plague tax authorities under current income tax regimes.[17] Moreover, although the treatment of debt transactions and interest would be initially unfamiliar and puzzling under both versions of the consumption-based tax, it appears that it would be somewhat more difficult to gain taxpayer acceptance of the inclusion of principal in taxable income under the ICF/RF base than of the disallowance of interest deductions under the ITP/R base; this would be most likely to be true in countries that already have provisions for the disallowance of certain forms of interest under the income tax. In addition, it seems almost certain that a more extensive educational campaign would be required under the ICF approach, since the inclusion of the proceeds of loans in the tax base would represent such a significant change from current practice.

The treatment of loans under the ICF approach also provides possibilities for tax abuse that do not occur under the ITP base. For example, loans at below-market interest rates could be made to children or other family members in order to shift income to taxpayers subject to lower marginal tax rates.[18] There would be similar opportunities for tax arbitrage involving loans - especially reciprocal loans at different interest rates - between taxpayers with different rates and between taxpayers and tax-exempt institu-

---

[17] Note however that the more complete "paper trail" left under the ICF consumption tax implies that auditing loans would be somewhat easier than under the income tax. Specifically, interest payments should be deducted only if the proceeds of the loan were previously included in the tax base, and deductions for the making of loans should be accompanied by subsequent interest receipts.

[18] Note that such loans at market rates of interest would not reduce tax liability in present value terms (but would alter the timing of tax payments), as long as the tax rates for each party to the transaction were constant over the duration of the loan.

tions. No such abuses are possible under the ITP approach to the taxation of consumption.

The greatest public outcry against either approach would almost certainly involve the tax treatment of home mortgages and mortgage interest. Under the ICF approach, any deviations from standard rules or special averaging provisions for withdrawals from qualified accounts to fund down payments on home purchases would create complexity and opportunities for abuse. By comparison, the elimination of deductions for home mortgage interest under the ITP approach would add relatively little to complexity. Note however that any special provisions favoring investment in owner-occupied housing - such as partial mortgage interest deductions under the ITP approach or partial exclusion of the proceeds of home mortgage loans under the ICF approach - would open opportunities for abuse through borrowing home equity in order to make non-housing investments and would require potentially complicated anti-abuse provisions.

In addition, accurate withholding under the ICF approach would require withholding - presumably at some "average" tax rate - on loans and "negative withholding" on repayment of loans. Such provisions would result in significant added complexity, and would also represent a significant departure from current practices. Alternatively, a withholding system under an ICF base that simply ignored loans would be extremely inaccurate for many taxpayers.

Recognizing that ICF treatment of loans might pose significant compliance problems, especially for small taxpayers, some proponents of ICF/RF taxes propose that a limited amount of loans be accorded ITP treatment.[19] Although such treatment would simplify compliance for small taxpayers, it would cause some additional administrative problems. One potential avenue for abuse would involve simultaneous borrowing from tax-exempt institutions or foreigners at an above-market interest rate on an ICF basis and at a below-market rate on an ITP basis. In addition, taxpayers would have to keep records to ensure that the loan limit was not exceeded and to identify "ICF" loans and interest payments and "ITP" loans and interest payments. Moreover, tax authorities would have to ensure that the loan limit was enforced and that interest payments and

---

[19] For example, Aaron and Galper recommend (optional) ITP treatment for up to $20,000 in outstanding loans.

repayment of principal on ITP loans were not illegally deducted from the tax base; both tasks would appear to be difficult at best.[20]

In addition to problems associated with the treatment of loans, it appears that there are substantially greater opportunities for tax evasion under the ICF approach than under the ITP method. For example, assets of all types could be shifted to family members subject to low marginal tax rates, in order to have interest, dividends, and capital gains taxed at lower rates. This would be especially problematical to the extent gifts are untaxed, or subject to generous exclusions, or are not reported to tax authorities. Such problem would not arise under the ITP approach, since all these types of income would be exempt from taxation when received by individuals.

Since withdrawals from qualified accounts would be subject to full taxation under the ICF approach, the incentive to evade taxation by not reporting such withdrawals would be great; in particular, it would be greater than under current income taxes, where only the real or nominal gain on the asset is subject to tax. This suggests that one could expect substantial attempts at tax evasion, especially in the absence of withholding.[21] Accordingly, monitoring systems under the ICF approach would have to be quite comprehensive to ensure full reporting of all amounts withdrawn from qualified accounts. Again, such issues do not arise under the ITP approach.

International capital transactions by sophisticated taxpayers would pose some problems under the ICF approach. At a minimum, such taxpayers would have considerable discretion in the timing of their tax payments (without reducing the present value of their tax burden). For example, one could borrow abroad and deposit the proceeds in a domestic qualified account; this would have the effect of reducing current taxes, with tax subsequently due when funds were withdrawn from the qualified account. If tax rates were constant over time, only the timing of the tax payment - but not its present

[20] Note however that there is no difference in present value terms between the two methods of accounting for loans if tax rates are constant. Thus, taxpayers would benefit from schemes involving "excessive" borrowing on an ITP basis to fund deposits in an ICF account only if their tax rates were lower at the time if withdrawal of the funds from the account. That is, such taxpayers would have greater access to an averaging mechanism than would their counterparts who were unwilling to engage in such transactions.

[21] Evasion of capital gains tax is reportedly a significant problem under U.S. income tax, even though only gain is subject to taxation - formerly at a preferential rate.

value - would be changed. However, if the individual's tax rate were lower at the time of withdrawal, such borrowing would reduce the present value of tax liability; that is, individuals with access to foreign borrowing would have better averaging opportunities than other taxpayers.

The tax treatment of foreign portfolio investment is likely to be problematical under any circumstances [Musgrave (1969)], but the issues it raises seem to be relatively less troublesome under the ITP approach. Unless deductions for foreign portfolio investment were not allowed under the ICF approach, it would be a fairly simple matter for taxpayers to take deductions for such investments but to avoid tax on foreign source income (or withdrawals from foreign qualified accounts); altogether too many foreign institutions and governments would be happy to cooperate in making such abuse possible. Since the ITP approach exempts both domestic and foreign source capital income and allows no deductions for saving, it would be simpler than either the ICF approach or the income tax, as it would eliminate the need to monitor foreign portfolio investment - a difficult task at best.

Finally, the ICF/RF approach would present opportunities for tax avoidance if individuals could transfer funds from qualified accounts out of the country, emigrate, and then fund consumption without paying tax to the home country. To prevent such activities, transfers abroad would presumably be treated as taxable consumption. For example, Aaron and Galper recommend that qualified accounts be restricted to domestic institutions and that transfers to individuals or businesses with a foreign residence be subject to withholding at the maximum individual rate. Such measures would complicate the administration of an ICF/RF tax. Since capital income is not taxed at the individual level under an ITP/R tax, these issues do not arise.

B. Business Tax Issues

The advantages of the R base over the RF base are significant. Most importantly, there is no distinction between debt and equity under the R base. That is, neither the proceeds of borrowing nor contributions of equity capital have any tax consequences under the R base, and there is no deduction for either interest expense or dividends paid. By comparison, under the RF base the distinction between debt and equity can be crucial, since debt proceeds and interest are taxable (and repayment of debt and interest expense are deductible), whereas contributions of equity capital are not taxable and dividends are not deductible. By eliminating this distinction, the R base eliminates the need for regulations and monitoring and enforcement efforts designed to prevent attempts to convert debt into equity and dividends into interest in order to reduce tax liability. Such attempts are quite difficult to police; efforts at preventing the conversion of dividends into interest give rise to many troublesome and complex issues under the income tax.

For the reasons given above, the treatment of debt is also administratively much simpler under the R base than under the RF base. In addition, because such treatment is consistent with that for individuals, there are no possibilities for evasion or avoidance resulting from inconsistent treatment across individual and business taxpayers.

As noted in the previous discussion of business and individual tax integration, the taxation of returns to entrepreneurship poses a potential problem under the ICF approach. Since firms are not able to "expense" the investment of entrepreneurial skills in a venture, the income from such investment would be fully taxed at the business level. Moreover, to the extent such returns were paid as dividends to individuals or realized as capital gains, they would be subject to a second tax at the individual level. Thus, the returns to entrepreneurship could be subject to double taxation under the ICF/RF base. (This problem could be avoided only if all returns to entrepreneurship were distributed to individuals as wages - which are deductible to the firm - rather than as dividends.) No such problem arises under the ITP/R approach. Returns are taxed only at the business level, since no tax is levied on dividends received or business activities at the individual level. If such returns were distributed as wages, they would be deductible to the business and thus taxed only at the individual level, at the marginal tax rate of the individual taxpayer.

V. Problems of the ITP/R Approach

Although the ITP/R approach has numerous administrative advantages over the ICF/RF plan, several administrative issues are more troublesome under the former approach. We first consider some problems raised by the treatment of interest and then turn to several other issues, including those that would be raised during the transition from an income-based tax to a consumption-based tax.

A. Problems Related to the ITP/R Treatment of Interest

Although the treatment of debt and interest under the ITP/R approach is generally simpler than under the ICF/RF approach, this is not universally the case. Particular problems arise when there are transactions between business taxpayers and parties that are not subject to tax, including foreigners, tax-exempt organizations and, in some cases, individuals. These problems arise only if the party is not subject to the ITP/R tax system and also is indifferent between interest receipts (expense) and other types of income (deductions).

Any transaction in which a purchase and a lending arrangement are involved has opportunities for abuse. If a seller/lender is subject to the ITP/R tax, it has an incentive to understate the price and overstate interest, in order to shift receipts from taxable sales receipts to tax-exempt interest income. If it is a buyer/borrower that is subject to tax, it has an incentive to overstate the price to get larger deductions, and to understate interest expense, which is not deductible in any event. Parties engaging in simultaneous leases and borrowing arrangements can exploit a similar type of abuse. For example, a taxable lessor/borrower has an incentive to inflate lease payments and arrange for a below-market interest rate in order to increase its deductions. In all these cases, under the circumstances described above, the business taxpayer can reduce its tax liability without any adverse effects on the other party to the transaction. In contrast, these problems do not arise under the ICF/RF approach, since interest receipts are included in the tax base and interest payments are fully deductible.

Installment sales to parties that are not subject to the consumption-based business tax involve a slightly different problem. If the interest component of installment payments is ignored, as is conceptually proper under the ITP/R approach, the seller defers taxes. As the buyer is indifferent between cash and installment sales, such sales become an effective tax avoidance device. This problem does not arise under the ICF/RF tax, since the entire installment payment, including the interest component, is included in the tax base. (Note that this problem could be avoided under the ITP/R approach - at the cost of introducing some additional complexity - if installment sales were accorded cash flow treatment.)

Finally, the treatment of loan defaults would be somewhat more complicated under the ITP/R approach. In principle, a borrower who defaults on a loan should include the outstanding loan balance in his tax base; similarly, the lender should receive a deduction in the same amount. Under the cash flow accounting for loans required by the ICF/RF approach, such treatment occurs automatically. In contrast, since loans have no tax consequences under the ITP/R approach, special provisions would be required to deal with defaults.

B. Other Structural Issues

A particularly important problem under the ITP/R approach - though not necessarily an administrative one - involves the tax treatment of financial institutions. Since interest income is exempt and interest expense is not deductible, the entire spread of financial institutions would be tax exempt. While fully consistent with the conceptual rationale underlying the consumption-based tax, one can readily imagine such an outcome being unacceptable on political grounds. Moreover, any attempt to assure taxation of the profits of financial institutions - say, through cash flow treatment of their lending/borrowing transactions - would create complexity, in addition to being inconsistent with the basic conceptual foundation underlying the ITP/R consumption-based alternative.

The problem of losses discussed above would be particularly troublesome under the R base. In present value terms, the combination of expensing and the tax treatment of debt and interest are equivalent under the R and RF bases. However, the timing of deductions differs considerably. Under the RF base, the inclusion of the proceeds of borrowing offsets the expensing of asset purchases financed by debt. Since there is no such offset under the R base, losses can be expected to occur much more commonly than under either the ICF/RF consumption tax or the income tax. Thus the ITP/R consumption tax is more complicated than its ICF/RF counterpart to the extent that monitoring and enforcement of loss carryforward/carryback provisions (including those dealing with the liquidation of companies with accumulated losses) creates administrative problems and/or if any special provisions are enacted to allow limited "pass through" treatment of business losses to individual taxpayers.[22]

Another potential complication under the ITP/R approach arises from the fact that individuals receive tax prepayment treatment of all investment, while businesses must use cash flow accounting. It would clearly be desirable to limit opportunities for tax abuses that involve two accounts for related investments, with deductions assigned to business cash flow accounts and receipts included under the individual tax base [Graetz (1979)]. In order to prevent such "gaming" of the tax system, it would be necessary to define business activities very broadly under the ITP/R approach. (For example, transactions in real estate by an investor not undertaking such transactions as part of a trade or business would nevertheless be considered to constitute a business for tax purposes.)

This implies that many individual taxpayers would need to file business returns, as well as individual returns, under the ITP/R approach. Such treatment appears to be more complicated than under the ICF/RF consumption-based tax - where this issues does not arise since both businesses and individuals are taxed on a cash flow basis - or under the income tax. However, the difference may not be as great as it appears. Many of the activities and transactions that would be reported on business tax returns under the ITP/R tax would be reported on schedules attached to the individual tax return under the ICF/RF tax. Indeed, it might be possible under the ITP/R tax to utilize a simplified business tax return that, in essence, would be no more than a schedule attached to the individual return. Note that any such business returns would actually be substantially simpler than the corresponding schedule under the ICF/RF tax (or the income tax), because of the simpler treatment of debt and interest (and the existence of expensing).

Another advantage of the ICF approach arises from the fact that the individual tax base is essentially consumption; by comparison, under the ITP approach the tax base is labor income plus gifts and inheritances received, to the extent such transfers are

---

[22] Bradford (1990) notes that losses could be limited under an R base tax by disallowing the deduction for wages at the firm level. Under this approach, there would be a flat rate of tax on wages; progressivity under the individual tax system would be achieved by granting individuals wage credits that varied inversely with the size of the individual tax base.

taxable. Since the ICF consumption base is substantially more stable than the ITP alternative (at least if one ignores the purchase of consumer durables financed by withdrawals from qualified accounts), there is relatively more need for income averaging under the ITP approach. Any averaging provisions added to the ITP/R tax would result in additional complexity. However, one might argue that sufficient opportunities for averaging would exist as long as cash flow treatment were allowed for pensions; such treatment is in fact commonly recommended for pensions by proponents of the ITP approach.

In principle, the base of a consumption tax should include all compensation for labor effort. The returns to certain forms of labor effort, especially home production, are not likely to be taxed under either form of consumption tax or under the income tax. However, certain additional issues are raised by the fact that the individual tax base of the ITP/R tax exempts capital income. Specifically, the returns to labor efforts at portfolio management (if successful) are not taxed under the ITP/R approach but appear as dividends and/or capital gains under the ICF/RF base.[23] Any attempts to tax such returns under the individual tax of the ITP/R approach would add complexity and raise difficult classification issues. However, note that this issue would probably arise only for relatively small investors; for sufficiently large investors, portfolio management would be treated as a business activity and would be subject to cash flow taxation under the business tax.

C. Transitional Issues

The transitional issues raised by a movement from an income tax to a consumption-based tax are commonly viewed as particularly troublesome. Since most "income" taxes are in fact hybrid taxes that combine elements of income-based and consumption-based taxation, it is far from clear that the transitional issues raised by a movement to a consumption tax are in fact worse than those that would be associated with other comprehensive tax reforms, such as a movement to a tax on real economic income. In

[23] Note that a similar issue arises with respect to labor efforts devoted to repairing/improving owner-occupied housing and consumer durables. However, it seems likely that most if not all the capital gains on such activities would also go untaxed under an ICF/RF tax (or the income tax). For a discussion of these issues, see Gordon (1988).

any case, it does not appear that there are significant differences between the ICF/RF and ITP/R taxes in terms of relative administrative simplicity during transition. In particular, it is difficult to distinguish between the two approaches on these grounds, since rules that would normally be associated with one approach could easily be used as a transition mechanism under the alternative approach.[24]

Since both the ICF/RF and ITP/R taxes call for a cash flow tax at the business level, the transitional issues associated with reform of the business tax would be roughly similar under both approaches. The primary difference would be in the treatment of interest on debt outstanding at the time of implementation of reform. Under either approach, rules would have to be devised to determine how much of interest income (payments) attributable to "old" or pre-existing debt would be included in (deducted from) the tax base of the lender (borrower). The same issue - and presumably the same transition rules - would also arise for the treatment of old debt at the individual level.

The treatment of capital gains would also have to be specified. Under the ICF/RF approach, rules would have to be devised to determine how much of withdrawals from "old" savings accounts represent savings out of after-tax dollars and thus should be exempt from tax; under the ITP/R approach, some means of taxing accrued gains (on which income tax had been deferred) would be desirable. Since both cases would require a determination of the basis of capital assets existing prior to the enactment of reform, the transitional rules used could be quite similar. For example, under either the ICF/RF or the ITP/R approach, capital gains on pre-existing assets could be included in the tax basis on a cash flow basis during the transition period.

The final major transitional issue for the individual tax would be the treatment of dividends paid from income accumulated prior to the date of enactment of a movement to a consumption-based tax. If no dividend relief were provided under the pre-reform tax structure, no special transition rules would be required under the ICF/RF tax but some attempt to tax such dividends would probably be made under the ITP/R tax; in this case, the former approach is clearly superior on grounds of administrative simplicity during the transition. However, if the pre-reform tax structure provided for divi-

[24] For example, the Aaron and Galper (1985) version of an ICF/RF tax includes a transition rule that would provide for ITP treatment of existing debt.

dend relief at the individual level and it was deemed desirable to replicate approximately the tax burden that would have occurred under the pre-reform tax structure, transition rules would be quite complicated under both approaches.

VI. Conclusion

Although early discussions of the relative merits of income and consumption taxes emphasized efficiency and horizontal equity issues, attention has recently focused on the administrative advantages and disadvantages of these two competing forms of direct taxation. In addition, proponents of consumption taxes have debated the relative merits of alternative forms of consumption-based direct taxation.

In this paper, we argue that taxation on the basis of consumption is superior to income-based taxation because of important advantages in two critical areas. First, the need to measure changes in net wealth under the income tax results in a wide variety of "timing" issues that greatly complicate income tax administration; these issues disappear under consumption-based taxation, since purchases of real assets are treated on a cash flow basis (expensed), and financial transactions are also treated on a cash flow basis or they are simply ignored. Second, a conceptually sound income tax should be based on real or inflation-adjusted economic income; however, the measures required to ensure accurate accounting for the effects for inflation would also greatly complicate income tax administration. Again, these issues generally do not arise under a consumption-based tax, since all elements of the tax base are appropriately measured in monetary units of the current accounting period. Our view regarding the superiority of the consumption tax in terms of the criterion of administrative simplicity is not reversed by a wide variety of less critical considerations that both support and challenge this basic conclusion.

A separate issue is the relative merits on administrative simplicity grounds of two alternative methods of implementing consumption-based direct taxation. The "ICF/RF" approach would require cash flow accounting at the individual level coupled with cash flow accounting for real and certain financial transactions at the business level. The alternative "ITP/R" approach would exempt capital income at the individual level and require cash flow accounting for only real transactions at the business level. In our view, the latter approach is preferable on simplicity grounds because it would require far less record-keeping and monitoring and enforcement efforts - especially in treating loans and interest income and expense and in differentiating between debt and equity finance - and would present fewer opportunities for tax avoidance and abuse.

Appendix
Income and Consumption Taxes: Structural Issues[25]

This appendix provides background information on a variety of structural issues in the taxation of income and consumption. The first section considers the role of a business tax in a consumption-based system of direct taxation. The following section provides several simple numerical examples that illustrate the basic differences between an income-based and a consumption-based business tax. The third section provides numerical examples that illustrate the differences between two alternative ways of implementing consumption-based direct taxation of individuals - the individual cash flow (ICF) and individual tax prepayment (ITP) approaches discussed in the text. The final section discusses the treatment of gifts and bequests under the individual tax.[26]

A. Consumption vs. Income Tax Treatment of Businesses

Some consumption tax advocates support complete elimination of taxation at the business level. In principle, this is consistent with the notion of taxation of consumption since, neglecting problems of personal consumption disguised as business expenditures, only individuals consume. However, it is fairly easy to design a business tax that is generally consistent with consumption tax principles. Moreover, for the reasons detailed below, such a "consumption-based" business tax provides an important complement to consumption taxation at the individual level.

Such a consumption-based business tax would allow immediate expensing for all business-related expenditures, including additions to inventories and purchases of depreciable assets and other expenditures that might normally be capitalized or amor-

[25] This appendix is based on material presented in Zodrow and McLure (1988).

[26] Kay (in this volume) provides a more formal discussion of many of the points discussed in this appendix.

tized over several years under ordinary accounting principles. (For expositional convenience we will generally use the term "depreciable assets" to refer to all expenditures of the latter type in what follows.) Such a tax is commonly described as being based on the real cash flow of a business.[27] This terminology arises from the fact that the tax base is defined to include receipts and allow deductions for non-financial business-related expenditures on a cash flow basis; this is in contrast to an income tax where receipts and expenditures are in principle treated on an accrual basis. As will be demonstrated below, the implication of such treatment is that, in present value terms, capital income is exempt from tax.

We believe such a business tax is desirable within a consumption tax framework for at least five reasons. First, the government will obtain positive revenue in present value terms from the taxation of economic rents and from above-normal returns to the government's "share" of risky investments[28]; moreover, such a tax is likely to be a relatively efficient source of revenue. The business tax thus supplements the revenue raised from taxes on individual consumption and allows lower and thus less distortionary tax rates on such consumption.

Second, in a system of direct taxation the existence of a business tax is probably indispensable from a political standpoint. The perception problems associated with complete elimination of business taxation would be enormous in most if not all countries.

Third, such a tax provides a convenient means for taxing foreign investors if such taxation is deemed desirable. Revenues are raised from investments generating economic rents - which may be an important component of much foreign investment in many countries - simply by applying the rules of the consumption-based business tax to foreign-owned branches and subsidiaries. If deemed desirable, additional withholding taxes on dividends or interest remitted abroad can also be assessed.

[27] For the present, we ignore the tax treatment of borrowing and lending and of interest income and expense. As described in the text and explained in more detail below, debt and interest may be ignored for tax purposes (the "real" or R base) or treated on a cash flow basis (the "real plus financial" or RF base).

[28] Expensing implies that the government effectively acts as a "silent partner" in risky investments; this point is discussed further below.

Fourth, in the absence of a business tax it would be difficult to prevent owners of businesses from disguising personal consumption expenditures as business purchases. The cash flow business tax provides a vehicle for preventing such abuses, since personal consumption expenses theoretically would not be deductible from the business tax base. Of course, structuring rules that differentiate between legitimate business expenses and disguised personal expenditures is not simple under either a consumption tax or an income tax. Denial (partial or full) of business deductions for expenditures on fringe benefits that are tax exempt when received by individuals also provides a means of limiting this form of tax avoidance.

Finally, a business tax is desirable because it makes it possible to assess taxes on income from investments made under the pre-reform tax regime and thus prevent the enactment of a consumption tax from conferring a windfall gain to the owners of capital existing at the time of enactment. The magnitude of such taxes would obviously depend on the transition rules applied to receipts from and deductions related to investments made under the pre-reform regime.

In our view, these reasons for maintaining a separate business tax within any direct consumption tax framework are compelling. Accordingly, we restrict our discussion of consumption tax alternatives to those plans that include a consumption-based business tax. In addition, we believe that such a tax should be characterized by the following three features.

First, businesses should get a deduction for pension contributions, with pension benefits being included in the individual tax base when received. Such treatment provides an important and administratively simple form of averaging for individual taxpayers. Moreover, it is similar to treatment already provided under many income tax systems.

Second, the business tax rate should equal the maximum individual tax rate and should be applied to all elements of the business tax base. Such a rate structure eliminates the potential for tax avoidance schemes based on differences (in either direction) between the maximum individual and business rates, as well as the inequities and distortions caused by preferential rates that favor investment by "small" businesses. In the aggregate, this choice almost certainly provides desirable protection for the progressivity of the tax system. However, in certain cases, it is likely to violate vertical equity by subjecting income attributable to low-income taxpayers who own corporate shares (or participate in the earnings of non-corporate businesses subject to the cash flow business tax) to the top marginal rate.

Third, all businesses should be subject to the same business tax, regardless of their form of organization (corporation, partnership, proprietorship, etc.). This means that no organizational forms are provided with special tax treatment that allows them to avoid the business tax by passing through income and losses to their owners. Such treatment avoids tax-induced distortions in the form of business organization and the economic distortions that may result if certain activities must, for non-tax reasons, employ a particular form of organization. It also improves both equity and the perception of equity by providing for uniform treatment of all business activity, thereby preventing affluent taxpayers from using tax-preferred business forms as tax shelters. Finally, it simplifies the tax code in two important ways. First, it eliminates the need to define and enforce the rules that distinguish which entities qualify for "pass-through" treatment. Second, it eliminates the complexities associated with auditing many partners rather than a single firm.

B. The Treatment of Business Investment and Debt

Given the decision to include a business tax of the type specified above in the consumption tax framework, the primary differences in the tax treatment of businesses under an income tax and a consumption tax are in the tax treatments accorded purchases of depreciable assets and the principal and interest on loans. We consider first the treatment of equity-financed purchases of depreciable assets, and then discuss how debt finance affects the analysis.

The conventional Schanz-Haig-Simons definition of the tax base under a tax on real economic income is the sum of consumption plus changes in net wealth. For firms, this definition implies that the purchase of a depreciable asset, in and of itself, should generate no deduction; since money is exchanged for an asset of equal value, there is no immediate change in net wealth. Accordingly, deductions should be allowed only to the extent that loss in the economic value of the asset results in changes in the net wealth of the firm. Thus, in any single year, a deduction is allowed only for the estimated economic depreciation - the loss in economic value - of the asset. These deductions can be used to offset gross returns to the investment, which are included in the tax base upon receipt. For example, consider an all equity-financed purchase of a $1,000 asset that depreciates $100 in the first year of use. Under an income tax, the expenditure of $1,000 in the first year is largely offset by an increase in the firm's holdings of fixed assets of $900; thus, a deduction of only $100 is allowed against the returns generated by the asset in the first year of operation, with subsequent deductions similarly based on the further economic depreciation of the asset. In marked contrast, under a consumption-based business tax, all expenditures on depreciable assets are deducted in the year of purchase, or "expensed." In terms of the example above, a deduction for the entire purchase price of $1,000 would be allowed in year one.

The effects of these two alternative treatments of business investment can be demonstrated with a simple two-period model of investment in a competitive economy. In the discussion of this model only the tax levied at the business level is considered; individual taxes levied on bondholders and shareholders are not considered. Although highly stylized, the model captures the essential differences between income and consumption tax treatment of investment.

Consider an asset purchased on December 31 of Year 1 for $1,000 that lasts exactly one year and has no residual value. The asset generates gross receipts of $1,100 in Year 2, so that the real internal rate of return to the investment is 10 percent.[29] This rate is also the discount rate used by the firm to calculate present values of future cash flows; this assumption implies that the investment is marginal in that the rate of return is exactly equal to the opportunity cost of funds.

In order to compare expenditures and receipts occurring in the two different years, it is necessary to convert all monetary quantities into present values of one of the years. Since all returns and deductions except the deduction for expensing occur in Year 2, it is convenient to measure all monetary quantities in present values of Year 2, rather than following the usual practice of measuring all quantities in Year 1 present values. An analysis in Year 1 present values would, of course, yield identical qualitative results.

The marginal tax rate faced by the firm is assumed to be 30 percent, and the firm is assumed to have other sources of income that may be offset by the deductions generated by the investment. Expensing under the consumption tax alternative results in a

[29] Note that all returns are assumed to be real. Inflation is a separate issue that is ignored in the analysis below. For a discussion of the effects of inflation within the context of this model, see McLure (1987b).

Year 1 deduction of $1,000, which has a Year 2 value of $1,100. Economic depreciation allowances under the income tax alternative results in a Year 2 deduction of $1,000.

The results for the two cases are as follows. For the income tax, gross receipts in Year 2 of $1,100 less a deduction of $1,000 for economic depreciation result in taxable income of $100. Taxable income thus equals economic income, which is equal to the internal rate of return of 10 percent times the investment of $1,000. The tax paid in Year 2 is $30. Thus, the effective tax rate, defined as the tax paid divided by economic income, is equal to the statutory income tax rate of 30 percent (0.30 = 30/100).

The results are quite different in the consumption tax case where expensing is allowed. The Year 2 value of expensing ($1,100) equals the value of gross receipts. Thus, the present value of the business tax base under the consumption tax is zero, which in turn implies a zero effective tax rate.

This simple example demonstrates the sense in which a business tax that allows expensing is consistent with the notion of taxing personal consumption. That is, the business tax imposes no tax burden in present value terms on income from marginal investments; if all investments were marginal, the entire burden of such a tax system, again in present value terms, would be due to the consumption-based tax assessed at the individual level.

Another way of viewing the effects of expensing is also instructive. Expensing costs the government $300 in Year 1 since the firm's taxes are reduced by that amount. In Year 2, the government receives $330 in tax revenue. This "tax revenue" is best viewed as a return on the government's "share" of the investment purchased through the reduction in the firm's taxes in Year 1; the government in effect is a "silent partner" in the venture, sharing in both the risk and the return. On a marginal investment such as the one analyzed, the present value of taxes on gross receipts generated by the investment exactly equals the present value of the foregone revenue; that is, the government's share of the investment earns the same 10 percent return earned by the investor. (Note that the investor effectively invests only $700 in Year 1 and earns net receipts of $770 in Year 2. That the investor receives the full 10 percent return on the $700 investment further demonstrates that the effective tax rate is zero.) Viewing the government's participation in investment implied by expensing in this way helps to reconcile the apparent inconsistency between the result of a zero marginal effective tax rate and the fact that tax revenue is being collected under such a system.[30]

This example is easily modified to analyze the effects of expensing for an investment with a rate of return that exceeds the discount rate. Consider the above example when the investment results in gross receipts of $1,200, so that the gross rate of return is 20 percent. Under the income tax, gross receipts less economic depreciation yield taxable and economic income of $200 in Year 2, implying taxes of $60. The effective tax rate is again equal to the statutory rate of 30 percent (0.30=60/200).

For the consumption tax, gross receipts of $1,200 less a deduction for expensing equal to $1,100 in Year 2 dollars results in a business tax base equal to $100 and a tax of $30. This result can be interpreted in a number of ways. The *average* effective tax rate, again defined as tax paid divided by economic income, is 15 percent (0.15=30/200). Alternatively, the business tax can be viewed as assessing tax at the statutory rate on above-normal returns; that is, the tax rate on the above-normal return of $100 is 30 percent (0.30=30/100). The *marginal* effective tax rate (on the normal returns to the investment) is still zero, as in the previous example.

However, the most instructive way to interpret the results in the case of consumption tax treatment of an investment that yields above-normal returns is as follows. Recall that under the "government risk-sharing" interpretation of the effects of expensing, the government's share of the $1,000 investment is $300, and the investor's share is the remaining $700. Consider the returns to these two components of the investment. The investor receives $840 in Year 2 ($1,200 in gross receipts less $360 in taxes paid under the consumption-based business tax). Thus, the investor receives the full 20 percent return on his investment of $700. Simultaneously, the government receives $360 on its "investment" of $300; thus, like the private investor, the government earns 20 percent on its investment. In short, the government is a partner in the above-normal returns to investment, as well as in the marginal returns.[31]

---

[30] Whether any revenue is collected in the steady state depends on whether the internal rate of return exceeds the growth rate of investment; see McLure (1987b).

[31] The government receives $330 in present values of Year 1. This implies that the government receives revenue that is positive in present value terms; that is, net revenue in Year 1 present values is $30. The most straightforward interpretation of this result is that the government earns - in the form of revenue that is positive in present value terms - the above-normal return on its share of the investment (30=300x(0.2-0.1)).

To summarize, the government risk-sharing interpretation of the effects of expensing implies that both normal and above-normal private returns to investment are exempt under a consumption-based business tax. Thus, the income attributable to capital investments that qualify for expensing is effectively exempt from tax; that is, in present value terms, the consumption-based business tax does not impose a tax burden on such income. The government does receive net positive revenue in present value terms under such a consumption-based business tax. This net positive revenue arises only in the case of investments that yield above-normal returns; it equals the above-normal returns on the government's share of the investment.

Analogous results can be obtained when debt finance is considered. However, the tax treatment of debt is quite different under the income and consumption tax approaches. Under the income tax, interest payments are deductible from the business tax base (and interest receipts are taxable). Consider the first example above (with gross receipts of $1,100) when the investment is 80 percent debt-financed and the interest rate is 10 percent. Gross receipts of $1,100 are offset by a deduction for economic depreciation of $1,000 and an interest deduction of $80. Taxable income (which is equal to economic income) is only $20 and tax is $6. However, the equity invested in the project is only $200, so that the after-tax return to equity is 7 percent (0.07 = 14/200). This implies that the effective tax rate on equity is again equal to the statutory rate of 30 percent (0.30 = 6/20). (Recall, however, that this approach calculates effective tax rates at the firm level, and thus neglects additional individual taxes paid on interest and on the return to equity.)

Under the consumption-based business tax, there are two alternative methods of treating principal and interest on loans; neither alters the results presented above. The simplest method - which in the terminology used in the text results in a business tax with an "R base" - is to ignore loan proceeds and repayments and interest payments and receipts altogether. This approach obviously has no effect on the calculations of effective tax rates presented above.[32]

Alternatively, the government does not merely receive the value of its original investment of $300 (which equals $330 in Year 2 present values); it also earns an additional $30 in Year 2 - the amount of above-normal return on its share of the investment.

[32] This method of treating debt corresponds to the treatment of debt under the individual tax prepayment (ITP) approach discussed in the text and described below.

The alternative approach is to include the proceeds of loans in the business tax base, but to allow a deduction for both interest and the repayment of principal. Such treatment clearly has a zero net effect in present value terms on the business tax base. In the example described above, $800 would be included in the business tax base in Year 1, but a deduction of $880 (principal plus interest) would be allowed in Year 2; these quantities are equal in present value terms and thus have no effect on tax burdens or effective tax rates on capital income.[33]

To summarize, allowing debt finance has no effect on the results presented in the previous subsection, as long as interest payments are treated correctly. This result holds for both the income and consumption taxes, although the correct treatment of interest is different for the two taxes. It also holds for both of the two alternative treatments of interest available under the business tax component of the consumption tax.

C. Consumption vs. Income Tax Treatment of Individuals

The essential difference between income and consumption taxation of individuals is the tax treatment of saving and the return to saving and of borrowing and interest expenses. Under an income tax, no deduction is allowed for saving and the annual return to saving is included in the tax base. In contrast, under an individual cash flow (ICF) consumption tax, a deduction is allowed for saving placed in so-called "qualified accounts" and withdrawals from such accounts, including earnings thereon, are included in the tax base. (Qualified accounts can be defined loosely as any legitimate investment account.) Thus interest, dividends, rents, and capital gains, as well as the original investment, are taxed only when withdrawn from a qualified account. Loans are also treated on a cash flow basis, as the proceeds of loans are included in the tax base, but repayment of interest and principal is deductible.[34]

The "cash flow" terminology follows from the fact that the individual tax base is net cash flow, defined as cash receipts less cash saving. The tax base is consumption

---

[33] This method of treating debt corresponds to the treatment of debt under the individual cash flow (ICF) approach discussed in the text and described below.

[34] One well-known version of this type of tax is the "cash flow lifetime income tax" proposed by Aaron and Galper (1985); another is the cash flow portion of the consumption tax plan recommended by the U. S. Treasury (1977).

because wages and salaries are taxed only if consumed, and capital earnings are taxed only if withdrawn from a qualified account to finance consumption. Note that the proceeds of a loan used to finance consumption are included in the tax base, while proceeds that are used to finance an investment produce an offsetting deduction due to the expensing of investment, so that the loan/investment combination has no immediate tax consequences.

A critical question in the design of such a tax is whether gifts and bequests are to be treated as consumption of the donor. This section considers a model that neglects gifts and bequests; the following section turns to the question of the appropriate treatment of gifts and bequests and the effects of such treatment.

An ICF consumption tax is sometimes characterized as exempting capital income received by individuals from tax, or applying a zero effective tax rate to such capital income. The rationale underlying this characterization is analogous to that presented above in the discussion of a business tax which allows expensing. Specifically, if tax rates are constant and the rate of return equals the discount rate, the tax benefit of the deduction for saving equals in present value terms the tax cost of including both principal and interest in the tax base when savings are withdrawn. As a result, the effective tax rate on capital income is zero. These points can be illustrated with the following simple numerical example.

Consider a two-period life-cycle model of individual behavior where consumption in the two periods is denoted as C1 and C2; in this model each of the two periods may consist of many years. Individual wage earnings in the two periods are W1 = \$4,000 and W2 = \$2,000. The interest rate is assumed to equal the discount rate and to be one; it is relatively large to reflect the fact that the periods are relatively long rather than a single year. The tax rate is assumed to be constant over the individual's lifetime and equal to 30 percent.[35] In this example, period two values are discounted to period one present-value equivalents.

If consumption equals spending in both periods, the present value of tax paid (PVT) under the income tax would simply be \$1,500, since

$$PVT = 0.3(4000) + 0.3\,(2000)/2 = 1500\ .$$

[35] The implications of this assumption are discussed below.

In this case, the PVT under the income tax is equal to the product of the tax rate (t) and the present value of the individual's "lifetime endowment" (PVE), which is defined as the present value of earnings, or

$$\text{PVE} = 4000 + 2000/2 = 5000 \ ,$$

and

$$\text{PVT} = t\,(\text{PVE}) = 0.3\,(5000) = 1500 \ .$$

A tax in which the base equals the PVE, which can be referred to an endowment tax, provides a convenient benchmark for the subsequent analysis. For the case in which consumption equals earnings in each period and the individual saves nothing in the first period, the tax burdens under the income and consumption taxes are the same; thus, the actual tax equals the endowment tax in present value terms under both the income and consumption taxes.

The differences between the income and consumption taxes are brought out only when the individual saves during the first period for consumption during the second. Suppose he wishes to consume \$2,100 in period one and save the rest of after-tax earnings for period two consumption. Under the income tax, saving in the first period (S1) would be \$700 (700=0.7x4000-2100). Period two consumption is thus the sum of after-tax wage earnings in period two, the amount saved in period one (which is untaxed in period two since it represents return of principal), and the after-tax return on savings, or

$$\text{C2} = 0.7(2000) + 700 + 0.7(700) = 2590 \ .$$

Thus, the present value of taxes under the income tax in this case is

$$\text{PVT} = 0.3(4000) + 0.3(2000+700)/2 = 1605 \ ,$$

which represents a 7 percent tax increase relative to the endowment tax of \$1,500. The \$105 difference in present value of taxes paid arises purely from the taxation of interest income in period two (105=0.3x700/2).

Under the cash flow consumption tax, the individual again consumes $2,100 in the first period, which implies he is able to save $1,000 (C1 = 0.7(4000-1000) = 2100). (Note that S1 = $1,000 is deducted from the tax base.) Second period consumption is thus

$$C2 = 0.7(2000) + 0.7(2000) = 2800 ,$$

where the first term reflects after-tax wage earnings and the second term reflects consumption funded from the after-tax proceeds of withdrawing gross savings of $2,000, consisting of $1,000 of principal and $1,000 of interest. The present value of ICF taxes paid is

$$PVT = 0.3(4000\text{-}1000) + 0.3(2000+2000)/2 = 1500 .$$

This is again equal to the value of the endowment tax.[36]

Thus, in contrast to the income tax, the cash flow tax has the effect of exempting the yield from capital income from tax. This occurs because the value of the tax reduction resulting from the period one deduction for saving (300 = 0.3x1000) is exactly equal in present value terms to the tax burden imposed by the taxation of the withdrawal of principal and interest in period two (300 = 0.3x2000/2). Alternatively, the individual forgoes $700 of consumption in period one by saving $1000 (700 = 0.7x1000) in order to fund consumption of $1400 in period two (1400 = 0.7x2000). Because he realizes the full 100 percent return on his investment, the return to saving is said to be untaxed.

---

[36] However, note that the equivalence between the present values of the tax burdens under a cash flow consumption tax and under an endowment tax depends on the assumption of a constant tax rate over the individual's lifetime. Matters are much less clear with progressive marginal tax rates. In this case, calculation of the present value of the endowment tax would presumably require the application of a progressive rate structure to a tax base equal to the present value of each individual's lifetime endowment. Since consumption tends to be relatively smooth over time (in comparison to the time path of wage earnings), the tax paid under the cash flow consumption tax would be likely to correspond fairly closely to that assessed under a tax on the present value of the endowment. (In a steady state, this would be true if consumption were equalized over the lifetime.) In this case, the income tax would result in a tax burden higher than would a lifetime endowment tax to the extent that (1) the return to savings were taxed, and (2) individuals with variable wage earnings paid higher taxes because they were subject to relatively high marginal tax rates in high-wage years.

The fact that, under the appropriate assumptions, the ICF approach effectively exempts from tax the yield to capital income can be demonstrated in an even more straightforward fashion. Suppose that the yield to capital income is explicitly excluded from the tax base; that is, suppose no deduction is given for saving, but the return to saving is untaxed. The effects of such an approach in the two-period example are straightforward. With no deduction for saving, $S1 = 0.7(4000) - 2100 = 700$. With no taxation of capital income, $C2 = 0.7(2000) + 1400 = 2800$. The present value of taxes paid is

$$PVT = 0.3(4000) + 0.3(2000)/2 = 1500 ,$$

or the value of the endowment tax. Thus consumption in both periods is the same as with the ICF tax, and the PVT is the same, although the time path of tax receipts is different. It is in this sense that an individual cash flow tax is equivalent to a tax which exempts the yield from capital income.[37]

This equivalence suggests that an alternative method of implementing a consumption-based tax at the individual level would be to exclude the yield to capital income from the tax base. That is, in contrast to the ICF approach, both saving and the receipt of capital income at the individual level would simply be ignored for tax purposes. Interest income, dividends, and capital gains would not be included in the individual tax base; symmetrically, interest payments would not be deductible. Loans would thus have no tax consequences. As a result, the individual tax base would consist of only labor income - wages and salaries plus any other labor-related payments including pension receipts.[38] Such a method of implementing a consumption-based tax is the individual tax prepayment (ITP) approach discussed in the text.[39]

One well-known version of the ITP approach is the "flat tax" plan proposed by Hall and Rabushka (1983, 1985). Under this approach all of the individual tax base, after

---

[37] Once again, this equivalence obtains only with constant tax rates. Under a cash flow consumption tax, capital income is subsidized (taxed) if the tax rate at the time the deduction is taken is higher (lower) than the tax rate at the time savings are withdrawn and consumed.

[38] As noted in the text, proponents of ITP taxes typically recommend that pensions be treated on a cash flow basis. The treatment of gifts and inheritances is discussed below.

[39] For further discussion of why a system consisting of an ITP tax coupled with the consumption-based business tax described above is in fact a tax on consumption, see Bradford (1988).

personal exemptions and a standard deduction, would be taxed at a single tax rate. A multi-rate variant of this approach is the so-called "Plan X" proposed by Bradford (1986) and the "Simplified Alternative Tax" described by McLure, Mutti, Thuronyi and Zodrow (1988). It can also be viewed as the "yield exemption" portion of the consumption tax plan described by the U.S. Treasury (1977).

In comparison to the ICF approach, no deduction is allowed for saving under the ITP approach, so that period one taxes are larger; on the other hand, no tax is assessed on the return to saving, so period two taxes are smaller. The tax that would be paid on the withdrawal from savings of principal and interest under the ICF tax is thus "prepaid" by virtue of the absence of a deduction for saving under the ITP approach. Turning around the argument made above, the cost of the lost deduction is equal in present value terms to the benefit of the exemption of future capital earnings. (In anticipation of the discussion in the following section, note that the "tax prepayment" reasoning applies regardless of whether the funds saved are consumed or used to fund the making of gifts and bequests.)

To summarize, an ICF tax differs from an income tax in that a deduction for saving is allowed, with all proceeds of dissaving subject to tax. With constant tax rates and a rate of return equal to the discount rate, this is equivalent to exempting capital income from tax. As a result, another way of achieving a tax base similar in present value terms to that under the ICF consumption tax is to exempt capital income from taxation at the individual level; this is the ITP approach to taxation on the basis of consumption.

D. The Treatment of Gifts and Bequests

There are two very diverse views among consumption (and income) tax advocates regarding the appropriate tax treatment of gifts and bequests.[40] Most observers agree that gifts and inheritances received represent potential consumption and thus should be included in the consumption tax base of the recipient. The contentious issue is the treatment of gifts and bequests given.

---

[40] The proper tax treatment of charitable donations is a separate issue. Deductions for charitable donations can be allowed under both the ICF and ITP consumption taxes, as under an income tax, if such treatment is deemed to be a desirable and effective means of stimulating contributions to socially beneficial activities.

Under one view, gifts and bequests made represent one form of consumption among many alternatives and thus should be subject to tax. This view requires taxation of such transfers to both the donor and the recipient. Under the ICF approach, it implies that a withdrawal from a qualified account to fund the making of a gift or bequest constitutes consumption and should thus be included in the tax base of the donor (as well as in the tax base of the recipient).

Under the ITP approach, however, no tax is due when savings are withdrawn for any purpose, including the making of gifts and bequests. (Recall that such treatment is appropriate since, relative to the ICF approach, the tax has been "prepaid," as no deduction was allowed for saving.) Thus, taxation to both the donor and recipient is achieved automatically as long as gifts and bequests are included in the recipient's tax base. Note that under both the ICF and ITP approaches, this treatment can be summarized as including gifts and inheritances received in the tax base of the recipient, but allowing no deduction to the donor for amounts transferred through gifts and bequests.

The lifetime tax base under such a plan is equal to all of the resources under the individual's control, including gifts and inheritances received, as well as wages, salaries and pensions, regardless of whether some of those resources are used to fund the making of gifts and bequests. Thus, this approach is consistent with a "lifetime endowment" view of tax equity, under which an individual's lifetime command over resources is seen to be the proper basis for taxation of individuals.

The alternative view is that a consumption tax should exclude gifts and bequests given; such transfers would be subject to tax only when actually consumed by the recipient. Under both the ICF and ITP approaches, this view implies that gifts and inheritances received should be included in the tax base, but deductions should be allowed for gifts and bequests made. Note that under the ICF approach, the deduction for the gift or bequest offsets the inclusion in the tax base of the withdrawal from the qualified account. In contrast, under the ITP approach, deductions for gifts and bequests made would offset compensation and, because tax has been prepaid, would in many cases require refunds to the donor.

Under this view, the lifetime tax base is appropriately consumption narrowly defined, with tax on gifts and bequests paid only upon actual consumption by the recipient or heir. Thus, this approach is consistent with a "dynastic" view of tax equity, under which it is appropriate for only a single tax to be paid, when resources are actually consumed by some member of a multi-generational family.

An alternative way to approximate fair treatment according to the dynastic view of tax equity involves allowing no deduction for gifts and bequests made. In this case, the tax paid by the donor should not be viewed as a tax paid on his consumption, since under the dynastic view the donor theoretically should not pay tax on gifts and bequests given. Instead, the tax on the donor should be viewed as a proxy tax paid on behalf of the recipient; accordingly, gifts and inheritances received should not be included in the recipient's tax base. Note that the proxy tax will be too high (too low) according to the dynastic view if the tax rate of the donor is greater than (less than) that of the recipient. Under this approach, gifts and bequests are completely ignored in the calculation of the tax base of both the donor and the recipient. This simple (but generally inaccurate) treatment contrasts sharply with the direct method of implementing the dynastic view described above. The direct approach requires inclusion of gifts and inheritances in the tax base of the recipient and deductions from the tax base of the donor for all gifts and bequests made. Such treatment would clearly be difficult to enforce and administer.

The choice between these two views of the proper treatment of gifts and bequests depends on a host of economic and philosophical issues. However, in our view, countries considering consumption-based direct tax alternatives should adopt the lifetime endowment viewpoint and consider only reforms consistent with that viewpoint. This belief is based on four considerations.

First, the vertical equity goals of most if not all countries - a fair distribution of tax burdens across income classes - are likely to call for a tax burden across income classes that is mildly progressive, or at least not regressive. Given the common practice of relying heavily on regressive indirect taxes, these goals can be achieved much more easily if the lifetime endowment view is adopted; indeed, it may be very difficult, as well as costly in terms of reduced economic incentives and increased tax avoidance and evasion due to higher tax rates on wealthy individuals, to achieve any particular vertical equity goals under a consumption-based direct tax without adopting this viewpoint. Thus, we believe that adopting the lifetime endowment view of tax equity (and taking steps necessary to enforce the tax provisions it implies) is critical to ensuring the vertical equity of a consumption tax system.

Second, such a system will arguably be fairer, and in any case, will certainly be perceived as being fairer, than the dynastic alternative described above. Most observers are probably accustomed to thinking about vertical equity in terms of annual tax burdens of individuals. Though the lifetime perspective implicit in the discussion above represents a significant departure from this convention, it can plausibly be explained as necessary to achieve horizontal equity between taxpayers with equal lifetime endowments, as well as vertical equity. By comparison, a multi-generational or dynastic view of equity represents a much greater departure from conventional views, since it effectively defines vertical equity over an infinite time horizon for a group of donors and donees (typically a multi-generational family group), rather than over an individual's lifetime or a single year (or several years). Some prominent tax experts are unconvinced that a lifetime view of tax equity is preferable to a standard of equity based on a much shorter time period.[41] In light of this skepticism, it seems unlikely that most observers would be sympathetic to a view of equity based on an infinite time horizon. Accordingly, the dynastic view of equity would probably be unconvincing as a rationale underlying the tax treatment of gifts and bequests.

In addition, allowing wealthy heirs to consume tax-free (under the "proxy tax" alternative version of the dynastic view) would probably be perceived as grossly unfair, even if donors had been taxed on the transfers. (It might be argued that such perception problems are not significant since the income taxes in most countries generally tax gifts and bequests lightly without provoking public outcry. However, contrary to the situation under the consumption tax, income from capital is commonly subject to income tax. The taxation of capital income under the income tax provides an indirect means of taxing gifts and bequests; that is, income taxation reduces the return to wealth and thus reduces funds available for the making of gifts and bequests. Moreover, in some countries, the income tax is supplemented by a wealth tax or a gift/estate tax.) For all of these reasons, it seems unlikely that the dynastic view of tax equity could provide a rationale for the design of a tax structure that would be widely acceptable.

Third, the argument (frequently made by income tax proponents) that the accumulation of wealth confers status, power, and peace of mind to the owner and thus should be included in measures of ability to pay, surely has some validity, especially in

---

[41] See Goode (1980).

countries in which wealth differentials are very great. This point supports the notion of taxing all individual wealth at least once during each generation.

Fourth, the existence of wealth, estate and gift taxes in many countries, as well as a history of progressive income taxes, suggests that such taxation conforms with societal norms in those countries.

It should be noted that implementing a consumption tax based on the lifetime endowment view would not be without costs. In particular, administrative costs would be high. The most important problems would occur because it is notoriously difficult to ensure that gifts and bequests received are reported in the tax base of the recipient; this is especially true for gifts among family members. It is unclear what types of administrative measures would be most effective in improving compliance in this area. Monitoring of such transfers would be simplified in those cases in which the transfers were recorded by some governmental agency for reasons unrelated to the national tax system (such as property transfers recorded by local officials for property tax or other reasons); alternatively, rules requiring reporting (either by individuals or by institutions) of all transfers of certain types of assets could be implemented in the hope of generating a "paper trail" that would help identify gifts and bequests. A separate estate tax could be implemented, with bequests taxed at the highest individual marginal tax rate under the consumption tax system; heirs could be allowed a credit under the consumption tax for taxes paid on their behalf by the testator. Note also that the likelihood that significant amounts of gifts and bequests will not be reported under a consumption tax based on the lifetime endowment view provides a justification - though a somewhat tenuous one - for a separate tax on individual net wealth. Specifically, such a tax may indirectly offset the effects of undertaxation of gifts and bequests received by reducing the wealth of the donors and recipients of such transfers. Of course, all such measures would increase the complexity of a consumption tax system, while still leaving a significant portion of such transfers untaxed.

In addition to the tax evasion problem of non-reporting of gifts and inheritances received, in many cases, problems in determining the value of gifts and inheritances would be significant even when such transfers were reported. Accurate valuations would be particularly difficult for transfers of ownership interests in closely-held businesses or for assets that are unique or infrequently traded, such as art and other collectibles. Measures designed to improve valuation techniques would add complexity and would undoubtedly be somewhat unproductive in the cases of certain types of assets.

Another familiar problem associated with taxing gifts and inheritances arises in those cases in which the asset transferred is a family business (such as a family farm) and a portion of the asset might have to be sold in order to pay the tax liability. To the extent this is perceived to be a problem, special measures allowing installment payments of taxes (including interest payments at a market rate) could be provided. Such measures of course add complexity to the tax system, and are arguably inequitable since such treatment would apply only to certain elements of the individual tax base.[42]

Despite all of these difficulties[43], we feel that the arguments for the lifetime endowment view are compelling. Thus, to improve the equity of a system of consumption taxation, every effort should be made to administer and enforce as effectively as possible the treatment of gifts and bequests implied by adoption of the lifetime view of tax equity.

It is interesting to note that the above numerical analyses of individual income and consumption taxation are basically unchanged when gifts and bequests are considered. That is, as long as gifts and bequests received are included in the tax base and there are no deductions for gifts and bequests given (which are thus treated as consumption of the donor under the ICF tax), the numerical comparisons of the income and ICF and ITP consumption taxes are basically unchanged.

To see this, note that gifts or bequests received would simply be included in the tax base and in the calculation of the present value of the individual's endowment. In terms

---

[42] Adopting the lifetime view of tax equity would also have efficiency costs. Individual decisions regarding gifts and bequests, as well as their nature (e.g., cash vs. "in kind" transfers such as expensive educations), would be distorted. In addition, taxation of gifts and bequests would generally involve taxation of the return to saving; this in turn implies that some of the intertemporal neutrality benefits of reducing the taxation of capital income under a consumption tax would be reduced.

[43] Note that these problems are not unique to the consumption tax. That is, very similar problems arise if the lifetime endowment criterion is adopted under an income tax, since gifts and bequests received should be included in the tax base, with no offsetting deduction under the income tax for donors. The only important difference is that deficiencies in the taxation of gifts and bequests are offset in a rather indirect fashion under the income tax by the taxation of the capital income of the donors and recipients of such transfers.

of the two-period example analyzed above, gifts and inheritances received could be included by separating W1 into $3,000 of wages and $1,000 of inheritance. Since no deduction is allowed for gifts and bequests made, the division of C2 into a consumption and a bequest component has no tax consequences. Thus, all results regarding the differences between income and consumption taxes, as well as the similarities between the ICF and ITP approaches, obtain when gifts and bequests are treated as specified above.

Comments by Wolfram F. Richter

Early economic discussions of the direct taxation of consumption as a potential alternative to the direct taxation of income have commonly focussed on equity and economic efficiency. The hope for efficiency gains in fact motivated the consideration of the consumption tax.

I must confess, that I would readily join the consumption party if a clear case could be made on efficiency grounds. Alas, the case is not that clear and McLure and Zodrow do not even try to make an efficiency argument. They neither appeal to equity. Their intention is to justify the choice of a consumption tax on the field of administrative simplicity.

The attempt deserves credit since simplicity is a truely important objective. The discussion of consumption taxation so far greatly suffered from ignoring aspects of tax administration. Too often, to my view, the obvious defects of income taxation in practice have been contrasted with the advantages of an ideal consumption tax. I therefore appreciate McLure and Zodrow's work as a careful and detailed analysis of the administrative difficulties that we may have to face under consumption taxation. I would not know of any other attempt to derive such a fair account of the pros and cons.

And still, I do not feel convinced by their conclusions. To say it frankly: Even after reading the paper I do not feel convinced that we should join the consumption party for reasons of administrative simplicity. I suspect that the complicating timing issues of income taxation do not really disappear. They only appear in another form and it is far from clear which form produces more or less administrative problems. Admittedly, we would not have to bother about depreciation allowances if we followed the paper's suggestions. On the other hand, interest rates gain a much more important role as I am still going to explain. Unfortunately, McLure and Zodrow say little about the correct choice of interest rates for consumption tax administration. My thesis is that all the timing issues reappear at this point. Let me show how they come in.

McLure and Zodrow do not simply plead for consumption taxation. They favour a special institutional structure. Thus they first explain why they would not do without a business tax even under consumption taxation. The reasons are convincing. The authors next present two basic forms: "ICF/RF" and "ITP/R". The first form couples cash flow accounting at the individual levels with cash flow accounting for real and financial transactions at the business level. As the authors consider this form the inferior option I may concentrate in my remarks on ITP/R. The letters stand for individual tax prepayment which is coupled with a business tax on real cash flows. This indirect form of personal consumption taxation has been popularized by Hall and Rabushka (1983, 1985) and Bradford (1986).

For Europeans it may help if they think about ITP/R in terms of a value-added tax (VAT). ITP/R in fact amounts to a value-added tax where tax rates are not differentiated among goods but according to life-time income. Intertemporal consuption decisions remain undistorted. There is however a discrimination against the use of labour in production. VAT is a tax on labour income and producers' rent.

The major policy problem with VAT comes from equity. VAT is at best regarded to be proportional if not regressive. In order to alleviate the regressive effects the European countries usually tax favoured forms of consumption more lightly. McLure and Zodrow would prefer a VAT that is designed as a personal tax. The idea is simple. Withhold producers' rent at the business level and tax it at a rate that equals the top marginal rate applied to individual labour income. Marginal rates on labour income may be minimally differentiated as under the Hall and Rabushka plan. (These authors propose a flat rate of 19 percent which is complemented by a personal exemption in order to reach redistributive effects.) Or marginal tax rates may be differentiated more and openly as suggested by Bradford. This is also the preferred option of McLure and Zodrow.

The problem with differentiated marginal tax rates is that it makes averaging devices necessary. This holds in particular for ITP/R which taxes periodic income although life-time income is the declared ideal. One might argue that if averaging were not allowed for tax purposes then firms would develop instruments of workers' compensation that - like pension schemes - provide implicit averaging.

The argument however ignores the self-employed. If explicit averaging must therefore be accepted interest rates have to be fixed in a second step. Any possibility of carrying forward tax credits and liabilities has to be accompanied by appropriate discounting.

The wish to combine VAT with personally differentiated marginal tax rates is however not the only reason that makes the compounding of interest necessary in tax assessment. The need is enforced by the fighting of tax abuse. Let me only discuss two avenues of tax abuse which I see greatly accentuated under cash-flow taxation:

i) hobby farms

and

ii) the profitable transformation of real transactions into financial ones.

One might argue that every tax, the income tax included, has to face the problem of tax abuse. The argument however ignores that cash-flow taxation for systematic reasons not only increases the profitability of various forms of tax abuse but also weakens the prerequisites for successful auditing. The mentioned avenues of tax abuse might more easily be fought if tax authorities could audit the economic profitability of business activities directly. It is however the declared advantage of cash-flow taxation that it works without the determination of economic income. Direct ways of auditing economic profitability should therefore not be taken into regard. We would have to rely on more indirect methods. And that is where interest rates become important.

The problem is well-known from the financial sector. The common pricing of services does not allow to distinguish there between real and financial transactions. This is why the Meade Committee (1978) searched for consumption based taxes that do not rely on the restricted taxation of real cash flows. Clearly, if financial transactions are tax free and if tax authorities fail to distinguish between financial and real ones then there will be scope for systematic tax abuse whenever one transactor is tax free and the other one not. Zodrow and McLure, in a 1988 Paper, discuss various forms that such tax abuse can take on. I would expect that they would become very popular under ITP/R. "Solutions to these problems are far from obvious" as Zodrow and McLure (1988, p.73) admit. One would have to observe market rates of interest, well structured with respect to maturity and risk characteristics - no easy task.

A related problem arises under the heading of "hobby farms". Clearly, every personal tax knows the difficulty of distinguishing between hobby activities and legitimate business ventures. However, the opportunities for tax abuse are greatly accentuated by expensing as McLure and Zodrow admit (1989, p. 15). The only effective way of fighting this form of tax abuse is the denial of tax refunding. Claims that result from negative cash flows should only be carried forward and offset against later tax liabilities. This has in fact been proposed by Garnaut and Clunies Ross (1975) and also by Kay and King (1978). The proposal however raises servere problems when tax claims are never redeemed. Not only are risky legitimate investments discouraged. The interest rates by which tax credits are carried forward would correctly have to include risk premia reflecting the risk characteristics of the specific investment under consideration [Fane, (1987); Summers (1987)]. This is hardly an appealing implication.

Let me summarize: The alleged administrative advantage of cash-flow taxation relies on not auditing economic profitability. I cannot see however how one should successfully fight tax abuse under such circumstances. If one refuses to determine economic income the correct determination of interest rates gains crucial importance. For systematic reasons it would not suffice to introduce just one interest rate for tax assessment. One would have to consider the full range of market interest rates. I cannot see why this should be administratively more attractive than the consideration of market prices for assets as required under an ideal income tax. In summary, I highly appreciate McLure's and Zodrow's analysis but I hesitate to follow their conclusions. I cannot see how one could justify the substitution of the income tax by ITP/R with sole regard to administrative simplicity.

References

Aaron, H.J. / Galper, H. (1985), Assessing Tax Reform, Washington,D.C.: The Brookings Institution.

Andrews, W.D. (1974), A Consumption-Type or Cash Flow Personal Income Tax, Harvard Law Review 87, pp. 1113-1188.

Bradford, D.F. (1986), Untangling the Income Tax, Cambridge: Harvard University Press.

Bradford, D.F. (1988), What are Consumption Taxes and Who Pays Them?, Tax Notes 39, pp. 383-391.

Bradford, D.F. (1990), Die X-Steuer: Ein Weg zur Steuervereinfachung, in: M.Rose (ed.), Konsumorientierte Neuordnung des Steuersystems, Berlin, Heidelberg.

Economic Council of Canada (1987), Road Map for Tax Reform, Ottawa: Ministry of Supply and Services.

Eigner, E.M. (1959), Indian Income, Wealth and Expenditure Taxes: Integration and Administration, National Tax Journal 12, pp. 151-162.

Fane, G. (1987), Neutral Taxation under Uncertainty, Journal of Public Economics 33, pp. 95-105.

Garnaut, R. / Clunies Ross, A. (1975), Uncertainty, Risk Aversion and the Taxing of Natural Resource Projects, Economic Journal 85, pp. 272-287.

Gordon, R.H. (1988), Notes on Cash-Flow Taxation, paper prepared for World Bank Workshop on the Implementation of Cash Flow Company Taxation.

Goode, R.A. (1960), New System of Direct Taxation in Ceylon, National Tax Journal 13, pp. 329-340.

Goode, R.A. (1980), The Superiority of the Income Tax, in: J. A. Pechman, ed., What Should be Taxed: Income or Expenditure?, Washington, D.C.: The Brookings Institution, pp. 49-73.

Graetz, M.J. (1979), Implementing a Progressive Consumption Tax, Harvard Law Review 92, pp. 1575-1661.

Hall, R.E. / Rabushka, A. (1983), Low Tax, Simple Tax, Flat Tax, New York: McGraw-Hill.

Hall, R.E. / Rabushka, A. (1985), The Flat Tax, Stanford: Hoover Institution Press.

Institute for Fiscal Studies (1978), The Structure and Reform of Direct Taxation, Report of a committee chaired by professor J.E. Meade, London: Allen and Unwin.

Kaldor, N. (1955), An Expenditure Tax, London: Allen and Unwin.

Kay, J.A. / King, M.A. (1978), The British Tax System, Oxford: Oxford University Press.

Lodin, S.-O. (1978), Progressive Expenditure Tax. An Alternative?, Stockholm: LiberForlag.

McLure, C.E., Jr. (1979), Must Corporate Income be Taxed Twice?, Washington: The Brookings Institution.

McLure, C.E., Jr. (1987a), The Value Added Tax: Key to Deficit Reduction? Washington: American Enterprise Institute.

McLure, C.E., Jr. (1987b), Illustration of Effects of Expensing (first-year write-off) of Investment, With and Without Debt Finance, Jamaica Tax Structure Examination Project, Metropolitan Studies Program, Syracuse University.

McLure, C.E., Jr. (1988), The 1986 Tax Act. Tax Reform's Finest Hour or Death Throes of the Income Tax? National Tax Journal 41, pp. 303-315.

McLure, C.E., Jr. / Mutti, J. / Thuronyi, V. / Zodrow, G.R. (1988), The Taxation of Income from Business and Capital in Colombia, Bogota, Colombia: Ministerio de Hacienda Y Credito Publico, and forthcoming, Duke University Press.

Meade-Committee (1978), The Structure and Reform of Direct Taxation, report of a committee chaired by Professor J.E. Meade, Institute for Fiscal Studies, London: Allen and Unwin.

Mieszkowski, P. (1977), The Cash Flow Version of an Expenditure Tax, U.S. Treasury Department Office of Tax Analysis Paper No. 26.

Mieszkowski, P. (1980), The Advisability and Feasibility of an Expenditure Tax System, in: H.J. Aaron / M.J. Boskin (eds.), The Economics of Taxation, Washington, D.C.: The Brookings Institution, pp. 179-201.

Musgrave, P.B. (1969), United States Taxation of Foreign Investment Income: Issues and Arguments, Cambridge: Harvard Law School International Tax Program.

Shoup, C.S. (forthcoming), Criteria for Choice Among Types of Value Added Tax, in: M. Gillis / C. Shoup / G.P. Sicat (eds.), Value Added Taxation in Developing Countries, Duke University Press.

Summers, L.H. (1987), Investment Incentives and the Discounting of Depreciation allowances, in: M. Feldstein, (ed.), University of Chicago Press, The Effects of Taxation on Capital Accumulation, pp. 295-304.

Tait, A.A., (forthcoming), The Value-Added Tax: Revenue, Inflation, and the Foreign Trade Balance, in: M. Gillis / C. Shoup / G.P. Sicat (eds.), Value Added Taxation in Developing Countries, Duke University Press.

U.S. Department of the Treasury (1977), Blueprints for Basic Tax Reform, Washington, DC: U.S. Government Printing Office; also available as D. F. Bradford and the U.S. Treasury Department Staff (1984), Blueprints for Basic Tax Reform, Arlington, VA: Tax Analysts.

U.S. Department of the Treasury (1984), Tax Reform for Fairness, Simplicity, and Economic Growth, Washington, D.C.: U.S. Government Printing Office.

Zodrow, G.R. (1987), Alternative Approaches to Progressive Expenditure Taxation, Proceedings of the 1986 Annual Conference on Taxation, National Tax Association-Tax Institute of America, pp. 125-134.

Zodrow, G.R. (forthcoming), The Individual Tax Base: Efficiency and Horizontal Equity Aspects of the Choice Between Income and Consumption, in: S. Cnossen / R.M. Bird (eds.), The Personal Income Tax: Phoenix from the Ashes? Amsterdam: North-Holland.

Zodrow, G.R. / McLure, Jr., C.E. (1988), Implementing Direct Consumption Taxes in Developing Countries, Policy, Planning, and Research Working Paper Number WPS 131, Washington: World Bank, Public Economics Division, Country Economics Department.

Henry J. Aaron

Alternate Roads to Consumption Taxation - Administration versus Tax Structure

The debate about the theoretical and practical advantages of taxing income or consumption will no doubt outlive us all. In this paper I shall not try to resolve - or even advance - that debate. Rather I shall focus on a subsidiary question. If it is decided that consumption is a more appropriate tax base than income, how would administrative considerations influence the choice among alternative ways to tax consumption? Judgments about the administrative ease of shifting from income to consumption taxation would bulk large even if the theoretical debate were resolved. Absent such a conclusive outcome, they are likely to be dominant.

I shall suggest that a switch to consumption taxes will not spare governmental authorities the need to calculate income for a sizeable minority of the population, that entity-level consumption taxes are no more capable than entity-level income taxes of dealing with the growing problems posed by international trade and capital movements, and that several issues of design in personal consumption taxes that are normally treated separately should be considered jointly.

I. Background Issues

Three sets of issues not normally combined with the income-consumption tax debate are of considerable practical significance. One concerns policy regarding transfer payments. A second arises from the increasing openness of economies to international capital movements. And the third concerns withholding.

A. Transfer Payments

Transfers, as every textbook emphasizes, are simply negative taxes. The linear income tax, for example, is nothing but a lump-sum entitlement combined with a proportional income tax. One would think, therefore, that the income-consumption tax debate would have a counterpart in debates about transfer policy.

Such is not the case. Cash transfers are based sometimes on categorical entitlement (childrens' allowances or unemployment benefits) or on some combination of categorical entitlement and either earnings (old-age benefits) or income and wealth (assistance in cash to the poor). Similar considerations govern the distribution of benefits in kind.

No large scale program of cash transfers is based on consumption, however. The very concept of basing cash transfers or subsidies in cash or in kind on total consumption seems peculiar, since the purpose of cash transfers is to enable more *consumption* than the recipient's *income* is sufficient to sustain. A person with ample income who elects to consume little may be regarded with curiosity, but rarely with pity.

Because consumption services and consumption outlays may be largely unrelated for extended periods, a consumption-calibrated transfer system would be a practical, as well as a theoretical, monstrosity. Furthermore, assistance based on low consumption would be susceptible to manipulation. By minimizing consumption for a stipulated period, those close to eligibility could maximize the aid they receive in increasing consumption.

This line of argument does not prove that consumption is necessarily an inappropriate basis for determining *positive* taxes. But it does mean that even if the income tax were entirely supplanted by a consumption tax, the need to measure income for the sizeable minority of the population deemed eligible for assistance would remain. In short, transfers related to income will survive even under a consumption tax. If transfers are regarded as simply negative income taxes, the tax system broadly defined will unavoidably remain in part an income tax system.

B. Open Economies

An increasing proportion of tax-relevant transactions cross international borders. International trade as a fraction of gross national product has risen significantly in the past few decades and international capital movements have grown even more. Between 1964 and 1985 gross world domestic product outside the socialist bloc grew at a compound rate of 10.4 percent, international trade in goods and services grew at a compound rate of 12.4 percent, and international banking grew at a compound rate of 25.8 percent according to the Bank for International Settlements and 26.1 percent according to Morgan Guaranty.[1] These trends significantly complicate the already formidable task of accurately assessing income taxes. The reasons are straightforward and well known. Companies can manipulate prices at which trade is recorded among subsidiaries located in different countries to minimize tax - the so-called "transfer-pricing" problem. Effective rates of tax on different forms of capital income vary within and across countries, making the computation of foreign tax credits inevitably arbitrary. And fluctuations in exchange rates complicate the determination of profits and tax credits. These problems mean that tax systems can distort real decisions by multinational corporations about where to produce and from which subsidiary or branch to buy, thus adding a new form of potential excess burden and expanding old opportunities for tax avoidance and evasion. Some authors have argued that the difficulty of taxing international transactions and their growing importance pose a threat to the long run viability of income taxes at either the personal or entity level.[2]

A critical test for the long-run appeal of consumption taxation will be whether consumption tax rules can be fashioned to deal better with international trade and capital movements than income taxes can. These problems operate at both the personal and business levels.

At the personal level, Bird and McLure have pointed out the havoc wrought by the coexistence of source and destination tax rules for the taxation of capital income. These problems vanish if capital income is untaxed at the personal level, as it would be under

---

[1] See Bryant (1987, table 3-1, p.22).

[2] Bird and McLure, Jr. (1988) argue that international transactions jeopardize personal income taxes. Aaron (1987) argues that international transactions jeopardize entity-level income taxes.

a personal consumption tax - explicitly under the tax-prepayment approach, implicitly under the qualified-accounts approach.

At the business level the problem is more serious. While elimination of entity-level taxation under a consumption tax is imaginable, business taxes make both theoretical and practical sense under a consumption tax.[3] The theoretical case arises from the simple proposition that, even if investments are expensed, an entity-level tax on cash flow captures for the government a part of returns accruing at rates in excess of the government's rate of discount. Viewed from the company standpoint, such a tax falls on rents or monopoly profits and revenues from such taxes impose no excess burdens.

The practical case for an entity-level cash-flow tax rests on two considerations. First, repeal of any pre-existing corporation or business income tax would give rise to windfall capital gains arising from any front-loaded investment incentives, such as investment credits, initial allowances, or accelerated depreciation. Having received deductions or credits that understated economic income early in the life of particular investments, repeal of entity-level taxes would then spare businesses the compensating taxes later in the lives of the relevant assets. Second, in the absence of an entity-level tax business owners would have a strong incentive to conceal personal consumption or earnings within the business. An entity-level tax can be used to discourage such evasion. Whether or not an entity-level tax is imposed, tax collections from businesses will fall during the transition to a consumption tax. If the entity-level tax is repealed, the source of the decline is clear. Even if it is retained, revenues would fall because the front-loaded deductions for the cost of investments would substantially offset taxable income under the previous tax system.

If an entity-level tax exists, a cash-flow tax has some administrative advantages over an income tax. Investments could be expensed instead of capitalized and depreciated. And accounting could be managed consistently on a cash, rather than accrual, basis.

With respect to international transactions, however, neither approach skirts the most important complexities. Determination of transfer prices remains as difficult under a consumption tax as it is under an income tax. Some form of credit for taxes paid in one country on earnings repatriated to another would still have to be provided. Unless all countries taxed all classes of economic activity at similar rates, the problems

[3] See Zodrow / McLure Jr. (1988).

of calculating and limiting the proper amounts of such credits that have bedeviled tax writers since the birth of the foreign tax credit would persist. Fluctuations in exchange rates would continue to magnify these difficulties.

C. Withholding

For most households, withholding would pose no greater problem under a consumption tax than it does under an income tax. Most households receive little income other than from earnings, and annual consumption differs little from income, except when the taxpayer buys an automobile or, less frequently, a house. Since income, consumption, and earnings are similar, a withholding system based solely on earnings would work as well under a consumption tax as under an income tax.

For households who finance more than a trivial part of their consumption from unearned income (including pensions), a personal consumption tax would require the taxpayer to estimate annual consumption and make estimated tax payments. This process would necessitate a direct estimate of planned consumption outlays. For most tax units the calculations would be similar to those made under personal income taxes - the summation of estimated earned and unearned income - plus an estimate of planned saving. If withholding is collected not only from earnings, but also from capital income and transfer payments not based on current income of the tax unit, relatively few families would have to file estimated returns. If taxes are withheld only from earnings, such estimates would be required not only for the relatively small fraction of earners whose unearned income represents more than, say, 10 percent of earnings, but also by retirees and others who are out of the labor force who finance consumption from transfer payments, pensions, or other forms of capital income.

The problem of withholding could be minimized if consumption were taxed through a combination of a value-added tax imposed at a rate deemed to be the basic personal consumption tax rate and a personal consumption tax that applied only to a small fraction of high-bracket taxpayers. The value-added tax would be, in effect, the bottom bracket of the personal consumption tax. The additional tax paid by such families would correspond to surtax rates. As will be indicated below, the choice between these two approaches to withholding is closely related to other issues in design of a consumption tax.

II. Administrative Considerations in Selecting Among Personal Consumption Taxes

If a country decides to rely on consumption, rather than income, as the base for personal taxation, administrative considerations should influence three important aspects of design. The first concerns the choice between taxing consumption directly, as the difference between comprehensive income and net saving, and taxing earnings only. If consumption is taxed directly, the tax base can be defined to exclude all cash flows associated with borrowing or to include the proceeds of loans and to permit deductions for loan repayments. The former approach is sometimes called the "tax prepayment" approach; the latter, the "qualified accounts" approach.[4] Because lawyers have found it impossible to devise a viable distinction between debt and equity, I shall disregard the former option.

As an alternative, consumption can be taxed indirectly by taxing earnings. The equivalence between the direct taxation of consumption and an earnings tax is based on the proposition that under certain conditions the present value of life-time earnings equals the present value of life-time consumption. One of the conditions is that neither bequests nor inheritances occurs.[5]

Because bequests and inheritances account for a large part of the lifetime resources of a small, but economically important, minority of the population, the second major issue, both for policy and for administration, is whether to include inheritances and bequests in the personal tax base. The direct taxation of consumption and the taxation of earnings remain equivalent in present value within a single life if bequests are treated as consumption under the former and inheritances are treated as earnings under the latter. In either case, the tax base accurately represents lifetime income, provided that consumption is discounted at the rate of return the taxpayer earns on his or her investments. Consumption of households that plan with a life-cycle horizon will be undistorted by either tax. If households plan consumption with an infinite time hori-

[4] U.S. Department of the Treasury (1977).

[5] Other conditions include the existence of perfect capital markets and the persistence throughout the taxpayers life of constant proportional tax rates that satisfy the condition that $(1 - t_W) = (1 - t_C)^{-1}$, where t_W is the tax rate on earnings and t_C is the tax exclusive rate on consumption.

zon, consumption will be undistorted only if wealth transfers are excluded from the tax base. While the consumption plan of life-cycle planners will be the same under either consumption or wage taxes, the macroeconomic effects of these two taxes have been shown to be quite different from one another.[6] Furthermore, doubt is accumulating rapidly that the life-cycle model is a poor approximation to the way in which consumption is determined by many families viewed individually or by nations as a whole.[7] In particular, simulations based on plausible parameter values of the effects of switching from an income tax to a consumption tax leads to higher saving, a larger capital stock, and increased earnings and welfare than does a switch to an earnings tax.[8] The price of this gain is reduced welfare for a transitional cohort of relatively old workers and retirees who, in effect, make a lump-sum capital transfer during the transition to all future cohorts.

Given a decision to rely on consumption taxes, the third major issue concerns the relative reliance to be placed on personal consumption taxes and on broad commodity taxes, such as a value-added tax or a retail sales tax.[9] Personal consumption taxes permit rate variation on the basis of the size of each filing unit's tax base. Commodity taxes permit some minor variation in effective rates through variations in rates on classes of commodities, but the amount of such variation is quite limited and, more importantly, it is imperfectly correlated with the variation that would result from explicit consideration of a tax unit's ability to pay. Thus, a trade-off exists between the more refined measurement of ability to pay under a personal consumption tax and the simpler administration under a commodity tax.

The first and third of these issues are related. The chief administrative problem with the use of the direct taxation of consumption is that taxpayers must keep records of all capital transactions. In addition, taxpayers who finance consumption with debt must be prepared to borrow enough not only to pay for the commodities, but also for

[6] Auerbach / Kotlikoff (1987).

[7] Carroll / Summers (1989).

[8] These results depend on the assumed parameters and do not follow from pure theory, as demonstrated by Sandmo / Atkinson (1980, pp. 529-549).

[9] I shall not go into the relative administrative advantages of sales and value-added taxes.

the tax, a significant issue in the real world of high borrowing rates and borrowing limits.

Both problems are particularly burdensome for tax payers with few resources. Surveys in the United States indicate that few households have liquid assets equaling as much as one year's income. Well-to-do taxpayers in developed countries normally maintain adequate records of capital transactions for their own purposes and have sufficient assets to handle temporary bulges in consumption. Thus, limiting a personal tax to households with relatively high consumption would drastically attenuate the administrative disadvantages of the direct taxation of consumption through the qualified account approach.

This line of argument leads to the conclusion that if consumption is taxed directly through the qualified accounts approach, the tax would have to be limited to perhaps the upper 5 to 10 percent of the economic distribution. If taxes on consumption were to produce considerable revenue, however, such a tax would have to be supplemented by a value-added or retail sales tax.

Reliance on the tax-prepayment approach raises problems of perception regarding the free-ride for capital income. While the consumption tax in any form has no effect on the rate of return to saving, the fact that capital income is untaxed is transparent under a wage tax, thus heightening concern that a consumption tax will lead to large concentrations of wealth.[10] If the amount that a taxpayer can invest is constrained by outside limits, then the wage tax can result in greater concentrations of wealth, since large percentage gains will go untaxed at consumption. Thus, use of the tax prepayment approach would increase pressure to include inheritances in the tax base, a move that is necessary if one is to measure life-time income accurately. While an earnings tax is certainly easy to administer at the personal level, the analytical case for including inheritances in the base would be stiffened by the practical concern over wealth inequality.

This line of reasoning suggests that a country considering a shift from income to consumption taxation should choose among two broad options.

[10] As long as investments can be made in any amount, a consumption tax and a wage tax should lead to identical investments if the investments are $(1 - t_c)^{-1}$ times as large under a consumption tax as under an earnings tax. Since investors take a deduction for the investment, the net cost to the investor per unit of investment is 1.

- If all or most consumption tax revenues are to be raised from personal taxes, the tax prepayment method should be used. The base of such a tax would include inheritances to minimize the perception and the reality that accumulations of wealth could be transferred from generation to generation and consumed without tax.

Whether a separate tax on bequests would be desirable depends on considerations other than the objective of correctly measuring and taxing lifetime resources. Note that since correct measurement of lifetime resources requires the addition of inheritances to earnings in the personal tax base, a separate accessions tax on wealth transfers could be approximated by including inheritances in the tax base at some multiple of actual value, thereby taxing them at a higher rate than is applied to earnings. If such a tax were to generate sufficient revenue, exemptions would be relatively modest. Assistance would be necessary for families with incomes too low to support sufficient consumption, but nothing would have to be done to offset tax burdens of commodity taxes since such taxes would be nonexistent. Thus, the assistance systems and the positive tax system would not need to overlap, a circumstance that would permit an integrated tax and transfer system in which few households or none at all would simultaneously be eligible for assistance and face positive taxes.

- If the qualified accounts approach is employed, it should be limited to perhaps the upper 5 to 10 percent of the economic distribution, by exempting a relatively high base level of consumption. To raise a large part of the government's revenues from the consumption base, such a tax would have to be supplemented by a value-added or retail sales tax. And because of the burdens such commodity taxes would place on households with few resources, this approach would increase the importance of various kinds of assistance in cash or in kind.

Freeing taxpayers of modest means from filing tax returns would reduce administrative inconvenience. As a matter of politics, pressure to include bequests in the base of a direct consumption tax would not be so strong as the pressure to include inheritances would be under the earnings tax of the prepaid tax approach, although the analytical case for their inclusion is in no way diminished. High progressive rates on consumption would appear to reach large investment gains, while an earnings tax would not. The assistance system would be used not only to supplement low earnings, but also to offset the burdens that commodity taxes would impose on households with low earnings. Thus, while households of modest means would be freed from filing personal consumption tax returns, more would have to apply for assistance than under the first approach. Furthermore, since assistance would be based on income or on income and wealth, while taxes would be based on consumption, the two systems would be likely to overlap.

III. Conclusion

In this paper I have argued that a move to consumption taxation is unlikely to ameliorate the major emerging problem in entity-level taxation, the proper measurement of income arising from international trade and capital movements. At the personal level, I have suggested that the choice between the method of assessing a personal consumption tax is intimately related to the degree to which a country relies on commodity taxation. In general, the greater the reliance on commodity taxes, the smaller the scope for personal consumption taxation and the larger the scope for *income-related* assistance. Moreover, heavy reliance on personal consumption taxes is likely to necessitate either indirect taxation of consumption through a tax on earnings or on earnings plus inheritances; of, if consumption is to be taxed directly, the tax would be limited to a small proportion of relatively well-to-do taxpayers, while the consumption of most households would be reached through a tax on value added. An entity-level tax would still be required, but this tax would enjoy no important administrative advantage over the corporation income tax other than the avoidance of the need to capitalize and depreciate assets. In particular, a consumption tax will not free tax administrators from the increasingly vexatious complexities introduced by the increasing prevalence of businesses operating subject to dissimilar tax systems of two or more sovereign states.

Comments by Sven-Olof Lodin

Professor Aaron's paper covers a wide range of questions. This makes the nature of the paper rather general. The reader has to be quite familiar with the subject in order to understand all the implications involved and make an evaluation of the arguments.

Professor Aaron's paper is divided into two parts. The first concerns the problems of combining a consumption tax with a system of transfer payments, the problems of international capital movements and withholding of taxes. The second part deals with the type of personal consumption tax that is preferable for administrative reasons.

Transfer Payments

Professor Aaron rightly points out that consumption is not a feasible base for transfer payments/negative taxes. But will this really cause any problem? The answer is no, as in any personal consumption tax system the income before savings/dissavings will be included in the tax return in such a way that it will easily be identified, separated and usable as a base for transfer payments to the same extent as in the existing income tax systems. No extra reporting will be necessary.

International Problems

a. Entity Business Tax

There seems to be a common agreement that a personal consumption tax should be combined with a cash flow corporate tax. The question is whether a cash flow tax can cope better or worse with the transfer pricing problem and other international problems. As I can see it, the transfer pricing problem will be exactly the same as in the existing income tax system.

If various countries have very different tax systems (broad/narrow base, high/low tax rate, income tax/cash flow tax), this always gives some room for international tax arbitrage. But this is due to the differences as such not to the special cash flow tax technique. In countries having considered a cash flow type of corporate tax, the most serious international obstacle for introducing it has been the uncertainty of whether this tax would be recognized as an income tax with regard to tax treaties and foreign tax credit. Because, if this were not the case, this would seriously hurt international investments.

b. Personal Consumption Taxes

It is true that the international problems created by a "tax-prepayment" or earnings type of consumption tax are rather small. If the "qualified-accounts" approach is chosen, emigration will cause very severe problems. This system will most probably need an emigration tax which means a tax on all savings earlier deducted. This is administratively burdensome but will also create serious political and psychological problems. (Otherwise a "cash flow"-country will attract capital. But then the problem of taxing the foreign capital has to be solved.)

The transitional problems caused by "front-loaded" investment incentives are not really a cash flow tax problem. It is a general problem of changing the tax base. The same problem - but the other way round as a disadvantage for companies - occurred in Britain and in the United States when these countries changed to a broad based income tax. In my opinion a business cash flow tax must mean great administrative advantages.

Withholding

I agree with professor Aaron that for most households withholding would pose no greater problem under a consumption tax than under an income tax. Moreover, using the prepayment method the accuracy of withholding will be greatly improved. If the qualified account method is used, withholding on pensions is easy to introduce. In other cases where the PAYE-system is not accurate enough the declared consumption for preceeding year is a feasible basis for estimated tax collection.

Professor Aaron recommends as a solution of the withholding tax problems and several other problems (which I do not believe are of a magnitude justifying special measures) that a value added tax be introduced as a basic consumption tax. Then the personal consumption tax should be imposed only on the small fraction of the tax payers having sizable unearned cash flow. I do not believe this to be a very realistic proposal for most industrialized countries. Most of them - excluding USA - considering an expenditure tax already have a VAT or similar indirect consumption tax with rates not possible to increase very much.

The industrialized countries having seriously considered an expenditure tax have opted for broadbased general consumption taxes including most taxpayers because the expenditure tax is looked upon as replacing the income tax - not replacing other consumption taxes. Another reason is that administrative reasons speak in favour of a general tax. It is very important to limit the possibilities of tax arbitrage between the taxed and the untaxed sector. One example is the interests problems in the earnings tax. Therefore, the smaller the untaxed sector is the better. That is also one reason why I would prefer the qualified account method to the prepayment method. If a deduction of one taxpayer results in a taxable income for another, the possibilities of tax evasion and arbitrage are limited. This is also the reason why interest payments will cause special problems in the prepayment method where this balance does not exist but not in the qualified account method where the balance is found. It must be recognized that the gain of underreporting unearned income under the qualified account method is limited. If you do not report your interest income you cannot claim a deduction for your savings. If you want a deduction for interest costs you must also report the loan and be taxed for it. Thus, these to some extent self controlling elements will help to simplify administration. No interest problem will occur and no gain will be caused by conversion of earned income into unearned.

The qualified account method also taxes windfall gains in a much more appropriate way. If consumed the gains are subject to progressive taxation.

The qualified account method does not require more information than what has to be submitted already in Sweden in the income tax and net wealth tax return, although the information has to be structured in another way.

Although the possibility offered by the prepayment method to exclude taxpayers of modest means from the duty of filing tax returns would reduce administrative inconvenience, I nevertheless believe that the qualified account approach is preferable for a general tax.

However, for developing countries the prepayment method seems to be the better choice, as these countries may have limited administrative resources. The same seems to be true also when only a small part of the taxpayers are to be subject to the tax.

Thus, my conclusion concerning the choice of method is almost the opposite to Professor Aaron's proposal - as should be expected from a discussant.

In Sweden a general progressive expenditure tax has been seriously considered to replace the personal income tax. Two thorough Government studies [SOU (1976, p.62) and SOU (1986, p. 40)] have been produced. Both studies recommended the qualified account method. Finally, however, the expenditure tax was rejected by the Government mainly because of three major problems involved.

1. The problems caused by emigration and immigration - especially the introduction of an emigration tax.
2. The transitional problems - especially the psycological and optical effects caused by the technique for the transition.
3. The problems of family taxation. In Sweden spouses are separately taxed. However, in a progressive expenditure tax system separate taxation of spouses opens great opportunities for tax arbitrage between the spouses with regard to deductions for savings and taxation of dissavings and loans. If joint taxation is applied these problems will disappear. The introduction of joint taxation has for other reasons, however, not been considered politically desirable in Sweden.

If we look at the new general development of personal income taxes towards a broadbased more comprehensive tax with considerable reductions in tax rates and progressivity it must be admitted that the need for replacing the personal income tax with a personal consumption tax is much less than before this development of the income tax took place. Although a personal consumption tax has many advantages compared with an income tax this development implies that the gains that could be made by a transition to a personal consumption tax will be smaller although the transitional costs and administrative problems will stay unchanged.

References

Aaron, H.J. (1987), Some Observations on Taxation and International Economic Transactions, paper prepared for Conference on Tax Policy, Caserta, Italy, June 11-13, 1987.

Auerbach, A.J. / Kotlikoff, L.J. (1987), Dynamic Fiscal Policy, Cambridge: Cambridge University Press.

Bird, R.M. / McLure, C.E. Jr., (1989), The Personal Income Tax in an Interdependent World, paper prepared for International Seminar in Public Economics, January 5-6, 1989.

Bryant, R.C. (1987), International Financial Intermediation, Brookings.

Carroll, C. / Summers, L.H. (1989), Consumption Growth Parallels Income Growth: Some New Evidence, National Bureau of Economic Research, Working Paper No. 3090, September 1989.

Sandmo, A. / Atkinson, A.B. (1980), Welfare Implications of the Taxation of Savings, Economic Journal, September 1980.

SOU: Statens offentliga utredningar, Stockholm

U.S. Department of the Treasury (1977), Blueprints for Basic Tax Reform, Washington, D.C., January 17, 1977.

Zodrow G.R. / McLure, C.E. Jr. (1988), Implementing Direct Consumption Taxes in Developing Countries, Policy, Planning, and Research Working Papers, WPS 131, The World Bank, December 1988.

Christian Seidl

Administration Problems of an Expenditure Tax*

I. Administration: The Achilles' Heel of an Expenditure Tax

An expenditure tax has been endorsed at various times by a respectable number of most notable scholars such as Thomas Hobbes, John Revans, John Stuart Mill, Eduard Pfeiffer, Alfred Marshall, Francis Ysidro Edgeworth, Arthur Cecil Pigou, Irving Fisher, Luigi Einaudi, Joseph A. Schumpeter, Nicholas Kaldor, and James Edward Meade, to name only the most prominent ones. Over the years several motions have been proposed to enact an expenditure tax, or to consider it for possible enactment. Such proposals include John Stuart Mill's famous suggestion to the *Select Committee on Income and Property Tax* in 1861[1], the considerations of the Colwyn Committee on National Debt and Taxation[2], Congressman Ogden L. Mills' motion of a spending tax bill put before the U.S. House of Representatives in 1921[3], Mr. Morgenthau's proposal

* I am indebted to Robin Boadway, John Kay, and Wolfram Richter for helpful comments and to Elizabeth Harrison for her efforts to improve my English style.

[1] Cf. Kaldor (1955, p. 11).

[2] Cf. Kaldor (1955, p. 12).

[3] Congressman Mills' spendings tax bill (H.R. 7867) was introduced to the U.S. Congress in July 20, 1921, and was discussed in Congress in August 17, 1921. But it was not enacted. Mr. Mills did not pursue his proposal any further when he became Secretary of the Treasury. At the 1932 Congressional Hearings on Revenue Revision he renounced his former motion saying that he had been very wrong. This occurred obviously under the influence of the Great Depression. However, in 1937 he told Irving Fisher that the time was now ripe again for a spendings tax. Fisher/Fisher (1942) dedicated their famous book to the memory of Ogden L. Mills. Cf. Mills (1922) and Fisher/Fisher (1942, p. 208 seq.). Mills' forerunner in the United States was Beale (1911). Mills himself was obviously influenced by Adams (1921).

of an expenditure tax to pay for the war submitted to the Finance Committee of the Senate of the United States in September 1942[4], the suggestion of an expenditure tax by the Danish Commission on Tax Reform in 1958[5] and by the Swedish Government Commission on Taxation in 1972[6], by the British Meade Committee in (1978), the Blueprints of the U.S. Treasury (1977/1984), the Information Report of the U.S. Advisory Commission on Intergovernmental Relations (1974), and - let us not forget - the discussions within the Royal Commission on the Taxation of Profits and Income, appointed in 1950[7], which provided much of the material leading to Kaldor's well-known book published in 1955. None of these numerous attempts at establishing an expenditure tax was ever adopted, save for rather short interludes of expenditure tax enactment in India and Sri Lanka[8].

The main preference among economists for an expenditure tax over an income tax[9] was given on grounds of greater equity, more efficiency, greater welfare (in the sense of less excess burden), or better economic incentives[10]. Among Business School professors

[4] Cf. Morgenthau (1942); for details of this proposal cf. Haensel (1942); Buehler (1950).

[5] Cf. Philip, etc. (1958).

[6] Cf. Lodin (1978).

[7] Cf. Kaldor (1955), preface; cf. also Radcliffe Report (1955).

[8] These experiments resulted, however, in complete failures, which was certainly also a consequence of the backward state of the economy and the tax administration in these countries. Cf.,e.g., Eigner (1959); Kelley (1970, pp. 248 seqq.); Prakesh (1958).

[9] Or over an even more demanding comprehensive income tax; cf. expecially Carter Commission (1966).

[10] A sharply progressive expenditure tax had also been endorsed for purposes of war finance only as a more elegant device as compared with compulsory loans, etc. It should have helped to reduce spending during the war period and shift it to the peace period in order to direct funds to war financing by means of public borrowing. Indeed, war financing was the main goal of Mr. Morgenthau's (1942) motion. The expenditure tax discussion continued during World War II. Wallis (1942) proposed it on precisely these grounds, and Friedman (1943), then a member of the U.S. Treasury Department's Division of Tax Research, strongly advocated it as well. However, Friedman (1943, p. 61 seq., note 12) was reluctant to adopt an expenditure tax in peacetime: "The case for a spendings tax in peacetime does not seem satisfactory; and its substitution for the income tax, far from improving the tax structure, would, in the opinion of the present writer, make it a good deal worse." Haensel (1942), on the contrary, rejected an expenditure tax as an appropriate instrument for war financing (as it soaks only the very rich), though he conceded that it may become an appropriate tax regime in peacetime.

and accountants, however, an expenditure tax has been enthusiastically welcomed mainly on grounds of alleged administrative superiority as compared with an income tax, or an income tax possibly supplemented by a corporation tax. Dieter Schneider, one of the most prominent experts on business taxation in Germany, maintained: "Gesetzt den Fall, wir kämen zu der Einsicht, daβ steuerliche Leistungsfähigkeit durch die persönlichen Konsumausgaben zu messen sei und auch praktisch gemessen werden könne, dann hätte die betriebswirtschaftliche Steuerlehre das Idealziel einer jeden Wissenschaft erreicht. Sie hätte sich selbst überflüssig gemacht! Denn würde steuerliche Leistungsfähigkeit allein in den persönlichen Konsumausgaben gemessen, dann gäbe es keine Unternehmensbesteuerung.[11]" It seems also that these quarters entertained confidence that all those tricky accountancy problems caused by the needs of taxation would suddenly disappear if only the income tax and the corporation tax were replaced by an expenditure tax[12].

This switch of taxation systems was expected to take the heavy burden of taxation off the business sector and shift it to private households. Private households would, however, not be significantly more inconvenienced because they have now to complete an expenditure tax return instead of an income tax return. This greater administrative comfort is reaped even in addition to the realization of greater equity, greater efficiency, greater welfare, and better economic incentives. Notice that even no less an authority such as Kaldor (1955, p. 146) reinforced this belief[13]: "It follows ... that the justification for company taxation would disappear if the principle of taxing income were abandoned in favour of taxing expenditure."

It is true, the justification of company taxation would disappear under an expenditure tax regime. But the need to maintain meticulous bookkeeping on the part of corporations and all noncorporate businesses for purposes of tax inspection and tax auditing

---

Similarly Buehler (1950) considered an expenditure tax an inappropriate instrument for war financing.

[11] Schneider (1978, p. 27); cf. also Schneider (1971, pp. 355-372); Moxter (1982, pp. 209 seqq., 231).

[12] This view was even shared by experts such as Harberger (1958, p. 84), and Mieszkowski (1978, pp. 36-37). Cf. even some views expressed in the Blueprints, e.g. Bradford and Staff (1984, p. 9, pp. 39 seqq., p. 107).

[13] Cf. also Advisory Commission (1974, p. 14).

would in no way be diminished under an expenditure tax regime, as will be explained below. Notice, however, that an expenditure tax puts the question of the *taxation of nonprofit organizations* on the agenda. Most of the activities of nonprofit organizations such as political parties, charitable organizations, religious organizations, trade unions, private clubs, etc., represent in fact *consumption activities.* Saving and investment is done only to a much lesser extent. It is not only for the sake of avoiding tax evasion (e.g., by shifting private consumption to private clubs if the latter were not liable to an expenditure tax), but also for the sake of equal tax treatment of expenditure for consumption purposes, that an expenditure tax is required to encompass also the consumption of nonprofit institutions. A personal expenditure tax requires thus a *corporate expenditure tax* on nonprofit organizations as a companion, a fact which is overlooked by virtually all authors in this field. In this paper, for the sake of brevity I shall confine myself to the administration problems of a personal expenditure tax. The reader should not conclude, however, that the issues which are addressed in this paper are the *only* administrative problems which an expenditure tax harbours.

Although I am rather sceptical as to the alleged superiority of an expenditure tax over an income tax with respect to equity, efficiency, welfare, and incentives[14], I do not deny that a case can be made for an expenditure tax on precisely these grounds[15]. I think, however, that the administration of an expenditure tax is its real Achilles' heel[16]. This paper does not deal with my other objections to an expenditure tax, but confines itself wholly to problems of its administration. It will also disregard problems of the

---

[14] Cf.,e.g., Seidl (1985); Prest (1956) and Musgrave (1957) are early sources of similar scepticism. Cf. also Goode (1980).

[15] For a rather concise account cf., e.g., Little (1956).

[16] It is not surprising that some partisans of an expenditure tax have overemphasized its alleged administrative simplicity. Fisher/Fisher (1942, p. 34), e.g., contend: "No other income tax can approach the yield tax in simplicity either as to concept or as to administration. Ogden L. Mills, than whom there could be no better judge, six weeks before he died, wrote to the author approving the spendings tax essentially as here proposed, and commended it especially for its simplicity." Even Little (1956, p. 120), cares little for the question of whether or not an expenditure tax works; he considers this "the least interesting" question. Quite recently, Fullerton (1985, pp. 6-7), adduces as the first out of seven arguments in favour of an expenditure tax that it "would be immensely *easier to administer*."

possible introduction of an expenditure tax alongside with an income tax[17] or with a general wealth tax. Throughout this paper it is assumed that an expenditure tax regime should replace the income tax regime[18]. Moreover, problems which plague income and expenditure taxes alike will largely be disregarded, as they can neither be avoided, nor would they additionally occur when switching from one tax regime to the other. Before delving into greater detail, let us review some other voices which have judged the administrative difficulties of an expenditure tax.

As early as 1955, Kaldor (1955, p. 222) himself was honest enough to admit "that a personal expenditure tax would undoubtedly be a more complicated tax to administer than the present type of income tax". But on the whole he was rather optimistic concerning the administration of an expenditure tax[19]. More than two decades later, and after the failure of the expenditure tax experiments in India and Sri Lanka, we witness a complete change of Kaldor's mind. Rather bitterly he remarked in 1978: "What I feel about the recent advocates of the changeover from income to expenditure as the basis of personal taxation - on both sides of the Atlantic - is the same as what I now think about my own writing of twenty-five years ago. They both show a lack of awareness (or at least of sufficient awareness) of the political and sociological problems involved in closing tax loop-holes. A highly distorted and loophole-ridden income tax is compared with an expenditure tax drawn up on the right principles and free of distortions and of anomalous concessions from political pressures. In fact ... it is just as easy to make a mockery of an expenditure tax as it has been with progressive income tax.[20]"

---

[17] This was proposed by scholars such as Kaldor (1955) and Slitor (1973).

[18] Otherwise a considerable number of possible combinations of tax systems would have had to be investigated. Therefore, I restricted myself to the analysis of adopting an expenditure tax in lieu of the present income tax. This means, of course, that some administrative problems outlined below might possibly be avoided by more sophisticated tax systems to replace the present income tax.

[19] When reviewing Kaldor's book, Musgrave (1957, p. 201), was more sceptical, remarking that "he seems to overstate the difficulties of the income tax and to understate those of the spendings tax."

[20] Kaldor (1980, p. 238). Notice, however, that Musgrave (1957, p. 202), had predicted such administrative difficulties quite at the outset of Kaldor's work: "The proof of the pudding, of course, is not in comparing a perfect income tax with a perfect spendings tax, but in comparing both as they turn out in practice. Again, Kaldor tends to overstate

Whereas Kaldor addressed more the political problems of introducing an evasion-proof expenditure tax, other authors considered more directly the problems of administrating an expenditure tax. Zumstein, one of the most competent authors in this respect, estimated the effort to produce an expenditure tax return to be two or three times greater than that to prepare an income tax return[21] and Slitor (1973, p. 258) concluded "that a comprehensive, progressive approach to taxation of consumption involves... the acceptance of mass problems of paper work, information returns, electronic data processing, and a new range of complications in tax reporting under an essentially fragile self-assessment system for taxpayers whose desire for simplification has been almost continually disappointed and frustrated since World War II." Keynes held that an expenditure tax was "perhaps theoretically sound [but] ... practically impossible[22]". In 1942 one member of the Finance Committee of the U.S. Senate described an expenditure tax as the "most complicated monstrosity" he had ever seen[23].

Although being rather sceptical himself with respect to the practicability of an expenditure tax, Prest has warned that "It is only too easy to pour cold water on a scheme on the grounds that it is impracticable. The cynic might in fact say that this is the favourate device of academic economists who are unable or unwilling to face up to the implications of a new idea![24]" Therefore rejecting a proposed tax system on grounds of insuperable problems of administration requires a careful examination of the administrative properties of an expenditure tax.

Many administrative problems result from a new challenge posed to tax administration, viz. the necessity of a sharp distinction between consumption and saving. Prest noted that the "identification of some forms of saving is an extremely treacherous operation. ... One cannot help feeling that the evaluation of saving is even more difficult

---

the administrative difficulties of improving the income tax, while understating those involved in the spendings tax."

21 Zumstein (1977, p. 406; cf. also p. 223 seq. and pp. 334-336).

22 Quoted from Kaldor (1955, p. 12). Cf. also Slitor (1973, p. 230); Slitor (1973, p. 229-230) reports that Pigou was rather sceptical too as regards administrability of an expenditure tax.

23 Quoted from Kaldor (1955, p. 16, note 1).

24 Prest (1956, p. 46).

than Mr. Kaldor admits it to be.[25]" Along the same lines Musgrave (1957, p. 203) has rather forcefully argued "that Kaldor shows little recognition of the host of administrative difficulties inherent in a spendings tax." Such difficulties are bound to occur not the least as we are "saddled with a new problem, not encountered in the income tax, of having to distinguish between consumption and saving.[26]" E.M. Sunley, a former deputy assistant secretary of the U.S. Department of Treasury reported [in his discussion of the Fullerton paper (1985, p. 20)] on the reasons which induced the Treasury to discard the expenditure tax, so dearly recommended in the Blueprints: "The progressive tax on consumed income was rejected because of international implications and transitional and administrative problems."

We shall next look at the methods and thereafter investigate the pitfalls of expenditure tax administration.

II. Methods of Expenditure Tax Administration

An expenditure tax requires the calculation of period expenditure and its subsequent taxation, which can basically be performed by at least five methods[27], viz.

(1) the *direct method*, which requires the taxpayer to give a direct account of all items consumed during the taxation period;

and four *indirect* methods of expenditure calculation and taxation:

(2) the *cash-flow method*, which computes period expenditure as period income less net savings (including changes in cash and bank deposits);

(3) the *wealth-accrual method*, which computes period expenditure as period income less period accrual of the taxpayer's net wealth;

[25] Prest (1956, p. 48).

[26] Musgrave (1957, p. 202). Slitor (1973, p. 247) has also warned that many consumption expenditures might be disguised as investment or business acquisitions, such as hunting grounds or a beach home. A complaisant tenant may give the owner liberal access to the property.

[27] Zumstein (1977, p. 256) mentions three of them.

(4) the *tax-prepayment method*, which taxes expenditure and saving from current labour income alike, but exempts all returns on capital (for whatever purposes they are used) and all unsaving from taxation;

(5) the *taxing-business-cash-flows-cum-wages method*, which taxes wages and business cash flows computed as business returns less investment and wages.

A. The Direct Method of Expenditure Tax Administration

The direct method had been ruled out by all partisans of an expenditure tax on grounds of alleged administrative infeasibility[28]. For that very reason, Irving Fisher's (1937; 1942) work has been celebrated for having removed the decisive obstacle to administrative feasibility of an expenditure tax by having first shown the way to calculate expenditure indirectly. Even as late a statement as that of the Advisory Commission on Intergovernmental Relations of 1974 traces the administrative feasibility of an expenditure tax back to Fisher's discovery: "The administration of an expenditure tax has always been considered its major drawback. When Irving Fisher realized that expenditures would not have to be reported individually, a major part of the problem was solved.[29]"

With hindsight this view seems to be rather outdated. Credit cards and electronic data processing are powerful tools which could be employed to manage the vast problems of direct calculation of individual period expenditure. There can be no doubt about that: all one has to do is to replace anonymous money (banknotes and coins) by individualized money (that which is held in the form of accounts only) and to assign a personal number to any resident of the country. Economic transactions must not be paid for with cash; instead all transactions must be paid for with cheques, credit cards, or similar devices, all carrying the individual's personal number. All objects of economic transactions may easily be classified and earmarked as to whether they are liable to an expenditure tax or not. All other administrative problems are then simply reduced to being a matter of electronic data processing.

[28] This view was even shared by an authority such as Graetz (1980, p. 163): "No one suggests direct accounting for consumption expenditures of individuals as a practical approach to a progressive tax on consumption."

[29] Advisory Commission (1974, p. 33).

One may object that this invokes images of a Leviathan state with strong intervention into the private spheres of its residents, but we will see that both other methods of expenditure calculation also require a similar level of interloping with respect to individual wealth and its composition. Moreover, the prevailing income tax has also been driven so far in some countries as to subject taxpayers to virtually complete official control[30]. Notice that the decisive prerequisite for the application of the direct method of expenditure calculation is the *complete absence of anonymous money* or its close substitutes (e.g., gold coins, foreign exchange, etc.). The presence of anonymous money allows expenditure to be "depersonalized", i.e. the purchaser must not necessarily be identified with the expenditure. Cash payments would clearly paralyze the functioning of the direct method of expenditure calculation. The possibilities recently opened up by electronic data processing do not allow us to discard the direct method of expenditure calculation from the outset, as is done in the bulk of the literature[31].

When there is little scope for exchanges in kind of investment goods or consumer durables for consumer goods, the direct method of expenditure calculation does not require *asset registers* on the part of individuals. This represents a definite administrative advantage of the direct method of expenditure calculation over the indirect calculation methods. Asset registers are, however, necessary for businesses in order to avoid untaxed flows of goods in kind from a business to the households of its owners.

B. The Cash-Flow Method of Expenditure Tax Administration

The cash-flow method of expenditure tax administration is the classical method as it had been proposed by Irving Fisher, Kaldor, and most other proponents of an expenditure tax. In this method period expenditure is computed as period income from all sources less gross savings plus all dissavings. The administration of an expenditure tax following this method requires the keeping of meticulous asset registers (and for most variants also of registers of consumer durables) on the part of all taxpayers to control

---

[30] Unfortunately, the here aptly descriptive German term "gläserner Steuerzahler" does not exist in English.

[31] The recent British Green Paper on the Reform of Personal Taxation (1986) stresses the opportunity opened up by computerization for fundamental tax reforms. However, the Green Paper pursues another goal, viz. to adopt independent taxation of couples for the income tax.

for current consumption financed by dissaving. Otherwise a taxpayer could evade the expenditure tax completely by saving all income earned in the period t and financing expenditures by dissaving the income earned and saved in period $(t-1)$ or in earlier periods.

Under the cash-flow method, the registers are kept in nominal terms. This means they are kept in terms of the historical market prices or initial costs until new transactions of the respective items occur at actual market prices. These in turn enter into all subsequent calculations. This means that the cash-flow method takes into account only *realized* capital gains or windfall gains in the very period when they are realized.

As most of this paper deals with the cash-flow method, this short characterization of this method suffices for the moment.

C. The Wealth-Accrual Method of Expenditure Tax Administration

The wealth-accrual method of expenditure tax administration is virtually the same as the cash-flow method save that the wealth-accrual method requires that the asset register be kept in terms of current market prices, i.e. "replacement" prices.

Let us illustrate the difference between this and the cash-flow method of expenditure calculation with a simple example. We consider a taxpayer who holds shares bought several periods ago. Assume now that these shares experience a sudden capital gain in some period t. Assume further that the taxpayer is not going to sell any of these shares in period t. According to the cash-flow method, the capital gain does not affect period expenditure. Only when the shares are actually sold and the receipts or a part thereof is used for purposes of consumption is there any effect upon period expenditure and thus upon taxation. The effects of the capital gain are in any case deferred until its realization.

The wealth-accrual method follows a different philosophy. When the shares appreciate in value, part of them could have been sold (so as to leave the stock of the taxpayer's wealth unchanged) and consumption could have been increased accordingly. Insofar as this does not take place, saving of the capital gain has occurred, which in turn reduces period expenditure. A capital loss, on the other hand, would mean that adequate extra saving should occur in order to keep the taxpayer's wealth unchanged. When this extra saving does not occur, the taxpayer is supposed to have dissaved an additional amount equal to the capital loss, which increases expenditure accordingly. Notice that the wealth-accrual method implies asymmetric treatment of profits paid out as dividends and of withheld profits which cause capital gains of the shares. Assume that distributed profits are saved. This is tax neutral under both indirect methods of expenditure calculation. However, when the share values increase because of withheld profits, the wealth-accrual method allows for a corresponding reduction of expenditure, which the cash-flow method does not. When shares are finally sold and proceeds from the sale are consumed, taxpayers are taxed alike under both methods. This illustrates the asymmetric treatment saving experiences under the wealth-accrual method[32].

Notice that the wealth-accrual method requires rather complicated revaluations of all taxpayers' wealth at the end of any period. This implies also a periodic reassessment of the market value of all firms. Because of this rather formidable task most proposals of an expenditure tax rely on the cash-flow method of expenditure calculation.

Notice also that neither the cash-flow method nor the wealth-accrual method of expenditure calculation can afford to forgo meticulous accounting and adequate control by tax inspectors in order to prevent untaxed flows of funds or commodities in kind from businesses to the households of the firm owners. At the same time, these controls prevent the booking of private consumption to a firm's expense account. As we encounter this very same motive under an expenditure tax as under an income tax, the checks and balances must also remain the same. Subsequently we cannot expect much administrative relief for the business sector.

D. The Tax-Prepayment Method of Expenditure Tax Administration

This paper shows the considerable administrative difficulties of the cash-flow method and even more so of the wealth-accrual method of expenditure tax administration. Therefore the profession[33] has looked for methods to facilitate administration of an expenditure tax. In doing so, an approach of striking simplicity has been suggested.

Suppose an asset for $ 1,000 with a rate of return of 20 per cent is bought under the cash-flow method. Assume that it is sold after one year and the proceeds are fully

[32] For a similar argument cf. Kelley (1970, p. 242).

[33] Warren (1975); Bradford and Staff (1984, pp. 107 seqq.); Mieszkowski (1978, pp. 43 seqq.); Advisory Commission (1974, pp. 37-38.).

consumed. We assume further that an expenditure tax exists which has a marginal rate amounting to 50 per cent. In this case no expenditure tax is paid for the purchase of this asset in the first year. In the second year \$ 800 of the proceeds are consumed, and \$ 400 are paid in expenditure tax.

Alternatively, when tax exemption of the acquisition of the particular asset is not granted in the first period, \$ 666.67 out of the respective \$ 1,000 can be saved, and \$ 333.33 are paid in expenditure tax. Assume now that unsaving of assets inclusive of their return is exempt from taxation, then the taxpayer is free to consume \$ 800 [\$ 666.67 plus a return of 20 per cent] in the second year without any further tax burden on this amount.

Notice that both methods are equivalent for the taxpayer as well as for the tax authorities. The tax authorities could also purchase part of the same asset with the \$ 333.33 in tax revenue they received in the first period and gain \$ 400 [\$ 333.33 plus a return of 20 per cent] in the second period. As this second method restricts taxation to current labour income only, we see that it seems to avoid much record-keeping and yet attain the same result as the first method. It has therefore been regarded as a significant administrative relief.

Some authors suggested the tax-prepayment method as a universal approach for an expenditure tax administration, others would like to restrict the tax-prepayment method to consumer durables only, others to consumer durables and to those assets for which control raises major problems. But as "tagging" of every asset[34] with regard to its eligibility for tax-prepayment or not would rehash the administrative problems of an expenditure tax, it seems expedient either to apply the tax-prepayment method throughout or else to settle altogether for the cash-flow method.

The adoption of the tax-prepayment method would imply that savings are not deductible from the tax base and loans are not taxable when they are raised. On the other hand, dissaving of assets and consumer durables (including returns of assets, capital gains and windfall gains) are not taxable and repayment of loans and interest payments are not tax-deductible. This means in effect that taxation is neither concerned with capital income nor with savings and dissavings, but only with *labour income.* The great bulk of administrative difficulties of an expenditure tax would indeed disappear if

[34] Cf. Mieszkowski (1978, p. 46).

we could only rely that a tax on labour income would do the required job. But, alas, the equivalence of the cash-flow method and the tax-prepayment method presupposes a set of conditions to hold which is rather unlikely in the real world.

This is best shown by adducing a somewhat lengthy quotation from Graetz: "If the equivalence between immediate deduction and exemption of yield holds, an expenditure tax should be equivalent to a tax on wages under which all income from savings is excluded from the base. It would then be a matter of indifference whether the base for an expenditure tax is computed by deducting amounts saved or by exempting investment sales and yield.

A consumption tax will indeed be equivalent to a wage tax under the following set of unrealistic conditions:

1. There is no initial period wealth.
2. The system is closed: the taxpayer exhausts his wealth by death, or the system classifies all remaining capital balances (all bequests) as consumption in the taxpayer's final tax return, or an identical tax is subsequently imposed on bequests in some other way.
3. Tax rates are not progressive; moreover, they do not change over time.
4. There exists a perfect capital market with no uncertainty: all taxpayers can borrow and lend unlimited amounts at a risk-free interest rate.
5. All income can be classified as one of two types: wage income or income to capital accumulated during and after the initial period.

Under these conditions a wage tax and a consuption tax are equivalent: the discounted present value of a wage base equals the discounted present value of a consumption base when viewed from the perspective of the opening or closing period. When the conditions are relaxed, however, the equivalence disappears.

The set of conditions required for this equivalence simply will not exist when an expenditure tax is acutally implemented. Under the consumption tax set forth in Blueprints, for example, rates are progressive and likely to vary over time, capital markets are imperfect and the future uncertain, and the system is open at the beginning. Progressivity alone, which is central to the decision to impose an expenditure tax, defeats the equivalence. The immediate deduction-yield exemption equivalence therefore will not hold ex post in practice and should not serve as the basic guide to implementation decisions.

Perhaps most important, with uncertainty and progressive rates the distributional consequences of the two methods would be different. With a progressive rate structure, the cash-flow version of the tax would narrow the after-tax differences between the lucky and unlucky investor in ways that the omission alternative would not."[35]

We have little to add, but must correct Graetz insofar as it is, strictly speaking, not wage income which is to be taxed under the tax-prepayment approach, but *labour income*. This would lead to another problem, viz. many taxpayers would try to declare as much as possible of their income to be attributable to their capital invested and as little as possible to be attributable to their work effort. This would confront tax administration with the formidable problem of separating capital income from labour income where the taxpayers are the far better informed party.

As we may confidently assume that the conditions listed above are never satisfied in real life, the tax-prepayment approach is no longer equivalent to expenditure taxation, but is, in fact, an income tax restricted, however, to labour income only. Saving is taxed when it is done out of labour income, and consumption is tax exempt when it is financed from capital income or from dissaving. Or, to put it in less agreeable terms, the rich are legally tax-free, whereas the major tax burden is shifted to the wage earners (who cannot claim that their income is attributable to capital). This conforms much better to the French *ancien régime* than to modern tax states. Therefore, we discard the tax-prepayment method from further consideration.

E. The Taxing-Business-Cash-Flows-Cum-Wages Method of Expenditure Tax Administration

This method is obviously induced by considerations of national accounting. Starting from the identity

$$Y - I = C \; ,$$

we have immediately

$$(Y - I - L) + L = C \; .$$

[35] Graetz (1980, pp. 172-173).

This suggests that consumption can be taxed equally as well by taxing business cash flows and wages.

As macroeconomic identities hardly ever translate immediately into individual tax bases, the apparent smoothness of the above argument should certainly alarm us. It is readily seen that this method of expenditure taxation violates *personal identity*. Everything goes well as long as wage-earners consume all income and it is only entrepreneurs who possibly save. In this case (Y-I-L) is roughly equivalent to that part of profits which is consumed by the entrepreneurs.[1]

But when a wage earner saves part of his income and invests it into an enterprise, *his* tax burden is not reduced, as should properly take place under an expenditure tax. Rather the tax burden of the *enterprise* into which his savings were invested is reduced instead. As the investor has no claim to a tax credit vis-à-vis the tax authorities, he must negotiate with the firm in which he invests for his tax credit. Assume the tax rate is 25 per cent, then a wage earner who invests $ 750 in a firm should be credited $ 1,000, because the firm may buy, say, machinery for $ 1,000 and finance it through the investor's contribution amounting to $ 750 and through a tax reduction amounting to $ 250. This presupposes, however, immediate tax credits for investment; otherwise the question arises as to who finances the tax credit during the interim between investment and final tax payment. When the share is repaid, the firm withholds the cash-flow tax on business, even if the cash-flow happens to be negative in that particular year. The concomitant problems are still aggravated when the wage earner does not invest directly into a firm, but opens a savings account with a bank and the bank invests in the firm, or when the wage earner makes a loan to the firm.

Although we could imagine a lot more difficulties, we will cut ourselves short by observing that all those mutual tax credits to compensate for the different impact incidences of the tax burden work only in the special case in which the expenditure tax is *proportional* without any tax exemptions (e.g., for subsistence, etc.). But in such a case a correspondingly higher rate of the value-added tax would perform much better from an administrative point of view than would an expenditure tax plagued with the above sketched troubles. Therefore, we also discard the taxing-business-cash-flows-cum-wages method from further consideration.

In the next section of this paper we shall concentrate primarily on the direct method and on the cash-flow method of expenditure tax administration. Whenever indirect methods of expenditure tax administration are henceforth addressed, they refer only to the cash-flow method or to the wealth-accrual method. We are now ready to investigate the administrative problems associated with an expenditure tax[36] in greater detail.

III. Consumer Durables: The Main Administrative Blunder of an Expenditure Tax

The greatest administrative complication of an expenditure tax is without a doubt the treatment of consumer durables[37]. Such goods are bought in one period; however, they create a consumption stream which extends over subsequent periods[38]. Even under a proportional expenditure tax the entire tax must be paid in the period of acquisition, well in advance of the greater part of consumption. This effect is reinforced under a progressive expenditure tax which implies an exorbitant tax burden in the period of acquisition of consumer durables. It is obvious that it would be rather arbitrary and unfair to tie expenditure taxation to the volatility of irregular acquisition of consumer durables.

Several methods have been proposed to gear the periods of the virtual consumption stream to the time pattern of taxation:

(1) *Tax averaging:* all consumer goods are taxed in the period of acquisition. There is, however, a tax averaging such as that suggested by Vickrey (1947, chapter 6). Using this method one is able to eliminate fluctuations in taxation due to irregular

[36] Cf. in particular Fisher/Fisher (1942, pp. 3-36, and 201-208); Poole (1943); Vickrey (1947, pp. 345-348, and 354-359); Kaldor (1955); Slitor (1973); Advisory Commission (1974); Bradford and Staff (1977/1984); Zumstein (1977); Lodin (1978); Meade Committee (1978); Peffekoven (1980); Andrews (1974; 1980); Bradford (1980); Mieszkowski (1977; 1978; 1980); Graetz (1980); Committee on Simplification (1981/82).

[37] At former stages of the expenditure tax discussion there was some ambiguity as to whether consumer durables were to be treated as investment or as consumption. Consumer durables are indeed located on the fringe between investment and consumption. This makes their treatment under an expenditure tax rather complicated, as Musgrave (1957, p. 202), so wisely predicted. The great challenge of an expenditure tax is indeed that of making a rather sharp distinction between consumption and saving. Notice that nowadays nobody ever questions that consumer durables form part of private consumption.

[38] This situation is similar to the treatment of depreciation allowances under an income tax.

acquisition of consumer durables; it is not possible, however, to eliminate the systematic bias inherent in consumer durables, as the period of acquisition precedes the periods representing the greater part of the consumption stream. This method is, nevertheless, appropriate to smooth the fluctuations of a progressive expenditure tax. Judged from an administrative point of view, this seems to be the least demanding method.

(2) *Depreciation method:* this method allows the taxpayer to spread the amount expended on consumer durables over a greater number of periods. The number of periods is chosen either at the discretion of the taxpayer[39] or following some guidelines issued by the tax authorities.

(3) *User charges:* for very expensive consumer durables, such as housing[40], or for consumer durables which are not subject to wear and tear, such as jewelry, antiques, paintings by old masters, private parks, etc., an annual user charge should serve to capture the consumption stream of a period and should form part of period expenditure. Kaldor (1955, p. 200) suggested a fixed percentage of the purchase price along the order of 5 per cent[41].

(4) *Method of registered and unregistered assets*[42]*:* the indirect methods of expenditure calculation require an asset register. In order to keep the asset register to a manageable size, the Meade Committee suggested that all assets be divided into two groups: registered and unregistered assets. The acquisition of unregistered assets is not tax-deductible and, therefore, does not decrease expenditure[43]. On the other hand, the sale of unregistered assets is not regarded as dissaving and does not,

---

[39] Cf. Kaldor (1955, p. 197).

[40] Poole (1943, pp. 70-73), deals in rather great detail with the problems of treating houses under an expenditure tax. He too favours user charges by *imputing a rent* to owner-occupied housing. Cf. also Advisory Commission (1974, pp. 27-29, 38-42), and Slitor (1973, pp. 239-240).

[41] Cf. Advisory Commission (1974, pp. 23 seqq.), for an economic rationale of this procedure.

[42] Meade Committee (1978, pp. 175-183).

[43] Notice that this method relies in this respect on the tax-prepayment method, although restricted to a specified set of items.

therefore, increase expenditure. The very existence of unregistered assets would allow taxpayers to accumulate wealth in the form of unregistered assets (after they have been subject to expenditure taxation). When taxpayers later decide to acquire consumer durables, they may finance these by selling unregistered assets, thus avoiding the burden of a progressive expenditure tax. According to the Meade Committee, consumer durables, with the exception of houses, are regarded as unregistered assets. Only if a considerable capital gain is realized on these unregistered assets should this capital gain be counted as an expenditure.

Notice that the methods (1) and (4) represent higher administrative convenience. This is bought, however, at the price of unequal treatment of different kinds of expenditure; these methods harbour the tendency to tax expenditure for consumer durables more heavily than expenditure for nondurable consumer goods[44]. This drawback is largely avoided in methods (2) and (3), but also at a rather high price, viz. these methods require a complete register of consumer durables on the part of the taxpayer. On top of that, method (2) also requires the registration of past depreciation for any durable consumer good. Any sale of a durable consumer good has to be reported as well, not only to document its elimination from the taxpayer's wealth, but also to check for the realization of capital gains which have to be added to the taxpayer's inflow of funds.

This notable inconvenience for the taxpayer of registering all consumer durables is increased in the case of inflation or if particular items of consumer durables experience capital or windfall gains or losses. If the depreciation rates or the user charges are computed from the lower initial outlay for these goods, period expenditure is underestimated. Whereas the taxpayer has every reason to underrate the actual values of consumer durables under an expenditure tax, the tax authorities have every reason to estimate the actual values of consumer durables as closely as possible. This will, as I suspect, become a major battlefield with taxpayers on the one side, and the tax authorities on the other. Everyone who is aware of the difficulties of asset valuation will acknowledge that a routine revaluation of all consumer durables for purposes of taxation cannot be done save for in the roughest way. But this would again introduce a lot of arbitrariness into taxation. It seems that the burden of asset valuation is only largely

[44] Because the whole expenditure tax has to be paid earlier. This burden is reinforced in case of a progressive expenditure tax.

removed from the business sector in order to place it more heavily (and accompanied with more red tape than before) on private households.

Notice also that an expenditure tax requires some safeguard against small leasing[45] firms. Imagine that five families decide to establish a small leasing firm for automobiles and that this firm buys five identical cars and rents them for $ 200 per month to each family. As these car rentals are insufficient to cover operation costs, the firm is run at a loss of, say $ 12,000 per year. Each of the five entrepreneurs compensates the firm for his share of the loss, which amounts to $ 2,400. But when the firm's losses are covered by its owners, this counts as saving in the owners' expenditure tax returns! Furthermore, this would mean that half of the firm owners' expenditures on cars would de facto be exempt from expenditure taxation. As similar examples may readily be invented[46], an expenditure tax requires some safequards against loss compensation of firms by private households for purposes of transferring taxable expenditures into tax-deductable loss compensation paid into the firm as fresh money. This would involve many controls by tax inspectors, which further aggravates the administrative difficulties of an expenditure tax. Notice that the problems caused by consumer durables are the same in the direct and the indirect methods of expenditure calculation.

In methods (1) and (4) it is implied that the purchase of consumer durables forms part of expenditure in the period of their acquisition. By contrast, in methods (2) and (3) the purchase of consumer durables is deducted from period expenditure to give taxable expenditure; only the period depreciation or the period user charges form part of the period expenditure. This different tax treatment of consumer durables also requires a different treatment of the *sale* of consumer durables. Under methods (1) and (4), the sale of consumer durables is considered as *"negative consumption"*[47], i.e. the period expenditure is reduced by the proceeds of consumer durables to give taxable expenditure. This treatment seems to be warranted, because the total value of consumer durables has already been taxed. If they are now sold, this means that they have not

---

[45] Leasing of consumer durables would in any case increase when they are treated according to methods (1) or (4) under an expenditure tax.

[46] Think also of consumers' cooperatives.

[47] Cf. Advisory Commission (1974, pp. 22-23). Of course, negative consumption may give rise to negative expenditure tax in some period when substantial sales of consumer durables occur.

been consumed in full, but only in part, whereas they have been taxed in full. Subtracting the proceeds of the sale of the consumer durables from period expenditure undoes this double taxation. This seems to be fairly easy. But, alas, windfall gains (losses) on consumer durables would cause distortions: they imply that too much (less) has been deducted as negative consumption[48]. Therefore, we encounter the problem of separating windfall gains (losses) from the negative consumption proper, which amounts to calculating the book value of the consumer durable involved by appropriate depreciation rates. The difference between the proceeds of the sale of a consumer durable and this book value is then a windfall gain which must not be deducted from taxable expenditure (insofar as it is not saved). In methods (2) and (3) the expenditure tax is paid only on that part of the durable consumer good which is actually consumed. The purchase of consumer durables does not affect taxable expenditure; therefore, the proceeds from the sale of consumer durables is treated as an inflow of funds. It is only exempted from taxation insofar as it is actually saved. Notice that in this case we need not separate out book value, on the one hand, and windfall gains, on the other.

Before proceeding further, let us halt for a short digression to the traditional income tax. Consumer durables pose indeed some rather difficult problems also for an income tax. Suppose someone invests his other capital at the market rate of return and rents a house with the post-tax return on capital. Suppose someone else buys a house instead and the tax law of the respective country contains no provisions for taxing an imputed rent on the house. Then the second person is obviously better off, because he can either live in a better house tying up the same amount of capital, or he needs only a smaller sum to buy an equivalent house which the first person rents, leaving him some extra funds to invest or to buy some other consumer durables.

---

[48] Contrastingly, the Advisory Commission (1974, pp. 26-27), maintains that the negative consumption should "be based on the resale price irrespective of whether it is higher or lower than the original purchase price." The Advisory Commission argues in favour of such a tax treatment of windfall gains or losses by stressing the investment element reflected in part by consumer durables. Yet this stance would in fact allow substantial amounts of windfall gains on consumer durables to escape expenditure taxation when they are being fully consumed. Inasmuch as they are saved, the treatment recommended in the present paper provides for tax deductibility of the respective share of the windfall gains. The Advisory Commission's proposal, on the other hand, implies that saved windfall gains are twice deductible: first as a negative consumption, second as a saving. This does not sound very convincing.

These considerations carry over to other forms of consumer durables as well. Whenever consumer durables are acquired, this means acquisition of a consumption stream extending into the future. The economic agent will acquire the consumer durable only if its present value is nonnegative. But in order to be treated consistent with capital goods, the interest associated with the future consumption streams of consumer durables should also be taxed under an income tax. Otherwise, an income tax will be allocationally distortive and distributionally inequitable.

Notice that although problems associated with consumer durables plague an income tax as well, the problem is less severe in this case, because it is only the "interest" and not, as in the case of an expenditure tax, the "capital" which calls for appropriate treatment with respect to taxation. On the other hand, a wealth tax which is in force in many countries in addition to an income tax is able to successfully complement an income tax for precisely the interest part of consumption streams which would otherwise escape taxation.

IV. Gifts, Bequests, and Exchanges

Following the pure theory of an expenditure tax, gifts should be tax-deductible by the donor and should increase the inflow of funds on the part of the donee. But imagine a rich man who lives next to a poor widow. The rich man is subject to a marginal expenditure tax rate of 50 per cent; the poor widow's period expenditures, however, lie well below the tax-free threshold. Suppose the rich man offers the poor widow a gift of $ 1,000 in exchange for a (tax-deductable) receipt signed by the widow. Furthermore, imagine that there are informal strings attached to this gift: the rich man allows the widow to keep $ 100 for her own in exchange for purchasing a score of bottles of good Bordeaux wine for him with the remaining $ 900. Had the expenditure on his wine been taxed accordingly at the official tax schedule, he would have had to pay $ 1,350 ($ 900 plus 50 per cent expenditure tax). Thus the "gift" to the poor widow saves him $ 350. Notice that this also works more generally whenever the marginal expenditure tax rates differ for two parties. Tax arbitrage may also avail itself of the instrument of making *interpersonal loans* instead of outright gifts. Ultimate bancruptcy of the borrower eventually transforms loans into one-sided transfers for purposes of expenditure tax cosmetics. Interpersonal loans will be used as a means of tax evasion when gifts are not allowed to be tax-deductible on the part of the donor[49].

An expenditure tax must, therefore, depart from a theoretically correct treatment of gifts. Kaldor (1955, pp. 201-205) suggested that only one-sided transfers which are either ordered by courts (such as alimony), or transfers for the support of aged or incapacitated relatives who have only insufficient means of their own support, should be tax-deductible. All other gifts should not be tax-deductible, neither for the donor nor for the donee. The possibility of widespread tax arbitrage, not only in connection with gifts, would nevertheless suggest treating families as the taxpaying units. This requires, of course, some provision to mitigate tax progressivenes in the case of large families. Therefore, some kind of splitting would have to be adopted under an expenditure tax regime[50].

Bequests pose problems of a somewhat different kind. Assets and (depending on the method applied) consumer durables have been accumulated tax-free. According to the pure theory of an expenditure tax, they should form part of the inflow of funds on the part of the heirs. But when the heirs decide not to consume the bequest and keep it instead, or save it in some other form, it escapes taxation under an expenditure tax. This may lead to substantial concentration of wealth among certain dynasties. This led Kaldor (1955, p. 100 seq. and pp. 201-204) and Mieszkowski (1978, p. 31) to call for a tax on gifts and inheritances to complement an expenditure tax. This will, according to Mieszkowski (1978, p. 31) establish intertemporal equity: "Yet, on a life-cycle basis, the miser who consumes virtually nothing, and the individual who consumes all of his wage income as soon as it is received, pay the same tax calculated on a present value basis, *as long as the miser's estate is taxed* as consumption at the time of death. The miser accumulates wealth at a very rapid rate and will pay a large tax at the time of death."

We may agree that this is a sound practical measure, yet it is alien to the basic philosophy of an expenditure tax. As long as no consumption occurs, economic transactions should not be subject to taxation[51]. The Exchequer would have to wait until a spendthrift is born to the dynasty. But this period may turn out to be far too long for the

---

49 Cf. Slitor (1973, p. 247).

50 Cf. Poole (1943, p. 68).

51 Such procedure is accordingly endorsed by the Advisory Commission (1974, p. 37).

Exchequer. Practical reasons may therefore suggest that consumption be fictionalized on the part of the heirs and that inheritance be taxed along with current consumption or under a special inheritance tax. In the first case provisions of tax averaging are, of course, needed under a progressive expenditure tax.

Exchanges of ordinary consumer goods cause no problems, as such exchanges do not alter expenditures of either of the parties to an exchange. However, when assets or consumer durables are exchanged for consumer goods, the exchange becomes important for purposes of taxation. As registration of assets and consumer durables is required by the method of indirect expenditure calculation, there is sufficient safeguard that such exchanges will be adequately reflected in period expenditures. But this cannot be relied upon in the method of direct expenditure calculation, as this method usually works without asset registers. Remember that all goods can be purchased only with nonanonymous money, which makes asset registering (though not necessarily registering of consumer durables) dispensable. This opens up a tax loophole, however, when certain assets (for example, shares) may be exchanged against consumer goods, for this would entail consumption which is not reflected in nonanonymous money transfers. Therefore, an expenditure tax relying on the method of direct expenditure calculation has to allow for safeguards against the underreporting of expenditures due to exchanges of assets for consumer goods.

V. Interest Payments

If someone purchases an asset with a return of 10 per cent by taking out a loan at an interest rate of 6 per cent, the difference of 4 per cent represents the increase in his net wealth if the net return of this asset is saved rather than consumed. On the other hand, if someone makes a trip around the world and finances it through credit, this credit would count as dissaving in the first period and subsequent repayment of the credit would count as saving in following periods. But the expenditure for traveling around the world is in fact - due to the interest paid for the credit - higher than the amount spent in the first period. Therefore interest payments for consumer loans should not be deemed as being deductible under an expenditure tax[52].

---

[52] Cf. in the same sense Advisory Commission (1974, p. 30); Slitor (1973, p. 241).

So far, the theory of an expenditure tax is clearcut. But, alas, money - like dead men - tells no tales! Everyone possessing any assets can claim under fairly weak conditions that these assets were financed by credit up to the face value of the assets. This renders an adequate assignment of interest payments to the wealth sphere, on the one hand, and to the consumption sphere, on the other, largely impossible. Therefore, for administrative reasons, there are only two options for an expenditure tax, viz. either consider all interest payments to be tax-deductible, or else treat interest payments generally to be non-tax-deductible[53]. Both options are incorrect from a systematic point of view. Therefore, an expenditure tax may, with respect to interest payments, either discriminate against the savers (non-tax-deductible interest payments), or favour the consumers (fully tax-deductible interest payments). Both options imply inequity of an expenditure tax.

VI. Insurance, Social Security Contributions, Lotteries, and Necessitous Expenditures

Some insurance contracts are substitutes for own *saving*. Private pension insurance and life insurance, in particular, are of this type. These insurance contracts fit well into the philosophy of an expenditure tax: the premiums should be tax-deductible, whereas payments coming from the insurance company should be fully liable to the expenditure tax. Things become rather different in the case of a *risk insurance*, say an insurance against burglary. If we apply the very same treatment, we could allow deduction of an insurance premium of, say $ 300 per period. Imagine now that a burglary occurs causing $ 100,000 of damage. Can we sensibly argue that the insurance company's indemnity payment should be subject to an expenditure tax? Is it justified to tax some other noninsured household which has to replace the goods which were lost by burglary? The answer to this question depends largely on which method is applied for the treatment of consumer durables. Methods (2) and (3) will facilitate their handling, because there is no expenditure tax on the purchase of consumer durables. In this case insurance indemnity payments may be treated as an ordinary inflow of funds. As the consumer durables are replaced, the amount spent for them is fully tax-deductible. This

[53] The Advisory Commission (1974, p. 43), suggests tax-deductibility of interest payments up to the amount of indebtedness which equals the wealth of the taxpayer's assets.

offsets the increase of the tax base by the indemnity payments. But if methods (1) and (4) are applied for the tax treatment of consumer durables, special provisions have to be made for risk insurance and for the treatment of persons who fall victim to crime or to catastrophes which destroy their fortune or part thereof[54]. This means that the treatment of insurance premiums must be in accord with the treatment of wealth damages in the absence of insurance contracts.

Unfortunately, not all cases of risk insurance are covered by the method of tax treatment of consumer durables. Consider a third-party indemnity insurance, such as a car accident liability insurance. Assume an insured person damages the car of a third party and his insurance company pays damage indemnities to the third party. Certainly the third party experiences an inflow of funds, but should this flow be liable to expenditure taxation? Of course not. This suggests, however, that indemnity payments received from third parties should be exempt from taxation. On the contrary, indemnity payments made by a (noninsured) person who has caused the damage can be considered to be part of his consumption. They should, therefore, not be tax-deductible. In the framework of a third-party indemnity insurance this means that insurance premiums should be subject to taxation whereas indemnity payments received from third parties or from their insurance companies should be exempt from taxation subject that they are used to restore the damaged objects.

It remains to be seen whether an expenditure tax law is successful in clearly distinguishing all those cases requiring different treatment under an expenditure tax.

Social security contributions[55] pose similar problems. There can be no doubt that social security contributions for old age pensions should be tax-deductible and old age pensions should be subject to an expenditure tax inasmuch as they increase expenditure. The same applies to unemployment insurance. But the situation is completely different for health insurance. It does not seem appropriate to put a heavy expenditure tax burden on the miserable patient. Health insurance is a type of a risk insurance, which means that health insurance premiums and social health insurance contributions

---

[54] Buehler (1950, p. 15), has also addressed such events as major problems under an expenditure tax.

[55] The treatment of social security contributions under an expenditure tax should extend also to the employer's share. It should be imputed to the employee for purposes of expenditure tax assessment.

should be regarded as consumption and therefore not be tax-deductible. Accordingly, health treatment paid by insurance institutions should not be taxable. Notice, however, that health treatment which is not paid by insurance institutions, but by uninsured patients themselves, must be deemed period consumption and be fully liable to an expenditure tax[56]. This corresponds to tax liability of the health insurance contributions (or premiums) in the case of insured persons.

Winning a lottery or a bet causes an inflow of funds. Buying a lottery ticket or staking a bet is, on the other hand, an expenditure. The logic of an expenditure tax now has the option of declaring lottery prizes or bet winnings as being tax-liable (inasmuch as they are not saved); this would imply tax deductability of buying lottery tickets and of the stakes of bets. Otherwise the expenditure of buying lottery tickets and staking bets may be declared as subject to an expenditure tax; this would imply tax-exemption for lottery prizes and the winning of bets. It is not only inconsistent, but also unfair that most expenditure tax proposals treat both the stakes and the proceeds of bets and lotteries as liable to expenditure taxation. This can be justified only on grounds of avoiding tax arbitrage between two taxpayers with different marginal expenditure tax rates.

Some of the cases addressed above have been summed up by Kaldor under the headline "*necessitous expenditures*"[57] and he advocated that they be tax-exempt. I do not agree with Kaldor in that, because the amounts involved are rather considerable and because this would make an expenditure tax rather inconsistent and arbitrary. Many tax loopholes would be opened up by too generous concepts of necessitous expenditures. But some items (partly not addressed by Kaldor) certainly deserve special treatment which should exempt them from taxation. There is certainly a case for making professional expenditures tax-deductible if they have not already been taken into account. The question of the tax-deductibility of professional expenditures is closely connected with the question of the tax-deductibility of investment in human capital. Investment in human capital is a form of saving which elicits higher future income. As this investment

---

[56] Slitor (1973, pp. 248-249), on the contrary, argues in favour of tax-deductibility of medical expenses because of the financial hardships which taxation of medical expenditure would inflict upon the persons affected. Notice, however, that this is not in line with an expenditure tax regime and contributes to the erosion of the tax base, thus necessitating a higher tax rate to raise a given sum of tax revenue.

[57] Kaldor (1955, pp. 209-212); cf. also Fisher/Fisher (1942, p. 8).

expenditure detracts from available current expenditure, a case can be made to make investment expenditure in human capital tax-exempt[58]. On the other hand, investment in human capital opens up greater pleasures of consumption, and such expenditures do not warrant tax-exemption. An expenditure tax legislation would, in any case, have to solve questions relating to the tax treatment of investment in human capital.

There is certainly also room for expenditures which a taxpayer is virtually forced to incur by the society in which he lives. These may be contributions to trade unions, religious institutions, etc. Such forced expenditures are largely culturally conditioned and need to be carefully defined for each expenditure tax legislation. This category should be kept as narrow as possible, because these expenditures harbour a tendency to erode the tax base and thereby paralyze any tax system once they escape close control.

VII. What must be Registered?

An expenditure tax requires extensive registering[59]. The method of direct expenditure calculation requires no asset register, but this is bought at the price of registering any item of expenditure (separating out nonconsumption expenditure) and relying on nonanonymous money only. The advantage of this method is that the powerful engine of electronic data processing can be employed to solve this vast registration problem. Both methods of indirect expenditure calculation require asset registers to keep trace of each item of assets to insure that dissaving in any period is properly entered into period expenditure and that any saving is actually reflected as an increase in some item(s) of assets[60]. Secret borrowing from taxpayers with a low marginal rate of expenditure tax might otherwise be used to bolster the end-of-year cash holdings or bank deposits in order to reduce the expenditure tax base.

---

[58] This applies more to the United States than to Europe. Most European countries do heavily subsidize human capital formation which can then be regarded as a tax credit to offset higher future taxation due to income-tax progressiveness.

[59] For a general account cf. Kelley (1970, pp. 241-242); Poole (1943, p. 69); Slitor (1973, pp. 237-238 and 243).

[60] An expenditure tax induces taxpayers otherwise to overstate savings, as this would reduce taxable expenditure. Cf. Kelley (1970, p. 244); Advisory Commission (1974, pp. 46-47); Slitor (1973, pp. 237-238). Slitor (1973, pp. 254-254), even comes to examine a voucher system for investment as a ready method of checking reported investment.

Notice that the wealth-accrual method needs even more than that; it needs an asset register in which the values of all items of assets are revaluated for each period.

The method suggested by the Meade Committee (1978; pp. 175-183) reduces the scope of the asset register by requiring that only those assets falling under the category of "registered assets" be actually registered. However, the price of this is that substantial amounts of saving (in unregistered assets) are taxed as if they were current expenditure, whereas substantial amounts of dissaving (from unregistered assets) escapes expenditure taxation. When there are only a few items which are deemed to be registered assets, this would paralyze the expected performance of an expenditure tax.

Particular problems would be raised by the need to show evidence for the amount of cash held at the beginning and at the end of each period. Who knows whether cash holdings are exactly reported or whether they are exaggerated or understated by the taxpayer? It is hardly possible to check the validity of taxpayers' reports by immediate inspection, say on December 31st of each year. Even in that case the same cash may be used by different taxpayers and presented to the tax inspectors, or some cash may be hidden from inspection. Reliable controls must indeed employ rather draconian measures such as a complete change of coins and notes for every period or stamps placed on the banknotes to renew their validity for the next period. Otherwise cash-holdings could become a major tool of expenditure tax evasion.

As to the registration of consumer durables, we can see immediately that the depreciation method (2) and the method of user charges (3) require a register of consumer durables, possibly including a revaluation of the consumer durables in any period. It is not only for purposes of computing depreciation and user charges for which a register of consumer durables is needed, but also for the registration of consumer durables which are being sold. This is necessary to guarantee that the proceeds of the consumer durables sold are entered as inflows of funds; otherwise some room is cleared for untaxed expenditure by selling (partly untaxed) consumer durables. Notice, however, that we also need a register when applying methods (1) and (4) to consumer durables, because we have to check for negative consumption (to be deducted from period expenditure), on the one hand, and for windfall gains (to be added to period expenditure), on the other. This makes a register of consumer durables in any case fairly indispensable[61].

Thus far, it seems that an expenditure tax has shifted most of the nasty accountancy problems from the business sector to private households. An expenditure tax would inevitably induce any household liable to the expenditure tax to maintain a household bookkeeping[62]. It would force whole nations to become populations of accountants[63]. It seems that this would, on balance, increase the total transaction costs in society, but the business sphere, at least, would stand to gain. Unfortunately, this hope is also frustrated.

An expenditure tax can hardly work without meticulous computation of all sources of income. Otherwise it would invite tax evasion; any undisclosed income allows untaxed consumption, at least when an indirect method of expenditure calculation applies. Consider, for example, income from a small business. Any unregistered transfer of funds from the business to its owner's household means expenditure tax evasion, as do any shifts from private expenditure to business expenditure[64]. In addition, there is the problem of (the owner's) private consumption of products from the business (notably for agriculture)[65]. Finally, a business may offer goods or services, the proceeds

---

[61] Mieszkowski (1978, p. 44), on the contrary, recommends method (1) (without tax averaging) mainly for reasons of avoiding too much registering on the part of taxpayers. But this hope is rather unwarranted.

[62] Cf. Zumstein (1977, p. 355): "Um die im obigen Steuererklärungsschema erforderlichen Eintragungen machen zu können, muss der Steuerpflichtige während des ganzen Jahres zahlreiche das Einkommen und die Einkommensverwendung betreffende Tatbestände entweder selber schriftlich festhalten oder durch Quittungen und Bestätigungen belegen." Cf. also Slitor (1973, p. 237): "The enforcement of the spending tax would probably call for a considerable extension of the reporting mechanisms and requirements in order to cover money receipts or payments and capital transactions that are not now included in the information-return system for the income tax."

[63] Slitor (1973, p. 243), also concluded: "Perhaps complete balance-sheet reporting for higher-bracket taxpayers might be appropriate..." Cf. also Slitor (1973, pp. 252-253).

[64] Cf. Slitor (1973, p. 246). Any perquisites and any income in kind given to employees cause similar problems as under an income tax regime.

[65] Notice that an expenditure tax, like an income tax, can neither tax home production nor leisure. Therefore, as Mieszkowski (1978, p. 38), noted, one common feature of both tax regimes is that either of them distorts the choice between work and leisure. "It is theoretically possible that, even though an income tax distorts both work choice and savings decisions, it is superior to a consumption-based system from an efficiency

from which are paid into the owner's private purse. These problems, while well known from the income tax, will occur with an expenditure tax as well.

With respect to cross-checking and auditing by tax inspectors, the expenditure tax does not differ fundamentally from the income tax. Only the scope of such controls is much larger under an expenditure tax, as it must extend not only to income, but (if methods of indirect expenditure calculation are being applied) also to savings, dissavings, and wealth in the form of assets and consumer durables.

VIII. Problems of International Taxation

Tourism does not pose particular difficulties for an expenditure tax. Applying the method of direct expenditure calculation makes expenditures incurred abroad subject to the domestic expenditure tax if they were paid for by credit cards or cheques (notice that registering is done by domestic institutions). Any purchase of foreign exchange is also registered by domestic institutions due to the absence of anonymous money; therefore, it may also be subject to the domestic expenditure tax. Indirect expenditure calculation makes no distinction whatsoever between domestic and foreign expenditures, which means that an expenditure tax may cope with tourism very well. There is virtually only one major possibility of tax evasion via tourism: a tourist may for whatever reason possess foreign wealth. When foreign wealth is brought home undetected, it can be transformed into consumption which is not registered under the domestic expenditure tax. Notice that the indirect methods of expenditure calculation are more susceptible to this kind of tax evasion than is the direct method of expenditure calculation. In the latter case tax evasion requires taking consumption goods in kind (e.g. jewelry) from abroad. This possibility implies in any case rather meticulous customs control for tourists returning home.

More difficult problems arise when profits are earned by domestic branches of foreign companies. The pure theory of an expenditure tax would require that such profits be

---

standpoint if the savings distortion somehow offsets or moderates the work-effort distortion." For a more formal analysis of these distortions cf. Seidl (1985). Slitor (1973, pp. 245-246), expressed concern that widespread home production in response to an expenditure tax "would tend to discourage the supposedly more efficient exchange economy."

completely exempt from taxation. It would, therefore, be inconsistent if such profits were to be taxed in an expenditure tax system under a special tax[66]. Double taxation agreements should in any case rely on the domicile principle of taxation. Any income earned by nonresidents should be completely exempted from domestic taxation. The same should apply to any consumption by nonresidents; they should not be liable to domestic expenditure tax. This principle would reconcile an expenditure tax system applicable in a country with an income tax system applicable in another country. Income flows from an expenditure tax country into an income tax country should be exempt from any taxation in the expenditure tax country and should be fully subject to income taxation in the income tax country. Income flows from an income tax country into an expenditure tax country should be fully exempt from taxation in the income tax country. These income flows may either accrue to business, in which case they are not affected by an expenditure tax, or they may accrue to private households, in which case they increase the inflow of funds and are taxed insofar as they are not saved. Any other arrangement would introduce distortions into international tax relations. Such regulations could, however, require an intensive exchange of controls and cross-checking of information among the tax authorities involved, otherwise there would be great potential for tax evasion. The absence of double taxation agreements[67] would, therefore, indeed suggest some special tax on income transferred abroad, but we should keep in mind that this is basically an alien component of an expenditure tax system.

Still more difficult, however, are problems concerning *emigration* and *immigration* of residents[68]. Such problems arise even among countries when both have expenditure tax systems if the tax schedules differ. This applies even more so when we compare a country with an expenditure tax to a country adhering to an income tax. Obviously there are incentives for well-off taxpayers to work and save in an expenditure tax country and

---

[66] Cf., e.g., Rose (1987, pp. 877-878): "Ein Gewinntransfer ins Ausland müßte allerdings durch eine Sondersteuer erfaßt werden, um insbesondere auch einer Steuerhinterziehung durch Konsum der ausgeschütteten Gewinne außerhalb des Inlandsbereichs entgegenzuwirken. Angesprochen wird hier die nicht ganz unproblematische, aber unabdingbare Außensteuerlösung für jede Form einer persönlichen Konsumsteuer."

[67] Mieszkowski (1978, pp. 49-50), also stresses that a tight network of double taxation agreements is indispensable for an expenditure tax to work.

[68] Notice that severe difficulties are bound to arise when dealing with the question of whether permanent residence has been established or not.

then move to an income tax country for their retirement period and consume the fruits of their tax-exempt savings without being liable to any income tax or expenditure tax. It is obvious that these incentives run counter to the intentions of the tax authorities in both countries and induce them to take precautions against such behaviour.

Basically there are two methods of settlement of the different tax burdens under the two tax regimes in cases of migration:

(1) Income tax adjustment method: Assume first that a person emigrates from an expenditure tax country to an income tax country. The income tax adjustment method implies that he can take his assets free of charge or tax with him, but has to subject his fortune (evaluated at current market prices) to the income tax upon entering his new country of residence. On the other hand, a person emigrating from an income tax country into an expenditure tax country is reimbursed for all income tax previously paid while accumulating his fortune. He is thus reinstated the gross value of the parts of his past income he has saved and can start from scratch in the expenditure tax country. This simulates a situation of his ever having lived in this country.

(2) Expenditure tax adjustment method: Under this method a person emigrating from an expenditure tax country can take his fortune (evaluated at current market prices) with him only after it has been subject to an expenditure tax. The remaining wealth may then be consumed tax-free in the income tax country. When, on the other hand, a person from an income tax country immigrates to an expenditure tax country, he is reimbursed his future expenditure tax burden at the moment of entry, i.e., he receives a capital subsidy on his fortune (evaluated at current market prices), the accumulation of which had been impaired by his former domicile's income tax.

Obviously the first method places the burden of tax adjustment on the income tax country, whereas the second method places it on the expenditure tax country. Moreover, a great many other determinants may overshadow these simple adjustment methods and may leave a country with considerable net costs for subsidies to emigrants (first method) or to immigrants (second method) without adequate tax revenue from migration. Moreover, income tax countries may be tempted to attract well-off emigrants from expenditure tax countries for reasons of the positive external effects they exert upon the economy of the host country. This will induce these countries to relinquish collecting income tax based on the fortune of those emigrants at the moment of their immigration to the income tax country.

Therefore, most expenditure tax proposals rely on the second method and require an emigration tax levied on the fortune of their emigrants[69]. This should replace the expenditure tax which had not been collected when the emigrants were accumulating their fortunes. Curiosly enough, these proposals usually overlook that the complementary measure to taxing the fortunes of emigrants would be subsidizing the fortunes of immigrants coming from income tax countries or from expenditure tax countries with an emigration tax. This asymmetric tax treatment causes a lock-in effect for residents of an expenditure tax country. It detracts much from their human right to settle in any country of their choice.

Yet these suggestions do not seem to be very promising either. They overlook that taxpayers planning to leave their resident expenditure tax country after retirement have other alternatives. If there is an emigration tax they will try not to accumulate savings in their domicile. Instead they will make use of the numerous possibilities of international tax avoidance. They can, for example, found a firm in a tax haven country and export to third-party countries only via this firm. This firm is charged artificially low prices for asset or inventory acquisitions and issues invoices at market prices for the recipient of the exported goods in the third country. In that way profits are accumulated in the tax haven. Losses which occur in the domestic firm are covered by its owners and are treated as tax-deductible saving under an expenditure tax regime. This procedure allows funds to be shifted into tax havens so that they may escape expenditure taxation. When the taxpayer finally emigrates from the expenditure tax country to enjoy his retirement, he has little domestic fortune to take with him. The emigration tax will thus not inflict much harm. But when he arrives in the tax haven or in some income tax country, he may enjoy expenditure-tax free the fruits accumulated in long decades when he was working in the expenditure tax country. Profit shifting will thus pay, not only under an income tax regime, but also under an expenditure tax regime.

---

[69] Cf. Meade Committee (1978, pp. 438-442); Lodin (1978, pp. 108-114). - Goode (1980, p. 66, note 27), reports that Canada already taxes unrealized capital gains (or losses) which are deemed to be realized upon emigration.

IX. Problems of Regime Transition

The most elegant procedure to alleviate transition from an income tax to an expenditure tax would consist of a subsidy on all wealth present in an economy. This is to compensate for past income tax which has burdened the accumulation of that wealth by means of saving out of taxed income. Unfortunately, this method is not feasible, first because of the immense cost that would have to be incurred to finance this task; and second, because rather different amounts of income tax burden may be contained in different fortunes even of the same size, due to the preferential tax treatment of some forms of accumulation (remember, e.g., capital gains). As current wealth is the product of different histories of accumulation, it would be next to impossible to determine even approximately the amounts of income tax contained in the fortunes of the taxpayers.

Therefore we must apply another method, viz. we must provide for two asset registers and two registers of consumer durables for each taxpayer. The first register should contain assets and consumer durables relevant to pre-expenditure-tax periods. These items may be dissaved and consumed without any expenditure tax consequences. The items in this register may only be "used up". The tax law may contain a deadline after which all those items are regarded as liable to expenditure tax. The second register should contain all items of assets and consumer durables which were acquired after the introduction of the expenditure tax. This method is feasible, though it requires administrative duplication during a (probably rather long) period of transition.

But this second method is costly, too. In fact, it means that during a possibly rather long period of transition substantial parts of current consumption may legitimately escape expenditure taxation. Revenue considerations may therefore suggest that a switch be made to an expenditure tax regime without employing some of the above mentioned means of smoothing the transition, differing between tax regimes. But such a rather rigid stance overriding taxpayers' good faith in the past would give rise to severe problems of tax evasion in connection with the transition of tax regimes. It is then in the interest of any taxpayer to hide as many assets and consumer durables (jewelry, art, antiques) as possible from being registered for purposes of the expenditure tax. When a taxpayer succeeds in hiding many assets, he can de facto increase his expenditure over a couple of periods without being taxed on the expenditure coming from hidden sources.

The method of direct expenditure calculation is not very exposed to this danger, because of the non-existence of anonymous money in the economy. Notice, however, that the incentive to hide consumer durables from the tax authorities is present also under the method of direct expenditure calculation.

Both methods of indirect expenditure calculation are, on the contrary, also susceptible to the concealment of assets at the moment of transition to an expenditure tax. The type of assets most likely to be concealed is, of course, anonymous money[70]. This disturbance of a smooth transition to an expenditure tax has led Poole (1943, p. 67) and Kaldor (1955, p. 221) to consider even "the more drastic step of calling in all bank notes and reissuing them in a new form at a date subsequent to the introduction of the tax, so that all cash hoards would be automatically disclosed."

X. Evaluation of an Expenditure Tax

This paper has demonstrated that the administration of an expenditure tax is its Achilles' heel. An expenditure tax harbours substantial possibilities for tax evasion and associates greater gains to tax evasion due to the higher expenditure tax rates as compared with an income tax (notice that consumption is usually smaller than income in an economy). It requires a nation of accountants on the one hand and omnipotent and omniscient tax authorities on the other. It works well only in a world of highly controlled taxpayers who are willing to sacrifice much of their leisure time for the purpose of smooth tax administration. On the part of the bureaucracy, an expenditure tax requires a meddlesome state which, by necessity of tax administration, must interlope in the privacy of each of its residents. On careful reflection it seems that a well-working expenditure tax[71] is bought at the price of living in an Orwellian world.

---

[70] Due to the large amount of registering under an expenditure tax hiding of undisclosed assets other than anonymous money will become increasingly difficult. Cf. Kelley (1970, pp. 247-248); Poole (1943, p. 67); Slitor (1973, p. 244).

[71] Cf. also Slitor (1973, p. 257): "On the basic question of whether a spendings tax is practicable, this chapter reaches the qualified conclusion that it probably is practicable within a relatively restricted scope of high-income, substantial-wealth taxpayers. The risk of excessive cost, substantial breakdown, and even an administrative debacle would probably increase if the tax were applied on a broad scale approaching that of the personal income tax." In other words, Slitor too considers an expenditure tax regime as

Comments by Albert J. Rädler

First of all, I would like to compliment the organizers of this conference for "pairing" Professor Seidl and myself. The reason for this compliment is that there are many conclusions of his which I do not agree with. Perhaps this is due to the fact that I belong to both groups which Prof. Seidl feels are especially attracted by consumption tax, i.e. business school professors and accountants. We seem to agree, however, but for different reasons, that a personal consumption tax will be extremely difficult to introduce.

I cannot concur that the administration would be the Achilles' heel of a personal consumption tax. Its introduction would certainly reduce a number of tax problems connected with an income tax, because cash flow is much easier to establish than net income. On the other hand it would create a number of severe new problems, especially in the international field, as we will see later on. A great number of tax problems under the existing income tax will simply continue; many of which are mentioned in Prof. Seidl's paper as a deterrent to a consumption tax.

Let me briefly explain my point of view:

If we double the rates of VAT, and extend the base, for example by including rents, and abolish income tax and corporate income tax altogether, we would have a good example

being impotent to replace the income tax regime. On p. 258 he expresses doubt whether an expenditure tax will work even if restricted to high-income taxpayers only: "Even on this basis, there are unpleasant possibilities of intolerable complexity and taxpayer resistance."

Graetz (1980, p. 276), after an impressive investigation of an expenditure tax design, comes to conclude: "Given the practical difficulties, proponents of an expenditure tax should be required to demonstrate that its claimed advantages in terms of equity and economic efficiency are real and cannot be achieved in a simpler fashion... Unless and until this burden is met, replacing the income tax with a progressive personal tax on consumption should remain low on the list of political priorities, and the principal utility of expenditure tax analysis should continue to lie in illuminating issues of income taxation and increasing our understanding of tax policy."

of a consumption tax system (although not of a personal consumption tax). There are no doubts that this would result in a substantial reduction in administrative work forindividual taxpayers, businesses and tax administration alike.

In my opinion it would not be viable to introduce a direct method for establishing the base of a personal consumption tax, because this would indeed necessitate total supervision of taxpayers by tax inspectors, a situation which Prof. Seidl clearly rejects in his paper in another context.

The failure of personal consumption tax systems in Sri Lanka and in India is in my view no proof for the administrative failure of such a tax; I would assume that these countries also have many problems in the administration of an ordinary income tax.

Contrary to Prof. Seidl I cannot see a big problem in the requirement that non-business taxpayers also would have to register their assets under a personal consumption tax. This is an absolutely normal procedure in any country which taxes personal capital gains and would not bring much change for those German taxpayers which are subject to net-worth taxation.

The inclusion of gifts and inheritances in a personal consumption tax system is another conceptual issue, for which, however, in my view the administrative aspects are not the decisive ones.

In my view the greatest obstacles against the introduction of personal consumption tax arise in the international field. It could not be avoided that the transfer of assets abroad must be deemed consumption; correspondingly the transfer of assets from abroad must be deemed investment. The problems which arise are obvious. The mobility of individuals to move to another country would be extremely limited. I would not go as far, however, as to see human rights endangered, when capital gains are taxed when somebody leaves the country. This, for example, is done in Canada today. I also disagree with the concept that double taxation agreements should rely on the domicile principle. The domicile principle can only work under the assumption that there is a prior right of taxation for the country from which, for example, business income originates. This prior taxing right cannot be taken away from the country where substantial economic activities are performed. In summary, I would conclude that nowadays it would be almost impossible for a country such as Germany to introduce a personal consumption tax without the same changeover taking place in the other Member-States of the European Communities.

A technical aspect might be that the Common Market legislation, in particular the Sixth VAT-directive, limits the rights of the Member-States to levy a general consumption tax other than VAT. There is no doubt that a general personal consumption tax would be somewhat different from VAT. However, in my view it can not be excluded that the European Court of Justice would decide against a Member-State which introduced a personal consumption tax.

I would also like to add that in my view the problem of international transfer pricing would continue to exist under a personal consumption tax system as it does today under an income tax system; theoretically this problem could be solved by the replacement of the arm's length concept by unitary taxation, a step which the Common Market member-States might be ready to take in ten years at the earliest; but this has nothing to do with the use of personal consumption tax or a personal income tax.

I can also not concur with one of Prof. Seidl's final conclusions that a consumtion tax will require a nation of accountants and an omnipotent tax administration. In my view, there would be no basic change in this aspect. Perhaps, there would even be a small reduction in tax work force. Instead I come to the final conclusion that from a purely domestic administrative point of view a system of personal consumption tax would be viable. However, in my view, the two main obstacles are conceptual:

- There is the distributional aspect that the part of the population which has to consume most of its income would be hit harder than the more prosperous one,
- and there is the international aspect of emigration which would severely limit the possibilities of moving freely from one country to another.

So the "ball is back in the yard" of public finance.

References

Adams, T.S. (1921), Fundamental Problems of Federal Income Taxation, Quarterly Journal of Economics 35, pp. 527-556.

Advisory Commission on Intergovernmental Relations (1974), The Expenditure Tax: Concept, Administration and Possible Applications, Information Report M-84 (Washington, D.C.).

Andrews, W.D. (1974), Consumption-Type or Cash Flow Personal Income Tax, Harvard Law Review 87, pp. 1113-1188.

Andrews, W.D. (1980), A Supplemental Personal Expenditure Tax, in: J.A. Pechman (ed.), What Should Be Taxed: Income or Expenditure? (The Brookings Institution, Washington, D.C.), pp. 127-157.

Beale, T. (1911), The Measurement of Income for Taxation, Journal of Political Economy 19, pp. 655-675.

Bradford, D.F. (1980), The Case for a Personal Consumption Tax, in: J.A. Pechman (ed.), What Should Be Taxed: Income or Expenditure? (The Brookings Institution, Washington, D.C.), pp. 75-113.

Bradford, D.F./ U.S. Treasury Tax Policy Staff (1977/1984), Blueprints for Basic Tax Reform (Washington, D.C. / Tax Analysts, Arlington, Virginia).

Buehler, A. (1950), The Spendings Tax, Public Finance 5, pp. 8-22.

Carter Commission (1966), Report of the Royal Commission on Taxation (Queen's Printer and Controller of Stationary, Ottawa).

Committee on Simplification, Selection of Taxation, American Bar Association (1981/82), Complexity and the Personal Consumption Tax, Tax Lawyer 35, pp. 415-442

Eigner, E.M. (1959), Indian Income, Wealth and Expenditure Taxes: Integration and Administration, National Tax Journal 12, pp. 151-162.

Elster, K. (1913), Eine Reichsaufwandsteuer? Jahrbücher für Nationalökonomie und Statistik 101, pp. 785-796.

Fisher, I. (1937), Income in Theory and Income Taxation in Practice, Econometrica 5, pp. 1-55.

Fisher, I. / Fisher, H.W. (1942), Constructive Income Taxation, A Proposal for Reform (Harper, New York-London).

Friedman, M. (1943), The Spendings Tax as a Wartime Fiscal Measure, The American Economic Review 33, pp. 50-62.

Fullerton, D. (1985), The Consumption Tax versus the Income Tax, in: J.H. Makin (ed.), Real Tax Reform, Replacing the Income Tax (American Enterprise Institute, Washington, D.C.), pp. 5-13.

Goode, R. (1980), The Superiority of the Income Tax, in: J.A. Pechman (ed.), What Should Be Taxed: Income or Expenditure? (The Brookings Institution, Washington, D.C.), pp. 49-73.

Graetz, M.J. (1980), Expenditure Tax Design, in: J.A. Pechman (ed.), What Should Be Taxed: Income or Expenditure? (The Brookings Institution, Washington, D.C.), pp. 161-276.

Haensel, P. (1942), The Spendings Tax and the Victory Tax: A Critique, Taxes, The Tax Magazine 20, pp. 614-619.

Haensel, P. (1943), Constructive Income Taxation: A Proposal for Reform. By Irving Fisher / Herbert W. Fisher, The American Economic Review 33, pp. 162-164.

Harberger, A.C. (1958), An Expenditure Tax. By Nicholas Kaldor, Journal of Political Economy 66, pp. 84-85.

Kaldor, N. (1955), An Expenditure Tax (George Allen & Unwin Ltd., London).

Kaldor, N. (1980), Reports on Taxation I, Papers Relating to the United Kingdom (Duckworth, London).

Kelley, P.L. (1970), Is an Expenditure Tax Feasible?, National Tax Journal 23, pp. 237-253.

Little, I.M.D. (1956), An Expenditure Tax. By Nicholas Kaldor, The Economic Journal 66, pp. 116-120.

Lodin, S.-O. (1978), Progressive Expenditure Tax - An Alternative?, A Report of the 1972 Government Commission on Taxation (Liber Förlag, Stockholm).

Meade, J.E., Chairperson (1978), Committee Report on the Structure and Reform of Direct Taxation (George Allen & Unwin, London-Boston-Sydney).

Mieszkowski, P. (1977), The Cash Flow Version of An Expenditure Tax, Office of Tax Analysis Papers, Paper No. 26, Department of the Treasury, August 1977.

Mieszkowski, P. (1978), The Choice of Tax Base: Consumption versus Income Taxation, in: M.J. Boskin (ed.), Federal Tax Reform: Myths and Realities (Institute for Contemporary Studies, San Francisco), pp. 27-53.

Mieszkowski, P., (1980), The Advisability and Feasibility of an Expenditure Tax System, in: H.J. Aaron, M.J. Boskin (eds.), The Economics of Taxation (The Brookings Institution, Washington, D.C.), pp. 179-201.

Mills, O.L. (1922), The Spendings Tax, Proceedings of the Fourteenth Annual Conference on Taxation held at Bretton Woods, N.H., September 12-16, 1921 (National Tax Association, New York), pp. 327-331.

Mitschke, J. (1976), Über die Eignung von Einkommen, Konsum und Vermögen als Bemessungsgrundlage der direkten Besteuerung, Eine meßtechnische Analyse (Duncker & Humblot, Berlin).

Mombert, P. (1916), Eine Verbrauchseinkommensteuer für das Reich als Ergänzung zur Vermögenszuwachssteuer (Duncker & Humblot, Tübingen).

Morgenthau, H. (1942), Statement to the Senate Finance Committee on Proposals for a Spending Tax and other changes in the Tax Bill, New York Times, Sept. 4th, p. 16.

Moxter, A. (1982), Betriebswirtschaftliche Gewinnermittlung (J.C.B. Mohr (Paul Siebeck), Tübingen).

Musgrave, R.A. (1957), An Expenditure Tax. By Nicholas Kaldor, The American Economic Review 47, pp. 200-205.

Peffekoven, R. (1980), Persönliche allgemeine Ausgabensteuer, in: F. Neumark / N. Andel / H. Haller (eds.), Handbuch der Finanzwissenschaft, 3rd ed., Vol. II (J.C.B. Mohr (Paul Siebeck), Tübingen), pp. 417-452.

Pfeiffer, E. (1866), Die Staatseinnahmen. Geschichte, Kritik und Statistik derselben, Vol. II (Verlag von A. Kröner, Stuttgart und Leipzig).

Philip, K. / Gelting, J. / Christiansen, K. etc. (1958), Betaenkning om Forbrugsbeskatning, Betaenkning 202 (Statens Trykningskontor, Copenhagen).

Poole, K.E. (1943), Problems of Administration and Equity under a Spendings Tax, American Economic Review 33, pp. 63-73.

Prakesh, O. (1958), An Indian View of the Expenditure Tax, Manchaster School of Economic and Social Studies 26, pp. 48-67.

Prest, A.R. (1956), A Tax on Expenditure? Lloyd's Bank Review 42, pp. 35-49.

The Reform of Personal Taxation (1986), (Her Majesty's Stationary Office, Cmnd. 9756, London)

Revans, J. (1847), A Per Centage Tax on Domestic Expenditure to supply the whole of the Public Revenue: The Customs, Excise, Stamp, Legacy, Assess, Income, and all other Government Taxes, and Tax Establishments; together with the Coast Guard and the Revenue Cruisers to be Abolished. By which Two Millions and a half will be annually saved in the cost of Collection; and Trade and Production be Rendered Perfectly Free. (John Hatchford and Son, London).

Rose, M. (1987), Plädoyer für eine konsumorientierte Steuerreform, in: R. Henn (ed.), Technologie, Wachstum und Beschäftigung, Festschrift für Lothar Späth (Springer-Verlag, Berlin), pp. 869-883.

Royal Commission on the Taxation of Profits and Income (1955), Final Report (Radcliffe Report), (Her Majesty's Stationary Office, Cmnd. 9474, London).

Schneider, D. (1971), Gewinnermittlung und steuerliche Gerechtigkeit, Zeitschrift für betriebswirtschaftliche Forschung 23, pp. 352-394.

Schneider, D. (1978), Steuerbilanzen. Rechnungslegung als Messung steuerlicher Leistungsfähigkeit (Betriebswirtschaftlicher Verlag Dr. Th. Gabler, Wiesbaden).

Schumpeter, J.A. (1929/30), Ökonomie und Soziologie der Einkommensteuer, Der deutsche Volkswirt 4, pp. 380-385.

Seidl, C. (1985), Effizienz und Steuerreform: Umfassende Einkommensteuer oder Konsumsteuer?, Das öffentliche Haushaltswesen in Österreich 26, pp. 180-197.

Slitor, R.E. (1973), Administrative Aspects of Expenditure Taxation, in: R.A. Musgrave (ed.), Broad-Based Taxes. New Options and Sources (John Hopkins University Press, Baltimore-London), pp. 227-263.

Vickrey, W. (1947), Agenda for Progressive Taxation (The Ronald Press Company, New York).

Wallis, W.A. (1942), How to Ration Consumer Goods and Control their Prices, The American Economic Review 32, pp. 501-512.

Warren, A.C. (1975), Fairness and a Consumption-Type or Cash Flow Personal Income Tax, Harvard Law Review 88, pp. 931-958.

Zumstein, P. (1977), Die Ausgabensteuer, Volkswirtschaftliche Begründung und praktische Durchführbarkeit (Verlag Rüegger, Diessenhofen).

PART SIX

Taxing Consumption from an International Point of View

Peggy B. Musgrave

International Coordination Problems of Substituting Consumption for Income Taxation*

Worldwide interest in consumption taxation in recent years has largely been focused on domestic considerations of growth, efficiency, revenue, equity, and stabilization [Mieszkowski (1980); Hall and Rabushka (1983); Bradford (1984); Aaron and Galper (1985); McLure (1987a)]. To the extent that international considerations have been included in the discussion, it has largely been by way of effects on the balance of payments or on the competitive trade position of the country contemplating adoption of a consumption-based tax. For instance, among the reasons given on behalf of adoption of value-added taxes in the United States and Japan has been the desire to gain comparable competitive advantage with the European Common Market [Aaron (1981); Weidenbaum et al. (1989)]. Thus the adoption of consumption-based taxation has rarely been seen in the context of an international tax order within which differences in fiscal systems might be coordinated to mutual advantage. Since the European Community has been for long involved in a process of fiscal coordination, it is appropriate and perhaps not surprising that this conference should be the first, so far as I know, to give some attention to the problem of the international coordination of consumption taxes.

In this paper, section I briefly lays the conceptual foundation for exploring the economic role which taxes play in a multiunit setting, and the issues and objectives involved in the process of fiscal coordination. Section II then discusses the requirements for coordination of symmetrical income tax systems with and without integration

* The author wishes to express appreciation for the useful comments made by the discussant, Norbert Andel.

of the corporate and personal income taxes. Even though the novel problem to be considered deals with the case of consumption taxes, this will prove useful in providing a background and permitting a comparison. Section III turns to an exploration of coordination of symmetrical general consumption taxes, including those of the *in rem* as well as the personal type and in the latter case, in combination with a business cash-flow tax. Section IV then goes on to consider coordination problems in a world of non-symmetrical income and consumption taxes. A summary and the conclusions are presented in section V.

I. Role of Taxes and Tax Coordination in International Setting

We begin with a brief discussion of certain fundamental questions regarding the role of taxation in a world in which national economies are becoming increasingly open one to another, reflected in the increasing volume of trade and mobility of factors, residents and consumers, and the need for coordinating diverse fiscal systems which display the varying public-sector preferences of each country's citizenry.

A. Types of Tax and Base Assignment

Until recent decades, the only tax which was the subject of serious policy concern for its role in international economic relations was the tariff. Happily by now tariffs have diminished in relative importance in national revenue structures, but other taxes and international differentials between them have increased. At the same time, international mobility of resources, particularly of capital, has risen sharply and this mobility now is of as much concern as are trade flows. These two developments have lent an additional international dimension to the design of tax policy.

The role of taxes in interjurisdictional economic relationships differs with the nature of the tax. As shown in the rows of Table 1, taxes may be imposed on income, consumption or wealth. They may be personal in their application (such as the individual income tax, the tax on net worth, and the personal expenditure tax) or they may be impersonal or *in rem* in type (such as the value-added tax, the corporation income tax, the withholding tax or the property tax). Where the subject or transaction to be taxed crosses borders, there is the further question in which country the tax is to be applied.

The appropriate forms of tax-base assignment are shown in the columns of the table and differ for various taxes. Income may be taxed where it arises by the country of source of that income and it may be taxed by the country of residence of the recipient. Taxes on income at source must necessarily be of the *in rem* type, such as the corporation income tax, the payroll tax, or the withholding tax. Personal taxes, on the other hand may only be applied by the country of residence since, if global in nature, such taxes will apply to income from all sources. The corporation tax may be applied according to both principles, with residence defined as the place of incorporation or location of management. Just as taxes on income may be divided into those applied to persons in their country of residence (primary tax allegiance) and those applied as impersonal taxes by the country of source, so may taxes on consumption be conceptually divided into personal expenditure taxes and *in rem* taxes. Like the personal income tax, the personal expenditure tax is only applicable by the country of residence of the consumer, since consumption in all locations must be included in the tax base. *In rem* taxes such as the value-added tax of the consumption type and the retail sales tax, may be imposed either at the point of production (at origin) or at point of final purchase (at destination). A value-added tax without border tax adjustments (BTAs) is an example of the former and the retail sales tax of the latter. These various patterns may be perused further in Table 1.

B. Coordination and its Objectives

In the domestic setting, tax policy has to be concerned with (1) providing the needed revenue, (2) maintaining standards of equity and (3) minimizing inefficiencies which result from distorting effects on resource use. In the international setting, each country will continue to be concerned with these objectives, but additional considerations enter and, as we shall see, have to be met by measures of coordination.

1. Internation Equity: Entitlement to Tax Bases

A fundamental concern of international tax coordination has to be that of internation equity. This concept which plays an important role in our analysis recognizes the entitlement to tax income at its source or real property at its situs. The exercise of this

Table 1: Classification of Taxes in Multiunit Setting

	Source Principle	Residence Principle	Origin Principle	Destination Principle
Income Taxes				
In Rem	Corporation Income Tax Payroll Tax VAT-Income Type Withholding Tax	Corporation Income Tax	VAT-Income Type	VAT-Income Type with BTAs
Personal	not applicable	Individual Income Tax	not applicable	not applicable
Consumption Taxes				
In Rem	not applicable	not applicable	VAT- Cons. Type	VAT- Cons. Type with BTAs Retail Sa-les Tax
Personal	not applicable	Personal Exp. Tax	not applicable	not applicable
Wealth Taxes				
In Rem	Property Tax	not applicable	not applicable	not applicable
Personal	not applicable	Personal Net Worth Tax	not applicable	not applicable

entitlement is most effectively applied by the use of *in rem* taxes at source of income, such as a payroll tax or a value-added tax of the origin and income type. It is generally thought reasonable to permit the country of income source or product origin to take a "fair" tax share in the income value arising within it, even though owned by foreign residents. The appropriate magnitude of that share depends on an international view of property rights but a reasonable standard of internation equity would suggest that such taxes should be applied at reciprocally equal rates, whether on a bilateral or multilateral basis. It is to be noted that this reciprocity of rates may have to override the commonly accepted rule of non-discrimination as between taxes applied by the source country to income accruing to non-residents and those applied to residents. In some cases internation equity may not be attained without the use of international transfers of revenues.

The question may be raised whether the entitlement principle may also be expressed as entitlement to tax the export of products as in the case of an origin-type VAT thereby burdening the foreign consumers of domestic products, rather than the foreign participants in domestically created income. For various reasons, this would be an inferior formulation of the entitlement claim. Entitlement, it would seem, is more appropriately related to the foreign share in income rather than to foreign absorption of part of the country's gross product, including depreciation as well as income. For this reason, entitlement in the following analysis will be viewed in terms of claim to a share in the income base at source.

2. Internation Equity: Burden Shifting

A second problem also bearing on internation equity arises from the possibility of burden shifting across jurisdictions. In the closed economy context, a tax imposed on X may be shifted to Y, an outcome important for the resulting burden distribution among residents. In the international context, a tax imposed by country A on transactions which also involve country B may initially yield revenue to A, yet the burden may come to be borne by residents of B as would be the case with an origin-type value-added tax. Such burden export distorts product flows and creates an internation inequity as the cost of providing public services in the exporting country is partly shifted to foreigners.

This is inappropriate, especially in view of our earlier conclusion that entitlement claims should be defined in terms of an income, rather than a production base.

3. Allocative Efficiency

Tax policy should avoid interference with efficient resource use. This task is difficult enough in the domestic context as has been well shown by the burgeoning literature on optimal taxation. The potential for distortion is magnified in the international setting. First, differentials in effective tax rates from one country to another can influence the flow of goods and services, of factors of production, and the choices of individuals to reside and consume in one country or another.[1] Thus international differentials in product taxes imposed at origin may affect the pattern of trade and in turn the allocation of resources between domestic and traded goods.[2] On the other hand, differences in rates of retail sales taxes (product taxes imposed on a destination basis) may encourage transborder shopping on the part of consumers. Differentials in effective rates of corporate tax, if unmatched by corresponding differentials in subsidies offered to intermediate inputs in the corporate sector, will influence the choice of production location. In addition, personal income taxes on financial flows of dividends, interest, royalties and rents may apply differentially to individuals receiving capital income from foreign sources and those receiving such income from domestic sources, thereby influencing international financial flows. Similarly, labor movements may be induced by differentials in fiscal treatment, including income and payroll taxes as well as government pension and other transfer plans. Finally, differentials in the combined array of taxes can have a bearing on the choice of residence of individuals. This consideration may reinforce the choice of location of where to work, or may be a choice open only to recipients of capital income, such as retirees.

---

[1] More accurately, differences in "fiscal residues", i.e. allowing for the incidence of both benefits of government expenditures and of tax burdens, is the relevant variable. However, for purposes of this paper we are assuming that the two are comparable and we focus only on effective tax rate differentials.

[2] It is widely accepted that differentials in general, origin-based product taxes can be compensated for by offsetting adjustments in exchange rates thus neutralizing any adverse allocative effects. However, product taxes are not likely to be universally general in nature, exchange rates may be "sticky" and for these and other reasons it is unrealistic to assume such a perfectly flexible system.

These and other tax-induced distortions in the allocation of resources will carry an efficiency cost, reducing the level of international welfare, even though the countries which are the recipients of increased capital inflows or of improved terms of trade may experience a net gain. Furthermore, such allocative changes are likely to carry with them strong redistributive implications in each country. Thus, a tax-induced capital outflow may be expected to be harmful to labor in the exporting country, but helpful to capital owners, with the opposite effect in the capital-importing country. Similarly, an immigration of foreign labor will be relatively beneficial to capital in the country of immigration, but again with opposite effect in the country of labor outflow. With capital by far the most mobile factor, differentials in the taxation of capital income are of particcular importance.

To avoid these distortions, coordination should secure a neutral fiscal environment in which goods and services can be exchanged and factors of production move across boundaries in ways which are not dictated by fiscal concerns. This requires the consumers of any unit to pay the same tax on the goods which they consume whether produced in their own jurisdiction or another; and it also requires that investors and workers should face the same effective tax rates on their returns whether they choose to invest or work at home or abroad. In the absence of such neutrality, the flow of consumer goods and the location of production will be diverted from their efficient patterns. Nor should fiscal differentials affect the location of residency and thus introduce a further interference with individual choice.

4. Interresident Equity

As distinct from internation equity which is subject to agreement among nations, any one jurisdiction will wish to implement its own concept of interpersonal equity. In the absence of benefit taxation, this requires that people in equal positions (capacity to pay) should pay the same tax and calls for payments among unequals to differ in line with what each electorate may consider a fair distribution of burdens. This pattern tends to be interfered with in an open economy setting since trade and factor movements among jurisdictions raise the possibility of either over- or under-taxation of the taxpayers of a particular unit. This means that residents of one unit who choose to work, invest or consume in another may be subject to higher or lower tax burdens than those who choose to do so within their own country. As a result, the effect on the distribution of tax liabilities among persons becomes a major concern as do resulting effects on factor movements. Once more, the exceptionally high mobility of capital and hence of the source of capital income is of particular importance. Thus it is generally agreed that residents of one country who choose to transact abroad should pay the same as their fellow residents who do not. It is for coordination to show how this may be implemented.

C. Coordination or Competition?

It is apparent that the co-existence of differing national fiscal systems in a world increasingly open to movements of commodities, capital and people, presents problems of internation equity, allocative efficiency and taxpayer equity, problems that need to be dealt with. Until quite recently, it was taken for granted that it was desirable for both economic and political reasons to do so by coordination. For the economist, such coordination suggested the removal of fiscal barriers or inducements to the flow of goods, capital and labor, thus promoting an efficient use of resources within and across jurisdictions. Traditionally, interest has been focused on the removal of barriers to trade flows through the mutual reduction of tariffs, a central objective of the postwar General Agreement on Tariffs and Trade, a form of international coordination. There has also been some historical concern with tax barriers to the free international flow of capital, leading to the prewar work of the League of Nations, later taken up by the United Nations and the OECD in promoting international tax treaties to prevent "double taxation" of international capital.[3] The emergence of the European Economic Community after World War II has given much impetus to fiscal coordination. Its goals were soon seen to require not only coordination through the removal of internal tariffs and the equalization of external tariffs, but also the coordination of commodity and company taxes [Andel (1983)].

These approaches rest on the premise that fiscal differentials among countries should be coordinated, either by removing the differentials themselves or by harmo-

[3] There has always been more concern with the problem of so-called "double taxation" of capital income caused by overlapping claims to tax base than with the problem of under-taxation of capital income due to avoidance of taxes by operation in low- or zero-tax jurisdictions.

nizing arrangements which would neutralize the effects on resource allocation. In recent years, however, the desirability of fiscal coordination has been challenged, based on the argument that as commodity, labor and capital markets open up one to another, superior public sector performance will be rewarded by attracting resources, residents and trade, just as the superior performance of firms in the market results in increased profits. According to this view, harmonization may be counter-productive since it insulates government budgets from the discipline of international competition, and may be likened to collusion of firms in the private sector. Seen from this perspective, the application of normative fiscal rules as traditionally developed becomes invalid and is replaced by a very different set of requirements. Instead, fiscal competition, by wooing resources through offer of lower tax rates is to serve as a means of checking overexpansion in the public sector. Even if this "Leviathan" concept of government [Brennan and Buchanan (1978)] were correct, fiscal competition in my view would be an inefficient way of correcting overexpansion. Moreover, it would fail to deal with the problems noted in the preceding section [P. Musgrave (1989)]. We therefore proceed on the premise that coordination is needed, although it may take various forms.

D. Harmonization, Equalization or Centralization?

One approach to coordination lies in centralization of those taxes and fiscal functions which, if applied differentially by separate nation states will induce misallocations of resources. Although this remedy is appropriate in the case of those operations which carry large spillovers of benefits and costs, in other areas centralization may eliminate the benefits to be derived from the expression of heterogeneous preferences among jurisdictions. This diversity extends from the choice of level and mix of public services as well as of redistributive policies and of the tax structure.

Coordination may alternatively seek to maintain a decentralized fiscal structure, but with the goal of equalizing tax rates to secure neutrality. Again, diversity in the expression of fiscal preferences would be violated, although the choice of tax rates would have to be agreed upon by all participating units. In all, there would seem to be little advantage in this form of coordination over the centralization model. Coordinating policies within the European Community have largely been aimed at equalizing rates of origin-type commodity taxes and adoption of source-based company-tax systems, together with a common form of corporate-individual income tax integration. I believe both these approaches are flawed since they do not sufficiently protect fiscal diversity among nations.

The third and more fruitful approach to coordination is that of harmonization, under which taxes are equalized only when it is administratively too costly to apply neutralizing arrangements to differential rates, or when equal rates are called for on grounds of internation equity.[4] This is the approach which will be followed here and will now be applied to both income- and consumption- based taxes.

II. Coordination of Symmetrical Income Tax Systems

We consider first a world in which corporation and individual income taxes are universally applied, though at different effective rates. Such taxes reduce the returns to investment (real and financial) and to work effort and without coordination varying effective rates of tax from one country to another will influence the choice of location of investment, work and residence. Additionally, overlapping claims to tax base by the countries of source of income and of residence of taxpayer can result in double taxation thus impeding free factor movements. Such tax-distorted choices will lead to inefficient international resource allocation both in private and public sectors. As a factor of production, capital is separable from its ownership and therefore, unlike labor, can move without the need for its owners to change their residence. This confers a high degree of mobility on capital and has strong implications for the equity of tax-induced capital movements [P. Musgrave (1989)]. Thus the application of corporation income taxes has a particularly important role to play in international resource allocation which in turn places high priority on the coordination of corporate tax systems.

A. Individual Income Tax

The income tax is a personal tax and therefore calls for a global base, including income from both domestic and foreign sources. Because of this it must be imposed by the country of residence. Inclusion in the tax base of financial income earned abroad poses

[4] This interpretation of the term "harmonization" was introduced by Douglas Dosser [Shoup (1967)].

considerable problems of administration and thus calls for administrative cooperation of the countries concerned.

While the country of source cannot tax income flowing to foreigners on a personal basis, it can impose an *in rem* tax on such income to claim its entitlement to a share in that tax base. In the case of wage income, this may take the form of a payroll tax. In the case of capital income, with dividends reached already under the corporation income tax, a withholding tax on interest only need be added. In line with internation equity, income flowing abroad should be taxed at equal rates by source countries. The country of residence, finally, would include foreign income gross of the foreign tax in its own tax base and then credit the foreign tax against its tax. Given such crediting, horizontal equity among residents would be assured and the tax would be neutral regarding the choice of whether to earn income at home or abroad. But differentials in tax rates may still have a distorting effect on the choice of residency. This has become of increasing importance (e.g. the popularity of Monte Carlo) and cannot readily be taken care of by coordination measures. Perhaps some check might be applied by linking tax allegiance to citizenship.

B. Absolute Corporation Income Tax

In order to bring about a neutral tax environment for international investment, corporations "resident" in any one country should face the same effective rate of tax on their income whether arising at home or abroad. This effective rate of tax includes the corporation tax itself and any withholding taxes at source on income remitted to the country of "residence". This "capital-export neutrality" can be achieved by universal application of the principle of global income taxation by the country of residence, in which all income, both domestic and foreign in source, is included gross of foreign taxes , the residence country's rate applied and a credit is then provided for foreign taxes. Profits of foreign affiliates have to be included when earned, whether distributed or retained, without deferral of tax on retained earnings. This system of global-residence taxation, with foreign tax credit implies that corporations will pay the higher of the home or foreign rates on their foreign investments. It will remove tax inducements to investing abroad but not remove tax impediments to so doing. The foreign tax credit for corporations also proves to be in practice a cumbersome and administratively complex instrument of coordination. As evident in the case of the United States, there is considerable resistance to the taxation of profits as earned, without deferral, by foreign incorporated subsidiaries. More important, the corporation income tax is an *in rem* tax applied at source of income and as such is a major instrument of source entitlement. As suggested above, there is then a strong case to be made for equalizing rates of corporation tax among countries and applying them on the source principle. Such equalization would simultaneously achieve internation equity and allocative neutrality, while not interfering with interresident tax equity (which is determined by the application of the individual income tax) and would be administratively simpler. If all countries apply the corporate tax as an absolute tax (deductible only from dividends), then dividends to domestic shareholders would be taxed under the individual income tax in the usual way, i.e. net of corporate tax. Alternatively, as a second-best solution, if countries retain their varying rates of corporation tax, withholding taxes might be applied to remitted income at varying rates to bring the combined taxes up to the equal agreed-upon level. Thus, for countries A and B, $t_c^A + t_w^A(1 - t_c^A) = t_c^B + t_w^B(1 - t_c^B)$ where t_c and t_w are the rates of corporation and withholding taxes respectively. Under such a system, residence-global taxation would be needed, again without deferral, but both internation equity and allocative neutrality would be improved by the use of the compensating withholding tax [P. Musgrave (1987)].

C. Integrated Corporation Tax

Now let us consider the outlines of well-coordinated income tax systems in which the corporation tax is integrated with the individual income tax. Note that in the international setting the corporation tax not only acts as a withholding tax on shareholders' income (as in the closed economy case) but also as the means of exercising source entitlement. Again, there is a strong case to be made for equalization of corporate tax rates across countries. If that is done, the corporation tax can be applied on the source principle. Consider first full integration whereby all corporate profits are imputed to the shareholder, and the corporate tax credited against the individual income tax. Clearly, this would be very difficult to implement for corporate income earned abroad, without close international administrative cooperation. Now suppose that partial integration is applied by means of a "dividends -paid credit", i.e. dividends paid are relieved of the corporate tax. Shareholders resident in A will face the same corporate tax rate applied to their foreign retained earnings as to their domestic earnings, although the disparity between that common rate and the shareholder's marginal rate of individual income tax will vary from one residence country to another depending on their individual income tax schedules. Their dividends received from abroad, however, will be free of foreign (B's) tax and would be included in full in taxable income in A. This mode of integration, however, violates internation equity by denying B, the source country, its entitlement to tax corporate source income remitted to A. Partial integration, however, might alternatively follow the "dividends-received credit" system whereby the corporate tax on the profits underlying the dividends is credited by the shareholder against his/her individual income tax applied to the dividends gross of the foreign tax. This system presents some of the same enforcement and compliance difficulties as in the case of full imputation, but has the major advantage of allowing the source country to claim its full tax entitlement.

One interesting point to note is that integrated and non-integrated income tax systems can coexist without presenting coordination problems, if corporate rates are equalized. Whether a country has an integrated system or not and whatever the form of integration may be, so long as it applies a global individual income tax with the foreign and domestic corporate taxes treated in the same way vis-a-vis the individual income tax, its individual investors will face the same tax treatment whether they choose to invest at home or abroad, and the system will be neutral as to investment location choice. Uniformity in the tax treatment of individuals *among* countries is not required. However, in the interest of internation equity, partial integration, if applied, should follow the dividends-received credit method.

III. Coordination of Symmetrical Consumption Tax Systems

As was noted in section I, consumption taxes can take a variety of forms and the kinds of coordinating measures required to meet efficiency and equity criteria differ accordingly [OECD (1988)]. The discussion will be focused on the principles involved and no attention will be given to the many complex issues arising in transition from an income to a consumption tax system, nor will there be much attention given to the many interesting administrative and technical problems of implementing those principles.

A. In Rem Consumption Taxes

In rem consumption taxes of the destination type are applied as retail sales taxes and serve to tax consumption by residents. As such they cannot be adapted to the taxpayer's ability-to-pay. Thus, if income is considered to be the "correct" index of ability-to-pay, such impersonal consumption taxes are inferior in terms of both vertical and horizontal equity. Even if consumption is considered to be the appropriate index, these taxes also fail to meet the usual standards of vertical equity.

As noted before, an *in rem* consumption tax of the origin type burdens foreign consumers but is not an appropriate instrument for implementing source entitlement. Moreover, the tax violates allocative efficiency unless imposed at universally equal rates, a requirement that may be inefficient since it restricts freedom of choice of individual countries. As against these disadvantages of the origin-type value-added tax, the latter has the advantage of avoiding fiscal frontiers, which have to be dealt with by destination value-added taxes. This, it appears, was the reason for the original intent of the European Community to impose equal-rate, origin-type value-added taxes, a goal which is now being reconsidered because of new administrative solutions to applying border tax adjustments without fiscal frontiers. If, however, the goal is destination-type taxation, it may well be argued that a retail sales tax approach is the more obvious solution. It may also be noted that this discussion has been in terms of consumption-type value-added taxes. If an income-type value-added tax were used, there would be a direct similarity to exercising entitlement via withholding in the context of a source-type income tax.

1. Coordination Requirements: Internation Equity

A destination-based VAT is in line with internation equity since each country bears its own burden, whereas an origin-based VAT is not. Imposed by one country only, it offends internation equity since it permits the exporting country to burden the consumers of the importing country. We have also argued that implementation of entitlement should be via income-based taxes so that the origin-type VAT should not be used for this purpose. In short, such a tax is disqualified on internation equity as well as on other grounds.

Does the same conclusion apply if such a tax is imposed by both trading countries and at the same rate? If trade is in balance, neither country enjoys a net burden export and internation equity is not violated. If, however, trade is in imbalance, the country with export surplus continues to enjoy net burden export. It is thus only in the special case of equal tax rates and balanced trade that the origin tax does not offend considerrations of internation equity.

2. Coordination Requirements: Neutrality

The primary allocative effects of general *in rem* consumption taxes differs sharply, depending on whether they are applied at origin or destination. While the latter is neutral in its effect on international trade, the former is not. Nonneutralities will arise from differential price effects on consumer goods of domestic and foreign origin. If all countries apply the retail sales tax (a destination form of product tax), no such differential will apply and no coordination is needed to neutralize differences in tax rates. Most economists also agree that a uniform and general, origin-type *in rem* consumption tax is also neutral with respect to trade flows if exchange rates are flexible. Introduction of such a tax would have the immediate effect of raising the price of exports while leaving imports untaxed. This would lead to a deterioration in the balance of payments and a resulting decline in the exchange rate of the taxing country, until the export/import price ratio is restored to its pre-tax position. According to this view, no coordinating adjustments would then be needed [Gravelle (1986)]. However, product taxes are never completely general in their application, exchange rates may be sticky and capital flows may interfere with the adjustment process. For these and other reasons, origin-type product taxes which are applied at differing rates and with differing coverages need to be coordinated to render them neutral with respect to trade flows. This may be done by converting them to the destination basis by application of border tax adjustments, as in the European Common Market. Thus trade neutrality is met, even if tax rates differ among countries, with the use of destination-based product taxes such as the retail sales tax or a destination-type value-added tax. While the latter has the administrative advantage of ensuring superior compliance, it has the disadvantage of requiring "fiscal frontiers" in the application of the border tax adjustment. This problem evidently could be solved via international cooperation in tax clearing arrangements for imported commodities [Cnossen and Shoup (1987)].

Use of destination-based product taxes will not however, achieve neutrality with respect to all individual choices. Such taxes affect the real income of consumers from the uses side of their accounts and may induce cross-border, mail order or tourist shopping whereby residents of the higher-tax country may choose to shop in the lower-tax country, thus leading to inefficiencies in both private and public sectors.[5] Substantial differentials in sales tax rates may theoretically perform as differentials in income taxes on the sources side of taxpayers' accounts and induce a change of residence into the low-tax jurisdiction. In the case of personal taxes, tax allegiance may be linked to citizenship as well as residency and thus discourage this type of tax-induced migration. However, this is not readily done with respect to *in rem* taxes, so that consumption and residency mobility may remain a problem unless countries can cooperate in imposing sales taxes on non-residents at rates prevailing in the country of residency.[6]

B. Personal Consumption Taxes

Now consider a world of personal consumption or "expenditure" taxes rather than *in rem* product taxes, a matter which has received much attention in recent years [Pechman, ed. (1980); Aaron and Pechman, eds. (1988)]. In an open economy setting, problems of compliance and enforcement are likely to be more severe than in the case of income taxes, but it will be seen that coordination problems are of a different nature and depend on how the personal consumption tax is applied, i.e. whether as an individual cash-flow (ICF) tax [U.S. Department of the Treasury (1984)] or in the individual tax prepayment (ITP) form. We assume, to begin with, that all countries apply the same form of personal consumption tax though at different rates. We also initially assume that there is no supplementary business cash flow tax, introducing the latter in a subsequent section.

---

[5] The phenomenon of cross border shopping is analagous to the case of capital export whereby individuals may live and vote in one country while avoiding the taxes needed to pay for public services, thus leading to inefficient public sector choices.

[6] This process has not been notably successful in the United States where there is now legislation pending to require mail-order establishments to collect tax on behalf of the purchaser's state of residence.

Under the ICF approach, all kinds of cash receipts are included. This includes wages, interest and other forms of capital income, as well as proceeds of loans and sale of equity, while excluding loan repayments and purchases of equity. In addition, interest payments are deducted. This netting out of cash flow incomings and outgoings leaves the tax base to equal consumption expenditures. It may be viewed as an equivalent, though administratively more feasible way of arriving at the tax base by direct reporting of consumption expenditures. The ITP approach, in turn, disregards loan and equity transactions as well as receipts of interest and other forms of capital income and the deduction of interest payments, leaving the tax base simply to equal current wage receipts. The term "prepayment" is used to indicate that the tax is paid before consumption takes place. The ICF approach thus defines the tax base in terms of consumption, whereas the ITP approach defines it in terms of wage income. Both approaches meet the complaint that income taxation discriminates against future consumption, the one by way of taxing consumption only when it occurs and the other by exempting capital income. Another way of putting it is that the two bases are in fact the same since (assuming all wages to be consumed during the course of the taxpayer's life), the present value of tax payments under ICF equals their present value under ITP [Stiglitz (1986); Musgrave and Musgrave (1989)]. All this, of course, simplifies matters and overlooks quite major transition problems, but nevertheless brings out the basic equivalence between the wage and consumption taxes. However, at a more practical level, it may be noted that the two approaches differ. The ITP approach is much easier to administer since it does not require the "qualified accounts" system, essential to ICF. Since the accounts system would seem extremely difficult to monitor in the international setting, a point which has been given inadequate attention, ITP gains a major administrative advantage.

1. Coordination Requirements: Internation Equity

We have advanced the proposition that internation equity would assign each country a "source entitlement", and that each would claim a reciprocally equal share of income (value) arising within it and accruing to non-residents. The picture with regard to either form of personal consumption tax is a straightforward one. Such a tax, whether it be of the ICF or ITP type, amounts to a wage tax. The former applies as earnings are consumed and the latter as wages are earned. In the absence of any other supplementary taxes (such as the business cash flow tax discussed below), each country surrenders its claim on capital income whether earned by residents or foreign investors (individuals or corporations) within its borders. Furthermore, since the tax is a personal tax, countries of source will be unable to claim a share of labor income earned by foreign workers who are border-crossing commuters in the absence of a withholding tax applied to labor income at source. Thus, if countries are to exercise any source entitlements, reciprocally equal withholding taxes would be needed on both capital and labor income paid to non-residents. However, such withholding taxes would have to be credited in the country of residence of workers and investors to ensure allocative neutrality. In the absence of global income taxation, such crediting could not readily be implemented. Thus neutrality and internation equity requirements come into conflict in the case of the personal consumption tax.

2. Coordination Requirements: Neutrality

As noted earlier, we are concerned here with tax neutrality with respect to (1) trade flows, (2) the location of consumption, (3) location of investment, (4) the location of labor, and (5) choice of residency location.

Regarding (1), a personal consumption tax will provide the same neutrality with respect to trade flows as does the retail sales tax or the destination-based value-added tax. This is true for both the ICF and the ITP forms of the tax.

However, with regard to (2), there is one very significant difference between the *in rem* and personal types of consumption taxes in the international setting and that is the fact that a personal consumption tax cannot be readily imposed on non-residents. There will then be a strong incentive for consumers in all countries to spend abroad as tourists or as migratory consumers for tax avoidance purposes. This incentive will be far stronger than in the previous case of *in rem* consumption taxes universally applied, where the consumption tax is applied at the point of purchase and consumption abroad merely offers the advantage of a rate differential. It is therefore crucial for neutrality with respect to location of consumption (and taxpayer equity) that the personal consumption tax be residence-based and applied to worldwide consumption expenditures. Under the ICF version of the personal consumption tax, the base can be globalized by treating all changes in foreign asset holdings and the receipt and payment of foreign investment income in the same way as for those of domestic origin. Thus, net increases in holdings of foreign assets are deducted and net receipts of foreign investment income are included. In this way, all consumption expenditures, whether domestic or foreign, in principle become taxable. Unfortunately, compliance with such a global approach is not readily attained, given the ease with which domestic assets can be converted to foreign assets and later drawn down for consumption purposes abroad without detection. Receipt of foreign investment income can also go unreported. Further, the system of "qualified accounts" which determines the eligibility of asset acquisition as a deduction, is not readily transferable to foreign institutions. The ITP version of the tax, on the other hand, is not as afflicted with these administrative difficulties since the net acquisition of assets, whether domestic or foreign, are not deductible and receipt of interest and other capital income is not included (making explicit the nature of the personal expenditure tax as a tax on wages). Thus tax on future consumption of such assets is "prepaid" and the taxpayer gains nothing by drawing down foreign assets for consumption purposes abroad. Because of this and other administrative advantages, it has been suggested that the ITP version of the personal consumption tax be adopted by developing countries [McLure et al. (1987b); Zodrow and McLure (1989)].

Turning to (3), neutrality with respect to capital flows, the personal consumption tax universally applied attains neutrality simply by taxing capital income at a zero rate. Certain distorting effects on capital flows may arise in the case of the ICF version of the tax due to the administrative weaknesses of that tax, as discussed above. Since acquisitions of foreign assets are deductible, foreign investment will be attractive for reasons of the tax evasion which it makes possible. Again, the ITP form of the tax will be largely free of this problem. Of course, varying rates of consumption tax from country to country will have differential income effects on the supply of saving and investment in each country and this in turn may affect the amount and distribution of national ownership of world capital. However, this is not a neutrality problem for location choices which will not be distorted by these differentials.

The principal problem with regard to neutrality of the personal consumption tax will arise with respect to (4) i.e. neutrality with respect to location of work. Since the personal consumption tax, in either the ICF or ITP form amounts to a tax on wages (explicitly so in the case of the ITP), differentials in rates might induce labor migration.

We might expect this effect to be particularly strong in the case of highly paid professionals. This problem can be taken care of if workers retain their residency in one country while earning income in another (the border-crossing commuter case), by including foreign earnings in the tax base and permitting a credit for any foreign source withholding tax on such earnings. But as in the case of residency migration, there is no way to neutralize such distortions if workers change their residency along with their place of work. In this case, application of the personal consumption tax on the basis of citizenship may be helpful but would be very difficult to implement without close cooperation by the tax administrations of the countries of emigration and immigration.

Finally, with regard to (5), neutrality with respect to residency choice, differentials in personal consumption taxes cannot be neutralized any more than can differentials in income taxes unless such foreign residency is of a temporary nature. Permanent shift of residency for tax purposes cannot be avoided. However, use of citizenship rather than residency as the test of tax allegiance might go some way in avoiding this non-neutrality, so that in order to enjoy lower tax rates the taxpayer must change both place of residence and citizenship. Again, however, a large degree of international cooperation in tax administration would be needed.

C. Business Cash Flow Tax

Most proposals for personal consumption-based taxes include a business tax component [Bradford (1984); Meade (1978); Aaron and Galper (1985); Hall and Rabushka (1983); McLure et al. (1987b) ; Bird and McLure (1989)], sometimes (and in my view, misleadingly) referred to as the "business consumption tax". It is a cash-flow tax which in its most usual form incorporates expensing of investment expenditures with non-deductibility of interest and dividend payments and non-inclusion of capital income receipts. The tax has been advocated for a number of reasons. Even though expensing effectively excludes all normal returns to depreciable assets from the base, the business component is said to make the personal expenditure tax politically more acceptable. Politics aside, the supplement of a business tax is also said to be needed to prevent the avoidance or evasion of the personal consumption tax through the use of business accounts. Another rationale for adding a business tax may be seen to arise in the international context where (in the absence of income taxation) such a tax may be seen as providing a way of implementing some degree of source entitlement, particularly with respect to resource rents. On closer consideration, the latter is a weak argument since the Treasury's gain from such a tax is quite limited if compared with that of a corporation income tax.[7]

The business cash flow tax may be applied either by including the proceeds of loans in the tax base and then deducting interest payments (the cash-flow method) or excluding the loan proceeds and including interest payments, the latter being the tax prepayment method. The two methods give identical results and to simplify the presentation we follow the latter.

Let me spell out in more detail the nature of the business cash flow tax and how it compares with the corporation income tax and a no-tax situation before exploring the international aspects. Consider a one-period investment with an initial purchase of Z in depreciable assets at the beginning of the year and a gross return of $(1 + r)Z$ at the end of that year, yielding an economic rate of return of r (allowing for economic depreciation). A business cash flow tax at rate t is applied under which the investment is expensed with the tax value of the expensing ($= tZ$) immediately refundable, and tax due at the end of the year of $t(1 + r)Z$.

Expensing of depreciable assets may be looked at in either of two ways. First, the tax refund may be seen as a cash grant by government, so that the present value of tax equals $t(1 + r)Z/(1 + i) - tZ = tZ(r - i)/(1 + i)$, with i the market rate of interest. The tax, in effect applies only to returns in excess of the interest or discount rate. Alternatively, the refund may be regarded as a government advance to the firm equal to a part tZ of its investment expenditure. The remainder $(1 - t)Z$ is either loan or equity financed by the investor. At the end of the year the investor reaps an after-tax return on his share of the investment equal to $(1 - t)(1 + r)Z$ which is equivalent to a return of r on his share of the investment cost, $(1- t)Z$. In this sense, the investor's rate of return is unaffected by imposition of the tax. However, this tax-free return is obtained on a smaller investment base ($= (1 - t)Z$). The tax he pays is merely a return to the government for its interest-free loan on the original investment provided through expensing. With continuous reinvestment of the government's share of the investment, however,

[7] This statement does not apply to the tax on already existing capital to which the benefits of expensing do not of course apply. However, this is of only transitional significance.

the investor will ultimately provide the full cost Z of the investment on which he will obtain a tax-free rate of return of *r*. Now consider the government's position. It provides initially a share of the investment equal to tZ, and in return collects tax equal to t(1 + r)Z. It therefore also obtains a return of *r* on its share of the investment cost. However, the government will have to borrow funds to cover its tax refund tZ at the market rate of interest *i*. Inclusion of this component is essential, although it frequently tends to be overlooked. Thus the net budgetary return will be (r - i). In other words, positive tax revenue will only be obtained if r > i. For purposes of this paper we will take the first view of the tax which concludes that it applies to returns in excess of the interest rate or the normal rate of return applied to the entire investment.

Table 2: Comparison of Business Income and Cash Flow Taxes (one period investment)

	P.V. Net Tax	After-tax Rate of Return
No Tax	0	r
Corporation Income Tax		
Equity financed	$t_c r/(1+i)$	$(1-t_c)\, r$
Debt financed		
Interest deductible	$t_c(r-i)/(1+i)$	$(1-t_c)r + t_c i$
Interest not deductible	$t_c r/(1+i)$	$(1-t_c)r$
Business Cash Flow Tax	$t_f(1+r)/(1+i) - t_f$	$(1-t_f)r + t_f i$

i = market rate of interest, discount rate and normal rate of return
r = economic rate of return to depreciable assets (based on economic depreciation)
Z = investment in depreciable assets
t_c = rate of corporation income tax
t_f = rate of business cash flow tax

Table 2 compares the effects on government and investor of the cash flow tax imposed at rate t_f with those of a corporate income tax of rate t_c. Under the corporation income tax the results differ depending on whether the corporation is equity- or debt-financed, and in the latter case, whether interest is deductible. With equal-rate corporate and business cash flow taxes, the latter leaves the investor with the same after-tax rate of return as does a corporate income tax (based on economic depreciation) with investment fully debt-financed and interest fully deductible. The same result would be achieved if the corporate tax were applied only to profits in excess of the interest rate.

1. Coordination Requirements: Internation Equity

As it has been earlier argued, the country of source is entitled to a share in the total profits of foreign investment within its borders, and in practice this is a major consideration by the capital-importing countries in designing their tax systems. I have also argued that the corporation income tax is an appropriate means of claiming a share of capital income arising at its source. In the case of the corporation tax with interest payments deductible, a withholding tax on the interest paid abroad is needed, imposed at a rate in line with the mutually agreed standard of internation equity. No withholding tax on dividends would be needed unless necessary to supplement the rate of corporation income tax again in line with internation equity. Under the cash flow tax, no burden is imposed on the foreign investor's normal return, the tax being limited to "excess" profits, rents and other returns to non-depreciable assets such as entrepreneurship. The source country's Treasury shares in the return to foreign capital only to the extent that the yield exceeds the normal return. This base of excess gains is much less than that of total profits as reached under the corporation tax in combination with the withholding tax on interest. Since entitlement calls for a share in total profits, the cash flow tax should therefore be supplemented by a withholding tax applied to the economic return on the total investment which accrues to non-residents. Such a withholding tax would clearly present severe difficulties of implementation, including a required dual accounting system. It therefore appears that the cash flow tax by itself is inadequate when it comes to implementing source-country entitlement. This is not surprising since it is, after all, designed to implement a domestic consumption (not income) tax, and thus belongs in an entirely different framework.

2. Coordination Requirements: Neutrality

Substitution of a business cash-flow tax for a corporate income tax would remove from tax a major part of business profits and if universally applied would thereby reduce international average rate differentials and in that sense improve neutrality. Furthermore, to the extent the remaining tax applies to rents, such differentials which remained would not have adverse allocative implications. If this were all to it, the business cash flow tax could be applied according to the source principle only without seriously impeding neutrality. However, the "excess" profits to which the tax would apply include returns to entrepreneurship and other non-depreciable assets the location of which is likely to be sensitive to tax rate differentials. Moreover, if rates of cash-flow tax are adjusted to generate the same revenue as the corporate tax which it replaces, such rates and differentials among countries are likely to be considerably higher than under a corporate tax regime. It is therefore quite possible that there would be even greater need for a business cash flow tax to be applied under a global-residence principle with foreign tax credit in order to preserve neutrality with respect to investment location.

As discussed in the last section, countries of source would probably wish to impose withholding taxes on remitted income to compensate for the foregone tax on normal returns. While more or less satisfying source entitlement, such taxes would lead to non-neutralities since only foreign investment income would be subject to tax and the foreign withholding tax could not be readily credited against tax in the country of residence both because it is a tax on income and there would be no corresponding tax in the country of residence against which it might be credited. The compatibility of the exercise of source entitlement with international neutrality with respect to capital flows made possible with the use of either (1) the global-residence income tax with foreign tax credit, or (2) equal-rate source-based business income taxation, breaks down in the case of the business cash flow and personal consumption tax. In this case, source-entitlement taxation leads to non-neutralities which cannot be resolved through coordinating measures. Uniform withholding taxes on all payments of investment income, to residents as well as non-residents would be needed, but this would combine an income tax with a consumption tax system.

Whereas the business cash flow tax in the domestic context is seen as a protection against abuse of the personal consumption tax, this would scarcely be the case with the foreign business cash flow tax. A major problem in preserving the integrity of a personal consumption tax is the protection against use of foreign assets to finance consumption abroad. The foreign cash flow tax, even of the tax prepayment type which we have been discussing, would not be helpful in this respect.

IV. Coordination of Consumption Taxes with Income Taxes

We now consider the coordination problem in a more realistic setting, namely when one country alone (which we will designate country A) substitutes a business cash-flow/ personal consumption tax for corporate and individual income taxes while country B applies an income tax system. The latter could take various forms but here we will confine ourselves to an absolute corporation tax with the individual income tax (classical system).

A. Coordination Requirements: Internation Equity

In order for country A to exercise its source entitlement, a withholding tax should be applied to the normal return on investment which accrues to foreign residents. To meet the reciprocity standard of internation equity, this rate of this tax would be equal to B's rate of corporation income tax. A more readily implemented, but second-best procedure would be to apply the withholding tax only to payments of dividends, interest and branch profits to non-resident corporations and individuals resident in B. With interest deductible under B's corporation income tax, country B would then apply a withholding tax only to interest payments to A at its own corporate tax rate. In line with our earlier discussion of the personal consumption tax, wages and salaries earned by non-residents in country A would have to be subject to a flat-rate payroll tax, again to allow exercise of source entitlement, and this should approximate the average rate of personal income tax in B as it applies to foreign residents. Thus a withholding tax system applied to income accruing to non-residents would have to be grafted on to A's consumption/cash flow tax system with rates aligned with those of B's income taxes as applied to non-residents.

B. Coordination Requirements: Neutrality

If withholding taxes in both countries were equal to B's corporate rate, the corporate tax in B could be applied on the source principle without sacrifice of neutrality for B's investors. However, if not equal, country B could neutralize matters with respect to capital flow by applying its corporate income tax on a global basis and allowing a credit for A's withholding tax. There has been much interest in the question of whether a country such as B with a global corporation income tax should also grant a credit for country A's business cash flow tax.[8] The answer would seem to be in the negative, since the two taxes are not applied to the same base. Indeed, it might be argued that with continuous reinvestment of the government's advance under expensing, the business cash-flow tax is a non-tax which leaves investors with an unchanged after-tax rate of return, even though the government collects a modest return on its share of the investment; with this line of argument, crediting would not be called for.

In spite of B's global income tax with credit for A's withholding tax, there would remain a strong inducement for B's corporations to shift their registration to country A where their income would largely be free of tax. As pointed out earlier, there is no protection against this form of non-neutrality, and the outflow of resources from B may ultimately compel it to follow A in converting to a consumption-based system. Country A's investors will also face a strong tax penalty on investment in country B as against that made in their own country. Again, no coordinating measures are available to repair this non-neutrality other than for B to grant an exemption from its corporate tax to investors from abroad. Developing countries, heavily dependent on investment from abroad and on the tax revenue which that investment generates would be particularly disadvantaged by the conversion to a consumption-based system on the part of their capital suppliers. They would find themselves in a catch-22 situation - retention of the income tax would reduce the inflow of foreign capital, while adoption of a consumption

---

[8] McLure et al. (1987b) and Zodrow and McLure (1989) discuss at some length the question of the creditability of a business cash flow tax against the U.S. corporate income tax, in the context of the U.S. statutes and regulations pertaining to the foreign tax credit.

tax to maintain that inflow would surrender their important source entitlement. Perhaps one of the least helpful policies of developed countries with respect to the development of low-income countries would be conversion to a cash flow consumption tax. On the other hand, unilateral adoption of a cash flow tax by a developing country while capital-exporting countries retain their corporate taxes would attract capital inflow, while sacrificing revenue, the net gain being somewhat uncertain.

Since the individual income tax in country B is a personal tax, it must be applied on a global basis to include labor income earned in A. This then would call for a credit against that tax for A's payroll withholding tax. It is noteworthy that the coordination of an asymmetric system of a cash-flow consumption tax in one country and an income tax system in the other of the kind described presents a serious problem of non-neutrality for capital flows which is not readily corrected by coordinating measures. However, the non-neutrality for labor flow is much less serious, not only because labor is the less mobile factor, but also because the burden differential between the personal income tax in B and that of the personal consumption tax in A will be much less than the differential between the near-zero tax on capital income in A and the income tax rate in B. It is also to be noted that unilateral adoption of a consumption-based system will not only introduce irremedial distortions in international resource allocation, but also impose serious damage to the integrity of the income-tax systems of other countries whose residents can avail themselves of tax exemption on their capital income by investing or residing abroad.

V. Summary and Conclusion

This paper has proposed that fiscal coordination should seek to equalize only those taxes which apply to the most mobile of factors and which serve as instruments of source entitlement. Such is the case with the corporation income tax which, if equalized, might be applied on the source principle thus avoiding the complications inherent in a residence-based global tax. This approach would allow diversity among countries in personal income taxes as well as in the degree of integration with the corporate tax, provided such integration were implemented at the shareholder level (i.e. in the country of residence). Protection of diversity in fiscal choices might also call for *in rem* consumption taxes such as the retail sales tax or value-added taxes applied on the destination principle, for such taxes need not be applied at equal rates. European Common Market thinking may point in the wrong direction by turning towards rate equalization of origin taxes and imposition of uniform types of income tax integration at the corporation level.

It was a general conclusion of the paper that the substitution of a cash flow consumption tax (including a business tax component) for income-based personal taxation, whatever its merits in the closed economy setting, introduces serious difficulties in international tax relationships in an open economy setting and these difficulties are not easily remedied. This will be the case especially if unilateral substitution is made by a single country. There will then be a serious breach of tax neutrality with resulting inefficiency as well as of individual taxpayer equity. Such will be the case particularly with respect to capital flows which will be attracted into the consumption-tax country. This is due to the fact that the consumption tax (ICP or ITP), even with a business cash flow component, implies a near-zero tax on capital income. Capital will then flow from income-tax to consumption-tax countries. While this may be mitigated at the personal level by use of a residence-based, global income tax in other countries, that will not prevent tax-induced corporate migrations into the consumption tax country, nor prevent a tax deterrence to investors in that country from putting their resources to more productive use abroad. There will be strong pressure on other countries to protect themselves from loss of resources by also moving to a consumption-based system. One would expect this kind of development to be particularly strong in a common market setting with a high degree of business mobility.

General substitution of cash-flow consumption-based systems for income-based systems will not generate this distortion of capital flows, but serious shortcomings with regard to internation equity and entitlement remain. Under a personal consumption tax the source country cannot reach the income earned by non-residents nor can it implement entitlement from the consumption side. This carries particularly adverse implications for low-income, developing countries for which the exercise of source entitlement is of major importance. Coordinating remedies would then require that the cash flow tax be supplemented either by an *in rem* source-based income tax such as a corporation income tax on foreign capital, or a withholding tax applied to all income accruing to non-residents. This means that introduction of the cash flow tax will not be a simplifying substitution for income-based taxation since the latter has to be retained as a supplement and applied selectively to non-residents. Given these complications, the case for a cash flow tax is weakened substantially as one turns from the closed to the open economy setting.

Comments by Norbert Andel

All of us who take some interest in problems of co-ordinating direct taxes internationally are in debt to Peggy Musgrave. Like no other scholar of public finance before, she has analysed systematically a field up to then dominated nearly monopolistically by lawyers. The way she structured the problem has been adopted by many other scholars, including myself. In the paper presented today, after reviewing rather well-known aspects in the first parts, she pioneers into the new field of co-ordination problems in a world of personal consumption and cash flow taxes.

My first remark is related to tax principles. I think in the case of indirect taxes levied at one stage in the production process, like a retail sales tax or a tobacco tax collected from the producer, the meaning of *origin principle* (imposition at the point of production) and of *destination principle* (imposition at the point of final purchase) is clear and covers the alternatives.

But in the case of *multi-stage taxes* like a value-added tax of the income type, we need a third principle, for which in the context of the EEC the expressions "community principle" and "common market principle" (Dieter Biehl) have been proposed. Contrary to table 1 (p. 456) the "VAT-Income Type" cannot be realized by use of the origin principle only. There is not a single point of production in the exporting country, and in the importing country the tax also has to be collected at all stages and not just at the point of final purchase.

The community principle received some attention in the EEC recently in connection with the proposed change from traditional border tax adjustment to "adjustment" within the importing firm by way of tax deduction. However, it was connected with a clearing mechanism.

My next point concerns entitlement to tax bases. Intitlement to tax base is interpreted as permitting "the country of income source or product origin to take a "fair" tax share in the income value arising within, it even though owned by foreign residents" (p. 457). To require from foreign residents a tax share of their *income* received in the source country may be reasonable in a world of income taxation. But it is less obvious in a world of personal consumption taxes where income received in the source country may not become part of the tax base in the residence country, or, to put it in a different way, in a world where the personal consumption tax is interpreted as a tax on wages only.

But what is the justification for letting the source country's Treasury participate? Probably some notion of benefit principle: Those who as earners of income enjoy advantages of public expenditure should also contribute in the form of paying taxes. Given the technical difficulties of implementing the benefit principle in an exact manner, one may take recourse to lump-sum measures, for instance, in the form of a reciprocally equal withholding tax even if levels and structures of public expenditure differ. But in that case should not source taxes be *deducted* rather than *credited* in the country of residence?

However, such a procedure would imply discrimination of international transactions as long as income flowing to residents is taxed in the usual way, that is to say, without requiring special (deductible) levies for government services.

This leads me to the question raised by Musgrave, whether the entitlement principle may also be expressed as entitlement to tax the export of products, for instance, "as in the case of an origin-type VAT thereby burdening the foreign consumers of domestic products, rather than the foreign participants in domestically created income" (p. 457). But she concludes: "For various reasons, this would be an inferior formulation of the entitlement claim" (p. 457). It would be interesting to learn what these reasons are. After all, the idea to implement the benefit principle by use of a value-added tax has a long history [see Clara K. Sullivan, The Tax on Value Added (1965, pp. 156-169)] and is also influential in our days. Of course, one should not consider indirect taxation of exports a specific substitute for levying a withholding tax on income flowing to non-residents. The question is rather whether the entitlement based on benefit considerations should be implemented by general product-related taxes instead of by special withholding taxes on foreign income. The former are especially justified if the advantages of expenditure are shifted in the form of lower prices. In addition, all products would be taxed equally, irrespective of the nationality of the owners of factors of production.

There is another aspect of entitlement, mentioned only in sections concerning allocative efficiency. In order to reduce the tendency to take advantage of lower taxes abroad, Musgrave mentions several times the possibility of linking tax allegiance to citizenship (p. 463, 472). This reduces tax-induced distortions; however, it would hardly be compatible with proper entitlement from the point of view of residence countries. I think the right to levy comprehensive personal taxes like personal income or personal consumption taxes should be given to the country of residence, not only because of administrative reasons, but also because the revenue should go to the country where a person has its centre of vital interests.

With respect to an *absolute corporation income tax*, Musgrave sees a strong case to be made for equalizing corporation tax rates among countries. Of course, this would imply neutrality between corporations located in different countries. But contrary to what is stated on p. 464, last sentence, first paragraph, this may interfere with interresident tax equity which is not only determined by the application of the individual income tax but also by the relation between individual income tax rates and corporation income tax rates. In countries where the latter are lower, as happens often, the rich owner of a corporation is offered the possibility to accumulate at favourable special rates.

Really comprehensive personal consumption taxes are difficult to enforce - as are personal income taxes. Musgrave seems to see more enforcement problems in the former case. I wonder which channels she has in mind when she mentions the "ease with which domestic assets can be converted to foreign assets and later drawn down for consumption purposes without detection" (p. 471). If they are transferred from qualified accounts, they are taxed unless reinvested in the approved forms. If they are unknown to the Treasury, they can be consumed free of tax at home anyway. In case the later use for assets cannot be checked sufficiently, the tax prepayment method should indeed be used - despite its disadvantages in other respects: It is not an exact consumption tax, but a standard tax, the consumption-type counterpiece of a standard income tax (Sollertragsteuer).

As Peggy Musgrave has shown, in case some countries start replacing income taxes by personal consumption and cash flow taxes, there surely will be new and some hardly solvable problems - and let me add, certainly one group of beneficiaries: those distinguished lawyers and officials, for instance, associated with the International Fiscal Association, accustomed to meet at the most beautiful places of the world. They will have many new and very interesting problems to tackle.

Comments by Klaus Vogel

Consumption Tax in the International Field

Let me begin by stating that I am, for the most part, in accordance with Professor Musgrave's results, and that I cannot but compliment her for the stringency of her reasoning. As some may know, I was daring enough last year to challenge some of her basic assumptions in the context of international income taxation with a paper which was published in Intertax. Don't fear that I am going to repeat this discussion. It was based on a slightly different understanding of neutrality and on a more detailed analysis of the equity concept; should someone be interested in that, I shall be glad to supply him with an off-print. But it does not relate to anything specific to consumption taxation. Therefore, I shall not touch it today.

Being a lawyer I prefer a somewhat different wording here and there than Professor Musgrave does. I have no problem to call a tax imposed on the income of non-residents, if it is levied parallel to the income tax from residents, an income tax as it is called by legislators all over the world. Similarly, within the framework of expenditure taxation (or in other words, of a direct tax on consumption) I have no problem to consider the counterpart to the expenditure tax imposed on residents an expenditure tax on non-residents. Of course there will be differences between such branches of expenditure taxation. We cannot expect a State to forgo taxing income which has been raised in its territory by non-residents; States will not be prepared to do this, not even in the context of an expenditure tax. The State of source may defer that taxation as long as the income in question is invested in its own territory, as it defers taxation of income raised by residents as long as it is invested. But at least when the income of the non-resident is remitted to his State of residence, the State of source will want to tax that income even if it is invested again, now in the State of residence. In other words: remittance of income to another State, in particular to the taxpayer's State of residence, will be taxed by the State of source as if it were consumption, it will be considered "constructive consumption".

Now, if the State of residence is an income tax State, a technical consideration will support Professor Musgrave's results. Let us assume income earned and invested in year 1 to be disinvested and remitted to the State of residence in year 10. Even if the State of residence may be willing to grant a credit on its income tax for expenditure tax paid abroad, there is, in year 10, no income in the State of residence and consequently no income tax against which the expenditure tax *could* be credited. True, the State of residence could provide for a carry-back of the credit. But it is highly improbable that it will be prepared to do so. I do not know of any example in current income tax legislation; States are extremely reluctant even to grant a carry-forward of credits. If, however, no carry-back is provided for by the State of residence, the expenditure tax levied by the State of source will be a forceful disincentive against remitting the income to the residence State, a disincentive which will be in some way comparable to exchange control regulations prohibiting such remittance. It is possible that this may deter the taxpayer from investing in the source State at all. Then the non-creditability of the expenditure tax in year 10 would counteract the incentive to invest in the State of source which the expenditure tax normally provides. But assuming that the investment has already been made, the same consideration will induce the taxpayer not to remit the income, it may eventually induce him to consume it in the State where it has been raised. In any case, without carry-back the expenditure tax will affect and distort the international capital flow.

Now let us consider the reverse situation: let us assume that the State of residence is the one to apply an expenditure tax. This State may impose the tax on a worldwide basis and it is conceivable that it permits deduction of income invested or otherwise saved, even if it is saved abroad. This is, however, not a matter of course. There are important reasons which may impel the State of residence to deny such deduction of foreign savings. This State may just want to prevent loss of revenue. Or it may consider the expenditure tax system to be a subsidy which it wants to limit to its own territory. And even if it recognizes foreign investment in principle, it will, as a rule, not recognize so many foreign investments as being "qualified accounts" because it cannot control them. In all these events foreign investment will be hampered by the expenditure tax, and such obstacles may even exist if the other State, too, has introduced an expenditure tax. Professor Musgrave has discussed the tax prepayment method as an alternative to the qualified accounts concept. But she certainly is aware of the enormous political opposition that would be raised if foreign investment were declared tax-free in general. However, let us set aside all these impediments and let us assume that the State of residence recognizes foreign investments and permits their deduction as if they were domestic, and let us assume that the same State grants a credit even for foreign income tax. In this situation, again, it is the time difference that may prevent making use of the credit. For the income tax State (the State of source) taxes the income when it is raised, whereas the expenditure tax State (the State of residence) defers taxation until the income is dissaved. In this situation a carry-forward will be necessary which is more likely to be admitted than in the reverse situation a carry-back. But even if the carry-forward is provided unlimited in time, the taxpayer who invests in an income tax country will experience a temporal loss of liquidity and a definite loss of interest because he cannot use the credit before the time of consumption.

(In Munich we discussed giving out vouchers for unused carry-forwards to overcome this obstacle. But this does not seem advisable because it would give the taxpayer a possibility to circumvent the tax credit limitation, i.e. the maximum credit, which has its sound reasons.)

Thus, I agree that the distortion which the expenditure tax may bring to capital flows can only be eliminated by cooperation, in particular by treaties.

References

Andel, N. (1983), Directions of Tax Harmonization in the EEC, in Cnossen, S. (ed.), Comparative Tax Studies (North-Holland, Amsterdam).

Aaron, H.J. (ed.) (1981), The Value Added Tax: Lessons from Europe (Brookings Institution, Washington, D.C.).

Aaron, H.J. / Galper, H. (1985), Assessing Tax Reform (Brookings Institution, Washington, D.C.).

Aaron, H.J. / Pechman, J.A. (eds.) (1988), Uneasy Compromise: Problems of a Hybrid Income-Consumption Tax (Brookings Institution, Washington, D.C.).

Bird, R.M. / McLure, Jr., C.E. (1989), The Personal Income Tax in an Interdependent World" in: S. Cnossen (ed.), (title forthcoming).

Bradford, D.F. / The U.S. Treasury Tax Policy Staff (1984), Blueprints for Basic Tax Reform (Tax Analysts, Arlington, Virginia).

Brennan, G. / Buchanan, J.M. (1980), The Power to Tax: Analytic Foundations of a Fiscal Constitution (Cambridge University Press, Cambridge).

Cnossen, S. / Shoup, C.S. (1987), Coordination of Value-Added Taxes, in: S. Cnossen (ed.), Tax Coordination in the European Community (Kluwer, Antwerp).

Department of the Treasury (1984), Tax Reform for Fairness, Simplicity, and Growth, Volume 3: The Value-Added Tax, (U.S. Department of the Tre asury, Washington, D.C.).

Graetz, M.J. (1980), Expenditure Tax Design, in J.A. Pechman (ed.), What Should Be Taxed: Income Or Expenditure? (Brookings Institution, Washington, D.C.).

Gravelle, J.G. (1986), Corporate Tax Reform and International Competitiveness, in Congressional Research Service Report No. 86-42E (Library of Congress, Washington D.C), February 25.

Hall, R.E. / Rabushka, A. (1983), Low Tax, Simple Tax, Flat Tax (McGraw-Hill, New York).

McLure, C.E. Jr. (1987a), The Value-Added Tax: Key to Deficit Reduction? (American Enterprise Institute, Washington, D.C.).

McLure, C.E. Jr. / Mutti, J. / Thuronyi, V. / Zodrow, G.R. (1987b), The Taxation of Income from Business and Capital in Colombia (Ministerio de Hacienda y Credito Publico, Bogota, Colombia).

Meade, J.E., (Chairman), (1978), The Structure and Reform of Direct Taxation, Report of a IFS Committee (Unwin, London).

Mieszkowski, P. (1980), The Advisability and Feasibility of an Expenditure Tax System in: Aaron and M.J. Boskin (eds.), The Economics of Taxation (Brookings Institution, Washington, D.C.).

Musgrave, P.B. (1987), Interjurisdictional Coordination of Taxes on Capital Income, in: S. Cnossen (ed.), Tax Coordination in the European Community (Kluwer, Antwerp).

Musgrave, P.B. (1989), Fiscal Coordination and Competition in an International Setting, in volume on Retrospectives on Public Finance (Duke University Press, forthcoming).

Musgrave, R.A. / Musgrave, P.B. (1989), Public Finance in Theory and Practice, 5th edition (McGraw Hill, New York).

Organization for Economic Cooperation and Development (1988), Taxing Consumption (OECD, Paris).

Pechman, J.A. (ed.) (1980), What Should Be Taxed: Income Or Expenditure? (Brookings Institution, Washington, D.C.).

Shoup, C.S. (ed.) (1967), Fiscal Harmonization in Common Markets, (Columbia University Press, New York).

Stiglitz, J.E. (1986), Economics of the Public Sector, (W.W. Norton, New York).

Weidenbaum, M.L. / Raboy, D.G. / Christian, Jr., E.S. (eds.) (1989), The Value Added Tax: Orthodoxy and New Thinking (Kluwer, Boston).

Zodrow, G.R. / McLure, Jr., C.E. (1989), Implementing Direct Consumption Taxes in Developing Countries, WPS 131 (Country Economics Department, The World Bank, Washington, D.C.).

Gerold Krause-Junk

Problems of International Tax Coordination under Alternative Consumption Tax Regimes

I. Introduction

1. There are many arguments pro and contra a change from income to consumption taxation. In what follows, attention is given only to aspects connected with the fact that economies have international economic relations.

2. Nowadays there are quite a lot of consumption tax models, not all of which, clearly, can be investigated in a paper as such. We will concentrate on a direct personal consumption tax, because with respect to equity it seems to be the most appropriate candidate to replace the personal income tax. We will not discuss indirect consumption tax models nor tax systems which macro-economically put the tax burden on aggregate consumption.[1]

3. If one wants to consider a realistic alternative to the present income tax, one has to acknowledge that most of the consumption tax suggestions imply the introduction of certain supplementary taxes, e.g. a real asset tax, a business cash-flow tax, a tax on gifts and bequests [Meade-Report (1978)] and some kind of a withholding tax [Aaron/Galper (1985, p. 73)]. We have to decide which of those should be included in the analysis.

[1] Such is the case, e.g. with an income tax combined with immediate depreciation. Cf. Meade-Report (1978, chapter 8); H.-W. Sinn (1985).

4. From an equity point of view, it seems desirable to supplement a consumption tax by a real asset tax as far as one considers ability to pay also a function of accumulated capital [Haller (1988)]. But a real asset tax which is supposed to be neutral with respect to all kinds of assets, i.e. has regard to real economic values of houses, business firms, valuables or even human capital, is a very complicated and costly matter [Wissenschaftlicher Beirat beim Bundesministerium der Finanzen (1989)]. Besides, such a tax would have to handle most of the problems which gave reason to look for a substitution for the income tax. I am therefore not considering any asset tax.

5. Still, from an equity point of view it seems to be unbearable to leave capital accumulation tax-free for ever. It, therefore, seems appropriate - as has been often suggested - to include gifts, donations and bequests into the consumption tax base [Meade-Report (1978)]. Of course, such a provision again causes all kinds of assessment problems. But compared with annual asset taxation, fiscal administration costs seem tolerable.

6. A supplementary cash-flow business tax is meant to play a similar role within a consumption tax system like the corporation tax within the income tax system. But contrary to the corporation tax, the cash-flow tax is supposed to be neutral with respect to intersectoral and intertemporal allocation of capital. Supposedly, neutrality is accomplished because the cash-flow tax puts the burden on old and on inframarginal capital returns only. Also, unlike the corporation tax, the main purpose of which is to tax retained profits, a cash-flow tax lays hold on distributions only, be it the net outflow of equity capital alone, or the net outflow of all capital ("S-based" or "R-based" cash-flow tax respectively [Meade-Report (1978, chapter 23); H.-W. Sinn (1984, p. 331)]).

In a closed economy with private households being the capital investors, the business cash-flow is part of the consumption tax base and the business cash-flow tax simply puts an additional burden on that part. One can argue in favour or against that kind of double taxation by much the same reasoning traditionally directed pro or contra the classical corporation tax system. As I personally favour the imputation system, I don't see much sense either in double taxation of all or certain net cash-flows within a personal consumption tax system. If one wants to have non-personal and possibly different tax-rates on the consumption of capital income compared with labour income, one should combine a business cash-flow tax with a personal labour income tax (as suggested by Bradford (1986)), but if one wants to have a synthetic taxation of all consumed income, then there is simply no room for a supplementary business cash-flow tax. Of course, one must not overlook capital returns flowing outside the country. But these can be taken care of by a proper withholding tax system (see below).

7. I could not imagine the functioning of a personal consumption tax without provision of a proper withholding device. The vast majority of taxpayers would not be able to save enough income (in the necessary liquid form) to pay the personal consumption tax whenever it is fixed by the fiscal authorities.[2] There are two possible withholding schemes, an income source tax and an indirect consumption tax. The income tax, naturally, might not get hold of all kinds of income - especially because administration costs have to be kept low - but that does not seem to be necessary either, because the withholding tax mainly ought to take care of steady and tax-base-oriented tax payments of the mass of taxpayers. We are going to consider (below) the income withholding tax also as an element of an internationally workable consumption tax system.

The second withholding scheme makes use of an indirect consumption tax.[3] Ideally, tax-rates are to be fixed such that for most of the personal consumption taxpayers, the indirect tax burden comes close to their personal tax duty. But this, of course, is difficult or rather impossible to accomplish the more the personal consumption tax takes aspects of individual ability-to-pay into account. We are going to discuss international aspects of both schemes.

8. The personal consumption tax base is the difference between income and net savings of a taxpayer. The taxpayer therefore has to furnish evidence of his net savings. The fiscal authority can use this evidence to estimate (or control) future capital returns. So, the taxpayer trying to evade taxes seems to be in a jam: either he declares savings and, consequently, future capital returns, or he tries to hide capital returns, but then he better not declare capital accumulation. But in reality, the fiscal authorities might not find it that easy to uncover all capital returns, even if they have learnt about the capital

---

[2] Of course, the fiscal authority could require monthly provisional payments according to the last consumption tax assessment. But this seems to create all kinds of problems, if tax authorities try to keep up with actual consumption.

[3] That is essentially, what the Meade-Report's two-tier tax system comes to.

accumulation. Therefore, it has been suggested to permit exemption only with respect to certain savings on controlled or qualified accounts [Meade-Report (1978, chapter 9)]. All other savings are to be taxed as consumption, the respective dissavings or capital returns being put tax-free.

The first method may be called taxation "ex post", the second taxation "ex ante".[4] Both methods are equivalent under very restrictive assumptions. The (subjective) present value of future taxpayments with respect to capital returns and dissavings must equal the present tax on savings. This, in any case, might be true only with respect to the marginal investment of a risk-neutral person as with ex-post taxation where the fiscus also participates in infra-marginal profits. So, this two-fold way of taxation is certainly not what one ideally aspires to with a change to consumption tax. But it is part of a realistic concept, especially because returns of many investments are difficult to calculate [Bradford (1986)].

9. So by now we know what we are looking at:

- A personal progressive expenditure tax without any additional business taxation.
- A tax which defines consumption in a way that donations, gifts and bequests are included.
- A tax which, principally, allows for two different ways of defining the periodical tax base. Either savings are excluded and capital returns from these savings are included, or savings are included but capital returns thereof are not.
- A tax which is collected by utilization of a withholding tax, either on labour and capital income or on all domestic consumption.

II. International Problems

A. The Structure of Problems

1. International problems seem to be quite different in a world of consumption taxation compared with a world in which a single country (C-tax-country) turns to the consumption tax, whereas all other countries keep their traditional income tax systems. So we

[4] These terms are used in analogy to the terms "nachgelagertes Verfahren" and "vorgelagertes Verfahren", both terms used by the Wissenschaftliche Beirat (1986).

have to discuss both settings separately (B, C), starting, first, under the assumption that all countries cooperate in the search for a consistent consumption tax solution whereas later, a single C-tax-country is assumed to make the best of it in an income tax world.

2. As difficult it might generally be to determine individual consumption adequately so that the purpose of consumption taxation is properly served, here we can only focus on whatever additional problems arise with respect to international relations. Now, as individual consumption (C) is defined as the difference of individual income (Y) and individual net savings (S), international problems may result from the fact that

- C may take place at home or abroad,
- S may be invested at home or abroad and
- Y may be generated at home or abroad.

We are going to discuss each case in that order.

3. In a well-established tradition [Sato/Bird (1975); Musgrave/Musgrave (1972)], international taxation is evaluated according to three different criteria, namely

- international allocation of resources,
- personal equity (with respect to people with international economic activity and with purely domestic activity, respectively) and
- internation equity (i.e. a fair participation in the tax bases of all countries affected by international activity).[5]

In principle, all three kinds of problems (mentioned in 2.) are to be evaluated by all three kinds of criteria.

B. World-wide Consumption Taxation

1. Consumption

1. Starting with a C-tax world and assuming an individual's Y and S given, the first question to ask is how to tax international consumption expenditures. Under world-wide consistency assumptions a single country might tax either consumption of

[5] I am using the Musgrave/Musgrave notation in a slightly different way [Musgrave/Musgrave (1972, p. 68)].

residents (nationals[6]) at home and abroad or national consumption (of residents and non-residents).

Which of the two demarcations should be used under the allocational view is a function of what kind of individual decisions are going to be distorted. If a person's residency could be assumed given, his world consumption should be the consumption tax base, lest differences in the national tax-rates should drive him into foreign consumption places.[7] This does not necessarily imply that a country does not levy any taxes on national consumption of non-residents, as it is going to happen, if, for instance, an indirect consumption tax is used as a withholding tax and not rebated to foreigners. But in that case, for allocational reasons, the residence country should credit the tax against the personal consumption tax.

If residency is flexible, i.e. people can actually or formally change residency, then the residence principle will lose its appeal. From a welfare point of view it might even be less costly to discriminate against the locus of consumption than to discriminate against residency, which would drive people out of the country. Generally, though, people seem to be more reluctant to change residency than to change consumption places.

Now, of course, change of residency is something which principally could be made a tax base by itself. We will have to discuss that possibility in more detail under equity considerations. From an allocational point of view, one could imagine an emigration tax which somehow neutralizes any C-tax differentials. But caution is to be taken not to overdo it, creating a locking-in effect instead. Besides, it seems to come heavily accross the basic right of the freedom of movement.

2. From an equity point of view one first has to decide on the equity criterion itself. Clearly, as a personal C-tax is thought of as replacing the personal income tax, ability-to-pay comes into the picture. But there is also the Kaldor word, well-considered among C-tax supporters, that people should be taxed "according to the amount which

---

[6] As in income taxation, the full tax liability of a person to a certain country can either be founded on his residency or his nationality. We consider explicitly residency as the crucial criterion, but most of what follows would also be valid - mutis mutandis -, if nationality drew the dividing line.

[7] There is also the question of how to define a consumption place, i.e. where consumption actually takes place or where consumption goods are bought.

they take out of the common pool, and not according to what they put into it ... it is only by spending, not by earning or saving, that an individual imposes a burden on the rest of the community..." [Kaldor (1955, p. 53)]. Though that idea occasionally, seems to be considered as quite in line with a refined ability to pay-principle [Rose (1987)], I personally prefer to put it into another box.

As far as the good old ability-to-pay-priciple is concerned, there should be no doubt, that a person's consumption must be taken as a whole, not drawing any line between C at home and abroad. It especially, does not matter whether a person gets less benefits from his domestic country, if he is spending most of his money on consumption abroad. Ability-to-pay-considerations have nothing to do with that: Someone is a taxpayer because he is considered a member of the community and his consumption serves just as an indicator of his ability to contribute to the common need.

One might come to another conclusion if one follows the Kaldor-rationale of a personal consumption tax. The question is whether someone puts his claims on the social product of his domestic country, if he consumes abroad. To my mind, of course, he does - as he is going to spend national income. On the other hand, there is still the possibility that the foreign country does not use its in-traded income for consumption, but instead uses the money to acquire investment goods within the consumer's country. Now, does that mean that our consumer after all has not laid his claims on the national product as it is so far going to be used for capital accumulation rather than being consumed? I would still stick to my first judgement, but I also see to what most peculiar consequences the Kaldor criterion might lead someone to.

There is still the possibility that the Kaldor principle serves just as a proxy to benefit taxation, which might really be aimed at. A person's private consumption goes always along with the consumption of public goods and it is for that reason that he should pay consumption taxes. Now, though I consider that reasoning more in line with an indirect C-tax, it still might be used to justify a personal consumption tax. In consequence, whatever a person consumes abroad would have to be left tax-free by his residence country and to be taxed by the respective foreign country.

Now, one might wonder whether that kind of tax rule would not equally be valid under allocational considerations, as assumingly the consumer is going to consume public goods. The answer depends on the character of these public goods. Precisely: if, and as far as a foreign private consumer causes any additional public costs, e.g. if the production of public goods has to be extended because of his individual private consumption, then he should be made to pay for it, also from an allocational point of view. If, on the other hand, the public goods production costs are really overhead and not to be attributed to an individual consumer, then the benefit principle is not to serve any allocational purpose.

Let us now turn to the case that someone is going to change his residency. Clearly, there is no tax problem if C-taxes are not levied according to the residence principle but to the principle of local consumption. (I hesitate to call that "source principle"-taxation, as obviously the source of income has nothing to do with it.) But generally, there is more in favour of the residence principle. Now, is there a case for some kind of emigration tax on equity grounds?

To my mind, the answer is "yes". By the very ideology of a personal consumption tax, taxation of income is not entirely cancelled but rather postponed up to the moment when income is consumed. As discussed above, that does not even imply exempting capital accumulation for ever but taxing gifts, donations and bequests, considering them in a way as consumption. Now, it seems to be in the same line to assume fictitious consumption in the case of change of residency. If a person waives his residency, the mere postponement of taxes turns into a cancellation (as far as the tax-rates of his old domicile country exceed the rates of his new one). This seems to be not only unfavourable under allocational but also under equity considerations. To see this most clearly, consider a person close to death who is changing (or made to change) his residency just to save consumption taxation on his bequest. The solution seems to be to define change of residency as another case of fictitious consumption and to levy an "equalization tax", i.e. to tax away any possible tax gains with respect to the accumulated capital. This still leaves the question open what to do, if the tax-rates of the new residence country happen to be higher than the old ones.

3. The last case brings us close to internation equity considerations. I personally feel that the former home country is entitled to collect all the postponed taxes on accumulated capital, but I have to admit that one might consider that view as very much "income tax-distorted". In other words: if one is ready to forget where any consumption tax system comes from and to evaluate C-tax on its own, one can, in fact, fail to see consumption tax as postponed income tax. In that case, one might argue: too bad for a

country if it loses a rich inhabitant; but if he decides to die elsewhere, then it is his business alone, and the former residence country has no business to collect any taxes from him any more.

There are other more fundamental problems of personal consumption taxation under the criterion of a fair distribution of the tax bases (or tax yields) among all countries involved. For the time being, we will still concentrate on the case of international consumption, which means there is first a country of residence, and second a country where consumption takes place.[8] The question is really whether the second one should get any part of the tax yield.

There are arguments in favour and arguments against. I already mentioned a possible benefit consideration. And even apart from any public goods consumption: why should a country, qualifying as a favourite consumption place, not participate in any taxes coming along with that consumption. (It might even be that the consumption would not have taken place at all, had it not been for the atmosphere of the respective country.) If, for instance, international tax law acknowledges the priority of the source country to tax any income generated within its jurisdiction [cf. Debatin (1983, p. 283)], why deny a similar right to tax any national consumption?

On the other hand, one must not overlook the very special character of a personal consumption tax. Consumption is only meant as an indicator of personal ability to pay taxes, the true tax subject being the member of a national (or rather residing) community. (There is, to my mind, nothing like a "consumers' community"). Therefore, the very personal C-tax should be reserved for the residence country. But I could imagine some kind of international crediting system, if, for instance, countries use an indirect consumption tax as a withholding device.

2. Savings

1. Like consumption capital accumulation can also be either national or international. Precisely, international aspects come into picture if capital allocated abroad is transferred home or if old domestic or newly formed capital is transferred abroad. The

[8] There is, of course, also a country where consumption goods were produced. But that country seems not to be entitled to any tax yields in a consumption tax world. "A destination basis appears to be the natural approach to a graduated personal consumption tax ..." [Bradford (1986, p. 87)].

question to be answered seems to be: is capital formation abroad to be included into gross saving and is liquidization of foreign capital included in gross dissaving? Clearly, in an all C-tax world, the answer should either be "yes" in both cases or "no" in both cases.

Why should someone exclude capital accumulation abroad from gross saving? Because possibly he does not like the allocative effects. He might consider stimulating national investments as a very important target of consumpton taxation which - at least prima facie - seems to be failed, when capital is flowing abroad. And there is another very practical reason to include capital formation abroad into the consumption formula: As long as there is no definite guarantee that capital returns and capital withdrawals from abroad were properly declared,[9] consumption taxation may prove to be much rather a renunciation than the intended postponement of income taxation. On the other hand - and in as far as international cooperation prevents any tax evasion - there seems to be good reason to handle capital accumulation abroad not differently from capital accumulation at home. For one thing: if consumption taxation is to stop discrimination of savings, there is no point in drawing new lines of discrimination as between national and international capital formation. The economy, after all, gets capital returns from both. At least from a world-wide perspective, international capital allocation should not be distorted.

To reach full capital export neutrality, it takes, of course, more than equal treatment of savings: also, respective capital returns would have to be taxed equally. We will postpone that point up to the discussion of income determination below.

We must also consider the case that even nationally only certain registered savings accounts qualify for exemption, whereas the capital returns to all other savings are tax-free. Now, while that kind of differentiation generally is not neutral (cf. above, p. 494), there should be no question that international capital formation would fall into the non-qualified category. But one also has to consider people having claims to national registered accounts to emigrate. In that case, dissavings from foreign registered accounts are possible. Again, some kind of "emigration tax" seems necessary, and be it

[9] "Depletion of unrecorded savings, e.g. running down holdings in foreign bank accounts" is a major general objection against a personal consumption tax. [OECD (1988, p. 225)].

in the form of a withholding tax on withdrawings from registered assets held by non-residents [Bruce (1986, p.7)].

2. Equity considerations do not seem to bring up any additional aspects. There is no general personal advantage or disadvantage in putting savings into foreign instead of national accounts. So, ability to pay or other equity criteria will generally forbid any differential tax treatment of the two kinds of savings.

3. The internation equity criterion might arouse the question, how the two countries involved gain from international capital transfer. Clearly, the capital import country can be happy if additional savings from the capital export country keep flowing in, undistorted by any differential tax advice. There might be a point in giving the capital export country some kind of reward. The opportunity will be, when taxing the returns from international capital.

3. Income

1. Turning to the definition an proper handling of income within a personal consumption tax system, again we will discuss only international problems, i.e. problems which arise from the existence of income originating in one country and accruing to people residing in another one.

To begin with, one might not expect any problems with international income within a tax system in which income as a tax base is substituted in favour of consumption. But one must not forget that consumption is to be calculated as a residual out of income on one side and net savings on the other. The question then is: what is income proper in that calculation, especially, does it include international as well as national income of a resident?

From an allocational point of view, the answer is "yes". If international income were exempted, capital (and labour) export would be favoured. Possible benefits from foreign public goods don't matter, as long as exported capital (or labour) does not generate any additional public production cost within the foreign country. So, it looks as if treating international income within a world-wide C-tax system has to follow more or less the same rules as within an international income tax system. But, certainly, there are some differences. Compared with the traditional income tax, consumption tax has one advantage: one does not have to worry about any international income not transferred to the resident consumer.

But with respect to transferred foreign income, the problem of proper tax implementation, so badly solved within the existing system prevails. The solution can only be an effective withholding tax on income at its origin, mind you without any differences between active or passive income, i.e. dividend or interest income, respectively. The withholding tax (by its very idea) clearly, is to be fully credited against the main or final tax, i.e. the consumption tax considered here. Though this may create problems of international tax-sharing (to be discussed later), no allocational problem would arise from a proper international extension of the withholding tax system with full scale international crediting.

As far as the two-way system (exemption of qualified savings or of all capital returns from non-qualified savings) is concerned, international income does not seem to create any problems: as international capital placements are not likely to qualify for exemption, all international capital returns are to be put tax-free anyway. So, whereas different taxation of qualified and non-qualified savings is likely to create misallocations, there seems to be no discrimination between international income and income from domestic non-qualified accounts.

Problems might result from quite a different dilemma. Even if the whole world turns to consumption tax, it is by no means sure that all source countries - in the traditional sense of source of income - are going to waive their tax claims. They are much rather to postulate their share in national income accruing to foreigners and be it in that part of income which is not going to be reinvested in the source country.

So it seems difficult to determine the source country's fair share. Possibly, the capital return is consumed, possibly reinvested somewhere else. If the source country levies a withholding tax - which is quite in line with international precautions against tax evasion - the withholding tax is to be credited against the personal consumption tax. The amount of consumption tax actually to be paid depends, of course, on the propensity to spend and on the progressivity of the tax rates. So it may well be that foreign withholding tax exceeds the consumption tax liability. Then either foreign-sourced income is discriminated against or the residence country pays back taxes which another country received.

Things are even worse when a country uses the ex ante tax method, i.e. taxes residentials' savings which are used for foreign investments and leaves the capital returns tax-free. If the source country still levies a withholding tax, the residence country might be forced to rebate the tax if it wants to preserve capital export neutrality.

So, there seems to be after all an allocational problem with respect to the international tax treatment within the consumption tax world.

2. There is not much to be said with respect to personal equity. I think it is obvious that, especially from the equity point of view, foreign sourced income is not to be taxed differrently from domestic income. [For another view, cf. Vogel (1985, p. 26)]. Surely, to earn income abroad might be more risky and more difficult than to earn income at home. But comprehensive income tax theory does not tell us to tax income in relation to risk and effort taken by the income recipient. It simply cannot be done even by the most eager fiscal administration.

3. Internation equity seems easy to accomplish if all countries agree to tax personal consumption only. But as already mentioned, I wonder if all source countries go along with that. Especially if a withholding tax on income at the source is to be levied anyway, one can hardly imagine source countries not to claim at least part of that tax yield. This would deprive residence countries of much of their consumption tax yields, if they were giving full credit on the foreign withholding tax. So after all, it might be even more difficult to find an international credit system in the consumption tax world than in the present income tax world.

C. Unilateral C-taxation

1. Consumption

In a way, the all-consumption tax world serves only as a point of reference; clearly, in the real world any change to a C-tax would occur unilaterally. Someone would just have to take the lead. In what follows, emphasis is laid on those special problems which arise when - different from what has been considered so far - all the world around the C-tax country sticks to good old income taxation. In that special setting one cannot assume the C-tax country to handle outgoing and incoming C, S and Y symmetrically, but looking, separately, for the best possible solution which is agreeable to the Y-tax world.

As far as taxation of international consumption is concerned, little differences to the all C-tax world exist from a normative point of view. Again, all three criteria for optimal international taxation demand cross-border shoppings of C-country's residents included in the tax base. But implementation might prove much more difficult. This is due to the fact, that taxation in different countries now differs not only in tax-rates, but systematically.

Consider the model of a general indirect consumption tax as a withholding tax (to be credited against the direct consumption tax). If the Y-tax world around does not have an indirect consumption tax, nothing less than controlling all cross-border shoppings would do. Moreover: as it is not conceivable that the Y-tax world gives any credit on indirect consumption taxes, borne by its citizen shopping in the C-tax country, that country must either rebate the tax at the border or discriminate against its own consumption place. Both results are highly unsatisfactory.

Even more difficult is C-tax policy, if change of residency must be considered a realistic reaction of the taxpayers. Whereas in a C-tax world only tax differentials matter and have to be somehow taken care of (as discussed above), now literally all taxation could be avoided by someone who is moving out of a C-tax country the moment he retires and is living from thereon on dissavings. The C-tax country would have all reason either to levy an emigration tax or to put a withholding tax on domestic dissavings of non-residents [Bruce (1985)].

2. Savings

A single country turning to C-taxation in a Y-tax world faces a problem not known (or at least not as relevant) in a C-tax world: The country is kept alone inducing saving[10] and it is therefore likely to create capital transfers to the rest of the world.

[10] Whereas it is more or less common belief that a switch from income to consumption taxation stimulates savings, J. Frenkel and A. Razin (1989) recently came to the opposite conclusion with respect to a country which runs a trade balance deficit. That, indeed, is surprising and would need a thorough revaluation of consumption taxation, if the two authors would not have argued under a set of very strange assumptions. They, in fact, consider not an income tax but an income tax allowing immediate (100 %) de-

Now, from a welfare point of view that might well have advantages for the C-tax country. The time preference of residents is made equal to the domestic gross rate of return of capital as well as to the world interest rate, which seems to be the principal target of C-taxation anyway. If the C-tax country is capital importing, national savers take the place which was before taken by foreigners, and a larger part of domestic capital returns accrue to residents.

But these results might, after all, not be in accordance with what a C-tax country was striving for. In a way, it might feel deprived of the fruits of its efforts: while savings are increased, domestic investment and labour productivity - at least for a small country - might not be affected at all [Whalley (1985)]. And if the country happens to be a large one and capital exporting, then the additional capital export might let the world interest rate decrease and thus, possibly, foreign earned capital income [Hamada (1966), Krause-Junk (1988)]. It is for that reason, that the C-tax country might consider taxing its residents' capital export, or, more specifically, not to exclude gross capital accumulation abroad from the consumption tax base while including any foreign dissavings. That comes to regard capital transfers abroad for the purpose of taxation - like gifts and bequests - as fictitious consumption.

---

preciation, i.e. a tax which for a closed economy and equal tax rates would be identical with a consumption tax. Differences in the tax bases occur only for an open economy if foreign trade is not balanced. They further assume a two period world in which any country's trade deficit (surplus) in the first period is compensated by a surplus (deficit) in the second period (interest payments included). And finally, they assume a government which is strictly running a periodically balanced budget. So now, if the country running a trade deficit in the first period turns from income to consumption taxation, it actually increases its tax base in the first and decreases its tax base in the second period. Still, to run a periodically balanced budget, the government is forced to lower the C-tax rate in the first and to increase the C-tax rate in the second period. No wonder the tax reform seems to be anti- much rather than pro-savings. But I think the assumptions are not such that one would have to revise the common belief in the pro savings effect of tax reform in question.

But will the Y-tax countries tolerate as obvious a discrimination, refraining from any retaliation measures? Now, the C-tax country can point out that it does not do to foreign capital accumulation anything different from what the Y-world is doing to its own savings: putting a tax on it, the name of which does not matter much. But it remains the fact that savings would be treated differently according to the place where they are invested.

Problems are quite the same if the ex-ante method is used and instead of savings thereof capital returns are put tax-free. Again, allocational and equity considerations would call for an equal treatment of capital investments at home and abroad. And again, that might cause an increase in capital exports much rather than additional formation of real capital at home.

Now, considering a country dropping income taxation and crowding out instead of attracting capital seems rather odd and definitely to be in need for further explanation. Indeed, one would expect that any positive effect on capital export which additional saving might create, should be washed out by resulting net income differentials for foreign capital owners. But the opposite seems to be true, as we will argue in a moment.

3. Income

A single C-tax country in a Y-tax world has not only to decide on the taxation of its residents' foreign income but also on the taxation of the domestic income, accruing to non-residents (mind you, there is no symmetry in taxing the two income streams as it would be in an ideal C-tax world!).

Should all residents' foreign income appear as a positive element within the C-tax base formula? The general positive answer found for a C-tax world needs reconsideration as foreign income now might be submitted to a foreign income tax. Including foreign income into the tax base then seems to insinuate crediting foreign income tax against domestic consumption tax, which, indeed, would put a high fiscal burden on the C-tax country, especially unbearable if foreign income is not consumed and therefore adding nothing to the national tax yield. On the other hand, if the foreign income tax is generally not credited, then consumption of foreign income clearly leads to double-taxation. That seems to suggest a differential taxation, according to whether foreign income is consumed or not. But such a solution certainly is not a practical one and will break down whenever a person has income from different countries.

Now, actually not all foreign income is taxed by the source country. So, what was said above is valid only with respect to so-called active income which generally is taxed according to the source principle. Passive income, i.e. interest payments, is generally left tax-free at the source. That seems to make it easier on the C-tax country - if it were not for another problem.

Most Y-countries allow for depreciation substantially faster than economically called for. In so far tax exemption of interest payments really comes to subsidizing imported debt capital [Bird (1988)]. Now, as in the C-tax countries depreciation no longer matters, there is clearly an incentive to place debt capital abroad. If capital export is not included in the tax base, foreign subsidies together with a general increase in the residents' savings ratio are really endangering the C-tax country to lose much rather than to attract capital.

There is, of course, a chance that with respect to equity capital it just goes the other way round - and much more to the expectations of a country turning to C-taxation. As active foreign income in most parts of the world is exempted by the residence country or at least residence taxes are deferred, the C-tax country is about to become a favourite place for direct investments. It might hope to gain in equity capital what it loses in debt capital, a change - as widely considered - for the better. But that might prove too good to be true. If the C-tax country is not taxing any income accrued to foreigners, then, to the present international tax system, it is going to be considered a tax haven which implies that it is no longer granted a favourable tax treatment by the residence countries which may turn to full-size residence taxation.

So, what is the C-tax country supposed to do? The best way I can see is to put a substantial withholding tax on all income to be credited against the personal consumption tax and not to be rebated to foreigners. There is a chance that the Y-world will tolerate the withholding tax and continuing favourable tax treatment of capital invested in the C-tax country. This country, after all, would have a share in domestic income accrued to foreigners.

III. Conclusion

A personal consumption tax is a very complicated matter also from an international point of view. But I hesitate to recommend no further thought should be given to a C-tax introduction. After all: the contemporary income taxation with respect to international incomes could hardly be worsened. So, while international aspects certainly are not suggesting the introduction of a consumption tax, the present shape of the international income tax order is nothing which could not be put at a risk.

Comments by Rolf Caesar

Indeed, discussion on consumption taxes has widely left out problems resulting from the fact that national economies have international relations. This point is of particular relevance when looking at the international interdependencies between countries which have been constantly increasing during the last two decades. Therefore, it is certainly interesting to take a closer look at the international aspects of consumption taxation as it is done in the stimulating paper of Gerold Krause-Junk. I shall confine my comments on it to five points.

Firstly, a terminological remark may be necessary. It is true, the topic of international policy coordination has been most popular in recent debates on the academic as well as on the political level. But this discussion has focused on the interaction of national politicians' decisions referring to macroeconomic policies. Similar reasoning on consumption taxes would lead to the discussion of explicit versus implicit coordination of national decisions on (consumption) taxes. In this context it may be more correct to speak of a question relating to a "harmonization" problem.

Secondly, with respect to the general structure of the paper Mr. Krause-Junk discusses C, S, and Y separately as more or less independent parameters in the context of consumption taxation. However, this seems to pose a problem of consistency. From a theoretical point of view, C ought to be the appropriate dimension to be discussed entailing strong implications for the definition of S and Y. Instead, from a pragmatic point of view, it might be easier to approach the determination of C indirectly by looking at S and Y (though even S and Y may be interdependent as to the treatment of savings on the one hand and income from savings on the other). Now it may be more appropriate to choose the first or the second strategy depending on the specific purposes of the analysis. But to pursue both ways at the same time is certainly not possible without problems.

Thirdly, turning to Mr. Krause-Junk's concrete analysis, one should point out an underlying assumption that seems to be of decisive importance for the argumentation of the paper. I.e., any allocational distortion in the C-world presupposes that there are differences in the consumption tax rates of the countries concerned and that the differences are high enough to cover the costs of internationalizing consumption and/or of changing residence. Without such differences there will be no specific problems of international resource allocation connected with a consumption tax. Now starting from this assumption of sufficiently high differences in tax rates some specific questions about the allocational properties of alternative tax designs could be asked: Is it possible to differentiate that clearly between a discrimination of places of consumption and of places of residence, respectively? There rather seems to be a high degree of interdependence between both criteria. Furthermore, is Mr. Krause-Junk's analysis concerned primarily with immediate adjustments to changes in tax rates differences or with the ultimate effects of tax rate differences on capital flows or growth rates in the long run? Finally, of what relevance are these differences if the monetary sphere is taken into account? In particular, differences in the rate of inflation and expectations may well dominate real interest rate effects at least in the short or middle run.

As a fourth point, I should like to emphasize my doubt on the usefulness of the "inter-nation equity" criterion as such. As there is no objective indicator for determining the possible degree of such an "equity", any reflections referring to it must be very arbitrary. Hence, one is left in the unsatisfactory position to accept or not to accept an argument merely on grounds of personal estimation. But taking the inter-nation equity criterion as it is, one should expect the problem of an emigration tax to be discussed under this heading and not so much with respect to allocational and personal equity criteria as Mr. Krause-Junk did.

Finally, as to the factual relevance of the terminological demarcations (resulting from the residence principle chosen as the crucial criterion in the paper) it could be interesting to look at some figures. E.g., international direct consumption of German private households amounted to 46 billion DM in 1987, or only 4.1 percent of total private consumption in Germany, respectively. A similar dimension can be found with regard to international income flows. I.e., income of German residents from abroad totalled 61 billion DM, or 3.9 percent of national income, in 1987. Thus, compared to the domestic requirements of a consumption tax international problems connected with such a tax in a C-world, or even within a C-Y-world, may allow a substantial degree of pragmatic reasoning concerning the tax design.

References

Aaron, H.J. / Galper, H. (1985), Assessing Tax Reform (The Brookings Institution, Washington, D.C.).

Bird, R.M. (1988), Shaping a New International Tax Order, in: Bulletin for International Fiscal Documentation, Vol. 42 (July 1988), pp. 292-299.

Bradford, D.F. (1986), Untangling the Income Tax (Harvard University Press, Cambridge, Mass. and London).

Bruce, N. (1985), Remarks on the Design of an Expenditure Tax in Canada, in: J. Mintz (1985), pp. 5-9.

Debatin, H. (1983), Probleme der internationalen Doppelbesteuerung, in: Handbuch der Finanzwissenschaft, Band IV, 3. Aufl., pp. 269-309.

Hamada, K. (1966), Strategic Aspects of Taxation on Foreign Investment Income, in: Quarterly Journal of Economics, Vol. 80, pp. 361-375.

Haller, H. (1988), Bemerkungen zu einigen Ergebnissen der Optimal Taxation- und Excess Burden-Analysen, in: Finanzarchiv, N.F., Bd. 46, pp. 236-251.

Institute for Fiscal Studies (1978), The Structure and Reform of Direct Taxation, Report of a Committee chaired by Professor J.E. Meade (London).

Kaldor, N. (1955), An Expenditure Tax (London).

Mintz, J. (1985), Report of the Policy Forum on Tax Reform and the Consumption Tax (John Deutsch Institute for the Study of Economics Policy, Queen's University, Kingston, Ontario, Policy Forum Series -5-), pp. 5-9.

Musgrave, P.B. / Musgrave, R.A. (1972), Internation Equity, in: Bird, R.M. and Head, J.G. (eds.), Modern Fiscal Issues, Essays in honor of Carl S. Shoup (Toronto and Buffalo), pp. 63-85.

OECD (1988), Taxing Consumption (Paris).

Razin, A. / Fenkel, J.A. (1989), International Effects of Tax Reforms, in: The Economic Journal, 99 (Conference 1989), pp. 38-58.

Rose, M. (1987), Plädoyer für eine Konsumorientierung bei der Reform des Steuersystems, in: Volkswirtschaftliche Korrespondenz der Adolf-Weber-Stiftung, 26. Jg. Nr.2.

Sato, M. / Bird, R.M. (1975), International Aspects of the Taxation of Corporations and Shareholders, in: IMF Staff Papers, pp. 384-455.

Sinn, H.-W. (1984), Neue Wege der Unternehmensbesteuerung, Wirtschaftsdienst, 64. Jg. Nr. 7, pp. 328-334.

Sinn, H.-W. (1985), Kapitaleinkommensbesteuerung (Tübingen).

Vogel, K. (1985), Die Besteuerung von Auslandseinkünften - Prinzipien und Praxis, in: Vogel, K. (ed.), Grundfragen des internationalen Steuerrechts (Köln), pp. 3-31.

Whalley, J. (1985), Allocative and Distributive Effects of Consumption Taxation, in: J. Mintz, (1985), pp. 13-17.

Wissenschaftlicher Beirat beim Bundesministerium der Finanzen (1986), Gutachten zur einkommensteuerlichen Behandlung von Alterseinkünften (Schriftenreihe des Bundesministeriums der Finanzen, Heft 38, Bonn).

Wissenschaftlicher Beirat beim Bundesministerium der Finanzen (1989), Die Einheitsbesteuerung in der Bundesrepublik Deutschland - Mängel und Alternativen, Gutachten (Schriftenreihe des Bundesministeriums der Finanzen, Heft 41, Bonn).

Bernd Genser

Do International Tax Relations Impede a Shift towards Expenditure Taxation?*

I. Introduction

The eighties showed a worldwide discussion of tax reform scenarios, based on the theoretical and empirical evidence that national income tax regimes suffered from major shortcomings. The criticism is not new that the system of direct taxes needed adaptation in order to achieve the goals of an equitable distribution of tax burdens and net personal income, of avoiding allocative distortions and welfare losses for the society and of low costs of information, compliance, administration and control. All this has led to changes in the tax systems in the past. In the last three decades major reform steps have included measures to integrate corporate and personal income taxes, indexation rules to mitigate inflationary distortions or the introduction of assignment rules for household income in order to escape undesirable progressivity effects.

These traditional targets are also present in the recent reform debate, but there seems to be one further aspect which might be responsible for the international coincidence of tax reform considerations in nearly all major industrialized countries, namely the awareness of the interdependence of national tax systems in our increasingly integrated world economy [cf. OECD (1987a), Pechman (1988), Summers (1988), Tanzi 1988)].

* For helpful and critical remarks I give thanks to Werner Ebke, Andreas Haufler (both University of Konstanz) and to the participants of the seminar session in Heidelberg, especially to my discussant Klaus Vogel.

Nevertheless this international view of domestic tax regimes is not novel at all. International factor mobility and resulting income flows have caused international negotiations to tackle the double taxation problem as early as in the last century and in every industrialized country forty or more bilateral double taxation treaties complement domestic tax law. Depending on the goals aimed at these arrangements reflect the structure of the national tax systems at the time when the treaties were negotiated or amended.

The existence of the tax treaties has to be considered if the national tax system is to be reformed. If a new tax system is introduced there might be a necessity to adapt tax treaties as well. On the other hand the tremendous problem caused by the necessity to renegotiate bilaterally a double digit series of tax treaties might very well be regarded as a major constraint to national tax reform plans and may make the tax policy maker discard tax reform proposals which are not in accord with the prevailing system of international tax relations.

My interest in this topic arose, when I noticed that objections to expenditure tax proposals stressed the problems of international relations and their constraints for tax reforms [cf. Mieszkowski (1977, p. 48), Goode (1980, pp. 65 seq.), Henderson (1984, pp. 90 seq.)]. In fact, income tax reforms have been implemented recently in accordance with the traditional Schanz/Haig/Simons comprehensive income concept in Europe as well as overseas, dismissing expenditure tax alternatives.

The question I want to address in my paper is whether these political decisions could be justified by the existence of international tax relations, which are assumed to be unchangeable in the short run.

The paper is organized as follows. In chapter II the notion of international tax relations is defined and illustrated. Expenditure tax scenarios are explained in chapter III. Chapters IV, V and VI try to explain in which way international tax relations might cause problems with respect to a unilateral step towards an expenditure tax regime. In chapter VII a political economy view of tax reforms in open economies raises the question of whether or not tax relations inhibit a change towards expenditure taxation as a result of legal rigidities, or economic benefits, as perceived by multinational firms. There seem to be arguments that an expenditure tax regime is not particularly advantageous to international firms if one takes into consideration loopholes in international income taxation open to them nowadays. Chapter 8 gives a short summary of the interrelationship between tax treaties and the outcome of recent tax reforms.

II. The Range of International Tax Arrangements

From a legal perspective international tax law in Germany [cf. Fischer/Warneke (1988, pp. 10 seqq.)] is based on

(a) international public law,

(b) European Community law,

(c) national foreign tax law (Außensteuerrecht),

(d) double taxation treaties.

a) Within this legal hierarchy international public law contains general rules, such as national tax sovereignty or ban of arbitrariness in international taxation. Furthermore, the model conventions, worked out by the OECD and by the UN as a guideline for bilateral double taxation treaties are related to international tax law. The "Model Convention for the Avoidance of Double Taxation with Respect to Taxes on Income and on Capital" [OECD (1977)] aims at the harmonization of tax treaties between industrialized countries, whereas the UN model should do the same for contracts between developed and developing countries. An international treaty which contains general regulations concerning taxes including tariffs, which may be considered as taxes on traded goods, is the "General Agreement on Tariffs and Trade".

b) The Treaty of Rome provides different rules to harmonize indirect taxes and direct taxes (Art. 99 and 100) in the member countries of the European Community. Up to now the supranational authority has passed a series of directives, which set tax policy targets to be met by national governments of the EC member countries.

c) National foreign tax law includes all regulations which are relevant for tax problems when the power to tax is shared with a foreign tax authority. German tax laws determine unrestricted and restricted tax liability for income, wealth and inheritance taxes as well as unilateral concessions to avoid international double taxation. Special regulations to eliminate distortionary consequences of international tax avoidance are included in separate laws on the taxation of foreign relations (Außensteuergesetz).

d) For more than 150 years, double taxation treaties have been recognized as a means of reducing the tax burden for economic transactions, where two national authorities might exercise their power to tax[1]. With the rise of the number of bilateral treaties following the growth of trade several attempts have been undertaken to standardize these treaties. A number of model treaties[2] have provided a guideline for new treaties as well as for renegotiations of existing ones.

Under the German constitution double taxation treaties do not have the status of international law, but belong to a group of self-executing agreements, which become German law by approval, without further legal transformation [cf. Fischer/Warneke (1988, p. 12)]. This status even gives priority to double taxation treaties as compared to domestic legislation.

By 1988 Germany had approved 56 double taxation agreements concerning income and wealth taxes (negotiations with another 7 countries had already started) and 5 treaties concerning inheritance taxes [cf. Finanznachrichten (1/88, pp. 3 seqq.)]. Due to Ger-many's position in the world market the network of bilateral tax relations is quite elaborate but the situation does not differ markedly from other industrialized countries.

III. Expenditure Tax Scenarios

In order to analyze the constraints placed by the existing network of international tax relations on a tax reform, dubbed a "switch towards an expenditure tax system", one has to have a closer look at the "expenditure tax scenario". Kaldor's expenditure tax concept [cf. Kaldor (1955)] was aimed at replacing the personal income tax by a personal consumption tax. This switch is rather easy to grasp in a single tax model economy. But real world scenarios must catch the whole tax system of direct and indirect taxes.

---

[1] Ross (1988, p. 91), mentions a double taxation agreement between France and Belgium signed in 1843 to be the first modern tax convention.

[2] League of Nations Model Convention 1928; Model Convention of Mexico 1943; Model Convention of London 1946; OECD Recommendation Concerning Double Taxation 1955; OECD Draft Double Taxation Convention on Income and Capital 1963; OECD Model Double Taxation Convention on Income and on Capital 1977; United Nations Model Taxation Convention between Developed and Developing Countries 1980. [Cf. Debatin (1983, pp. 291 seqq.)].

With respect to recent reform proposals I will distinguish three types of expenditure tax scenarios reshaping traditional tax systems:

(a) partial replacement of traditional tax revenues by a consumption type Value Added Tax,

(b) replacement of the corporate income tax by a cash-flow business tax,

(c) replacement of the personal income tax by a graduated personal expenditure tax.

This classification does not exactly meet the proposals discussed in the relevant literature. Lodin (1978) and Meade (1978) concentrate on direct taxes leaving commodity taxes apart. On the other hand their recommendation for an expenditure tax regime in accordance with scenarios (b) and (c) also includes a complementary tax on net wealth.

Bradford (1986, pp. 312 seqq.) suggests three different plans to follow a consumption strategy of tax reform. His Plan 1 converts the tax base of existing US individual and corporate income taxes to a cash-flow base. Plan 2 introduces a VAT on an add-on basis, as a substitute for a share of current taxes on individual and corporate income by reducing the tax rates and introducing some payroll tax credits to compensate low income earners for the effects of regressiveness. Plan 3 is a two-tier cash-flow tax consisting of a flat rate business tax and of a graduated compensation tax on wages, salaries and pension receipts[3].

Kay and King (1986) plead for a shift to a lifetime expenditure tax in the UK including a corporate tax transformed into a cash-flow tax. In their analysis of the British tax system one can also find some implicit recommendations towards VAT when the authors argue that "there are reasons for supposing that the UK would do better to rely rather more on indirect taxes than it does at present" [Kay/King (1986, p. 139)].

Considering the variety of reform plans we will regard any shift in accordance with (a), (b) or (c) as a step towards expenditure taxation. I further assume that the cash-flow versions of corporate and personal income can be implemented in accordance with constitutional regulations and double taxation agreements. I therefore exclude expenditure tax models which are designed in a way that the question of whether the new taxes can be regarded as "similar to their income tax counterparts" is answered in the negative from a legal point of view [cf. Birk (1989, this conference)].

---

[3] This Plan 3 version is closely related to the Simple Flat Tax promoted by Hall/Rabushka (1985). In an unpublished 1988 paper Bradford dubbed this Plan Three "X-Tax" and proposed an equivalent Earned-Income-Credit version, the EICX-Tax.

IV. International Tax Relations and Value Added Tax

VAT has been a point of recent discussion with respect to income versus expenditure tax scenarios in Canada, Japan and the US, whereas it had already been implemented in most of the industrialized European countries as well as in many developing countries in Latin America and Africa by the end of the seventies[4]. By 1988, 18 out of 24 OECD members had a VAT system to tax private consumption, and another three (Canada, Iceland and Japan) are expected to follow in the near future [Messere/Norregard (1989, p. 25 seq.)]. Only Australia, Switzerland and the United States seem to refuse VAT and to rely on their traditional sales taxes.

A first look at OECD figures of consumer taxes shows that the successive change towards VAT has increased the share of general consumption taxes compared to total taxes from 11.7 % in 1965 to 15.5 % in 1986, whereas within the same period the ratio of all consumption taxes dropped from 34.8 % to 28.4 % [OECD (1988)].

A closer look at single countries shows that those countries which had not introduced VAT by 1986 have the lowest share of general consumption taxes. Related to national GDP the general consumption tax quota in the US (2.2 %), in Australia (2.4 %) and in Switzerland (3.0 %) was less than half the 1986 average OECD quota of 6 % (or 7 % within the EC). This development will most likely continue and become even stronger due to income tax cuts, harmonization measures in the EC and the introduction of VAT in the three other OECD countries.

Implementation of VAT in the OECD countries as a substitute for the former sales and turnover taxes is based on the GATT and its implicit recommendation for the destination principle[5]. Besides a transparent calculation of equalisation charges for imports and of tax rebates for exports to meet the non-discrimination target, Article IV requires bilateral transparency by entitling contracting countries to retaliate with a

---

[4] Tait (1988, pp. 10 seqq.) offers a list of 50 countries applying a VAT by 1988.

[5] Article III prohibits tax discrimination of imported goods as compared to domestic ones. The supplementary provision to Article XVI permits refunds of indirect taxes on exported goods as "the remission of such duties and taxes in amounts not in excess of those which have accrued, shall not be deemed as a subsidy". So tax rebates for exports are in accordance with GATT although export subsidies are prohibited.

countervailing duty on imports if duties or taxes in the exporting country have been refunded in excess of the permitted amount. This arithmetical transparency can only be met by a VAT. The GATT thus seems to have stimulated the acceptance of a VAT and brought about a shift towards expenditure taxation.

As regards the 12 EC countries, who have signed the GATT, the change to the VAT system is based on the Treaty of Rome. The demand for a unified system of indirect taxes (Art. 99) has led the EC to require all member countries to follow the VAT line. In a number of VAT directives the unification of the national VAT systems was aimed at, the most important being the 6th directive (1977) on the harmonization of the tax bases. These international arrangements have forced the countries joining the EC to introduce a VAT system, but they also made them use the new tax as a powerful source of government revenue. Apart from France, in all VAT countries the share of general consumption taxes has risen faster than in non-VAT countries within the last ten years.

Although the EC directives are relevant for EC countries only, they have the character of an interpretation of the GATT rules for non-EC countries. GATT does not recommend a VAT, but the EC multi-stage system with border tax adjustment is in full accordance with the GATT rules and will have been introduced in more than 50 countries, among them 9 out of 12 non-EC OECD countries by the end of the decade. Thus a look at indirect taxation offers evidence that a shift towards consumption taxes has taken place as a consequence of tax rules included in international agreements. International tax relations have forced this development rather than prohibited it.

V. International Tax Relations and Cash-Flow Company Taxes

Taxation of international investment income is usually governed by double taxation treaties. Although the actual methods by which double taxation relief is granted vary considerably from country to country [cf. Alworth (1988), Debatin (1983)], basically the residence principle is applied if income is repatriated to the home country, whereas the source principle is chosen for foreign income accumulation.

In an open economy setting efficient allocation of capital requires an equalization of gross marginal returns on investment at home and abroad. International taxation, creating a wedge between gross and net returns to the investor will distort capital allocation and reduce global welfare, unless "capital export neutrality" holds, viz. income from marginal investment is taxed at the same rate irrespective in which country investment takes place. It can be shown that an ideal comprehensive income tax system is able to ensure capital export neutrality, provided that international personal as well as corporate taxation follows the residence principle, income is defined comprehensively and corporate and income taxes are fully integrated [cf. Sinn (1985)]. Nevertheless none of these requirements are met in real income taxation, due to difficulties in calculating true depreciation comprehensive income, to nonimputation of undistributed profits and to the taxation of foreign affiliates at arms' length[6].

Basically double taxation treaties do adhere to the residence principle by crediting withheld taxes on interests and dividends as well as by exempting source taxes on royalties or independent personal services. On the other hand foreign corporate income from retained earnings and realized capital gains are subject to tax under the foreign income tax regime and exempt in the home country. Here the arms' length view of foreign affiliates causes a deviation from the residence principle, responsible for distortionary effects within a traditional income tax regime.

Although a pure expenditure tax system could abolish corporate taxes completely, as companies do not consume but distribute profits to shareholders only [cf. Kaldor (1955, p. 146)], most recent expenditure tax scenarios adhere to flat rate company taxes either as a withholding tax in an integrated personal expenditure tax regime or as a measure to capture revenues from foreign capital income[7]. But they recommend a change in the tax base from company income to cash flow.

Meade (1978, pp. 228 seqq.) has discussed three different kinds of cash-flow taxes for corporations:

- the R-base tax, whose tax base is the difference of sales of real goods and services R_i and purchases of real goods and services R_o,

[6] Boadway/Bruce (1988) have demonstrated the welfare consequences of a full integration of corporate and personal income on accrual in an open economy setting. Still, the investment decision remains distorted by the corporate income tax unless the corporate tax can be levied on a destination basis.

[7] Further arguments are taxation of rents, avoidance of windfall capital gains or discouragement of expenditure tax evasion within companies. [Cf. Aaron (1989, pp. 3 seqq.) or Boadway/Bruce (1988, p. 27)].

- the (R+F)-base tax, whose tax base is the difference of real and financial inflows (R_i+F_i) and outflows (R_o+F_o),
- the S-base tax, whose tax base is the difference of outflows S_o and inflows S_i associated with share transactions and with dividend payments to resident companies and resident shareholders.

The different tax bases are related by the fundamental cash-flow identity

$$R_i+F_i+S_i+T_i = R_o+F_o+S_o+T_o$$

where T_o and T_i are taxes paid and repaid to the fiscus respectively. Thus the (R+F)-base and the S-base only differ by the tax term

$$(R_i\text{-}R_o)+(F_i\text{-}F_o) = (S_o\text{-}S_i)+(T_o\text{-}T_i)$$

and may be regarded as being equivalent apart from a tax inclusive versus tax exclusive calculation of tax rates.

The efficiency gain of a global switch to cash-flow corporation taxes can be fully captured in an international setting, if the residence principle is universally applied. Then capital export neutrality will prevail, if the credit system absorbs differences in national corporation tax rates. But efficient capital allocation can also be reached in a world, where only one country introduces a cash-flow system whereas other countries keep their income tax, provided that the application of the residence principle ensures that income taxes in the source country are credited against domestic cash-flow taxes [cf. Sinn (1987, pp. 35 seqq.)].

Double taxation relief that is granted in existing treaties for different types of company income under the prevailing income tax regime, will be granted for different types of company cash flows under the expenditure tax regime. In general, repatriation of income to the domestic parent by means of royalties or purchases of goods and services are tax-exempt in the source country but taxed in the destination country, where these flows increase the tax base. Dividends and interest payments by the foreign subsidiary are included in the F-base and taxed according to the cash-flow concept chosen. Withheld foreign taxes on these flows should be credited against domestic company taxes.

Income taxation according to the residence principle is not applicable to retained earnings and realized capital gains, where double taxation relief is provided by exemption in the residence country. With respect to these income flows source taxation under an income tax regime may differ considerably from source taxation under an expenditure tax regime, even if tax rates are close. But a deviation from neutrality due to exemption cannot be regarded as a specific expenditure tax problem. It is relevant for income tax systems as well and it will remain if both countries switch to an expenditure tax regime.

Whether this allocative distortion introduced by the arms' length principle should be tolerated as a trade-off between efficiency in international capital markets and national independence of tax administrations must be answered again in an expenditure tax world. Meade (1978, pp. 412 seq.) seems to prefer an arms' length rule by restricting the deductibility of real investments to domestic ones. Foreign investment returns would therefore be subject to company taxation in advance, whereas repatriation of returns will be tax-exempt by crediting foreign source taxes. This regulation would require no amendment of existing tax treaties but could be implemented within the scope of domestic company tax law.

VI. International Tax Relations and a Personal Expenditure Tax

A change from the existing personal income tax regime towards an expenditure tax basically results in exempting personal saving from the existing income tax base, irrespective of the specific form of a personal expenditure tax scenario. Contrary to company taxation, the personal expenditure tax should exhibit some progressivity. In an open economy setting a graduated expenditure tax makes sense only in combination with the residence principle. Domestic as well as foreign personal expenditures of any resident form the tax base to which the tax schedule is applied in such a way as to meet horizontal as well as vertical equity targets. A pure residence principle would require that foreign cash-flow income to residents is taxed by granting a tax credit on income taxes withheld abroad thus compensating the domestic tax liability that arises when these cash flows are not invested in qualified domestic assets but consumed. If according to existing treaties double taxation relief is granted by exclusive source taxation, this might be regarded as an administrative compromise and national equity targets revealed in the graduation of the tax schedule are partly met by the progressivity proviso clause.

Further problems arise if expenditure taxation is introduced in one country whereas the other keeps its income tax regime. Here again foreign income taxes on dividends and interests can be credited and other income flows are exempted in the source country. In this case the residence principle absorbs any difference in tax bases between the two countries. But on the other hand there are foreign income taxes on capital income, wages, pensions, and realized capital gains, which are taxed abroad with tax bases and tax rates differing from the domestic expenditure regime. Since for these income flows the credit system is not agreed upon in existing tax treaties, there is only an economic incentive to escape detrimental taxation by repatriation and accumulation of foreign income in domestic savings to qualify for expenditure tax exemption.

This implicit use of tax crediting by substitution does not avoid the efficiency loss due to the different treatment of income flows in the source and the residence country, but on the other hand it may help to outweigh the most important discriminating element of foreign source taxation within an income tax regime.

The application of the expenditure tax regime to non-residents would require taxing them on a cash-flow basis, exempting accrued income such as pension rights or unrealized capital gains and if desirable also savings in tax-exempt assets. The non-resident's tax base thus would include consumption expenditures in the source country as well as repatriated cash flows.

One item of the expenditure tax base which is supposed to create difficulties is consumption financed by foreign assets. If two countries apply an expenditure tax, then dissaving of foreigners will be regarded as a taxable activity, which due to a residual item clause in the treaties is tax exempt in the source country and taxable in the residence country. Since dissaving is not subject to tax under an income tax regime, the residence country does not have to provide any credit mechanism. On the other hand there will be a strong incentive for residents to evade domestic expenditure taxation by consuming abroad, especially in income tax countries where the tax authority has no obligation to check dissavings. This loophole nevertheless may be closed by applying the prepayment method for foreign saving restricting tax exempt saving to domestic registered assets.

One problem which has been a major point of discussion in Lodin (1978, pp. 108 seqq.) and Meade (1978, pp. 419 seqq.) is migration. A shift towards an expenditure tax regime offers an incentive to residents to emigrate in order to consume tax-exempt assets in an income tax country. On the other hand there also exists a disincentive to immigrate from an income tax country, if accumulated wealth out of already taxed income might be subject to the expenditure tax as well. In my view both problems do not conflict with tax treaties. Emigration means withdrawal from qualified accounts, which like consumption expenditures lead to expenditure tax liability. Lodin's "emigration tax" is another form of expenditure tax prepayment which has been suggested for consumer durables to avoid the problem of imputing consumption flows over the years of utilization. Progressivity peaks might be avoided by some kind of averaging according to domestic regulations.

Immigrants on the other hand should be made to register their assets in qualified accounts by granting them a fair tax credit which again is to be regarded as a prepayment of taxes to the foreign fiscus and which can be used up if future consumption is financed through dissaving. There is an incentive to register for immigrants in order to avoid double taxation which would occur if liquidation of assets for consumption purposes would give rise to expenditure taxation once they are residents.

A switch towards a personal expenditure tax does not necessarily seem to require amendments to existing double taxation agreements, although a revision would be desirable in the long run to introduce explicitly some special expenditure tax regulations mentioned above. In addition an expenditure tax reform will neither require a simultaneous international harmonization of national tax regimes nor cause higher costs for international administration and control. As regards efficiency again the question must be posed, whether deviation from the residence principle, which according to existing double taxation treaties is tolerated for the current income tax regimes, might be tolerated as a minor administration/efficiency trade-off for the expenditure tax regime as well.

VII. A Political Economy View of Tax Reforms in Open Economies

Considering the impediments which international tax relations may set against a switch towards an expenditure tax regime, I do not see a serious obstacle as long as cash-flow taxes are treated as "modified income taxes". Although the residence principle is not applied generally in tax treaties, both cash-flow company taxation as well as cash-flow personal expenditure taxation can be implemented within the existing framework of international tax relations even if there is only a unilateral shift to such a new system.

The theoretical argument in favour of the switch towards expenditure taxation is a welfare gain caused by avoiding tax distortions. Efficiency can be improved by eliminating allocative distortions in domestic savings and investments as well as distortions in international investments.

A switch to cash-flow company taxation therefore should prove attractive to enterprises investing in international markets. Nevertheless tax reform proposals in favour of a change in the tax regime did not gain a majority in the political process and furthermore didn't even receive decisive support from multinational enterprises.

This is all the more surprising as the importance of the multinationals as well as the mobility of capital have grown considerably within the industrialized world. Nevertheless there is a rather simple explanation why multinationals do not lobby for a tax reform based on cash-flow concepts. They benefit from the existing network of tax treaties in a way, which does not make them appreciate an expenditure tax regime as an attractive alternative[8].

Tax treaties prevent double taxation of income flows between two countries. To reach this target double taxation agreements between two countries contain rules which limit the national power of the two countries involved in levying taxes. This attempt to escape the welfare loss which accompanies discriminatory taxation in the presence of international factor mobility offers enterprises the possibility of not only benefitting from bilateral treaties, but also from the whole network of existing treaties and the regulations contained therein by exploiting the differences between various bilateral treaties.

Basically three types of strategies might be followed by multinational companies to make use of tax preferences in addition to a simple bilateral double taxation relief:

[8] The existence of tax loopholes in the income tax regime may also be the reason why domestic enterprises hardly lobby for an expenditure tax regime, but prefer to apply for traditional tax preferences, usually more favourable depreciation rules etc.

a) "zero taxation"

Instead of repatriating capital income from a firm in country A to the shareholder in country B income may be collected temporarily in a base company in country C. By placing base companies in suitable tax havens (e.g. the Bahamas or the Channel Islands) as "exempt companies", tax liabilities in the countries A and B can be avoided [cf. OECD (1987b, pp. 60 seqq.), Grundy (1984, pp. 57 seqq.)]. Base companies are frequently found in the Netherlands where dividends of foreign subsidiaries are not taxed, if the company qualifies for the "participation exemption", or in Belgium where tax preferences apply if a company acts as a "coordination centre" [cf. Giovanini (1989, pp. 14 seqq.)]. Usually the shareholder will benefit from a tax deferral, as income flowing from the base company to the shareholder will only be subject to tax in some future period. But there may also exist an opportunity for a second sheltering which leads to a permanent exemption.

b) "treaty shopping"

Instead of using a tax haven a shareholder in country B may also benefit from a double taxation treaty between country A and C [cf. Becker (1985, pp. 171 seqq.), Piltz (1987, pp. 36 seqq.)]. To become entitled to this form of double taxation relief a conduit company may be placed in country C and the income flow from A to B is channelled via country C. The conduit company in country C serves as a stepping stone to take advantage of the tax preferences of the bilateral treaty [cf. OECD (1987b, pp. 88 seqq.)]. The stepping stone approach may be extended by using a series of treaties sequentially to arrive at the most favourable tax treatment ("stepping stone conduit").

c) "rule shopping"

Rule shopping makes use of the different treatment of transnational income flows in double taxation treaties [cf. Piltz (1987, pp. 49 seq.)]. Within a multinational firm income flows show a high degree of fungibility. In any suitable stepping stone country the conduit company can be used to transform a certain flow of income into another one, e.g. royalties into interests, in order to reduce the overall tax burden.

International tax relations thus create economic rents which can be exploited by multinational firms through tax avoidance strategies. These rents do not only include reduced tax burdens, but they also offer multinationals a comparative advantage with respect to national competitors who cannot escape taxation through double taxation treaties.

Multinational companies will have an incentive to lobby for the continuance of national income tax systems and international tax relations as the source of their rents. Furthermore, other enterprises becoming aware of these rents will invest resources in rent-seeking activities which create opportunity costs and reduce global welfare, but offer a chance to participate in rent sharing.

I must admit that this explanation of a resistance of the multinationals to switch to an expenditure tax system is not based on quantitative empirical data. Nevertheless a variety of case studies [cf. Grundy (1984) or Piltz (1987)] support the view that prevailing tax systems are "highly ineffective in reaching foreign-source investment income" [Bird/McLure (1988, p. 31)]. Alworth (1988) has provided some figures to illustrate tax options for multinationals although statistical evidence on the actual amount of tax avoidance is still lacking. This is a new field to apply the political economy approach and to test its explanatory power.

VIII. Conclusion

One of the obstacles to change from the existing income tax regime to an expenditure tax regime can be seen in the existence of a highly complex network of bilateral double taxation treaties, negotiated and implemented in countries with traditional income tax systems. Nevertheless the hypothesis that the legal constraints of international tax relations have had a decisive influence on the dismissal of expenditure tax alternatives in recent tax reforms in industrialized countries should be rejected. A closer look at the proposals shows that international tax relations have pushed ahead the introduction of consumer type VAT systems and their fiscal importance, and this is a step towards expenditure taxation. A change from the existing personal and corporate income taxes towards cash-flow taxes on companies and households recommended by theoretical analysis did not fail due to incompatibilities with the existing structure of bilateral tax treaties, which would have allowed a single country expenditure tax reform in an income tax world.

Nevertheless another impediment for an expenditure tax reform may be attributed to international tax relations. Existing regulations and treaties provide an incentive for rent seeking by multinational firms to avoid taxes and to exploit rents. Thus one important target group of an expenditure tax reform, multinational firms, does not necessarily appreciate tax relief in an efficient expenditure tax regime compared to existing benefits from tax loopholes in our income tax world.

Majority assistance for expenditure taxation seems to require that consumers are convinced of the beneficial effects of such a reform. Thus it is necessary to fight the view that expenditure taxation would primarily relieve the entrepreneur and the rentier by exempting their savings and to demonstrate more clearly that international taxation of income is a poor concept which is neither efficient nor equitable.

Comments by Francesco Forte

1. Genser deals with three types of tax changes of different kind: those relating to increase or introduction of VAT which implies an extended taxable basis as compared to the "old" single wage sales and excise taxes; those relating to unilateral introduction of cash flow concepts in corporate taxation which implies three possible different taxable bases or combinations of them; those relating to unilateral shift from personal progressive income taxes based on accrued income to personal progressive expenditure taxation which implies a smaller taxable basis and higher rates, allowing for future extension of the basis with the same rate.

I will introduce another - less dramatic and more gradualistic - possible shift toward expenditure taxation, at the personal or corporate income tax level; i.e. rate reduction or exemption of income saved up to a given amount or derived from given kinds of savings, which is practically important and does not call for difficult adjustments at the international tax relations level. In other words, as the comprehensive income tax is only a theoretical model, the expenditure tax may be simply considered as a "reference" model, to be adapted to reality in a second best condition as for the tax optimality.

At the end I will comment on Genser's statement about multinational apparent aversion to the cash flow model, as for corporate taxation.

2. No doubt VAT can be easily accommodated under existing international tax rules, namely - in this case - GATT rules and EEC rules on tax neutrality as for international economic flows, through the border tax adjustment (BTA) mechanism. It is also true that the recognition of this mechanism as for VAT, in the GATT rules, stimulates a shift of taxation from other kinds of taxes, not only the profit taxation and income taxation but also the payroll social security contributions to VAT. Through BTA it is possible to achieve a better forward shifting of the tax burden. This fact corresponds with the fact that BTA allows a better competitive situation in international trade without currency devaluation, in promoting the introduction of value added taxation in several tax systems which rely on a different proportion among income, profit and payroll taxation on one side and consumption taxation on the other side.

Clearly, countries of the EEC with lower VAT rates, as Germany shifting emphasis to the VAT, will increase the harmonization level in the common market. Similarly will do countries like Italy which extensively apply exemption and rate reductions. Abolition of borders or their harmonization therefore will become easier, even if not too much emphasis should be put on rates differentials in the range of 5 % in this respect.

On the other hand development of VAT to replace single stage sales taxes and excises is not caused by particularly favourable GATT rules. Retail sales tax do not need any BTA and wholesale or production sales and excise taxes, whether specific or ad valorem, are allowed BTA by existing GATT and EEC rules. The shift from these narrow based excises and sales taxes to VAT implies, for the government, a broadening of the taxable matter which extends its tax power in the consumption taxation area. Whether this power will be exerted to change the composition of the aggregate tax burden or to increase its level is a question which may well have a different answer in the short and in the long run. The positive theory of tax Leviathan as a maximizing monopolist may lead to argue that in the longer run this will imply a higher taxation level. The normative theory of taxation of consumption as a meanss to keep a high level of welfare expenditure while fostering economic growth, may lead to an increase of (future) tax burden in comparison with the level which, otherwise, would have been considered as optimal. This does not imply that tax burden will increase but that it may not decrease.

3. Considering now the shift from the income concept to the expenditure concept in personal progressive income taxation, Genser *prima facie* is right in maintaining that existing international tax rules relating to the residence principle as for personal income taxation do not constrain this change.

Income perceived from abroad will be taxable in the country of residence of the taxpayer applying the expenditure tax model by crediting the tax withhold abroad on interests and dividends. But since only income not saved will be taxed domestically, this credit will be applicable to the tax due on expenditure. Suppose, however, that we are considering a rich taxpayer who gets 90 % of his income from abroad and only consumes one tenth of his income (particularly because he does a lot of his consumption within the corporations he works for and controls). He could hardly apply successfully the credit of, let us say, 20 % for taxes levied by foreign states on income earned abroad, from his tax obligation, even if the marginal rate is very high and the progressivity very steep. Even with an average burden of, let us say, 70 % which is an enormous burden, the 20 % credit on 90 % is 18 % as against a tax obligation of 7 % of the considered income.

Thus, this tax payer will either shift his residence abroad, to a country applying a progressive income tax model without high marginal rates or will shift his investments from abroad to avoid that tax credit.

The other possibililty is to reimburse the rich taxpayer the 20 % withholding tax payed abroad: something hard to be understood by an ordinary taxpayer who bears the progressive consumption tax.

4. On the other hand, a tax on emigration is suggested to avoid the incentive of moving to countries which apply the income tax with a comprehensive income model from countries which adopt the expenditure model, as for citizens who decide to change their residence. But would this tax be considered constitutional, in view of the principle of freedom of movements within a community of states like the EEC?

And what about savings sent or made abroad? If they are exempted, how to check consumption from them? But if they are not exonerated, is this internationally justifiable?

Would states, which tax income saved, accept an outflow of citizens to states which follow the other scheme? The fact that existing tax rules do not prevent this kind of favourable treatment relates to the existing situation in which the so-called fiscal heavens are a limited amount and mostly small motions which merely practice tourism or financial intermediation. The situation might differ for dramatic changes of tax models, as among industrialized countries. Certainly this would not be allowed under the EEC general principles of tax harmonization, which are particularly sensitive to capital taxation issues.

5. This last reflection allows us to rapidly consider the issues of a cash flow corporation taxation.

As Professor Genser rightly says, no problem *per se* is raised by this different method of taxing profits as far as tax credits to domestic shareholders by foreign companies and exemptions of earnings made in other countries or tax credits on foreign subsidiaries are concerned.

But the problem is that this kind of taxation diminishes the existing burden on corporate capital substantially, thus creating distortions in the investments. Again this may not be considered to be acceptable among industrialized countries, while it is normally tolerated or even stimulated as for the underdeveloped countries and some particular underdeveloped region (not without severe limitations, now, in the EEC).

The concept of distortion of competition as applied in the internal market rules of the EEC is relevant here.

6. A final point has to do with the reason why multinationals do not show any particular interest in the change from the present profit basis to the cash flow concepts as for corporate income taxation.

It seems to me that a simple public choice explanation may be offered here, without being forced to argue that this new way of taxing them is *per se* less favourable to them than the present model.

To get fiscal rents, pressure groups must invest a considerable effort in terms of money, time, and personnel (experts, public relations people and so on).

If the present situation as for corporation taxation has been adapted to the needs of the multinationals through a considerable investment by their pressure groups, that investment would be lost through a change to another model of taxation.

This however does not imply that if the change is done, rent seeking will not develop, after an initial stage, to manipulate the taxable basis, the rates, the assessment and other crucial concepts as that of "resident", to get benefits from the new model. R. Wagner's analysis on this point seems relevant here.

To sum up, what I want to argue is simply that it seems hard to adopt these big changes in income and profit tax concepts, within the existing international frame, if the changes are unilateral. The VAT case is much more straightforward. This does not imply that tax incentives enticing savings in personal income taxation or new technological investments in corporations taxation could not be suggested and introduced without creating an "international case".

And this seems to me what we may derive as a suggestion from the articulate Genser analysis of the avenues which present international rules, happily, leave open to adjust fiscal autonomous choices to the interconnections of the international economic and fiscal game.

Comments by Klaus Vogel

I spent last weekend in company of a dozen of students discussing in all detail the effects of existing double taxation treaties on a hypothetical personal (direct) expenditure tax. The result is that all existing treaties would have to be renegotiated, and this thoroughly. Let me give you the reasons:

First, it is by no means clear that existing treaties could be applied to an expenditure tax of the Kaldor type at all. Usually, treaties enumerate the existing taxes of the two contracting States to which they apply and used to include a general clause according to which the treaty shall also apply "to any identical or substantially similar taxes". But is an expenditure tax "substantially similar" to an income tax? In addition, the

OECD and UN models used to include a general clause defining "income taxes" to be "all taxes imposed on total income ... or on elements of income ..., including taxes on ..." (now certain items of income are listed). This definition, however, is not incorporated into very many treaties. And again it does not answer the question whether an expenditure tax may be called a tax on income or on elements of income. If not, the treaty is not applicable, double taxation would persist. Unilateral measures may alleviate it, but would be insufficient.

But let us assume that by common consent of all States concerned expenditure taxes are held to be "substantially similar" to income taxes, in other words that the treaties are considered to remain applicable. Then the *second* problem to be solved is how *dissavings* shall be dealt with under a treaty. Double taxation conventions are organised according to items of income; they have different distributive rules relating to different items of income, e.g. business profits, dependent and independent services, dividends, interest, royalties, etc. Finally, they have a catchall clause saying that all items of income not expressly dealt with in foregoing articles are taxable in the taxpayer's State of residence. Now dissavings - in other words: the cash flow resulting from sale of equity, repayment of loans, dissolution of savings accounts etc. - within an expenditure tax system clearly would constitute an element of the annual tax base. We may choose whether to consider them an item of income of their own, then the aforementioned catchall clause would apply. Or we may qualify them for treaty purposes according to the type of income which was used to acquire the original asset, the "saving", from which they are derived. This latter solution, however, would be extremely impractical. It would require tracing back savings up to the time when they were originally acquired. And if income of different types has been saved on the same account, and part of it is dissaved now, we would need a particular rule for attributing the dissaving to the original types of income. This certainly would not be feasible. On the other hand, treating dissavings as if they were an item of income and applying the catchall clause to them would not be feasible, either. For it would give the taxpayer an opportunity to avoid taxation by the State of source of an item of income whenever the State of residence's tax rate is lower. By saving the income in question and then dissaving it the taxpayer could always bring in the catchall clause which attributes taxation to the residence State. Thus, the only feasible solution is to devise a new treaty rule for dissavings.

Nobody, however, has brought forward any idea until now as to how such a rule might be shaped.

Third, if one contracting State introduces an expenditure tax and the other one sticks to its income tax the treaty's credit mechanism must be revised to take care of the fact that income is taxable in the two contracting States at different periods. As I mentioned before, a credit for expenditure tax paid in the source State may be impossible because the income expended had been taxed years before in the State of residence. Or a credit for an income tax paid in the source State may not be obtained because the income has been saved in the State of residence and, therefore, there is no expenditure tax due in that State. Here extensive carry-backs and carry-forwards must be provided for by the treaties. (Note that similar problems arise if the tax prepayment method is adopted by the State of residence, whereas the State of source adheres to the income tax or to a Kaldor type expenditure tax.)

Finally, in many treaties double taxation is avoided today not by credit, but by exemption. This has been the traditional method used to prevent double taxation in continental Europe and it is predominantly applied still, e.g., by Austria, France, Germany, the Netherlands and Switzerland. Within an income tax setting I, personally, prefer exemption to credit, because in my opinion this method is more in accordance with efficiency and with equity, too. But within an expenditure tax setting exemption would lead to serious disturbances of capital allocation. Thus, when adopting an expenditure tax this method would have to be abolished.

Today there are about 950 income tax treaties that I know of, there may be even hundreds of them more. The United Kingdom has about 85 treaties, France has about 75, Germany about 60. All these treaties would have to be renegotiated. And do not think that renegotiating them is a simple matter. Tax treaty negotiations are hard, extended and sometimes wily battles. And they take their time: after introduction of corporation tax imputation in Germany it took twelve years to renegotiate Germany's treaties with the United States and with Switzerland.

This is just sordid reality. I agree that pure theory may have much more beauty. But at least once I wanted to show you the real picture.

References

Alworth, J. (1988), The Finance, Investment and Taxation Decisions of Multinationals (Blackwell, Oxford).

Becker, H. (1985), Erschleichung der Abkommensberechtigung durch Zwischenpersonen, in: K. Vogel (ed.), Grundfragen des Internationalen Steuerrechts (Schmidt, Köln), pp. 171-193.

Bird, R. (1988), Shaping a New International Tax Order, Bulletin of the International Bureau of Fiscal Documentation 42, pp. 292-299.

Bird, R. / McLure, Ch. (1988), The Personal Income Tax in an Interdependent World, mimeo.

Birk, D. (1989), Verfassungsrechtliche Grenzen der Konsumbesteuerung, in: M. Rose (ed.) (1990), Konsumorientierte Neuordnung des Steuersystems (Springer-Verlag, Berlin-Heidelberg).

Boadway, R. / Bruce, N. (1988), Problems with Integrating Corporate and Personal Income Taxes in an Open Economy, mimeo.

Bradford, D. (1986), Untangling the Income Tax (Harvard University Press, Cambridge).

Bradford, D. (1988), A Consumed-Income Tax: What is it? Is There a Role for it after Tax Reform? mimeo.

Bundesministerium der Finanzen (1988), Finanznachrichten 1/88.

Debatin, H. (1983), Probleme der internationalen Doppelbesteuerung, in: F. Neumark et al. (eds.), Handbuch der Finanzwissenschaft, Vol. 4, pp. 269-309.

Fischer, L. / Warneke, P. (1988), Internationale Betriebswirtschaftliche Steuerlehre, 3rd ed., (Schmidt, Berlin).

GATT (1969), Basic Instruments and Selected Documents, Vol. 4 (Geneva).

Giovanini, A. (1989), National Tax Systems vs. The European Capital Market, mimeo.

Goode, R. (1980), The Superiority of the Income Tax, in: J. Pechman (ed.), What Should Be Taxed: Income or Expenditure? (The Brookings Institution, Washington, D.C.), pp. 49-73.

Grundy, M. (1984), The World of International Tax Planning (Cambridge University Press, Cambridge).

Hall, R. / Rabushka, A. (1985), The Flat Tax (Hoover Institution Press, Stanford).

Henderson, G. (1984), Alternatives to the Income Tax, in: J. Pechman (ed.), Options to Tax Reform (The Brookings Institution, Washington, D.C.), pp. 78-105.

Kay, J. / King, M. (1986), The British Tax System, 4th ed. (Oxford: Oxford University Press).

Krause-Junk, G. (1989), Problems of International Coordination Under Alternative Consumption Tax Regimes, this volume.

Lodin, S.-O. (1978), Progressive Expenditure Tax - an Alternative? (LiberFörlag, Stockholm).

McLure, Ch. (1988), The 1986 Act: Tax Reform's Finest Hour or Death Throes of the Income Tax? National Tax Journal 41, pp. 303-315.

Meade, J. (1978) (ed.), The Structure and Reform of Direct Taxation (The Institute for Fiscal Studies, London).

Messere, K. / Norregaard, J. (1989), Taxing Consumption, The OECD Observer, No. 156, pp. 24-27.

Mieszkowski, P. (1977), The Cash Flow Version of an Expenditure Tax, Office of Tax Analysis Paper 26, (Washington).

Musgrave, P. (1989), International Coordination Problems of Substituting Consumption for Income Taxation, this volume.

OECD (1977), Model Double Taxation Convention on Income and on Capital (Paris).

OECD (1986), Personal Income Tax Systems under Changing Economic Conditions (Paris).

OECD (1987a), Taxation in Developed Countries (Paris).

OECD (1987b), International Tax Avoidance and Evasion (Paris).

OECD (1988), Revenue Statistics of OECD Member Countries 1965-1987 (Paris).

Peffekoven, R. (1983), Probleme der internationalen Finanzordnung, in: F. Neumark et al. (eds.), Handbuch der Finanzwissenschaft, Vol. 4, pp. 219-268.

Piltz, D. (1987), Doppelbesteuerungsabkommen und Steuerumgehung - unter besonderer Berücksichtigung des treaty-shopping, Hefte zur Internationalen Besteuerung 25 (Universität Hamburg) mimeo.

Ross, St. (1988), International Tax Law: The Need for Constructive Change, in: H. Stein (ed.), pp. 87-100.

Sinn, H.-W. (1985), Kapitaleinkommensbesteuerung. Eine Analyse der intertemporalen, internationalen und intersektoralen Allokationswirkungen (J.C.B. Mohr (Paul Siebeck), Tübingen).

Sinn, H.-W. (1987), Alternativen zur Einkommensteuer, in Steuersystem und wirtschaftliche Entwicklung, in Beihefte der Konjunkturpolitik 33 (Duncker & Humblot, Berlin), pp. 11-50 .

Stein, H. (1988) (ed.), Tax Policy in the Twenty-First Century (Wiley, New York).

Summers, L. (1988), Taxation in a Small World, in: H. Stein (ed.), pp. 64-75.

Tait, A. (1988), Value Added Tax. International Practice and Problems (International Monetary Fund, Washington).

Tanzi, V. (1988), Tax Reform in Industrial Countries and the Impact of the U.S. Tax Reform Act of 1986. Bulletin of the International Bureau of Fiscal Documentation 42, pp. 51-64.

Participants

Aaron, Henry J. The Brookings Institution, Washington

Ahlheim, Michael Universität Heidelberg

Ahsan, Syed M. Concordia University Montreal

Albrecht, Peter Universität Heidelberg

Andel, Norbert Johann Wolfgang Goethe-Universität Frankfurt

Ballard, Charles L. Michigan State University

Bernholz, Peter Universität Basel

Birk, Dieter Westfälische Wilhelms-Universität Münster

Blankart, Charles B. Technische Universität Berlin

Boadway, Robin W. Queen's University Kingston/Kanada

Bös, Dieter Rheinische Friedrich Wilhelms-Universität Bonn

Bradford, David F. Princeton University

Brennan, H. Geoffrey The Australian National University Canberra

Buchanan, James M. George Mason University Virginia

Caesar, Rolf Ruhr-Universität Bochum

Cnossen, Sijbren Erasmus-Universiteit Rotterdam

Conrad, Klaus Universität Mannheim

Dziadkowski, Dieter Universität Essen

Folkers, Cay Universität Hohenheim

Forte, Francesco Università Degli Studi Di Roma

Genser, Bernd Universität Konstanz

Hackmann, Johannes Universität der Bundeswehr in Hamburg

Häuser, Karl Johann Wolfgang Goethe-Universität Frankfurt

Haller, Heinz Technische Hochschule Zürich

Hardorp, Benediktus Wirtschaftsprüfer-Steuerberater Heidelberg

Head, John G. Monash University Melbourne

Hinterberger, Friedrich Universität Gießen

Kanniainen, Vesa L. University of Helsinky

Kay, John Center for Business Strategy London

Keuschnigg, Christian Universität Innsbruck

Krause-Junk, Gerold Universität Hamburg

Lang, Joachim Universität Köln

Littmann, Konrad Hochschule für Verwaltungswissenschaften Speyer

Lodin, Sven-Olov University of Stockholm

McLure jr., Charles E. Hoover Institution, Stanford University

Mitschke, Joachim Universität Frankfurt

Mueller, Dennis C. University of Maryland/USA

Müller, Matthias Universität Gieβen

Musgrave, Peggy B. University of California Santa Cruz

Musgrave, Richard A. University of California Santa Cruz

Pestieau, Pierre Université de Liegè/Belgien

Petersen, Hans-Georg Universität Gieβen

Pohmer, Dieter Universität Tübingen

Pollak, Helga Universität Göttingen

Rädler, Albert Universität Hamburg

Recktenwald, Horst Claus Universität Erlangen-Nürnberg

Richter, Wolfram Universität Dortmund

Rose, Manfred Universität Heidelberg

Roskamp, Karl W. Wayne State University Detroit

Schlicht, Ekkehart Technischen Hochschule Darmstadt

Schlieper, Ulrich Universität Mannheim

Schmidt, Kurt Universität Mainz

Schneider, Dieter Ruhr Universität Bochum

Schneider, Helmut Universität Zürich

Schwinger, Reiner Eberhard-Karls-Universität Tübingen

Seidl, Christian Universität Kiel

Siegel, Theodor Technische Universität Berlin

Sinn, Hans-Werner Universität München

Sørensen, Peter Birch University of Copenhagen

Stephan, Gunter Universität Bern

Swoboda, Peter Karl-Franzenz-Universität Graz

Tolkemitt, Georg Universität Hamburg

Trzaskalik, Christoph Universität Mainz

Vogel, Klaus Universität München

Wagenhals, Gerhard Universität Heidelberg

Wagner, Franz W. Eberhard-Karls-Universität Tübingen

Wagner, Richard E. George Mason University Virginia

von Weizsäcker, Carl Christian Universität Köln

Werner, Götz W. dm-drogerie märkte Karlsruhe

Wickström, Bengt-Arne Universität Linz

Wiegard, Wolfgang Universität Regensburg

van Winden, Frans Universiteit van Amsterdam

Zodrow, George R. Rice University Houston

MIX
Papier aus verantwortungsvollen Quellen
Paper from responsible sources
FSC® C105338

If you have any concerns about our products,
you can contact us on
ProductSafety@springernature.com

In case Publisher is established outside the EU,
the EU authorized representative is:
Springer Nature Customer Service Center GmbH
Europaplatz 3, 69115 Heidelberg, Germany

Printed by Libri Plureos GmbH
in Hamburg, Germany